T0234015

Lecture Notes in Computer Science　　12174

More information about this series at http://www.springer.com/series/7410

Abderrahmane Nitaj · Amr Youssef (Eds.)

Progress in Cryptology - AFRICACRYPT 2020

12th International Conference on Cryptology in Africa
Cairo, Egypt, July 20–22, 2020
Proceedings

 Springer

Editors
Abderrahmane Nitaj 🆔
Mathematics, LMNO
Université de Caen
Caen, France

Amr Youssef
School of Engineering
and Computer Science
Concordia University
Montreal, QC, Canada

ISSN 0302-9743   ISSN 1611-3349   (electronic)
Lecture Notes in Computer Science
ISBN 978-3-030-51937-7   ISBN 978-3-030-51938-4   (eBook)
https://doi.org/10.1007/978-3-030-51938-4

LNCS Sublibrary: SL4 – Security and Cryptology

This Springer imprint is published by the registered company Springer Nature Switzerland AG
The registered company address is: Gewerbestrasse 11, 6330 Cham, Switzerland

Preface

This volume contains the papers accepted for presentation at the 12th International Conference on the Theory and Application of Cryptographic Techniques (Africacrypt 2020). The aim of this series of conferences is to provide an international forum for practitioners and researchers from industry, academia, and government agencies from all over the world for a wide-ranging discussion of all forms of cryptography and its applications. The initiative of organizing Africacrypt started in 2008 where it was first held in Morocco. Subsequent yearly events were held in Tunisia, South Africa, Senegal, Morocco, and Egypt. This year, on the initiative of the organizers from Zewail City of Science and Technology, Africacrypt 2020, which is organized in cooperation with the International Association for Cryptologic Research (IACR), was planned to be held in Cairo, Egypt, during July 20–22. Unfortunately, because of the COVID-19 outbreak, the physical event had to be canceled.

We received 49 submissions authored by researchers from 36 different countries. After a reviewing process that involved 37 Program Committee members and 34 external reviewers, the Program Committee went through a significant online discussion phase before deciding to accept 21 papers. All submitted papers received at least three reviews. We are indebted to the members of the Program Committee and the external reviewers for their diligent work and fruitful discussions. We are also grateful to the authors of all submitted papers for supporting the conference. The authors of accepted papers are thanked again for revising their papers according to the suggestions of the reviewers. Apart from one conditionally accepted paper, the revised versions were not checked again by the Program Committee, so authors bear full responsibility for their content. The general chair, Dr. Ashraf Badawi, and the local Organizing Committee from Zewail City of Science and Technology were, as always, a pleasure to work with. We are deeply thankful for their effort in the planning phase of the conference. We are also thankful to the staff at Springer for their help with producing the proceedings and to the staff of EasyChair for the use of their conference management system.

May 2020

Abderrahmane Nitaj
Amr Youssef

Organization

Africacrypt 2020 was organized by Zewail City of Science and Technology, Giza, Egypt, in cooperation with the International Association for Cryptologic Research (IACR).

General Chair

Ashraf Badawi   Zewail City of Science and Technology, Egypt

Program Chairs

Abderrahmane Nitaj   University of Caen Normandie, France
Amr Youssef   Concordia University, Canada

Organizing Committee

Ashraf Badawi (Chair)   Zewail City of Science and Technology, Egypt
Ahmed Eldakrory   Zewail City of Science and Technology, Egypt
Nourhan Magdy   Zewail City of Science and Technology, Egypt

Program Committee

Riham Altawy   University of Victoria, Canada
Elena Andreeva   Danish Technical University, Denmark
Muhammad Rezal   Universiti Putra Malaysia, Malaysia
  Kamel Ariffin
Hatem M. Bahig   Ain Shams University, Egypt
Magali Bardet   University of Rouen Normandie, France
Lejla Batina   Radboud University, The Netherlands
Hussain Ben-Azza   ENSAM Meknes, Morocco
Olivier Blazy   University of Limoges, France
Sébastien Canard   Orange Labs, France
Nicolas Courtois   University College London, UK
Joan Daemen   Radboud University, The Netherlands
Luca De Feo   IBM Research, Switzerland
Milena Dukanovic   University of Montenegro, Montenegro
Nadia El Mrabet   SAS, CGCP, EMSE Saint-Étienne, France
Guang Gong   University of Waterloo, Canada
Aline Gouget   Thales DIS, France
Kishan Gupta   Indian Statistical Institute Kolkata, India
Javier Herranz   Universitat Politècnica de Catalunya, Spain

Sorina Ionica	University of Picardie, France
Tetsu Iwata	Nagoya University, Japan
Juliane Krämer	TU Darmstadt, Germany
Fabien Laguillaumie	University of Lyon, LIP, France
Subhamoy Maitra	Indian Statistical Institute Kolkata, India
Abderrahmane Nitaj	University of Caen Normandie, France
Yanbin Pan	Chinese Academy of Sciences, China
Christophe Petit	University of Oxford, UK
Elizabeth Quaglia	Royal Holloway, University of London, UK
Palash Sarkar	Indian Statistical Institute Kolkata, India
Alessandra Scafuro	North Carolina State University, USA
Ali Aydin Selçuk	TOBB University, Turkey
Djiby Sow	University Cheikh Anta Diop, Senegal
Pantelimon Stanica	Naval Postgraduate School in Monterey, USA
Noah Stephens-Davidowitz	Massachusetts Institute of Technology, USA
Willy Susilo	University of Wollongong, Australia
Joseph Tonien	University of Wollongong, Australia
Vanessa Vitse	University of Grenoble Alpes, France
Amr Youssef	Concordia University, Canada

Additional Reviewers

Khalid Abdelmoumen	Kalikinkar Mandal
Simon Abelard	Simon-Philipp Merz
Amira Barki	Romy Minko
Andreas Brasen Kidmose	Murat Osmanoglu
Guilhem Castagnos	Ayoub Otmani
Dung Hoang Duong	Carles Padró
Muhammad Elsheikh	Simon Pontié
Ashley Fraser	Francisco Rodríguez Henríquez
Shihui Fu	Raghvendra Rohit
Stefan-Lukas Gazdag	Arnab Roy
Adel Hamdi	Niels Samwel
Turgut Hanoymak	Patrick Struck
Murat Burhan İlter	Léo Weissbart
David Jao	Charlotte Weitkämper
Guillaume Kaim	Julian Wälde
Orhun Kara	Oğuz Yayla
Liliya Kraleva	Mahmoud Yehia
Zhen Liu	

Contents

Zero Knowledge

QA-NIZK Arguments of Same Opening
for Bilateral Commitments

Carla Ràfols and Javier Silva[✉]

Universitat Pompeu Fabra, Barcelona, Spain
{carla.rafols,javier.silva}@upf.edu

Abstract. Zero-knowledge proofs of satisfiability of linear equations over a group are often used as a building block of more complex protocols. In particular, in an asymmetric bilinear group we often have two commitments in different sides of the pairing, and we want to prove that they open to the same value. This problem was tackled by González, Hevia and Ràfols (ASIACRYPT 2015), who presented an aggregated proof, in the QA-NIZK setting, consisting of only four group elements. In this work, we present a more efficient proof, which is based on the same assumptions and consists of three group elements. We argue that our construction is optimal in terms of proof size.

Keywords: Pairing-based cryptography · Zero-knowledge proofs · Commitments

1 Introduction

Bilinear groups have been used to design countless cryptographic protocols, some of them with no equivalent in other settings. In particular, such groups have been very useful to design non-interactive zero-knowledge (NIZK) proofs in the common reference string (CRS) model. The first works to realize that pairings allowed for the construction of efficient NIZK proofs were [5,17,19,20], culminating in the work of Groth–Sahai [21]. The latter presents a NIZK proof system for satisfiability of most types of linear and quadratic equation in bilinear groups, in the CRS model and under standard, constant size and weak assumptions. Groth–Sahai proofs are one of the fundamental building blocks in pairing-based cryptography, with well-known applications as anonymous credentials [13], e-Cash [3], ring-signatures [8], shuffles [18], signatures of knowledge [4], and tight CCA encryption [22].

Groth–Sahai proofs follow the usual commit-and-prove paradigm: first, the prover commits to the solution of the equation, and then produces a "proof" formed of some group elements, which the verifier uses together with the commitments to get convinced of the satisfiability of the equation. The commit-and-prove framework is used implicitly in the original work of Groth and Sahai [21], and formalized explicitly in [10,13]. In this view, a NIZK proof proves some property of a committed value, and many different statements about a

© Springer Nature Switzerland AG 2020
A. Nitaj and A. Youssef (Eds.): AFRICACRYPT 2020, LNCS 12174, pp. 3–23, 2020.
https://doi.org/10.1007/978-3-030-51938-4_1

single committed value can be proven.[1] This formalization is also a conceptually cleaner approach. It allows to differentiate clearly between the "commit" and the "proof" part among all the elements computed by the prover. In this work we also make the separation between commitment and proof, so when we discuss proof sizes we refer exclusively to the latter part.

For many equation types, the Groth–Sahai proof system is still the state of the art. Few improvements are known, like the general techniques to replace dual mode commitments by ElGamal ciphertexts [10], aggregation of many Groth–Sahai proofs [16,24], which are of limited applicability, or some techniques to encode partial satisfiability [30].

A notable exception are quasi-adaptive NIZK (QA-NIZK) arguments of membership in linear spaces over a source group [24,26,27], introduced by Jutla–Roy [23], which allow to prove satisfiability of linear equations. More precisely, let $e : \mathbb{G}_1 \times \mathbb{G}_2 \to \mathbb{G}_T$ be an asymmetric bilinear group equipped with a pairing. We use implicit notation as in [12], where $[\boldsymbol{y}]_1 \in \mathbb{G}_1^n$ denotes a vector $(y_1 \mathcal{P}, \ldots, y_n \mathcal{P})$, for $\mathcal{P}$ a generator of $\mathbb{G}_1$. Such QA-NIZK arguments allow to prove that a vector $[\boldsymbol{y}]_1 \in \mathbb{G}_1^n$ is of the form $\boldsymbol{y} = \mathbf{M}\boldsymbol{w}$, for some public matrix $[\mathbf{M}]_1 \in \mathbb{G}_1^{n \times t}$. These arguments are extremely efficient: under an assumption weaker than DDH, their size is only 1 group element, for most distributions of $[\mathbf{M}]_1$.[2] The same statement proven with Groth–Sahai proofs requires $O(t)$ elements for committing to $\boldsymbol{w}$ and $O(n)$ elements to prove that $\boldsymbol{y}$ is of this form.

Because of their efficiency, these arguments have many applications, for instance to different flavors of identity-based encryption [23] or group signatures [28]. These arguments also have a close relation to structure-preserving signatures [1,2,25]. Membership in linear spaces naturally encodes statements about ciphertexts and commitments: for example, two ElGamal ciphertexts (or more generally, any 'algebraic' commitment scheme, like Pedersen or Groth–Sahai commitments) encrypt the same message if their difference is in a certain linear space dependent of the public key. More generally, QA-NIZK arguments allow to aggregate proof easily: proving that two vectors of ElGamal commitments open pairwise to the same value requires only one group element, using the constructions of Kiltz-Wee [26], and the security relies on Kernel assumptions [29]. On the other hand, with the Groth–Sahai proof system, this requires two elements of each group $\mathbb{G}_1, \mathbb{G}_2$ for each pair of ciphertexts.

In this paper, we consider the problem of proving that two commitments, one in $\mathbb{G}_1$ and one in $\mathbb{G}_2$, open to the same value. This statement appears naturally when one wants to prove quadratic relations in asymmetric bilinear groups. Indeed, suppose that we want to prove that a commitment opens to a bit, that is, that the opening of some commitments satisfies the quadratic equation $X(X - 1) = 0$. This often appears as part of a larger proof, for example in ring signatures [8,14,15], e-voting [7] or range proofs [6]. To prove that a commitment opens to a bit, Groth–Sahai proofs proceed as follows:

---

[1] In contrast, if one thinks of Groth–Sahai proofs as NIZK proofs of satisfiability of quadratic equations, formally commitments cannot be reused across proofs.

[2] More precisely, $[\mathbf{M}]_1$ should be taken from a witness sampleable distribution.

1. Rewrite the equation as $X(Y - 1) = 0$.
2. Commit to a solution: $[c]_1 = \mathsf{Com}(x; r)$ and $[d]_2 = \mathsf{Com}(y; s)$.
3. Prove satisfiability of the equation $X(Y - 1) = 0$ using the commitments c, d and providing some additional proof elements.
4. Prove that the commitments c, d open to the same value.

We note that step 4 is proving the linear equation $X = Y$. Informally, the idea is that step 3 is a quadratic check which requires commitments in different groups, and step 4 makes sure there is some consistency between these values. Formally, the need for it arises from the fact that Groth–Sahai proofs work for disjoint sets of variables in $\mathbb{G}_1$ and $\mathbb{G}_2$.

This is one of the main techniques for proving quadratic equations in $\mathbb{Z}_p$ in bilinear groups (in the CRS model and under standard assumptions), and any efficiency improvement in the same opening step (4) would have a direct impact on the overall efficiency. We note that there is another construction, introduced very recently in [9], that proves that a commitment over $\mathbb{G}_1$ opens to either 0 or 1. Their approach consists of using a pairing to compile interactive arguments into non-interactive ones, and they manage to prove that a commitment opens to a bit with 7 group elements. For comparison, the Groth–Sahai approach requires 10 group elements using our approach. Groth–Sahai proofs still seem better for proving that n commitments to a bit: in [9] the proof scales linearly, whereas if we use the aggregated version of our scheme, n proofs require $6n + 3$ elements.

1.1 Our Results

To the best of our knowledge, there are two ways of proving step 4. One is to use standard Groth–Sahai proofs, which requires 2 group elements in each of $\mathbb{G}_1$ and $\mathbb{G}_2$. The alternative is to use QA-NIZK arguments of membership in linear spaces. However, because the statement is split between $\mathbb{G}_1$ and $\mathbb{G}_2$, we need to resort to arguments of membership in bilateral spaces, which show, for two vectors $[\boldsymbol{x}]_1, [\boldsymbol{y}]_2$, and some matrices $[\mathbf{M}]_1, [\mathbf{M}]_2$ that there exists some $\boldsymbol{w}$ such that $\boldsymbol{x} = \mathbf{M}\boldsymbol{w}$ and $\boldsymbol{y} = \mathbf{N}\boldsymbol{w}$. These were constructed by González et al. [16] under some computational assumption in bilinear groups.[3] However, this does not improve step (4) over the cost of Groth–Sahai proofs. The proof of González et al. only improves on the state of the art for the aggregated case, namely to show that n pairs of commitments open (pairwise) to the same value with a proof made of 2 elements in $\mathbb{G}_1$ and 2 elements in $\mathbb{G}_2$, independent of n. However, this is not an improvement for a single pair of commitments.

Noticing the gap between one element for one-sided proofs and four elements for bilateral proofs, a natural question is how much we can reduce the proof size in the bilateral case. In this paper, we give a construction which reduces the

---

[3] Standard QA-NIZK arguments can be proven sound under Kernel Matrix Diffie-Hellman Assumptions (KerMDH) [29], and bilateral arguments can be proven sound under Split KerMDH, a natural generalization to bilinear groups. In its weakest and most efficient instatiation, KerMDH is weaker than DDH, and SKerMDH is weaker than 2-Lin.

proof size of [16] to three elements, while maintaining the same computational assumption in the soundness proof.

We note that this is the first concrete improvement for step (4) since the publication of the work of Groth–Sahai. Our result is a sophisticated combination of the techniques of Kiltz–Wee [26] and González et al. [16]. Additionally, we argue that our constructions are optimal, by showing that any two-element proof is vulnerable to a simple attack.

1.2   Our Techniques

We briefly review the linear space membership proof of Kiltz–Wee [26]. Their core idea is a clever translation to the bilinear group setting of a hash proof system, which is essentially a NIZK proof in the symmetric key setting. Given a matrix $\mathbf{M} \in \mathbb{Z}_p^{m \times t}$, the starting point is a proof system for the language

$$\mathcal{L}_{\mathbf{M}} = \{[c]_1 \leftarrow \mathbb{G}_1^m \mid \exists \boldsymbol{w} \text{ s. t. } \boldsymbol{c} = \mathbf{M}\boldsymbol{w}\}$$

which works as follows: prover and verifier share a key $\mathbf{K} \leftarrow \mathbb{Z}_p^{m \times (k+1)}$, where k will depend on the hardness assumption used to ensure soundness. The projection $[\mathbf{M}^\top \mathbf{K}]_1$ is published in the CRS. The prover sends $[\boldsymbol{\pi}]_1 = \boldsymbol{w}^\top [\mathbf{M}^\top \mathbf{K}]_1$, and the verifier checks that

$$[\boldsymbol{c}^\top]_1 \mathbf{K} \overset{?}{=} [\boldsymbol{\pi}]_1.$$

Intuitively, the proof is sound because if $\boldsymbol{c}$ is not in $\mathbf{Im}(\mathbf{M})$ then $\boldsymbol{c}^\top \mathbf{K}$ is uniformly random given $\mathbf{M}^\top \mathbf{K}$, and thus there is no way for the prover to produce such a proof.

Kiltz–Wee take this idea and remove the need for a shared secret key by using a bilinear group. Now the CRS includes $[\mathbf{A}, \mathbf{K}\mathbf{A}]_2$, for a matrix $\mathbf{A} \in \mathbb{Z}_p^{(k+1) \times k}$. This partially fixes $\mathbf{K}$ without revealing it, the goal being that the verifier can use these elements to verify without needing to know $\mathbf{K}$ as before. The proof is still the same, but the verification is now

$$e([\boldsymbol{c}^\top]_1, [\mathbf{K}\mathbf{A}]_2) \overset{?}{=} e([\boldsymbol{\pi}]_1, [\mathbf{A}]_2).$$

By assuming the hardness of a Kernel problem on $\mathbf{A}$, i.e., it is hard to find non-trivial cokernel elements of $\mathbf{A}$, we are essentially back to the argument of the hash proof system. For the right choice of distribution of $\mathbf{A}$, the assumption is believed to hold starting at $k = 1$, so in this case we have that the proof is formed of 2 group elements.

However, this can be taken one step further. Assuming that the distribution of $[\mathbf{M}]_1$ is witness sampleable, that is, that we can efficiently sample $\tilde{\mathbf{M}}$ such that $[\tilde{\mathbf{M}}]_1$ is distributed as $[\mathbf{M}]_1$, then it is enough to use the truncated matrix $\overline{\mathbf{A}} \in \mathbb{Z}_p^{k \times k}$ instead of $\mathbf{A}$, thus using $\mathbf{K} \in \mathbb{Z}_p^{m \times k}$, which yields proofs consisting of only one group element.

We now consider the natural generalization of this approach to bilateral proofs, as developed by González et al. [16].[4] Consider the following language:

$$\mathcal{L}_{\mathbf{M},\mathbf{N}} = \{([\boldsymbol{c}]_1, [\boldsymbol{d}]_2) \leftarrow \mathbb{G}_1^m \times \mathbb{G}_2^n \mid \exists \boldsymbol{w} \text{ s. t. } \boldsymbol{c} = \mathbf{M}\boldsymbol{w}, \boldsymbol{d} = \mathbf{N}\boldsymbol{w}\}.$$

To account for two-sided statements, we consider one key $\mathbf{K}$ for $\mathbb{G}_1$ and one key $\mathbf{L}$ for $\mathbb{G}_2$, and so we publish the following elements in the CRS:

$$[\mathbf{M}^\top \mathbf{K} + \mathbf{Z}, \mathbf{A}, \mathbf{LA}]_1, [\mathbf{N}^\top \mathbf{L} - \mathbf{Z}, \mathbf{A}, \mathbf{KA}]_2,$$

where $\mathbf{Z} \in \mathbb{Z}_p^{t \times k}$. The prover produces the proofs $[\boldsymbol{\pi}]_1 = \boldsymbol{w}^\top [\mathbf{M}^\top \mathbf{K} + \mathbf{Z}]_1$ and $[\boldsymbol{\theta}]_2 = \boldsymbol{w}^\top [\mathbf{N}^\top \mathbf{L} - \mathbf{Z}]_2$, and the verifier checks the equation

$$e([\boldsymbol{c}^\top]_1, [\mathbf{KA}]_2) + e([\mathbf{LA}]_1, [\boldsymbol{d}]_2) \stackrel{?}{=} e([\boldsymbol{\pi}]_1, [\mathbf{A}]_2) + e([\mathbf{A}]_1, [\boldsymbol{\theta}]_2). \tag{1}$$

Intuitively, the term $\mathbf{Z}$ in the CRS elements produces terms in the verification equation that will not cancel out unless $\boldsymbol{w}$ is the same in both sides. In a similar way as above, the soundness of this scheme reduces to the hardness of a Split Kernel problem, which is a Kernel problem with the solution split between $\mathbb{G}_1$ and $\mathbb{G}_2$. However, Split Kernel problems are easy for $k = 1$, and so we must take at least $k = 2$. This has a direct impact on the sizes of the keys $\mathbf{K}$ and $\mathbf{L}$, and so this approach yields proofs of two group elements in $\mathbb{G}_1$, and two in $\mathbb{G}_2$, and two verification equations.

Our strategy to reduce the proof size is to use only one element in $\mathbb{G}_2$, so instead of having $\boldsymbol{\theta} = (\theta, \hat{\theta})$ as above, we reuse the same θ. To make it work, we require the condition that the columns of $\mathbf{N}^\top \mathbf{L}$ are equal, so that $\boldsymbol{\theta} = (\theta, \theta)$, and it is enough to send it once. This introduces extra complexity in the CRS generation, and the simulation of the CRS for the adversary in the soundness security reduction, particularly in the aggregated case. We present the proof directly for the most efficient case, $k = 2$.

To solve these new issues, we need to reformulate the problem slightly. Instead of considering the pair of commitments $([\boldsymbol{c}]_1, [\boldsymbol{d}]_2)$ as the statement, we consider just $[\boldsymbol{c}]_1$, and build a proof of F-knowledge of $F(\boldsymbol{w}) = [\boldsymbol{w}]_{1,2}$. Indeed, in applications the commitment $[\boldsymbol{d}]_2$ is an artifact of the proof, as when proving quadratic statements we need to split the commitments between $\mathbb{G}_1$ and $\mathbb{G}_2$ to exploit the pairing. Regarding zero-knowledge, this change implies that the simulator knows the opening of one of the commitments. We note that both openings are required for proving zero-knowledge in Groth–Sahai proofs.

We stress that our modified formalization is due to the intricacies of the soundness reduction, and has no actual impact in most applications. This is because, as we have seen in the proof of $X(X - 1) = 0$ above, the commitment in $\mathbb{G}_2$ is a byproduct of the proof, and thus can be seen as part of it, while the 'meaningful' statement is about the commitment in $\mathbb{G}_1$.

Interestingly, our trick of reusing θ does not work for both sides, and in fact in Sect. 5 we show an attack for any two-element proof of this form. We argue

---

[4] The actual construction requires some masking terms to ensure zero-knowledge, but we omit these for simplicity of the presentation.

that the general form of any proof of bilateral same opening consisting of only two elements must have a verification equations that looks essentially like Eq. (1) above, but with π, θ scalars instead of vectors; then we show a simple algebraic attack that exploits the two-sided nature of the proof.

2   Preliminaries

Let $\mathcal{G}$ be some probabilistic polynomial time algorithm which on input 1^λ, where λ is the security parameter, returns the *group key* which is the description of an asymmetric bilinear group $gk := (p, \mathbb{G}_1, \mathbb{G}_2, \mathbb{G}_T, e, \mathcal{P}_1, \mathcal{P}_2)$, where $\mathbb{G}_1, \mathbb{G}_2$ and $\mathbb{G}_T$ are additive groups of prime order p, the elements $\mathcal{P}_1, \mathcal{P}_2$ are generators of $\mathbb{G}_1, \mathbb{G}_2$ respectively, $e : \mathbb{G}_1 \times \mathbb{G}_2 \to \mathbb{G}_T$ is an efficiently computable, non-degenerate bilinear map, and there is no efficiently computable isomorphism between $\mathbb{G}_1$ and $\mathbb{G}_2$.

Elements in $\mathbb{G}_\gamma$ are denoted implicitly as $[a]_\gamma := a\mathcal{P}_\gamma$, where $\gamma \in \{1, 2, T\}$ and $\mathcal{P}_T := e(\mathcal{P}_1, \mathcal{P}_2)$. For simplicity, we often write $[a]_{1,2}$ for the pair $[a]_1, [a]_2$, and $[a, b]_\gamma$ for $([a]_\gamma, [b]_\gamma)$. The pairing operation will be written as a product, that is, $[a]_1 \cdot [b]_2 = [a]_1[b]_2 = e([a]_1, [b]_2) = [ab]_T$. Vectors and matrices are denoted in boldface. Given a matrix $\mathbf{T} = (t_{i,j})$, $[\mathbf{T}]_\gamma$ is the natural embedding of $\mathbf{T}$ in $\mathbb{G}_\gamma$, that is, the matrix whose (i, j)th entry is $t_{i,j}\mathcal{P}_\gamma$. We denote by $|\mathbb{G}_\gamma|$ the bit-size of the elements of $\mathbb{G}_\gamma$.

2.1   Quasi-Adaptive Non-interactive Zero-Knowledge Proofs

A Quasi-Adaptive NIZK proof system [23] enables to prove membership in a language defined by a relation $\mathcal{R}_\rho$, which is in turn determined by some parameter ρ sampled from a distribution $\mathcal{D}_{gk}$. We say that $\mathcal{D}_{gk}$ is *witness sampleable* if there exists an efficient algorithm that samples (ρ, ω) from a distribution $\mathcal{D}_{gk}^{\mathsf{par}}$ such that ρ is distributed according to $\mathcal{D}_{gk}$, and membership of ρ in the *parameter language* $\mathcal{L}_{\mathsf{par}}$ can be efficiently verified with ω. While the Common Reference String (CRS) can be set based on ρ, the zero-knowledge simulator is required to be a single PPT algorithm that works for any relation $\mathcal{R}_{gk}$. We assume that CRS contains an encoding of ρ, which is thus available to V.

A tuple of algorithms $(\mathsf{K}_0, \mathsf{K}_1, \mathsf{P}, \mathsf{V})$ is called a QA-NIZK proof system for witness-relations $\mathcal{R}_{gk} = \{\mathcal{R}_\rho\}_{\rho \in \sup(\mathcal{D}_{gk})}$ with parameters sampled from a distribution $\mathcal{D}_{gk}$ over the parameter language $\mathcal{L}_{\mathsf{par}}$, if there exists a PPT simulator $(\mathsf{S}_1, \mathsf{S}_2)$, such that for all non-uniform PPT adversaries $\mathcal{A}_1, \mathcal{A}_2, \mathcal{A}_3$ we have:

Quasi-adaptive Completeness:

$$\Pr\left[\begin{array}{l} gk \leftarrow \mathsf{K}_0(1^\lambda); \rho \leftarrow \mathcal{D}_{gk}; \mathsf{CRS} \leftarrow \mathsf{K}_1(gk, \rho); \\ (x, w) \leftarrow \mathcal{A}_1(gk, \mathsf{CRS}); \pi \leftarrow \mathsf{P}(\mathsf{CRS}, x, w) \end{array} : \mathsf{V}(\mathsf{CRS}, x, \pi) = 1 \text{ if } \mathcal{R}_\rho(x, w) \right] = 1.$$

Computational Quasi-adaptive Soundness:

$$\Pr\left[\begin{array}{l} gk \leftarrow \mathsf{K}_0(1^\lambda); \rho \leftarrow \mathcal{D}_{gk}; \\ \mathsf{CRS} \leftarrow \mathsf{K}_1(gk, \rho); (x, \pi) \leftarrow \mathcal{A}_2(gk, \mathsf{CRS}) \end{array} : \begin{array}{l} \mathsf{V}(\mathsf{CRS}, x, \pi) = 1 \text{ and} \\ \neg(\exists w : \mathcal{R}_\rho(x, w)) \end{array} \right] \approx 0.$$

Perfect Quasi-adaptive Zero-Knowledge:

$$\Pr[gk \leftarrow \mathsf{K}_0(1^\lambda); \rho \leftarrow \mathcal{D}_{gk}; \mathsf{CRS} \leftarrow \mathsf{K}_1(gk, \rho) : \mathcal{A}_3^{\mathsf{P}(\mathsf{CRS}, \cdot, \cdot)}(gk, \mathsf{CRS}) = 1]$$
$$= \Pr[gk \leftarrow \mathsf{K}_0(1^\lambda); \rho \leftarrow \mathcal{D}_{gk}; (\mathsf{CRS}, \tau) \leftarrow \mathsf{S}_1(gk, \rho) : \mathcal{A}_3^{\mathsf{S}(\mathsf{CRS}, \tau, \cdot, \cdot)}(gk, \mathsf{CRS}) = 1]$$

where
- $\mathsf{P}(\mathsf{CRS}, \cdot, \cdot)$ emulates the actual prover. It takes input (x, w) and outputs a proof π if $(x, w) \in \mathcal{R}_\rho$. Otherwise, it outputs $\perp$.
- $\mathsf{S}(\mathsf{CRS}, \tau, \cdot, \cdot)$ is an oracle that takes input (x, w). It outputs a simulated proof $\mathsf{S}_2(\mathsf{CRS}, \tau, x)$ if $(x, w) \in \mathcal{R}_\rho$ and $\perp$ if $(x, w) \notin \mathcal{R}_\rho$.

We will prove that our schemes have F-knowledge soundness, which we define in the context of witness sampleable distributions. Intuitively, F-knowledge means that, with access to some extraction key, it is possible to extract a function F of the witness from the statement and the proof. We note that our definition differs from the definition in [10], as we give the extraction key generator access to the witness ω that proves membership of ρ in $\mathcal{L}_{\mathsf{par}}$ (in practice, this means that it has access to the discrete logarithms of the commitment key) and allow to extract information from not only the statement, but also the proof.

Given a function F, a scheme is F-knowledge sound if there exist a soundness PPT extraction key generator E_1 and a DPT extractor E_2 such that for any non-uniform PPT adversary $\mathcal{A}_2$, we have:

Computational Quasi-adaptive F-knowledge Soundness:

$$\Pr \begin{bmatrix} gk \leftarrow \mathsf{K}_0(1^\lambda); \rho \leftarrow \mathcal{D}_{gk}; \\ (\mathsf{CRS}, xk) \leftarrow \mathsf{E}_1(gk, (\rho, \omega)); \\ (x, \pi) \leftarrow \mathcal{A}_2(gk, \mathsf{CRS}) \end{bmatrix} : \begin{matrix} \mathsf{V}(\mathsf{CRS}, x, \pi) = 1 \text{ and} \\ \mathsf{E}_{2xk}(x, \pi) \neq F(x, w) \end{matrix} \end{bmatrix} \approx 0,$$

and the distributions of the CRS produced by K_1 and E_1 are the same.

We also define a stronger notion of zero-knowledge, called composable zero-knowledge [17]. Essentially, this means that real and simulated proofs are indistinguishable even when the simulation trapdoor is known. More formally, a scheme is composable zero-knowledge if there exists a PPT simulator $(\mathsf{S}_1, \mathsf{S}_2)$ such that for any non-uniform PPT adversary $\mathcal{A}_3$ we have:

Composable Quasi-adaptive Zero-Knowledge:

$$\Pr \begin{bmatrix} gk \leftarrow \mathsf{K}_0(1^\lambda); \rho \leftarrow \mathcal{D}_{gk}; (\mathsf{CRS}, \tau) \leftarrow \mathsf{S}_1(gk, \rho); \\ (x, w) \leftarrow \mathcal{A}_3(gk, \mathsf{CRS}, \tau); \pi \leftarrow \mathsf{P}(gk, \mathsf{CRS}, x, w) \end{bmatrix} : \mathcal{A}_3(\pi) = 1 \end{bmatrix}$$
$$= \Pr \begin{bmatrix} gk \leftarrow \mathsf{K}_0(1^\lambda); \rho \leftarrow \mathcal{D}_{gk}; (\mathsf{CRS}, \tau) \leftarrow \mathsf{S}_1(gk, \rho); \\ (x, w) \leftarrow \mathcal{A}_3(gk, \mathsf{CRS}, \tau); \pi \leftarrow \mathsf{S}_2(gk, \mathsf{CRS}, \tau, x) \end{bmatrix} : \mathcal{A}_3(\pi) = 1 \end{bmatrix}.$$

and the CRS produced by K_1 and S_1 are indistinguishable.

2.2   Assumptions

Definition 1. *Let $\ell, k \in \mathbb{N}$. We call $\mathcal{D}_{\ell,k}$ a matrix distribution if it outputs (in PPT time, with overwhelming probability) matrices in $\mathbb{Z}_p^{\ell \times k}$. We define $\mathcal{D}_k := \mathcal{D}_{k+1,k}$.*

The following applies for $\mathbb{G}_\gamma$, where $\gamma \in \{1, 2\}$.

Assumption 1 (Matrix Decisional Diffie-Hellman Assumption in $\mathbb{G}_\gamma$ [11]). *For all non-uniform PPT adversaries $\mathcal{A}$,*

$$|\Pr[\mathcal{A}(gk, [\mathbf{A}, \mathbf{Aw}]_\gamma) = 1] - \Pr[\mathcal{A}(gk, [\mathbf{A}, \mathbf{z}]_\gamma) = 1]| \approx 0,$$

where the probability is taken over $gk \leftarrow \mathcal{G}(1^\lambda)$, $\mathbf{A} \leftarrow \mathcal{D}_{\ell,k}, \mathbf{w} \leftarrow \mathbb{Z}_p^k, [\mathbf{z}]_\gamma \leftarrow \mathbb{G}_\gamma^\ell$ and the coin tosses of adversary $\mathcal{A}$.

Intuitively, the $\mathcal{D}_{\ell,k}$-MDDH assumption means that it is hard to decide whether a vector is in the image space of a matrix or it is a random vector, where the matrix is drawn from $\mathcal{D}_{\ell,k}$. In this paper we will refer to the following matrix distributions:

$$\mathcal{L}_k : \mathbf{A} = \begin{pmatrix} a_1 & 0 & \dots & 0 \\ 0 & a_2 & \dots & 0 \\ \vdots & \vdots & \ddots & \vdots \\ 0 & 0 & \dots & a_k \\ 1 & 1 & \dots & 1 \end{pmatrix}, \qquad \mathcal{RL}_k : \mathbf{A} = \begin{pmatrix} a_1 & 0 & \dots & 0 \\ 0 & a_2 & \dots & 0 \\ \vdots & \vdots & \ddots & \vdots \\ 0 & 0 & \dots & a_k \\ r_1 & r_2 & \dots & r_k \end{pmatrix},$$

where $a_i, r_i \leftarrow \mathbb{Z}_p$ for $i = 1, \dots, k$. The $\mathcal{L}_k$-MDDH Assumption is the k-linear family of Decisional Assumptions and corresponds to the Decisional Diffie-Hellman (DDH) Assumption in $\mathbb{G}_\gamma$ when $k = 1$. The SXDH Assumption states that DDH holds in $\mathbb{G}_\gamma$ for $\gamma = 1, 2$.

Additionally, we will be using the following family of computational assumptions:

Assumption 2 (Kernel Diffie-Hellman Assumption in $\mathbb{G}_\gamma$ [29]). *For all non-uniform PPT adversaries $\mathcal{A}$:*

$$\Pr\left[[\mathbf{x}]_{3-\gamma} \leftarrow \mathcal{A}(gk, [\mathbf{A}]_\gamma) : \mathbf{x} \neq 0 \wedge \mathbf{x}^\top \mathbf{A} = 0\right] \approx 0,$$

where the probability is taken over $gk \leftarrow \mathcal{G}(1^\lambda)$, $\mathbf{A} \leftarrow \mathcal{D}_{\ell,k}$ and the coin tosses of adversary $\mathcal{A}$.

The $\mathcal{D}_{\ell,k}$-KerMDH$_{\mathbb{G}_\gamma}$ Assumption is not stronger than the $\mathcal{D}_{\ell,k}$-MDDH$_{\mathbb{G}_\gamma}$ Assumption, since a solution to the former allows to decide membership in $\mathbf{Im}([\mathbf{A}]_\gamma)$. In asymmetric bilinear groups, there is a natural variant of this assumption.

Assumption 3 (Split Kernel Diffie-Hellman Assumption [16]). *For all non-uniform PPT adversaries $\mathcal{A}$:*

$$\Pr\left[[\mathbf{r}]_1, [\mathbf{s}]_2 \leftarrow \mathcal{A}(gk, [\mathbf{A}]_{1,2}) : \mathbf{r} \neq \mathbf{s} \wedge \mathbf{r}^\top \mathbf{A} = \mathbf{s}^\top \mathbf{A}\right] \approx 0,$$

where the probability is taken over $gk \leftarrow \mathcal{G}(1^\lambda)$, $\mathbf{A} \leftarrow \mathcal{D}_{\ell,k}$ and the coin tosses of adversary $\mathcal{A}$.

While the Kernel Diffie-Hellman Assumption says one cannot find a non-zero vector in one of the groups which is in the co-kernel of $\mathbf{A}$, the split assumption says one cannot find different vectors in $\mathbb{G}_1^\ell \times \mathbb{G}_2^\ell$ such that the difference of the vector of their discrete logarithms is in the co-kernel of $\mathbf{A}$. As a particular case, [16] considers the *Split Simultaneous Double Pairing Assumption in* $\mathbb{G}_1, \mathbb{G}_2$ (SSDP) which is the $\mathcal{RL}_2$-SKerMDH Assumption.

3 Linear Relations in a Bilinear Group

3.1 Algebraic Commitment Schemes

We present the type of commitments for which our QA-NIZK arguments can be used. These generalize many common schemes, like (multi-)Pedersen commitments and Groth–Sahai commitments. Our commitments are in the source groups, $\mathbb{G}_\gamma$ for $\gamma = 1, 2$, of a bilinear group. Let $\mathbf{F} \in \mathbb{Z}_p^{m \times n}$ and $\mathbf{U} \in \mathbb{Z}_p^{m \times \ell}$ be full-rank matrices. The commitment key is $ck = [\mathbf{F}, \mathbf{U}]_\gamma$, and the commitment to a message $\boldsymbol{x} \in \mathbb{Z}_p^n$ with randomness $\boldsymbol{r} \in \mathbb{Z}_p^\ell$ is defined as

$$\mathsf{Com}_{ck}(\boldsymbol{x}; \boldsymbol{r}) = [\mathbf{F}\boldsymbol{x} + \mathbf{U}\boldsymbol{r}]_\gamma.$$

Choosing the appropriate distributions for $([\mathbf{F}]_\gamma, [\mathbf{U}]_\gamma)$, we can have two commitment keys, one that produces a perfectly binding commitment scheme and one that produces a perfectly hiding commitment scheme, and these two key distributions are computationally indistinguishable under a MDDH assumption (see [11] for details). In the description of our schemes and the soundness proofs we will use the perfectly binding key, switching to perfectly hiding to argue that our schemes are zero-knowledge.

The most well-known example is Groth–Sahai commitments to integers: given $x \in \mathbb{Z}_p$ and randomness $r \in \mathbb{Z}_p$, this is an instantiation of the commitment defined above, with the matrices $\mathbf{F} \leftarrow \mathbb{Z}_p^2, \mathbf{U} \leftarrow \mathbb{Z}_p^2$ when in perfectly binding mode, and $\mathbf{F} \leftarrow \mathbb{Z}_p^2, \mathbf{U} = \lambda \mathbf{F}$ for $\lambda \leftarrow \mathbb{Z}_p$, when in perfectly hiding mode.

3.2 Linear Equations in a Bilinear Group

A set of linear equations split between the two sides of a bilinear group can be written as

$$\begin{pmatrix} [\boldsymbol{c}]_1 \\ [\boldsymbol{d}]_2 \end{pmatrix} = \begin{pmatrix} [\mathbf{M}]_1 \\ [\mathbf{N}]_2 \end{pmatrix} \boldsymbol{X},$$

where $\boldsymbol{X}$ is the vector of unknowns, $[\boldsymbol{c}, \mathbf{M}]_1$ are the coefficients in $\mathbb{G}_1$ and $[\boldsymbol{d}, \mathbf{N}]_2$ are the coefficients in $\mathbb{G}_2$. Thus, proving satisfiability of this system is equivalent to proving that there exist some vector $\boldsymbol{w}$ such that

$$\boldsymbol{w} \in \mathbf{Im}\begin{pmatrix} \mathbf{M} \\ \mathbf{N} \end{pmatrix}.$$

Thus, these proofs are usually seen as proofs of membership in a linear subspace, in this case split between $\mathbb{G}_1$ and $\mathbb{G}_2$. The problem of same opening of two algebraic commitments,

$$[\boldsymbol{c}]_1 = \mathsf{Com}_{ck_1}(\boldsymbol{x}; \boldsymbol{r}) = [\mathbf{F}\boldsymbol{x} + \mathbf{U}\boldsymbol{r}]_1, \qquad [\boldsymbol{d}]_1 = \mathsf{Com}_{ck_2}(\boldsymbol{x}; \boldsymbol{s}) = [\mathbf{G}\boldsymbol{x} + \mathbf{V}\boldsymbol{s}]_2$$

can be seen in this framework of membership in linear spaces, where

$$\begin{pmatrix} [\boldsymbol{c}]_1 \\ [\boldsymbol{d}]_2 \end{pmatrix} = \begin{pmatrix} [\mathbf{F}\,|\,\mathbf{U}\,|\,\mathbf{0}]_1 \\ [\mathbf{G}\,|\,\mathbf{0}\,|\,\mathbf{V}]_2 \end{pmatrix} \begin{pmatrix} \boldsymbol{x} \\ \boldsymbol{r} \\ \boldsymbol{s} \end{pmatrix}.$$

Since we are particularly interested in the case of same opening, we present our constructions directly for this application, although it would be easy to generalize to any matrices $[\mathbf{M}]_1, [\mathbf{N}]_2$, as long as they verify some conditions on their dimensions. As a warm-up, we develop first a non-aggregated version of the proof, as the main ideas are easier to visualize in this case.

4 Non-aggregated Scheme

Given $x \in \mathbb{Z}_p$ and two commitments $[\boldsymbol{c}]_1, [\boldsymbol{d}]_2$ to x, we provide a proof of both commitments opening to the same element x. More precisely, given a group description gk and commitment keys $ck_1 = [\boldsymbol{f}, \boldsymbol{u}] \in \mathbb{G}_1^{2 \times 2}$ and $ck_2 = [\boldsymbol{g}, \boldsymbol{v}]_2 \in \mathbb{G}_2^{2 \times 2}$, we want to prove F-knowledge in the language

$$\mathcal{L}_{gk,ck_1} = \{[\boldsymbol{c}]_1 \in \mathbb{G}_1^2 \mid \exists x, r \text{ s. t. } [\boldsymbol{c}]_1 = \mathsf{Com}_{ck_1}(x; r) = [x\boldsymbol{f} + r\boldsymbol{u}]_1\},$$

where $F(x, r) = [x]_{1,2}$.

- $gk := (p, \mathcal{P}_1, \mathcal{P}_2, \mathbb{G}_1, \mathbb{G}_2, \mathbb{G}_T, e) \leftarrow \mathcal{G}(1^\lambda)$.
- $\mathsf{K}_0(gk)$: set $ck_1 = [\boldsymbol{f}, \boldsymbol{u}]_1 \leftarrow \mathcal{D}_{\mathsf{par}}$, where $\mathcal{D}_{\mathsf{par}}$ is witness sampleable, that is, there exists an efficiently sampleable distribution $\tilde{\mathcal{D}}_{\mathsf{par}}$ outputting $(\tilde{\boldsymbol{f}}, \tilde{\boldsymbol{u}})$ such that $[\tilde{\boldsymbol{f}}, \tilde{\boldsymbol{u}}]_1$ is distributed as $[\boldsymbol{f}, \boldsymbol{u}]_1$.
- $\mathsf{K}_1(gk, ck_1)$: set $ck_2 = [\boldsymbol{g}, \boldsymbol{v}]_2$, where $\boldsymbol{g}, \boldsymbol{v} \leftarrow \mathbb{Z}_p^2$. Choose $a_1, a_2 \leftarrow \mathbb{Z}_p$ and also $\boldsymbol{k}_u, \hat{\boldsymbol{k}}_u, \boldsymbol{l}_v, \hat{\boldsymbol{l}}_v \leftarrow \mathbb{Z}_p^2$ conditioned on

$$\boldsymbol{l}_v^\top \boldsymbol{v} = \hat{\boldsymbol{l}}_v^\top \boldsymbol{v}, \tag{2}$$

Finally, choose $z_2 \leftarrow \mathbb{Z}_p$ and set

$$w = \frac{\boldsymbol{k}_u^\top \boldsymbol{f}}{\boldsymbol{l}_v^\top \boldsymbol{g}}, \qquad\qquad z_1 = z_2 w,$$

$$\hat{w} = \frac{\boldsymbol{k}_u^\top \boldsymbol{f}}{\hat{\boldsymbol{l}}_v^\top \boldsymbol{g}}, \qquad\qquad \hat{z}_1 = z_2 \hat{w}.$$

Algorithm K_1 outputs the following CRS:

$$\begin{pmatrix} gk, ck_1, [\boldsymbol{k}_u^\top \boldsymbol{u}]_1, [\hat{\boldsymbol{k}}_u^\top \boldsymbol{u}]_1, [a_1 w]_1, [a_2 \hat{w}]_1, [a_1 w \boldsymbol{l}_v]_1, [a_2 \hat{w} \hat{\boldsymbol{l}}_v]_1, [z_1]_1, [\hat{z}_1]_1, \\ ck_2, [\boldsymbol{l}_v^\top \boldsymbol{v}]_2, [a_1]_2, [a_2]_2, [a_1 \boldsymbol{k}_u]_2, [a_2 \hat{\boldsymbol{k}}_u]_2, [z_2]_2 \end{pmatrix}.$$

- $P(CRS, ([c]_1, x, r) \in \mathcal{R})$: commit to x in $\mathbb{G}_2$ by choosing $s \leftarrow \mathbb{Z}_p$ and setting

$$[d]_2 = \text{Com}_{ck_2}(x, s) = [xg + sv]_2.$$

Choose $\delta \leftarrow \mathbb{Z}_p$ and output $[d]_2$ and

$$[\pi]_1 = [rk_u^\top u + \delta z_1]_1, \qquad\qquad [\theta]_2 = [sl_v^\top v + \delta z_2]_2,$$
$$[\hat{\pi}]_1 = [r\hat{k}_u^\top u + \delta \hat{z}_1]_1,$$

- $V(CRS, [c]_1, ([d, \theta]_2, [\pi, \hat{\pi}]_1)$: The algorithm outputs 1 iff the following equations hold:

$$e\left([c^\top]_1, [a_1 k_u]_2\right) - e([a_1 wl_v^\top]_1, [d]_2) \stackrel{?}{=} e([\pi]_1, [a_1]_2) - e([a_1 w]_1, [\theta]_2),$$
$$e\left([c^\top]_1, [a_2 \hat{k}_u]_2\right) - e([a_2 \hat{w} \hat{l}_v^\top]_1, [d]_2) \stackrel{?}{=} e([\hat{\pi}]_1, [a_2]_2) - e([a_2 \hat{w}]_1, [\theta]_2).$$

Completeness. Both equations are analogous, and it is easy to see that for honest provers, using that $f^\top k_u = w(l_v^\top g)$, we have that

$$c^\top (a_1 k_u) - (a_1 wl_v^\top)d = (xf^\top + ru^\top)(a_1 k_u) - (a_1 wl_v^\top)(xg + sv)$$
$$= a_1 xf^\top k_u - a_1 x(wl_v^\top g) + (ru^\top k_u)a_1 - a_1 w(sv^\top l_v) = \pi a_1 - a_1 w\theta.$$

F-extractor. We now define the algorithm that, given the extraction key $xk = (f, g, u, v)$, outputs a function of the witness, in this case $F(x, r) = [x]_{1,2}$.

- $\text{Ext}_{xk}([c]_1, [d]_2)$: knowing f, u, we can find a vector $u^\perp$ such that $u^\top u^\perp = 0$ and $f^\top u^\perp = 1$, and compute $[c^\top]_1 u^\perp = [x]_1$. Similarly, we obtain $[x]_2$ from $[d]_2$, using g, v.

Theorem 1. *The above scheme is computationally F-knowledge sound under the $\mathcal{RL}_2$-SKerMDH assumption. More precisely, there exists an adversary $\mathcal{B}$ against the $\mathcal{RL}_2$-SKerMDH problem such that for any PPT adversary $\mathcal{A}$, we have that*

$$\text{Adv}_{F-\text{KnowledgeSoundness}}(\mathcal{A}) \leq \text{Adv}_{\mathcal{RL}_2\text{-SKerMDH}}(\mathcal{B}).$$

Proof. We assume the existence of an adversary $\mathcal{A}$ against the F-knowledge soundness of the scheme (that is, $\mathcal{A}$ is able to produce a statement and an accepting proof such that $\text{Ext}_{xk}([c]_1, [d]_2) = ([x]_1, [y]_2)$ and $x \neq y$), and we use it to build an adversary $\mathcal{B}$ against the $\mathcal{RL}_2$-SKerMDH problem. $\mathcal{B}$ receives the challenge matrix

$$[\mathbf{A}]_{1,2} = [a_1 \| a_2]_{1,2} = \begin{bmatrix} a_1 & 0 \\ 0 & a_2 \\ r_1 & r_2 \end{bmatrix}_{1,2},$$

and builds the environment for $\mathcal{A}$ as follows. $\mathcal{B}$ samples $f, u \leftarrow \tilde{\mathcal{D}}_{\text{par}}$ and $k_u', \hat{k}_u' \leftarrow \mathbb{Z}_p^2$, and $u^\perp \leftarrow \mathbb{Z}_p^2$ conditioned on $u^\top u^\perp = 0$. Implicitly, $\mathcal{B}$ defines

$$k_u = k_u' + a_1^{-1} r_1 u^\perp, \qquad \hat{k}_u = \hat{k}_u' + a_2^{-1} r_2 u^\perp.$$

Observe that this implies that

$$a_1 \boldsymbol{k}_u = a_1 \boldsymbol{k}'_u + r_1 \boldsymbol{u}^\perp, \qquad a_2 \hat{\boldsymbol{k}}_u = a_2 \hat{\boldsymbol{k}}'_u + r_2 \boldsymbol{u}^\perp, \tag{3}$$

which $\mathcal{B}$ can compute in $\mathbb{G}_2$. For the other side, $\mathcal{B}$ samples $\boldsymbol{g}, \boldsymbol{v} \leftarrow \mathbb{Z}_p^2$ and $\boldsymbol{l}'_v \leftarrow \mathbb{Z}_p^2$, and let $\boldsymbol{v}^\perp \in \mathbb{Z}_p^2$ be the unique vector such that $\boldsymbol{v}^\top \boldsymbol{v}^\perp = 0$ and

$$\boldsymbol{f}^\top \boldsymbol{u}^\perp = \boldsymbol{g}^\top \boldsymbol{v}^\perp. \tag{4}$$

$\mathcal{B}$ defines

$$w = \frac{\boldsymbol{k}'^\top_u \boldsymbol{f}}{\boldsymbol{l}'^\top_v \boldsymbol{g}}, \qquad \hat{w} = \frac{\hat{\boldsymbol{k}}'^\top_u \boldsymbol{f}}{\boldsymbol{l}'^\top_v \boldsymbol{g}}, \tag{5}$$

(note that $\boldsymbol{l}'_v$ is the same in both), and implicitly

$$\boldsymbol{l}_v = \boldsymbol{l}'_v + (a_1 w)^{-1} r_1 \boldsymbol{v}^\perp, \qquad \hat{\boldsymbol{l}}_v = \boldsymbol{l}'_v + (a_2 \hat{w})^{-1} r_2 \boldsymbol{v}^\perp,$$

which means that

$$a_1 w \boldsymbol{l}_v = a_1 w \boldsymbol{l}'_v + r_1 \boldsymbol{v}^\perp, \qquad a_2 \hat{w} \hat{\boldsymbol{l}}_v = a_2 \hat{w} \boldsymbol{l}'_v + r_2 \boldsymbol{v}^\perp, \tag{6}$$

and these can be computed in $\mathbb{G}_1$. Note that, by construction,

$$\frac{a_1 \boldsymbol{f}^\top \boldsymbol{k}_u}{a_1 w \boldsymbol{g}^\top \boldsymbol{l}_v} = \frac{a_1 \boldsymbol{f}^\top \boldsymbol{k}'_u + r_1 \boldsymbol{f}^\top \boldsymbol{u}^\perp}{a_1 w \boldsymbol{g}^\top \boldsymbol{l}'_v + r_1 \boldsymbol{g}^\top \boldsymbol{v}^\perp} = 1,$$

where we have used equalities (5) and (4), and therefore $w = \frac{\boldsymbol{f}^\top \boldsymbol{k}_u}{\boldsymbol{g}^\top \boldsymbol{l}_v}$. A similar argument shows that $\hat{w} = \frac{\boldsymbol{f}^\top \hat{\boldsymbol{k}}_u}{\boldsymbol{g}^\top \hat{\boldsymbol{l}}_v}$. $\mathcal{B}$ can also compute

$$[\boldsymbol{k}_u^\top \boldsymbol{u}]_1 = [\boldsymbol{k}'^\top_u \boldsymbol{u}]_1, \qquad [\hat{\boldsymbol{k}}_u^\top \boldsymbol{u}]_1 = [\hat{\boldsymbol{k}}'^\top_u \boldsymbol{u}]_1, \qquad [\boldsymbol{l}_v^\top \boldsymbol{v}]_2 = [\boldsymbol{l}'^\top_v \boldsymbol{v}]_2 = [\hat{\boldsymbol{l}}_v^\top \boldsymbol{v}]_2.$$

Finally, choose $z_2 \leftarrow \mathbb{Z}_p$ and set

$$z_1 = w z_2, \qquad \hat{z}_1 = \hat{w} z_2,$$

completing the CRS. The CRS is then sent to adversary $\mathcal{A}$, who outputs a statement $[\boldsymbol{c}]_1$ and a proof $[\boldsymbol{d}]_2, [\pi]_1, [\hat{\pi}]_1, [\theta]_2$ such that

$$\boldsymbol{c}^\top (a_1 \boldsymbol{k}_u) - (a_1 w \boldsymbol{l}_v^\top) \boldsymbol{d} = \pi a_1 - (a_1 w) \theta,$$
$$\boldsymbol{c}^\top (a_2 \hat{\boldsymbol{k}}_u) - (a_2 \hat{w} \hat{\boldsymbol{l}}_v^\top) \boldsymbol{d} = \hat{\pi} a_2 - (a_2 \hat{w}) \theta.$$

Notice that, using the equalities (3) and (6), we can rewrite these expressions in terms of the columns of $\mathbf{A}$. Indeed, these are equivalent to

$$\boldsymbol{c}^\top (\boldsymbol{k}'_u || \hat{\boldsymbol{k}}'_u || \boldsymbol{u}^\perp) \boldsymbol{a}_1 - \boldsymbol{d}^\top (w \boldsymbol{l}'_v || \hat{w} \boldsymbol{l}'_v || \boldsymbol{v}^\perp) \boldsymbol{a}_1 = (\pi, \hat{\pi}, 0) \boldsymbol{a}_1 - (w\theta, \hat{w}\theta, 0) \boldsymbol{a}_1,$$
$$\boldsymbol{c}^\top (\boldsymbol{k}'_u || \hat{\boldsymbol{k}}'_u || \boldsymbol{u}^\perp) \boldsymbol{a}_2 - \boldsymbol{d}^\top (w \boldsymbol{l}'_v || \hat{w} \boldsymbol{l}'_v || \boldsymbol{v}^\perp) \boldsymbol{a}_2 = (\pi, \hat{\pi}, 0) \boldsymbol{a}_2 - (w\theta, \hat{w}\theta, 0) \boldsymbol{a}_2.$$

We rearrange this as a solution of the $\mathcal{RL}_2$-SKerMDH problem that the reduction $\mathcal{B}$ can compute:

$$e([(\boldsymbol{c}^\top \boldsymbol{k}'_u - \pi || \boldsymbol{c}^\top \hat{\boldsymbol{k}}'_u - \hat{\pi} || \boldsymbol{c}^\top \boldsymbol{u}^\perp)]_1, [\mathbf{A}]_2) = e([(w(\boldsymbol{d}^\top \boldsymbol{l}'_v - \theta) || \hat{w}(\boldsymbol{d}^\top \boldsymbol{l}'_v - \theta) || \boldsymbol{d}^\top \boldsymbol{v}^\perp)]_2, [\mathbf{A}]_1).$$

It remains to argue that this is not the trivial solution. To do so, we look at the third component. As $\{\boldsymbol{f}, \boldsymbol{u}\}$ and $\{\boldsymbol{g}, \boldsymbol{v}\}$ are bases of $\mathbb{Z}_p^2$, we can write $\boldsymbol{c} = x\boldsymbol{f} + r\boldsymbol{u}$ and $\boldsymbol{d} = y\boldsymbol{g} + s\boldsymbol{v}$ for some $x, y, r, s \in \mathbb{Z}_p$. Since the proof provided by the adversary is false, it must be that $x \neq y$. Then, in the first equation, the third component on the left is $\boldsymbol{c}^\top \boldsymbol{u}^\perp = x\boldsymbol{f}^\top \boldsymbol{u}^\perp$, while the corresponding component on the right is $\boldsymbol{d}^\top \boldsymbol{v}^\perp = y\boldsymbol{g}^\top \boldsymbol{v}^\perp$. Since $\boldsymbol{f}^\top \boldsymbol{u}^\perp = \boldsymbol{g}^\top \boldsymbol{v}^\perp$ and $x \neq y$, these values are different. We conclude that we have found a nontrivial solution of the $\mathcal{RL}_2$-SKerMDH problem. □

Theorem 2. *The above scheme is composable zero-knowledge, with simulation trapdoor $\tau = (\boldsymbol{k}_u, \hat{\boldsymbol{k}}_u, \boldsymbol{l}_v)$.*

Proof. We switch to a game in which the commitments in $\mathbb{G}_2$ are perfectly hiding instead of perfectly binding, and prove that in this case the scheme has perfect zero-knowledge. The CRS simulator generates the CRS as in the honest execution of the protocol, and also outputs $\tau = (\boldsymbol{k}_u, \hat{\boldsymbol{k}}_u, \boldsymbol{l}_v)$ as the simulation trapdoor. The proof simulator chooses $\delta \leftarrow \mathbb{Z}_p$ and uses τ to produce:

$$[\boldsymbol{d}_{\mathsf{sim}}]_2 = \mathsf{Com}_{ck_2}(0; s) = s[\boldsymbol{v}]_2$$

$$[\pi_{\mathsf{sim}}]_1 = [\boldsymbol{c}^\top]_1 \boldsymbol{k}_u + \delta[z_1] \qquad [\theta_{\mathsf{sim}}]_2 = [\boldsymbol{d}_{\mathsf{sim}}^\top]\boldsymbol{l}_v + \delta[z_2]$$

$$[\hat{\pi}_{\mathsf{sim}}]_1 = [\boldsymbol{c}^\top]_1 \hat{\boldsymbol{k}}_u + \delta[\hat{z}_1]$$

We have that $\boldsymbol{d}_{\mathsf{sim}}$ is distributed as $\boldsymbol{d}$, as the commitment is perfectly hiding, and $\pi_{\mathsf{sim}}, \hat{\pi}_{\mathsf{sim}}, \theta_{\mathsf{sim}}$ are uniformly random elements conditioned on satisfying the verification equations for any fixed $\boldsymbol{c}, \boldsymbol{d}$, which is the same distribution that $\pi, \hat{\pi}, \theta$ have in an honest execution. □

5 Aggregated Scheme

Given $\boldsymbol{x} \in \mathbb{Z}_p^n$ and two commitments $[\boldsymbol{c}]_1, [\boldsymbol{d}]_2$ to $\boldsymbol{x}$, we provide a proof of both commitments opening to the same vector $\boldsymbol{x}$. More precisely, given a group description gk and commitment keys $ck_1 = [\mathbf{F}, \mathbf{U}]_1$, and $ck_2 = [\mathbf{G}, \mathbf{V}]_2$, where $\mathbf{F} \in \mathbb{Z}_p^{m_1 \times n}, \mathbf{G} \in \mathbb{Z}_p^{m_2 \times n}$ and $\mathbf{U} \in \mathbb{Z}_p^{m_1 \times \ell_1}, \mathbf{V} \in \mathbb{Z}_p^{m_2 \times \ell_2}$, we want to prove F-knowledge in the language

$$\mathcal{L}_{gk, ck_1} = \{[\boldsymbol{c}]_1 \in \mathbb{G}_1^{m_1} \mid \exists \boldsymbol{x}, \boldsymbol{r} \text{ s. t. } [\boldsymbol{c}]_1 = \mathsf{Com}_{ck_1}(\boldsymbol{x}; \boldsymbol{r})\},$$

where $F(\boldsymbol{x}, \boldsymbol{r}) = [\boldsymbol{x}]_{1,2}$.

- $gk := (p, \mathcal{P}_1, \mathcal{P}_2, \mathbb{G}_1, \mathbb{G}_2, \mathbb{G}_T, e) \leftarrow \mathcal{G}(1^\lambda)$.

- $K_0(gk)$: set $ck_1 = [\mathbf{F}, \mathbf{U}]_1 \leftarrow \mathcal{D}_{par}$, where $\mathcal{D}_{par}$ is witness sampleable, that is, there exists an efficiently sampleable distribution $\tilde{\mathcal{D}}_{par}$ outputting $(\tilde{\mathbf{F}}, \tilde{\mathbf{U}})$ such that $[\tilde{\mathbf{F}}, \tilde{\mathbf{U}}]_1$ is distributed as $[\mathbf{F}, \mathbf{U}]_1$.
- $K_1(gk, ck_1)$: set $ck_2 = [\mathbf{G}, \mathbf{V}]_2$, where $\mathbf{G} \leftarrow \mathbb{Z}_p^{m_2 \times n}, \mathbf{V} \leftarrow \mathbb{Z}_p^{m_2 \times \ell_2}$. Also choose $a_1, a_2 \leftarrow \mathbb{Z}_p$ and $\boldsymbol{k}_u, \hat{\boldsymbol{k}}_u \leftarrow \mathbb{Z}_p^{m_1}$. Set $\boldsymbol{l}_v, \hat{\boldsymbol{l}}_v \leftarrow \mathbb{Z}_p^{m_2}$ conditioned on

$$\boldsymbol{l}_v^\top \mathbf{V} = \hat{\boldsymbol{l}}_v^\top \mathbf{V}, \qquad \boldsymbol{k}_u^\top \mathbf{F} = w(\boldsymbol{l}_v^\top \mathbf{G}), \qquad \hat{\boldsymbol{k}}_u^\top \mathbf{F} = \hat{w}(\hat{\boldsymbol{l}}_v^\top \mathbf{G}), \qquad (7)$$

for some $w, \hat{w} \leftarrow \mathbb{Z}_p$. Choose $z_2 \leftarrow \mathbb{Z}_p$ and set

$$z_1 = wz_2, \qquad \hat{z}_1 = \hat{w}z_2.$$

Algorithm K_1 outputs the following CRS:

$$\begin{pmatrix} gk, [\mathbf{U}^\top \boldsymbol{k}_u]_1, [\mathbf{U}^\top \hat{\boldsymbol{k}}_u]_1, [a_1 w]_1, [a_2 \hat{w}]_1, [a_1 w \boldsymbol{l}_v]_1, [a_2 \hat{w} \hat{\boldsymbol{l}}_v]_1, [z_1]_1, [\hat{z}_1]_1, \\ [\mathbf{V}^\top \boldsymbol{l}_v]_2, [a_1]_2, [a_2]_2, [a_1 \boldsymbol{k}_u]_2, [a_2 \hat{\boldsymbol{k}}_u]_2, [z_2]_2 \end{pmatrix}.$$

- $P(\text{CRS}, ([\boldsymbol{c}]_1, (\boldsymbol{x}, \boldsymbol{r})) \in \mathcal{R})$: commit to $\boldsymbol{x}$ in $\mathbb{G}_2$ as $[\boldsymbol{d}]_2$. Choose $\delta \leftarrow \mathbb{Z}_p$ and output $[\boldsymbol{d}]_2$ and

$$[\pi]_1 = [\boldsymbol{r}^\top \mathbf{U}^\top \boldsymbol{k}_u + \delta z_1]_1, \qquad\qquad [\theta]_2 = [\boldsymbol{s}^\top \mathbf{V}^\top \boldsymbol{l}_v + \delta z_2]_2,$$
$$[\hat{\pi}]_1 = [\boldsymbol{r}^\top \hat{\mathbf{U}}^\top \boldsymbol{k}_u + \delta \hat{z}_1]_1,$$

- $V(\text{CRS}, [\boldsymbol{c}]_1, ([\boldsymbol{d}, \theta]_2, [\pi, \hat{\pi}]_1))$: The algorithm outputs 1 iff the following equations hold:

$$e\left([\boldsymbol{c}^\top]_1, [a_1 \boldsymbol{k}_u]_2\right) - e([a_1 w \boldsymbol{l}_v^\top]_1, [\boldsymbol{d}]_2) \stackrel{?}{=} e([\pi]_1, [a_1]_2) - e([a_1 w]_1, [\theta]_2),$$
$$e\left([\boldsymbol{c}^\top]_1, [a_2 \hat{\boldsymbol{k}}_u]_2\right) - e([a_2 \hat{w} \hat{\boldsymbol{l}}_v^\top]_1, [\boldsymbol{d}]_2) \stackrel{?}{=} e([\hat{\pi}]_1, [a_2]_2) - e([a_2 \hat{w}]_1, [\theta]_2).$$

Completeness. It is easy to check that, if the prover is honest,

$$\boldsymbol{c}^\top (a_1 \boldsymbol{k}_u) - (a_1 w \boldsymbol{l}_v^\top)\boldsymbol{d} = (\boldsymbol{x}^\top \mathbf{F}^\top + \boldsymbol{r}^\top \mathbf{U}^\top)(a_1 \boldsymbol{k}_u) - (a_1 w \boldsymbol{l}_v^\top)(\mathbf{G}\boldsymbol{x} + \mathbf{V}\boldsymbol{s})$$
$$= a_1 \boldsymbol{x}^\top \mathbf{F}^\top \boldsymbol{k}_u - a_1(w \boldsymbol{l}_v^\top \mathbf{G})\boldsymbol{x} + a_1 \boldsymbol{r}^\top \mathbf{U}^\top \boldsymbol{k}_u - a_1 w \boldsymbol{l}_v^\top \mathbf{V}\boldsymbol{s} = \pi a_1 - a_1 w \theta.$$

We have used that $\boldsymbol{k}_u^\top \mathbf{F} = w(\boldsymbol{l}_v^\top \mathbf{G})$. The second equation is completely analogous.

Note on Dimensions. For this scheme to work and be secure, we require some relations between the dimensions of the different elements involved.

(1) We want our commitments to be perfectly binding to be able to open the commitments in the source groups, so we require that $m_i \geq n + \ell_i$, for $i = 1, 2$.

(2) To be able to find $l_v, \hat{l}_v$ verifying the Eq. (7), we need to solve the linear system

$$\begin{pmatrix} \mathbf{G}^\top & \mathbf{0} \\ \mathbf{0} & \mathbf{G}^\top \\ \mathbf{V}^\top & -\mathbf{V} \end{pmatrix} \begin{pmatrix} l_v \\ \hat{l}_v \end{pmatrix} = \begin{pmatrix} \mathbf{F}^\top k_u \\ \mathbf{F}^\top \hat{k}_u \\ \mathbf{0} \end{pmatrix}.$$

Since $\mathbf{F}$ is only known in $\mathbb{G}_1$, the system cannot be fully solved over $\mathbb{Z}_p$. However, we do not need the full solution over $\mathbb{Z}_p$, as only the projection $\mathbf{V}^\top l_v$ needs to be given in $\mathbb{G}_2$, while the full l_v is necessary in $\mathbb{G}_1$. Thus we proceed as follows: we start by sampling $t \leftarrow \mathbb{Z}_p^{\ell_2}$ and setting $\mathbf{V}^\top l_v = \mathbf{V}^\top \hat{l}_v = t$. Then we consider the system

$$\begin{pmatrix} \mathbf{G}^\top & \mathbf{0} \\ \mathbf{0} & \mathbf{G}^\top \\ \mathbf{V}^\top & \mathbf{0} \\ \mathbf{0} & \mathbf{V} \end{pmatrix} \begin{pmatrix} l_v \\ \hat{l}_v \end{pmatrix} = \begin{pmatrix} \mathbf{F}^\top k_u \\ \mathbf{F}^\top \hat{k}_u \\ t \\ t \end{pmatrix}.$$

The matrix is known over $\mathbb{Z}_p$ and the right hand side is known over $\mathbb{G}_1$ (since $\mathbf{F}$ is known over $\mathbb{G}_1$ and the rest is known over $\mathbb{Z}_p$), so the system can be solved over $\mathbb{G}_1$ using Gaussian elimination. The system has solutions if $2m_2 \geq 2n + 2\ell_2$, which is implied by condition (1) above.

(3) In the proof of the zero-knowledge property, we want to be able to switch the commitment in $\mathbb{G}_2$ to perfectly hiding, so we need to ensure that it has enough randomness. Thus $\ell_2 \geq n$.

(4) Consider the matrices $(\mathbf{F}\|\mathbf{U})$ and $(\mathbf{G}\|\mathbf{V})$. These are of size $m_i \times (n + \ell_i)$, for $i = 1, 2$, respectively. In the soundness reduction we will be interested in finding nonzero vectors $u^\perp, v^\perp$ such that $w^\top u^\perp = 0$ for any vector w outside of the span of the columns of $\mathbf{F}$, and the same for $v^\perp$ and $\mathbf{G}$. Additionally, we will require that

$$\mathbf{F}^\top u^\perp = \mathbf{G}^\top v^\perp.$$

As we have already established that $m_i \geq n + \ell_i$, we might need to add more columns to the matrices $(\mathbf{F}\|\mathbf{U})$ and $(\mathbf{G}\|\mathbf{V})$ so that they form bases of $\mathbb{Z}_p^{m_i}$, so let $\overline{\mathbf{U}}, \overline{\mathbf{V}} \in \mathbb{Z}_p^{m_i \times (m_i - n)}$ be the augmented matrices such that $(\mathbf{F}\|\overline{\mathbf{U}})$ and $(\mathbf{G}\|\overline{\mathbf{V}})$ are bases of $\mathbb{Z}_p^{m_i}$ for $i = 1, 2$, respectively. Then the vectors $u^\perp, v^\perp$ are given by the nontrivial solutions of the linear system

$$\begin{pmatrix} \overline{\mathbf{U}}^\top & \mathbf{0} \\ \mathbf{0} & \overline{\mathbf{V}}^\top \\ \mathbf{F}^\top & -\mathbf{G}^\top \end{pmatrix} \begin{pmatrix} u^\perp \\ v^\perp \end{pmatrix} = \mathbf{0}.$$

This matrix is of size $(m_1 + m_2 - n) \times (m_1 + m_2)$, and therefore it has nontrivial solutions.

F-extractor. We now define the algorithm that, given the extraction key $xk = (\mathbf{F}, \mathbf{G}, \mathbf{U}, \mathbf{V})$, outputs a function of the witness, in this case $F(x, r) = [x]_{1,2}$.

– $\text{Ext}_{xk}([c]_1, [d]_2)$: as above, consider $\overline{\mathbf{U}}, \overline{\mathbf{V}}$ so that $(\mathbf{F}||\overline{\mathbf{U}})$ and $(\mathbf{G}||\overline{\mathbf{V}})$ are bases of $\mathbb{Z}_p^{m_i}$ for $i = 1, 2$, respectively. Knowing $\mathbf{F}, \overline{\mathbf{U}}$, we can find a matrix $\mathbf{U}^\perp \in \mathbb{Z}_p^{m_1 \times n}$ such that $\overline{\mathbf{U}}^\top \mathbf{U}^\perp = \mathbf{0}$ and $\mathbf{F}^\top \mathbf{U}^\perp = \mathbf{I}$, and compute $[c^\top]_1 \mathbf{U}^\perp = [x]_1$. Similarly, we obtain $[x]_2$ from $[d]_2$, using $\mathbf{G}, \overline{\mathbf{V}}$.

Theorem 3. *The above proof system is computationally F-knowledge sound under the $\mathcal{RL}_2$-SKerMDH assumption. More precisely, there exists an adversary $\mathcal{B}$ against the $\mathcal{RL}_2$-SKerMDH problem such that for any PPT adversary $\mathcal{A}$, we have that*

$$\text{Adv}_{F-\text{KnowledgeSoundness}}(\mathcal{A}) \leq \text{Adv}_{\mathcal{RL}_2\text{-SKerMDH}}(\mathcal{B})$$

Proof. Assume that there is an adversary $\mathcal{A}$ against the soundness of the scheme ($\mathcal{A}$ is able to produce a statement and an accepting proof such that $\text{Ext}_{xk}([c]_1, [d]_2) = ([x]_1, [y]_2)$ and $x \neq y$). We use it to build an adversary $\mathcal{B}$ against the $\mathcal{RL}_2$-SKerMDH problem. $\mathcal{B}$ receives the challenge matrix

$$[\mathbf{A}]_{1,2} = [a_1 || a_2]_{1,2} = \begin{bmatrix} a_1 & 0 \\ 0 & a_2 \\ r_1 & r_2 \end{bmatrix}_{1,2},$$

and builds the environment for $\mathcal{A}$ as follows. We sample $\mathbf{G} \leftarrow \mathbb{Z}_p^{m_2 \times n}, \mathbf{V} \leftarrow \mathbb{Z}_p^{m_2 \times \ell_2}$, and let $\overline{\mathbf{V}}$ be as in (4) above. We choose $w, \hat{w} \leftarrow \mathbb{Z}_p$ and $l_v' \leftarrow \mathbb{Z}_p^{m_2}$ Let $v^\perp \in \mathbb{Z}_p^{m_2}$ such that $\overline{\mathbf{V}}^\top v^\perp = 0$. Implicitly set

$$l_v = l_v' + (a_1 w)^{-1} r_1 v^\perp, \qquad \hat{l}_v = l_v' + (a_2 \hat{w})^{-1} r_2 v^\perp.$$

Observe that this implies that

$$a_1 w l_v = a_1 w l_v' + r_1 v^\perp, \qquad a_2 \hat{w} \hat{l}_v = a_2 \hat{w} l_v' + r_2 v^\perp, \tag{8}$$

which we can compute over $\mathbb{G}_1$. For the other side, we sample $(\mathbf{F}, \mathbf{U}) \leftarrow \tilde{\mathcal{D}}_{\text{par}}$ and define $\overline{\mathbf{U}}$ as in (4) above. We also sample $k_u', \hat{k}_u' \leftarrow \mathbb{Z}_p^{m_1}$ conditioned on

$$k_u'^\top \mathbf{F} = w(l_v'^\top \mathbf{G}), \qquad \hat{k}_u'^\top \mathbf{F} = \hat{w}(\hat{l}_v'^\top \mathbf{G}). \tag{9}$$

Let $u^\perp \in \mathbb{Z}_p^{m_1}$ such that $\overline{\mathbf{U}}^\top u^\perp = 0$ and

$$\mathbf{F}^\top u^\perp = \mathbf{G}^\top v^\perp. \tag{10}$$

We implicitly define

$$k_u = k_u' + a_1^{-1} r_1 u^\perp, \qquad \hat{k}_u = \hat{k}_u' + a_2^{-1} r_2 u^\perp.$$

which means that

$$a_1 k_u = a_1 k_u' + r_1 u^\perp, \qquad a_2 \hat{k}_u = a_2 \hat{k}_u' + r_2 u^\perp. \tag{11}$$

Note that, by construction,

$$a_1 w \mathbf{G}^\top \boldsymbol{l}_v = a_1 w \mathbf{G}^\top \boldsymbol{l}'_v + r_1 \mathbf{G}^\top \boldsymbol{v}^\perp = a_1 \mathbf{F}^\top \boldsymbol{k}'_u + r_1 \mathbf{F}^\top \boldsymbol{u}^\perp = a_1 \mathbf{F}^\top \boldsymbol{k}_u$$

where we have used equalities (9) and (10), and therefore $\mathbf{F}^\top \boldsymbol{k}_u = w(\mathbf{G}^\top \boldsymbol{l}_v)$ A similar argument shows that $\mathbf{F}^\top \hat{\boldsymbol{k}}_u = \hat{w}(\mathbf{G}^\top \hat{\boldsymbol{l}}_v)$. We can also compute

$$[\boldsymbol{k}_u^\top \mathbf{U}]_1 = [\boldsymbol{k}'^\top_u \mathbf{U}]_1, \qquad [\hat{\boldsymbol{k}}_u^\top \mathbf{U}]_1 = [\hat{\boldsymbol{k}}'^\top_u \mathbf{U}]_1, \qquad [\boldsymbol{l}_v^\top \mathbf{V}]_2 = [\boldsymbol{l}'^\top_v \mathbf{V}]_2 = [\hat{\boldsymbol{l}}_v^\top \mathbf{V}]_2.$$

Finally, choose $z_2 \leftarrow \mathbb{Z}_p$ and set

$$z_1 = w z_2, \qquad \hat{z}_1 = \hat{w} z_2,$$

completing the CRS. The CRS is then sent to adversary $\mathcal{A}$, who outputs a statement $[\boldsymbol{c}]_1, [\boldsymbol{d}]_2$ and a proof $[\pi]_1, [\hat{\pi}]_1, [\theta]_2$ such that

$$\boldsymbol{c}^\top(a_1 \boldsymbol{k}_u) - (a_1 w \boldsymbol{l}_v^\top)\boldsymbol{d} = \pi a_1 - (a_1 w)\theta,$$
$$\boldsymbol{c}^\top(a_2 \hat{\boldsymbol{k}}_u) - (a_2 \hat{w} \hat{\boldsymbol{l}}_v^\top)\boldsymbol{d} = \hat{\pi} a_2 - (a_2 \hat{w})\theta.$$

Notice that, using equalities (11) and (8), we can rewrite these expressions in terms of the columns of $\mathbf{A}$. Indeed, these are equivalent to

$$\boldsymbol{c}^\top(\boldsymbol{k}'_u \| \hat{\boldsymbol{k}}'_u \| \boldsymbol{u}^\perp)\boldsymbol{a}_1 - \boldsymbol{d}^\top(w \boldsymbol{l}'_v \| \hat{w} \boldsymbol{l}'_v \| \boldsymbol{v}^\perp)\boldsymbol{a}_1 = (\pi, \hat{\pi}, 0)\boldsymbol{a}_1 - (w\theta, \hat{w}\theta, 0)\boldsymbol{a}_1,$$
$$\boldsymbol{c}^\top(\boldsymbol{k}'_u \| \hat{\boldsymbol{k}}'_u \| \boldsymbol{u}^\perp)\boldsymbol{a}_2 - \boldsymbol{d}^\top(w \boldsymbol{l}'_v \| \hat{w} \boldsymbol{l}'_v \| \boldsymbol{v}^\perp)\boldsymbol{a}_2 = (\pi, \hat{\pi}, 0)\boldsymbol{a}_2 - (w\theta, \hat{w}\theta, 0)\boldsymbol{a}_2,$$

We rearrange this as a solution of the $\mathcal{RL}_2$-SKerMDH problem that the reduction can compute:

$$e([(\boldsymbol{c}^\top \boldsymbol{k}'_u - \pi \| \boldsymbol{c}^\top \hat{\boldsymbol{k}}'_u - \hat{\pi} \| \boldsymbol{c}^\top \boldsymbol{u}^\perp)]_1, [\mathbf{A}]_2) = e([(w(\boldsymbol{d}^\top \boldsymbol{l}'_v - \theta) \| \hat{w}(\boldsymbol{d}^\top \boldsymbol{l}'_v - \theta) \| \boldsymbol{d}^\top \boldsymbol{v}^\perp)]_2, [\mathbf{A}]_1).$$

It remains to argue that this is not the trivial solution. To do so, we look at the third component. As the columns of $(\mathbf{F} \| \overline{\mathbf{U}})$ and $(\mathbf{G} \| \overline{\mathbf{V}})$ are bases of $\mathbb{Z}_p^{m_i}$ for $i = 1, 2$, respectively, we can write $\boldsymbol{c} = \mathbf{F}\boldsymbol{x} + \overline{\mathbf{U}}\boldsymbol{r}$ and $\boldsymbol{d} = \mathbf{G}\boldsymbol{y} + \overline{\mathbf{V}}\boldsymbol{s}$ for some $\boldsymbol{x}, \boldsymbol{y} \in \mathbb{Z}_p^n, \boldsymbol{r}, \boldsymbol{s} \in \mathbb{Z}_p^\ell$. Since the proof provided by the adversary is false, it must be that $\boldsymbol{x} \neq \boldsymbol{y}$. Then, in the first equation, the third component on the left is $\boldsymbol{c}^\top \boldsymbol{u}^\perp = \boldsymbol{x}^\top \mathbf{F}^\top \boldsymbol{u}^\perp$, while the corresponding component on the right is $\boldsymbol{d}^\top \boldsymbol{v}^\perp = \boldsymbol{y}^\top \mathbf{G}^\top \boldsymbol{v}^\perp$. Since $\mathbf{F}^\top \boldsymbol{u}^\perp = \mathbf{G}^\top \boldsymbol{v}^\perp$ and $\boldsymbol{x} \neq \boldsymbol{y}$, these values are different. We conclude that we have found a nontrivial solution of the $\mathcal{RL}_2$-SKerMDH problem. $\square$

Theorem 4. *The above proof system is composable zero-knowledge, with simulation trapdoor* $\tau = (\boldsymbol{k}_u, \hat{\boldsymbol{k}}_u, \boldsymbol{l}_v)$.

The proof is completely analogous to the proof of Theorem 2.

6 Optimality of Our Constructions

We argue that our constructions are optimal in terms of proof size, at least based
on this general strategy of commit-and-prove schemes, and where the prover is
limited to linear algebraic operations on the group elements, and verification is
a pairing equation. To the best of our knowledge, this is the approach that is
always taken in the literature. We prove optimality by arguing that any such
proof formed of two elements (plus the commitments) is vulnerable to an attack.

We now consider any proof in which we have two commitments $[c]_1$ and $[d]_2$
to the values x and y, respectively, and we have a two-element proof $[\pi]_1, [\theta]_2$
of same opening, that is, $x = y$. We consider a CRS formed of elements in
$\mathbb{G}_1$ and $\mathbb{G}_2$, and we assume that each side of the CRS is closed under linear
combination. We can do this without loss of generality, since given the CRS it
is easy to compute linear combinations of its elements.

Then the general verification equation of such a proof looks like this:

$$e([\boldsymbol{c}^\top]_1, [\boldsymbol{k}_1]_2) + e([\boldsymbol{k}_2^\top]_1, [\boldsymbol{d}]_2) + e([\pi]_1, [k_3]_2) + e([k_4]_1, [\theta]_2) = [0]_T, \qquad (12)$$

where $[\boldsymbol{k}_1, k_3]_2, [\boldsymbol{k}_2, k_4]_1$ are elements (some of them vectors of elements) of the
CRS. We note two omissions from this general equation: there is no affine term
and there are no "quadratic" terms, i.e., terms in $\boldsymbol{c}^\top\boldsymbol{d}, \pi\boldsymbol{d}, c\theta$ or $\pi\theta$. This is
because the linear terms (those in Eq. (12)) force π and θ to be linear in the
witness, and so the terms above are quadratic. The quadratic condition causes
the appearance of terms with coefficient xy, which must cancelled out with other
quadratic terms of the same coefficient. We note that, unlike in the linear part,
this check does not make a distinction when $x = y$ or $x \neq y$, so we conclude that
these quadratic terms do not contribute to achieving soundness. The intuition
behind this is that we are proving membership in a linear space, and non-linear
operations take us out of the space.

This leaves us with the Eq. (12) above. We now observe a very simple attack
on any scheme with a verification equation like this. We set

$$[\boldsymbol{c}]_1 = \boldsymbol{\alpha}[k_4]_1, \qquad\qquad [\boldsymbol{d}]_2 = \boldsymbol{\beta}[k_3]_2,$$
$$[\pi]_1 = -\boldsymbol{\beta}^\top[\boldsymbol{k}_2]_1, \qquad\qquad [\theta]_2 = -\boldsymbol{\alpha}^\top[\boldsymbol{k}_1]_2,$$

where $\boldsymbol{\alpha}, \boldsymbol{\beta} \leftarrow \mathbb{Z}_p^2$. It is trivial to verify that the first term in the equation
cancels out with the fourth and the second with the third, and with overwhelming
probability the openings of $[\boldsymbol{c}]_1$ and $[\boldsymbol{d}]_2$ do not match. Intuitively, this attack
works because of the two-sided nature of the proof: the elements that are given
in the CRS to ensure verifiability in one side are used to fool the other. Indeed,
in an honest execution the first term is expected to cancel out with the third,
and the second with the fourth, while in this attack the pairs are jumbled.

One could also consider one-sided two-element proofs, i.e., of the form
$[\pi_1, \pi_2]_1$ or $[\theta_1, \theta_2]_2$, but these can be handled in a very similar way. For example,
in the first case, the general verification equation would be

$$e([\boldsymbol{c}^\top]_1, [\boldsymbol{k}_1]_2) + e([\boldsymbol{k}_2^\top]_1, [\boldsymbol{d}]_2) + e([\pi_1]_1, [k_3]_2) + e([\pi_2]_1, [k_4]_2) = [0]_T, \qquad (13)$$

and the attack would consist of setting

$$[\boldsymbol{c}]_1 = \alpha[\boldsymbol{k}_2]_1, \qquad\qquad [\boldsymbol{d}]_2 = \beta(r[k_3]_2 + s[k_4]_2) - \alpha[\boldsymbol{k}_1]_2,$$
$$[\pi_1]_1 = -r\boldsymbol{\beta}^\top[\boldsymbol{k}_2]_1, \qquad\qquad [\pi_2]_1 = -s\boldsymbol{\beta}^\top[\boldsymbol{k}_2]_1,$$

for $\beta \leftarrow \mathbb{Z}_p^2, \alpha, r, s \leftarrow \mathbb{Z}_p$. Thus we conclude that, with this approach, there is no possible proof of same opening of commitments in different groups which consists of less than three group elements, making our constructions optimal.

Acknowledgements. The second author was supported by a PhD grant from the Spanish government, co-financed by the ESF (Ayudas paracontratos predoctorales para la formación de doctores 2016).

References

1. Abe, M., Ambrona, M., Ohkubo, M., Tibouchi, M.: Lower bounds on structure-preserving signatures for bilateral messages. In: Catalano, D., De Prisco, R. (eds.) SCN 2018. LNCS, vol. 11035, pp. 3–22. Springer, Cham (2018). https://doi.org/10.1007/978-3-319-98113-0_1

2. Abe, M., Jutla, C.S., Ohkubo, M., Roy, A.: Improved (almost) tightly-secure simulation-sound QA-NIZK with applications. In: Peyrin, T., Galbraith, S. (eds.) ASIACRYPT 2018, Part I. LNCS, vol. 11272, pp. 627–656. Springer, Cham (2018). https://doi.org/10.1007/978-3-030-03326-2_21

3. Belenkiy, M., Chase, M., Kohlweiss, M., Lysyanskaya, A.: Compact E-cash and simulatable VRFs revisited. In: Shacham, H., Waters, B. (eds.) Pairing 2009. LNCS, vol. 5671, pp. 114–131. Springer, Heidelberg (2009). https://doi.org/10.1007/978-3-642-03298-1_9

4. Bernhard, D., Fuchsbauer, G., Ghadafi, E.: Efficient signatures of knowledge and DAA in the standard model. In: Jacobson, M., Locasto, M., Mohassel, P., Safavi-Naini, R. (eds.) ACNS 2013. LNCS, vol. 7954, pp. 518–533. Springer, Heidelberg (2013). https://doi.org/10.1007/978-3-642-38980-1_33

5. Boyen, X., Waters, B.: Full-domain subgroup hiding and constant-size group signatures. In: Okamoto, T., Wang, X. (eds.) PKC 2007. LNCS, vol. 4450, pp. 1–15. Springer, Heidelberg (2007). https://doi.org/10.1007/978-3-540-71677-8_1

6. Camenisch, J., Chaabouni, R., Shelat, A.: Efficient protocols for set membership and range proofs. In: Pieprzyk, J. (ed.) ASIACRYPT 2008. LNCS, vol. 5350, pp. 234–252. Springer, Heidelberg (2008). https://doi.org/10.1007/978-3-540-89255-7_15

7. Chaidos, P., Cortier, V., Fuchsbauer, G., Galindo, D.: BeleniosRF: a non-interactive receipt-free electronic voting scheme. In: Weippl, E.R., Katzenbeisser, S., Kruegel, C., Myers, A.C., Halevi, S. (eds.) ACM CCS 2016, Vienna, Austria, 24–28 October 2016, pp. 1614–1625. ACM Press (2016)

8. Chandran, N., Groth, J., Sahai, A.: Ring signatures of sub-linear size without random oracles. In: Arge, L., Cachin, C., Jurdziński, T., Tarlecki, A. (eds.) ICALP 2007. LNCS, vol. 4596, pp. 423–434. Springer, Heidelberg (2007). https://doi.org/10.1007/978-3-540-73420-8_38

9. Couteau, G., Hartmann, D.: Shorter non-interactive zero-knowledge arguments and zaps for algebraic languages (2020)

10. Escala, A., Groth, J.: Fine-tuning Groth-Sahai proofs. In: Krawczyk, H. (ed.) PKC 2014. LNCS, vol. 8383, pp. 630–649. Springer, Heidelberg (2014). https://doi.org/10.1007/978-3-642-54631-0_36

11. Escala, A., Herold, G., Kiltz, E., Ràfols, C., Villar, J.: An algebraic framework for Diffie-Hellman assumptions. In: Canetti, R., Garay, J.A. (eds.) CRYPTO 2013, Part II. LNCS, vol. 8043, pp. 129–147. Springer, Heidelberg (2013). https://doi.org/10.1007/978-3-642-40084-1_8

12. Escala, A., Herold, G., Kiltz, E., Ràfols, C., Villar, J.L.: An algebraic framework for Diffie-Hellman assumptions. J. Cryptol. **30**(1), 242–288 (2017)

13. Fuchsbauer, G.: Commuting signatures and verifiable encryption. In: Paterson, K.G. (ed.) EUROCRYPT 2011. LNCS, vol. 6632, pp. 224–245. Springer, Heidelberg (2011). https://doi.org/10.1007/978-3-642-20465-4_14

14. Ghadafi, E.M.: Sub-linear blind ring signatures without random oracles. In: Stam, M. (ed.) IMACC 2013. LNCS, vol. 8308, pp. 304–323. Springer, Heidelberg (2013). https://doi.org/10.1007/978-3-642-45239-0_18

15. González, A.: Shorter ring signatures from standard assumptions. In: Lin, D., Sako, K. (eds.) PKC 2019. LNCS, vol. 11442, pp. 99–126. Springer, Cham (2019). https://doi.org/10.1007/978-3-030-17253-4_4

16. González, A., Hevia, A., Ràfols, C.: QA-NIZK arguments in asymmetric groups: new tools and new constructions. In: Iwata, T., Cheon, J.H. (eds.) ASIACRYPT 2015, Part I. LNCS, vol. 9452, pp. 605–629. Springer, Heidelberg (2015). https://doi.org/10.1007/978-3-662-48797-6_25

17. Groth, J.: Simulation-sound NIZK proofs for a practical language and constant size group signatures. In: Lai, X., Chen, K. (eds.) ASIACRYPT 2006. LNCS, vol. 4284, pp. 444–459. Springer, Heidelberg (2006). https://doi.org/10.1007/11935230_29

18. Groth, J., Lu, S.: A non-interactive shuffle with pairing based verifiability. In: Kurosawa, K. (ed.) ASIACRYPT 2007. LNCS, vol. 4833, pp. 51–67. Springer, Heidelberg (2007). https://doi.org/10.1007/978-3-540-76900-2_4

19. Groth, J., Ostrovsky, R., Sahai, A.: Non-interactive zaps and new techniques for NIZK. In: Dwork, C. (ed.) CRYPTO 2006. LNCS, vol. 4117, pp. 97–111. Springer, Heidelberg (2006). https://doi.org/10.1007/11818175_6

20. Groth, J., Ostrovsky, R., Sahai, A.: Perfect non-interactive zero knowledge for NP. In: Vaudenay, S. (ed.) EUROCRYPT 2006. LNCS, vol. 4004, pp. 339–358. Springer, Heidelberg (2006). https://doi.org/10.1007/11761679_21

21. Groth, J., Sahai, A.: Efficient non-interactive proof systems for bilinear groups. In: Smart, N. (ed.) EUROCRYPT 2008. LNCS, vol. 4965, pp. 415–432. Springer, Heidelberg (2008). https://doi.org/10.1007/978-3-540-78967-3_24

22. Hofheinz, D., Jager, T.: Tightly secure signatures and public-key encryption. Des. Codes Crypt. **80**(1), 29–61 (2015). https://doi.org/10.1007/s10623-015-0062-x

23. Jutla, C.S., Roy, A.: Shorter quasi-adaptive NIZK proofs for linear subspaces. In: Sako, K., Sarkar, P. (eds.) ASIACRYPT 2013, Part I. LNCS, vol. 8269, pp. 1–20. Springer, Heidelberg (2013). https://doi.org/10.1007/978-3-642-42033-7_1

24. Jutla, C.S., Roy, A.: Switching lemma for bilinear tests and constant-size NIZK proofs for linear subspaces. In: Garay, J.A., Gennaro, R. (eds.) CRYPTO 2014, Part II. LNCS, vol. 8617, pp. 295–312. Springer, Heidelberg (2014). https://doi.org/10.1007/978-3-662-44381-1_17

25. Kiltz, E., Pan, J., Wee, H.: Structure-preserving signatures from standard assumptions, revisited. In: Gennaro, R., Robshaw, M. (eds.) CRYPTO 2015, Part II. LNCS, vol. 9216, pp. 275–295. Springer, Heidelberg (2015). https://doi.org/10.1007/978-3-662-48000-7_14

26. Kiltz, E., Wee, H.: Quasi-adaptive NIZK for linear subspaces revisited. In: Oswald, E., Fischlin, M. (eds.) EUROCRYPT 2015, Part II. LNCS, vol. 9057, pp. 101–128. Springer, Heidelberg (2015). https://doi.org/10.1007/978-3-662-46803-6_4
27. Libert, B., Peters, T., Joye, M., Yung, M.: Non-malleability from malleability: simulation-sound quasi-adaptive NIZK proofs and CCA2-secure encryption from homomorphic signatures. In: Nguyen, P.Q., Oswald, E. (eds.) EUROCRYPT 2014. LNCS, vol. 8441, pp. 514–532. Springer, Heidelberg (2014). https://doi.org/10.1007/978-3-642-55220-5_29
28. Libert, B., Peters, T., Yung, M.: Short group signatures via structure-preserving signatures: standard model security from simple assumptions. In: Gennaro, R., Robshaw, M. (eds.) CRYPTO 2015, Part II. LNCS, vol. 9216, pp. 296–316. Springer, Heidelberg (2015). https://doi.org/10.1007/978-3-662-48000-7_15
29. Morillo, P., Ràfols, C., Villar, J.L.: The kernel matrix Diffie-Hellman assumption. In: Cheon, J.H., Takagi, T. (eds.) ASIACRYPT 2016, Part I. LNCS, vol. 10031, pp. 729–758. Springer, Heidelberg (2016). https://doi.org/10.1007/978-3-662-53887-6_27
30. Ràfols, C.: Stretching Groth-Sahai: NIZK proofs of partial satisfiability. In: Dodis, Y., Nielsen, J.B. (eds.) TCC 2015, Part II. LNCS, vol. 9015, pp. 247–276. Springer, Heidelberg (2015). https://doi.org/10.1007/978-3-662-46497-7_10

Signatures of Knowledge for Boolean Circuits Under Standard Assumptions

Karim Baghery[1,2]($\boxtimes$), Alonso González[3]($\boxtimes$), Zaira Pindado[4]($\boxtimes$), and Carla Ràfols[4]($\boxtimes$)

[1] imec-COSIC, KU Leuven, Leuven, Belgium
karim.baghery@kuleuven.be
[2] University of Tartu, Tartu, Estonia
[3] ENS de Lyon, Laboratoire LIP (U. Lyon, CNRS, ENSL, INRIA, UCBL),
Lyon, France
alonso.gonzalez@ens-lyon.fr
[4] Universitat Pompeu Fabra, Barcelona, Spain
{zaira.pindado,carla.rafols}@upf.edu

Abstract. This paper constructs unbounded simulation sound proofs for boolean circuit satisfiability under standard assumptions with proof size $O(n + d)$ bilinear group elements, where d is the depth and n is the input size of the circuit. Our technical contribution is to add unbounded simulation soundness to a recent NIZK of González and Ràfols (ASIACRYPT'19) with very small overhead. Our new scheme can be used to construct the most efficient Signature-of-Knowledge based on standard assumptions that also can be composed universally with other cryptographic protocols/primitives.

Keywords: NIZK · Signatures · Bilinear groups

1 Introduction

As one of the essential tools in modern cryptography, Non-Interactive Zero-Knowledge (NIZK) proof systems allow a party to prove that for a public statement $\vec{x}$, she knows a witness $\vec{w}$ such that $(\vec{x}, \vec{w}) \in \mathcal{R}$, for some relation $\mathcal{R}$, without leaking any information about $\vec{w}$ and without interaction with the verifier. Due to their impressive advantages and functionalities, NIZK proof systems are used ubiquitously to build larger cryptographic protocols and systems [2,16]. Among the various constructions of NIZK arguments, there is usually a trade-off between several performance measures, in particular, between efficiency, generality and the strength of the assumptions used in the security proof.

Zero-knowledge Succinct Argument of Knowledge (zk-SNARKs) [8,13] are among the most practically interesting NIZK proofs. They allow to generate succinct proofs for NP-complete languages (3 group elements for CircuitSat [13]) but they are constructed based on non-falsifiable assumptions (e.g. knowledge assumptions [6]). A well-known impossibility result of Gentry and Wichs [9]

© Springer Nature Switzerland AG 2020
A. Nitaj and A. Youssef (Eds.): AFRICACRYPT 2020, LNCS 12174, pp. 24–44, 2020.
https://doi.org/10.1007/978-3-030-51938-4_2

shows that this is unavoidable if one wants to have succinctness for general languages. Thus, non-falsifiable assumptions are an essential ingredient to have very efficient constructions, while falsifiable assumptions give stronger security guarantees and more explicit and meaningful security reductions [22].

Groth-Sahai proofs [15] also allow to prove general languages[1] under standard assumptions non-succinctly, trading security for succinctness. On the other extreme, some constructions of Quasi-Adaptive NIZK (QA-NIZK) generate very efficient proofs based on falsifiable assumptions for very specific statements (e.g. membership in linear spaces).

Somewhere in between, recent work by González and Ràfols [11] constructs a NIZK argument for boolean CircuitSat under falsifiable assumptions by combining techniques of QA-NIZK arguments and zk-SNARKs of size $O(n + d)$ group elements, where n is the length of the input and d is the depth of the circuit.

The primary requirements in a NIZK argument are *Completeness*, *Zero-Knowledge* (ZK), and *Soundness*. Completeness guarantees that if both parties honestly follow the protocol, the prover will convince the verifier. Zero-knowledge preserves prover's privacy and ensures that the verifier will not learn more than the truth of the statement from the proof. Soundness guarantees that a dishonest prover cannot convince an honest verifier. However, in practice usually bare soundness is not sufficient and one might need stronger variations of it, known as *Knowledge Soundness*, *Simulation Soundness* or *Simulation Knowledge Soundness* (a.k.a. Simulation Extractability) [12,24]. Knowledge soundness ensures that if an adversary manages to come up with an acceptable proof, he must *know* the witness. Simulation soundness (a.k.a. unbounded simulation soundness) ensures that an adversary cannot come up with valid proof for a false statement, even if he has seen an arbitrary number of simulated proofs. This notion basically guarantees that the proofs are sound and non-malleable. The strongest case, Simulation Extractability (SE) implies that an adversary cannot come up with a *fresh* valid proof unless he knows a witness, even if he has seen an arbitrary number of simulated proofs. In both notions knowledge soundness and simulation extractability the concept of *knowing* is formalized by showing that there exists an extraction algorithm, either non-Black-Box (nBB) or Black-Box (BB), that can extract the witness from the proof.

Zk-SNARKs (either knowledge sound ones [8,13], or SE ones [1,14]) are the best-known family of NIZK arguments that achieve nBB extraction which is achieved under non-falsifiable assumptions. While SE with nBB extraction is a stronger notion in comparison with (knowledge) soundness, it is still not sufficient for UC-security and needs to be lifted. The reason is that in UC-secure NIZK arguments, to simulate the corrupted parties, the ideal-world simulator should be able to extract witnesses without getting access to the source code of environment's algorithm, which is only guaranteed is BB SE [4,12].

---

[1] GS proofs allow to prove satisfiability of any quadratic equation over $\mathbb{Z}_p$, where p is the order of a bilinear group. In particular, this can encode CircuitSat. The size of the resulting proof is linear in the total number of wires.

SE NIZK arguments have great potential to be deployed in practice [18,20], or construct other primitives such as Signature-of-Knowledge (SoK) [5]. In an SoK, a valid signature of a message M for some statement $\vec{x}$ and a relation $\mathcal{R}$ can only be produced if the signer knows a valid witness $\vec{w}$ such that $(\vec{x}, \vec{w}) \in \mathcal{R}$. Groth and Maller [14] constructed a SE zk-SNARK and a generic construction of an SoK from any SE NIZK argument, resulting in an SoK for CircuitSat. While their construction is for general NP relations and it is also succinct, it also relies on non-falsifiable assumptions and cannot be used in the UC framework.

Briefly speaking, this paper constructs a SE NIZK argument with BB extraction for Boolean CircuitSat which is secure under falsifiable assumptions. The proposed construction is based on the result of [11]. We show that the proposed construction adds minimal overhead to the original construction, resulting in a SE NIZK argument with BB extraction and proof size $O(n + d)$. That the proposed construction also allows one to construct a (universally composable) SoK of roughly the same size. A comparison of our SoK with prior schemes can be found in Table 1.

Table 1. A comparison of our proposed SoK with prior schemes, where n_s the secret input size in a boolean circuit, d the depth of the circuit, n_{PPE} is the number of pairing product equations (each multiplication gate in an arithmetic circuit can be encoded as a pairing product equation, in such case $n_{PPE} = n$), n_X, n_Y are the number of variables in all the pairing product equations in $\mathbb{G}_1, \mathbb{G}_2$, respectively, ℓ_K is the size of the output of a hash function. PE: Pairing Equations, SAP: Square Arithmetic Equations, QE: Quadratic Equations.

Construction	Language	Signature Size	Assumption
BFG [3]	PE	$(n_{PPE}n_X, n_{PPE}n_Y) + \ell_K$	Falsifiable
GM [14]	SAP	3	Non-falsifiable
Sect. 3.2	QE	$(2n_s + 6d + 13, 2d + 11) + \ell_K$	Falsifiable

1.1 Our Contribution

Trivial Approach for Boolean CircuitSat. Let ϕ some boolean circuit, and let a_i, b_i, c_i be the left, right and output wires of gate i. An argument for Boolean CircuitSat, where the prover shows knowledge of some secret input satisfying the circuit, can be divided into three sub-arguments:

1) an argument of knowledge of some boolean input: to prove that the secret input is boolean, the prover must show that each input value satisfies some quadratic equation,
2) a set of linear constraints, which proves "correct wiring", namely that a_i, b_i are consistent with $\vec{c}$ and the specification of the circuit,
3) a set of quadratic constraints, which proves that for all i, a_i, b_i and c_i are in some quadratic relation which expresses correct evaluation of gate i.

It is straightforward to prove CircuitSat by computing perfectly binding commitments to all the wires a_i, b_i, c_i and use, for example, GS NIZK proofs for each of the three sub-arguments. However, the proof size is obviously linear in the number of wires.

New Techniques. In a recent result, González and Ràfols [11] give a proof for Boolean CircuitSat of size $O(n + d)$ group elements. We now give an overview of their techniques, which is the main building block of our paper. The key to their result is to prove 2) and 3) succinctly for each level of the circuit. More specifically (ignoring zero-knowledge, momentarily), if L_j (resp. R_j, O_j) is a shrinking (non-hiding, deterministic) commitment to all left (resp. right, output) wires at depth j, they construct:

2') an argument that shows that the opening of L_j is in the correct linear relation (given by the wiring constraints in the circuit specification) with the input and the openings of $O_1, \ldots, O_{j-1}$,

3') an argument that shows that the opening of O_j is in the correct quadratic relation (which depends on the type of gates at level j) with the opening of L_j and R_j.

The abstraction given above of the results of [11] hides an important subtlety: "the opening of L_j" (and similarly for the other shrinking commitments O_j, R_j) is not well defined, as many openings are possible, so it is unclear what it means for these sub-arguments to be sound. However, as the authors of [11] observe when we are using these as part of a global proof of CircuitSat, "the opening of L_j" to which we intuitively refer is well defined in terms of the openings in previous levels. In other words, in the soundness proof, 2') can be used to prove that if the reduction can extract an opening of $O_1, \ldots, O_{j-1}$ consistent with the input and the circuit, it can also extract a consistent opening of L_j (and similarly R_j). On the other hand, 3') shows that if the reduction can extract an opening of L_j and R_j consistent with the input and the circuit, it can also extract an opening of O_j. For this reason, González and Ràfols informally called 2') and 3') "arguments of knowledge transfer" (linear and quadratic, respectively): given knowledge of the input, arguments 2') and 3') can be used alternatively to transfer this knowledge to lower levels of the circuit.

Promise Problems. To formalize this intuitive notion, the authors of [11] define their sub-arguments 2') and 3') as arguments (with completeness and soundness) for certain promise problems:

2') Given the input $\vec{c}_0$ and openings $(\vec{c}_1, \ldots, \vec{c}_{j-1})$ of $O_1, \ldots, O_{j-1}$, the argument shows that L_j can be opened to some $\vec{a}_j$ with the correct linear relation to $(\vec{c}_1, \ldots, \vec{c}_{j-1})$ (similarly for R_j).

3') Given $\vec{a}_j$ and $\vec{b}_j$, openings of L_j and R_j, the argument shows that there is an opening $\vec{c}_j$ of O_j that is in the correct quadratic relation (which depends on the type of gates at level j) with $\vec{a}_j$ and $\vec{b}_j$.

From an efficiency point of view, the interesting thing is that the arguments are of constant size. This explains the proof size $O(n+d)$: $O(n)$ is for committing to the input (with extractable commitments, which exist under falsifiable assumptions because the input is boolean), and d is the cost of doing 2') and 3') repeatedly for each level. At a conceptual level, the key issue is that the verifier never checks that the openings are correct (i.e. in 2') it never checks that $\vec{c}_i$ is a valid opening of O_i, and in 3') that $\vec{a}_j$, $\vec{b}_j$ are valid openings of L_j, R_j), which is *the promise*. Soundness is only guaranteed if the promise holds, and nothing is said when it does not hold (when the given openings are invalid). In fact, the verifier does not need these openings, they are just part of the statement to define soundness in a meaningful way, reflecting the fact that in the global argument for boolean circuit sat, the openings at level j are uniquely determined by transferring the knowledge of the circuit to lower levels. So excluding the need to read the statement, the verifier works in constant time (it would work in linear time if it verified the statement). In particular, when using the sub-arguments in a global proof, verification of each of the sub-arguments is constant size, and the global verifier runs in time $O(n + d)$.

Security Proof. The sub-arguments 2') and 3') of [11] are not new. More specifically, for 2') the authors just use the QA-NIZK argument of linear spaces for non-witness samplable distributions of Kiltz and Wee [19], a generalization of [17,21] and for 3') they use techniques appeared in the context of zk-SNARKs (as e.g. [8]) to write many quadratic equations as a single relation of polynomial divisibility that can be proven succinctly. The challenge they solve is to give a proof that 2') and 3') are sound for the aforementioned promise problems under falsifiable assumptions. For 2'), they prove that soundness holds under some decisional assumption related to the matrix which defines the linear relations and for 3') they prove this is a straightforward consequence of a q-type assumption in bilinear groups.

Our Techniques: General Approach. This paper builds a SE NIZK for CircuitSat under falsifiable assumptions building on the work of [11]. There are several generic techniques to solve this problem. To the best of our knowledge, existing generic solutions are variations of the following approach, described for example in [12]: build an OR proof that given some circuit ϕ and a public input $\vec{x}_p$, either the circuit is satisfiable with public input x_p or a signature of $M = (\phi, \vec{x}_p)$ is known. The simulator uses as a trapdoor the signature secret key. We note that this approach results in a considerable (although also constant) overhead (around 20 group elements).[2] Our approach is based on the following observation: to compute "fake proofs" of satisfiability, a simulator just needs to lie either about the satisfiability of quadratic equations or linear equations, but not both. Further, it is sufficient to lie in the last gate. In particular, we choose

---

[2] Using OR proofs (the less efficient construction for PPE given in [23] or adding a bit as an auxiliary variable) plus the Boneh-Boyen signature for adaptive soundness.

the following strategy to simulate a proof for a circuit ϕ and a public input $\vec{x}_p$: complete the input arbitrarily, compute consistent assignments to all gates but choose the last left and right wire arbitrarily so that the last gate outputs one. Thus the simulator outputs only honest proofs except for the last linear relation, which is a simulated proof for a false statement, i.e. the simulator does not need the simulation trapdoor for sub-arguments 1) and 3') and standard soundness is sufficient. To be consistent with this strategy, our SE NIZK for boolean CircuitSat uses the construction of [11] but replaces 2'), the proof that the linear relation holds, with 2") an unbounded simulation sound proof for the same promise problem.

Recall that the argument 2') of [11] is just the QA-NIZK argument for membership in linear spaces of Kiltz and Wee for non-witness samplable distributions with a security proof is adapted for promise problems (non-trivially). We take the most efficient USS QA-NIZK argument of membership in linear spaces in the literature, also due to Kiltz and Wee [19] and we adapt the USS argument to work for bilateral linear spaces (linear spaces split among the two source groups in a bilinear group) as in [10] and for promise problems as in [11]. The overhead of the construction with respect to the original CircuitSat proof is minimal $(3|\mathbb{G}_1|)$. BB extractability is achieved because of the soundness of the argument which proves that the input is boolean and the fact that ElGamal ciphertexts of 0 or 1 are BB extractable (the extraction trapdoor is the secret key). Using the generic transformation of Groth and Maller [14], the result gives directly an SoK for boolean CircuitSat.

Generalization of Our Techniques. The observation that to add unbounded simulation soundness to NIZK arguments which prove both quadratic and linear equations it suffices to have USS in the linear part can have other applications. For example, a direct application is to give USS to the construction of Daza et al. [7], which gives a compact proof that a set of perfectly binding commitments open to 0 or 1. Second, we observe that the advantage of our approach is that to get tight security we only need to construct a tight USS for promise problems in bilateral linear spaces, which we leave for future work. The result would be a signature of knowledge for circuits with a loss of d (the circuit depth) in the reduction (inherited from [11]).

2 Preliminaries

Let PPT denote probabilistic polynomial-time, and NUPPT denote non-uniform PPT. Let $\lambda \in \mathbb{N}$ be the information-theoretic security parameter, say $\lambda = 128$. All adversaries will be stateful. For an algorithm $\mathcal{A}$, let $\mathbf{Im}(\mathcal{A})$ be the image of $\mathcal{A}$, i.e., the set of valid outputs of $\mathcal{A}$. By $y \leftarrow \mathcal{A}(x; r)$ we denote the fact that $\mathcal{A}$, given an input x and a randomizer r, outputs y. We denote by $negl$ an arbitrary negligible function. For distributions A and B, $A \approx_c B$ means that they are computationally indistinguishable.

In pairing-based groups, a *bilinear group generator* $\mathsf{BGgen}(1^\lambda)$ is a PPT algorithm returns the *group key* $gk := (p, \mathbb{G}_1, \mathbb{G}_2, \mathbb{G}_T, e, \mathcal{P}_1, \mathcal{P}_2)$, the description of an asymmetric bilinear group, where $\mathbb{G}_1, \mathbb{G}_2$ and $\mathbb{G}_T$ are additive groups of prime order p, the elements $\mathcal{P}_1, \mathcal{P}_2$ are generators of $\mathbb{G}_1, \mathbb{G}_2$ respectively, $e : \mathbb{G}_1 \times \mathbb{G}_2 \to \mathbb{G}_T$ is an efficiently computable, non-degenerate bilinear pairing, and there is no efficiently computable isomorphism between $\mathbb{G}_1$ and $\mathbb{G}_2$. Elements in $\mathbb{G}_\gamma$ are denoted implicitly as $[a]_\gamma := a\mathcal{P}_\gamma$, where $\gamma \in \{1, 2, T\}$ and $\mathcal{P}_T := e(\mathcal{P}_1, \mathcal{P}_2)$. For simplicity, we often write $[a]_{1,2}$ for the pair $[a]_1, [a]_2$. The pairing operation will be written as a product $\cdot$, that is $[a]_1 \cdot [b]_2 = [a]_1[b]_2 = e([a]_1, [b]_2) = [ab]_T$. Vectors and matrices are denoted in boldface. Given a matrix $\mathbf{T} = (t_{i,j})$, $[\mathbf{T}]_\gamma$ is the natural embedding of $\mathbf{T}$ in $\mathbb{G}_\gamma$, that is, the matrix whose (i, j)th entry is $t_{i,j}\mathcal{P}_\gamma$. We denote by $|\mathbb{G}_\gamma|$ the bit-size of the elements of $\mathbb{G}_\gamma$.

2.1 Definitions

We recall the formal definition of QA-NIZK proofs. A QA-NIZK proof system [17] enables to prove membership in a language defined by a relation $\mathcal{R}_\rho$, which is determined by some parameter ρ sampled from a distribution $\mathcal{D}_{gk}$. While the CRS can be constructed based on ρ, the simulator of zero-knowledge is required to be a single PPT algorithm that works for the whole collection of relations $\mathcal{R}_{gk}$. For witness-relations $\mathcal{R}_{gk} = \{\mathcal{R}_\rho\}_{\rho \in \sup(\mathcal{D}_{gk})}$ with parameters sampled from a distribution $\mathcal{D}_{gk}$ over associated parameter language $\mathcal{L}_{\mathsf{par}}$, a QA-NIZK argument system Π consists of tuple of PPT algorithms $\Pi = (\mathsf{K}_0, \mathsf{K}_1, \mathsf{P}, \mathsf{V}, \mathsf{S}_0, \mathsf{S}_1, \mathcal{E})$, defined as follows,

Parameter generator, $gk \leftarrow \mathsf{K}_0(1^\lambda)$: K_0 is a PPT algorithm that given 1^λ generates group description gk.

CRS generator, $\mathsf{crs} \leftarrow \mathsf{K}_1(gk, \rho)$: K_1 is a PPT algorithm that given gk, sample string $\rho \leftarrow \mathcal{D}_{gk}$, and then uses gk, ρ and generate $(\mathsf{crs}, \mathsf{tr}_s, \mathsf{tr}_e)$; finally output crs (that also contains parameter ρ) and store *simulation* trapdoor tr_s and *extraction* trapdoor tr_e as the trapdoors of CRS.

Prover, $\pi \leftarrow \mathsf{P}(\mathsf{crs}, \vec{x}, \vec{w})$: P is a PPT algorithm that, given $(\mathsf{crs}, \vec{x}, \vec{w})$, where $(\vec{x}, \vec{w}) \in \mathcal{R}$, outputs an argument π. Otherwise, it outputs $\perp$.

Verifier, $\{0, 1\} \leftarrow \mathsf{V}(\mathsf{crs}, \vec{x}, \pi)$: V is a PPT algorithm that, given $(\mathsf{crs}, \vec{x}, \pi)$, returns either 0 (reject) or 1 (accept).

CRS Simulator, $(\mathsf{crs}, \mathsf{tr}_s, \mathsf{tr}_e) \leftarrow \mathsf{S}_1(gk, \rho)$: S_1 is a PPT algorithm that, given (gk, ρ), output $(\mathsf{crs}, \mathsf{tr}_s, \mathsf{tr}_e)$, where tr_s is *simulation* trapdoor and tr_e is the *extraction* trapdoor.

Prover Simulator, $\pi \leftarrow \mathsf{S}_2(\mathsf{crs}, \vec{x}, \mathsf{tr}_s)$: S_2 is a PPT algorithm that for valid statements, given $(\mathsf{crs}, \vec{x}, \mathsf{tr}_s)$, output a simulated argument π.

Extractor, $\vec{w} \leftarrow \mathcal{E}(gk, \mathsf{crs}, \vec{x}, \pi, \mathsf{tr}_e)$: $\mathcal{E}$ is a PPT algorithm that, given $(\mathsf{crs}, \vec{x}, \pi, \mathsf{tr}_e)$ extracts the witness $\vec{w}$; where tr_e is the extraction trapdoor.

We require an argument QA-NIZK system Π to be *quasi-adaptive complete, computationally quasi-adaptive sound* and *perfectly quasi-adaptive zero-knowledge*, as defined below.

Definition 1 (Quasi-Adaptive Completeness). *A quasi-adaptive argument Π is perfectly complete for $\mathcal{R}_\rho$, if for all λ, and all $(\vec{x}, \vec{w}) \in \mathcal{R}_\rho$,*

$$\Pr\left[\begin{array}{l} gk \leftarrow \mathsf{K}_0(1^\lambda), \ \rho \leftarrow \mathcal{D}_{gk}, \\ \mathsf{crs} \leftarrow \mathsf{K}_1(gk, \rho), \pi \leftarrow \mathsf{P}(\mathsf{crs}, \vec{x}, \vec{w}) \end{array} : \mathsf{V}(\mathsf{crs}, \vec{x}, \pi) = 1\right] = 1.$$

Definition 2 (Computational Quasi-Adaptive Soundness). *A quasi-adaptive argument Π is computationally quasi-adaptive sound for $\mathcal{R}_\rho$, if for all λ, and for all non-uniform PPT $\mathcal{A}$,*

$$\Pr\left[\begin{array}{l} gk \leftarrow \mathsf{K}_0(1^\lambda), \ \rho \leftarrow \mathcal{D}_{gk}, \\ \mathsf{crs} \leftarrow \mathsf{K}_1(gk, \rho), \ (\vec{x}, \pi) \leftarrow \mathcal{A}(gk, \mathsf{crs}) \end{array} : \begin{array}{c} \mathsf{V}(\mathsf{crs}, \vec{x}, \pi) = 1 \ \wedge \\ (\vec{x}, \vec{w}) \notin \mathcal{R}_\rho \end{array}\right] \approx 0$$

Definition 3 (Perfectly Quasi-Adaptive Zero-Knowledge). *A quasi-adaptive argument Π is perfectly quasi-adaptive zero-knowledge for $\mathcal{R}_\rho$, if for all λ, and for all non-uniform PPT $\mathcal{A}$,*

$$\Pr\left[\begin{array}{l} gk \leftarrow \mathsf{K}_0(1^\lambda), \rho \leftarrow \mathcal{D}_{gk}, \\ \mathsf{crs} \leftarrow \mathsf{K}_1(gk, \rho) : \\ \mathcal{A}^{\mathsf{P}(\mathsf{crs}, \cdot, \cdot)}(gk, \mathsf{crs}) = 1 \end{array}\right] = \Pr\left[\begin{array}{l} gk \leftarrow \mathsf{K}_0(1^\lambda), \rho \leftarrow \mathcal{D}_{gk}, \\ (\mathsf{crs}, \mathsf{tr}_s, \mathsf{tr}_e) \leftarrow \mathsf{S}_1(gk, \rho) : \\ \mathcal{A}^{\mathsf{S}_2(\mathsf{crs}, \mathsf{tr}_s, \cdot, \cdot)}(gk, \mathsf{crs}) = 1 \end{array}\right]$$

where $\mathsf{P}(\mathsf{crs}, \cdot, \cdot)$ emulates the actual prover, and given $(\mathsf{crs}, \vec{x}, \vec{w})$ outputs a proof π if $(\vec{x}, \vec{w}) \in \mathcal{R}_\rho$, otherwise it outputs $\perp$; and $\mathsf{S}_2(\mathsf{crs}, \mathsf{tr}_s, \cdot, \cdot)$ is an oracle that given $(\mathsf{crs}, \mathsf{tr}_s, \vec{x}, \vec{w})$, it outputs a simulated proof $\mathsf{S}_2(\mathsf{crs}, \mathsf{tr}_s, \vec{x})$ if $(\vec{x}, \vec{w}) \in \mathcal{R}_\rho$ and $\perp$ if $(\vec{x}, \vec{w}) \notin \mathcal{R}_\rho$.

We also consider Simulation Soundness for our proofs, we take the next definition from Kiltz and Wee [19].

Definition 4 (Unbounded Simulation Adaptive Soundness). *A quasi-adaptive argument Π is unbounded simulation adaptive sound for $\mathcal{R}_\rho$, if for all λ, and for all non-uniform PPT $\mathcal{A}$,*

$$\Pr\left[\begin{array}{l} gk \leftarrow \mathsf{K}_0(1^\lambda), \rho \leftarrow \mathcal{D}_{gk}, \\ (\mathsf{crs}, \mathsf{tr}) \leftarrow \mathsf{S}_1(gk, \rho); \\ (\vec{x}^*, \tau^*, \pi^*) \leftarrow \mathcal{A}^{O(\cdot)}(gk, \mathsf{crs}, \rho) \end{array} : \begin{array}{c} (\vec{x}^*, \pi^*) \notin \mathcal{Q}_{tags} \ \wedge \ (\vec{x}, \vec{w}) \notin \mathcal{R}_\rho \\ \wedge \ \mathsf{V}(\mathsf{crs}, \vec{x}^*, \pi^*) = 1 \end{array}\right] \approx 0,$$

where $O(\vec{x})$ returns $(\vec{x}, \pi) \leftarrow \mathsf{S}_2(\mathsf{crs}, \mathsf{tr}, \tau, \vec{x})$ and adds τ to the set $\mathcal{Q}_{tags}$.

Now we define a variation of definition *BB simulation extractability* for QA-NIZKs that is used in the construction of new schemes. To the best of our knowledge, this is the first time that this definition is defined for QA-NIZKs.

Definition 5 (Quasi-Adaptive BB Simulation Extractability). *A non-interactive argument scheme Π is quasi-adaptive black-box simulation-extractable for $\mathcal{R}_\rho$, if for all λ, and for all non-uniform PPT $\mathcal{A}$, there exists a black-box extractor $\mathcal{E}$ such that,*

$$\Pr\left[\begin{array}{l} gk \leftarrow \mathsf{K}_0(1^\lambda), \ \rho \leftarrow \mathcal{D}_{gk}, \\ (\mathsf{crs}, \mathsf{tr}_s, \mathsf{tr}_e) \leftarrow \mathsf{S}_1(gk, \rho); \\ (\vec{x}^*, \pi^*) \leftarrow \mathcal{A}^{O(\cdot, \cdot)}(gk, \mathsf{crs}, \rho), \\ \vec{w} \leftarrow \mathcal{E}(gk, \mathsf{crs}, \vec{x}^*, \pi^*, \mathsf{tr}_e) \end{array} : \begin{array}{c} \mathsf{V}(\mathsf{crs}, \vec{x}^*, \pi^*) = 1 \\ \wedge \ (\vec{x}, \vec{w}) \notin \mathcal{R}_\rho \wedge \ (\vec{x}^*, \pi^*) \notin \mathcal{Q} \end{array}\right] \approx 0,$$

where $O(\vec{x})$ returns $(\vec{x}, \pi) \leftarrow S_2(\mathsf{crs}, \vec{x}, \mathsf{tr}_s)$ and adds $(\vec{x}, \pi)$ to the set of simulated proofs Q.

A key note about Definition 5 is that the extraction procedure is black-box and the extractor $\mathcal{E}$ works for all adversaries.

2.2 Boolean Circuits

As in González and Ràfols [11], we *slice* a boolean circuit in layers according to the level of each gate. Throughout the paper, $\phi : \{0,1\}^n \rightarrow \{0,1\}$ is a boolean circuit with m gates of fan-in two and d is the depth. To simplify the exposition of our result in limited space, we consider only NAND gates, but it is immediate to extend our result to include gates of ϕ of any type as was done in fact in [11].

The gates of ϕ are indexed by a pair (i, j), where i denotes the gate depth and j is some index in the range $1, \ldots, n_i$, where n_i is the number of gates at level i.

In Lemma 1 we now express in equations what it means for a tuple $(\vec{a}, \vec{b}, \vec{c})$ to be a valid assignment to the left, right and output wires of ϕ respectively, where $\vec{a} = (\vec{a}_1, \ldots, \vec{a}_d)$, $\vec{b} = (\vec{b}_1, \ldots, \vec{b}_d)$ and $\vec{c} = (\vec{c}_0, \vec{c}_1, \ldots, \vec{c}_d)$ and $\vec{y}_i = (y_{i,1}, \ldots, y_{i,n_i})$ for all $\vec{y} \in \{\vec{a}, \vec{b}, \vec{c}\}$. A valid assignment should give $a_{i,j}$, $b_{i,j}$ and $c_{i,j}$ the values of the left, right and output wires of the gate indexed by (i, j) and $c_{0,1}, \ldots, c_{0,n}$ some boolean values which represent a satisfying input.

Lemma 1 breaks down CircuitSat in different items which reflect the different building blocks used by [11] and also our work. The input vector $\vec{x}$ (which corresponds to $\vec{c}_0$) is divided in two parts, the first n_p components being the public input $\vec{x}_p$ and the rest is the secret input $\vec{x}_s$ of length n_s. The main achievement of [11] is to do two aggregated proof of all the constraints at the same depth with just two constant size proofs, one for the multiplicative and the other for the linear constraints. Therefore, items $c)$ (resp. $d)$) require that for each $i = 1, \ldots, d$, a set of quadratic (resp. linear) equations holds. In the next two subsections (Sect. 2.3, 2.4) we sketch the aggregated proofs of the sets of equations described in $c)$ and $d)$.

Lemma 1. *Let $\phi : \{0,1\}^n \rightarrow \{0,1\}$, be a circuit with m NAND gates. Then, for any public input $\vec{x}_p \in \{0,1\}^{n_p}$, $(\vec{a}, \vec{b}, \vec{c})$ is a valid input for satisfiability of $\phi(\vec{x}_p, \cdot)$ if and only if:*

a) $(c_{0,1}, \ldots, c_{0,n_p}) = (\vec{x}_p)$.
b) Boolean secret input: $(c_{0,n_p+1}, \ldots, c_{0,n}) = (\vec{x}_s) \in \{0,1\}^{n_s}$.
c) Correct gate evaluation at level i, for $i = 1, \ldots, d$:

$$c_{i,j} = 1 - a_{i,j} b_{i,j}, \qquad j = 1, \ldots, n_i,$$

d) Correct "wiring" (linear constraints) at level i:

$$a_{i,j} = c_{k_L, \ell_L}, \qquad b_{i,j} = c_{k_R, \ell_R},$$

for some indexes $0 \leq k_L, k_R < i$, $\ell_L \in \{1, \ldots, n_{k_L}\}$ and $\ell_R \in \{1, \ldots, n_{k_R}\}$. In other words, for all i, there exist some matrices $\mathbf{F}_i, \mathbf{G}_i$ such that $\vec{a}_i = \mathbf{F}_i \vec{c}_{|i-1}$ and $\vec{b}_i = \mathbf{G}_i \vec{c}_{|i-1}$, where $\vec{c}_{|i-1}^\top = (\vec{c}_0^\top, \ldots, \vec{c}_{i-1}^\top)$.
e) Correct output: $c_{d,1} = 1$.

2.3   Aggregated Proofs of Quadratic Equations

We now describe the construction proposed in González and Ràfols [11] to prove correct gate evaluation at level i, for $i = 1, \ldots, d - 1$, i.e. a proof that $c_{i,j} = 1 - a_{i,j}b_{i,j}$, for all $j = 1, \ldots, n_i$. It consists, for $k = 1, 2$, of a Groth-Sahai NIZK Proof that some secret values $[L_{i,k}]_1, [R_{i,k}]_2, [O_{i,k}]_1, [O^*_{i,k}]_2, [H_{i,k}]_1$ satisfy the following relation[3]:

$$[1]_T - e([L_{i,k}]_1, [R_{i,k}]_2) - e([O_{i,k}]_1, [1]_2) = e([H_{i,k}]_1, [t_k]_2), \tag{1}$$

$$e([O_{i,j}]_1, [1]_2) = e([1]_1, [O^*_{i,j}]_2). \tag{2}$$

where if $t(X) = \prod_{r \in \mathcal{R}}(X - r)$, $t_k = t(s_k)$ and $\lambda_i(X) = \prod_{j \in \mathcal{R} \setminus \{r_i\}} \dfrac{(X - r_j)}{(r_i - r_j)}$ is the ith Lagrangian polynomial associated to $\mathcal{R}$, a set of $W = \max_{i=1,\ldots,d} n_i$ points used for interpolation, then

$$L_{i,k} = \sum a_j \lambda_j(s_k), \quad R_{i,k} = \sum b_j \lambda_j(s_k), \quad C_{i,k} = \sum c_j \lambda_j(s_k), \quad H_{i,k} = h_i(s_k),$$

where s_1, s_2 are random secret points specified in the CRS, and $h_i(X) = (1 - (\sum a_j \lambda_j(X))(\sum b_j \lambda_j(X)) - \sum c_j \lambda_j(s_k))/t(X)$. Alternatively, for each n_i we define $\mathbf{\Lambda}_{n_i} = \begin{pmatrix} \lambda_1(s_1) \ldots \lambda_{n_i}(s_1) \\ \lambda_1(s_2) \ldots \lambda_{n_i}(s_2) \end{pmatrix}$,

$$[\vec{L}_i]_1 = [\mathbf{\Lambda}_{n_i} \vec{a}_i]_1, [\vec{R}_i]_2 = [\mathbf{\Lambda}_{n_i} \vec{b}_i]_2, [\vec{O}_i]_1 = [\mathbf{\Lambda}_{n_i} \vec{c}_i]_1,$$

and $\mathbf{\Lambda}$ is called Lagrangian Pedersen commitment in [11].

To the reader familiar with the literature, it is obvious that Eq. (1) uses SNARK techniques originally appeared in [8] (what we could call "polynomial aggregation") for proving many quadratic equations simultaneously. What is new in [11], is the security analysis, which avoids non-falsifiable assumptions.

GS proofs are necessary for zero-knowledge because $\vec{L}_i, \vec{R}_i, \vec{O}_i$ need to be deterministic for the proof to work. The authors of [11] use this proof as a building block in a larger proof, and for this they prove the following: "if $(\vec{a}_i, \vec{b}_i)$ are valid openings of $[L_{i,k}]_1, [R_{i,k}]_2$ for $k = 1, 2$ then $1 - \vec{a}_i \circ \vec{b}_i$ is a valid opening of $O_{i,k}$."

Formally, the authors define the languages

$$\mathcal{L}^{\text{quad}}_{\text{YES}} = \left\{ \begin{array}{c} (\vec{a}, \vec{b}, [\vec{L}]_1, [\vec{R}]_2, [\vec{O}]_1) : \vec{1} - \vec{a} \circ \vec{b} = \vec{c}, \\ \left[\vec{L}\right]_1 = [\mathbf{\Lambda}]_1 \vec{a}, \left[\vec{R}\right]_2 = [\mathbf{\Lambda}]_2 \vec{b}, \left[\vec{O}\right]_1 = [\mathbf{\Lambda}]_1 \vec{c} \end{array} \right\}$$

---

[3] The second equation is added to have the element $O_{i,j}$ in both groups $\mathbb{G}_1, \mathbb{G}_2$. This will allow us to use simple QA-NIZK proofs of membership in linear spaces in $\mathbb{G}_1$ and $\mathbb{G}_2$ for the linear constraints, instead of using proofs of membership in bilateral spaces (spaces with parts in $\mathbb{G}_1$ and in $\mathbb{G}_2$.).

$$\mathcal{L}_{\text{NO}}^{\text{quad}} = \left\{ \begin{array}{l} (\vec{a}, \vec{b}, [\vec{L}]_1, [\vec{R}]_2, [\vec{O}]_1) : \vec{1} - \vec{a} \circ \vec{b} = \vec{c}, \\ \left[\vec{L}\right]_1 = [\boldsymbol{\Lambda}]_1 \vec{a}, \left[\vec{R}\right]_2 = [\boldsymbol{\Lambda}]_2 \vec{b}, \left[\vec{O}\right]_1 \neq [\boldsymbol{\Lambda}]_1 \vec{c} \end{array} \right\}.$$

The argument consists of giving some values $\vec{H}, \vec{O}^*$ chosen by the prover which satisfy Eq. (1) for $\vec{L}, \vec{R}, \vec{O}$. *Completeness* holds for $\mathcal{L}_{\text{YES}}^{\text{quad}}$ and *soundness* for values $\mathcal{L}_{\text{NO}}^{\text{quad}}$ under the $(\mathcal{R}, m)$-Rational Strong Diffie-Hellman assumption [11]. When (1) are proven with GS proofs, they argue that *zero-knowledge* also holds.

Note that the fact $[\vec{L}]_1 = [\boldsymbol{\Lambda}]_1 \vec{a}$, or $[\vec{R}]_2 = [\boldsymbol{\Lambda}]_2 \vec{b}$ is never checked by the verifier, this is the promise. The argument does not give any guarantee when this does not hold.

2.4 Aggregated Proofs of Linear Equations

In this section we explain the technique used in González and Ràfols [11] to prove correct "wiring" at level i, for $i = 1, \ldots, d-1$, i.e. an aggregated proof for linear constraints. As we have seen in Lemma 1, we can express linear constraints at level i as:

$$\vec{a}_i = \mathbf{F}_i \vec{c}_{|i-1}, \quad \vec{b}_i = \mathbf{G}_i \vec{c}_{|i-1} \text{ for all } i = 1, \ldots, d. \tag{3}$$

Then at level i left and right constraints can be expressed, respectively as:

$$\begin{pmatrix} \vec{O}_{|i-1} \\ \vec{L}_i \end{pmatrix} = \begin{pmatrix} \mathbf{C}_i \\ \tilde{\mathbf{F}}_i \end{pmatrix} (\vec{c}_{|i-1}), \quad \begin{pmatrix} \vec{O}_{|i-1} \\ \vec{R}_i \end{pmatrix} = \begin{pmatrix} \mathbf{C}_i \\ \tilde{\mathbf{G}}_i \end{pmatrix} (\vec{c}_{|i-1}) \tag{4}$$

where $\mathbf{C}_i = \begin{pmatrix} \mathbf{I} & \vec{0} & \cdots & \mathbf{0} \\ \mathbf{0} & \boldsymbol{\Lambda}_{n_1} & \cdots & \vec{0} \\ \mathbf{0} & \mathbf{0} & \ddots & \mathbf{0} \\ \mathbf{0} & \mathbf{0} & \cdots & \boldsymbol{\Lambda}_{n_{i-1}} \end{pmatrix}$, $\tilde{\mathbf{F}}_i = \boldsymbol{\Lambda}_{n_i} \mathbf{F}_i$, $\tilde{\mathbf{G}}_i = \boldsymbol{\Lambda}_{n_i} \mathbf{G}_i$ and $\boldsymbol{\Lambda}_{n_i}$ is the matrix of the Lagrangian Pedersen commitment key defined in last section, and $\vec{O}_0$ is just the input of the circuit.

To make the argument zero-knowledge, the prover does never give $\vec{O}_i, \vec{L}_i$ or $\vec{R}_i$ in the clear, but rather, for $k = 1, 2$ and any $i \in [d]$, it gives GS commitments $[\vec{z}]_1$ to the input (i.e. to all components of $\vec{O}_0 = \vec{c}_0$), to the vector $\vec{O}_i$ as $[\vec{z}_{O,i}]_1$, to the vector $\vec{L}_i$ as $[\vec{z}_{L,i}]_1$ and to the vector $\vec{R}_i$ as $[\vec{z}_{R,i}]_2$ (a part from other GS commitments necessary for the quadratic proof). The matrices which define the linear relation between committed values are defined from $\mathbf{C}_i$, $\tilde{\mathbf{F}}_i = \boldsymbol{\Lambda}_{n_i} \mathbf{F}_i$, $\tilde{\mathbf{G}}_i = \boldsymbol{\Lambda}_{n_i} \mathbf{G}_i$ adding columns and rows to accommodate for the GS commitment keys in the relevant groups (see full details in [11]). We denote these matrices $\mathbf{M}_i^L, \mathbf{N}_i^L$ for the left constraints and $\mathbf{M}_i^R, \mathbf{N}_i^R$ for the right constraints.

González and Ràfols prove that the QA-NIZK argument of Kiltz and Wee [19] (with standard soundness) for membership in linear spaces for non-witness samplable distributions is an argument for the following promise problem:

$$\mathcal{L}_{\text{YES}}^{\text{Lin}} = \left\{ (\vec{w}, [\vec{x}]_1, [\vec{y}]_1) : \begin{array}{l} [\vec{x}]_1 = [\mathbf{M}]_1 \vec{w} \text{ and} \\ [\vec{y}]_1 = [\mathbf{N}]_1 \vec{w} \end{array} \right\}$$

$$\mathcal{L}_{\mathsf{NO}}^{\mathsf{Lin}} = \left\{ (\vec{w}, [\vec{x}]_1, [\vec{y}]_1) : \begin{array}{c} [\vec{x}]_1 = [\mathbf{M}]_1 \vec{w} \text{ and} \\ [\vec{y}]_1 \neq [\mathbf{N}]_1 \vec{w} \end{array} \right\}$$

parametrized by matrices $\mathbf{M}, \mathbf{N}$.

If we use this construction for matrices $\mathbf{M}_i^L$ and $\mathbf{N}_i^L$ (similarly for right side), this argument can be used to prove that, if we can extract $\vec{c}_{|i-1}$, then we can extract an opening $\vec{a}_i$ of $\vec{L}_i$ which is in the correct linear relation with $\vec{c}_{|i-1}$.

The authors prove completeness of the argument for statements in $\mathcal{L}_{\mathsf{YES}}^{\mathsf{Lin}}$ and soundness for $\mathcal{L}_{\mathsf{NO}}^{\mathsf{Lin}}$ under $\mathcal{M}_L^\top$-MDDH, $\mathcal{M}_R^\top$-MDDH and KerMDH assumption, where $\mathcal{M}_L$ (resp. $\mathcal{M}_R$) is the distribution of matrices $\mathbf{M}_i^L$ (resp. $\mathbf{M}_i^R$) described above[4].

We note that for simplicity, we have explained the result of [11] as proving a linear system of constraints for each level and each side (left or right), but in fact a single QA-NIZK argument for bilateral spaces for non-witness samplable distributions [10] is used in [11] to gain efficiency (the proof requires then only 2 elements in $\mathbb{G}_1$ and $\mathbb{G}_2$ instead of $O(d)$ elements).

3   SE NIZK Argument for Boolean CircuitSat

We present our Quasi-Adaptive argument for Boolean CircuitSat for the language defined as

$$\mathcal{L}_\phi = \left\{ (\vec{x}_p) \middle| \exists \vec{x}_s \in \{0,1\}^{n_s} \text{ s.t. } \phi(\vec{x}_p, \vec{x}_s) = 1 \right\}.$$

As consequence of Lemma 1 the language $\mathcal{L}_{\phi,ck}$ can be equivalently defined as

$$\mathcal{L}_\phi = \left\{ (\vec{x}_p) \middle| \begin{array}{l} \exists \vec{x}_s \text{ s.t. } \vec{x}_s \circ (\vec{x}_s - \vec{1}) = \vec{0}; \\ \vec{c}_0 := (\vec{x}_p, \vec{x}_s); \\ \forall i \in [d], \exists \vec{a}_i, \vec{b}_i, \vec{c}_i \in \mathbb{Z}_p^{n_i} \text{ s.t. }; \\ \vec{a}_i = \mathbf{F}_i \vec{c}_{|i-1}, \vec{b}_i = \mathbf{G}_i \vec{c}_{|i-1} \in \mathbb{Z}_p^{n_i}, \\ 1 - \vec{a}_i \circ \vec{b}_i = \vec{c}_i. \end{array} \right\}.$$

In the following Π_Q denotes the argument for Quadratic Equations described in Sect. 2.3, Π_L the USS membership argument for linear spaces presented in Sect. 4 and Input an argument to prove that some BB extractable commitments to integers open to binary values.

$\mathsf{K}_0(\lambda, W, \mathcal{R})$: On input some set $\mathcal{R} \subset \mathbb{Z}_p$ of cardinal W, choose a bilinear group gk and output (gk, W).

$\mathcal{D}_{gk,W,\mathcal{R}}$: Pick commitment keys $(ck_1, ck_2) = ([\mathbf{\Lambda}]_1, [\mathbf{\Lambda}]_2)$ that are the Lagrangian Pedersen commitment keys associated to $\mathcal{R}$. Output $(ck_1, ck_2, \mathsf{crs}_{\mathsf{GS}})$.

---

[4] An important point is that these MDDH assumptions can be reduced to a decisional assumption in bilinear groups which does not depend on the circuit. In fact, $\mathbf{M}_i^L$ only depends on $n, n_1, \ldots, n_s$, and the assumption can be reduced to a decisional assumption which only depends on $\mathbf{\Lambda}$ and the GS commitment key.

$K_1 (gk, \phi)$: Given $(ck_1, ck_2, \mathsf{crs_{GS}}) \leftarrow \mathcal{D}_{gk,W}$ and $\phi : \{0,1\}^n \to \{0,1\}$ of maximum width W. For each $i \in [d]$ define matrices $[\mathbf{M}_i^L]_1$, $[\mathbf{M}_i^R]_2$, $[\mathbf{N}_i^L]_1$, $[\mathbf{M}_i^R]_2$ as explained in Sect. 2.4. Let $\mathsf{crs_{Input}}$ the crs of the argument Input for a vector of size n_s is binary. Let crs_Q the crs of Π_Q for proving correct evaluation of (at most) W gates. For each $i \in [d]$, let $\mathsf{crs}_{L,i}^L$ ($\mathsf{crs}_{L,i}^R$) the crs for the USS argument of linear knowledge transfer Π_L of left (right) wires at depth i. Let $\mathsf{crs}_L = \{\mathsf{crs}_{L,i}^L, \mathsf{crs}_{L,i}^R\}_{i \in [d]}$ and $\mathsf{tr}_L = \{\mathsf{tr}_{L,i}^L, \mathsf{tr}_{L,i}^R\}_{i \in [d]}$, where $\mathsf{tr}_{L,i}^L$ ($\mathsf{tr}_{L,i}^R$) are the trapdoors of the Π_L arguments of left (right) wires at depth i.

Output $\mathsf{crs} = (ck_1, ck_2, \mathsf{crs_{GS}}, \mathsf{crs_{Input}}, \mathsf{crs}_Q, \mathsf{crs}_L)$, $\mathsf{tr} = \mathsf{tr}_L$.

$P\left(\mathsf{crs}, \vec{x}_s, \vec{r}, \vec{a}, \vec{b}, \vec{c}, \vec{x}_p\right)$: Computes the commitment of the secret input $[\vec{z}]_1 = \mathsf{com}_{ck_1, ck_2}(\vec{x}_s, \vec{r})$ and constructs the proof Input for $[\vec{z}]_1$. For each $i \in [d]$ compute Lagrangian Pedersen commitments to the wires $[\vec{O}_i]_{1,2}, [\vec{L}_i]_1, [\vec{R}_i]_2$, give a GS proof $\Pi_{Q,i}$ that they satisfy Eq. (1) and let $[\vec{z}_{O,i,k}]_1, [\vec{z}_{O,i,k}^*]_2, [\vec{z}_{L,i,k}]_1, [\vec{z}_{R,i,k}]_2$ the correspondent GS commitments to $\vec{O}, \vec{L}, \vec{R}$, for $k = 1, 2$. Compute proofs $\Pi_{L,i}$ of correct wiring and $\Pi_{L,0}$ that the opening of $[\vec{z}]_1$ is correctly assigned to $[\vec{z}_{O,0}]_1$. Outputs $\pi = \left([\vec{z}]_1, \mathsf{Input}, [\vec{z}_O]_1, [\vec{z}_L]_1, [\vec{z}_O^*]_2, [\vec{z}_R]_2, \vec{\Pi}_L, \Pi_{L,0}, \vec{\Pi}_Q\right)$.

$V(\mathsf{crs}, \vec{x}_p, \pi)$: Verify all the proofs in π with the corresponding verification algorithms V_{Input}, V_{Π_L} and check Eq. (1).

$S(\mathsf{crs}, \vec{x}_p, \mathsf{tr})$: Extend the input with zeros, $\vec{x} = (\vec{x}_p, 0, \ldots, 0)$ and evaluate the circuit honestly with this input to obtain the corresponding $\vec{a}_i, \vec{b}_i, \vec{c}_i$ for each $i = 1, \ldots, d$. Change the last gate values, i.e. the right and left values of the last gate at level d to $\hat{a}_d = 0$, $\hat{b}_d = 1$, $\hat{c}_d = 1$. Compute the commitment $[\vec{z}]_1 = \mathsf{com}_{ck_1, ck_2}(\vec{0}, \vec{r})$, honest proofs Input and $\Pi_{Q,i}$ and commitments $[\vec{z}_{O,i,k}]_1, [\vec{z}_{L,i,k}]_1, [\vec{z}_{O,i,k}^*]_2, [\vec{z}_{R,i,k}]_2$ for each $i = 1, \ldots, d$. Run the simulator S_{Π_L} to obtain d simulated $\Pi_{L,i}^S, \Pi_{R,i}^S$ together with $\Pi_{L,0}^S$. Finally, $\pi^S = ([\vec{z}]_1, \mathsf{Input}, [\vec{z}_O]_1, [\vec{z}_L]_1, [\vec{z}_R]_2, [\vec{z}_O^*]_2, \Pi_L^S, \Pi_{L,0}^S, \Pi_Q)$.

Completeness and Zero-Knowledge are directly from the completeness and zero-knowledge of the respective subarguments.

Unbounded Simulation Extractable Adaptive Soundness is proved in the following theorem.

Theorem 1. *If $\mathcal{A}$ is an adaptive adversary against the Unbounded Simulation BB Extractability Soundness of the Boolean CircuitSat argument described in Sect. 3 that makes at most Q queries to S, then there exist PPT adversaries $\mathcal{B}_1$, $\mathcal{B}_2$, $\mathcal{B}_3$ against the BB Extractable Soundness of Input, the Unbounded Simulation Soundness of Π_L argument and the soundness of Π_Q argument, respectively, such that*

$$\mathsf{Adv}_{USS}(\mathcal{A}) \leq \mathsf{Adv}_{ES\text{-}Input}(\mathcal{B}_1) + d\mathsf{Adv}_{USS\text{-}\Pi_L}(\mathcal{B}_2) + 2d\mathsf{Adv}_{Sound\text{-}\Pi_Q}(\mathcal{B}_3).$$

Proof (sketch). The simulator algorithm generates honestly the Input and Π_Q arguments and an adversary sees only simulated proofs of the linear argument Π_L. Therefore, an adversary that creates a new proof for an invalid statement breaks either the knowledge soundness of the Input, the soundness of the Π_Q arguments, or the USS of the linear arguments Π_L.   □

3.1   Concrete USES QA-NIZK for Boolean CircuitSat

For the scheme described above, one can take as Input, and Π_Q the same building blocks as [11], namely the bitstring argument of Daza et al. [7] and the argument described in Sect. 2.3. The USS for promise problems given in Sect. 4.

To simplify the exposition we have ommitted many details that actually make the proof more efficient. In particular, instead of using two linear arguments for each depth of the circuit, we can use the linear argument for all the linear constraints of the circuit at once (as it is also done in the original work). First, it is easy to see one can prove all the left (and right) constraints together, by considering a larger matrix. Second, left and right constraints can be merged in a single matrix which consists of elements in both groups, and using an argument for some promise problem in *bilateral* linear spaces. This also makes the auxiliary variable O^* (and related equations) unnecessary.

Efficiency. Then, the building blocks (1), (2) of our instantiation are exactly the same as in González and Ràfols [11]. The cost of committing to the input plus proving it is boolean with the argument of [7] is $(2n_s + 4)|\mathbb{G}_1| + 6|\mathbb{G}_2|$. We take the same quadratic constraints proof from [11] with Zero-Knowledge that is $12d|\mathbb{G}_1| + 4d|\mathbb{G}_2|$ for the commitments and $8d|\mathbb{G}_1| + 4d|\mathbb{G}_2|$ for the GS proofs. This is the same cost as in [11], but in the full version we will give different tradeoffs to reduce the proof size at the cost of increasing the common reference string. In any case, the overhead of using an USS argument for promise problems in bilateral spaces as opposed to the argument for bilateral spaces with standard soundness used in González and Ràfols [11] is only $3|\mathbb{G}_1|$.

3.2   Universally Composable Signature of Knowledge

Following the same approach as Groth and Maller [14], the SE NIZK argument with BB extractability together with a universal one-way hash function allows to construct a UC secure SoK for boolean CircuitSat based on falsifiable assumptions in bilinear groups in a straightforward way. The full details of this construction will appear in the full version of the paper.

4   USS QA-NIZK Arguments of Knowledge Transfer for Linear Spaces

In this section we prove that the USS argument for membership in linear spaces of Kiltz and Wee also satisfies the "knowledge transfer" property, or more technically, that it has soundness for the same promise problem described in Sect. 2.4.

We give the argument for membership in linear spaces in one group in detail in Sect. 4.1 and we present the scheme for the bilateral version in Sect. 4.2.

4.1   USS $\mathsf{Lin}_{\mathcal{D}_k}$ Argument

In this section we present $\mathsf{Lin}_{\mathcal{D}_k}$, a quasi-adaptive USS argument of membership in linear spaces in the group $\mathbb{G}_1$ for the promise problem defined by languages

$$\mathcal{L}_{\text{YES}}^{\text{Lin}} = \left\{ (\vec{w}, [\vec{x}]_1, [\vec{y}]_1) : \begin{array}{l} [\vec{x}]_1 = [\mathbf{M}]_1 \vec{w} \text{ and} \\ [\vec{y}]_1 = [\mathbf{N}]_1 \vec{w} \end{array} \right\}$$

$$\mathcal{L}_{\text{NO}}^{\text{Lin}} = \left\{ (\vec{w}, [\vec{x}]_1, [\vec{y}]_1) : \begin{array}{l} [\vec{x}]_1 = [\mathbf{M}]_1 \vec{w} \text{ and} \\ [\vec{y}]_1 \neq [\mathbf{N}]_1 \vec{w} \end{array} \right\}$$

parameterized by matrices $\mathbf{M} \in \mathbb{Z}_p^{\ell_1 \times n}, \mathbf{N} \in \mathbb{Z}_p^{\ell_2 \times n}$ sampled from some distributions $\mathcal{M}, \mathcal{N}$. Completeness holds for YES instances, and soundness guarantees that NO instances will not be accepted. That is, as in [11], we assume $[\vec{x}]_1 = [\mathbf{M}]_1 \vec{w}$ holds when proving soundness. In the CircuitSat context, this can be assumed because the idea is that this is proven by first proving knowledge of the input and then by "transferring" this knowledge to the lower layers via the quadratic or the linear argument we have presented. We consider the general language $\mathcal{L}$ that includes all tuples $(\vec{w}, \vec{x}, \vec{y})$ of the right dimension, some of them which are outside of $\mathcal{L}_{\text{YES}}^{\text{Lin}} \cup \mathcal{L}_{\text{NO}}^{\text{Lin}}$. We allow simulation queries for any tuple in $\mathcal{L}$. Note that it would be enough to allow the adversary just to ask for queries in $\mathcal{L}_{\text{NO}}^{\text{Lin}}$ in some contexts, as in Sect. 3 for CircuitSat, but we define for general statements.

Scheme Definition. The argument is presented in Fig. 1 and is just the USS QA-NIZK argument of [19] written in two blocks, which adds a pseudorandom MAC to the basic (not simulation sound, just sound) QA-NIZK argument of membership linear spaces for non-witness samplable distributions also given in [19]. If in the basic arguments proofs are of the form $[\vec{x}^\top, \vec{y}^\top]_1(\mathbf{K}_1, \mathbf{K}_2)$, in the USS variant they are given by

$$\left(\left[(\vec{x}^\top, \vec{y}^\top)(\mathbf{K}_1, \mathbf{K}_2) + \vec{r}^\top \mathbf{\Lambda}(\mathbf{\Lambda}_0 + \tau \mathbf{\Lambda}_1) \right]_1, \left[\vec{r}^\top \mathbf{\Lambda}^\top \right]_1 \right).$$

Our contribution is not in the scheme but in the security analysis. Our proof follows [11] that proved that the basic argument in [19] is complete and sound for the same promise problem under some MDDH and KerMDH assumptions related to the matrix $\mathcal{M}$. Our contribution is to modify their analysis to adapt it to simulation soundness for the scheme of Fig. 1.

Perfect Completeness, Perfect Zero-Knowledge. Our language $\mathcal{L}_{\text{YES}}^{\text{Lin}}$ is the same language for membership proofs in a linear space $[\mathbf{M}, \mathbf{N}]_1^\top$ used in [19]: $\left\{ (\vec{w}, [\vec{x}, \vec{y}]_1) : [\vec{x}^\top, \vec{y}^\top]_1^\top = [\mathbf{M}, \mathbf{N}]_1^\top \vec{w} \right\}$, so perfect completeness and perfect zero-knowledge are immediate.

$\mathrm{K}\,(gk, [\mathbf{M}]_1, [\mathbf{N}]_1):$

$\mathbf{K}_1 \leftarrow \mathbb{Z}_p^{\ell_1 \times (k+1)}, \mathbf{K}_2 \leftarrow \mathbb{Z}_p^{\ell_2 \times (k+1)},$

$\mathbf{K}^\top = \left(\mathbf{K}_1^\top, \mathbf{K}_2^\top \right)$

$\mathbf{A}, \boldsymbol{\Lambda} \leftarrow \mathcal{D}_k,$

$\boldsymbol{\Lambda}_0, \boldsymbol{\Lambda}_1 \leftarrow \mathbb{Z}_p^{(k+1) \times (k+1)}$

$\mathbf{C}_1 = \mathbf{K}_1 \mathbf{A}, \mathbf{C}_2 = \mathbf{K}_2 \mathbf{A},$

$[\mathbf{B}]_1 = \left[\mathbf{M}^\top \mathbf{K}_1 + \mathbf{N}^\top \mathbf{K}_2 \right]_1$

$(\mathbf{P}_0, \mathbf{P}_1) = (\boldsymbol{\Lambda}^\top \boldsymbol{\Lambda}_0, \boldsymbol{\Lambda}^\top \boldsymbol{\Lambda}_1)$

$(\mathbf{Q}_0, \mathbf{Q}_1) = (\boldsymbol{\Lambda}_0 \mathbf{A}, \boldsymbol{\Lambda}_1 \mathbf{A})$

Return $\mathsf{crs} = \left(gk, [\mathbf{B}]_1, [\mathbf{A}]_2, [\mathbf{P}_0]_1, \right.$

$[\mathbf{P}_1]_1, [\mathbf{Q}_0]_2, [\mathbf{Q}_1]_2, [\mathbf{C}_1]_2, [\mathbf{C}_2]_2, [\boldsymbol{\Lambda}]_1)$

$\mathsf{tr} = (\mathbf{K}_1, \mathbf{K}_2)$

$\mathrm{P}\,(\mathsf{crs}, \tau, [\boldsymbol{x}]_1, [\boldsymbol{y}]_1, \boldsymbol{w}):$

Pick $\vec{r} \leftarrow \mathbb{Z}_p^k$ and return

$\vec{\pi} = \left(\boldsymbol{w}^\top [\mathbf{B}]_1 + \vec{r}^\top [\mathbf{P}_0 + \tau \mathbf{P}_1]_1, \right.$

$\left. [\vec{r}^\top \boldsymbol{\Lambda}^\top]_1 \right).$

$\mathrm{V}\,(\mathsf{crs}, \tau, [\boldsymbol{x}]_1, [\boldsymbol{y}]_1, \vec{\pi}):$

Check if:

$e\,(\vec{\pi}_1, [\mathbf{A}]_2) - e\left([\boldsymbol{x}^\top, \boldsymbol{y}^\top]_1, [\mathbf{C}]_2 \right)$

$= e\,(\vec{\pi}_2, [\mathbf{Q}_0 + \tau \mathbf{Q}_1]_2)$

$\mathrm{S}\,(\mathsf{crs}, \tau, [\boldsymbol{x}]_1, [\boldsymbol{y}]_1, \mathsf{tr}):$

Sample $\vec{r} \leftarrow \mathbb{Z}_p^k$ and return

$\vec{\pi} = \left([\vec{x}^\top, \vec{y}^\top]_1 \mathbf{K} + \vec{r}^\top [\mathbf{P}_0 + \tau \mathbf{P}_1]_1, \right.$

$\left. [\vec{r}^\top \boldsymbol{\Lambda}^\top]_1 \right).$

Fig. 1. The $\mathsf{Lin}_{\mathcal{D}_k}$ argument for proving membership in linear spaces in blocks $[\vec{x}, \vec{y}]_1 \in \mathrm{Im}[\mathbf{M}, \mathbf{N}]_1$ where $\mathbf{M} \in \mathbb{Z}_p^{\ell_1 \times n}, \mathbf{N} \in \mathbb{Z}_p^{\ell_2 \times n}$.

Unbounded Simulation Soundness. For any adversary $\mathcal{A}$ that sends any number Q of queries $(\vec{w}^i, [\vec{x}^i, \vec{y}^i]_1) \in \mathcal{L}$ to the query simulator oracle S, receives simulated proofs $\{\vec{\pi}^i\}_{i=1}^Q$ as described in Fig. 1, the probability that the adversary $\mathcal{A}$ comes up with a proof $\vec{\pi}^*$ for a statement $(\vec{w}^*, [\vec{x}^*, \vec{y}^*]_1) \in \mathcal{L}_{\mathrm{NO}}^{\mathsf{Lin}}$ different of the queried ones and different tag τ^*, such that $\mathrm{V}(\mathsf{crs}, \tau^*, [\vec{x}^*, \vec{y}^*]_1, \vec{\pi}^*) = 1$ is negligible.

We use Definition 4 and our proof is analogous to USS proof of [19], where the authors argue that partial information about matrix $\mathbf{K}$ is hidden across all the simulated proofs which fits perfectly with the soundness argumentation in [11], where the authors prove the block $\mathbf{K}_{2,2}$ is hidden from the adversary. We need an extra change of games because our matrices admit more rows than columns and we have to assure the projection of our matrices does not reveal information of $\mathbf{K}_2$.

For the following theorem, we use the Computational Core Lemma of Kiltz and Wee in Sect. 4.1. of [19], which is independent of $\mathcal{M}, \mathcal{N}$, it just assumes the $\mathcal{D}_k$-$\mathsf{MDDH}_{\mathbb{G}_1}$, so we can use it directly in our proof.

Theorem 2. *The* $\mathsf{Lin}_{\mathcal{D}_k}$ *scheme in Fig. 1 is a Quasi-adaptive Non-Interactive Zero-Knowledge Argument with Unbounded Simulation Soundness such that for any adversary $\mathcal{A}$ that makes at most Q queries to S there exist adversaries $\mathcal{B}_1$, $\mathcal{B}_2$, $\mathcal{B}_3$ against the $\mathcal{D}_k$-KerMDH, $\mathcal{M}^\top$-MDDH assumptions in $\mathbb{G}_1$ for which the advantage of $\mathcal{A}$ is bounded by*

$$\mathsf{Adv}_{\mathsf{USS}\text{-}\mathsf{Lin}_{\mathcal{D}_k}}(\mathcal{A}) \leq \mathsf{Adv}_{\mathcal{D}_k-\mathsf{KerMDH}_{\mathbb{G}_1}}(\mathcal{B}_1) + 2Q\mathsf{Adv}_{\mathcal{D}_k\text{-}\mathsf{MDDH}_{\mathbb{G}_1}}(\mathcal{B}_2)$$

$$+ \mathsf{Adv}_{\mathcal{M}^\top\text{-}\mathsf{MDDH}_{\mathbb{G}_1}}(\mathcal{B}_3) + \frac{Q+1}{p}.$$

Proof. Let $\mathcal{A}$ be an adversary that plays the game described in USS Definition 4. We will proceed by changing to indistinguishable games in order to bound the advantage of $\mathcal{A}$. Let Game_0 be the real game and Adv_i the advantage of winning Game_i.

- Game_1 is the same as Game_0 except the verification algorithm V is changed to

$$\frac{\mathrm{V}^*(\mathsf{crs}, \tau, [\vec{x}, \vec{y}]_1, \vec{\pi}):}{\text{Check: } \vec{\pi}_1 = [\vec{x}^\top, \vec{y}^\top]_1 \mathbf{K} + \vec{\pi}_2(\mathbf{\Lambda}_0 + \tau\mathbf{\Lambda}_1).}$$

If a tuple $([\vec{x}, \vec{y}]_1, \vec{\pi})$ passes verification of V but does not pass verification of V^*, it means that the value $\vec{\pi} - [\vec{x}^\top, \vec{y}^\top]_1\mathbf{K} - \vec{\pi}_2(\mathbf{\Lambda}_0 + \tau\mathbf{\Lambda}_1) \in \mathbb{G}_1^{k+1}$ is a non-zero vector in the cokernel of $\mathbf{A}$. Thus, there exists an adversary $\mathcal{B}_1$ against $\mathsf{KerMDH}_{\mathbb{G}_1}$ such that

$$|\mathsf{Adv}_0 - \mathsf{Adv}_1| \leq \mathsf{Adv}_{\mathcal{D}_k-\mathsf{KerMDH}_{\mathbb{G}_1}}(\mathcal{B}_1).$$

- Game_2 is the same as Game_1 except the simulation algorithm S is changed to

$$\frac{\mathrm{S}^*(\mathsf{crs}, \tau, [\vec{x}, \vec{y}]_1, \mathsf{tr}):}{\vec{r} \leftarrow \mathbb{Z}_p^k, \mu \leftarrow \mathbb{Z}_p} ,$$
$$\text{Return: } \vec{\pi} = ([(\vec{x}^\top, \vec{y}^\top)\mathbf{K} + \mu\vec{a}^\perp + \vec{r}^\top(\mathbf{P}_0 + \tau\mathbf{P}_1)]_1, [\vec{r}^\top\mathbf{\Lambda}]_1)$$

where $\vec{a}^\perp$ is an element from the Kernel of $\mathbf{A}$. Let $\mathcal{B}_2$ be an adversary against $\mathcal{D}_k\text{-}\mathsf{MDDH}_{\mathbb{G}_1}$. $\mathcal{B}_2$ picks $\mathbf{K}$ itself and answers queries $(\tau_i, \vec{w}_i, [\vec{x}_i, \vec{y}_i]_1)$ from $\mathcal{A}$:
  - if $\tau_i \neq \tau^*$: $\mathcal{B}_2$ queries the oracle $\mathcal{O}_b$, defined in the core lemma [19], who simulates S if $b = 0$, or S^* if $b = 1$.
  - if $\tau_i = \tau^*$: $\mathcal{B}_2$ samples $\vec{r} \leftarrow \mathbb{Z}_p$ and computes $([(\vec{x}_i^\top, \vec{y}_i^\top)\mathbf{K} + \vec{r}^\top(\mathbf{P}_0 + \tau_i\mathbf{P}_1)]_1, [\vec{r}^\top\mathbf{\Lambda}_0^\top]_1)$.

Then $\mathcal{B}_2$ queries V^* to simulate verification of the final message of $\mathcal{A}$, $(\tau^*, \vec{w}^*, [\vec{x}^*, \vec{y}^*]_1)$. Now, it is easy to check if $(\vec{w}^*, [\vec{x}^*, \vec{y}^*]_1) \in \mathcal{L}_{\mathsf{NO}}^{\mathsf{Lin}}$ by computing $[\mathbf{M}]_1\vec{w}^*$ and $[\mathbf{N}]_1\vec{w}^*$. The difference between respective advantages is bounded using the core lemma of [19] as

$$|\mathsf{Adv}_1 - \mathsf{Adv}_2| \leq 2Q\mathsf{Adv}_{\mathcal{D}_k-\mathsf{MDDH}_{\mathbb{G}_1}}(\mathcal{B}_2) + \frac{Q}{p}.$$

- Game_3 is the same as Game_2 except the matrix $\mathbf{K} \leftarrow \mathbb{Z}_p^{(\ell_1+\ell_2)\times(k+1)}$ is changed in K to $\mathbf{K} = \mathbf{K}' + \vec{b}\vec{a}^\perp$ where $\mathbf{K}' \leftarrow \mathbb{Z}_p^{(\ell_1+\ell_2)\times(k+1)}$, $\vec{b}_1 \leftarrow \mathbb{Z}_p^{\ell_1}$, $\vec{b}_2 \leftarrow \mathbb{Z}_p^{\ell_2}$, $\vec{b}^\top = (\vec{b}_1^\top, \vec{b}_2^\top)$ and $\mathbf{B} = (\mathbf{M}^\top, \mathbf{N}^\top)\mathbf{K} + (\vec{z} + \mathbf{N}^\top\vec{b}_2)\vec{a}^\perp$, where $\vec{z} = \mathbf{M}^\top\vec{b}_1$. It is direct to see that both $\mathbf{K}, \mathbf{K}'$ are uniformly distributed in $\mathbb{Z}_p^{(\ell_1+\ell_2)\times(k+1)}$, so the advantages of both games are equivalent.
- Game_4 is the same as Game_3 except that now $\vec{z} \leftarrow \mathbb{Z}_p^{\ell_1}$. Let $\mathcal{B}_3$ be an adversary against $\mathcal{D}_k\text{-}\mathsf{MDDH}_{\mathbb{G}_1}$ that receives $([\mathbf{M}^\top]_1, [\vec{z}]_1)$ as a challenge and computes the crs as in previous game with this $[\vec{z}]_1$ in $\mathbf{B}$ and runs $\mathcal{A}$ as in Game_3. Finally, when the advantage of $\mathcal{B}_3$ to distinguish between Game_3 and Game_4 is bounded by the probability of distinguishing between a random vector from the image of the matrix $\mathbf{M}^\top$, so

$$|\mathsf{Adv}_3 - \mathsf{Adv}_4| \leq \mathsf{Adv}_{\mathbf{M}^\top-\mathsf{MDDH}_{\mathbb{G}_1}}(\mathcal{B}_3).$$

Now we bound the advantage of adversary $\mathcal{A}$ in winning Game_4. Firstly, we show what is leaked about vector $\vec{b}$ for the adversary's view:

- the matrix $\mathbf{C} = (\mathbf{K}' + \vec{b}\vec{a}^{\perp})\mathbf{A}$ completely hides the vector $\vec{b}$,
- the output of S^*, $(\vec{x}, \vec{y})^{\top}(\mathbf{K}' + \vec{b}\vec{a}^{\perp}) + \mu\vec{a}^{\perp}$ completely hides $\vec{b}$ because μ masks $(\vec{x}^{\top}, \vec{y}^{\top})\vec{b}$,
- the matrix $\mathbf{B}$ contains information about $\vec{z} + \mathbf{N}^{\top}\vec{b}_2$, but $\vec{z}$ is uniformly random and independent of $\vec{b}_2$, so $\vec{z}$ masks $\vec{b}_2$.

Note that if the adversary $\mathcal{A}$ passes the verification V^* with some $\vec{\pi}^*$ for an statement $(\vec{w}^*, \vec{x}^*, \vec{y}^*) \in \mathcal{L}_{\mathsf{NO}}^{\mathsf{Lin}}$, it can also construct a valid proof $\pi = (\vec{\pi}_1^* - \vec{w}^*\mathbf{B}, \vec{\pi}_2^*)$ for the statement $(\vec{w}^*, \vec{0}, \vec{y} - \vec{y}^*) \in \mathcal{L}_{\mathsf{NO}}^{\mathsf{Lin}}$ where $\vec{y} = \mathbf{N}\vec{w}^*$. It must hold that

$$\pi = (0, \vec{y} - \vec{y}^*)(\mathbf{K}' + \vec{b}\vec{a}^{\perp}) = (\vec{y} - \vec{y}^*)\mathbf{K}_2' + (\vec{y} - \vec{y}^*)\vec{b}_2\vec{a}^{\perp}, \qquad (*)$$

Note $\vec{y} - \vec{y}^*$ is not zero because $\vec{y} \neq \vec{y}^*$. Since $\vec{b}_2$ remains completely hidden to the adversary and $\mathbf{K}_2'$ is independent of $\vec{b}_2$, the probability that equation $(*)$ holds is less that $1/p$. $\qquad\square$

$\underline{\mathrm{K}\,(gk, [\mathbf{M}]_1, [\mathbf{N}]_1, [\mathbf{P}]_2):}$
$\mathbf{K}_1 \leftarrow \mathbb{Z}_p^{\ell_1 \times (k+1)}, \mathbf{K}_2 \leftarrow \mathbb{Z}_p^{\ell_2 \times (k+1)},$
$\mathbf{K}_3 \leftarrow \mathbb{Z}_p^{\ell_3 \times (k+1)},$
$\mathbf{A}, \mathbf{\Lambda} \leftarrow \mathcal{D}_k, \mathbf{\Gamma} \leftarrow \mathbb{Z}_p^{n \times (k+1)},$
$\mathbf{\Lambda}_0, \mathbf{\Lambda}_1 \leftarrow \mathbb{Z}_p^{(k+1) \times (k+1)}$
$\mathbf{C}_1 = \mathbf{K}_1 \mathbf{A}, \mathbf{C}_2 = \mathbf{K}_2 \mathbf{A}, \mathbf{C}_3 = \mathbf{K}_3 \mathbf{A},$
$[\mathbf{B}]_1 = [\mathbf{M}^{\top}\mathbf{K}_1 + \mathbf{N}^{\top}\mathbf{K}_2 + \mathbf{\Gamma}]_1$
$[\mathbf{D}]_2 = [\mathbf{P}^{\top}\mathbf{K}_3 - \mathbf{\Gamma}]_2$
$(\mathbf{P}_0, \mathbf{P}_1) = (\mathbf{\Lambda}^{\top}\mathbf{\Lambda}_0, \mathbf{\Lambda}^{\top}\mathbf{\Lambda}_1)$
$(\mathbf{Q}_0, \mathbf{Q}_1) = (\mathbf{\Lambda}_0 \mathbf{A}, \mathbf{\Lambda}_1 \mathbf{A})$
Return $\mathsf{crs} = (gk, [\mathbf{B}]_1, [\mathbf{A}]_{1,2}, [\mathbf{P}_0]_2,$
$[\mathbf{P}_1]_2, [\mathbf{Q}_0]_1, [\mathbf{Q}_1]_1, [\mathbf{C}_1]_2, [\mathbf{C}_2]_2,$
$[\mathbf{C}_3]_1, [\mathbf{\Lambda}]_1)$
$\theta = [\vec{y}]_2 \mathbf{K}_3^{\top}.$
$\mathsf{tr} = (\mathbf{K}_1, \mathbf{K}_2, \mathbf{K}_3)$

$\underline{\mathrm{P}\,(\mathsf{crs}, \tau, [\boldsymbol{x}_1]_1, [\boldsymbol{x}_2]_1, [\boldsymbol{y}]_2, \boldsymbol{w}):}$
Pick $\vec{r} \leftarrow \mathbb{Z}_p^k$ and return
$\vec{\pi} = (\boldsymbol{w}^{\top}[\mathbf{B}]_1 + \vec{r}^{\top}[\mathbf{P}_0 + \tau\mathbf{P}_1]_1,$
$[\vec{r}^{\top}\mathbf{\Lambda}^{\top}]_1),$
$\theta = \boldsymbol{w}^{\top}[\mathbf{D}]_2.$
$\underline{\mathrm{V}\,(\mathsf{crs}, \tau, [\boldsymbol{x}_1]_1, [\boldsymbol{x}_2]_1, [\boldsymbol{y}]_2, \vec{\pi}, \theta):}$
Check if: $e(\vec{\pi}_1, [\mathbf{A}]_2) - e([\mathbf{A}]_1, \theta)$
$-e([\boldsymbol{x}_1^{\top}]_1, [\mathbf{C}_1]_2) - e([\boldsymbol{x}_2^{\top}]_1, [\mathbf{C}_2]_2)$
$+e([\mathbf{C}_3]_1, [\boldsymbol{y}^{\top}]_2) = e(\vec{\pi}_2, [\mathbf{Q}_0 + \tau\mathbf{Q}_1]_2)$
$\underline{\mathrm{S}\,(\mathsf{crs}, \tau, [\boldsymbol{x}_1]_1, [\boldsymbol{x}_2]_1, [\boldsymbol{y}]_2, \mathsf{tr}):}$
Sample $\vec{r} \leftarrow \mathbb{Z}_p^k$ and return
$\vec{\pi} = ([\vec{x}_1, \vec{x}_2]_1(\mathbf{K}_1^{\top}, \mathbf{K}_2^{\top})$
$+\vec{r}^{\top}(\mathbf{P}_0 + \tau\mathbf{P}_1), [\vec{r}^{\top}\mathbf{\Lambda}^{\top}]_1),$

Fig. 2. The $\mathsf{BLin}_{\mathcal{D}_k}$ argument for proving membership in linear spaces in blocks $([\vec{x}_1, \vec{x}_2]_1, [\vec{y}]_2) \in \mathrm{Im}([\mathbf{M}, \mathbf{N}]_1, [\mathbf{P}]_2,)$ where $\mathbf{M} \in \mathbb{Z}_p^{\ell_1 \times n}, \mathbf{N} \in \mathbb{Z}_p^{\ell_2 \times n}, \mathbf{P} \in \mathbb{Z}_p^{\ell_3 \times n}$.

4.2   USS $\mathsf{BLin}_{\mathcal{D}_k}$ Argument

In this section we present the USS argument for membership in linear spaces in groups $\mathbb{G}_1$, $\mathbb{G}_2$, which is just an extension to bilateral spaces of the USS $\mathsf{Lin}_{\mathcal{D}_k}$ argument presented in Sect. 4.1 for the promise problem defined by languages

$$\mathcal{L}_{\text{YES}}^{\text{Blin}} = \left\{ (\vec{w}, [\vec{x}_1]_1, [\vec{x}_2]_1, [\vec{y}]_2) : \begin{array}{l} [\vec{x}_1]_1 = [\mathbf{M}]_1\vec{w} \text{ and} \\ [\vec{x}_2]_1 = [\mathbf{N}]_1\vec{w}, [\vec{y}]_2 = [\mathbf{P}]_2\vec{w} \end{array} \right\}$$

$$\mathcal{L}_{\text{NO}}^{\text{Blin}} = \left\{ (\vec{w}, [\vec{x}_1]_1, [\vec{x}_2]_1, [\vec{y}]_2) : \begin{array}{l} [\vec{x}_1]_1 = [\mathbf{M}]_1\vec{w} \text{ and} \\ [\vec{x}_2]_1 \neq [\mathbf{N}]_1\vec{w} \text{ or } [\vec{y}]_2 \neq [\mathbf{P}]_2\vec{w} \end{array} \right\}$$

parameterized by matrices $\mathbf{M} \in \mathbb{Z}_p^{\ell_1 \times n}, \mathbf{N} \in \mathbb{Z}_p^{\ell_2 \times n}, \mathbf{P} \in \mathbb{Z}_p^{\ell_3 \times n}$ sampled from some distributions $\mathcal{M}, \mathcal{N}, \mathcal{P}$. This argument is presented in Fig. 2. QA-NIZK arguments of membership in linear spaces were extended to the bilateral case in [10] for both samplable and non-witness samplable distributions. In [11], the authors proved that the argument for non-witness samplable distributions of [10] is also sound and complete for this promise problem. Adding the pseudorandom MAC given in [19] we get USS. The proof is essentially the same as in Sect. 4.1, but now the linear spaces are split in two groups $\mathbb{G}_1$ and $\mathbb{G}_2$. The core lemma would be the analogous one and the reduction of the proof of USS is bounded by SKerMDH and $\mathcal{D}_k$-MDDH$_{\mathbb{G}_1}$ Assumptions.

Acknowledgement. Karim Baghery was supported by CyberSecurity Research Flanders with reference number VR20192203.

References

1. Baghery, K.: Subversion-resistant simulation (knowledge) sound NIZKs. In: Albrecht, M. (ed.) IMACC 2019. LNCS, vol. 11929, pp. 42–63. Springer, Cham (2019). https://doi.org/10.1007/978-3-030-35199-1_3

2. Ben-Sasson, E., et al.: Zerocash: decentralized anonymous payments from bitcoin. In: 2014 IEEE Symposium on Security and Privacy, pp. 459–474. IEEE Computer Society Press, May 2014

3. Bernhard, D., Fuchsbauer, G., Ghadafi, E.: Efficient signatures of knowledge and DAA in the standard model. In: Jacobson, M., Locasto, M., Mohassel, P., Safavi-Naini, R. (eds.) ACNS 2013. LNCS, vol. 7954, pp. 518–533. Springer, Heidelberg (2013). https://doi.org/10.1007/978-3-642-38980-1_33

4. Canetti, R., Lindell, Y., Ostrovsky, R., Sahai, A.: Universally composable two-party and multi-party secure computation. In: 34th ACM STOC, pp. 494–503. ACM Press, May 2002

5. Chase, M., Lysyanskaya, A.: On signatures of knowledge. In: Dwork, C. (ed.) CRYPTO 2006. LNCS, vol. 4117, pp. 78–96. Springer, Heidelberg (2006). https://doi.org/10.1007/11818175_5

6. Damgård, I.: Towards practical public key systems secure against chosen ciphertext attacks. In: Feigenbaum, J. (ed.) CRYPTO 1991. LNCS, vol. 576, pp. 445–456. Springer, Heidelberg (1992). https://doi.org/10.1007/3-540-46766-1_36

7. Daza, V., González, A., Pindado, Z., Ràfols, C., Silva, J.: Shorter quadratic QA-NIZK proofs. In: Lin, D., Sako, K. (eds.) PKC 2019, Part I. LNCS, vol. 11442, pp. 314–343. Springer, Cham (2019). https://doi.org/10.1007/978-3-030-17253-4_11

8. Gennaro, R., Gentry, C., Parno, B., Raykova, M.: Quadratic span programs and succinct NIZKs without PCPs. In: Johansson, T., Nguyen, P.Q. (eds.) EURO-CRYPT 2013. LNCS, vol. 7881, pp. 626–645. Springer, Heidelberg (2013). https://doi.org/10.1007/978-3-642-38348-9_37

9. Gentry, C., Wichs, D.: Separating succinct non-interactive arguments from all fal-sifiable assumptions. In: Fortnow, L., Vadhan, S.P. (eds.) 43rd ACM STOC, pp. 99–108. ACM Press, June 2011

10. González, A., Hevia, A., Ràfols, C.: QA-NIZK arguments in asymmetric groups: new tools and new constructions. In: Iwata, T., Cheon, J.H. (eds.) ASIACRYPT 2015, Part I. LNCS, vol. 9452, pp. 605–629. Springer, Heidelberg (2015). https://doi.org/10.1007/978-3-662-48797-6_25

11. González, A., Ràfols, C.: Shorter pairing-based arguments under standard assump-tions. In: Galbraith, S.D., Moriai, S. (eds.) ASIACRYPT 2019. LNCS, vol. 11923, pp. 728–757. Springer, Cham (2019). https://doi.org/10.1007/978-3-030-34618-8_25

12. Groth, J.: Simulation-sound NIZK proofs for a practical language and constant size group signatures. In: Lai, X., Chen, K. (eds.) ASIACRYPT 2006. LNCS, vol. 4284, pp. 444–459. Springer, Heidelberg (2006). https://doi.org/10.1007/11935230_29

13. Groth, J.: On the size of pairing-based non-interactive arguments. In: Fischlin, M., Coron, J.-S. (eds.) EUROCRYPT 2016, Part II. LNCS, vol. 9666, pp. 305–326. Springer, Heidelberg (2016). https://doi.org/10.1007/978-3-662-49896-5_11

14. Groth, J., Maller, M.: Snarky signatures: minimal signatures of knowledge from simulation-extractable SNARKs. In: Katz, J., Shacham, H. (eds.) CRYPTO 2017, Part II. LNCS, vol. 10402, pp. 581–612. Springer, Cham (2017). https://doi.org/10.1007/978-3-319-63715-0_20

15. Groth, J., Sahai, A.: Efficient non-interactive proof systems for bilinear groups. In: Smart, N. (ed.) EUROCRYPT 2008. LNCS, vol. 4965, pp. 415–432. Springer, Heidelberg (2008). https://doi.org/10.1007/978-3-540-78967-3_24

16. Hofheinz, D., Jia, D., Pan, J.: Identity-based encryption tightly secure under chosen-ciphertext attacks. In: Peyrin, T., Galbraith, S. (eds.) ASIACRYPT 2018, Part II. LNCS, vol. 11273, pp. 190–220. Springer, Cham (2018). https://doi.org/10.1007/978-3-030-03329-3_7

17. Jutla, C.S., Roy, A.: Shorter quasi-adaptive NIZK proofs for linear subspaces. In: Sako, K., Sarkar, P. (eds.) ASIACRYPT 2013, Part I. LNCS, vol. 8269, pp. 1–20. Springer, Heidelberg (2013). https://doi.org/10.1007/978-3-642-42033-7_1

18. Kerber, T., Kiayias, A., Kohlweiss, M., Zikas, V.: Ouroboros crypsinous: privacy-preserving proof-of-stake. In: 2019 IEEE Symposium on Security and Privacy, pp. 157–174. IEEE Computer Society Press, May 2019

19. Kiltz, E., Wee, H.: Quasi-adaptive NIZK for linear subspaces revisited. In: Oswald, E., Fischlin, M. (eds.) EUROCRYPT 2015, Part II. LNCS, vol. 9057, pp. 101–128. Springer, Heidelberg (2015). https://doi.org/10.1007/978-3-662-46803-6_4

20. Kosba, A.E., Miller, A., Shi, E., Wen, Z., Papamanthou, C.: Hawk: the blockchain model of cryptography and privacy-preserving smart contracts. In: 2016 IEEE Symposium on Security and Privacy, pp. 839–858. IEEE Computer Society Press, May 2016

21. Libert, B., Peters, T., Joye, M., Yung, M.: Linearly homomorphic structure-preserving signatures and their applications. In: Canetti, R., Garay, J.A. (eds.) CRYPTO 2013, Part II. LNCS, vol. 8043, pp. 289–307. Springer, Heidelberg (2013). https://doi.org/10.1007/978-3-642-40084-1_17

22. Naor, M.: On cryptographic assumptions and challenges. In: Boneh, D. (ed.) CRYPTO 2003. LNCS, vol. 2729, pp. 96–109. Springer, Heidelberg (2003). https://doi.org/10.1007/978-3-540-45146-4_6

23. Ràfols, C.: Stretching groth-sahai: NIZK proofs of partial satisfiability. In: Dodis, Y., Nielsen, J.B. (eds.) TCC 2015, Part II. LNCS, vol. 9015, pp. 247–276. Springer, Heidelberg (2015). https://doi.org/10.1007/978-3-662-46497-7_10
24. Sahai, A.: Non-malleable non-interactive zero knowledge and adaptive chosen-ciphertext security. In: 40th FOCS, pp. 543–553. IEEE Computer Society Press, October 1999

LESS is More: Code-Based Signatures
Without Syndromes

Jean-François Biasse[1], Giacomo Micheli[1], Edoardo Persichetti[2(✉)],
and Paolo Santini[2,3]

[1] University of South Florida, Tampa, USA
{biasse,gmicheli}@usf.edu
[2] Florida Atlantic University, Boca Raton, USA
epersichetti@fau.edu
[3] Universitá Politecnica delle Marche, Ancona, Italy
p.santini@pm.univpm.it

Abstract. Devising efficient and secure signature schemes based on coding theory is still considered a challenge by the cryptographic community. In this paper, we construct a signature scheme by exploring a new
approach to the area. To do this, we design a zero-knowledge identification scheme, which we then render static via standard means (e.g.
Fiat-Shamir). We show that practical instances of our protocol have the
potential to outperform the state of the art on code-based signatures,
achieving small data sizes with a low computational complexity.

Keywords: Post-Quantum · Code-Based · Code Equivalence ·
Signatures · Zero-Knowledge

1 Introduction

Digital signatures are arguably one of the most important cryptographic primitives in the modern times. Many famous examples include schemes based on
RSA, as well as discrete logarithm assumptions (DSA, ECDSA), all currently
standardized. However, none of the above will remain secure once a quantum
computer with sufficient power and stability becomes available, due to the sem-
inal work of Shor [34]. As a consequence, the cryptographic world is focusing
its efforts on producing *Post-Quantum* secure signature schemes. At present,
the scene is dominated by protocols based on lattice problems such as LWE and
SIS, as well as multivariate equations (MQ, UOV), with the noticeable exception
of isogeny-based signatures (e.g. [17,20]), a newer family of primitives with very
promising data size. Also, hash-based schemes such as SPHINCS [8] offer a conservative choice with reasonable performance and confidence in security. At the
contrary, the community is still struggling to produce efficient and consolidated
code-base signature schemes. A testament of this is given by the ongoing Post-
Quantum Standardization effort by NIST [27], where only 4 code-based signature
schemes were initially submitted, none of which progressed to further rounds of
the competition. Indeed, many code-based schemes have been proposed over the

© Springer Nature Switzerland AG 2020
A. Nitaj and A. Youssef (Eds.): AFRICACRYPT 2020, LNCS 12174, pp. 45–65, 2020.
https://doi.org/10.1007/978-3-030-51938-4_3

years, either following the hash-and-sign approach like CFS [11], or relying on the Fiat-Shamir transform [18] to convert an identification scheme into a signature scheme. Unfortunately, many of the various proposals have been broken, and all those that are still considered secure suffer from one or more flaws, be that a huge public key, a large signature or a slow signing algorithm, which ultimately make them unsuitable for practical applications.

Our Contribution. In this paper, we propose a signature scheme based on a novel approach from coding theory. The scheme is built upon an identification scheme that relies on the hardness of the Linear Code Equivalence problem; consequently, we name our protocol LESS as in Linear Equivalence Signature Scheme. This problem has been studied for a long time with regards to its application to the McEliece and Niederreiter cryptosystem but, to the best of our knowledge, no scheme has ever been instantiated on it as a stand-alone problem. In a 2013 paper [32], where the hardness of the problem is studied, there is a brief reference to zero-knowledge protocols, and the authors describe a version of Girault's identification scheme [21] using monomial matrices. However, this is still fundamentally a protocol based on the hardness of Syndrome Decoding, following the traditional approach of code-based cryptography. Our approach, on the other hand, does not involve syndromes and decoding at all, and is purely based on the hardness of determining the linear isometry between two codes. This allows us to choose parameters that are much smaller than those usually selected by schemes based on SDP, which have to protect against generic decoding attacks such as those in the Information-Set Decoding (ISD) family, or equivalent. As a consequence, we are able to design extremely practical instances, while at the same time setting up a new framework for code-based signatures.

The paper is organized as follows. In Sect. 2, we define our notation and give some preliminary definitions about coding theory and identification schemes. In Sect. 3, we present the central notion upon which our protocol is based, the Code Equivalence Problem. We then introduce our scheme, in Sect. 4, along with a proof of security. A careful security analysis and description of attack techniques is given in Sect. 5. In Sect. 6, we make further considerations about the problem, and we discuss the applicability of Quantum attacks. We briefly describe the Fiat-Shamir transform in Sect. 7, and give other details of how we can convert our identification scheme into a full-fledged signature scheme. In Sect. 8, we provide an accurate comparison with the state-of-the-art code-based signature schemes, present some performance figures, and explain our computational advantage. Finally, we conclude in Sect. 9.

2   Preliminaries

We denote scalars with lowercase letters, and sets with uppercase letters. Vectors and matrices are written in boldface, respectively lowercase and upper case. We will use $\otimes$ to denote the Kronecker product between matrices (or vectors). We write $\mathbf{a}$ for a function or relation, and $\mathcal{A}$ for an algorithm. I_n stands for the $n \times n$

identity matrix, and $[a; b]$ for the set of integers $\{a, a+1, \ldots, b\}$. Finally, we use $\mathbb{U}(A)$ to indicate the uniform distribution over the set A, and $\xleftarrow{\$} A$ for the action of sampling uniformly at random from A.

Let $\mathbb{F}_q$ be the finite field of order q. We write $\mathrm{GL}_k(q)$ for the set of invertible $k \times k$ matrices with elements in $\mathbb{F}_q$. Let S_n be the set of permutations over n elements. These can equivalently be described as functions $\pi : \mathbb{F}_q^n \to \mathbb{F}_q^n$ or in matrix form as $n \times n$ matrices with exactly one 1 per row and column. By analogy, we denote with $M_n(q)$ the set of monomial matrices with elements in $\mathbb{F}_q$, i.e. all the matrices of the form $\mathbf{Q} = \mathbf{D}\mathbf{P}$ where $\mathbf{P}$ is an $n \times n$ permutation matrix and $\mathbf{D} = \{d_{ij}\}$ is an $n \times n$ diagonal matrix such that $d_{ii} = d_i \in \mathbb{F}_q^*$. Given a vector $\mathbf{x} = (x_1, \cdots, x_n) \in \mathbb{F}_q^n$ and a permutation $\pi \in S_n$, we write the action of π on $\mathbf{x}$ as $\pi(\mathbf{x}) = (x_{\pi^{-1}(1)}, \cdots, x_{\pi^{-1}(n)})$.

2.1   Coding Theory

An $[n, k]$-*linear code* $\mathfrak{C}$ of length n and dimension k over $\mathbb{F}_q$ is a k-dimensional vector subspace of $\mathbb{F}_q^n$. It can be represented by a matrix $\mathbf{G} \in \mathbb{F}_q^{k \times n}$, called *generator matrix*, whose rows form a basis for the vector space. Then, the generator matrix defines the code as a mapping between vectors $\mathbf{u} \in \mathbb{F}_q^k$ and the corresponding words $\mathbf{u}\mathbf{G}$. Obviously, there exist more than one generator matrix for the same code, corresponding to different choices of basis. It follows that all generator matrices are connected via a change-of-basis matrix, i.e. an invertible matrix $\mathbf{S} \in \mathrm{GL}_k(q)$ such that $\mathbf{G}' = \mathbf{S}\mathbf{G}$. Alternatively, a linear code can be represented as the kernel of a matrix $\mathbf{H} \in \mathbb{F}_q^{(n-k) \times n}$, known as *parity-check matrix*, i.e. $\mathfrak{C} = \{\mathbf{x} \in \mathbb{F}_q^n : \mathbf{H}\mathbf{x}^T = 0\}$. Once again, the parity-check matrix of a code is not unique. For both cases, there exists a standard choice, called *systematic form*. For the generator matrix, this corresponds to $\mathbf{G} = (\mathbf{I}_k \mid \mathbf{M})$, which can be obtained as the row-reduced echelon form starting from any other generator matrix. The systematic form of the parity-check matrix is given by $\mathbf{H} = (-\mathbf{M}^T \mid \mathbf{I}_{n-k})$. Note that, in general, it is possible that computing the row-reduced echelon form of $\mathbf{G}$ returns a matrix that does not have full rank. If this is the case, there are procedures to obtain a matrix in systematic form by reducing with respect to a different minor (for example, the Round 2 specification document of [10] describes one that works in constant-time). We denote such a procedure with SF.

For every linear code, we can define the *dual code* as the set of words that are orthogonal to the code, i.e. $\mathfrak{C}^\perp = \{\mathbf{y} \in \mathbb{F}_q^n : \forall \mathbf{x} \in \mathfrak{C}, \ \mathbf{x} \cdot \mathbf{y}^T = 0\}$ It is then easy to see that a parity-check matrix of a linear code is a generator of its dual, and viceversa. In fact, it must be that $\mathbf{G} \cdot \mathbf{H}^T = \mathbf{0}_{k \times (n-k)}$. Codes that are contained in their dual, i.e. $\mathfrak{C} \subseteq \mathfrak{C}^\perp$, are called *weakly self-dual*, and codes that are equal to their dual, i.e. $\mathfrak{C} = \mathfrak{C}^\perp$, are called simply *self-dual*.

2.2   Identification Schemes and Zero-Knowledge Protocols

We now recall some standard cryptographic notions about the so-called Sigma protocols, and how to derive identification schemes from them. To do so, we follow the general outline given in [20], in turn based on definitions and notation from [1,5,12,23,37].

Definition 1 (Sigma Protocol). *Consider two sets X and Y parameterized by a security parameter λ. Let R be a relation on $X \times Y$ defining a language $L = \{y \in Y : \exists x \in X, R(x, y) = 1\}$. We call* witness *an element $x \in X$ such that, given $y \in L$, verifies $R(x, y) = 1$. We define a* Sigma Protocol *as a 3-round interactive protocol between two PPT algorithms, a* Prover $\mathcal{P}$ *and a* Verifier $\mathcal{V}$, *as described in Table 1 below.*

Table 1. Sigma protocol.

Prover Data   A witness x for $y \in L$.
Verifier Data $y \in L$.

PROVER		VERIFIER
$\alpha \leftarrow \mathcal{P}(x, y)$	$\xrightarrow{\alpha}$	
	$\xleftarrow{\beta}$	$\beta \leftarrow \mathcal{V}(\alpha, y)$
$\gamma \leftarrow \mathcal{P}(\alpha, \beta, x, y)$	$\xrightarrow{\gamma}$	$\{0, 1\} \leftarrow \mathcal{V}(\alpha, \beta, \gamma, y)$

The triple (α, β, γ) forms a *transcript* of the protocol, and the three values are usually known as *commitment, challenge* and *response*, respectively. A transcript for which the verifier outputs 1 (accept) is called *valid*.

Sigma protocols are often required to satisfy the following properties:

- *Completeness*: when $y \in L$, an honest prover is accepted with probability 1.
- *2-Special Soundness*: there exists an *extractor* algorithm $\mathcal{X}$ such that, for any $y \in L$, given two valid transcripts (α, β, γ) and $(\alpha, \beta', \gamma')$ with $\beta \neq \beta'$, the output $\mathcal{X}(\alpha, \beta, \gamma, \beta', \gamma')$ is a witness for R.
- *Honest-Verifier Zero-Knowledge*: there exists a *simulator* algorithm $\mathcal{S}$ such that, on input $y \in L$, is able to generate a valid transcript (α, β, γ) that is distributed identically to one obtained from a real execution of the protocol.

An identification scheme can be defined as a special type of Sigma protocol, where the relation R is defined over key pairs (sk, pk), and one can think of sk as a witness for pk.

Definition 2. *Let λ be a security parameter. A* Canonical Identification Scheme *is composed by a triple of PPT algorithms $(\mathcal{K}, \mathcal{P}, \mathcal{V})$, respectively Key Generator, Prover and Verifier, and a parameter ℓ, the length of the challenge, interacting as described in Table 2, below.*

As before, the exchanged data takes the name of commitment, challenge, and response. Note that we have made explicit the role of the randomness ρ in the generation of the challenge (remember that $\mathcal{P}$ is a probabilistic algorithm). The scheme is said to be *non-trivial* if $\ell \geq \lambda$.

Table 2. Canonical identification scheme.

Private Key   A private key sk output by $\mathcal{K}(1^\lambda)$.
Public Key   The public key pk corresponding to sk.

PROVER		VERIFIER
cmt $\leftarrow \mathcal{P}(\text{sk}, \text{pk}, \rho)$	$\xrightarrow{\text{cmt}}$	
	$\xleftarrow{\text{ch}}$	ch $\leftarrow \{0,1\}^\ell$
rsp $\leftarrow \mathcal{P}(\text{sk}, \text{pk}, \rho, \text{cmt}, \text{ch})$	$\xrightarrow{\text{rsp}}$	$\{0,1\} \leftarrow \mathcal{V}(\text{pk}, \text{cmt}, \text{ch}, \text{rsp})$

An *impersonator* $\mathcal{I}$ is a PPT adversary that aims to get verified by $\mathcal{V}$ without knowing the private key. The impersonator is able to observe a number of transcripts from honest executions, before producing a commitment, receiving a corresponding challenge, and finally outputting its response. The impersonator is commonly said to have *cheating probability* equal to $1/2^\ell$. We say that $\mathcal{I}$ *wins* if $\mathcal{V}(\text{pk}, \text{cmt}, \text{ch}, \text{rsp}) = 1$, and we define $\mathcal{I}$'s advantage as

$$\left| \mathsf{Adv}(\mathcal{I}, \lambda) = \Pr[\mathcal{I} \text{ wins}] - \frac{1}{2^\ell} \right|.$$

We say that an identification scheme is *secure against impersonation under passive attacks* if the advantage of any PPT impersonator is negligible.

Usually, identification schemes are defined using challenges that are too short to obtain a non-trivial instance, the most common case being, as in this paper, $\ell = 1$ (i.e. the challenge is a single bit). However, it is possible to obtain a non-trivial scheme by iterating the protocol t times (which can be done in parallel). Formally, the prover generates commitments cmt_i for $i = 1, \ldots, t$, then receives a challenge ch $\in \{0,1\}^{t\ell}$, parses it into t blocks ch_i of length ℓ each, and produces responses rsp_i for $i = 1, \ldots, t$. The verifier receives as input $(\text{pk}, \text{cmt}_1, \ldots, \text{cmt}_t, \text{ch}, \text{rsp}_1, \ldots, \text{rsp}_t)$ and accepts if and only if $\mathcal{V}(\text{pk}, \text{cmt}_i, \text{ch}_i, \text{rsp}_i) = 1$ for $i = 1, \ldots, t$. This reduces the cheating probability to $1/2^{t\ell}$, which makes the scheme non-trivial as long as $t \geq \lambda/\ell$.

3   The Code Equivalence Problem

In this section we introduce the ideas upon which we base the security of our protocol. We first formally define the notion of code equivalence.

Definition 3 (Permutation Code Equivalence). *We say that two codes $\mathfrak{C}$ and $\mathfrak{C}'$ are permutationally equivalent, and write $\mathfrak{C} \overset{\text{PE}}{\sim} \mathfrak{C}'$, if there is a permutation $\pi \in S_n$ that maps $\mathfrak{C}$ into $\mathfrak{C}$, i.e.*

$$\mathfrak{C}' = \{\pi(\boldsymbol{x}), \ \boldsymbol{x} \in \mathfrak{C}\}.$$

The previous notion of code equivalence can be extended using linear isometries. Indeed, let $\mu = (\boldsymbol{v}, \pi) \in \mathbb{F}_q^{*n} \rtimes S_n$ be an isometry μ, such that

$$\mu(\boldsymbol{x}) = (v_1 x_{\pi^{-1}(1)}, \cdots, v_n x_{\pi^{-1}(n)}).$$

We can then generalize the previous definition as follows.

Definition 4 (Linear Code Equivalence). *We say that two codes* $\mathfrak{C}$ *and* $\mathfrak{C}'$ *are linearly equivalent, and write* $\mathfrak{C} \overset{\text{LE}}{\sim} \mathfrak{C}'$, *if there is a linear isometry* $\mu = (\boldsymbol{v}; \pi) \in \mathbb{F}_q^{*n} \rtimes S_n$ *such that* $\mathfrak{C}' = \mu(\mathfrak{C})$, *i.e.* $\mathfrak{C}' = \{\mu(\boldsymbol{x}), \ \boldsymbol{x} \in \mathfrak{C}\}$.

It is clear the previous definitions can equivalently be stated in terms of generator (or parity-check) matrices; furthermore, the application of a permutation (resp. linear isometry) corresponds to the right multiplication by a permutation matrix $\boldsymbol{P}$ (resp. monomial matrix $\boldsymbol{Q}$).

Let $\mathfrak{C}$ and $\mathfrak{C}'$ be two codes with respective generator matrices $\boldsymbol{G}$ and $\boldsymbol{G}'$: we then have

$$\mathfrak{C} \overset{\text{PE}}{\sim} \mathfrak{C}' \iff \exists (\boldsymbol{S}, \boldsymbol{P}) \in \mathrm{GL}_k(q) \times S_n \ \text{s.t.} \ \boldsymbol{G}' = \boldsymbol{SGP},$$
$$\mathfrak{C} \overset{\text{LE}}{\sim} \mathfrak{C}' \iff \exists (\boldsymbol{S}, \boldsymbol{Q}) \in \mathrm{GL}_k(q) \times M_n(q) \ \text{s.t.} \ \boldsymbol{G}' = \boldsymbol{SGQ}.$$

Another notion of code equivalence (using *semilinear* isometries) is often found in the literature; however, it is not needed for our protocol, and therefore we do not present it here. We instead refer the interested reader to [32] for further details, and move on to present the hard problems connected to the notions we just described.

Problem 1 (Permutation Code Equivalence). *Let* $\boldsymbol{G}, \boldsymbol{G}' \in \mathbb{F}_q^{k \times n}$ *be two generator matrices for, respectively, linear codes* $\mathfrak{C}$ *and* $\mathfrak{C}'$. *Determine whether the two codes are permutationally equivalent, i.e. if there exist two matrices* $\boldsymbol{S} \in \mathrm{GL}_k(q)$ *and* $\boldsymbol{P} \in S_n$ *such that* $\boldsymbol{G}' = \boldsymbol{SGP}$.

Problem 2 (Linear Code Equivalence). *Let* $\boldsymbol{G}, \boldsymbol{G}' \in \mathbb{F}_q^{k \times n}$ *be two generator matrices for, respectively, linear codes* $\mathfrak{C}$ *and* $\mathfrak{C}'$. *Determine whether the two codes are linearly equivalent, i.e. if there exist two matrices* $\boldsymbol{S} \in \mathrm{GL}_k(q)$ *and* $\boldsymbol{Q} \in M_n(q)$ *such that* $\boldsymbol{G}' = \boldsymbol{SGQ}$.

The two problems above are clearly two different flavors of the same problem, namely, deciding whether two codes are equivalent, which differ according to which notion of code equivalence is considered. However, as we will see, the connection between the two is not as obvious as it seems.

3.1   Hardness

As proven in [28], the permutation equivalence problem is unlikely to be NP-complete, since this property would imply a collapse of the polynomial hierarchy. While the problem can be efficiently solved for some families of codes, there are however many instances that, after almost 40 years of study, are still intractable.

The first algorithm to solve this problem was proposed by Leon in 1982 [24], and is able to reconstruct the secret permutation from its action on the set of codewords with fixed weight. The permutation can efficiently be recovered when this set is not too large. The bottleneck is in the codewords search, whose time complexity is $nq^{O(k)}$. Thus, as noted in [4], Leon's algorithm is impractical, unless considering codes of small dimension defined over small finite fields.

The Support Splitting Algorithm (SSA), due to Sendrier [31,32], strongly improves upon Leon's algorithm. The algorithm is based on the concept of the hull, that is, the intersection between a code and its dual. The hull computation requires simple linear algebra while the time complexity of the whole algorithm essentially grows as q^h, where h is the hull's dimension. For random codes, this dimension is with high probability equal to a small constant [33], de facto making SSA a polynomial-time solver for permutation equivalence in many cases.

One case in which SSA fails is that of codes with a trivial (i.e. zero) hull. However, an efficient treatment of this situation has recently been provided [4] through a reduction, running in time $O(n^\omega)$ (with $2 \leq \omega \leq 3$), from permutation equivalence to an instance of the graph isomorphism problem between undirected weighted graphs. Another case which cannot efficiently be solved through SSA is that of codes with a large hull. In fact, since the time complexity is dominated by q^h, SSA becomes quickly unfeasible as h grows. This is, for instance, the case of self-dual (or weakly self-dual codes), for which $h = k$: for such codes, SSA can be made arbitrarily hard by choosing codes with a sufficiently large dimension. The hardness of such instances is corroborated by the reduction to graph isomorphism in [4] which, for non-trivial hulls, runs in time $O(hn^{\omega+h+1})$ and, as expected, becomes quickly unfeasible for large values of h.

We conclude this section with a note on the hardness of linear equivalence. As shown in [32], the problem of establishing the linear equivalence between two codes can always be reduced to that of finding a permutation equivalence between their closures. Thus, constructing the closures (as we detail in Sect. 5) and applying SSA is enough to solve the linear equivalence. However, when $q \geq 5$, the closure of a code is always weakly-self dual. It follows that such instances are exactly the hardest ones for SSA to solve. These results are confirmed by the analysis in [29], which includes a study of algebraic approaches to the code equivalence problem.

4 Protocol Description

We begin by describing the underlying identification scheme, in Table 3.

We now show that our protocol satisfies the necessary security requirements for identification schemes.

Completeness. It is immediate to check that the protocol is correct, and an honest prover always gets accepted. In fact, if $b = 0$ the verifier receives $\mu = \tilde{Q}$ and then obviously can check that $\mathsf{H}(\mathsf{SF}(G\mu)) = \mathsf{H}(\mathsf{SF}(G\tilde{Q})) = \mathsf{H}(\mathsf{SF}(\tilde{G})) = h$ since by construction $\tilde{G} = G\tilde{Q}$. On the other hand, if $b = 1$, then $\mu = Q^{-1}\tilde{Q}$ and we have $\mathsf{H}(\mathsf{SF}(G'\mu)) = \mathsf{H}(\mathsf{SF}(SGQQ^{-1}\tilde{Q})) = \mathsf{H}(\mathsf{SF}(S\tilde{G}))$, which is also equal to h since $S\tilde{G}$ generates the same code as $\tilde{G}$ and therefore the two matrices have the same systematic form.

Table 3. The LESS identification scheme.

Public Data	Parameters $q, n, k \in \mathbb{N}$, matrix $\boldsymbol{G} \in \mathbb{F}_q^{k \times n}$ and hash function H.
Private Key	Invertible matrix $\boldsymbol{S} \in \mathrm{GL}_k(q)$ and monomial matrix $\boldsymbol{Q} \in M_n(q)$.
Public Key	$\boldsymbol{G'} = \boldsymbol{SGQ}$.

PROVER		VERIFIER
Choose $\tilde{\boldsymbol{Q}} \xleftarrow{\$} \mathbb{F}_q^{n \times n}$ and set $\tilde{\boldsymbol{G}} = \boldsymbol{G}\tilde{\boldsymbol{Q}}$.	$\xrightarrow{h}$	
Set $h = \mathsf{H}(\mathsf{SF}(\tilde{\boldsymbol{G}}))$.		
	$\xleftarrow{b}$	$b \xleftarrow{\$} \{0,1\}$.
If $b = 0$ then $\mu = \tilde{\boldsymbol{Q}}$.	$\xrightarrow{\mu}$	Accept if $\mathsf{H}(\mathsf{SF}(\boldsymbol{G}\mu)) = h$.
If $b = 1$ then $\mu = \boldsymbol{Q}^{-1}\tilde{\boldsymbol{Q}}$.		Accept if $\mathsf{H}(\mathsf{SF}(\boldsymbol{G'}\mu)) = h$.

Honest-Verifier Zero-Knowledge. In this section we show that the produced responses do not leak information about the private key. We do this by proving that there exists a probabilistic polynomial time simulator algorithm $\mathcal{S}$ that, without the knowledge of the private key, is able to produce a transcript which is indistinguishable from one obtained after an interaction with an honest verifier. To this end, we introduce the following straightforward Lemma.

Lemma 1. *Let $M_n(q)$ be the set of monomial matrices as defined in Sect. 2. Then for any $\boldsymbol{A} \in M_n(q)$ and $\boldsymbol{B} \xleftarrow{\$} M_n(q)$, we have $\boldsymbol{A}^{-1}\boldsymbol{B} \sim \mathbb{U}(M_n(q))$.*

The simulator works as follows.

- When the challenge is $b = 0$, it can trivially simulate correctly by choosing a matrix $\tilde{\boldsymbol{Q}}$ uniformly at random. This, in fact, corresponds to a legitimate response for this challenge, and doesn't include the secret.
- When the challenge is $b = 1$, the simulator again chooses a matrix, say $\boldsymbol{Q}^*$, uniformly at random. By Lemma 1, we have seen that the product $\boldsymbol{Q}^{-1}\tilde{\boldsymbol{Q}}$ that would be output by an honest execution of the protocol is uniformly distributed among all monomial matrices. Therefore $\mathcal{S}$ is able to simulate correctly in this case.

This simple argument shows that both responses are actually indistinguishable from randomly generated ones, and thus do not reveal any secret.

Soundness. Finally, we prove that the protocol is 2-special sound. We do this by describing an extractor algorithm and showing that it is able to find a witness, i.e. solve the code equivalence problem. To this end, let $\mathcal{A}$ be an adversary that is given an instance $\{\boldsymbol{G}, \boldsymbol{G'}\}$ as in Problem 2. The algorithm proceeds as follows.

To begin, set $\boldsymbol{G}$ and $\boldsymbol{G'}$ as public data and public key for the identification scheme. Then, obtain a transcript $(\mathsf{cmt}, \mathsf{ch}_0, \mathsf{ch}_1, \mathsf{rsp}_0, \mathsf{rsp}_1)$ such that $\mathsf{ch}_0 \neq \mathsf{ch}_1$ and the verifier accepts $(\mathsf{cmt}, \mathsf{ch}_i, \mathsf{rsp}_i)$ for $i \in \{0, 1\}$: in other words, the transcript is such that both challenges are satisfied for the same commitment. Thus, the two responses must be two monomial matrices $\tilde{Q}$ and Q^* such that

$$\mathsf{H}(\mathsf{SF}(G\tilde{Q})) = \mathsf{H}(\mathsf{SF}(G'Q^*)).$$

Unless he is able to find a collision for the hash function, this means

$$\mathsf{SF}(G\tilde{Q}) = \mathsf{SF}(G'Q^*).$$

At this point, since two matrices with the same systematic form define the same linear code, we have that

$$\hat{S}G\tilde{Q} = G'Q^*$$

for some invertible matrix $\hat{S}$ or, if we write $\hat{Q} = \tilde{Q}(Q^*)^{-1}$,

$$\hat{S}G\hat{Q} = G'.$$

It is then easy to verify that $\hat{Q}$, which can be calculated immediately from the two responses, and $\hat{S}$, which can be then computed via linear algebra, provide the desired witness.

5   Security Analysis

In this section we assess the complexity of the state-of-the-art algorithms for solving the code equivalence problem. We begin by analyzing Leon's algorithm and SSA, which both originally target the permutation equivalence problem. We then describe how the algorithms can be applied to solve linear equivalence.

5.1   Leon's Algorithm

Leon's algorithm [24] solves permutation equivalence by analyzing its action on the subset of codewords with fixed weight ω. Once such a set is computed, it gets partitioned into smaller subsets, which are then used to retrieve the permutation mapping one code to the other. The partitioning phase has very low complexity, while finding all codewords of weight ω is the actual bottleneck of the algorithm. Usually ω is set as the minimum distance of the code (which, for random codes, can be estimated with the GV bound); if this set does not have sufficient structure, then ω is slightly increased. We now briefly describe how the codeword enumeration can be performed. Let G be the generator of a code $\mathfrak{C}$ of length n and dimension k, and $G_{\mathsf{SF}} = \mathsf{SF}(G)$. For $\delta \leq w$, and $i \leq k-\delta$, we define

$$U(\delta, i) = \left\{ u \in \mathbb{F}_q^k \text{ s.t. } \mathrm{wt}(u) = \delta, \ u_i = 1, \ u_j = 0 \ \forall j < i \right\}.$$

It can then be easily seen that, when $\omega \leq k$ (which is the case we consider in this paper) we have

$$\{c \in \mathfrak{C} \text{ s.t. } \mathrm{wt}(c) = \omega\} \subseteq \left\{ a(u G_{\mathsf{SF}}), \ a \in \mathbb{F}_q^* \setminus \{1\}, \ u \in \bigcup_{\delta=1}^{\omega} \bigcup_{i=0}^{k-\delta} U(\delta, i) \right\}.$$

From a practical point of view, the codeword search can be performed by testing all codewords of the form $\boldsymbol{u}\boldsymbol{G}_{\mathsf{SF}}$. Once a codeword of weight ω is found, then all of its scalar multiples are computed. In particular, few scalar multiples will be computed, with respect to the whole number of tested codewords, since we expect the set of weight-ω codewords to be relatively small; thus, we can neglect the computational cost of this step. For each candidate $\boldsymbol{u}$, we need to compute $n - k$ codeword symbols; when $\boldsymbol{u}$ has weight δ, this can be done with $\delta - 1$ multiplications (since the first non null entry of $\boldsymbol{u}$ is 1) and $\delta - 1$ sums in $\mathbb{F}_q$. Since all sets $U(\delta, i)$ are disjoint, it can be straightforwardly shown that the number of vectors $\boldsymbol{u}$ that are tested is $\sum_{\delta=1}^{\omega} \binom{k}{\delta}(q-1)^{\delta-1}$. Then, by neglecting the cost of the partitioning step, we have

$$C_{LEON} = O\left(4(n-k)\sum_{\delta=1}^{\omega}(\delta-1)\binom{k}{\delta}(q-1)^{\delta-1}\right). \tag{1}$$

One final remark is about eventual future developments regarding Leon's algorithm. Indeed, the algorithm is inefficient for large codes, or for large finite fields, since the codeword enumeration quickly becomes unfeasible. This step cannot be avoided, as the algorithm requires to find *all* the codewords of weight ω. We do not exclude the possibility of strong improvements in Leon's algorithm, leading to the possibility of operating with just a subset of all such codewords. In such a case, codewords of some weight ω can be efficiently determined by means of ISD algorithms which, at each call, randomly pick a codeword of the desired weight. Thus, multiple ISD calls can be used to find the required number of codewords of the desired weight. If this scenario ever became a concern, the issue could be entirely avoided by choosing code parameters such that even a single ISD call is computationally too expensive.

5.2   The Support Splitting Algorithm

A fundamental concept to analyze SSA is that of *signature function*, introduced in [31], which is defined in the following way.

Definition 5. *Let $\mathfrak{C}$ be a linear code of length n; we say that a function S is a signature function over a set F if it maps $\mathfrak{C}$ and a position $i \in [0; n-1]$ to F and is such that*

$$\mathsf{S}(\mathfrak{C}, i) = \mathsf{S}\big(\pi(\mathfrak{C}), \pi(i)\big), \quad \forall \pi \in S_n.$$

We say a signature function is fully discriminant *if $\mathsf{S}(\mathfrak{C}, i) \neq \mathsf{S}(\mathfrak{C}, j), \ \forall i \neq j$.*

Signature functions can be used to recover information about the permutation that is acting on the code; in particular, once in possession of a fully discriminant signature, the permutation π can immediately be recovered, since

$$\mathsf{S}(\mathfrak{C}, i) = \mathsf{S}(\mathfrak{C}', j) \iff j = \pi(i). \tag{2}$$

Assuming that such a fully discriminant function S is available, SSA corresponds to the trivial algorithm that searches for collisions between the sets of values $S(\mathfrak{C}, i)$ and $S(\mathfrak{C}', j)$, for $(i, j) \in [1; n] \times [1; n]$. We point out that the existence of such a function (and one that doesn't require unfeasible computation) is clearly not guaranteed for all pairs of codes. In such cases, SSA makes use of signatures refining, that is, new computations and combinations of signatures, that proceed until a fully discriminant function is obtained [32]. In this paper, with a conservative choice, we assume that the chosen signature function is fully discriminant for the pair of codes considered, and that the refining of signatures is never required. In this way, we are guaranteed to provide a lower bound on the actual complexity of SSA. The signature function proposed by Sendrier in [31] is based on the *hull space* of a code, which is defined as

$$\text{Hull}(\mathfrak{C}) = \mathfrak{C} \cap \mathfrak{C}^{\perp}.$$

An efficiently computable signature function, which at the same time is sufficiently discriminant, can be obtained from the weight enumerator function of the hull of a code (with some proper additional operations). For the complete details, we refer to reader to [31]; for the purpose of this paper, we are just interested in the associated complexity, which grows as $q^{d_{\text{Hull}}}$, where d_{Hull} denotes the dimension of the hull. Then, a conservative estimate for the complexity of using SSA to solve the Permutation Equivalence Problem is given by

$$C_{SSA} = O\left(n^3 + n^2 q^{d_{\text{Hull}}} \log n\right). \tag{3}$$

The leading term in Eq. (3) is clearly $q^{d_{\text{Hull}}}$. Thus, the dimension of the hull plays a central role in determining the complexity of the algorithm. As verified empirically in [31], the hull of random codes is very likely to have small dimension. Furthermore, it has been shown in [33] how, as n grows, the size of the hull of a random code approaches a small constant which depends only on q. It follows that, for random codes, Permutation Code Equivalence can be efficiently solved by SSA with high probability. However, for special choices such as weakly self-dual codes, the hull can be made arbitrarily large by increasing the code dimension. Thus, for such codes, SSA has exponential complexity.

5.3   Application to Linear Code Equivalence

We now describe how the algorithms can be used to tackle the linear equivalence problem. To do that, we need to introduce the concept of closure of a code.

Definition 6. *Let* $\mathbb{F}_q = \{a_0 = 0, a_1, \cdots, a_{q-1}\}$, *and* $\boldsymbol{a} = (a_1, \cdots, a_{q-1})$. *We define the* closure *of a linear code* $\mathfrak{C}$ *as*

$$\tilde{\mathfrak{C}} = \{\boldsymbol{c} \otimes \boldsymbol{a}, \ \boldsymbol{c} \in \mathfrak{C}\}.$$

As observed by Sendrier in [32], the linear equivalence problem between a pair of codes $\mathfrak{C}$ and $\mathfrak{C}'$ can be reduced to the permutation code equivalence problem between their closures $\tilde{\mathfrak{C}}$ and $\tilde{\mathfrak{C}}'$. We remark that the above definition for the closure is slightly different from the one considered in [32], since we consider a different order to build the closure's coordinates; clearly, this has no practical impact in the relation between the linear and permutation equivalence problems.

To use Leon's algorithm, it is necessary to enumerate all the low-weight codewords in the closures. Then, one can run the algorithm on the set of codewords of weight $\omega' = (q-1)\omega$, where ω can be approximated by the GV bound for parameters n, k and q. The time complexity can be estimated through Eq. (1) by setting $\omega = d_{GV}(n, k, q)$. To use SSA, instead, it is enough to apply the algorithm directly on the closures. However, a crucial result is that, for $q \geq 5$, closures of codes are always weakly self-dual, i.e., have a hull of maximum dimension k.

It is worth noting that an isometry between $\mathfrak{C}$ and $\mathfrak{C}'$ can be built (with simple linear algebra) from a linear equivalence between their duals $\mathfrak{C}^{\perp}$ and $\mathfrak{C}'^{\perp}$, whose closures have hull of dimension $n - k$. Thus, when $2k > n$, the optimal strategy is to attack the duals of the considered codes.

6 Quantum Attacks on the Code Equivalence Problem

To the best of our knowledge, there are no dedicated quantum algorithms for solving the Code Equivalence Problem. In here, we discuss the applicability of the usual quantum cryptanalysis approaches.

First, we consider the use of Grover's search algorithm [22], which is known to improve the cryptanalysis of a system in almost all cases. Indeed, the algorithm allows us to efficiently search an unsorted database X, consisting of N entries, for an element $x \in X$ such that $f(x) = 1$. The cost of the algorithm is in $O(\sqrt{N}C_f)$, where $f : X \rightarrow \{0,1\}$ and where C_f is the cost of implementing f. Note that here "cost" means either number of gates or execution time (i.e. circuit depth). With regards to Leon's algorithm, it can indeed be expected that an application of Grover can improve the search part of the algorithm, leading to the usual speedup which corresponds, in the worst case, to roughly halving the complexity exponent (if one ignores the remaining part). This is similar to what happens in the case of Information-Set Decoding (see for instance [7]). Interestingly, though, a Grover search over all possible secrets (i.e. $P \in S_n$) would not outperform the classical SSA because of the size of S_n.

In principle, it is also possible to use Grover's algorithm *within* SSA. Indeed, for each $i \in [1; n]$, the search for $j \in [1; n]$ such that $j = \pi(i)$ corresponds to finding $j \in [1; n]$ such that $f(j) = 1$, where the function $f : [1; n] \rightarrow \{0, 1\}$ is defined as

$$f(j) = \begin{cases} 1 \text{ if } \mathsf{S}(\mathfrak{C}', j) = \mathsf{S}(\mathfrak{C}, i) \\ 0 \qquad \text{otherwise} \end{cases}$$

for a fully discriminant function S. Following the application of Bennett's generic method [6] (which converts any algorithm taking time T and space S into a reversible algorithm taking time $T^{1+\varepsilon}$ and space $O(S \log T)$), the cost of a quantum circuit evaluating f is that of S, which is in $\tilde{O}(nq^{d_{\mathrm{Hull}}} \log n)$. Thus, the search for $j \in [1; n]$ such that $j = \pi(i)$ costs

$$O(\sqrt{|[1; n]|}C_f) = \tilde{O}(n^{3/2}q^{d_{\mathrm{Hull}}} \log n).$$

This process needs to be repeated $n/2$ times. Every time a pair $(i, \pi(i))$ is found, both elements can be removed from the search space. This means that, in the previous formulas, we replace $[1; n]$ with $[1; n]^{(k)}$, where $n - 2k \leq |[1; n]^{(k)}| \leq n - k$ (at each stage we remove either 1 or 2 elements depending on whether $\pi(i) = i$). Our total cost is

$$O\left(\left(\sum_{k \leq n/2} \sqrt{|[1; n]^{(k)}|}\right) C_f\right).$$

We can bound this using the fact that

$$\underbrace{\sum_{k=1}^{n/2} \sqrt{2k}}_{\Omega(n^{3/2})} \leq \sum_{k \leq n/2} \sqrt{|[1; n]^{(k)}|} \leq \underbrace{\sum_{k=n/2}^{n} \sqrt{k}}_{\Omega(n^{3/2})}.$$

In the end, the complexity of the overall procedure is $\tilde{O}(n^{5/2} q^{d_{\text{Hull}}} \log n)$, which does not outperform the classical method consisting in $2n$ evaluations of S followed by a matching of the values obtained.

The other famous family of algorithms for quantum cryptanalysis is based on quantum Fourier sampling. These algorithms can be seen as generalizations of Shor's algorithm for factoring and solving the Discrete Logarithm Problem [34]. The general approach is to rephrase a problem as the search for a secret subgroup H within a known "control group" G. The Quantum Fourier Transform (QFT) over G allows us to create a state whose measurement (hopefully) yields an element in $\hat{H}$. By repeating this operation and using ad-hoc methods depending on H, one can recover H and solve the problem. In [15] and in the follow up work [14], Dinh, Moore and Russell show that to use a similar approach for solving the Permutation Equivalence Problem, one would have to choose $G = (\text{GL}_k(q) \times S_n) \rtimes \mathbb{Z}_2$. A criterion is given in Corollaries 1 and 2 of [14] for linear codes to be *HSP-hard*, meaning that it does not reveal any information about $\hat{H}$. The criterion asks that the code has very high rate, namely, that $q^{k^2} \leq n^{0.2n}$, and that the automorphism group of the code has very small degree.

The authors give some concrete examples of families of codes that satisfy the criterion. This is the case, for instance, of Alternant codes and Goppa codes. For these families, it is possible to give explicit bounds on the size of the automorphism group. Moreover, since these codes are subfield subcodes of Generalized Reed-solomon codes, the criterion can be satisfied by considering a generator matrix over the extension field and referring to the dimension of the "parent" code. This makes it so that the resulting code does not need to have the very high rate mentioned above, thus generating practical cryptographic instances.

The results just presented naturally extend to the Linear Equivalence Problem via the use of the closure. We note that these conditions, as interesting as they are from a theoretical point of view, are not necessary for our codes to offer quantum resistance. Indeed, no attack relying on the quantum Fourier sampling has been described so far in literature. Interestingly, the conditions are also not sufficient to claim post-quantum resistance since other attacks not based on quantum Fourier sampling might exist. This is for example the case of certain Goppa codes which satisfy the conditions described in [15] showing the impossibility of using the quantum Fourier sampling method, despite being attacked by the classical SSA because their hull has a small dimension.

7   Signature Scheme

The usual security notion that is required for signature schemes is Existential Unforgeability against Chosen-Message Attacks, or simply EUF-CMA. The attack model allows an adversary to perform polynomially-many queries to a signing oracle, in order to obtain valid message-signature pairs that could be used to extrapolate information. The adversary's goal is to be able to produce a single valid message-signature pair (different than those queried).

There is a standard conversion mechanism due to Fiat and Shamir, that allows to transform a canonical identification scheme into a signature scheme. The idea of the so-called Fiat-Shamir transform [18] is to make the protocol non-interactive by having the prover run the scheme with itself, using a random oracle to generate the challenge. The prover can then send the whole transcript $(\mathsf{cmt}_1, \ldots, \mathsf{cmt}_t, \mathsf{rsp}_1, \ldots, \mathsf{rsp}_t)$ as a signature to the verifier, who accepts if and only if $\mathcal{V}(\mathsf{pk}, \mathsf{cmt}_i, \mathsf{ch}_i, \mathsf{rsp}_i) = 1$ for all $i = 1, \ldots, t$ (Table 4).

Table 4. The Fiat-Shamir transform.

Private Key   A (signing) private key sk output by $\mathcal{K}(1^\lambda)$.

Public Key   The (verification) public key pk corresponding to sk.

SIGNER	VERIFIER
Input message m	
$\mathsf{cmt}_i \leftarrow \mathcal{P}(\mathsf{sk}, \mathsf{pk}, \rho_i)$	
$\mathsf{ch} = \mathsf{H}(m, \mathsf{cmt}_1, \ldots, \mathsf{cmt}_t)$	
$\mathsf{ch}_i \in \{0,1\}^\ell \leftarrow \mathsf{ch}$	
$\mathsf{rsp}_i \leftarrow \mathcal{P}(\mathsf{sk}, \mathsf{pk}, \rho_i, \mathsf{cmt}_i, \mathsf{ch}_i)$	
$\sigma = (\mathsf{cmt}_1, \ldots, \mathsf{cmt}_t, \mathsf{rsp}_1, \ldots, \mathsf{rsp}_t)$ $\xrightarrow{\sigma}$	
	$\mathsf{ch} = \mathsf{H}(m, \mathsf{cmt}_1, \ldots, \mathsf{cmt}_t)$
	$\mathsf{ch}_i \in \{0,1\}^\ell \leftarrow \mathsf{ch}$
	$\{0,1\} \leftarrow \mathcal{V}(\mathsf{pk}, \mathsf{cmt}_i, \mathsf{ch}_i, \mathsf{rsp}_i)$

The following theorem was proved in [1] and states the security of the Fiat-Shamir transform in all generality.

Theorem 1. *Consider a non-trivial canonical identification protocol that is secure against impersonation under passive attacks. Then the signature scheme derived using the Fiat-Shamir transform is secure against chosen-message attacks in the random oracle model.*

In the attack scenario that includes a quantum adversary, able to make quantum queries to the random oracle, the Fiat-Shamir transform could in principle not suffice to guarantee security, as the strategy employed in the proof requires techniques that are not compatible (e.g. rewinding). As a consequence, Unruh designed an alternative transform [36], which is proved to be secure in the QROM. The transform is considerably less practical than Fiat-Shamir, and this prompted a follow-up body of work trying to analyze the situation. Recently, two contributions [16,25] appeared at CRYPTO 2019, explaining how it may be safe, in certain instances, to still employ Fiat-Shamir in the presence of a quantum adversary. In particular, in [16], the case of lattice signatures is analyzed explicitly, and the authors show that popular schemes, such as those based on the work of Lyubashevsky [26], satisfy the *collapsing* property necessary to achieve existential unforgeability in the QROM. This is done by introducing a (rather plausible) assumption, which is justified by the authors, mentioning that the separation between the collision resistance and collapsingness properties is usually only artificial. As a matter of fact, the former is already a feature in the majority of Sigma protocols that are used with Fiat-Shamir, since it is necessary to guarantee unforgeability, and our scheme is no exception. Following the arguments detailed in Sect. 4, we can argue that applying Fiat-Shamir to the LESS identification scheme is enough to preserve EUF-CMA security in the QROM.

8 Concrete Instances

In this section we present concrete instances of the LESS protocol, as well as a thorough comparison with the state of the art of code-based signatures. To highlight the novelty of our approach, we remind the reader that all existing schemes in literature are based on the traditional method in code-based cryptography, which relies on the hardness of the syndrome decoding problem.

Identification Schemes. The credit for the first code-based identification scheme is attributed to Stern [35]. The protocol, proposed in 1989, is a very simple 3-pass scheme with three commitments, and thus a cheating probability of $2/3$, which in turn means the number of rounds necessary to guarantee security is quite high. Since the size of the public key is also very large, the scheme is quite impractical, and remains in literature mostly as a reference. The scheme was then marginally improved by Véron [38], using a slightly different formulation for the private key. In 2010, Cayrel, Véron and El Yousfi introduce a new scheme [9] with a few interesting modifications, such as the use of q-ary codes and a 5-pass framework, leading to a cheating probability is $q/(2q-1)$ which, for large enough values of q, can be approximated as $1/2$. It follows that, despite the large alphabet size, the scheme performs better than its predecessors. The entire line of work can be further improved by using circulant matrices, as shown in [19], a variation of Stern's scheme instantiated with quasi-cyclic codes, and later by Aguilar, Gaborit and Schrek [2]. The latter, a 5-pass scheme similar to [9], is usually regarded as the most efficient proposal to obtain a signature scheme from an identification scheme. Yet, as we will see, the communication cost is still very high, leading to an impractical signature size.

Other Approaches. Two schemes have recently come to attention as promising solutions for code-based signatures. Wave [13] describes a family of trapdoor one-way preimage sampleable functions, following the CFS framework and utilizing a new class of codes known as *Generalized* $(U \mid U + V)$ *Codes* to sample preimages of high weight, rather than low weight as usual. This novel approach is extremely interesting, but is still far from practical, leading to a scheme with a huge public key (about 4 Mb) and a high-complexity signing algorithm (in the order of λ^3 for a security level of λ bits, as mentioned by the authors). Durandal [3] obtains a signature scheme applying the Fiat-Shamir transform to an identification scheme using codes in the *rank metric*. The scheme is based on the framework of Schnorr [30], successfully exploited by Lyubashevsky for the lattice case [26], and obtains relatively small keys and signature sizes. However, there are some concerns about security, mostly due to the lack of an explicit proof of leakage immunity and to a security reduction that relies on a new ad-hoc problem which is rather convoluted and not so well-studied.

8.1   Choice of Parameters

We now provide some concrete instances of the scheme, which we depict in Table 5. In light of what explained in Sect. 6, our main concern is the classical security, so we choose system parameters to achieve 128-bit security against Leon's algorithm and SSA.

Table 5. Proposed LESS instances, targeting 128-bit security.

	n	k	q	Type
LESS-I	54	27	53	MONO
LESS-II	106	45	7	MONO
LESS-III	60	25	31	PERM

Clearly, to instantiate the scheme we need to choose a public code which does not allow for an easy solution of the corresponding code equivalence problem. The first and most natural approach is to rely on the hardness of Linear Equivalence by using random codes over $\mathbb{F}_q$ with $q \geq 5$, and choose n and k such that the complexities of Leon's algorithm and SSA are above the desired security level. LESS-I and LESS-II instances have been designed with this criteria; in the last column of Table 5 we remark the fact that monomial matrices are used in the protocol. In particular, LESS-I parameters have been obtained with the goal of optimizing the trade-off between security and performance, by looking for the triplet of values (n, k, q) that minimizes the (maximum) communication cost per round and, at the same time, guarantees that the complexities of both Leon's algorithm and SSA are above the desired security level. Note that this is not the case in some of the previous works such as [9], where the *average* communication cost is considered, and the average is taken over the cost of different responses. However, when designing a signature scheme, one is only interested in the maximum size of the signature, and therefore we deem more relevant to take into the account the maximum cost for each round. On the other hand, LESS-II parameters have been obtained by seeking the best trade-off between the scheme security and the computational efficiency of the algebra in the underlying finite field: for this reason, the field size is relatively small (i.e., $q = 7$ versus $q = 53$ for LESS-I) and of practical use.

The final choice, aimed at obtaining a performance advantage, is to restrict the scheme to permutations. In this case, in fact, the communication cost is reduced by the amount of bits necessary to transmit the scaling factors in each monomial matrix. However, to provide security, random codes are no longer enough, since, as we have seen, they have usually a very small hull. Therefore, it becomes necessary to choose a weakly-self dual code. It is possible to show that such a code can be generated in polynomial time. We call this parameter set LESS-III, and remark the fact that it uses only permutations in the last column of Table 5.

8.2 Performance and Comparison

The maximum communication cost per round is calculated as follows. We denote by l_{Hash} and l_{Seed} the sizes of, respectively, a hash and a seed for a pseudorandom generator. In our scheme, the commitment is a hash value (thus, requiring l_{Hash} bits), and the challenge is a single bit. When $b = 0$, the reply is a random monomial matrix and can be compactly transmitted by sending the corresponding seed. This trick however cannot be applied in the case $b = 1$ which, requires the transmission of $n(\lceil \log_2 n \rceil + \lceil \log_2 (q - 1) \rceil)$ bits. Then, the maximum communication cost per round is

$$l_{\mathsf{Hash}} + 1 + \max \left\{ n(\lceil \log_2 n \rceil + b \lceil \log_2 (q - 1) \rceil), l_{\mathsf{Seed}} \right\},$$

where $b = 0$ or 1 depending on whether permutations or monomials are used.

Note that, in order to have a fair comparison, we had to scale up parameters for all the compared schemes, since those were given according to a variety of different metrics (none of which were sufficient to guarantee a secure signature scheme). This means for example that we require 128 bits of security against impersonation (commonly given at 2^{-16}), and assume that hash digests and seeds are 128 bits long. Following the suggestion of [20, Remark 2], we instantiate Fiat-Shamir with a number of rounds equal to the desired security level (in this case 128). The resulting signature scheme achieves 128-bit security with a signature size which, with respect to the AGS scheme, gets reduced by a factor which ranges from 57% for LESS-II to 82% for LESS-III (Table 6).

Table 6. Comparison between code-based signature schemes obtained from identification schemes, for 128-bit security. All sizes in bits, except where indicated.

	Véron [38]	CVE [9]	AGS [2]	LESS-I	LESS-II	LESS-III
Public Matrix	262,144	86,528	599	8,748	14,310	7,500
Public Key	1,024	832	599	8,748	14,310	7,500
Max. Comm. Cost per Round	2,434	3,593	2,792	777	1,189	489
Number of rounds	219	129	128	128	128	128
Signature size (kB)	66.63	57.94	44.67	12.43	19.02	7.82

Regarding a comparison with the two new approaches, the numbers are as follows. For Wave, the key size is given by $0.368n^2$ bits and the signature size by $2n$. The authors suggest using a code of length $n = 9,078$, which leads to 30,326,911 bits of public key, i.e. roughly 3.8 MB, and 2.2 kB of signature. Durandal features more practical sizes: two sets of parameters are proposed, the smallest of which has 121,961 bits of public key and 32,514 bits of signature, which corresponds to approximately 15 kB and 4 kB, respectively. The proposed LESS instances feature a much smaller public key, while the signature size is only a few times bigger.

9   Conclusion

In this paper, we have presented LESS, a new code-based signature scheme derived from a zero-knowledge identification scheme. Our protocol is based on an innovative use of a long-standing problem in code-based cryptography, the Code Equivalence problem. Rather than looking at this in the context of McEliece-like encryption, in fact, our scheme exploits the action of linear isometries on codes as a stand-alone tool to provide security. This problem and its hardness have been thoroughly studied over the years, and therefore it is possible to give an accurate security assessment.

Since our scheme doesn't involve syndromes and doesn't require any hardness assumptions or security results connected to decoding, we are able to choose, to our advantage, ad hoc parameters which would not normally be usable within the traditional code-based framework (due to poor error-correction capability). As a result, for instance, all the codes considered have very short lengths, which means the sizes of the objects involved in the signature scheme can be kept small. The public keys in our protocol are among the smallest in code-based cryptography, without needing to resort to families with special structure such as Quasi-Cyclic (QC) codes. Furthermore, the size of our signatures is as short a few Kilobytes (less than 8 for the LESS-III parameter set), in line with the major post-quantum signature schemes. Our design performs better than the traditional solutions based on identification schemes in nearly every aspect, and compares very well with modern approaches to code-based signatures such as Wave [13] and Durandal [3]. Finally, we expect to see very good performance from the computation point of view, due to the simplicity of the underlying arithmetic. Naturally, a full-fledged and optimized implementation will be the topic of a follow-up work. To conclude, we see our work as but the first step in paving the way for a new, very promising trend in code-based cryptography.

Acknowledgments. Jean-François Biasse was supported by the U.S. National Science Foundation under grant 1839805, and grant 1846166, by NIST under grant 60NANB17D184, and by a Seed Grant of the Florida Center for Cyber-security.

Edoardo Persichetti and Paolo Santini were supported by the U.S. National Science Foundation under grant 1906360.

References

1. Abdalla, M., An, J.H., Bellare, M., Namprempre, C.: From identification to signatures via the Fiat-Shamir transform: minimizing assumptions for security and forward-security. In: Knudsen, L.R. (ed.) EUROCRYPT 2002. LNCS, vol. 2332, pp. 418–433. Springer, Heidelberg (2002). https://doi.org/10.1007/3-540-46035-7_28
2. Aguilar, C., Gaborit, P., Schrek, J.: A new zero-knowledge code based identification scheme with reduced communication. In: 2011 IEEE Information Theory Workshop, pp. 648–652, October 2011. https://doi.org/10.1109/ITW.2011.6089577
3. Aragon, N., Blazy, O., Gaborit, P., Hauteville, A., Zémor, G.: Durandal: a rank metric based signature scheme. In: Ishai, Y., Rijmen, V. (eds.) EUROCRYPT 2019. LNCS, vol. 11478, pp. 728–758. Springer, Cham (2019). https://doi.org/10.1007/978-3-030-17659-4_25
4. Bardet, M., Otmani, A., Saeed-Taha, M.: Permutation code equivalence is not harder than graph isomorphism when hulls are trivial. In: IEEE ISIT 2019, pp. 2464–2468, July 2019
5. Bellare, M., Poettering, B., Stebila, D.: From identification to signatures, tightly: a framework and generic transforms. In: Cheon, J.H., Takagi, T. (eds.) ASIACRYPT 2016. LNCS, vol. 10032, pp. 435–464. Springer, Heidelberg (2016). https://doi.org/10.1007/978-3-662-53890-6_15
6. Bennett, C.H.: Time/space trade-offs for reversible computation. SIAM J. Comput. **18**(4), 766–776 (1989)
7. Bernstein, D.J.: Grover vs. McEliece. In: Sendrier, N. (ed.) PQCrypto 2010. LNCS, vol. 6061, pp. 73–80. Springer, Heidelberg (2010). https://doi.org/10.1007/978-3-642-12929-2_6
8. Bernstein, D.J., et al.: SPHINCS: practical stateless hash-based signatures. In: Oswald, E., Fischlin, M. (eds.) EUROCRYPT 2015. LNCS, vol. 9056, pp. 368–397. Springer, Heidelberg (2015). https://doi.org/10.1007/978-3-662-46800-5_15
9. Cayrel, P.-L., Véron, P., El Yousfi Alaoui, S.M.: A zero-knowledge identification scheme based on the q-ary syndrome decoding problem. In: Biryukov, A., Gong, G., Stinson, D.R. (eds.) SAC 2010. LNCS, vol. 6544, pp. 171–186. Springer, Heidelberg (2011). https://doi.org/10.1007/978-3-642-19574-7_12
10. https://classic.mceliece.org/
11. Courtois, N.T., Finiasz, M., Sendrier, N.: How to achieve a McEliece-based digital signature scheme. In: Boyd, C. (ed.) ASIACRYPT 2001. LNCS, vol. 2248, pp. 157–174. Springer, Heidelberg (2001). https://doi.org/10.1007/3-540-45682-1_10
12. Damgård, I.: On Σ-protocols. Lecture Notes, University of Aarhus, Department of Computer Science (2002)

13. Debris-Alazard, T., Sendrier, N., Tillich, J.-P.: Wave: a new family of trapdoor one-way preimage sampleable functions based on codes. In: Galbraith, S.D., Moriai, S. (eds.) ASIACRYPT 2019. LNCS, vol. 11921, pp. 21–51. Springer, Cham (2019). https://doi.org/10.1007/978-3-030-34578-5_2

14. Dinh, H., Moore, C., Russell, A.: Limitations of single coset states and quantum algorithms for code equivalence. Quantum Inf. Comput. 15(3–4), 260–294 (2015). ISSN 1533-7146

15. Dinh, H., Moore, C., Russell, A.: McEliece and niederreiter cryptosystems that resist quantum fourier sampling attacks. In: Rogaway, P. (ed.) CRYPTO 2011. LNCS, vol. 6841, pp. 761–779. Springer, Heidelberg (2011). https://doi.org/10.1007/978-3-642-22792-9_43

16. Don, J., Fehr, S., Majenz, C., Schaffner, C.: Security of the Fiat-Shamir transformation in the quantum random-oracle model. In: Boldyreva, A., Micciancio, D. (eds.) CRYPTO 2019. LNCS, vol. 11693, pp. 356–383. Springer, Cham (2019). https://doi.org/10.1007/978-3-030-26951-7_13

17. De Feo, L., Galbraith, S.D.: SeaSign: compact isogeny signatures from class group actions. In: Ishai, Y., Rijmen, V. (eds.) EUROCRYPT 2019. LNCS, vol. 11478, pp. 759–789. Springer, Cham (2019). https://doi.org/10.1007/978-3-030-17659-4_26

18. Fiat, A., Shamir, A.: How to prove yourself: practical solutions to identification and signature problems. In: Odlyzko, A.M. (ed.) CRYPTO 1986. LNCS, vol. 263, pp. 186–194. Springer, Heidelberg (1987). https://doi.org/10.1007/3-540-47721-7_12

19. Gaborit, P., Girault, M.: Lightweight code-based identification and signature. In: IEEE International Symposium on Information Theory, pp. 191–195. IEEE (2007)

20. Galbraith, S.D., Petit, C., Silva, J.: Identification protocols and signature schemes based on supersingular isogeny problems. In: Takagi, T., Peyrin, T. (eds.) ASIACRYPT 2017. LNCS, vol. 10624, pp. 3–33. Springer, Cham (2017). https://doi.org/10.1007/978-3-319-70694-8_1

21. Girault, M.: A (non-practical) three-pass identification protocol using coding theory. In: Seberry, J., Pieprzyk, J. (eds.) AUSCRYPT 1990. LNCS, vol. 453, pp. 265–272. Springer, Heidelberg (1990). https://doi.org/10.1007/BFb0030367

22. Grover, L.: A fast quantum mechanical algorithm for database search. In: Proceedings of the Twenty-Eighth Annual ACM Symposium on Theory of Computing. STOC 1996, Philadelphia, Pennsylvania, USA, pp. 212–219. ACM (1996). ISBN 0-89791-785-5. https://doi.org/10.1145/237814.237866

23. Katz, J.: Digital Signatures. Springer, Boston (2010). https://doi.org/10.1007/978-0-387-27712-7

24. Leon, J.: Computing automorphism groups of error-correcting codes. IEEE Trans. Inf. Theory 28(3), 496–511 (1982). https://doi.org/10.1109/TIT.1982.1056498. ISSN 1557-9654

25. Liu, Q., Zhandry, M.: Revisiting post-quantum Fiat-Shamir. In: Boldyreva, A., Micciancio, D. (eds.) CRYPTO 2019. LNCS, vol. 11693, pp. 326–355. Springer, Cham (2019). https://doi.org/10.1007/978-3-030-26951-7_12

26. Lyubashevsky, V.: Lattice signatures without trapdoors. In: Pointcheval, D., Johansson, T. (eds.) EUROCRYPT 2012. LNCS, vol. 7237, pp. 738–755. Springer, Heidelberg (2012). https://doi.org/10.1007/978-3-642-29011-4_43

27. https://csrc.nist.gov/Projects/post-quantum-cryptography/Post-Quantum-Cryptography-Standardization

28. Petrank, E., Roth, R.M.: Is code equivalence easy to decide? IEEE Trans. Inf. Theory 43(5), 1602–1604 (1997)

29. Saeed, M.A.: Algebraic approach for code equivalence. Ph.D. thesis (2017)

30. Schnorr, C.P.: Efficient signature generation by smart cards. J. Cryptol. **4**(3), 161–174 (1991). https://doi.org/10.1007/BF00196725
31. Sendrier, N.: The support splitting algorithm. IEEE Trans. Inf. Theory **46**, 1193–1203 (2000). https://doi.org/10.1109/18.850662
32. Sendrier, N., Simos, D.E.: The hardness of code equivalence over $\mathbb{F}_q$ and its application to code-based cryptography. In: Gaborit, P. (ed.) PQCrypto 2013. LNCS, vol. 7932, pp. 203–216. Springer, Heidelberg (2013). https://doi.org/10.1007/978-3-642-38616-9_14
33. Sendrier, N., Symbolique, P.: On the dimension of the hull. SIAM J. Discrete Math. **10**, 282–293 (1995). https://doi.org/10.1137/S0895480195294027
34. Shor, P.: Polynomial-time algorithms for prime factorization and discrete logarithms on a quantum computer. SIAM J. Comput. **26**(5), 1484–1509 (1997)
35. Stern, J.: A new identification scheme based on syndrome decoding. In: Stinson, D.R. (ed.) CRYPTO 1993. LNCS, vol. 773, pp. 13–21. Springer, Heidelberg (1994). https://doi.org/10.1007/3-540-48329-2_2
36. Unruh, D.: Non-interactive zero-knowledge proofs in the quantum random oracle model. In: Oswald, E., Fischlin, M. (eds.) EUROCRYPT 2015. LNCS, vol. 9057, pp. 755–784. Springer, Heidelberg (2015). https://doi.org/10.1007/978-3-662-46803-6_25
37. Venturi, D.: Zero-knowledge proofs and applications. Lecture Notes, Sapienza University of Rome, Department of Computer Science (2015)
38. Véron, P.: Improved identification schemes based on error-correcting codes. Appl. Algebra Eng. Commun. Comput. **8**(1), 57–69 (1997). https://doi.org/10.1007/s002000050053

UC Updatable Databases and Applications

Aditya Damodaran⬤ and Alfredo Rial⁽✉⁾⬤

SnT, University of Luxembourg, Esch-sur-Alzette, Luxembourg
{aditya.damodaran,alfredo.rial}@uni.lu

Abstract. We define an ideal functionality $\mathcal{F}_{\mathrm{UD}}$ and a construction Π_{UD} for an updatable database (UD). UD is a two-party protocol between an updater and a reader. The updater sets the database and updates it at any time throughout the protocol execution. The reader computes zero-knowledge (ZK) proofs of knowledge of database entries. These proofs prove that a value is stored at a certain position in the database, without revealing the position or the value.

(Non-)updatable databases are implicitly used as building block in priced oblivious transfer, privacy-preserving billing and other privacy-preserving protocols. Typically, in those protocols the updater signs each database entry, and the reader proves knowledge of a signature on a database entry. Updating the database requires a revocation mechanism to revoke signatures on outdated database entries.

Our construction Π_{UD} uses a non-hiding vector commitment (NHVC) scheme. The updater maps the database to a vector and commits to the database. This commitment can be updated efficiently at any time without needing a revocation mechanism. ZK proofs for reading a database entry have communication and amortized computation cost independent of the database size. Therefore, Π_{UD} is suitable for large databases. We implement Π_{UD} and our timings show that it is practical.

In existing privacy-preserving protocols, a ZK proof of a database entry is intertwined with other tasks, e.g., proving further statements about the value read from the database or the position where it is stored. $\mathcal{F}_{\mathrm{UD}}$ allows us to improve modularity in protocol design by separating those tasks. We show how to use $\mathcal{F}_{\mathrm{UD}}$ as building block of a hybrid protocol along with other functionalities.

Keywords: Vector commitments · ZK proofs · Universal composability

1 Introduction

In priced oblivious transfer (POT) [3], a provider offers N messages to a user. Each message m_i is associated with a price p_i ($\forall i \in [1, N]$). The user purchases a message m_i without disclosing i or p_i.

This research is supported by the Luxembourg National Research Fund (FNR) CORE project "Stateful Zero-Knowledge" (Project code: C17/11650748).

A. Nitaj and A. Youssef (Eds.): AFRICACRYPT 2020, LNCS 12174, pp. 66–87, 2020.
https://doi.org/10.1007/978-3-030-51938-4_4

In privacy-preserving billing (PPB) [25], a user receives meter readings from a meter that measures the consumption c of some service. The provider defines a tariff policy that typically consists of several functions. For example, a different rate r_i is applied depending on the time interval i of consumption. The user pays a price $p = r_i c$ for her consumption at time interval i and proves that p_i is correct without revealing c, r_i or i. Usually, multiple prices p are aggregated and paid together so that the aggregate reveals little information about each (c, r_i, i).

In POT [9,41] (resp. PPB [39,40]) protocols, the user frequently uses a zero-knowledge (ZK) proof to prove that p_i (resp. r_i) is correctly associated with i. The user discloses neither p_i (resp. r_i) nor i. Nevertheless, the user needs to prove in ZK statements about i and p_i (resp. r_i), such as proving that she retrieves m_i and that she has enough funds to pay p_i.

We can generalize the task of associating i with p_i (resp. r_i) as the task of proving that an entry is read from a database. Consider a database DB of N entries of the form $[i, vr_i]$ ($\forall i \in [1, N]$), where i is the position and vr_i the value stored at that position. The provider establishes the contents of DB, which are revealed to the user. Then the user proves knowledge of a database entry $[i, vr_i]$. The provider does not learn $[i, vr_i]$ but is guaranteed that $[i, vr_i]$ is stored in DB.

To allow the user to prove knowledge of an entry $[i, vr_i]$ from DB, DB needs to be stored into some data structure that allows for efficient ZK proofs. POT [9,41] and PPB [39,40] protocols typically use a signature scheme with efficient ZK proofs of signature possession. The provider computes signatures s_i on tuples $[i, vr_i]$ ($\forall i \in [1, N]$) and sends them to the user. Then the user proves knowledge of a signature s_i on $[i, vr_i]$ to prove that i and vr_i are stored together in DB.

Practical POT and PPB protocols require that the provider be able to update DB, so the data structure should allow efficient updates. However, if signatures are used, each time a database entry is updated, a signature revocation mechanism would be needed to revoke the signatures that sign old database entries.

In addition to proving that $[i, vr_i] \in$ DB, the user needs to prove other statements about i and vr_i. Very frequently, in cryptographic protocol design, these two types of statements are intertwined. I.e, protocols use ZK proofs that involve both statements to prove that the witness is stored in a data structure and statements to prove something else about the witness. To improve modularity in protocol design, we propose to separate those tasks.

Our Contribution: $\mathcal{F}_{UD}$. We use the universal composability (UC) framework [14] and define an ideal functionality $\mathcal{F}_{UD}$ for an updatable database (UD) in Sect. 3. We define UD as a two-party task between a reader $\mathcal{R}$ and an updater $\mathcal{U}$. $\mathcal{U}$ sets a database DB and updates it at any time. Both $\mathcal{R}$ and $\mathcal{U}$ know the content of DB. $\mathcal{R}$ reads in ZK an entry $[i, vr_i]$ from DB. $\mathcal{F}_{UD}$ ensures that it is not possible to prove that $[i, vr_i]$ is stored in DB if that is not the case.

In the UC framework, modular protocol design can be achieved by describing hybrid protocols. In a hybrid protocol, the protocol building blocks are described by their ideal functionalities, and parties in the real world invoke those ideal functionalities. We show how to use $\mathcal{F}_{UD}$ as building block in a protocol where

$\mathcal{F}_{UD}$ handles the tasks of storing a database DB and proving that an entry $[i, vr_i]$ is stored in DB, while the ideal functionality $\mathcal{F}_{ZK}^R$ for zero-knowledge is used to prove further statements about i and vr_i. One challenge when defining a hybrid protocol is to ensure that two functionalities receive the same input. To this end, $\mathcal{F}_{UD}$ uses the method proposed in [10], which consists in receiving committed inputs produced by a functionality $\mathcal{F}_{NIC}$ for non-interactive commitments. We show how to use $\mathcal{F}_{UD}$ as building block in a protocol designed modularly in Sect. 6.

The advantages of our modular design are threefold. First, it simplifies the security analysis because security proofs in the hybrid model are simpler and because, by separating the handling of the database from ZK proofs about other statements, each building block becomes simpler to analyze. Second, it allows multiple instantiations by replacing each of the ideal functionalities by any protocols that realize them. Third, it allows the study of the task of creating an updatable database in isolation, which eases the comparison of different constructions for it.

Our Contribution: Π_{UD}. In Sect. 4, we propose a construction Π_{UD} for $\mathcal{F}_{UD}$. Π_{UD} is based on non-hiding vector commitments (NHVC) [15,33]. A NHVC scheme allows us to compute a commitment *com* to a vector $\mathbf{x} = (\mathbf{x}[1], \ldots, \mathbf{x}[N])$. To open the value $\mathbf{x}[i]$ committed at position i, an opening w_i is computed. The size of w_i is independent of N.

Π_{UD} works as follows. $\mathcal{U}$ sends a database DB to $\mathcal{R}$, and both $\mathcal{U}$ and $\mathcal{R}$ map DB to a vector $\mathbf{x}$ and compute a commitment *com* to $\mathbf{x}$. To update an entry $[i, vr_i]$ to $[i, vr_i']$, $\mathcal{U}$ sends $[i, vr_i']$ to $\mathcal{R}$, and both $\mathcal{U}$ and $\mathcal{R}$ update *com* to obtain a commitment *com'* to a vector $\mathbf{x}'$ such that $\mathbf{x}'[i] = vr_i'$, while the other positions remain unchanged. Therefore, updates do not need any revocation mechanism. To prove in ZK that an entry $[i, vr_i]$ is in DB, $\mathcal{R}$ computes an opening w_i for position i and a ZK proof of knowledge of (w_i, i, vr_i) that proves that $\mathbf{x}[i] = vr_i$.

We discuss a variant of $\mathcal{F}_{UD}$ and Π_{UD} where $\mathcal{R}$ reads several entries simultaneously. We also discuss a variant where the database is of the form $[i, vr_{i,1}, \ldots, vr_{i,m}]$, i.e., a database where a tuple of values is stored in each entry.

We describe an efficient instantiation of Π_{UD} (and its variants) that uses a NHVC scheme based on the DHE assumption, similar to the mercurial VC scheme in [33]. The size of the public parameters of the scheme grows linearly with N. The size of *com* and w_i is constant and independent of i and N. The computation cost of *com* and w_i grows linearly with N. However, the cost of updating *com* and w_i grows only with the number of updated positions and is independent of N. Also, after w_i is computed, it can be reused to compute multiple ZK proofs. In our efficiency analysis in Sect. 5, we show that the size of a ZK proof that $[i, vr_i] \in$ DB is independent of the size N of the database. Moreover, when w_i is already computed (after the first proof for position i), the computation cost is also independent of N. We implement our instantiation of Π_{UD} and report timings for updating and reading DB, which attest that our solution is practical.

Π_{UD} can be regarded as an efficient way of implementing an OR proof, i.e., a ZK proof for a disjunction of statements. Namely, proving that $[i, vr_i]$ is in DB is equivalent to computing an OR proof where the prover proves that he knows at least one of the entries. Typically, the size of an OR proof would grow with N, while our proof is of size independent of N. In fact, Π_{UD} is suitable for databases of large sizes. We compare our construction with related work in Sect. 7.

2 Modular Design and $\mathcal{F}_{NIC}$

We refer to [14] for a description of the UC framework. An ideal functionality can be invoked by using one or more interfaces. In the notation in [10], the name of a message in an interface consists of three fields separated by dots, e.g., ud.read.ini in $\mathcal{F}_{UD}$ in Sect. 3. The first field indicates the name of $\mathcal{F}_{UD}$ and is the same for all interfaces. This field is useful for distinguishing between invocations of different functionalities in a hybrid protocol. The second field indicates the kind of action performed by $\mathcal{F}_{UD}$ and is the same in all messages that $\mathcal{F}_{UD}$ exchanges within the same interface. The third field distinguishes between the messages that belong to the same interface, and can take the following values. A message ud.read.ini is the incoming message received by $\mathcal{F}_{UD}$, i.e., the message through which the interface is invoked. ud.read.end is the outgoing message sent by $\mathcal{F}_{UD}$, i.e., the message that ends the execution of the interface. ud.read.sim is used by $\mathcal{F}_{UD}$ to send a message to the simulator $\mathcal{S}$, and ud.read.rep is used to receive a message from $\mathcal{S}$.

We use the method in [10] to allow $\mathcal{F}_{UD}$ to be used as building block in modularly-designed protocol. This method allows us to ensure, when needed, that $\mathcal{F}_{UD}$ and other functionalities receive the same input. In [10], a functionality $\mathcal{F}_{NIC}$ for non-interactive commitments is proposed. $\mathcal{F}_{NIC}$ consists of four interfaces:

1. Any party $\mathcal{P}_i$ uses the com.setup interface to set up the functionality.
2. Any party $\mathcal{P}_i$ uses the com.commit interface to send a message m and obtain a commitment com and an opening $open$. A commitment com consists of (com', $parcom$, COM.Verify), where com' is the commitment, $parcom$ are the public parameters, and COM.Verify is the verification algorithm.
3. Any party $\mathcal{P}_i$ uses the com.validate interface to send a commitment com to check that com contains the correct $parcom$ and COM.Verify.
4. Any party $\mathcal{P}_i$ uses the com.verify interface to send ($com, m, open$) to verify that com is a commitment to m with opening $open$.

To ensure that a party $\mathcal{P}_i$ sends the same input m to several functionalities, $\mathcal{P}_i$ first uses com.commit to get a commitment com to m with opening $open$. Then $\mathcal{P}_i$ sends ($com, m, open$) to each functionality, and each functionality runs COM.Verify to verify com. Finally, other parties receive com from each functionalities and use com.validate to validate com. Then, if com received from all the functionalities is the same, the binding property provided by $\mathcal{F}_{NIC}$ ensures that all the functionalities received the same input m. $\mathcal{F}_{UD}$ receives committed inputs as described in [10].

3 Functionality $\mathcal{F}_{\mathrm{UD}}$

$\mathcal{F}_{\mathrm{UD}}$ interacts with a reader $\mathcal{R}$ and an updater $\mathcal{U}$. $\mathcal{F}_{\mathrm{UD}}$ maintains a database DB that consists of N entries $[i, vr_i]$. $\mathcal{F}_{\mathrm{UD}}$ has two interfaces ud.update and ud.read:

1. $\mathcal{U}$ sends the ud.update.ini message on input $(i, vu_i)_{\forall i \in [1,N]}$. For all $i \in [1, N]$, $\mathcal{F}_{\mathrm{UD}}$ updates DB to contain value vu_i at position i. If $vu_i = \bot$, no update at position i takes place. $\mathcal{F}_{\mathrm{UD}}$ sends $(i, vu_i)_{\forall i \in [1,N]}$ to $\mathcal{R}$.
2. $\mathcal{R}$ sends ud.read.ini on input $(i, vr_i, com_i, open_i, comr_i, openr_i)$, where $[i, vr_i]$ is a DB entry and $(com_i, open_i)$ and $(comr_i, openr_i)$ are commitments and openings to i and vr_i. $\mathcal{F}_{\mathrm{UD}}$ verifies the commitments and checks that there is an entry $[i, vr_i]$ in DB. $\mathcal{F}_{\mathrm{UD}}$ sends $(com_i, comr_i)$ to $\mathcal{U}$.

$\mathcal{F}_{\mathrm{UD}}$ stores a counter cr for $\mathcal{R}$ and a counter cu for $\mathcal{U}$. These counters are used to check that $\mathcal{R}$ and $\mathcal{U}$ have the same version of DB. When $\mathcal{U}$ initiates the ud.update interface, cu is incremented. When $\mathcal{F}_{\mathrm{UD}}$ sends the update to $\mathcal{R}$, $\mathcal{F}_{\mathrm{UD}}$ checks that $cu = cr + 1$ and then increments cr. In the ud.read interface, $\mathcal{F}_{\mathrm{UD}}$ checks that $cu = cr$, which ensures that they have the same DB.

When invoked by $\mathcal{U}$ or $\mathcal{R}$, $\mathcal{F}_{\mathrm{UD}}$ first checks the correctness of the input and aborts if it does not belong to the correct domain. $\mathcal{F}_{\mathrm{UD}}$ also aborts if an interface is invoked at an incorrect moment in the protocol. For example, $\mathcal{R}$ cannot invoke ud.read if ud.update was never invoked.

The session identifier sid has the structure $(\mathcal{R}, \mathcal{U}, sid')$. Including the identities in sid ensures that any reader can initiate an instance of $\mathcal{F}_{\mathrm{UD}}$ with any updater. $\mathcal{F}_{\mathrm{UD}}$ implicitly checks that sid in a message equals the one received in the first invocation. Before $\mathcal{F}_{\mathrm{UD}}$ queries the simulator $\mathcal{S}$, $\mathcal{F}_{\mathrm{UD}}$ saves its state, which is recovered when receiving a response from $\mathcal{S}$. To match a query to a response, $\mathcal{F}_{\mathrm{UD}}$ creates a query identifier qid.

Description of $\mathcal{F}_{\mathrm{UD}}$. $\mathcal{F}_{\mathrm{UD}}$ is parameterised by a universe of values $\mathbb{U}_v$ and by a database size N.

1. On input $(\text{ud.update.ini}, sid, (i, vu_i)_{\forall i \in [1,N]})$ from $\mathcal{U}$:
   - Abort if $sid \notin (\mathcal{R}, \mathcal{U}, sid')$.
   - For all $i \in [1, N]$, abort if $vu_i \notin \mathbb{U}_v$.
   - If (sid, DB, cu) is not stored:
     - For all $i \in [1, N]$, abort if $vu_i = \bot$.
     - Set $\mathrm{DB} \leftarrow (i, vu_i)_{\forall i \in [1,N]}$ and $cu \leftarrow 0$ and store (sid, DB, cu).
   - Else:
     - For all $i \in [1, N]$, if $vu_i \neq \bot$, update DB with $[i, vu_i]$.
     - Increment cu and update DB and cu in (sid, DB, cu).
   - Create a fresh qid and store $(qid, (i, vu_i)_{\forall i \in [1,N]}, cu)$.
   - Send $(\text{ud.update.sim}, sid, qid, (i, vu_i)_{\forall i \in [1,N]})$ to $\mathcal{S}$.
S. On input $(\text{ud.update.rep}, sid, qid)$ from $\mathcal{S}$:
   - Abort if $(qid', (i, vu_i)_{\forall i \in [1,N]}, cu')$ such that $qid = qid'$ is not stored.

- If (sid, DB, cr) is not stored, set $\mathsf{DB} \leftarrow (i, vu_i)_{\forall i \in [1,N]}$ and $cr \leftarrow 0$ and store (sid, DB, cr).
- Else:
    - Abort if $cu' \neq cr + 1$.
    - For all $i \in [1, N]$, if $vu_i \neq \bot$, update DB with $[i, vu_i]$.
    - Increment cr and update cr and DB in (sid, DB, cr).
- Delete the record $(qid, (i, vu_i)_{\forall i \in [1,N]}, cu')$.
- Send $(\mathsf{ud.update.end}, sid, (i, vu_i)_{\forall i \in [1,N]})$ to $\mathcal{R}$.

2. On input $(\mathsf{ud.read.ini}, sid, i, vr_i, com_i, open_i, comr_i, openr_i)$ from $\mathcal{R}$:
    - Abort if (sid, DB, cr) is not stored.
    - Abort if $i \notin [1, N]$, or if $vr_i \notin \mathbb{U}_v$, or if $[i, vr_i] \notin \mathsf{DB}$.
    - Parse the commitment com_i as $(com_i', parcom, \mathsf{COM.Verify})$.
    - Parse the commitment $comr_i$ as $(comr_i', parcom, \mathsf{COM.Verify})$.
    - Abort if $\mathsf{COM.Verify}$ is not a ppt algorithm.
    - Abort if $1 \neq \mathsf{COM.Verify}(parcom, com_i', i, open_i)$.
    - Abort if $1 \neq \mathsf{COM.Verify}(parcom, comr_i', vr_i, openr_i)$.
    - Create a fresh qid and store $(qid, com_i, comr_i, cr)$.
    - Send $(\mathsf{ud.read.sim}, sid, qid, com_i, comr_i)$ to $\mathcal{S}$.

S. On input $(\mathsf{ud.read.rep}, sid, qid)$ from $\mathcal{S}$:
    - Abort if $(qid', com_i, comr_i, cr')$ such that $qid = qid'$ is not stored, or if $cr' \neq cu$, where cu is in (sid, DB, cu).
    - Delete the record $(qid, com_i, comr_i, cr')$.
    - Send $(\mathsf{ud.read.end}, sid, com_i, comr_i)$ to $\mathcal{U}$.

Variants of $\mathcal{F}_{\mathrm{UD}}$. It is straightforward to modify the ud.read interface of $\mathcal{F}_{\mathrm{UD}}$ to allow $\mathcal{R}$ to read a tuple $(i, vr_i, com_i, open_i, comr_i, openr_i)_{\forall i \in \mathbb{S}}$ ($\mathbb{S} \subseteq [1, N]$) of database entries simultaneously. This variant of $\mathcal{F}_{\mathrm{UD}}$ allows us to reduce communication rounds when a party in a protocol that uses $\mathcal{F}_{\mathrm{UD}}$ needs to read more than one value simultaneously, e.g. a buyer that purchases several items at once and reads the prices of those items from the database.

$\mathcal{F}_{\mathrm{UD}}$ can also be modified to store a database of the form $[i, vr_{i,1}, \ldots, vr_{i,m}]$, i.e., a database where a tuple of values is stored in each entry. In the ud.update interface, $\mathcal{U}$ sends $(i, vu_{i,1}, \ldots, vu_{i,m})_{\forall i \in [1,N]}$, and each value $vu_{i,j}$ ($j \in [1, m]$) can be updated or not independently of other values in the same entry. In the ud.read interface, $\mathcal{R}$ sends $(i, vr_{i,1}, \ldots, vr_{i,m})$ along with commitments and openings to the position and values, i.e., all the values in an entry are read. The position $j \in [1, m]$ of each value $vr_{i,j}$ is not hidden from $\mathcal{U}$. This variant of $\mathcal{F}_{\mathrm{UD}}$ is useful for protocols where a party needs to read a tuple of values and prove that they are stored in the same entry and that each $vr_{i,j}$ is stored at a certain position j within the entry, e.g. a user that consumes some utility and reads a pricing function that is represented by a tuple of values.

$\mathcal{F}_{\mathrm{UD}}$ can also be modified to interact with two parties such that both of them can read and update the database, or such that a party reads and updates and the other party receives read and update operations. Π_{UD} can be easily adapted to realize the variants of $\mathcal{F}_{\mathrm{UD}}$ discussed here.

4   Construction Π_{UD}

4.1   Building Blocks

Non-Hiding Vector Commitments. A non-hiding vector commitment (NHVC) scheme allows one to succinctly commit to a vector $\mathbf{x} = (\mathbf{x}[1], \ldots, \mathbf{x}[n]) \in \mathcal{M}^n$ such that it is possible to compute an opening w to $\mathbf{x}[i]$, with the size of w independent of i and n. The scheme consists of the following algorithms.

VC.Setup($1^k, \ell$). On input the security parameter 1^k and an upper bound ℓ on the size of the vector, generate the parameters of the vector commitment scheme *par*, which include a description of the message space $\mathcal{M}$.

VC.Commit($par, \mathbf{x}$). On input a vector $\mathbf{x} \in \mathcal{M}^n$ $(n \leq \ell)$, output a commitment *com* to $\mathbf{x}$.

VC.Prove($par, i, \mathbf{x}$). Compute an opening w for $\mathbf{x}[i]$.

VC.Verify(par, com, x, i, w). Output 1 if w is a valid opening for x being at position i and 0 otherwise.

VC.ComUpd(par, com, j, x, x'). On input a commitment *com* with value x at position j, output a commitment com' with value x' at position j. The other positions remain unchanged.

VC.WitUpd(par, w, i, j, x, x'). On input an opening w for position i valid for a commitment *com* with value x at position j, output an opening w' for position i valid for a commitment com' with value x' at position j.

A non-hiding VC scheme must be correct and binding [15].

Ideal Functionality $\mathcal{F}_{\mathrm{CRS}}^{\mathrm{CRS.Setup}}$. Our protocol uses the functionality $\mathcal{F}_{\mathrm{CRS}}^{\mathrm{CRS.Setup}}$ for common reference string generation in [14]. $\mathcal{F}_{\mathrm{CRS}}^{\mathrm{CRS.Setup}}$ interacts with any parties $\mathcal{P}$ that obtain the common reference string, and consists of one interface crs.get. A party $\mathcal{P}$ uses the crs.get interface to request and receive the common reference string crs from $\mathcal{F}_{\mathrm{CRS}}^{\mathrm{CRS.Setup}}$. In the first invocation, $\mathcal{F}_{\mathrm{CRS}}^{\mathrm{CRS.Setup}}$ generates crs by running algorithm CRS.Setup. The simulator $\mathcal{S}$ also receives crs.

Ideal Functionality $\mathcal{F}_{\mathrm{AUT}}$. Our protocol uses the functionality $\mathcal{F}_{\mathrm{AUT}}$ for an authenticated channel in [14]. $\mathcal{F}_{\mathrm{AUT}}$ interacts with a sender $\mathcal{T}$ and a receiver $\mathcal{R}$, and consists of one interface aut.send. $\mathcal{T}$ uses the aut.send interface to send a message m to $\mathcal{F}_{\mathrm{AUT}}$. $\mathcal{F}_{\mathrm{AUT}}$ leaks m to the simulator $\mathcal{S}$ and, after receiving a response from $\mathcal{S}$, $\mathcal{F}_{\mathrm{AUT}}$ sends m to $\mathcal{R}$. $\mathcal{S}$ cannot modify m. The session identifier sid contains the identities of $\mathcal{T}$ and $\mathcal{R}$.

Ideal Functionality $\mathcal{F}_{\mathrm{ZK}}^R$. Let R be a polynomial time computable binary relation. For tuples $(wit, ins) \in R$ we call wit the witness and ins the instance. Our protocol uses the ideal functionality $\mathcal{F}_{\mathrm{ZK}}^R$ for zero-knowledge in [14]. $\mathcal{F}_{\mathrm{ZK}}^R$ is parameterized by a description of a relation R, runs with a prover $\mathcal{P}$ and a verifier $\mathcal{V}$, and consists of one interface zk.prove. $\mathcal{P}$ uses zk.prove to send a witness wit and an instance ins to $\mathcal{F}_{\mathrm{ZK}}^R$. $\mathcal{F}_{\mathrm{ZK}}^R$ checks whether $(wit, ins) \in R$, and, in that case, sends the instance ins to $\mathcal{V}$. The simulator $\mathcal{S}$ learns ins but not wit.

We give the security definitions for non-hiding VC schemes and depict $\mathcal{F}_{\mathrm{CRS}}^{\mathrm{CRS.Setup}}$, $\mathcal{F}_{\mathrm{AUT}}$ and $\mathcal{F}_{\mathrm{ZK}}^R$ in the full version [17].

4.2 Description of Π_{UD}

In Π_{UD}, an NHVC *com* is used to commit to the database DB. To this end, *com* commits to a vector $\mathbf{x}$ such that $\mathbf{x}[i] = vr_i$ for all $i \in [1, N]$. $\mathcal{F}_{CRS}^{VC.Setup}$ is parameterized by VC.Setup and generates the parameters *par*.

In the ud.update interface, $\mathcal{U}$ uses $\mathcal{F}_{AUT}$ to send to $\mathcal{R}$ the update $(i, vu_i)_{\forall i \in [1,N]}$. In the first execution of this interface, $\mathcal{U}$ and $\mathcal{R}$ run VC.Commit to commit to $(i, vu_i)_{\forall i \in [1,N]}$. In the following executions, $\mathcal{U}$ and $\mathcal{R}$ update *com* by using VC.ComUpd. If $\mathcal{R}$ already stores openings w_i, $\mathcal{R}$ runs VC.WitUpd to update them.

In the ud.read interface, $\mathcal{R}$ uses $\mathcal{F}_{ZK}^R$ to prove that com_i and $comr_i$ commit to a position i and a value vr_i such that $\mathbf{x}[i] = vr_i$, where $\mathbf{x}$ is the vector committed in *com*. The witness of R includes an opening w_i. $\mathcal{R}$ runs VC.Prove to compute it if it is not stored.

Description of Π_{UD}. N denotes the database size. The universe of values $\mathbb{U}_v$ is given by the message space of the NHVC scheme.

1. On input (ud.update.ini, $sid, (i, vu_i)_{\forall i \in [1,N]}$):
   - If $(sid, par, com, \mathbf{x}, cu)$ is not stored:
     - $\mathcal{U}$ uses crs.get to obtain the parameters *par* from $\mathcal{F}_{CRS}^{VC.Setup}$. To compute *par*, $\mathcal{F}_{CRS}^{VC.Setup}$ runs VC.Setup($1^k, N$).
     - $\mathcal{U}$ initializes a counter $cu \leftarrow 0$ and a vector $\mathbf{x}$ such that $\mathbf{x}[i] = vu_i$ for all $i \in [1, N]$. $\mathcal{U}$ runs $com \leftarrow$ VC.Commit($par, \mathbf{x}$) and stores $(sid, par, com, \mathbf{x}, cu)$.
   - Else:
     - $\mathcal{U}$ sets $cu' \leftarrow cu + 1$, $\mathbf{x}' \leftarrow \mathbf{x}$ and $com' \leftarrow com$. For all $i \in [1, N]$ such that $vu_i \neq \bot$, $\mathcal{U}$ computes $com' \leftarrow$ VC.ComUpd($par, com', i, \mathbf{x}'[i], vu_i$) and $\mathbf{x}'[i] \leftarrow vu_i$.
     - $\mathcal{U}$ replaces the stored tuple $(sid, par, com, \mathbf{x}, cu)$ by $(sid, par, com', \mathbf{x}', cu')$.
   - $\mathcal{U}$ uses aut.send to send the message $\langle (i, vu_i)_{\forall i \in [1,N]}, cu' \rangle$ to $\mathcal{R}$.
   - If $(sid, par, com, \mathbf{x}, cr)$ is stored and $cu' \neq cr + 1$, $\mathcal{R}$ aborts.
   - For $j = 1$ to N, if (sid, j, w_j) is stored, $\mathcal{R}$ sets $w_j' \leftarrow w_j$ and, for all $i \in [1, N]$ such that $vu_i \neq \bot$, $w_j' \leftarrow$ VC.WitUpd($par, w_j', j, i, \mathbf{x}[i], vu_i$). $\mathcal{R}$ replaces (sid, j, w_j) by (sid, j, w_j').
   - $\mathcal{R}$ performs the same operations as $\mathcal{U}$ to set or update a tuple $(sid, par, com, \mathbf{x}, cr)$.
   - $\mathcal{R}$ outputs (ud.update.end, $sid, (i, vu_i)_{\forall i \in [1,N]}$).
2. On input (ud.read.ini, $sid, i, vr_i, com_i, open_i, comr_i, openr_i$):
   - $\mathcal{R}$ parses com_i as $(com_i', parcom, COM.Verify)$.
   - $\mathcal{R}$ parses $comr_i$ as $(comr_i', parcom, COM.Verify)$.
   - $\mathcal{R}$ aborts if COM.Verify is not a ppt algorithm.
   - $\mathcal{R}$ aborts if $1 \neq$ COM.Verify($parcom, com_i', i, open_i$).
   - $\mathcal{R}$ aborts if $1 \neq$ COM.Verify($parcom, comr_i', vr_i, openr_i$).
   - $\mathcal{R}$ takes the stored tuple $(sid, par, com, \mathbf{x}, cr)$ and aborts if $\mathbf{x}[i] \neq vr_i$.

- If (sid, i, w_i) is not stored, $\mathcal{R}$ runs $w_i \leftarrow$ VC.Prove$(par, i, \mathbf{x})$ and stores (sid, i, w_i).
- $\mathcal{R}$ sets the witness $wit \leftarrow (w_i, i, open_i, vr_i, openr_i)$ and the instance $ins \leftarrow (par, com, parcom, com'_i, comr'_i, cr)$. $\mathcal{R}$ uses zk.prove to send wit and ins to $\mathcal{F}^R_{\mathsf{ZK}}$. The relation R is

$$
R = \{(wit, ins) : \\
1 = \mathsf{COM.Verify}(parcom, com'_i, i, open_i) \wedge \\
1 = \mathsf{COM.Verify}(parcom, comr'_i, vr_i, openr_i) \wedge \\
1 = \mathsf{VC.Verify}(par, com, vr_i, i, w_i)\}
$$

- $\mathcal{U}$ receives $ins = (par', com', parcom, com'_i, comr'_i, cr)$ from $\mathcal{F}^R_{\mathsf{ZK}}$.
- $\mathcal{U}$ takes the stored tuple $(sid, par, com, \mathbf{x}, cu)$ and aborts if $cr \neq cu$, or if $par' \neq par$, or if $com' \neq com$.
- $\mathcal{U}$ sets $com_i \leftarrow (com'_i, parcom, \mathsf{COM.Verify})$ and $comr_i \leftarrow (comr'_i, parcom, \mathsf{COM.Verify})$. ($\mathsf{COM.Verify}$ is part of the description of R.)
- $\mathcal{U}$ outputs $(\mathsf{ud.read.end}, sid, com_i, comr_i)$.

Theorem 1. Π_{UD} *securely realizes* $\mathcal{F}_{\mathsf{UD}}$ *in the* $(\mathcal{F}_{\mathsf{CRS}}^{\mathsf{VC.Setup}}, \mathcal{F}_{\mathsf{AUT}}, \mathcal{F}^R_{\mathsf{ZK}})$*-hybrid model if the NHVC scheme is binding.*

We analyze in detail the security of Π_{UD} in the full version [17].

Variants of Π_{UD}. In Sect. 3, we describe a variant of $\mathcal{F}_{\mathsf{UD}}$ where $\mathcal{R}$ reads several database entries simultaneously, and another variant where the database entries are of the form $[i, vr_{i,1}, \ldots, vr_{i,m}]$. To construct the former, in the read phase, $\mathcal{R}$ simply needs to compute openings w_i for each entry read. Relation R replicates the equations described above for each entry read.

For the latter, com commits to a vector $\mathbf{x}$ of length $N \times m$ such that $\mathbf{x}[(i - 1)m + j] = vr_{i,j}$ for all $i \in [1, N]$ and $j \in [1, m]$. In the update phase, each vector component can be updated independently of others regardless of whether they belong to the same database entry. To read the database entry i, $\mathcal{R}$ needs to compute openings $(w_{(i-1)m+1}, \ldots, w_{im})$ to open the positions $[(i - 1)m + 1, im]$ of the committed vector $\mathbf{x}$. $\mathcal{R}$ must also prove that those positions belong to the database entry i. To this end, the relation R is modified to involve a witness $wit \leftarrow (i, open_i, \{w_{(i-1)m+j}, vr_{i,j}, openr_{i,j}\}_{\forall j \in [1,m]})$ and an instance $ins \leftarrow (par, com, parcom, com'_i, \{comr'_{i,j}\}_{\forall j \in [1,m]}, cr)$

$$
R = \{(wit, ins) : \\
1 = \mathsf{COM.Verify}(parcom, com'_i, i, open_i) \wedge \\
\{1 = \mathsf{COM.Verify}(parcom, comr'_{i,j}, vr_{i,j}, openr_{i,j}) \wedge \\
1 = \mathsf{VC.Verify}(par, com, vr_{i,j}, (i - 1)m + j, w_{(i-1)m+j})\}_{\forall j \in [1,m]}\}
$$

5   Instantiation and Efficiency Analysis

Bilinear Maps. Let $\mathbb{G}$, $\tilde{\mathbb{G}}$ and $\mathbb{G}_t$ be groups of prime order p. A map $e : \mathbb{G} \times \tilde{\mathbb{G}} \rightarrow \mathbb{G}_t$ must satisfy bilinearity, i.e., $e(g^x, \tilde{g}^y) = e(g, \tilde{g})^{xy}$; non-degeneracy, i.e., for all generators $g \in \mathbb{G}$ and $\tilde{g} \in \tilde{\mathbb{G}}$, $e(g, \tilde{g})$ generates $\mathbb{G}_t$; and efficiency, i.e., there exists an efficient algorithm $\mathcal{G}(1^k)$ that outputs the pairing group setup $grp \leftarrow (p, \mathbb{G}, \tilde{\mathbb{G}}, \mathbb{G}_t, e, g, \tilde{g})$ and an efficient algorithm to compute $e(a, b)$ for any $a \in \mathbb{G}$, $b \in \tilde{\mathbb{G}}$.

ℓ-Diffie-Hellman Exponent (DHE) Assumption. Let $(p, \mathbb{G}, \tilde{\mathbb{G}}, \mathbb{G}_t, e, g, \tilde{g}) \leftarrow \mathcal{G}(1^k)$ and $\alpha \leftarrow \mathbb{Z}_p$. Given $(p, \mathbb{G}, \tilde{\mathbb{G}}, \mathbb{G}_t, e, g, \tilde{g})$ and a tuple $(g_1, \tilde{g}_1, \ldots, g_\ell, \tilde{g}_\ell, g_{\ell+2}, \ldots, g_{2\ell})$ such that $g_i = g^{(\alpha^i)}$ and $\tilde{g}_i = \tilde{g}^{(\alpha^i)}$, for any p.p.t. adversary $\mathcal{A}$, $\Pr[g^{(\alpha^{\ell+1})} \leftarrow \mathcal{A}(p, \mathbb{G}, \tilde{\mathbb{G}}, \mathbb{G}_t, e, g, \tilde{g}, g_1, \tilde{g}_1, \ldots, g_\ell, \tilde{g}_\ell, g_{\ell+2}, \ldots, g_{2\ell})] \leq \epsilon(k)$.

NHVC Scheme. We use a NHVC scheme secure under the ℓ-DHE assumption [33].

VC.Setup$(1^k, \ell)$. Generate groups $(p, \mathbb{G}, \tilde{\mathbb{G}}, \mathbb{G}_t, e, g, \tilde{g}) \leftarrow \mathcal{G}(1^k)$, pick $\alpha \leftarrow \mathbb{Z}_p$ and compute $(g_1, \tilde{g}_1, \ldots, g_\ell, \tilde{g}_\ell, g_{\ell+2}, \ldots, g_{2\ell})$, where $g_i = g^{(\alpha^i)}$ and $\tilde{g}_i = \tilde{g}^{(\alpha^i)}$. Output $par \leftarrow (p, \mathbb{G}, \tilde{\mathbb{G}}, \mathbb{G}_t, e, g, \tilde{g}, g_1, \tilde{g}_1, \ldots, g_\ell, \tilde{g}_\ell, g_{\ell+2}, \ldots, g_{2\ell}, \mathcal{M} = \mathbb{Z}_p)$.

VC.Commit$(par, \mathbf{x})$. Let $|\mathbf{x}| = n \leq \ell$. Output $com = \prod_{j=1}^n g_{\ell+1-j}^{\mathbf{x}[j]}$.

VC.Prove$(par, i, \mathbf{x})$. Let $|\mathbf{x}| = n \leq \ell$. Output $w = \prod_{j=1, j \neq i}^n g_{\ell+1-j+i}^{\mathbf{x}[j]}$.

VC.Verify(par, com, x, i, w). Output 1 if $e(com, \tilde{g}_i) = e(w, \tilde{g}) \cdot e(g_1, \tilde{g}_\ell)^x$, else 0.

VC.ComUpd(par, com, j, x, x'). Output $com' = com \cdot g_{\ell+1-j}^{x'-x}$.

VC.WitUpd(par, w, i, j, x, x'). If $i = j$, output w, else $w' = w \cdot g_{\ell+1-j+i}^{x'-x}$.

This NHVC scheme is correct and binding under the ℓ-DHE assumption. This theorem is proven in the full version [17].

Commitment Scheme for $\mathcal{F}_{\text{NIC}}$. A commitment scheme consists of algorithms CSetup, Com and VfCom. CSetup(1^k) generates the parameters par_c, which include a description of the message space $\mathcal{M}$. Com(par_c, x) outputs a commitment com to $x \in \mathcal{M}$ and an opening $open$. VfCom$(par_c, com, x, open)$ outputs 1 if com is a commitment to x with opening $open$ or 0 otherwise.

We use the Pedersen commitment scheme [38]. CSetup(1^k) takes a group $\mathbb{G}$ of prime order p with generator g, picks random α, computes $h \leftarrow g^\alpha$ and sets the parameters $par_c \leftarrow (\mathbb{G}, g, h)$, which include a description of the message space $\mathcal{M} \leftarrow \mathbb{Z}_p$. Com$(par_c, x)$ picks random $open \leftarrow \mathbb{Z}_p$ and outputs a commitment $com \leftarrow g^x h^{open}$ to $x \in \mathcal{M}$ and an opening $open$. VfCom$(par_c, com, x, open)$ outputs 1 if $com = g^x h^{open}$. In [10], it is shown that any trapdoor commitment scheme, such as Pedersen commitments, realizes $\mathcal{F}_{\text{NIC}}$.

ZK Proof for $\mathcal{F}_{\text{ZK}}^R$. To instantiate $\mathcal{F}_{\text{ZK}}^R$, we use the scheme in [12]. In [12], a UC ZK protocol proving knowledge of exponents $(w_1, \ldots, w_n)$ that satisfy the formula $\phi(w_1, \ldots, w_n)$ is described as

$$\mathcal{A} \, w_1, \ldots, w_n : \phi(w_1, \ldots, w_n) \tag{1}$$

The formula $\phi(w_1, \ldots, w_n)$ consists of conjunctions and disjunctions of "atoms". An atom expresses *group relations*, such as $\prod_{j=1}^{k} g_j^{\mathcal{F}_j} = 1$, where the g_j's are elements of prime order groups and the $\mathcal{F}_j$'s are polynomials in the variables $(w_1, \ldots, w_n)$.

A proof system for (1) can be transformed into a proof system for more expressive statements about secret exponents *sexps* and secret bases *sbases*:

$$\Lambda \, sexps, sbases : \phi(sexps, bases \cup sbases) \tag{2}$$

The transformation adds an additional base h to the public bases. For each $g_j \in sbases$, the transformation picks a random exponent ρ_j and computes a blinded base $g_j' = g_j h^{\rho_j}$. The transformation adds g_j' to the public bases *bases*, ρ_j to the secret exponents *sexps*, and rewrites $g_j^{\mathcal{F}_j}$ into $g_j'^{\mathcal{F}_j} h^{-\mathcal{F}_j \rho_j}$.

The proof system supports pairing product equations $\prod_{j=1}^{k} e(g_j, \tilde{g}_j)^{\mathcal{F}_j} = 1$ in groups of prime order with a bilinear map e, by treating the target group $\mathbb{G}_t$ as the group of the proof system. The embedding for secret bases is unchanged, except for the case in which both bases in a pairing are secret. In this case, $e(g_j, \tilde{g}_j)^{\mathcal{F}_j}$ must be transformed into $e(g_j', \tilde{g}_j')^{\mathcal{F}_j} e(g_j', \tilde{h})^{-\mathcal{F}_j \tilde{\rho}_j} e(h, \tilde{g}_j')^{-\mathcal{F}_j \rho_j} e(h, \tilde{h})^{\mathcal{F}_j \rho_j \tilde{\rho}_j}$.

Signature Schemes. We use a signature scheme for the ZK proof for relation R in Sect. 5.1. A signature scheme consists of the algorithms KeyGen, Sign and VfSig. KeyGen(1^k) outputs a secret key sk and a public key pk, which include a description of the message space $\mathcal{M}$. Sign(sk, m) outputs a signature s on the message $m \in \mathcal{M}$. VfSig(pk, s, m) outputs 1 if s is a valid signature on m and 0 otherwise. This definition can be extended to blocks of messages $\bar{m} = (m_1, \ldots, m_n)$. In this case, KeyGen($1^k, n$) receives the maximum number n of messages as input. A signature scheme must be existentially unforgeable [23].

We use the structure-preserving signature (SPS) scheme in [2]. In SPSs, the public key, the messages, and the signatures are group elements in $\mathbb{G}$ and $\tilde{\mathbb{G}}$, and verification must consist purely in the checking of pairing product equations. We employ SPSs to sign group elements, while still supporting efficient ZK proofs of signature possession. In this SPS scheme, a elements in $\mathbb{G}$ and b elements in $\tilde{\mathbb{G}}$ are signed.

KeyGen(grp, a, b). Let $grp \leftarrow (p, \mathbb{G}, \tilde{\mathbb{G}}, \mathbb{G}_t, e, g, \tilde{g})$ be the bilinear map parameters. Pick at random $u_1, \ldots, u_b, v, w_1, \ldots w_a, z \leftarrow \mathbb{Z}_p^*$ and compute $U_i = g^{u_i}$, $i \in [1..b]$, $V = \tilde{g}^v$, $W_i = \tilde{g}^{w_i}$, $i \in [1..a]$ and $Z = \tilde{g}^z$. Return the verification key $pk \leftarrow (grp, U_1, \ldots, U_b, V, W_1, \ldots, W_a, Z)$ and the signing key $sk \leftarrow (pk, u_1, \ldots, u_b, v, w_1, \ldots, w_a, z)$.

Sign($sk, \langle m_1, \ldots, m_{a+b} \rangle$). Pick $r \leftarrow \mathbb{Z}_p^*$, set $R \leftarrow g^r$, $S \leftarrow g^{z-rv} \prod_{i=1}^{a} m_i^{-w_i}$, and $T \leftarrow (\tilde{g} \prod_{i=1}^{b} m_{a+i}^{-u_i})^{1/r}$, and output the signature $s \leftarrow (R, S, T)$.

VfSig($pk, s, \langle m_1, \ldots, m_{a+b} \rangle$). Output 1 if $e(R, V) e(S, \tilde{g}) \prod_{i=1}^{a} e(m_i, W_i) = e(g, Z)$ and $e(R, T) \prod_{i=1}^{b} e(U_i, m_{a+i}) = e(g, \tilde{g})$.

5.1   UC ZK Proof for Relation R

To instantiate $\mathcal{F}_{\text{ZK}}^{R}$ with the protocol in [12], we need to instantiate R with our chosen NHVC and commitment schemes. Then we need to express R following the notation for UC ZK proofs described above.

In R, we need to prove that the position i committed in com'_i equals the position opened in the NHVC com thorough the verification equation $e(com, \tilde{g}_i) = e(w, \tilde{g}) \cdot e(g_1, \tilde{g}_\ell)^x$. In our NHVC scheme, α is secret, which makes the relation between $\tilde{g}_i = \tilde{g}^{\alpha^i}$ and i not efficiently provable. To solve this problem, the public parameters are extended with SPSs that bind g^i with $\tilde{g}_i$. Given the parameters $par = (p, \mathbb{G}, \tilde{\mathbb{G}}, \mathbb{G}_t, e, g, \tilde{g}, g_1, \tilde{g}_1, \ldots, g_\ell, \tilde{g}_\ell, g_{\ell+2}, \ldots, g_{2\ell}, \mathcal{M} = \mathbb{Z}_p, \mathcal{R} = \mathbb{Z}_p)$, and the key pair (sk, pk), for $i \in [1, \ell]$, $\mathcal{F}_{\text{CRS}}^{\text{CRS.Setup}}$ computes $s_i \leftarrow \text{Sign}(sk, \langle g^i, g^{sid}, \tilde{g}_i \rangle)$, where sid is the session identifier. (We note that, in many practical settings, $\mathcal{U}$ can compute the parameters and signatures.) We remark that these signatures do not need to be updated when the database is updated.

Let (U_1, V, W_1, W_2, Z) be the public key of the signature scheme. Let (R, S, T) be a signature on $(g^i, g^{sid}, \tilde{g}_i)$. Let (g, h) be the parameters of the Pedersen commitment scheme. R involves proofs about secret bases and we use the transformation described above for those proofs. The base h is also used to randomize secret bases in $\mathbb{G}$, and another base $\tilde{h} \leftarrow \tilde{\mathbb{G}}$ is added to randomize bases in $\tilde{\mathbb{G}}$. Following the notation in [12], we describe the proof as follows.

$$\nexists i, open_i, v, openr_i, \tilde{g}_i, w, R, S, T :$$

$$com_i = g^i h^{open_i} \ \wedge \ comr_i = g^v h^{openr_i} \ \wedge \tag{3}$$

$$e(R, V)e(S, \tilde{g})e(g, W_1)^i e(g^{sid}, W_2)e(g, Z)^{-1} = 1 \ \wedge \tag{4}$$

$$e(R, T)e(U_1, \tilde{g}_i)e(g, \tilde{g})^{-1} = 1 \ \wedge \tag{5}$$

$$e(com, \tilde{g}_i)^{-1} e(w, \tilde{g})e(g_1, \tilde{g}_\ell)^v = 1 \tag{6}$$

Equation 3 proves knowledge of the openings of the Pedersen commitments com_i and $comr_i$. Equation 4 and Eq. 5 prove knowledge of a signature (R, S, T) on a message $\langle g^i, g^{sid}, \tilde{g}_i \rangle$. Equation 6 proves that the value v in $comr_i$ is equal to the value committed in the position i of the vector commitment com.

Instantiations of Variants of Π_{UD}. To instantiate the variant of Π_{UD} where several database entries are read simultaneously, we replicate the ZK proof described above for each entry read. To instantiate the variant with database entries $[i, vr_{i,1}, \ldots, vr_{i,m}]$, we compute signatures $s_i \leftarrow \text{Sign}(sk, \langle g^i, g^{sid}, \tilde{g}_{(i-1)m+1}, \ldots, \tilde{g}_{im} \rangle)$ to bind the entry i to the positions $[(i-1)m+1, im]$ that need to be opened in the committed vector. The public key of the signature scheme is now $(U_1, \ldots, U_m, V, W_1, W_2, Z)$. The ZK proof for relation R is:

$$\nexists\, i, open_i, \{vr_{i,j}, openr_{i,j}, \tilde{g}_{(i-1)m+j}, w_{(i-1)m+j}\}_{\forall j\in[1,m]}, R, S, T:$$
$$com_i = g^i h^{open_i} \;\wedge\; \{comr_{i,j} = g^{vr_{i,j}} h^{openr_{i,j}}\}_{\forall j\in[1,m]} \;\wedge$$
$$e(R,V)e(S,\tilde{g})e(g,W_1)^i e(g^{sid},W_2)e(g,Z)^{-1} = 1 \;\wedge$$
$$e(R,T)e(U_1,\tilde{g}_{(i-1)m+1})\cdots e(U_m,\tilde{g}_{im})e(g,\tilde{g})^{-1} = 1 \;\wedge$$
$$\{e(com,\tilde{g}_{(i-1)m+j})^{-1} e(w_{(i-1)m+j},\tilde{g})e(g_1,\tilde{g}_\ell)^{vr_{i,j}} = 1\}_{\forall j\in[1,m]}$$

The signature on $\langle g^i, g^{sid}, \tilde{g}_{(i-1)m+1}, \dots, \tilde{g}_{im}\rangle$ also binds the positions of the database entry i together and reveals the position $j \in [1,m]$ of each value $vr_{i,j}$ within the entry.

5.2 Efficiency Analysis

We analyze the storage, communication, and computation costs of our instantiation of Π_{UD}.

Storage Cost. $\mathcal{R}$ and $\mathcal{U}$ store the common reference string, whose size grows linearly with N. Throughout the protocol execution, $\mathcal{R}$ and $\mathcal{U}$ also store the last update of com and the committed vector. $\mathcal{R}$ stores the openings w_i. In conclusion, the storage cost is linear in N.

Communication Cost. In the ud.update interface, $\mathcal{U}$ sends $(i, vu_i)_{\forall i\in[1,N]}$ to $\mathcal{R}$. The communication cost is linear in the number of entries updated, except for the first update in which all entries must be initialized. In the ud.read interface, $\mathcal{R}$ sends an instance and a ZK proof to $\mathcal{U}$. The size of the witness and of the instance is constant and independent of N. Therefore, the communication cost of the proof is constant. In conclusion, after the first update phase, the communication cost does not depend on N.

Computation Cost. In the ud.update interface, $\mathcal{U}$ and $\mathcal{R}$ update com with cost linear in the number of updates (except for the first update where all the positions are initialized). $\mathcal{R}$ also updates the stored openings w_i with cost linear in the number of updates. In the ud.read interface, if w_i is not stored, $\mathcal{R}$ computes it with cost that grows linearly with N. However, if w_i is stored, the computation cost of the proof is constant and independent of N.

We note that it is possible to defer opening updates to the ud.read interface, so as to only update openings that are actually needed to compute ZK proofs. Thanks to that, the computation cost in the ud.update interface is constant. In the ud.read interface, if w_i is stored but needs to be updated, the computation cost grows linearly with the number of updates but it is independent of N. The only overhead introduced by deferring opening updates is the need to store the tuples $(i, vu_i)_{\forall i\in[1,N]}$ sent by $\mathcal{U}$.

In summary, after initializing com and the openings w_i, the communication and computation costs are independent of N, which makes our instantiation of Π_{UD} practical for large databases.

5.3   Implementation and Efficiency Measurements

We have implemented our instantiation of Π_{UD} in the Python programming language, using the Charm cryptographic framework [4], on a computer equipped with an Intel Core i5-7300U CPU clocked at 2.60 GHz, and 8 gigabytes of RAM. The BN256 curve was used for the pairing group setup.

To compute the UC ZK proofs for R, we use the compiler in [12]. The public parameters of the proof system contain a public key of the Paillier encryption scheme, the parameters for a multi-integer commitment scheme and the specification of a DSA group. (We refer to [12] for a description of how those primitives are used in the compiler.) The cost of a proof depends on the number of elements in the witness and of the number of equations composed by Boolean ANDs. The computation cost for the prover of a Σ-protocol for R involves one evaluation of each of the equations and one multiplication per value in the witness. The compiler in [12] extends a Σ-protocol and requires, additionally, a computation of a multi-integer commitment that commits to the values in the witness, an evaluation of a Paillier encryption for each of the values in the witness, a Σ-protocol to prove that the commitment and the encryptions are correctly generated, and 3 exponentiations in the DSA group. The computation cost for the verifier, as well as the communication cost, also depends on the number of values in the witness and on the number of equations. Therefore, as the number of values in the witness and of equations is independent of N in our proof for relation R, the computation and communication costs of our proof do not depend on N.

Table 1. Π_{UD} execution times in seconds

	1024 bit key		2048 bit key	
Interface	$N = 100$	$N = 1000$	$N = 100$	$N = 1000$
First update	0.6844	5.9952	0.7940	6.0822
Computation of com or w_i	0.0032	0.03787	0.0032	0.03787
1-entry update of com or w_i	0.0001	0.0001	0.0001	0.0001
Read	0.7496	0.7545	3.8945	3.5911

Table 1 lists the execution times of the update and read interfaces of the protocol, in seconds. The execution times of the interfaces of the protocol have been evaluated against the size N of the database, and against the security parameter of the Paillier encryption algorithm.

In the first update, the public parameters of all the building blocks are computed, and the database is set up by computing com. In the second row of Table 1, we show the cost of just computing com, which is virtually the same as that of computing an opening w_i. The computation time of com and w_i is very small. (As required by our applications in Sect. 6, the committed vector that we use consists of small numbers rather than random values in $\mathbb{Z}_p$.) In the 1-entry update, one database entry is modified and com is updated. The cost of updating an opening w_i is virtually the same. As can be seen, the cost of the first update grows linearly with the size N of the database, as does the cost of setting up com or w_i, whereas the cost of updating com or w_i is very small and independent of N. The execution times for the read interface depend greatly upon the security parameters for the Paillier encryption scheme. However, the execution time is independent of the database size N.

6   Modular Design with $\mathcal{F}_{\mathrm{UD}}$ and Applications

Consider the following relation R':

$$R' = \{(wit, ins) : [i, vr_i] \in \mathsf{DB} \ \wedge \ 1 = \mathrm{pred}_i(i) \ \wedge \ 1 = \mathrm{pred}_v(vr_i)\}$$

where the witness is $wit = (i, vr_i)$ and the instance is $ins = \mathsf{DB}$. pred_i and pred_v represent predicates that i and vr_i must fulfill, e.g., predicates that require i and vr_i to belong to a range or set of values.

We would like to construct a ZK protocol for R' that separates each of the equations of R'. We show how this protocol is constructed by using $\mathcal{F}_{\mathrm{UD}}$ and $\mathcal{F}_{\mathrm{NIC}}$ as building blocks, along with the functionalities $\mathcal{F}_{\mathrm{ZK}}^{R_i}$ and $\mathcal{F}_{\mathrm{ZK}}^{R_v}$.

1. On input DB, the verifier uses the ud.update interface to send DB to $\mathcal{F}_{\mathrm{UD}}$, which sends DB to the prover.
2. On input (i, vr_i), the prover checks that $[i, vr_i] \in \mathsf{DB}$.
3. The prover runs the com.setup interface of $\mathcal{F}_{\mathrm{NIC}}$. The prover uses the com.commit interface of $\mathcal{F}_{\mathrm{NIC}}$ on input i to obtain a commitment com_i with opening $open_i$. Similarly, the prover obtains from $\mathcal{F}_{\mathrm{NIC}}$ a commitment $comr_i$ to vr_i with opening $openr_i$.
4. The prover uses ud.read to send $(i, vr_i, com_i, open_i, comr_i, openr_i)$ to $\mathcal{F}_{\mathrm{UD}}$. $\mathcal{F}_{\mathrm{UD}}$ sends com_i and $comr_i$ to the verifier.
5. The verifier runs the com.setup interface of $\mathcal{F}_{\mathrm{NIC}}$. The verifier uses the com.validate interface of $\mathcal{F}_{\mathrm{NIC}}$ to validate the commitments com_i and $comr_i$. Then the verifier stores com_i and $comr_i$ and sends a message to the prover to acknowledge the receipt of the commitments.
6. The prover parses the commitment com_i as $(com_i', parcom, \mathsf{COM.Verify})$. The prover sets the witness $wit \leftarrow (i, open_i)$ and the instance $ins \leftarrow (parcom, com_i')$. The prover uses the zk.prove interface to send wit and ins to $\mathcal{F}_{\mathrm{ZK}}^{R_i}$, where R_i is

$$R_i = \{(wit, ins) : 1 = \mathsf{COM.Verify}(parcom, com_i', i, open_i) \ \wedge \ 1 = \mathrm{pred}_i(i)\}$$

7. The verifier receives ins from $\mathcal{F}_{\mathrm{ZK}}^{R_i}$. The verifier checks that the commitment in ins is equal to the stored commitment com_i. If it is equal, the binding property guaranteed by $\mathcal{F}_{\mathrm{NIC}}$ ensures that $\mathcal{F}_{\mathrm{UD}}$ and $\mathcal{F}_{\mathrm{ZK}}^{R_i}$ received as input the same position i.
8. The last two steps are replicated to prove that vr_i fulfills $1 = \mathrm{pred}_v(vr_i)$ by using $\mathcal{F}_{\mathrm{ZK}}^{R_v}$.

We think that a modular design has two advantages. First, it allows for a simple security analysis. A security proof of a protocol described in the hybrid model is much simpler than a proof that requires reductions to the security properties of different cryptographic primitives. Moreover, each of the building blocks realizes a simpler task and thus requires a simpler protocol with a less involved security analysis. Second, it facilitates the study in isolation of how to create efficient and secure ZK data structures. Namely, different constructions for $\mathcal{F}_{\mathrm{UD}}$ can easily be compared in terms of security and efficiency.

Application to POT. The POT protocols in [9, 41] are based on previously proposed oblivious transfer (OT) protocols. However, they do not use OT as a building block. Instead, the OT protocol is modified ad-hoc to create the POT protocol, and its security has to be reanalyzed when analyzing the security of the POT protocol.

$\mathcal{F}_{\mathrm{UD}}$ can be used to design a POT protocol modularly. The database DB consists of entries $[i, p_i]$, where p_i is the price to be paid for message m_i. To purchase m_i, the buyer uses the ud.read interface of $\mathcal{F}_{\mathrm{UD}}$ to read the entry $[i, p_i]$. The provider receives the commitments com_i to i and $comr_i$ to p_i. $comr_i$ is used as input to a functionality $\mathcal{F}_{\mathrm{ZK}}^{R_v}$ where the buyer proves that he subtracts the price p_i from his account. com_i is used as input to a functionality for oblivious transfer (modified to receive committed inputs as described in [10]) to allow the buyer to retrieve m_i.

Therefore, $\mathcal{F}_{\mathrm{UD}}$ allows the design of a POT protocol that uses a functionality for OT as building block. Thanks to that, the POT protocol can be instantiated with multiple OT schemes and their security does not need to be reanalyzed. Moreover, $\mathcal{F}_{\mathrm{UD}}$ allows the provider to update prices at any time.

Application to PPB. In the PPB protocols in [39, 40], a meter reading comprises the consumption c and the time interval i of consumption. The tariff policy associates a different function $p = f_i(c)$ to each time interval (and possibly to each consumption interval). $\mathcal{F}_{\mathrm{UD}}$ can be used to design a PPB protocol modularly, where the database DB consists of entries $[i, f_i]$. The PPB protocol works as follows. First, the meter outputs a signed meter reading (c, i). The user reads $[i, f_i]$ through $\mathcal{F}_{\mathrm{UD}}$, and the provider receives commitments com_i to i and $comr_i$ to f_i. com_i is used as input to a functionality $\mathcal{F}_{\mathrm{ZK}}^{R_i}$ to prove that i equals the value signed in the meter reading. $comr_i$ is used as input to a functionality $\mathcal{F}_{\mathrm{ZK}}^{R_v}$ to prove that $p = f_i(c)$. If f_i is represented by a tuple of values (e.g. the coefficients of a polynomial) the variant of $\mathcal{F}_{\mathrm{UD}}$ for databases of the form $[i, vr_{i,1}, \ldots, vr_{i,m}]$ should be used. If the formula f_i also changes with the consumption interval, the database can also store the minimum and maximum values of the consumption interval to allow the user to prove that he uses the right formula. Using $\mathcal{F}_{\mathrm{UD}}$ allows the design of PPB protocols modularly and allows the provider to modify the pricing policies efficiently and at any time.

7 Related Work

Accumulators. A cryptographic accumulator [6] allows us to represent a set X succinctly as a single accumulator value A. To prove that a value $x \in X$, a party computes a witness W_x whose size is independent of X. Some accumulator schemes are equipped with efficient ZK proofs to prove knowledge of W_x such that $x \in X$.

NHVC schemes are similar to accumulator schemes that use a trusted setup and are non-hiding [5,11,13,37], i.e., A does not hide X. (Recently, hiding accumulators [19,21] have been proposed.) The instantiation of NHVC schemes based on the DHE assumption resembles the accumulator scheme in [11]. The main difference between accumulators and NHVC schemes is that, while accumulators allow us to commit to a set, NHVC schemes allow us to commit to a vector of messages, where each message is committed at a specific position. This allows parties to prove statements about the position i and about the value vr_i stored at i, which is needed for $\mathcal{F}_{UD}$.

Vector Commitments. VC schemes [15,33] can be non-hiding and hiding, and can be based on different assumptions such as CDH, RSA and DHE. It would be possible to instantiate our construction under the more standard CDH or RSA assumptions. However, the instantiation of NHVC schemes based on DHE has efficiency advantages. A mercurial VC scheme based on DHE was proposed in [33], and subsequently non-hiding and hiding DHE VC schemes were used in [24,28,31]. In our instantiation of Π_{UD}, we use a NHVC scheme based on DHE that is extended with a ZK proof of knowledge of a witness w_i to prove that a value vr_i is stored at position i. For this proof, a signature scheme is used along with the NHVC scheme.

Recently, in [29], subvector commitments (SVC) are proposed. In SVC, a commitment can be opened to a set of positions such that the size of the opening does not depend on the size of the set. A construction for SVC secure under the cube Diffie-Hellman assumption is given, in which the public parameter size grows quadratically with the vector length. Our functionality $\mathcal{F}_{UD}$ only requires to open one vector component at a time. SVC may be used to construct the variant of $\mathcal{F}_{UD}$ where several positions are read simultaneously, or the variant where the database entries are of the form $[i, vr_{i,1}, \dots, vr_{i,m}]$. In the read phase, SVC would yield a ZK proof where one opening can be used to open several positions (at the expense of increasing the storage cost of the public parameters). Despite that SVC provides openings of size independent of the number of positions open, we note that the entire witness of the ZK proof would still grow with the number of positions opened, and thus the efficiency of those proofs would not be independent of the number of positions opened. In [7,29], constructions for SVC based on groups of hidden order are proposed, which are better suited for bit vectors.

Polynomial commitments allow a committer to commit to a polynomial and open the commitment to an evaluation of the polynomial. Polynomial commitments can be used as vector commitments by committing to a polynomial that interpolates the vector to be committed. In [26], a construction of polynomial commitments from the SDH assumption is proposed. The polynomial commitment scheme from SDH has the disadvantage that efficient updates cannot be computed without knowledge of the trapdoor. A further generalization of vector commitments and polynomial commitments are functional commitments [29,32].

Zero-Knowledge Data Structures. Zero-Knowledge Sets (ZKS) [35] allow a prover P to commit to a set X and to subsequently prove to a verifier V (non-) membership of an element x in X. Zero-Knowledge Databases (ZKDB) are similar to ZKS but each element $x \in X$ is associated with a value v, in such a way that a proof that $x \in X$ reveals v to V. Both ZKS and ZKDB are two-party protocols between a prover and a verifier. Zero-knowledge requires that proofs of (non-)membership reveal nothing else beyond (non-)membership, not even the set size.

A ZKS with short proofs for membership and non-membership is proposed in [33] and an updatable ZKDB with short proofs is proposed in [15]. In [26], constructions for "nearly" ZKS and ZKDB, which do not hide the size of the set or database, are given. In [22], a construction for zero-knowledge lists (ZKL) is proposed, where a list is defined as an ordered set. In contrast to our work, existing constructions for ZKS, ZKDB and ZKL are not updatable, with the exceptions of the ZKDB in [15,34].

The main difference between ZK data structures and our work is that ZK data structures hide the database content from the verifier, while in our work the database is public. Another difference is that our database is *oblivious* in the sense that it provides ZK proofs about a committed position i and value v, without revealing i or v. In existing ZK data structures, the prover reveals i and v along with the proof to the verifier. This property allows our database to be used as building block in privacy-preserving protocols where i and v must remain hidden from the verifier. As for modular design, in those works a method to integrate modularly the proposed ZK data structures as building blocks of other protocols is not given.

ZK Proofs for Large Datasets. In most ZK proofs, the computation and communication costs grow linearly with the size of the witness, which is inadequate for proofs about datasets of large size N. However, some techniques attain costs sublinear in N. Probabilistically checkable proofs [27] achieve verification cost sublinear in N, but the cost for the prover is linear in N. In succinct non-interactive arguments of knowledge [20], verification cost is independent of N, but the cost for the prover is still linear in N. ZK proofs for oblivious RAM programs [36] consist of a setup phase where the prover commits to the dataset, with cost linear in N for the prover and constant for the verifier. After setup, multiple proofs can be computed about the dataset with cost sublinear (proportional to the runtime of an ORAM program) for prover and verifier.

Our construction is somehow similar to [36], i.e. a database is committed, and then ZK proofs are computed. Storage cost is linear in N. However, the verification cost of a ZK proof is constant and independent of N. To compute a

ZK proof, only the cost of computing an opening w_i is linear in N, but w_i can be reused and updated with cost independent of N. Therefore, computing a ZK proof has an amortized cost independent of N, which makes our construction practical for large databases.

8 Conclusion and Future Work

We have proposed an ideal functionality $\mathcal{F}_{UD}$ and a construction Π_{UD} for an updatable database. In addition to POT and PPB, (non-)updatable databases are implicitly used as building blocks of other protocols. For example, many oblivious transfer with access control [1,8,16,30] protocols and other privacy preserving access control protocols [28] use a database that associates the index i of messages m_i with an access control policy ACP_i ($\forall i \in [1, N]$). As another example, privacy-preserving client-side profiling protocols [18] use a database that stores a codification of a profiling algorithm. These protocols also use signatures as a way of implementing the database. In those protocols, the reader needs to remain anonymous and unlinkable towards the updater. Therefore, to be used in those protocols, $\mathcal{F}_{UD}$ and Π_{UD} need to be modified to interact with multiple readers and to guarantee unlikability of readers towards the updater.

References

1. Abe, M., Camenisch, J., Dubovitskaya, M., Nishimaki, R.: Universally composable adaptive oblivious transfer (with access control) from standard assumptions. In: Proceedings of the 2013 ACM Workshop on Digital Identity Management, DIM 2013, pp. 1–12 (2013)
2. Abe, M., Groth, J., Haralambiev, K., Ohkubo, M.: Optimal structure-preserving signatures in asymmetric bilinear groups. In: Rogaway, P. (ed.) CRYPTO 2011. LNCS, vol. 6841, pp. 649–666. Springer, Heidelberg (2011). https://doi.org/10.1007/978-3-642-22792-9_37
3. Aiello, W., Ishai, Y., Reingold, O.: Priced oblivious transfer: how to sell digital goods. In: Pfitzmann, B. (ed.) EUROCRYPT 2001. LNCS, vol. 2045, pp. 119–135. Springer, Heidelberg (2011). https://doi.org/10.1007/3-540-44987-6_8
4. Akinyele, J.A., et al.: Charm: a framework for rapidly prototyping cryptosystems. J. Cryptogr. Eng. 3(2), 111–128 (2013)
5. Au, M.H., Tsang, P.P., Susilo, W., Mu, Y.: Dynamic universal accumulators for DDH groups and their application to attribute-based anonymous credential systems. In: Fischlin, M. (ed.) CT-RSA 2009. LNCS, vol. 5473, pp. 295–308. Springer, Heidelberg (2009). https://doi.org/10.1007/978-3-642-00862-7_20
6. Benaloh, J.C., de Mare, M.: One-way accumulators: a decentralized alternative to digital signatures (extended abstract). In: Helleseth, T. (ed.) EUROCRYPT 1993. LNCS, vol. 765, pp. 274–285. Springer, Heidelberg (1993). https://doi.org/10.1007/3-540-48285-7_24
7. Boneh, D., Bünz, B., Fisch, B.: Batching techniques for accumulators with applications to iops and stateless blockchains. In: Boldyreva, A., Micciancio, D. (eds.) CRYPTO 2019. LNCS, vol. 11692, pp. 561–586. Springer, Cham (2019). https://doi.org/10.1007/978-3-030-26948-7_20

8. Camenisch, J., Dubovitskaya, M., Neven, G.: Oblivious transfer with access control. In: Proceedings of the 2009 ACM Conference on Computer and Communications Security, CCS 2009, pp. 131–140 (2009)
9. Camenisch, J., Dubovitskaya, M., Neven, G.: Unlinkable priced oblivious transfer with rechargeable wallets. In: Sion, R. (ed.) FC 2010. LNCS, vol. 6052, pp. 66–81. Springer, Heidelberg (2010). https://doi.org/10.1007/978-3-642-14577-3_8
10. Camenisch, J., Dubovitskaya, M., Rial, A.: UC commitments for modular protocol design and applications to revocation and attribute tokens. In: Robshaw, M., Katz, J. (eds.) CRYPTO 2016. LNCS, vol. 9816, pp. 208–239. Springer, Heidelberg (2016). https://doi.org/10.1007/978-3-662-53015-3_8
11. Camenisch, J., Kohlweiss, M., Soriente, C.: An accumulator based on bilinear maps and efficient revocation for anonymous credentials. In: Jarecki, S., Tsudik, G. (eds.) PKC 2009. LNCS, vol. 5443, pp. 481–500. Springer, Heidelberg (2009). https://doi.org/10.1007/978-3-642-00468-1_27
12. Camenisch, J., Krenn, S., Shoup, V.: A framework for practical universally composable zero-knowledge protocols. In: Lee, D.H., Wang, X. (eds.) ASIACRYPT 2011. LNCS, vol. 7073, pp. 449–467. Springer, Heidelberg (2011). https://doi.org/10.1007/978-3-642-25385-0_24
13. Camenisch, J., Lysyanskaya, A.: Dynamic accumulators and application to efficient revocation of anonymous credentials. In: Yung, M. (ed.) CRYPTO 2002. LNCS, vol. 2442, pp. 61–76. Springer, Heidelberg (2002). https://doi.org/10.1007/3-540-45708-9_5
14. Canetti, R.: Universally composable security: A new paradigm for cryptographic protocols. In: FOCS 2001 (ePrint 2000/067 version 14-Dec-2005). pp. 136–145 (2001)
15. Catalano, D., Fiore, D.: Vector commitments and their applications. In: Kurosawa, K., Hanaoka, G. (eds.) PKC 2013. LNCS, vol. 7778, pp. 55–72. Springer, Heidelberg (2013). https://doi.org/10.1007/978-3-642-36362-7_5
16. Coull, S.E., Green, M., Hohenberger, S.: Controlling access to an oblivious database using stateful anonymous credentials. In: Jarecki, S., Tsudik, G. (eds.) PKC 2009. LNCS, vol. 5443, pp. 501–520. Springer, Heidelberg (2009). https://doi.org/10.1007/978-3-642-00468-1_28
17. Damodaran, A., Rial, A.: UC updatable databases and applications. http://hdl.handle.net/10993/42984
18. Danezis, G., Kohlweiss, M., Livshits, B., Rial, A.: Private client-side profiling with random forests and hidden Markov models. In: Fischer-Hübner, S., Wright, M. (eds.) PETS 2012. LNCS, vol. 7384, pp. 18–37. Springer, Heidelberg (2012). https://doi.org/10.1007/978-3-642-31680-7_2
19. Derler, D., Hanser, C., Slamanig, D.: Revisiting cryptographic accumulators, additional properties and relations to other primitives. In: Nyberg, K. (ed.) CT-RSA 2015. LNCS, vol. 9048, pp. 127–144. Springer, Cham (2015). https://doi.org/10.1007/978-3-319-16715-2_7
20. Gennaro, R., Gentry, C., Parno, B., Raykova, M.: Quadratic span programs and succinct NIZKs without PCPS. In: Johansson, T., Nguyen, P.Q. (eds.) EUROCRYPT 2013. LNCS, vol. 7881, pp. 626–645. Springer, Heidelberg (2013). https://doi.org/10.1007/978-3-642-38348-9_37
21. Ghosh, E., Ohrimenko, O., Papadopoulos, D., Tamassia, R., Triandopoulos, N.: Zero-knowledge accumulators and set algebra. In: Cheon, J., Takagi, T. (eds.) ASIACRYPT 2016. LNCS, vol. 10032, pp. 67–100. Springer, Heidelberg (2016). https://doi.org/10.1007/978-3-662-53890-6_3

22. Ghosh, E., Ohrimenko, O., Tamassia, R.: Zero-knowledge authenticated order queries and order statistics on a list. In: Malkin, T., Kolesnikov, V., Lewko, A., Polychronakis, M. (eds.) ACNS 2015. LNCS, vol. 9092, pp. 149–171. Springer, Cham (2015). https://doi.org/10.1007/978-3-319-28166-7_8
23. Goldwasser, S., Micali, S., Rivest, R.L.: A digital signature scheme secure against adaptive chosen-message attacks. SIAM J. Comput. 17(2), 281–308 (1988)
24. Izabachène, M., Libert, B., Vergnaud, D.: Block-wise P-signatures and non-interactive anonymous credentials with efficient attributes. In: Chen, L. (ed.) IMACC 2011. LNCS, vol. 7089, pp. 431–450. Springer, Heidelberg (2011). https://doi.org/10.1007/978-3-642-25516-8_26
25. Jawurek, M., Johns, M., Kerschbaum, F.: Plug-in privacy for smart metering billing. In: Fischer-Hübner, S., Hopper, N. (eds.) PETS 2011. LNCS, vol. 6794, pp. 192–210. Springer, Heidelberg (2011). https://doi.org/10.1007/978-3-642-22263-4_11
26. Kate, A., Zaverucha, G.M., Goldberg, I.: Constant-size commitments to polynomials and their applications. In: Abe, M. (ed.) ASIACRYPT 2010. LNCS, vol. 6477, pp. 177–194. Springer, Heidelberg (2010). https://doi.org/10.1007/978-3-642-17373-8_11
27. Kilian, J.: A note on efficient zero-knowledge proofs and arguments (extended abstract). In: ACM STOC 1992, pp. 723–732 (1992)
28. Kohlweiss, M., Rial, A.: Optimally private access control. In: WPES 2013, pp. 37–48 (2013)
29. Lai, R.W.F., Malavolta, G.: Subvector commitments with application to succinct arguments. In: Boldyreva, A., Micciancio, D. (eds.) CRYPTO 2019. LNCS, vol. 11692, pp. 530–560. Springer, Cham (2019). https://doi.org/10.1007/978-3-030-26948-7_19
30. Libert, B., Ling, S., Mouhartem, F., Nguyen, K., Wang, H.: Adaptive oblivious transfer with access control from lattice assumptions. In: Takagi, T., Peyrin, T. (eds.) ASIACRYPT 2017. LNCS, vol. 10624, pp. 533–563. Springer, Cham (2017). https://doi.org/10.1007/978-3-319-70694-8_19
31. Libert, B., Peters, T., Yung, M.: Group signatures with almost-for-free revocation. In: Safavi-Naini, R., Canetti, R. (eds.) CRYPTO 2012. LNCS, vol. 7417, pp. 571–589. Springer, Heidelberg (2012). https://doi.org/10.1007/978-3-642-32009-5_34
32. Libert, B., Ramanna, S.C., Yung, M.: Functional commitment schemes: from polynomial commitments to pairing-based accumulators from simple assumptions. In: ICALP 2016, pp. 30:1–30:14 (2016)
33. Libert, B., Yung, M.: Concise mercurial vector commitments and independent zero-knowledge sets with short proofs. In: Micciancio, D. (ed.) TCC 2010. LNCS, vol. 5978, pp. 499–517. Springer, Heidelberg (2010). https://doi.org/10.1007/978-3-642-11799-2_30
34. Liskov, M.D.: Updatable zero-knowledge databases. In: Roy, B. (ed.) ASIACRYPT 2005. LNCS, vol. 3788, pp. 174–198. Springer, Berlin, Heidelberg (2005). https://doi.org/10.1007/11593447_10
35. Micali, S., Rabin, M.O., Kilian, J.: Zero-knowledge sets. In: FOCS 2003, pp. 80–91 (2003)
36. Mohassel, P., Rosulek, M., Scafuro, A.: Sublinear zero-knowledge arguments for RAM programs. In: Coron, J.S., Nielsen, J. (eds.) EUROCRYPT 2017. LNCS, vol. 10210, pp. 501–531. Springer, Cham (2017). https://doi.org/10.1007/978-3-319-56620-7_18
37. Nguyen, L.: Accumulators from bilinear pairings and applications. In: Menezes, A. (ed.) CT-RSA 2005. LNCS, vol. 3376, pp. 275–292. Springer, Heidelberg (2005). https://doi.org/10.1007/978-3-540-30574-3_19

38. Pedersen, T.P.: Non-interactive and information-theoretic secure verifiable secret sharing. In: Feigenbaum, J. (ed.) CRYPTO 1991. LNCS, vol. 576, pp. 129–140. Springer, Heidelberg (1991). https://doi.org/10.1007/3-540-46766-1_9
39. Rial, A., Danezis, G.: Privacy-preserving smart metering. In: WPES 2011, pp. 49–60 (2011)
40. Rial, A., Danezis, G., Kohlweiss, M.: Privacy-preserving smart metering revisited. Int. J. Inf. Secur. **17**(1), 1–31 (2016). https://doi.org/10.1007/s10207-016-0355-8
41. Rial, A., Kohlweiss, M., Preneel, B.: Universally composable adaptive priced oblivious transfer. In: Shacham, H., Waters, B. (eds.) Pairing 2009. LNCS, vol. 5671, pp. 231–247. Springer, Heidelberg (2009). https://doi.org/10.1007/978-3-642-03298-1_15

Symmetric Key Cryptography

Impossible Differential Cryptanalysis of Reduced-Round Tweakable TWINE

Mohamed Tolba, Muhammad ElSheikh, and Amr M. Youssef[(✉)]

Concordia Institute for Information Systems Engineering, Concordia University,
Montréal, Québec, Canada
youssef@ciise.concordia.ca

Abstract. Tweakable TWINE (T-TWINE) is a new lightweight tweakable block cipher family proposed by Sakamoto *et al.* at IWSEC 2019. T-TWINE is the first Tweakable Block Cipher (TBC) that is built on Generalized Feistel Structure (GFS). It is based on the TWINE block cipher in addition to a simple tweak scheduling based on SKINNY's tweakey schedule. Similar to TWINE, it has two versions, namely, T-TWINE-80 and T-TWINE-128, both have a block length of 64 bits and employ keys of length 80 and 128 bits, respectively. In this paper, we present impossible differential attacks against reduced-round versions of T-TWINE-80 and T-TWINE-128. First, we present an 18-round impossible differential distinguisher against T-TWINE. Then, using this distinguisher, we attack 25 and 27 rounds of T-TWINE-80 and T-TWINE-128, respectively.

Keywords: Cryptanalysis · Impossible differential attacks ·
Tweakable · Block ciphers · TWINE · T-TWINE

1 Introduction

Tweakable Block Ciphers (TBCs) [11] differ from the conventional block ciphers since they accept an additional input called a tweak. Different specific keyed instances of the cipher can be generated by varying this tweak. TBCs allow new interesting highly-secure modes of operation and applications to become possible as they are designed to allow changing the tweak very efficiently compared to the key setup operation.

Block ciphers can be used to build TBCs through modes of operation such as LRW (Liskov, Rivest, and Wagner) and XEX (Xor-Encrypt-Xor) [14]. These modes of operations, for one TBC encryption/decryption, require few cipher calls. Therefore, they are efficient. However, their provable security guarantee, which is $2^{n/2}$ for n-bit block cipher, is not enough, in particular, for TBCs employed in modes of operation aiming to achieve "beyond-the-birthday-bound" (BBB) security. As a result, less efficient modes of operations [9,10], compared to LRW and XEX, are proposed to achieve BBB security guarantee.

Dedicated constructions is another approach to build efficient TBCs with an acceptable level of security guarantee. HPC [16], one of the submission to the

© Springer Nature Switzerland AG 2020
A. Nitaj and A. Youssef (Eds.): AFRICACRYPT 2020, LNCS 12174, pp. 91–113, 2020.
https://doi.org/10.1007/978-3-030-51938-4_5

AES competition, is the first proposal, where the tweak is called "spice". Three-fish [4], Deoxys-BC [7], SKINNY [2] and QARMA [1] are examples of recently proposed dedicated TBCs. Challenges such as designing efficient dedicated TBCs while having sufficient security guarantee is solved by the tweakey flamework [6] which is based on a Substitution Permutation Network (SPN).

Tweakable TWINE (T-TWINE) [15] is the first dedicated TBC that is based on Generalized Feistel Structure (GFS) [13,20]. The only work on GFS-based TBC, before the T-TWINE proposal, is done by Goldenberg et al. [5] and Mitsuda and Iwata [12] who focused on studding the provable security of the round functions that are instantiated by PRFs. TWINE, which is a GFS-based block cipher, was proposed by Suzaki et al. [18] after a comprehensive study done by Suzaki and Minematsu [17] showing the effect of the choice of sub-block permutation on the diffusion, the number of differential/linear active S-boxes, and the maximum numbers of rounds for impossible differential characteristics and saturation characteristics. The choice of the permutation of TWINE was a result of the work done in [17], it permutes over 16 nibbles to achieve the best characteristics.

T-TWINE [15] is built with the goal of reducing the cost of design, security evaluation, and implementation. As a result, TWINE was selected to be the basic building block of T-TWINE with extremely simple tweak scheduling. This tweak schedule is based on the SKINNY's [2] tweakey schedule. Similar to TWINE, T-TWINE has a block size of 64 bits and iterates using either 80-bit or 128-bit key over 36 rounds. It accepts an additional 64-bit tweak. It also uses independent key and tweak schedules where the tweak is mixed with the states by adding few nibble XORs to TWINE. Therefore, it has the same hardware cost of TWINE except for the additional tweak registers.

The designers of T-TWINE evaluated its security against differential, linear, impossible differential, and integral attacks in the chosen-tweak setting. However, they only presented distinguishers without converting any distinguisher to a key recovery attack. For impossible differential, they utilized the miss-in-the-middle approach to search the impossible differential characteristics that have one active nibble in the 16 tweak nibbles and one active nibble in 16 ciphertext nibbles at the decryption side. However, the 18-round impossible differential distinguisher that was proposed by the designers does not seem to be correct as we will illustrate in Sect. 3[1].

In this paper, we start by presenting an 18-round impossible differential distinguisher. Then, we use this distinguisher to launch a 25-round attack against T-TWINE-80 by pre-appending and appending 4 and 3 rounds, respectively. Finally, we launched a 27-round attack against T-TWINE-128, using the 18-round distinguisher, by pre-appending and appending 6 and 3 rounds, respectively. The data, time, and memory complexities of the 25-round (27-round) against T-TWINE-80 (T-TWINE-128) are $2^{61.5}$ (2^{60}) chosen plaintexts, $2^{70.86}$ 25-round ($2^{120.83}$ 27-round) encryptions, 2^{66} (2^{118}) 64-bit block, respectively.

---

[1] This has also been confirmed through personal communications with the designers.

The rest of the paper is organized as follows. Section 2 provides the notations used throughout the paper and a brief description of T-TWINE. In Sect. 3, we present the impossible differential distinguisher used in our attacks. The details of our attacks are presented in Sects. 4 and 5. Finally, the paper is concluded in Sect. 6.

2   Specifications of T-TWINE

The following notation will be used throughout the rest of the paper:

- K: The 80 or 128 bits master key.
- K_j: The jth nibble of K. The indices of the nibbles begin from 0.
- RK^i: The 32-bit round key used in round $i + 1$.
- RK^i_j: The jth nibble of RK^i. The indices of the nibbles begin from 0.
- T: The 64-bit tweak.
- T_i: The ith nibble of the tweak T.
- RT^i: The 24-bit round tweak used in round $i + 1$, where $RT^i \leftarrow t^i_0 \| t^i_1 \| t^i_2 \| t^i_3 \| t^i_4 \| t^i_5$, and t^i_j is the jth nibble of RT^i.
- X^i: The 16 4-bit nibbles output of round i.
- X_j^i: j^{th} nibble of X^i.
- $\Delta X^i, \Delta X^i_j$: The difference at state X^i and nibble X^i_j, respectively.
- $\oplus$: The XOR operation.
- $\|$: The concatenation operation.
- $Rotz(x)$: The z-bit left cyclic shift of x.

T-TWINE is based on TWINE [18]. T-TWINE-80/128 iterates 36 rounds over 64-bit block using 80/128-bit key, respectively, and 64-bit tweak T. The block cipher has three parts: data processing, key schedule, and tweak schedule. Except for the tweaks addition, T-TWINE-80/128 has the same data processing and key schedule of TWINE-80/128, respectively. Both T-TWINE-80 and T-TWINE-128 employ the same generalized Feistel structure and tweak schedule where the only difference between them is the key schedule.

Data Processing Part. As depicted in Fig. 1, the round function is based on a variant of Type-2 GFS with 16 4-bit nibbles [17]. It has four operations: 4-bit S-box (S, see Table 1), round key XOR, round tweak XOR, and a 16-nibble shuffle operation (π, see Table 2). Both versions of T-TWINE have the same number of rounds (36). The nibble shuffle operation in the last round is omitted.

Table 1. 4-bit S-box S in hexadecimal form

x	0	1	2	3	4	5	6	7	8	9	a	b	c	d	e	f
$S(x)$	c	0	f	a	2	b	9	5	8	3	d	7	1	e	6	4

Key Schedule. A round key RK^i of 8 nibbles is generated from the master key K for each round i, where $0 \leq i < 35$. Each version of T-TWINE has its own key

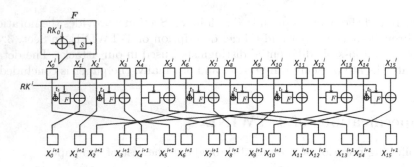

Fig. 1. The T-TWINE round function, for simplicity we use t_j instead of t_j^i. For example t_0 equivalent to t_0^i

schedule. Algorithm 1 and 2 show the details of T-TWINE-80/128, respectively, where CON_H^i and CON_L^i are predefined constants. For further details, the reader is referred to [15,18].

Tweak Schedule. A round tweak RT^i of 6 nibbles is generated from the tweak T for each round i, where $0 \leq i < 35$. Both versions of T-TWINE have the same tweak schedule, shown in Algorithm 3, where π^t is a 6-nibble permutation s.t. $(0, 1, 2, 3, 4, 5) \rightarrow (1, 0, 4, 2, 3, 5)$.

3   An Impossible Differential Distinguisher of T-TWINE

Impossible differential cryptanalysis was proposed independently by Knudsen [8] and Biham, Biryukov and Shamir [3]. It exploits a (truncated) differential characteristic of probability exactly 0 and thus acts as a distinguisher. Then, this distinguisher is turned into a key-recovery attack by prepending and/or appending additional rounds, which are usually referred to as the analysis rounds. The keys involved in the analysis rounds which lead to the impossible differential are wrong keys and thus are excluded. Miss-in-the-Middle is the general technique used to construct impossible differentials, where the cipher, E, is split such that $E = E_2 \circ E_1$, and we try to find two deterministic differentials, the first one covers E_1 and has the form $\Delta\delta \rightarrow \Delta\gamma$, and the second covers E_2^{-1}, and has the form $\Delta\beta \rightarrow \Delta\zeta$. When the intermediate differences $\Delta\gamma, \Delta\zeta$ do not match, the differential $\Delta\delta \rightarrow \Delta\beta$ that covers the whole cipher E holds with zero probability.

Table 2. Nibble shuffle π

h	0	1	2	3	4	5	6	7	8	9	10	11	12	13	14	15
$\pi[h]$	5	0	1	4	7	12	3	8	13	6	9	2	15	10	11	14
$\pi^{-1}[h]$	1	2	11	6	3	0	9	4	7	10	13	14	5	8	15	12

Algorithm 1: Key Schedule of T-TWINE-80

Data: The 80-bit master key K
Result: The round keys $RK = RK^0||RK^1||\cdots||RK^{35}$
$k_0||k_1||\cdots||k_{19} \leftarrow K$;
for $i \leftarrow 0$ *to* 34 **do**
    $RK^i \leftarrow k_1||k_3||k_4||k_6||k_{13}||k_{14}||k_{15}||k_{16}$;
    $k_1 \leftarrow k_1 \oplus S(k_0)$;
    $k_4 \leftarrow k_4 \oplus S(k_{16})$;
    $k_7 \leftarrow k_7 \oplus (0||CON_H^i)$;
    $k_{19} \leftarrow k_{19} \oplus (0||CON_L^i)$;
    $k_0||\cdots||k_3 \leftarrow Rot4(k_0||\cdots||k_3)$;
    $k_0||\cdots||k_{19} \leftarrow Rot16(k_0||\cdots||k_{19})$;
$RK^{35} \leftarrow k_1||k_3||k_4||k_6||k_{13}||k_{14}||k_{15}||k_{16}$;
$RK \leftarrow RK^0||RK^1||\cdots||RK^{35}$;

Algorithm 2: Key Schedule of T-TWINE-128

Data: The 128-bit master key K
Result: The round keys $RK = RK^0||RK^1||\cdots||RK^{35}$
$k_0||k_1||\cdots||k_{31} \leftarrow K$;
for $i \leftarrow 0$ *to* 34 **do**
    $RK^i \leftarrow k_2||k_3||k_{12}||k_{15}||k_{17}||k_{18}||k_{28}||k_{31}$;
    $k_1 \leftarrow k_1 \oplus S(k_0)$;
    $k_4 \leftarrow k_4 \oplus S(k_{16})$;
    $k_{23} \leftarrow k_{23} \oplus S(k_{30})$;
    $k_7 \leftarrow k_7 \oplus (0||CON_H^i)$;
    $k_{19} \leftarrow k_{19} \oplus (0||CON_L^i)$;
    $k_0||\cdots||k_3 \leftarrow Rot4(k_0||\cdots||k_3)$;
    $k_0||\cdots||k_{31} \leftarrow Rot16(k_0||\cdots||k_{31})$;
$RK^{35} \leftarrow k_2||k_3||k_{12}||k_{15}||k_{17}||k_{18}||k_{28}||k_{31}$;
$RK \leftarrow RK^0||RK^1||\cdots||RK^{35}$;

Algorithm 3: Tweak Schedule of T-TWINE

Data: The 64-bit tweak T
Result: The round tweaks $RT = RT^0||RT^1||\cdots||RT^{35}$
$t_0^0||t_1^0||\cdots||t_{16}^0 \leftarrow T$;
for $i \leftarrow 0$ *to* 35 **do**
    $RT^i \leftarrow t_0^i||t_1^i||t_2^i||t_3^i||t_4^i||t_5^i$;
    for $h \leftarrow 0$ *to* 5 **do**
        $t_{\pi^t[h]}^i \leftarrow t_h^i$;
    for $h \leftarrow 0$ *to* 15 **do**
        $t_{(h-6) \bmod 16}^{i+1} \leftarrow t_h^i$;
$RT \leftarrow RT^0||RT^1||\cdots||RT^{35}$;

The designers of T-TWINE in [15] presented an 18-round impossible differential distinguisher. They found this distinguisher using the Miss-in-the-Middle approach. The distinguisher begins at "1R" with zero differences and the tweak has a non-zero difference at the first nibble t_0. As mentioned above, this 18-round impossible differential distinguisher does not seem to be correct. In what follows, we list some of the problems (mistakes) we identified in this distinguisher (See Fig. 5): i) the numbers of rounds involved in the distinguisher is only 17 not 18 (as the plaintext is marked "1R" and the ciphertext is marked "18R"), ii) the tweaks used in the distinguisher are wrong. For example, the tweaks that are used in the seventh and ninth rounds are actually the tweaks of the sixth and seventh rounds, respectively, and iii) this distinguisher assumes that the tweak has difference at nibble "0" at the first round, then it appear again at nibble "0" at the nineteenth round, while it should appear again at the seventeenth round, after 16 rounds of the tweak schedule. Moreover, as shown in Figure 8 of [15] (See Fig. 5), the zero difference at "1R" associated with a non-zero difference at the first nibble t_0 of the tweak gives, after being propagated 7 rounds in the forward direction, the difference at "8R" in the form of $(1, 1, 1, 0, 0, ?, 0, 1, 1, ?, 0, 1, ?, ?, ?, ?)$. However, the correct difference should be in the form of $(?, 1, ?, 0, 1, ?, ?, 1, 1, ?, ?, 1, ?, ?, ?, ?)$.

In this section, we present an 18-round distinguisher that begins and ends with zero difference and has a difference at t_{12} at the first round, see Fig. 2. To the best of our knowledge, this is the first valid 18-round impossible differential distinguisher. This distinguisher is found using the Miss-in-the-Middle approach, where we propagate the difference in the tweak forward 8 rounds with probability 1 and propagate the difference in the tweak backward 10 rounds with probability 1, then match at the middle at the end of round 8. As seen in Fig. 2, there is a contradiction at nibble "6", where in the forward path, it should have a zero difference, while in the backward path, it should have a non-zero difference.

3.1   Observations

In this section, we present some useful observations that will be utilized in our attack.

Observation 1 [18,19]. *For any input difference $a(\neq 0)$ and output difference $b(\in \Delta S[a])$ of the S-box in TWINE, the average number of pairs that satisfy the differential characteristic $(a \rightarrow b)$ is $\frac{16}{7}$. Given an 8-bit pair (X_{2j}^i, X_{2j+1}^i) and $(X_{2j}^i \oplus a, X_{2j+1}^i \oplus b)$, the probability that RK_j^i leads to the S-box differential characteristic $(a \rightarrow b)$ is 7^{-1}.*

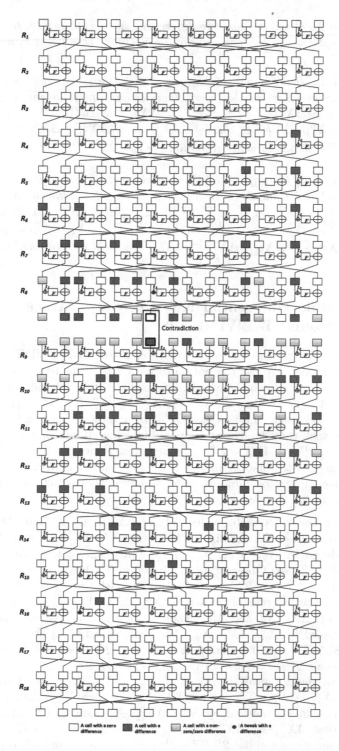

Contradiction

| | A cell with a zero difference | | A cell with a difference | | A cell with a non-zero/zero difference | | A tweak with a difference |

Fig. 2. An 18-round impossible differential distinguisher

Observation 2. *Given two nonzero differences Δi and Δo in $\mathbb{F}16$, the equation: $S(x) + S(x + \Delta i) = \Delta o$ has one solution on average. This property also applies to S^{-1}.*

Observation 3. *If the impossible differential illustrated in Fig. 2 is extended 6 rounds forward and 3 rounds backward, then we have the following relations, see Fig. 3: $\Delta X_3^0 \in S[\Delta X_2^0]$, $\Delta X_7^0 \in S[\Delta X_6^0]$, $\Delta X_{13}^0 \in S[\Delta X_{12}^0]$, $\Delta X_6^0 \in S[\Delta X_{11}^0]$, $\Delta X_{11}^0 \in S[\Delta X_2^0]$, $\Delta X_1^{27} \in S[\Delta T_2]$, $\Delta X_{15}^{27} \in S[\Delta X_{11}^{27}]$, $\Delta X_{14}^{27} \in S[\Delta X_{11}^{27}]$, $\Delta X_{11}^{27} \in S[\Delta T_2]$ that hold with probability $(\frac{7}{16})^9 = 2^{-10.734}$.*

Observation 4. *If the impossible differential illustrated in Fig. 2 is extended 4 rounds forward and 3 rounds backward, then we have the following relations, see Fig. 4: $\Delta X_1^0 \in S[\Delta X_0^0]$, $\Delta X_{11}^0 \in S[\Delta X_{10}^0]$, $\Delta X_{15}^0 \in S[\Delta X_{14}^0]$, $\Delta X_{14}^0 \in S[\Delta T_7]$, $\Delta X_0^0 \in S[\Delta X_3^0]$, $\Delta X_3^0 \in S[\Delta X_{10}^0]$, $\Delta X_{10}^0 \in S[\Delta T_7]$, $\Delta X_1^{25} \in S[\Delta T_7]$, $\Delta X_{14}^{25} \in S[\Delta X_{14}^{25}]$, $\Delta X_{14}^{25} \in S[\Delta X_{11}^{25}]$, $\Delta X_{11}^{25} \in S[\Delta T_7]$ that hold with probability $(\frac{7}{16})^{11} = 2^{-13.119}$.*

4   Impossible Differential Key-Recovery Attack on 27-Round T-TWINE-128

In this section, we present the first attack on 27-round T-TWINE-128 in the chosen-tweak model. We use the notion of data structures to generate enough pairs of messages to launch the attack. Our utilized structure takes all the possible values of the 12 nibbles X_2^0, X_3^0, X_4^0, X_5^0, X_6^0, X_7^0, X_8^0, X_9^0, X_{11}^0, X_{12}^0, X_{13}^0, X_{15}^0 while the remaining nibbles assume a fixed value. In addition, we choose the tweak T_2 such that it takes all its possible values. Thus, one structure generates $2^{4 \times 13} \times (2^{4 \times 13} - 1)/2 \approx 2^{103}$ possible pairs. Hence, we have 2^{103} possible pairs of messages satisfying the plaintext differences. In addition, we utilize the following pre-computation tables in order to efficiently extract/filter the round keys involved in the analysis rounds:

- H_1: For all the 2^{20} possible values of X_1^1, ΔX_1^1, X_4^1, t_4^0 and $RK_1^0 = K_3$, compute X_2^0, ΔX_2^0, X_3^0, and ΔX_3^0. Then, store X_1^1, ΔX_1^1, X_4^1, and $RK_1^0 = K_3$ in H_1 indexed by X_2^0, ΔX_2^0, X_3^0, ΔX_3^0, and t_4^0. ΔX_3^0 is chosen such that $\Delta X_3^0 \in S[\Delta X_2^0]$, see Observation 3. Therefore, H_1 has 7×2^{16} rows and on average about $2^{20}/(7 \times 2^{16}) = 16/7$ values in each row.
- H_2: For all the 2^{20} possible values of X_3^1, ΔX_3^1, X_8^1, t_3^0, and $RK_3^0 = K_{15}$, compute X_6^0, ΔX_6^0, X_7^0, and ΔX_7^0. Then, store X_3^1, ΔX_3^1, X_8^1, and $RK_3^0 = K_{15}$ in H_1 indexed by X_6^0, ΔX_6^0, X_7^0, ΔX_7^0, and t_3^0. ΔX_7^0 is chosen such that $\Delta X_7^0 \in S[\Delta X_6^0]$, see Observation 3. Therefore, H_2 has 7×2^{16} rows and on average about $2^{20}/(7 \times 2^{16}) = 16/7$ values in each row.
- H_3: For all the 2^{16} possible values of X_{10}^1, ΔX_{15}^1, X_{15}^1, and $RK_6^0 = K_{28}$, compute X_{12}^0, ΔX_{12}^0, X_{13}^0, and ΔX_{13}^0. Then, store X_{10}^1, ΔX_{15}^1, X_{15}^1, and $RK_6^0 = K_{28}$ in H_3 indexed by X_{12}^0, ΔX_{12}^0, X_{13}^0, and ΔX_{13}^0. ΔX_{13}^0 is chosen such that $\Delta X_{13}^0 \in S[\Delta X_{12}^0]$, see Observation 3. Therefore, H_3 has 7×2^{12} rows and on average about $2^{16}/(7 \times 2^{12}) = 16/7$ values in each row.

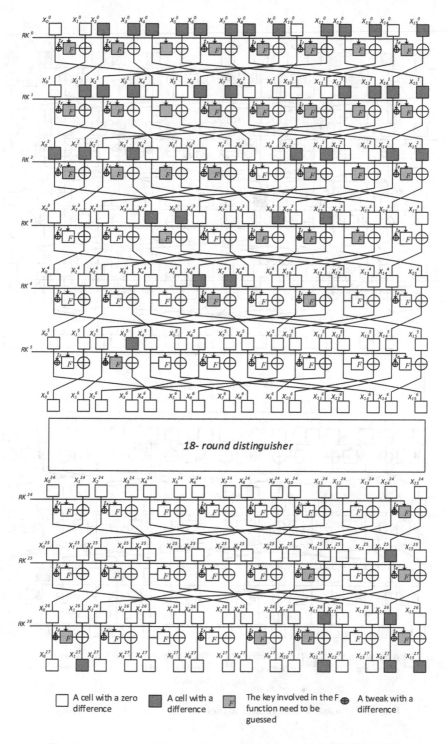

Fig. 3. Impossible differential attack on 27-round T-TWINE-128

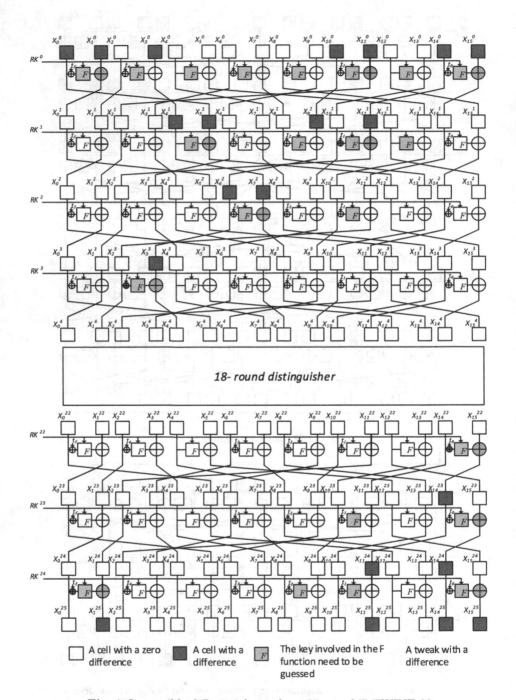

Fig. 4. Impossible differential attack on 25-round T-TWINE-80

- H_4: For all the 2^{32} possible values of X_1^2, ΔX_1^2, X_4^2, t_4^1, $RK_1^1 = K_7$, X_9^1, t_1^0, and $RK_5^0 = K_{18}$, compute $X_3^1 = X_6^0$, $\Delta X_3^1 = \Delta X_6^0$, X_{10}^0, X_{11}^0, and ΔX_{11}^0. Then, store X_1^2, ΔX_1^2, X_4^2, $RK_1^1 = K_7$, X_9^1, and $RK_5^0 = K_{18}$ in H_4 indexed by $X_3^1 = X_6^0$, $\Delta X_3^1 = \Delta X_6^0$, X_{10}^0, X_{11}^0, ΔX_{11}^0, t_4^1, and t_1^0. ΔX_6^0 is chosen such that $\Delta X_6^0 \in S[\Delta X_{11}^0]$, see Observation 3. Therefore, H_4 has 7×2^{24} rows and on average about $2^{32}/(7 \times 2^{24}) = (16/7) \times 2^4$ values in each row.
- H_5: For all the 2^{40} possible values of X_3^2, ΔX_3^2, X_8^2, t_3^1, $RK_3^1 = K_{19}$, X_{13}^1, ΔX_{13}^1, t_2^0, ΔT_2, and $RK_4^0 = K_{17}$, compute X_4^0, ΔX_4^0, X_8^0, ΔX_8^0, X_9^0, and ΔX_9^0. Then, store X_3^2, ΔX_3^2, X_8^2, $RK_3^1 = K_{19}$, X_{13}^1, ΔX_{13}^1, and $RK_4^0 = K_{17}$ in H_5 indexed by X_4^0, ΔX_4^0, X_8^0, ΔX_8^0, X_9^0, ΔX_9^0, t_3^1, t_2^0, and ΔT_2. H_5 has 2^{36} rows and on average about $2^{40}/2^{36} = 2^4$ values in each row.
- H_6: For all the 2^{44} possible values of X_0^3, X_5^3, ΔX_5^3, t_5^2, $RK_0^2 = K_{10}$, X_5^2, t_5^1, $RK_6^1 = K_6$, X_5^1, t_5^0, and $RK_0^0 = K_2$, compute X_1^2, $\Delta X_1^2 = \Delta X_{11}^0$, $X_1^1 = X_2^0$, $\Delta X_1^1 = \Delta X_2^0$, X_0^0, and X_1^0. Then, store X_5^3, ΔX_5^3, $RK_0^2 = K_{10}$, X_5^2, $RK_6^1 = K_6$, X_5^1, and $RK_0^0 = K_2$ in H_6 indexed by X_1^2, $\Delta X_1^2 = \Delta X_{11}^0$, $X_1^1 = X_2^0$, $\Delta X_1^1 = \Delta X_2^0$, X_0^0, X_1^0, t_5^0, t_5^1, and t_5^2. ΔX_{11}^0 is chosen such that $\Delta X_{11}^0 \in S[\Delta X_2^0]$, see Observation 3. Therefore, H_6 has 7×2^{32} rows and on average about $2^{44}/(7 \times 2^{32}) = (16/7) \times 2^8$ values in each row.
- H_7: For all the 2^{32} possible values of X_{10}^2, ΔX_{10}^2, X_{15}^2, ΔX_{15}^2, $RK_6^1 = K_1 + S(K_0)$, X_7^1, ΔX_7^1, and $RK_2^0 = K_{12}$, compute X_{13}^1, ΔX_{13}^1, X_4^0, ΔX_4^0, X_5^0, and ΔX_5^0. Then, store X_{10}^2, ΔX_{10}^2, X_{15}^2, ΔX_{15}^2, $RK_6^1 = K_1 + S(K_0)$, X_7^1, ΔX_7^1, and $RK_2^0 = K_{12}$ in H_7 indexed by X_{13}^1, ΔX_{13}^1, X_4^0, ΔX_4^0, X_5^0, and ΔX_5^0. H_7 has 2^{24} rows and on average about $2^{32}/2^{24} = 2^8$ values in each row.
- H_8: For all the 2^{36} possible values of X_{11}^2, ΔX_{11}^2, X_{14}^2, ΔX_{14}^2, t_0^1, $RK_7^1 = K_0$, X_{11}^1, t_7^0, and $RK_7^0 = K_{31}$, compute X_{15}^1, ΔX_{15}^1, X_{14}^0, X_{15}^0, and ΔX_{15}^0. Then, store X_{11}^2, ΔX_{11}^2, X_{14}^2, ΔX_{14}^2, $RK_7^1 = K_0$, X_{11}^1, and $RK_7^0 = K_{31}$ in H_8 indexed by X_{15}^1, ΔX_{15}^1, X_{14}^0, X_{15}^0, ΔX_{15}^0, t_0^1, and t_0^0. H_8 has 2^{28} rows and on average about $2^{36}/2^{28} = 2^8$ values in each row.
- H_9: For all the 2^{20} possible values of X_2^3, X_9^3, ΔX_9^3, t_1^2, and $RK_5^2 = K_{26}$, compute X_{10}^2, ΔX_{10}^2, X_{11}^2, and ΔX_{11}^2. Then, store X_9^3, ΔX_9^3, and $RK_5^2 = K_{26}$ in H_9 indexed by X_{10}^2, ΔX_{10}^2, X_{11}^2, ΔX_{11}^2, and t_1^2. H_9 has 2^{20} rows and on average about $2^{20}/2^{20} = 1$ value in each row.
- H_{10}: For all the 2^{20} possible values of X_{11}^3, ΔX_{11}^3, X_{14}^3, t_0^2, and $RK_7^2 = K_4 + S(K_{16})$, compute X_{14}^2, ΔX_{14}^2, X_{15}^2, and ΔX_{15}^2. Then, store X_{11}^3, ΔX_{11}^3, X_{14}^3, and $RK_7^2 = K_4 + S(K_{16})$ in H_{10} indexed by X_{14}^2, ΔX_{14}^2, X_{15}^2, ΔX_{15}^2, and t_0^2. H_{10} has 2^{20} rows and on average about $2^{20}/2^{20} = 1$ value in each row.
- H_{11}: For all the 2^{40} possible values of X_7^4, ΔX_7^4, X_{12}^4, $RK_2^3 = K_{24}$, X_1^3, t_4^2, $RK_1^2 = K_{11}$, X_9^2, t_1^1, and $RK_5^1 = K_{22}$, compute X_5^3, ΔX_5^3, X_3^2, ΔX_3^2, X_{10}^1, and X_{11}^1. Then, store X_7^4, ΔX_7^4, $RK_2^3 = K_{24}$, $RK_1^2 = K_{11}$, and $RK_5^1 = K_{22}$ in H_{11} indexed by X_5^3, ΔX_5^3, X_3^2, ΔX_3^2, X_{10}^1, X_{11}^1, t_4^2, and t_1^1. H_{11} has 2^{32} rows and on average about $2^{40}/2^{32} = 2^8$ values in each row.
- H_{12}: For all the 2^{12} possible values of X_7^2, X_{12}^2, and $RK_2^1 = K_{16}$, compute X_4^1, and X_5^1. Then, store X_7^2, X_{12}^2, and $RK_2^1 = K_{16}$ in H_{12} indexed by X_4^1, and X_5^1. H_{12} has 2^8 rows and on average about $2^{12}/2^8 = 2^4$ value in each row.

- H_{13}: For all the 2^{16} possible values of X_6^2, X_{13}^2, t_2^1, and $RK_4^1 = K_{21}$, compute X_8^1, and X_9^1. Then, store X_6^2, X_{13}^2, and $RK_4^1 = K_{21}$ in H_{13} indexed by X_8^1, X_9^1, and t_2^1. H_{13} has 2^{12} rows and on average about $2^{16}/2^{12} = 2^4$ value in each row.

- H_{14}: For all the 2^{28} possible values of X_2^4, X_9^4, t_1^3, ΔT_2, $RK_5^3 = K_{30}$, X_{15}^3, and $RK_6^2 = K_5 + S(K_4 + S(K_{16}))$, compute X_{11}^3, ΔX_{11}^3, X_{12}^2, and X_{13}^2. Then, store $RK_5^3 = K_{30}$, and $RK_6^2 = K_5 + S(K_4 + S(K_{16}))$ in H_{14} indexed by X_{11}^3, ΔX_{11}^3, X_{12}^2, t_1^3, ΔT_2, and X_{13}^2. H_{14} has 2^{24} rows and on average about $2^{28}/2^{24} = 2^4$ values in each row.

- H_{15}: For all the 2^{44} possible values of X_3^5, ΔX_3^5, X_8^5, t_3^4, $RK_3^4 = K_{31} + S(K_7)$, X_{13}^4, t_2^3, $RK_4^4 = K_{29}$, X_3^3, t_3^3, and $RK_3^2 = K_{23} + S(K_{30})$, compute X_7^4, ΔX_7^4, X_9^3, ΔX_3^3, X_6^2, and X_7^2. Then, store X_3^5, ΔX_3^5, $RK_4^3 = K_{29}$, and $RK_3^2 = K_{23} + S(K_{30})$ in H_{15} indexed by X_7^4, ΔX_7^4, X_9^3, ΔX_3^3, X_6^2, X_7^2, t_3^4, t_2^3, t_3^3, and $RK_3^4 = K_{31} + S(K_7)$. H_{15} has 2^{40} rows and on average about $2^{44}/2^{40} = 2^4$ values in each row.

- H_{16}: For all the 2^{48} possible values of X_1^6, X_4^6, t_4^5, ΔT_2, $RK_1^5 = K_{23} + S(K_{30})$, X_9^5, t_1^4, $RK_5^4 = K_3$, X_{15}^4, $RK_6^3 = K_9 + S(K_8 + S(K_{20}))$, X_7^3, and $RK_2^2 = K_{20}$, compute X_3^5, ΔX_3^5, X_{14}^3, X_8^2, X_4^2, and X_5^2. Then, store $RK_5^4 = K_3$, $RK_6^3 = K_9 + S(K_8 + S(K_{20}))$, and $RK_2^2 = K_{20}$ in H_{16} indexed by X_3^5, ΔX_3^5, X_{14}^3, X_8^2, X_4^2, X_5^2, $RK_1^5 = K_{23} + S(K_{30})$, $RK_5^4 = K_3$, t_4^5, ΔT_2, and t_1^4. H_{16} has 2^{44} rows and on average about $2^{48}/2^{44} = 2^4$ values in each row.

- H_{17}: For all the 2^{20} possible values of X_{14}^{26}, ΔX_{14}^{26}, X_{15}^{26}, t_0^{26}, and $RK_7^{26} = f_1(K_0, K_1, K_4, K_5, K_6, K_7, RK_6^3, K_{10}, K_{16}, K_{17}, K_{18}, K_{19}, K_{20}, K_{21}, K_{28}, K_{29}, K_{30})$, compute X_{14}^{27}, ΔX_{14}^{27}, X_{15}^{27}, and ΔX_{15}^{27}. Then, store X_{14}^{26} and ΔX_{14}^{26} in H_{17} indexed by X_{14}^{27}, ΔX_{14}^{27}, X_{15}^{27}, ΔX_{15}^{27}, RK_7^{26}, and t_0^{26}. ΔX_{15}^{27} is chosen such that $\Delta X_{15}^{27} \in S[\Delta X_{14}^{27}]$, see Observation 3. Therefore, H_{17} has 7×2^{20} rows and on average about $2^{20}/(7 \times 2^{20}) = (16/7) \times 2^{-4}$ values in each row.

- H_{18}: For all the 2^{20} possible values of X_0^{26}, X_1^{26}, t_5^{26}, ΔT_2, and $RK_0^{26} = f_2(K_0, K_1, K_3, K_{16}, K_{20}, K_{21}, RK_6^3, K_{27}, K_{28})$, compute X_0^{27}, ΔX_1^{27}, and X_1^{27}. Then, store RK_0^{26} in H_{18} indexed by X_0^{27}, ΔX_1^{27}, X_1^{27}, t_5^{26}, and ΔT_2. ΔX_1^{27} is chosen such that $\Delta X_1^{27} \in S[\Delta T_2]$, see Observation 3. Therefore, H_{18} has 7×2^{16} rows and on average about $2^{20}/(7 \times 2^{16}) = 16/7$ values in each row.

- H_{19}: For all the 2^{28} possible values of X_{10}^{25}, X_{11}^{25}, t_1^{25}, $RK_5^{25} = f_3(K_0, K_1, K_2, K_4, K_{12}, K_{13}, RK_6^3, K_{15}, K_{16}, K_{20}, K_{21}, K_{24}, K_{28})$, X_8^{26}, t_2^{26}, and $RK_4^{26} = f_4(K_0, K_4, K_5, K_{11}, K_{16}, K_{24})$, compute X_2^{27}, X_9^{27}, and X_8^{27}. Then, store X_{11}^{25} and RK_5^{25} in H_{19} indexed by X_2^{27}, X_9^{27}, X_8^{27}, RK_4^{26}, t_1^{25}, and t_2^{26}. H_{19} has 2^{24} rows and on average about $2^{28}/2^{24} = 2^4$ values in each row.

- H_{20}: For all the 2^{44} possible values of X_{14}^{24}, X_{15}^{24}, t_0^{24}, ΔT_2, $RK_7^{24} = f_5(K_0, K_1, K_2, K_{10}, K_{11}, K_{12}, K_{13}, RK_6^3, K_{20}, K_{21}, K_{22}, K_{24}, K_{28}, K_{29}, K_{30})$, X_{15}^{25}, t_0^{25}, $RK_7^{25} = f_6(K_0, K_1, K_2, K_3, K_4, K_5, K_6, K_{12}, K_{13}, K_{14}, K_{15}, K_{16}, K_{17}, K_{24}, K_{25}, K_{26}, K_{28})$, X_{10}^{26}, t_1^{26}, and $RK_5^{26} = f_7(0, K_1, K_4, K_5, K_6, K_8, K_{12}, K_{13}, K_{16}, K_{17}, K_{19}, K_{20}, K_{24}, K_{25}, K_{28})$, compute X_{11}^{25}, $X_{14}^{27} = X_{14}^{26}$, $\Delta X_{14}^{27} = \Delta X_{14}^{26}$, X_{11}^{27}, ΔX_{11}^{27}, and X_{10}^{27}. Then, store RK_7^{25}, RK_5^{26} in H_{20} indexed by X_{11}^{25}, X_{14}^{26}, ΔX_{14}^{26}, X_{11}^{27}, ΔX_{11}^{27}, X_{10}^{27}, t_0^{24}, ΔT_2, RK_7^{24}, t_0^{25}, and t_1^{26}. ΔX_{14}^{27} and

ΔX_{11}^{27} are chosen such that $\Delta X_{14}^{27} \in S[\Delta X_{11}^{27}]$ and $\Delta X_{11}^{27} \in S[\Delta T_2]$, recpectively, see Observation 3. Therefore, H_{19} has $7^2 \times 2^{36}$ rows and on average about $2^{44}/(7^2 \times 2^{36}) = (16/7)^2$ values in each row.

In the general approach, the round keys involved in the analysis rounds are guessed and the plaintext/ciphertext pairs are filtered to satisfy the differential path leading to the impossible differential distinguisher. Here, we use the above proposed pre-computation tables to deduce the round keys that lead a specific pair of plaintext/ciphertext to the impossible differential. Then, we exclude the deduced keys as they are wrong keys. Our attack proceeds as follows. We initialize an array H of $2^{31 \times 4 = 124}$ entries to "0", where each entry is 1-bit and the index of the array is 31 key nibbles involved in the attack, as we will see later. Then we generate 2^m structures as described above. Therefore, we have 2^{m+103} pairs of plaintext/ciphertext pairs generated using 2^{m+48} chosen plaintexts. Then, we ask the encryption oracle for their corresponding ciphertexts. The plaintext/ciphertext pairs that satisfy Observation 3 are $2^{m+103} \times 2^{-10.734} = 2^{m+92.266}$ pairs. After the ciphertext filtration, we have only $2^{m+92.266} \times 2^{-12 \times 4} = 2^{m+44.266}$ remaining pairs. For each remaining pair, we access the pre-computation tables in sequential order from table H_1 to H_{20} one by one in order to deduce 31 key nibbles that lead each remaining pair of plaintext/ciphertext to the impossible differential. Then, we mark them in H as invalid "1". Table 3 summarize these steps by identifying which table will be used and which key nibble is involved in this step in addition to the time complexity of each step.

Remarks on the analysis steps:

1. During steps 1–14 and step 18, we directly access the corresponding table to obtain the values of the involved key nibbles. For example, in step 1, we determine the number of possible values of $RK_1^0 = K_3$ that satisfy the path to the impassible differential by accessing H_1. Therefore, we have $(16/7)$ possible values for K_3.

2. During steps 15, 16, 17, 19, and 20, and because some combinations of the key nibbles determined during the previous steps are used in the indexing of the tables H_{15} to H_{20}, we firstly deduce these indices and then access the corresponding table. For example, during step 15, we deduce the value of $RK_3^4 = K_{31} + S(K_7)$ that is used in the indexing of table H_{15}, then determine the number of possible values of $RK_4^3 = K_{29}$ and $RK_3^2 = K_{23} + S(K_{30})$ that satisfy the path by accessing H_{15}. After that, the value of $RK_3^2 = K_{23} + S(K_{30})$ is used to deduce the value of K_{23} using the determined value of K_{30} from Step 14.

3. During steps 7 and 8, we determine the possible values of $RK_6^1 = K_1 + S(K_0)$ and $RK_7^1 = K_0$, respectively. Therefore, after step 8, we can deduce the values of K_1. In the same manner, we can deduce the values of K_4 and K_5 after steps 10, 12 and 14 where we determine the values of $RK_7^2 = K_4 + S(K_{16})$ and $RK_2^1 = K_{16}$, and $RK_6^2 = K_5 + S(K_4 + S(K_{16}))$, respectively.

4. During step 17, we deduce the value of $RK_7^{26} = f_1(K_0, K_1, K_4, K_5, K_6, K_7,$ $RK_6^3, K_{10}, K_{16}, K_{17}, K_{18}, K_{19}, K_{20}, K_{21}, K_{28}, K_{29}, K_{30})$, then determine the values of X_{14}^{26} and ΔX_{14}^{26} that satisfy the path by accessing H_{17}. Therefore, no new key nibbles are involved during this step but there is a filtration of some keys.

5. During steps 18 and 19, we can determine the values of $RK_0^{26} = f_2(K_0,$ $K_1, K_3, K_{16}, K_{20}, K_{21}, RK_6^3, K_{27}, K_{28})$ and $RK_5^{25} = f_3(K_0, K_1, K_2, K_4,$ $K_{12}, K_{13}, RK_6^3, K_{15}, K_{16}, K_{20}, K_{21}, K_{24}, K_{28})$, respectively. Therefore, we can deduce the values of K_{27} and K_{13}, respectively, since all the other key nibbles in f_2 and f_3 are determined during the previous steps.

6. After step 20, we have $2^{60} \times (16/7)^9$ possible values for $K_0, K_1, K_2, K_3,$ $K_4, K_5, K_6, K_7, K_9 + S(K_8 + S(K_{20})), K_{10}, K_{11}, K_{12}, K_{13}, K_{15}, K_{16}, K_{17}, K_{18},$ $K_{19}, K_{20}, K_{21}, K_{22}, K_{23}, K_{24}, K_{26}, K_{27}, K_{28}, K_{29}, K_{30}, K_{31}, RK_7^{25} = f_6(K_{14},$ $K_{25}), RK_5^{26} = f_7(K_8, K_{25})$. Hence, we marks them in H as invalid "1" in step 21.

Attack Complexity. As depicted in Fig. 3, we have 37 round keys involved in the analysis rounds. According to the key schedule, these 37 round keys take only 2^{124} possible values (see step 21 in Table 3). As mentioned in step 21, we remove on average $2^{60} \times (16/7)^9 = 2^{70.734}$ out of 2^{124} possible values of these 37 round keys involved in the attack for each pair of the $2^{m+44.266}$ remaining pairs. Hence, a wrong key is not discarded using one pair with probability $1 - 2^{70.734-124} = 1 - 2^{-53.266}$. Therefore, we have $2^{124} \times (1 - 2^{-53.266})^{2^{m+44.266}} \approx 2^{124} \times (e^{-1})^{2^{m+44.266-53.266}} \approx 2^{124} \times 2^{-1.4 \times 2^{m-9}}$ remaining candidates for 124-bit of the key, after processing all the $2^{m+44.266}$ remaining pairs. We evaluated the computational complexity of the attack as a function of m, as illustrated in Table 3, to determine the optimal value of m that leads to the best computational complexity. As steps 20 and 21 dominate the time complexity of the attack, see Table 3, we choose $m = 12$ in order to optimize the time complexity of the attack. Therefore, we have $2^{124} \times 2^{-1.4 \times 2^{12-9=3}} = 2^{124-11.2} = 2^{112.8}$ remaining candidates for 124-bit of the key. The remaining key nibbles can be retrieved by guessing K_8 and exhaustively searching the $2^{112.8}$ remaining key candidates using 2 plaintext/ciphertext pairs. This step requires $2 \times 2^4 \times 2^{112.8} = 2^{117.8}$ encryptions. Therefore, the time complexity of the attack is $2^{120.245} + 2^{119.245} + 2^{117.8} \approx 2^{120.83}$ encryptions. The data complexity of the attack is $2^{m+4 \times 13} = 2^{64}$ chosen tweak/plaintext combinations that can be generated using $2^{m+48} = 2^{60}$ chosen plaintexts. The memory complexity of the attack is dominated by the memory that is required to store H. Hence, the memory complexity is $2^{124} \times 2^{-6} = 2^{118}$ 64-bit blocks.

5   Impossible Differential Key-Recovery Attack on 25-Round T-TWINE-80

In this section, we present the first attack on 25-round T-TWINE-80 in the chosen-tweak model. We use the notion of data structures to generate enough pairs of messages to launch the attack. Our utilized structure takes all the possible values in 7 nibbles X_0^0, X_1^0, X_3^0, X_{10}^0, X_{11}^0, X_{14}^0, X_{15}^0 while the remaining nibbles take a fixed value. In addition, we choose the tweak T_7 such that it takes all the values. Thus, one structure generates $2^{4\times8} \times (2^{4\times8} - 1)/2 \approx 2^{63}$ possible pairs. Hence, we have 2^{63} possible pairs of messages satisfying the plaintext differences. In addition, we utilize the following pre-computation tables in order

Table 3. Time complexity of the different steps of the attack on 27-round T-TWINE-128, where NK denotes the number of keys to be excluded.

Step	Table	Key nibbles	Time complexity (in 27-round encryptions)	NK	$m = 12$
1	H_1	K_3	$2^{m+44.266} \times (16/7) \times \dfrac{4}{8 \times 27} \approx 2^{m+39.704}$	$(16/7)$	$2^{51.704}$
2	H_2	K_{15}	$2^{m+44.266} \times (16/7)^2 \times \dfrac{4}{8 \times 27} \approx 2^{m+40.896}$	$(16/7)^2$	$2^{52.896}$
3	H_3	K_{28}	$2^{m+44.266} \times (16/7)^3 \times \dfrac{4}{8 \times 27} \approx 2^{m+42.089}$	$(16/7)^3$	$2^{54.089}$
4	H_4	K_7, K_{18}	$2^{m+44.266} \times 2^4 \times (16/7)^4 \times \dfrac{6}{8 \times 27} \approx 2^{m+47.867}$	$2^4 \times (16/7)^4$	$2^{59.867}$
5	H_5	K_{17}, K_{19}	$2^{m+44.266} \times 2^8 \times (16/7)^4 \times \dfrac{7}{8 \times 27} \approx 2^{m+52.089}$	$2^8 \times (16/7)^4$	$2^{64.089}$
6	H_6	K_2, K_6, K_{10}	$2^{m+44.266} \times 2^{16} \times (16/7)^5 \times \dfrac{7}{8 \times 27} \approx 2^{m+61.282}$	$2^{16} \times (16/7)^5$	$2^{73.282}$
7	H_7	$K_1 + S(K_0), K_{12}$	$2^{m+44.266} \times 2^{24} \times (16/7)^5 \times \dfrac{8}{8 \times 27} \approx 2^{m+69.474}$	$2^{24} \times (16/7)^5$	$2^{81.474}$
8	H_8	K_0, K_1, K_{31}	$2^{m+44.266} \times 2^{32} \times (16/7)^5 \times \dfrac{7}{8 \times 27} \approx 2^{m+77.282}$	$2^{32} \times (16/7)^5$	$2^{89.282}$
9	H_9	K_{26}	$2^{m+44.266} \times 2^{32} \times (16/7)^5 \times \dfrac{3}{8 \times 27} \approx 2^{m+76.059}$	$2^{32} \times (16/7)^5$	$2^{88.059}$
10	H_{10}	$K_4 + S(K_{16})$	$2^{m+44.266} \times 2^{32} \times (16/7)^5 \times \dfrac{4}{8 \times 27} \approx 2^{m+76.474}$	$2^{32} \times (16/7)^5$	$2^{88.474}$
11	H_{11}	K_{11}, K_{22}, K_{24}	$2^{m+44.266} \times 2^{40} \times (16/7)^5 \times \dfrac{5}{8 \times 27} \approx 2^{m+84.796}$	$2^{40} \times (16/7)^5$	$2^{96.796}$
12	H_{12}	K_4, K_{16}	$2^{m+44.266} \times 2^{44} \times (16/7)^5 \times \dfrac{3}{8 \times 27} \approx 2^{m+88.059}$	$2^{44} \times (16/7)^5$	$2^{100.059}$
13	H_{13}	K_{21}	$2^{m+44.266} \times 2^{48} \times (16/7)^5 \times \dfrac{3}{8 \times 27} \approx 2^{m+92.059}$	$2^{48} \times (16/7)^5$	$2^{104.059}$
14	H_{14}	K_5, K_{30}	$2^{m+44.266} \times 2^{52} \times (16/7)^5 \times \dfrac{2}{8 \times 27} \approx 2^{m+95.474}$	$2^{52} \times (16/7)^5$	$2^{107.474}$
15	H_{15}	K_{23}, K_{29}	$2^{m+44.266} \times 2^{56} \times (16/7)^5 \times \dfrac{4}{8 \times 27} \approx 2^{m+100.474}$	$2^{56} \times (16/7)^5$	$2^{112.474}$
16	H_{16}	$RK_6^3 = K_9 + S(K_8 + S(K_{20})), K_{20}$	$2^{m+44.266} \times 2^{60} \times (16/7)^5 \times \dfrac{3}{8 \times 27} \approx 2^{m+104.059}$	$2^{60} \times (16/7)^5$	$2^{116.059}$
17	H_{17}	-	$2^{m+44.266} \times 2^{56} \times (16/7)^6 \times \dfrac{2}{8 \times 27} \approx 2^{m+100.667}$	$2^{56} \times (16/7)^6$	$2^{112.667}$
18	H_{18}	K_{27}	$2^{m+44.266} \times 2^{56} \times (16/7)^7 \times \dfrac{1}{8 \times 27} \approx 2^{m+100.860}$	$2^{56} \times (16/7)^7$	$2^{112.860}$
19	H_{19}	K_{13}	$2^{m+44.266} \times 2^{60} \times (16/7)^7 \times \dfrac{2}{8 \times 27} \approx 2^{m+105.860}$	$2^{60} \times (16/7)^7$	$2^{117.860}$
20	H_{20}	$RK_7^{25} = f_6(K_{14}, K_{25}), RK_5^{26} = f_7(K_8, K_{25})$	$2^{m+44.266} \times 2^{60} \times (16/7)^9 \times \dfrac{2}{8 \times 27} \approx 2^{m+108.245}$	$2^{60} \times (16/7)^9$	$2^{120.245}$
21	H	-	$2^{m+44.266} \times 2^{60} \times (16/7)^9 \times \dfrac{1}{8 \times 27} \approx 2^{m+107.245}$	$2^{60} \times (16/7)^9$	$2^{119.245}$

to efficiently extract/filter the round keys involved in the analysis rounds. Note that, for the 7 round keys that are involved in the 3 rounds below the distinguisher, we wrote them as 7 functions $f_1, f_2, f_3, f_4, f_5, f_6, f_7$ of the key nibbles that are not involved in the above analysis rounds, $K_0, K_2, K_5, K_7, K_9, K_{10}, K_{11}, K_{12}, K_{13}$, and ignored the other key nibbles as they are known.

- H_1: For all the 2^{20} possible values of $X_0^1, X_5^1, \Delta X_5^1, t_5^0$ and $RK_0^0 = K_1$, compute $X_0^0, \Delta X_0^0, X_1^0$, and ΔX_1^0. Then, store $X_5^1, \Delta X_5^1$, and $RK_0^0 = K_1$ in H_1 indexed by $X_0^0, \Delta X_0^0, X_1^0, \Delta X_1^0$, and t_5^0. ΔX_1^0 is chosen such that $\Delta X_0^0 \in S[\Delta X_0^0]$, see Observation 4. Therefore, H_1 has 7×2^{16} rows and on average about $2^{20}/(7 \times 2^{16}) = 16/7$ values in each row.

- H_2: For all the 2^{20} possible values of $X_2^1, X_9^1, \Delta X_9^1, t_1^0$, and $RK_5^0 = K_{14}$, compute $X_{10}^0, \Delta X_{10}^0, X_{11}^0$, and ΔX_{11}^0. Then, store $X_9^1, \Delta X_9^1$, and $RK_5^0 = K_{14}$ in H_2 indexed by $X_{10}^0, \Delta X_{10}^0, X_{11}^0, \Delta X_{11}^0$, and t_1^0. ΔX_{11}^0 is chosen such that $\Delta X_{11}^0 \in S[\Delta X_{10}^0]$, see Observation 4. Therefore, H_2 has 7×2^{16} rows and on average about $2^{20}/(7 \times 2^{16}) = 16/7$ values in each row.

- H_3: For all the 2^{20} possible values of $X_{11}^1, \Delta X_{11}^1, X_{14}^1, t_0^0$, and $RK_7^0 = K_{16}$, compute $X_{14}^0, \Delta X_{14}^0, X_{15}^0$, and ΔX_{15}^0. Then, store $X_{11}^1, \Delta X_{11}^1, X_{14}^1$, and $RK_7^0 = K_{16}$ in H_3 indexed by $X_{14}^0, \Delta X_{14}^0, X_{15}^0, \Delta X_{15}^0$, and t_0^0. ΔX_{15}^0 is chosen such that $\Delta X_{15}^0 \in S[\Delta X_{14}^0]$, see Observation 4. Therefore, H_3 has 7×2^{16} rows and on average about $2^{20}/(7 \times 2^{16}) = 16/7$ values in each row.

- H_4: For all the 2^{28} possible values of $X_7^2, \Delta X_7^2, X_{12}^2, RK_2^1 = K_8, X_1^1, t_4^0$, and $RK_1^0 = K_3$, compute $X_5^1 = X_0^0, \Delta X_5^1 = \Delta X_0^0, X_2^0, X_3^0$, and ΔX_3^0. Then, store $X_7^2, \Delta X_7^2, RK_2^1 = K_8$, and $RK_1^0 = K_3$ in H_4 indexed by $X_5^1 = X_0^0, \Delta X_5^1 = \Delta X_0^0, X_2^0, X_3^0, \Delta X_3^0$, and t_4^0. ΔX_0^0 is chosen such that $\Delta X_0^0 \in S[\Delta X_3^0]$, see Observation 4. Therefore, H_4 has 7×2^{20} rows and on average about $2^{28}/(7 \times 2^{20}) = (16/7) \times 2^4$ values in each row.

- H_5: For all the 2^{28} possible values of $X_2^2, X_9^2, t_1^1, \Delta T_7, RK_5^1 = K_{18}, X_{15}^1$, and $RK_6^0 = K_{15}$, compute $X_{14}^0 = X_{11}^1, \Delta X_{14}^0 = \Delta X_{11}^1, X_{12}^0$, and X_{13}^0. Then, store $RK_5^1 = K_{18}$ and $RK_6^0 = K_{15}$ in H_5 indexed by $X_{11}^1, \Delta X_{11}^1, X_{12}^0, X_{13}^0, t_1^1$, and ΔT_7. ΔX_{14}^0 is chosen such that $\Delta X_{14}^0 \in S[\Delta T_7]$, see Observation 4. Therefore, H_5 has 7×2^{20} rows and on average about $2^{28}/(7 \times 2^{20}) = (16/7) \times 2^4$ values in each row.

- H_6: For all the 2^{44} possible values of $X_3^3, \Delta X_3^3, X_8^3, t_2^2, RK_3^2 = K_{14}, X_{13}^2, t_2^1, RK_4^1 = K_{17}, X_3^1, t_3^0$, and $RK_3^0 = K_6$, compute $X_7^2, \Delta X_7^2 = \Delta X_3^0, X_9^1, \Delta X_9^1 = \Delta X_{10}^0, X_6^0$, and X_7^0. Then, store $X_3^3, \Delta X_3^3, RK_3^2 = K_{14}, RK_4^1 = K_{17}$, and $RK_3^0 = K_6$ in H_6 indexed by $X_7^2, \Delta X_7^2 = \Delta X_3^0, X_9^1, \Delta X_9^1 = \Delta X_{10}^0, X_6^0, X_7^0, t_3^2, t_2^1, t_3^0$, and $RK_3^2 = K_{14}$. ΔX_3^0 is chosen such that $\Delta X_3^0 \in S[\Delta X_{10}^0]$, see Observation 4. Therefore, H_6 has 7×2^{36} rows and on average about $2^{44}/(7 \times 2^{36}) = (16/7) \times 2^4$ values in each row.

- H_7: For all the 2^{48} possible values of $X_1^4, X_4^4, t_4^3, \Delta T_7, RK_1^3 = K_{15}, X_3^3, t_1^2, RK_5^2 = K_3, X_2^2, RK_6^1 = K_{19}, X_7^1$, and $RK_2^0 = K_4$, compute $X_3^3, \Delta X_{10}^0 = \Delta X_3^3, X_{14}^1, X_8^0, X_4^0$, and X_5^0. Then, store $RK_1^3 = K_{15}, RK_5^2 = K_3, RK_6^1 = K_{19}$, and $RK_2^0 = K_4$ in H_7 indexed by $X_3^3, \Delta X_{10}^0 = \Delta X_3^3, X_{14}^1, X_8^0, X_4^0, X_5^0, RK_1^3 = K_{15}, RK_5^2 = K_3, t_4^3, \Delta T_7$, and t_1^2. ΔX_{10}^0 is chosen such that $\Delta X_{10}^0 \in S[\Delta T_7]$, see Observation 4. Therefore, H_7 has 7×2^{40} rows and on average about $2^{48}/(7 \times 2^{40}) = (16/7) \times 2^4$ values in each row.

- H_8: For all the 2^{20} possible values of X_0^{24}, X_1^{24}, t_5^{24}, ΔT_7, and $RK_0^{24} = f_1(K_0, K_2, K_5, K_9, K_{10}, K_{12}, K_{13})$, compute X_0^{25}, ΔX_1^{25}, and X_1^{25}. Then, store RK_0^{24} in H_8 indexed by X_0^{25}, ΔX_1^{25}, X_1^{25}, t_5^{24}, and ΔT_7. ΔX_1^{25} is chosen such that $\Delta X_1^{25} \in S[\Delta T_7]$, see Observation 4. Therefore, H_8 has 7×2^{16} rows and on average about $2^{20}/(7 \times 2^{16}) = 16/7$ values in each row.

- H_9: For all the 2^{20} possible values of X_{14}^{24}, ΔX_{14}^{24}, X_{15}^{24}, t_0^{24}, and $RK_7^{24} = f_2(K_0, K_2, K_5, K_7, K_9, K_{10}, K_{11}, K_{12}, K_{13})$, compute X_{14}^{25}, ΔX_{14}^{25}, X_{15}^{25}, and ΔX_{15}^{25}. Then, store X_{14}^{24}, ΔX_{14}^{24}, and $RK_7^{24} = f_2(K_0, K_2, K_5, K_7, K_9, K_{10}, K_{11}, K_{12}, K_{13})$ in H_9 indexed by X_{14}^{25}, ΔX_{14}^{25}, X_{15}^{25}, ΔX_{15}^{25}, and t_0^{24}. ΔX_{15}^{25} is chosen such that $\Delta X_{15}^{25} \in S[\Delta X_{14}^{25}]$, see Observation 4. Therefore, H_9 has 7×2^{16} rows and on average about $2^{20}/(7 \times 2^{16}) = 16/7$ values in each row.

- H_{10}: For all the 2^{32} possible values of X_{14}^{23}, ΔX_{14}^{23}, X_{15}^{23}, t_0^{23}, $RK_7^{23} = f_3(K_0, K_2, K_5, K_7, K_9, K_{10}, K_{11}, K_{12}, K_{13})$, X_{10}^{24}, t_1^{24}, and $RK_5^{24} = f_4(K_0, K_2, K_5, K_7, K_9, K_{10}, K_{11}, K_{12}, K_{13})$, compute $X_{14}^{25} = X_{14}^{24}$, $\Delta X_{14}^{25} = \Delta X_{14}^{24}$, X_{11}^{25}, ΔX_{11}^{25}, and X_{10}^{25}. Then, store X_{14}^{23}, ΔX_{14}^{23}, $RK_7^{23} = f_3(K_0, K_2, K_5, K_7, K_9, K_{10}, K_{11}, K_{12}, K_{13})$, and $RK_5^{24} = f_4(K_0, K_2, K_5, K_7, K_9, K_{10}, K_{11}, K_{12}, K_{13})$ in H_{10} indexed by $X_{14}^{25} = X_{14}^{24}$, $\Delta X_{14}^{25} = \Delta X_{14}^{24}$, X_{11}^{25}, ΔX_{11}^{25}, X_{10}^{25}, t_0^{23}, and t_1^{24}. ΔX_{14}^{25} is chosen such that $\Delta X_{14}^{25} \in S[\Delta X_{11}^{25}]$, see Observation 4. Therefore, H_{10} has 7×2^{24} rows and on average about $2^{32}/(7 \times 2^{24}) = (16/7) \times 2^4$ values in each row.

- H_{11}: For all the 2^{44} possible values of X_{14}^{22}, X_{15}^{22}, t_0^{22}, ΔT_7, $RK_7^{22} = f_5(K_0, K_2, K_5, K_7, K_9, K_{10}, K_{11}, K_{12}, K_{13})$, X_{10}^{23}, t_1^{23}, $RK_5^{23} = f_6(K_0, K_2, K_5, K_7, K_9, K_{10}, K_{11}, K_{12}, K_{13})$, X_8^{24}, t_2^{24}, and $RK_4^{24} = f_7(K_0, K_2, K_5, K_9, K_{10}, K_{12}, K_{13})$, compute X_{14}^{23}, $\Delta X_{11}^{25} = \Delta X_{14}^{23}$, X_2^{25}, X_9^{25}, and X_8^{25}. Then, store $RK_7^{22} = f_5(K_0, K_2, K_5, K_7, K_9, K_{10}, K_{11}, K_{12}, K_{13})$, $RK_5^{23} = f_6(K_0, K_2, K_5, K_7, K_9, K_{10}, K_{11}, K_{12}, K_{13})$, and $RK_4^{24} = f_7(K_0, K_2, K_5, K_9, K_{10}, K_{12}, K_{13})$ in H_{11} indexed by X_{14}^{23}, $\Delta X_{11}^{25} = \Delta X_{14}^{23}$, X_2^{25}, X_9^{25}, X_8^{25}, t_0^{22}, ΔT_7, t_1^{23}, and t_2^{24}. ΔX_{11}^{25} is chosen such that $\Delta X_{11}^{25} \in S[\Delta T_7]$, see Observation 4. Therefore, H_{11} has 7×2^{32} rows and on average about $2^{44}/(7 \times 2^{32}) = (16/7) \times 2^8$ values in each row.

Our attack proceeds as follows. We initialize an array H of $2^{18 \times 4 = 72}$ entries to "0", where each entry is 1-bit and the index of the array is 18 key nibbles involved in the attack, as we will see later. Then, we generate 2^m structures as described above. Therefore, we have 2^{m+63} pairs of plaintext/ciphertext pairs generated using 2^{m+28} chosen plaintexts. Next, we ask the encryption oracle for their corresponding ciphertexts. The plaintext/ciphertext pairs that satisfy Observation 4 are $2^{m+63} \times 2^{-13.119} = 2^{m+49.881}$ pairs. After the ciphertext filtration, we have only $2^{m+49.881} \times 2^{-12 \times 4} = 2^{m+1.881}$ remaining pairs. For each remaining pair, we perform the following steps:

1. Determine the number of possible values of $RK_0^0 = K_1$ that satisfy the path by accessing H_1. Therefore, we have $(16/7)$ possible values for K_1.
2. Determine the number of possible values of $RK_5^0 = K_{14}$ that satisfy the path by accessing H_2. Therefore, we have $(16/7)^2$ possible values for K_1, K_{14}.
3. Determine the number of possible values of $RK_7^0 = K_{16}$ that satisfy the path by accessing H_3. Therefore, we have $(16/7)^3$ possible values for K_1, K_{14}, K_{16}.

4. Determine the number of possible values of $RK_2^1 = K_8, RK_1^0 = K_3$ that satisfy the path by accessing H_4. Therefore, we have $2^4 \times (16/7)^4$ possible values for $K_1, K_3, K_8, K_{14}, K_{16}$.

5. Determine the number of possible values of $RK_5^1 = K_{18}, RK_6^0 = K_{15}$ that satisfy the path by accessing H_5. Therefore, we have $2^8 \times (16/7)^5$ possible values for $K_1, K_3, K_8, K_{14}, K_{15}, K_{16}, K_{18}$.

6. Determine the number of possible values of $RK_3^2 = K_{14}, RK_4^1 = K_{17}, RK_3^0 = K_6$ that satisfy the path by accessing H_6. Therefore, we have $2^{12} \times (16/7)^6$ possible values for $K_1, K_3, K_6, K_8, K_{14}, K_{15}, K_{16}, K_{17}, K_{18}$.

7. Determine the number of possible values of $RK_1^3 = K_{15}, RK_5^2 = K_3, RK_6^1 = K_{19}, RK_2^0 = K_4$ that satisfy the path by accessing H_7. Therefore, we have $2^{16} \times (16/7)^7$ possible values for $K_1, K_3, K_4, K_6, K_8, K_{14}, K_{15}, K_{16}, K_{17}, K_{18}, K_{19}$.

8. Determine the number of possible values of RK_0^{24} that satisfy the path by accessing H_8. Therefore, we have $2^{16} \times (16/7)^8$ possible values for $K_1, K_3, K_4, K_6, K_8, K_{14}, K_{15}, K_{16}, K_{17}, K_{18}, K_{19}, RK_0^{24}$.

9. Determine the number of possible values of RK_7^{24} that satisfy the path by accessing H_9. Therefore, we have $2^{16} \times (16/7)^9$ possible values for $K_1, K_3, K_4, K_6, K_8, K_{14}, K_{15}, K_{16}, K_{17}, K_{18}, K_{19}, RK_0^{24}, RK_7^{24}$.

10. Determine the number of possible values of RK_7^{23}, RK_5^{24} that satisfy the path by accessing H_{10}. Therefore, we have $2^{20} \times (16/7)^{10}$ possible values for $K_1, K_3, K_4, K_6, K_8, K_{14}, K_{15}, K_{16}, K_{17}, K_{18}, K_{19}, RK_0^{24}, RK_7^{24}, RK_7^{23}, RK_5^{24}$.

11. Determine the number of possible values of $RK_7^{22}, RK_5^{23}, RK_4^{24}$ that satisfy the path by accessing H_{11}. Therefore, we have $2^{28} \times (16/7)^{11}$ possible values for $K_1, K_3, K_4, K_6, K_8, K_{14}, K_{15}, K_{16}, K_{17}, K_{18}, K_{19}, RK_0^{24}, RK_7^{24}, RK_7^{23}, RK_5^{24}, RK_7^{22}, RK_5^{23}, RK_4^{24}$.

12. The deduced $2^{28} \times (16/7)^{11}$ values for 18 key nibbles, $K_1, K_3, K_4, K_6, K_8, K_{14}, K_{15}, K_{16}, K_{17}, K_{18}, K_{19}, RK_0^{24}, RK_7^{24}, RK_7^{23}, RK_5^{24}, RK_7^{22}, K_5^{23}, RK_4^{24}$, involved in the attack are wrong keys. Hence, mark them in H invalid "1".

Attack Complexity. As depicted in Fig. 4, we have 22 round keys involved in the analysis rounds. According to the key schedule, these 22 round keys take only 2^{72} possible values (see step 12 in Table 4). As mentioned in step 12, we remove on average $2^{28} \times (16/7)^{11} = 2^{41.119}$ out of 2^{72} possible values of these 22 round keys involved in the attack for each pair of the $2^{m+1.881}$ remaining pairs. Hence, a wrong key is not discarded using one pair with probability $1 - 2^{41.119-72} = 1 - 2^{-30.881}$. Therefore, we have $2^{72} \times (1 - 2^{-30.881})^{2^{m+1.881}} \approx 2^{72} \times (e^{-1})^{2^{m+1.881-30.881}} \approx 2^{72} \times 2^{-1.4 \times 2^{m-29}}$ remaining candidates for 72-bit of the key, after processing all the $2^{m+1.881}$ remaining pairs. We evaluated the computational complexity of the attack as a function of m, as illustrated in Table 4, to determine the optimal value of m that leads to the best computational complexity. As steps 11 and 12 dominate the time complexity of the attack, see Table 4, we choose $m = 33.5$ in order to optimize the time complexity of the attack. Therefore, we have $2^{72} \times 2^{-1.4 \times 2^{33.5-29=4.5}} = 2^{72-31.678} = 2^{40.322}$ remaining candidates for 72-bit of the key. These 72-bit of the key include 11 master key nibbles and 7 round key nibbles. To retrieve the whole master key, we perform the following steps:

1. Retrieve K_{10} from RK_4^{24} by guessing the 6 key nibbles $K_0, K_2, K_5, K_9,$ K_{12}, K_{13}. Since this step includes 18 S-box operations, it requires $2^{40.322+24=64.322} \times \frac{18}{8 \times 25} \approx 2^{60.848}$ encryptions. Since RK_4^{24} and RK_0^{24} are functions in the same nibbles of the master key, we can compute RK_0^{24} using the retrieved K_{10} and then match the computed value with its value in the remaining candidate key. As a result, we have 4-bit filtration. Hence, we have only $2^{40.322+24-4=60.322}$ remaining key candidates. This step requires $2^{40.322+24=64.322} \times \frac{37}{8 \times 25} \approx 2^{61.888}$ encryptions.

2. Using the same technique, retrieve K_7 from RK_5^{23} by guessing K_{11}. This step requires $2^{60.322+4=64.322} \times \frac{90}{8 \times 25} \approx 2^{63.167}$ encryptions. Since RK_5^{24} is also a function in the same nibbles of the master key, we can compute it using the retrieved K_7 and compare it with its value in the remaining candidate. As a result, we have 4-bit filtration. Hence, we have only $2^{60.322+4-4=60.322}$ 80-bit remaining key candidates. This step requires $2^{60.322+4=64.322} \times \frac{112}{8 \times 25} \approx 2^{63.485}$. Then, we perform the previous filtration to the following round key nibbles RK_7^{22}, RK_7^{23}, and RK_7^{24}. Finally, we have another 3 4-bit filtrations. Therefore, we have only $2^{60.322-12} = 2^{48.322}$ remaining candidates for the whole master key. The time complexity of this step is dominated by $2^{64.335}$ encryptions.

The right master key can be retrieved by exhaustively searching the $2^{48.322}$ remaining key candidates using 2 plaintext/ciphertext pairs. This step requires $2 \times 2^{48.322} = 2^{49.322}$ encryptions. Therefore, the time complexity of the attack is dominated by steps 11 and 12 in Table 4 which requires $2^{70.441} + 2^{68.856} \approx 2^{70.86}$ encryptions, see Table 4. The data complexity of the attack is $2^{m+4 \times 8} = 2^{65.5}$ chosen tweak/plaintext combinations that can be generated using $2^{m+28} = 2^{61.5}$ chosen plaintexts. The memory complexity of the attack is dominated by the memory that is required to store H. Hence, the memory complexity is $2^{72} \times 2^{-6} = 2^{66}$ 64-bit blocks.

6   Conclusion

In this work, we presented two impossible differential attacks against reduced-round versions of T-TWINE. Both attacks use our proposed 18-round impossible differential distinguisher. To the best of our knowledge, this distinguisher is the first valid 18-round distinguisher. Utilizing this distinguisher, we launched 25-round and 27-round attacks on T-WINE-80 and T-TWINE-128, respectively. The presented attacks are the first published attacks against both versions of T-TWINE.

Table 4. Time complexity of the different steps of the attack on 25-round T-TWINE-80, where NK denotes the number of keys to be excluded.

Step	Time complexity (in 25-round encryptions)	NK	$m = 33.5$
1	$2^{m+1.881} \times (16/7) \times \dfrac{3}{8 \times 25} \approx 2^{m-2.985}$	$(16/7)$	$2^{30.515}$
2	$2^{m+1.881} \times (16/7)^2 \times \dfrac{3}{8 \times 25} \approx 2^{m-1.793}$	$(16/7)^2$	$2^{31.707}$
3	$2^{m+1.881} \times (16/7)^3 \times \dfrac{4}{8 \times 25} \approx 2^{m-0.185}$	$(16/7)^3$	$2^{33.315}$
4	$2^{m+1.881} \times 2^4 \times (16/7)^4 \times \dfrac{4}{8 \times 25} \approx 2^{m+5.008}$	$2^4 \times (16/7)^4$	$2^{38.508}$
5	$2^{m+1.881} \times 2^8 \times (16/7)^5 \times \dfrac{2}{8 \times 25} \approx 2^{m+9.200}$	$2^8 \times (16/7)^5$	$2^{42.700}$
6	$2^{m+1.881} \times 2^{12} \times (16/7)^6 \times \dfrac{5}{8 \times 25} \approx 2^{m+15.715}$	$2^{12} \times (16/7)^6$	$2^{49.215}$
7	$2^{m+1.881} \times 2^{16} \times (16/7)^7 \times \dfrac{4}{8 \times 25} \approx 2^{m+20.586}$	$2^{16} \times (16/7)^7$	$2^{54.086}$
8	$2^{m+1.881} \times 2^{16} \times (16/7)^8 \times \dfrac{1}{8 \times 25} \approx 2^{m+19.778}$	$2^{16} \times (16/7)^8$	$2^{53.278}$
9	$2^{m+1.881} \times 2^{16} \times (16/7)^9 \times \dfrac{3}{8 \times 25} \approx 2^{m+22.556}$	$2^{16} \times (16/7)^9$	$2^{56.056}$
10	$2^{m+1.881} \times 2^{20} \times (16/7)^{10} \times \dfrac{4}{8 \times 25} \approx 2^{m+28.164}$	$2^{20} \times (16/7)^{11}$	$2^{61.664}$
11	$2^{m+1.881} \times 2^{28} \times (16/7)^{11} \times \dfrac{3}{8 \times 25} \approx 2^{m+36.941}$	$2^{28} \times (16/7)^{11}$	$2^{70.441}$
12	$2^{m+1.881} \times 2^{28} \times (16/7)^{11} \times \dfrac{1}{8 \times 25} \approx 2^{m+35.356}$	$2^{28} \times (16/7)^{11}$	$2^{68.856}$

A   18-round Impossible Differential Characteristic as Depicted in Figure 8 of [15]

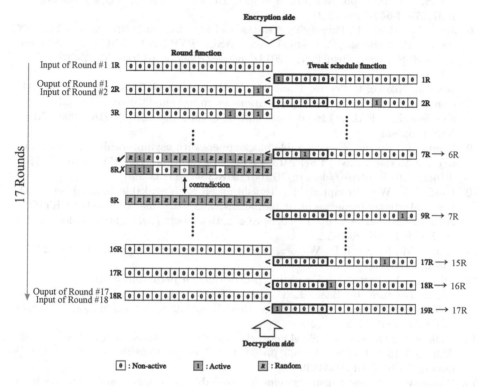

Fig. 5. 18-round impossible differential characteristic as depicted in Figure 8 of [15] with our comments.

References

1. Avanzi, R.: The QARMA block cipher family. Almost MDS matrices over rings with zero divisors, nearly symmetric even-mansour constructions with non-involutory central rounds, and search heuristics for low-latency S-boxes. IACR Trans. Symmetric Cryptol. 4–44 (2017)
2. Beierle, C., et al.: The SKINNY family of block ciphers and its low-latency variant MANTIS. In: Robshaw, M., Katz, J. (eds.) CRYPTO 2016. LNCS, vol. 9815, pp. 123–153. Springer, Heidelberg (2016). https://doi.org/10.1007/978-3-662-53008-5_5
3. Biham, E., Biryukov, A., Shamir, A.: Cryptanalysis of skipjack reduced to 31 rounds using impossible differentials. In: Stern, J. (ed.) EUROCRYPT 1999. LNCS, vol. 1592, pp. 12–23. Springer, Heidelberg (1999). https://doi.org/10.1007/3-540-48910-X_2

4. Ferguson, N., et al.: The SKEIN hash function family (2010). http://www.skeinhash.info
5. Goldenberg, D., Hohenberger, S., Liskov, M., Schwartz, E.C., Seyalioglu, H.: On tweaking Luby-Rackoff blockciphers. In: Kurosawa, K. (ed.) ASIACRYPT 2007. LNCS, vol. 4833, pp. 342–356. Springer, Heidelberg (2007). https://doi.org/10.1007/978-3-540-76900-2_21
6. Jean, J., Nikolić, I., Peyrin, T.: Tweaks and keys for block ciphers: the TWEAKEY framework. In: Sarkar, P., Iwata, T. (eds.) ASIACRYPT 2014. LNCS, vol. 8874, pp. 274–288. Springer, Heidelberg (2014). https://doi.org/10.1007/978-3-662-45608-8_15
7. Jean, J., Nikolić, I., Peyrin, T., Seurin, Y.: Deoxys v1.41. Submitted to CAESAR Competition (2016). https://competitions.cr.yp.to/round3/deoxysv141.pdf
8. Knudsen, L.: DEAL: a 128-bit block cipher. Complexity 258(2), 216 (1998). NIST AES Proposal
9. Lampe, R., Seurin, Y.: Tweakable blockciphers with asymptotically optimal security. In: Moriai, S. (ed.) FSE 2013. LNCS, vol. 8424, pp. 133–151. SPringer, Heidelberg (2014). https://doi.org/10.1007/978-3-662-43933-3_8
10. Landecker, W., Shrimpton, T., Terashima, R.S.: Tweakable blockciphers with beyond birthday-bound security. In: Safavi-Naini, R., Canetti, R. (eds.) CRYPTO 2012. LNCS, vol. 7417, pp. 14–30. Springer, Heidelberg (2012). https://doi.org/10.1007/978-3-642-32009-5_2
11. Liskov, M., Rivest, R.L., Wagner, D.: Tweakable block ciphers. J. Cryptol. 24(3), 588–613 (2010)
12. Mitsuda, A., Iwata, T.: Tweakable pseudorandom permutation from generalized feistel structure. In: Baek, J., Bao, F., Chen, K., Lai, X. (eds.) ProvSec 2008. LNCS, vol. 5324, pp. 22–37. Springer, Heidelberg (2008). https://doi.org/10.1007/978-3-540-88733-1_2
13. Nyberg, K.: Generalized feistel networks. In: Kim, K., Matsumoto, T. (eds.) ASIACRYPT 1996. LNCS, vol. 1163, pp. 91–104. Springer, Heidelberg (1996). https://doi.org/10.1007/BFb0034838
14. Rogaway, P.: Efficient instantiations of tweakable blockciphers and refinements to modes OCB and PMAC. In: Lee, P.J. (ed.) ASIACRYPT 2004. LNCS, vol. 3329, pp. 16–31. Springer, Heidelberg (2004). https://doi.org/10.1007/978-3-540-30539-2_2
15. Sakamoto, K., et al.: Tweakable TWINE: building a tweakable block cipher on generalized feistel structure. In: Attrapadung, N., Yagi, T. (eds.) IWSEC 2019. LNCS, vol. 11689, pp. 129–145. Springer, Cham (2019). https://doi.org/10.1007/978-3-030-26834-3_8
16. Schroeppel, R.: An overview of the hasty pudding cipher (1998). http://www.cs.arizona.edu/rcs/hpc
17. Suzaki, T., Minematsu, K.: Improving the generalized feistel. In: Hong, S., Iwata, T. (eds.) FSE 2010. LNCS, vol. 6147, pp. 19–39. Springer, Heidelberg (2010). https://doi.org/10.1007/978-3-642-13858-4_2
18. Suzaki, T., Minematsu, K., Morioka, S., Kobayashi, E.: TWINE: a lightweight block cipher for multiple platforms. In: Knudsen, L.R., Wu, H. (eds.) SAC 2012. LNCS, vol. 7707, pp. 339–354. Springer, Heidelberg (2013). https://doi.org/10.1007/978-3-642-35999-6_22

19. Zheng, X., Jia, K.: Impossible differential attack on reduced-round TWINE. In: Lee, H.-S., Han, D.-G. (eds.) ICISC 2013. LNCS, vol. 8565, pp. 123–143. Springer, Cham (2014). https://doi.org/10.1007/978-3-319-12160-4_8
20. Zheng, Y., Matsumoto, T., Imai, H.: Impossibility and optimality results on constructing pseudorandom permutations. In: Quisquater, J.-J., Vandewalle, J. (eds.) EUROCRYPT 1989. LNCS, vol. 434, pp. 412–422. Springer, Heidelberg (1990). https://doi.org/10.1007/3-540-46885-4_41

MixColumns Coefficient Property and Security of the AES with A Secret S-Box

Xin An[1,2], Kai Hu[1,2], and Meiqin Wang[1,2(✉)]

[1] School of Cyber Science and Technology, Shandong University,
Qingdao 266237, Shandong, China
{anxin19,hukai}@mail.sdu.edu.cn, mqwang@sdu.edu.cn
[2] Key Laboratory of Cryptologic Technology and Information Security of Ministry of
Education, Shandong University, Qingdao 266237, Shandong, China

Abstract. The MixColumns operation is an important component providing diffusion for the AES. The branch number of it ensures that any continuous four rounds of the AES have at least 25 active S-Boxes, which makes the AES secure against the differential and linear cryptanalysis. However, the choices of the coefficients of the MixColumns matrix may undermine the AES security against some novel-type attacks. A particular property of the AES MixColumns matrix coefficient has been noticed in recent papers that *each row or column of the matrix has elements that sum to zero*. Several attacks have been developed taking advantage of the coefficient property.

In this paper we investigate further the influence of the specific coefficient property on the AES security. Our target, which is also one of the targets of the previous works, is a 5-round AES variant with a secret S-Box. We will show how we take advantage of the coefficient property to extract the secret key directly without any assistance of the S-Box information. Compared with the previous similar attacks, the present attacks here are the best in terms of the complexity under the chosen-plaintext scenario.

Keywords: AES · MixColumns · Exchange attack · Key recovery attack · Secret S-Box

1 Introduction

The Advanced Encryption Standard (AES) [7] is designed to achieve good resistance against the differential [3] and linear cryptanalysis [13]. This includes the selection of the S-Box and linear components such as the MixColumns matrix. For the AES, the branch number of its MixColumns matrix is chosen as five then it ensures that any four continuous rounds of differential (linear) characteristics have at least 25 active S-Boxes [7,8]. Considering that the maximum correlation and the maximum difference propagation probability over the AES

© Springer Nature Switzerland AG 2020
A. Nitaj and A. Youssef (Eds.): AFRICACRYPT 2020, LNCS 12174, pp. 114–131, 2020.
https://doi.org/10.1007/978-3-030-51938-4_6

S-Box are 2^{-3} and 2^{-6}, respectively, there are no effective differential or linear characteristics for four or more rounds of the AES.

For the performance reasons, the coefficients of the AES MixColumns are chosen from a group of low-weight numbers. Therefore it is not surprising that there are elements in each row or column that will add up to zero. For example, its first row is $[02, 03, 01, 01]$ thus $01 \oplus 01 = 0$ and $01 \oplus 02 \oplus 03 = 0$. Several attacks have been developed facilitated by this property and show that the property can be a potential weakness [2,9,10,12,15]. For convenience, we conclude it into two types concretely as follows as did in [12],

Property 1. Each row or column of the MixColumns matrix has two elements that sum to zero.

Property 2. Each row or column of the MixColumns matrix has three elements that sum to zero.

At Crypto 2016, Sun et al. noticed Property 1 for the first time and established the first zero-correlation linear hull and the first integral distinguisher for the 5-round AES [15]. The two attacks exploited the existing 4-round corresponding properties and extended them one more round based on the MixColumns coefficient property. We take the 5-round zero-correlation linear hull as an example. As is well-known, the previous zero-correlation linear hull can cover at most 3.5 rounds of the AES (without last MixColumns) [4] which is illustrated in Fig. 1[1].

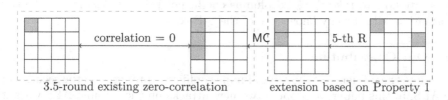

3.5-round existing zero-correlation   extension based on Property 1

Fig. 1. Extending 3.5-round zero-correlation linear hull for AES to 5 rounds exploiting Property 1

Let the first column of the input mask and the output mask of the Mix-Columns after the 3.5-round zero-correlation linear hull be Γ_{in} and Γ_{out}, respectively. According to the propagation of the mask over a linear map [4], we have $\Gamma_{in} = M_{AES}^T \Gamma_{out}$, where M_{AES}^T is the transpose of the matrix used by the AES MixColumns. Then if we can ensure that the two active masks of Γ_{out} are equal, we can make certain that Γ_{in} has only three active bytes like Fig. 1. Finally, the zero-correlation linear can be extended to 5 rounds.

Although the two distinguishers in [15] cost the whole codebook, they spawned a sequence of new fundamental results that are based on Property 1 or 2.

---

[1] In [4], the output mask of the 3.5-round zero-correlation linear hull has only one active byte, but it is easy to check that with 3 active byte in the output mask it is still a zero-correlation linear hull.

Soon after, two following improvements were proposed which aimed to reduce the complexities [6,12]. At FSE 2017, Grassi et al. took Property 1 proposing the first impossible differential distinguisher for the 5-round AES [10]. Later at CT-RSA 2018, the impossible differential distinguisher was further improved by Grassi exploiting Property 2 [9]. In the same paper, he also discussed the attacks on an AES variant with a secret S-Box. By combining the MixColumns coefficient property and the multiple-of-n attack [11], Grassi managed to extract the secret key from the 5-round AES without knowing any information of the S-Box or recovering it in advance as it was done in [16].

The security of the AES variant with a secret S-Box was firstly studied by Tiessen et al. at FSE 2015 [16]. Assuming that the choice of the S-Box is made uniformly at random from all 8-bit S-Boxes and keeping all other components unchanged, the size of the secret information increases from 128 bits to 1812 bits[2] (we focus on the AES-128). Generally speaking, a key-recovery attack requires the details of the S-Box since we have to peel off some key-involved components. Consequently, the authors of [16] needed to recover an equivalent S-Box by the square attack [16] and then found the equivalent secret key. However, the works in [9] showed that it is possible to recover the key information directly without recovering the S-Box in advance if we take advantage of Property 1 or 2 appropriately. At Africacrypt 2019, Bardeh and Rønjom further studied the influence of Property 1 under the adaptive-chosen-ciphertext scenario, which is the newest result in this direction. The AES variant with a secret S-Box has been a popular target for studying the MixColumns coefficient property. In this paper, we also study how to take the MixColumns coefficient property to extract the key information without any knowledge of the S-Box.

1.1   Our Contribution

To explore the influence of the MixColumns coefficient property on the security of the AES, in this paper we propose two new attacks on the 5-round AES variant with a secret S-Box based on Property 1 and 2 respectively. Our attacks are developed upon the newest technique called the exchange attack [1], we manage to transform the 5-round exchange attack to two key-recovery attacks. Compared with those previous attacks based on the MixColumns coefficient property, our 5-round attacks need only $2^{42.6}$ or 2^{46} chosen plaintexts, which are new records under the chosen-plaintext scenario. All the attacks on the 5-round AES related to the MixColumns coefficient property are listed in Table 1 for a convenient comparison.

Organization of This Paper

In Sect. 2, we introduce some background knowledge needed in this paper. In Sect. 3 and 4, we present two new attacks exploiting Property 1 and Property 2, respectively. We conclude this paper in Sect. 5.

---

[2] The number of all the 8-bit S-Boxes is $2^8!$ which is about $log_2^{(2^8!)} \approx 1684$ bits information. Totally, the security information is about $1684 + 128 = 1812$ bits.

Table 1. Attacks on the 5-round AES taking the mixcolumns coefficient property

Attack	Round	Data	Computation	Reference
Integral	5	2^{128} CC	$2^{129.6}$ XOR	[15]
Impossible differential	5	2^{102} CP	2^{107} M $\approx 2^{100.4}$ E*	[10]
Impossible differential	5	$2^{76.4}$ CP	$2^{81.5}$ M $\approx 2^{74.9}$ E	[9]
Integral	5	2^{96} CP	2^{96} E	[12]
Multiple-of-n	5	$2^{53.6}$ CP	$2^{55.6}$ M $\approx 2^{48.86}$ E	[9]
Zero difference	5	$2^{29.19}$ CP+2^{32}ACC	2^{31} XOR	[2]
Exchange	**5**	$\mathbf{2^{42.6}}$ CP	$2^{42.6}$ E	**Sect. 3**
Exchange	**5**	$\mathbf{2^{46}}$ CP	2^{46} E	**Sect. 4**

CC: chosen ciphertexts, CP: chosen plaintexts, ACC: adaptive chosen ciphertexts
M: memory access, XOR: XOR operation, E: 5-round AES encryption
*: In [9,10], the authors used the scale that 100 times of memory access are approximately equivalent to 1 times of 5-round AES. In this paper, we use the same scale.

2   Preliminary

2.1   Description of the AES

The AES (Advanced Encryption Standard) [7] is an iterated block cipher with the substitution-permutation network (SPN). It has three versions with the key size 128, 192, 256 bits and the number of rounds is 10, 12, 14, respectively. The length of the block cipher is 128-bit and it will be initialized as a 4×4 matrix of bytes as values in the finite field $\mathbb{F}_{2^8}$ defined over the the irreducible polynomial $x^8 + x^4 + x^3 + x + 1$ (AES finite field). The round function of the AES, except the last one, applies four operations to every state matrix:

- SubBytes (SB) - each of the 16 bytes in the state matrix is replaced by another value getting from an 8-bit S-Box. In our attack the adversary does not know the exact information about the S-Box.
- ShiftRows (SR) - the i-th ($0 \le i \le 3$) row of the state matrix is rotated to the left by i position(s).
- MixColumns (MC) - each column of the state matrix is multiplied by an MDS matric M_{AES} from the left over the AES finite field. The invertible matrix M_{AES} is shown as follows, each byte of matrix is presented as hexadecimal.

$$M_{AES} = \begin{bmatrix} 02 & 03 & 01 & 01 \\ 01 & 02 & 03 & 01 \\ 01 & 01 & 02 & 03 \\ 03 & 01 & 01 & 02 \end{bmatrix} \tag{1}$$

- AddRoundKey(AK) - the state of the AES is XORed with the 128-bit round key.

In the first round an additional AK will be applied to the plaintext ahead the SB operation. And in the last round the MixColumns operation is omitted for convenient decryption. In this paper, we focus on the 5-round AES variant where we consider the five full rounds of the AES keeping the last MC only for convenient description.

The AES Variant with A Secret S-Box. The target of this paper is an AES variant with a secret S-Box, i.e., the S-Box is replaced by a secret one and other structure and components are as the same as the original AES.

2.2 Notations

Let x denote a plaintext, a ciphertext, an intermediate state or a key. Then $x_{i,j}$ with $i, j \in \{0, 1, 2, 3\}$ denotes the byte located at the intersection of the i-th row and the j-th column. The secret key is usually denoted by k. We denote one round of the AES by R and denote r full rounds of the AES by R^{r}[3]. In this paper, we will also adopt the notations of the subspaces for the AES proposed initially in [10]. For a pair (x, x'), its dual pair $(\hat{x}, \hat{x}')$ is generated by exchanging the first diagonal between x and x'. We call a pair and its dual pair, i.e., $(x, x', \hat{x}, \hat{x}')$ a pair-of-pair. For a matrix or a vector v, we denote its transpose by v^{T}.

Subspaces of the AES. The subspace trial of the AES works with vectors and vector spaces over $\mathbb{F}_{2^8}^{4 \times 4}$. We denote the unit vectors of $\mathbb{F}_{2^8}^{4 \times 4}$ by $e_{0,0}, e_{0,1}, ..., e_{3,3}$ where $e_{i,j}$ has a single 1 in the intersection of the i-th row and the j-th column.

Definition 1 (Column Space [10]). *The column space C_i are defined as $C_i = \langle e_{0,i}, e_{1,i}, e_{2,i}, e_{3,i} \rangle$.*

Definition 2 (Diagonal and Inverse-Diagonal Space [10]). *The diagonal spaces D_i and inverse-diagonal spaces ID_i are defined as $D_i = \mathsf{SR}^{-1}(C_i)$ and $ID_i = \mathsf{SR}(C_i)$.*

Definition 3 (Mixed Space [10]). *The i-th mixed spaces M_i are defined as $M_i = \mathsf{MC}(ID_i)$.*

Definition 4 ([10]). *For $I \subseteq \{0, 1, 2, 3\}$ where $0 < |I| \leq 3$, let C_I, D_I, ID_I and M_I defined as*

$$C_I = \bigoplus_{i \in I} C_i, D_I = \bigoplus_{i \in I} D_i, ID_I = \bigoplus_{i \in I} ID_i, M_I = \bigoplus_{i \in I} M_i.$$

We refer readers to [10] for more details.

Next we introduce a useful one round subspace trail.

Lemma 1 ([10]). *For any coset $D_I \oplus a$ there exists a unique $b \in C_I^{\perp}$ such that after one round $R(D_I \oplus a)$ belongs to a coset of column space, i.e., $R(D_I \oplus a) = C_I \oplus b$. In other words, if $x \oplus x' \in D_I$, then $R(x) \oplus R(x') \in C_I$.*

---

[3] For the unity of description, we do not omit the last MC of R^r when we metion R^r.

2.3   Exchange Attack

The exchange attack is a new distinguisher proposed at Asiacrypt 2019 which can be used to attack the 5- and 6-round AES [1]. Since this paper only use the distinguishing attack on the 5-round AES, we only introduce some basic ideas about its application to the 5-round AES.

For a pair of states, if we exchange their first diagonals between the two values and get its dual pair, it is equivalent to swap the corresponding column after one round encryption. Furthermore, in some special cases, to exchange a column is equivalent to exchange a diagnoal. For example, if the difference of the state pair behaves like the rightmost state in Fig. 2, exchanging its first column is equivalent to exchange its first diagonal, because only the byte at the intersection of the first column and the first diagnoal is active.

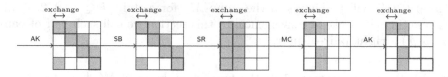

Fig. 2. Swapping the first column is equivalent to swap the first diagonal.

In [1], the authors modified a theorem from [14], which states an exchange-difference relation over 4 rounds of the AES.

Theorem 1 (4-round Exchange-Difference Relation [14]). *Let* $x, x' \in \mathbb{F}_{2^8}^{4 \times 4}$, *exchange some diagonals between* x *and* x' *and get* $\hat{x}, \hat{x}'$, *then for* $J \subseteq \{0, 1, 2, 3\}$ *and* $0 < |J| \leq 3$,

$$Pr(R^4(\hat{x}) \oplus R^4(\hat{x}') \in M_J | R^4(x) \oplus R^4(x') \in M_J) = 1.$$

According to the exchange attack illustrated in Fig. 2 [1], we choose a pair of plaintext $x, x' \in D_J \oplus a$ where $J = \{0, 1\}$, and exchange the first diagonal to get its dual pair $\hat{x}, \hat{x}' \in C_I \oplus a$. With some probability $x \oplus x'$ and $\hat{x} \oplus \hat{x}'$ may satisfy a special difference pattern making that it is equivalent to exchange some diagonals of $(R(x), R(x'))$ to get $(R(\hat{x}), R(\hat{x}'))$. Then it meets the starting condition of Theorem 1, we can get a 5-round exchange-equivalent relation for the AES.

3   Improved Key-Recovery Attack Based on Property 1

In this section, we show how to combine Property 1 with the exchange attack to establish an improved key-recovery attack on the 5-round AES with a secret S-Box. The basic idea of this attack is to extend the 4-round exchange-difference relation (Theorem 1) to 5 rounds. In the attack, we first choose two plaintexts

p, p' from a subspace $S_0 = a \oplus D_I$ where $I = \{0, 1\}$, and expect that $R(p), R(p')$ will be in a specific subspace $S_1 = b \oplus C_I$ as follows,

$$S_1 \triangleq \left\{ b \oplus \begin{bmatrix} x_1 & x_2 & 0 & 0 \\ 0 & 0 & 0 & 0 \\ 0 & x_3 & 0 & 0 \\ 0 & x_4 & 0 & 0 \end{bmatrix} \middle| x_1, x_2, x_3, x_4, b \in \mathbb{F}_{2^8} \right\}. \tag{2}$$

For two randomly drawn plaintexts $p, p' \in S_0$, the probability that $R(p) \oplus R(p') \in S_1$ is 2^{-32}. However, taking Property 1 into consideration and choosing p, p' carefully according to some secret key information, we can vary the probability of $R(p) \oplus R(p') \in S_1$ between the wrong and right key guess.

Once $R(p) \oplus R(p') \in S_1$, we can exchange the first diagonal between p and p' and get its dual pair $(\hat{p}, \hat{p}')$, thus $(R(p), R(p'))$ and $(R(\hat{p}), R(\hat{p}'))$ are two pairs satisfying the starting condition of Theorem 1. Hence, $R^5(p) \oplus R^5(p')$ and $R^5(\hat{p}) \oplus R^5(\hat{p}')$ will be always in the same M_J for certain $J \subseteq \{0, 1, 2, 3\}$ at the same time. For sake of convenience, in this section we call such pair-of-pair $(p, p', \hat{p}, \hat{p}')$ a **right pair-of-pair**.

Details. Based on Property 1, if the four input bytes of MC have two zero-difference values and the difference of the remaining two bytes are equal, the output vector will have one zero-difference byte with probability 1. Without loss of generality, we assume the input difference is $[a, 0, 0, a]^T$, then

$$\begin{bmatrix} 02 & 03 & 01 & 01 \\ 01 & 02 & 03 & 01 \\ 01 & 01 & 02 & 03 \\ 03 & 01 & 01 & 02 \end{bmatrix} \times \begin{bmatrix} a \\ 0 \\ 0 \\ a \end{bmatrix} = \begin{bmatrix} 3a \\ 0 \\ 2a \\ a \end{bmatrix}. \tag{3}$$

It can be seen that the second value of the output difference must be zero. Then if the second column of the input difference of MC is really the patten such as $[a, 0, 0, a]^T$ where $a \in \mathbb{F}_{2^8} \backslash \{0\}$, the probability that $R(p) \oplus R(p') \in S_1$ (Eq. 2) will be 2^{-24} rather than 2^{-32}. For this reason, we define the set $A_{z,\delta}$ as follows,

$$A_{z,\delta} \triangleq \left\{ a \oplus \begin{bmatrix} y_0 & z & 0 & 0 \\ 0 & y_1 & 0 & 0 \\ 0 & 0 & y_2 & 0 \\ z \oplus \delta & 0 & 0 & y_3 \end{bmatrix} \middle| \forall y_0, y_1, y_2, y_3, a \in F_{2^8} \right\} \text{ where } z, \delta \in F_{2^8}, \tag{4}$$

and then choose two different plaintexts $p \in A_{z_0, \delta}$ and $p' \in A_{z_1, \delta}$ where $z_0 \neq z_1$.

Let the two secret key bytes which are XORed with $p_{0,1}$ (Resp. $p'_{0,1}$) and $p_{3,0}$ (Resp. $p'_{3,0}$) be $k_{0,1}$ and $k_{3,0}$, respectively. After $f \triangleq SR \circ SB \circ AK$ operation, the second column of $f(p) \oplus f(p')$ is

$$(f(p) \oplus f(p'))_{C_1} = \begin{bmatrix} \text{S-Box}(z_0 \oplus k_{0,1}) \oplus \text{S-Box}(z_1 \oplus k_{0,1}) \\ 0 \\ 0 \\ \text{S-Box}(z_0 \oplus \delta \oplus k_{3,0}) \oplus \text{S-Box}(z_1 \oplus \delta \oplus k_{3,0}) \end{bmatrix}.$$

To meet the condition shown in Eq. 3, Eq. 5 should be met,

$$\text{S-Box}(z_0 \oplus k_{0,1}) \oplus \text{S-Box}(z_1 \oplus k_{0,1}) = \text{S-Box}(z_0 \oplus \delta \oplus k_{3,0}) \oplus \text{S-Box}(z_1 \oplus \delta \oplus k_{3,0}) \quad (5)$$

Since the S-Box is a secret permutation, Eq. 5 has only two solutions, i.e.,

$$\delta = k_{0,1} \oplus k_{3,0} \text{ or } \delta = z_0 \oplus z_1 \oplus k_{0,1} \oplus k_{3,0}.$$

If we let δ run through all values in $\mathbb{F}_{2^8}$, we can guarantee that there are at least two values of δ leading that Eq. 5 holds. For sake of simplicity, we call the two δ **right** δ and other values **wrong** δ. For right δ, the probability that $R(p) \oplus R(p') \in S_1$ will be 2^{-24}. For wrong δ, the probability is still 2^{-32}. Combinining with Theorem 1, we conclude the following proposition,

Proposition 1. *Let $p \in A_{z_0, \delta}$ and $p' \in A_{z_1, \delta}$. $(\hat{p}, \hat{p}')$ is the dual pair of (p, p'). If δ is right, for certain M_J with $|J| = 3$,*

$$Pr(R^5(p) \oplus R^5(p') \in M_J \wedge R^5(\hat{p}) \oplus R^5(\hat{p}') \in M_J) \approx 2^{-54}.$$

While for wrong δ,

$$Pr(R^5(p) \oplus R^5(p') \in M_J \wedge R^5(\hat{p}) \oplus R^5(\hat{p}') \in M_J) \approx 2^{-62}.$$

Proof. If two pairs satisfy the starting condition of Theorem 1, they will be in the same M_J at the same time after 4 rounds of encryption. Let $|J| = 3$, the probability for the two pairs being a right pair-of-pair is 2^{-30} since we have four choices of J.

For wrong δ, the starting condition of Theorem 1 is statisfied with probability 2^{-32}. Then, the probability for the two pairs being a right pair-of-pair is about 2^{-62}, which is consistent with the random case. While for right δ, the starting condition is met with probability 2^{-24}, so the probability for the two pairs being a right pair-of-pair is 2^{-54}. □

Finding δ Candidates. We can take advantage of Proposition 1 to find the right δ that implies $k_{0,1} \oplus k_{3,0}$. The process for finding δ is illustrated in Algorithm 1. For each candidate $\delta \in \mathbb{F}_{2^8}$, we find collision pairs and check whether there is at least one collision pair satisfying that its dual pair is also a collision pair. We explain briefly some crucial lines in Algorithm 1.

Line 4. For $A_{z_0, \delta}$ and $A_{z_1, \delta}$, we require that the i-th plaintexts in $A_{z_0, \delta}$ and $A_{z_1, \delta}$ should have the same value in the first diagonal. In this way, $(c_{z_0}^i, c_{z_1}^j)$ must be the dual pair of $(c_{z_1}^i, c_{z_0}^j)$. We can prepare a subset of D_0 with size 2^N and use it to generate the two sets $A_{z_0, \delta}$ and $A_{z_1, \delta}$ where $z_0 \neq z_1$.

Line 14. Since we have stored all the ciphertexts in tables, we only need to store the indexes of ciphertexts into the two hash tables. If the i-th lines of $\mathcal{T}_{z_0}$ and $\mathcal{T}_{z_1}$ are not empty simultaneously, we find a collision pair pointed by the corresponding indexes.

Algorithm 1. Finding δ Candidates (Property 1)

1: **procedure** CORE(z_0, z_1, r, c)   ▷ Return a set containing the possible right δ
2:     **for** Each $\delta \in \mathbb{F}_{2^8}$ **do**
3:         Initialize 2 sequence tables $\mathcal{C}_{z_0}, \mathcal{C}_{z_1}$, 1 table Δ
4:         Prepare two sets $A_{z_0, \delta}, A_{z_1, \delta}$ with 2^{29} plaintexts   ▷ Make sure $A_{z_0, \delta}[i]_{D_0} = A_{z_1, \delta}[i]_{D_0}$, according to Equation 4
5:         **for** $i = 0; i < 2^{29}; i = i + 1$ **do**
6:             **for** $j = 0; j < 2; j = j + 1$ **do**
7:                 $c_{z_j}^i \leftarrow R^5(p_{z_j}^i)$ ▷ $p_{z_j}^i$ is the i-th plaintext in $A_{z_j, \delta}$
8:                 $\mathcal{C}_{z_j}[i] \leftarrow c_{z_j}^i$ ▷ Store $c_{z_j}^i$
9:             **end for**
10:         **end for**
11:         **for** $k = 0; k < 4; k = k + 1$ **do**   ▷ For each M_k space, search for collisions
12:             Initialize 2 hash tables $\mathcal{T}_{z_0}, \mathcal{T}_{z_1}$
13:             **for** $i = 0; i < 2^{29}; i = i + 1$ **do**
14:                 **for** $j = 0; j < 2; j = j + 1$ **do**
15:                     $\mathcal{T}_{z_j}[\text{MC}^{-1}(c_{z_j}^i)_{ID_k}] \leftarrow \text{index}(c_{z_j}^i)$ ▷ $\text{index}(c_{z_j}^i) = i$
16:                 **end for**
17:             **end for**
18:             **for** $i = 0; i < 2^{32}; i = i + 1$ **do**   ▷ For each line of $\mathcal{T}_{z_0}$ and $\mathcal{T}_{z_1}$
19:                 **if** there is a collision pair with indexes (i_0, i_1) and $i_0 \neq i_1$ **then**
20:                     $c_{z_0}^{i_1} \leftarrow C_{z_0}[i_1], c_{z_1}^{i_0} \leftarrow C_{z_1}[i_0]$ ▷ $(c_{z_0}^{i_0}, c_{z_1}^{i_1})$ and $(c_{z_0}^{i_1}, c_{z_1}^{i_0})$ are dual pairs
21:                     **if** $c_{z_0}^{i_1} \oplus c_{z_1}^{i_0} \in M_k$ **then**   ▷ $(c_{z_0}^{i_1}, c_{z_1}^{i_0})$ is also collided
22:                         $\Delta \leftarrow \delta$
23:                     **end if**
24:                 **end if**
25:             **end for**
26:         **end for**
27:     **end for**
28:     **return** Δ
29: **end procedure**

Algorithm 2. Remove wrong δ

1: **procedure** REMOVE(Δ, z_0, z_1)
2:     **for** $\delta \in \Delta$ **do**
3:         **if** $\delta \oplus z_1 \oplus z_2 \notin \Delta$ **then**
4:             Remove δ from Δ
5:         **end if**
6:     **end for**
7:     **return** Δ
8: **end procedure**

Line 20. $(c_{z_0}^i, c_{z_1}^j)$ and $(c_{z_1}^i, c_{z_0}^j)$ are dual pairs, then we need to check if $c_{z_1}^i \oplus c_{z_0}^j \in M_k$.

Determine the Size of $A_{z_0,\delta}$ And $A_{z_1,\delta}$. For $A_{z_0,\delta}$ and $A_{z_1,\delta}$ with 2^N elements, we can obtain 2^{2N} pairs (p, p') by choosing $p \in A_{z_0,\delta}$ and $p' \in A_{z_1,\delta}$. By exchanging the first diagonal, we get 2^{2N-1} pair-of-pairs such as $(p, p', \hat{p}, \hat{p}')$.

For 5-round AES, these 2^{2N-1} pair-of-pairs can be regarded as 2^{2N-1} Bernoulli trials, and the number of right pair-of-pairs should obey Binomial distribution $\mathcal{B}(2^{2N-1}, 2^{-54})$ when δ is right. Otherwise, it will obey $\mathcal{B}(2^{2N-1}, 2^{-62})$. Let N_r and N_w be the number of right pair-of-pairs for right and wrong δ, respectively.

For right δ,

$$Pr(N_r \geq 1) = 1 - Pr(N_r = 0) = 1 - (1 - 2^{-54})^{2^{2N-1}} \approx 1 - exp(-2^{2N-1-54}).$$

For wrong δ,

$$Pr(N_w \geq 1) = 1 - Pr(N_w = 0) = 1 - (1 - 2^{-62})^{2^{2N-1}} \approx 1 - exp(-2^{2N-1-62}).$$

When we take $N = 29$, $Pr(N_r \geq 1) \approx 0.9997$ while $Pr(N_w \geq 1) \approx 0.0308$, which means we can distinguish the right δ from the wrong δ.

Determining the Exact $k_{0,1} \oplus k_{3,0}$. Either of the right δ including $\delta = k_{0,1} \oplus k_{3,0}$ and $\delta = k_{0,1} \oplus k_{3,0} \oplus z_0 \oplus z_1$ will bring at least one right pair-of-pair with probability about 0.9997. Therefore, they will be both returned by Algorithm 1 with probability $0.9997^2 \approx 0.9994$. At the same time, the probability for a wrong δ being recommended is 0.0308. For all the $2^8 - 2$ wrong δ, on average there will be $(2^8 - 2) \times 0.0308 \approx 8$ wrong δ which are also recommended. All the δ candidates are inserted into a set Δ, which is returned by Algorithm 1 finally.

To remove the wrong δ from Δ, we XOR $z_0 \oplus z_1$ with each value in Δ. For right δ, $\delta \oplus z_0 \oplus z_1$ should be also in Δ in a high probability (0.9994) while for wrong δ, the probability is about 2^{-8}. The method of removing wrong δ is shown in Algorithm 2.

Now the set Δ contains only $k_{0,1} \oplus k_{3,0}$ and $k_{0,1} \oplus k_{3,0} \oplus z_0 \oplus z_1$. To determine the exact right key byte, we have to call Algorithm 1 and Algorithm 2 again with (z_2, z_3) where $z_2 \oplus z_3 \neq z_0 \oplus z_1$. With $\Delta' = \{k_{0,1} \oplus k_{3,0}, k_{0,1} \oplus k_{3,0} \oplus z_2 \oplus z_3\}$ returned, we can easily determine the right $k_{0,1} \oplus k_{3,0}$ by comparing Δ and Δ'. Therefore we recover one byte key information with $0.9994^2 \approx 0.9988$ success probability. The process is illustrated in Algorithm 3.

The procedure RecoverKeyByte(r, c) (Algorithm 3) can be used to recover $k_{r,c} \oplus k_{r+1,c+1}$[4]. Since the equal bytes in MC matrix are all adjacent, for the i-th diagonal of the key state, we can recover $k_{0,i} \oplus k_{1,i+1}$, $k_{1,i+1} \oplus k_{2,i+2}$, $k_{2,i+2} \oplus k_{3,i+3}$ and $k_{3,i+3} \oplus k_{0,i}$. However, from any three out of the four values we can derive the remaining one, which means we can recover three bytes of useful key information for one diagonal. For the four diagonals of key state, we can recover 12 bytes of key information, i.e. we can get the secret key up to 2^{32} variants.

---

[4] In this paper, the addition of indexes are modulo 4.

Algorithm 3. Recover the real key $k_{r,c} \oplus k_{r+1,c+1}$ (Property 1)

1: **procedure** RECOVERKEYBYTE(r, c) ▷ Recover $k_{r,c} \oplus k_{r+1,c+1}$ with 99.88%
      probability
2:     Allocate z_0, z_1, z_2, z_3 s.t. $z_0 \oplus z_1 \neq z_2 \oplus z_3$
3:     $\Delta_0 \leftarrow \text{CORE}(z_0, z_1, r, c)$
4:     **if** $|\Delta_0| == 0$ **then**
5:         **return** $\bot$
6:     **else**
7:         $\Delta_0 \leftarrow \text{REMOVE}(\Delta_0, z_0, z_1)$
8:     **end if**
9:     $\Delta_1 \leftarrow \text{CORE}(z_2, z_3, r, c)$
10:     **if** $|\Delta_1| == 0$ **then**
11:         **return** $\bot$
12:     **else**
13:         $\Delta_1 \leftarrow \text{REMOVE}(\Delta_1, z_0, z_1)$
14:     **end if**
15:     **if** Δ_0, Δ_1 have the same value **then**
16:         **return** $\delta \leftarrow (\Delta_0, \Delta_1)$ ▷ Right $k_{r,c} \oplus k_{r+1,c+1}$ must lie in both set
17:     **else**
18:         **return** $\bot$
19:     **end if**
20: **end procedure**

Data Complexity. From Algorithm 1, for every $\delta \in \mathbb{F}_{2^8}$ we use four sets $A_{z_i, \delta}$ for $i = 0, 1, 2, 3$ each with 2^{29} plaintexts. Therefore we need $2^{29} \times 2^8 \times 4 = 2^{39}$ chosen plaintexts to recover one byte key. In order to recover 12 key bytes, the total data complexity is $2^{39} \times 12 \approx 2^{42.6}$ chosen plaintexts.

Computation Complexity. Firstly, we evaluate the complexity of Algorithm 1. For each possible $\delta \in \mathbb{F}_{2^8}$ we encrypt two sets $A_{z_0, \delta}$ and $A_{z_1, \delta}$ each with 2^{29} plaintexts, this operation needs $2^{29} \times 2 = 2^{30}$ 5-round encryptions. After obtaining 2^{30} ciphertexts, we insert them into C_{z_0} and C_{z_1} with 2^{30} table-lookups. To insert all the ciphertexts to T_{z_0} and T_{z_1}, we need 2^{30} table-lookups again. Then we compare each line of T_{z_0} and T_{z_1} to find collision pairs, it requires $2 \times 2^{32} = 2^{33}$ table-lookups. For the two sets $A_{z_0, \delta}$ and $A_{z_1, \delta}$ each with 2^{29} chosen plaintexts, on average we can obtain $2^{29} \times 2^{29} \times 2^{-32} = 2^{26}$ collision pairs. Once we find a collision pair $(c_{z_0}^i, c_{z_1}^j)$, we need a time of XOR to check whether $(c_{z_1}^i, c_{z_0}^j)$ is collided. These memory operations above need about 2^{33} table-lookups. Considering we have four possible M_k, the whole memory operations cost 2^{35} table-lookups. We use the convention that 100 times of table look-ups are equivalent to one time 5-round encryption. Hence, encrypting the plaintexts is dominant in the time complexity, which requires 2^{30} 5-round encryptions for each δ.

To determine the exact one byte information of key (Algorithm 3), the time complexity is $2^8 \times 2 \times 2^{30} = 2^{39}$ 5-round encryptions. Recovering 12 bytes key requires $2^{39} \times 12 \approx 2^{42.6}$ times of 5-round encryption.

Memory Complexity. We allocate 2 sequence tables with size 2^{29} and 2 hash tables with size 2^{32}. Since these tables can be reused, the total memory complexity is about $2^{32} \times 2 + 2^{29} \times 2 \approx 2^{33}$ 128-bit blocks.

Practical Verification. Using C/C++ implementation, we practically verified our key-recovery attack on a small-scale variant of the AES as presented in [5]. The block size of the small-scale AES is 64 bits, and each word is a 4-bit nibble in the state matrix. We simply recover one byte of the secret key XOR in our experiment. The experimental result supports our theory.[5]

4 Improved Key-Recovery Attack Based on Property 2

Similar to the exchange attack based on Property 1, we can also combine Property 2 of MC matrix with exchange attack to realize the key recovery attack with a secret S-Box. To exploit Property 2, we focus on another subspace S_1' that two plaintexts $p, p' \in D_I, I = \{0, 1\}$ should fall into after the first round encryption.

$$S_1' \triangleq \left\{ b \oplus \begin{bmatrix} a_1 & 0 & 0 & 0 \\ 0 & 0 & 0 & 0 \\ 0 & a_3 & 0 & 0 \\ a_2 & a_4 & 0 & 0 \end{bmatrix} \middle| a_1, a_2, a_3, a_4, b \in \mathbb{F}_{2^8} \right\}. \tag{6}$$

If we exchange the first diagonal between p and p', it is equivalent to exchange the first column between $R(p)$ and $R(p')$. Since $R(p), R(p') \in S_1'$, it is also equivalent to exchange the first and the fourth diagonals between $R(p)$ and $R(p')$.

Details. Property 2 of MC says that three elements in each row can be XORed to zero. If the input difference of the four bytes of MC has three equal values and the remaining one value is zero, the output difference will have two zero-difference byte with probability 1. Without loss of generality, we assume the input difference is $[a, a, a, 0]^T$, then

$$\begin{bmatrix} 02 & 03 & 01 & 01 \\ 01 & 02 & 03 & 01 \\ 01 & 01 & 02 & 03 \\ 03 & 01 & 01 & 02 \end{bmatrix} \times \begin{bmatrix} a \\ a \\ a \\ 0 \end{bmatrix} = \begin{bmatrix} 0 \\ 0 \\ 2a \\ 3a \end{bmatrix} \tag{7}$$

It can be seen that there are two zero-difference values in the output difference with probability 1. Then if the input difference of MC is really the pattern such as $[a, a, a, 0]^T$ for any $a \in \mathbb{F}_{2^8} \backslash \{0\}$. To achieve it, we define the set $A_{w, \delta_1, \delta_2}$ as follows,

$$A_{w, \delta_1, \delta_2} \triangleq \left\{ a \oplus \begin{bmatrix} y_1 & w & 0 & 0 \\ 0 & y_2 & w \oplus \delta_1 & 0 \\ 0 & 0 & y_3 & w \oplus \delta_2 \\ 0 & 0 & 0 & y_4 \end{bmatrix} \middle| \forall y_0, y_1, y_2, y_3 \in \mathbb{F}_{2^8} \right\} \tag{8}$$

$$\text{where } w, \delta_1, \delta_2 \in \mathbb{F}_{2^8}.$$

---

[5] https://github.com/anxin19/5-round-AES-keyrecoveryattack.git.

We choose two different plaintexts $p \in A_{w_0,\delta_1,\delta_2}, p' \in A_{w_1,\delta_1,\delta_2}$. Let the key bytes XORed with $p_{0,1}, p_{1,2}, p_{2,3}$ (Resp. $p'_{0,1}, p'_{1,2}, p'_{2,3}$) are $k_{0,1}, k_{1,2}, k_{2,3}$, respectively. After the operation $\mathsf{f} = \mathsf{SR} \circ \mathsf{SB} \circ \mathsf{AK}$, the difference between the second column of $\mathsf{f}(p)$ and $\mathsf{f}(p')$ is

$$\mathsf{f}(p)_{C_1} \oplus \mathsf{f}(p')_{C_1} = \begin{bmatrix} \text{S-Box}(w_0 \oplus k_{0,1}) \oplus \text{S-Box}(w_1 \oplus k_{0,1}) \\ \text{S-Box}(w_0 \oplus \delta_1 \oplus k_{1,2}) \oplus \text{S-Box}(w_1 \oplus \delta_1 \oplus k_{1,2}) \\ \text{S-Box}(w_0 \oplus \delta_2 \oplus k_{2,3}) \oplus \text{S-Box}(w_1 \oplus \delta_2 \oplus k_{2,3}) \\ 0 \end{bmatrix} \quad (9)$$

To meet the condition shown in Eq. 7, the following equation should be satisfied (denote S-Box$(\cdot)$ by S$(\cdot)$ for short),

$$\begin{cases} \text{S}(w_0 \oplus k_{0,1}) \oplus \text{S}(w_1 \oplus k_{0,1}) = \text{S}(w_0 \oplus \delta_1 \oplus k_{1,2}) \oplus \text{S}(w_1 \oplus \delta_1 \oplus k_{1,2}) \\ \text{S}(w_0 \oplus k_{0,1}) \oplus \text{S}(w_1 \oplus k_{0,1}) = \text{S}(w_0 \oplus \delta_2 \oplus k_{2,3}) \oplus \text{S}(w_1 \oplus \delta_2 \oplus k_{2,3}) \end{cases} \quad (10)$$

Since the S-Box is a secret permutation, there can be only four kinds of solutions,

$$\begin{aligned} (\delta_1, \delta_2) &= (k_{0,1} \oplus k_{1,2}, k_{0,1} \oplus k_{2,3}) \text{ or} \\ (\delta_1, \delta_2) &= (k_{0,1} \oplus k_{1,2}, w_0 \oplus w_1 \oplus k_{0,1} \oplus k_{2,3}) \text{ or} \\ (\delta_1, \delta_2) &= (w_0 \oplus w_1 \oplus k_{0,1} \oplus k_{1,2}, k_{0,1} \oplus k_{2,3}) \text{ or} \\ (\delta_1, \delta_2) &= (w_0 \oplus w_1 \oplus k_{0,1} \oplus k_{1,2}, w_0 \oplus w_1 \oplus k_{0,1} \oplus k_{2,3}) \end{aligned} \quad (11)$$

Similar with the attack in Sect. 3, we let (δ_1, δ_2) run through all possible values in $F_{2^8} \times F_{2^8}$. There will be at least four values of (δ_1, δ_2) that make Eq. 10 hold. We call the four (δ_1, δ_2) in Eq. 11 **right** (δ_1, δ_2) and the other values **wrong** (δ_1, δ_2). For right (δ_1, δ_2), the probability of $R(p^1) \oplus R(p^2) \in S'_1$ is 2^{-16} while for wrong (δ_1, δ_2) the probability is still 2^{-32}. Combining with Theorem 1, we conclude the following proposition.

Proposition 2. *Let $p \in A_{w_0,\delta_1,\delta_2}$ and $p' \in A_{w_1,\delta_1,\delta_2}$. $(\hat{p}, \hat{p}')$ is generated by exchanging the first diagonal between p and p'. If (δ_1, δ_2) is right, for certain M_J with $|J| = 3$,*

$$Pr(R^5(p) \oplus R^5(p') \in M_J \wedge R^5(\hat{p}) \oplus R^5(\hat{p}') \in M_J) \approx 2^{-46},$$

while for wrong (δ_1, δ_2),

$$Pr(R^5(p) \oplus R^5(p') \in M_J \wedge R^5(\hat{p}) \oplus R^5(\hat{p}') \in M_J) \approx 2^{-62}.$$

The proof of Proposition 2 is similar to the Proposition 1, we omit it here.

Finding (δ_1, δ_2) Candidates. We can also take advantage of Proposition 2 to find the right (δ_1, δ_2) which implies the key byte information $k_{0,1} \oplus k_{1,2}$ and $k_{0,1} \oplus k_{2,3}$. The process for finding (δ_1, δ_2) candidates is similar to Algorithm 1 except we need to guess two key byte difference. The process is illustrated in Algorithm 4.

Determine the Size of $A_{w_0,\delta_1,\delta_2}$ And $A_{w_1,\delta_1,\delta_2}$. If the size of $A_{w_0,\delta_1,\delta_2}$ and $A_{w_1,\delta_1,\delta_2}$ are both 2^M, we can obtain 2^{2M} pairs of (p,p') by choosing $p \in A_{w_0,\delta_1,\delta_2}$ and $p' \in A_{w_1,\delta_1,\delta_2}$. By exchanging the first diagonal, we can get totally 2^{2M-1} pair-of-pairs such as $(p,p',\hat{p},\hat{p}')$. If $R^5(p)\oplus R^5(p') \in M_J$ and $R^5(\hat{p})\oplus R^5(\hat{p}') \in M_J$ for $|J| = 3$ hold at the same time, then we call such $(p,p',\hat{p},\hat{p}')$ a **right** pair-of-pair. Consider the number of right pair-of-pairs,
For right (δ_1,δ_2),

$$Pr(M_r \geq 1) = 1 - Pr(M_r = 0) = 1 - (1 - 2^{-46})^{2^{2M-1}} \approx 1 - exp(-2^{2M-1-46}).$$

For wrong (δ_1,δ_2),

$$Pr(M_w \geq 1) = 1 - Pr(M_w = 0) = 1 - (1 - 2^{-62})^{2^{2M-1}} \approx 1 - exp(-2^{2M-1-62}).$$

When we take $M = 25$, $Pr(M_r \geq 1) \approx 0.9997$ while $Pr(M_w \geq 1) \approx 0.0001$ which means we can distinguish the right (δ_1,δ_2) from the wrong ones.

Determining $k_{0,1} \oplus k_{1,2}$ and $k_{0,1} \oplus k_{2,3}$. In this attack, we also have a probability $1 - (1 - 0.0001)^{2^{16}-4} \approx 0.9986$ nearly close to 1 to return at least one wrong (δ_1,δ_2). On average, approximately $(2^{16} - 4) \times 0.0001 \approx 7$ wrong (δ_1,δ_2) will be returned. To remove the wrong (δ_1,δ_2) from Δ, we XOR $w_0 \oplus w_1$ with the two components of each value in Δ and check whether the result is in Δ or not as Algorithm 5. To determine the exact $(k_{0,1} \oplus k_{1,2}, k_{0,1} \oplus k_{2,3})$, we need to use additional two sets $A_{w_2,\delta_1,\delta_2}$ $A_{w_3,\delta_1,\delta_2}$ where $(w_0,w_1) \neq (w_2,w_3)$ with 2^{25} plaintexts and do the same. Finally, the probability that we succeed to recover the two key bytes with probability $0.9997^{4\times2} \approx 0.9976$. The process is illustrated in Algorithm 6 .

After we recover two key bytes information, we can take the same strategy to recover another different key byte information in the same diagonal. At last we can recover 12 key byte difference, i.e., we can get the entire secret key up to 2^{32} variants.

Data Complexity. According to Algorithm 4, for each (δ_1,δ_2) we use two sets $A_{w_0,\delta_1,\delta_2}$ and $A_{w_1,\delta_1,\delta_2}$ each with 2^{25} plaintexts. Additional two sets $A_{w_2,\delta_1,\delta_2}$ and $A_{w_3,\delta_1,\delta_2}$ are also required to find the exact two key byte information. Therefore, totally we need $2^{25} \times 2^{16} \times 2 \times 2 = 2^{43}$ chosen plaintexts to recover two key bytes. To find the 12 bytes key information, the total data complexity is about $2^{43} \times 8 = 2^{46}$.

Computation Complexity. Encrypting two sets with 2^{25} plaintexts we need $2^{25} \times 2 = 2^{26}$ 5-round encryption which is the donimant in the complexity of Algorithm 4. The total time complexity is about $2^{26} \times 2^{16} \times 2 \times 8 = 2^{46}$ 5-round encryption.

Memory Complexity. We allocate two sequence tables with size 2^{25} to store the two ciphertext sets and additionally 2 hash tables with size 2^{32}. The memory complexity is finally 2^{33} 128-bit blocks.

Algorithm 4. Finding (δ_1, δ_2) Candidates (Property 2)

1: **procedure** CORE$'(w_0, w_1, r, c)$ ▷ Return a set containing possible (δ_1, δ_2)
2:     **for** Each $(\delta_1, \delta_2) \in \mathbb{F}_{2^8} \times \mathbb{F}_{2^8}$ **do**
3:         Initialize 2 sequence tables $\mathcal{C}_{w_0}$ and $\mathcal{C}_{w_1}$, 1 table Δ
4:         Prepare two sets $A_{w_0, \delta_1, \delta_2}, A_{w_1, \delta_1, \delta_2}$ with 2^{25} plaintexts each as Eq. 8
5:         **for** $i = 0; i < 2^{25}; i = i + 1$ **do**
6:             **for** $j = 0; j < 2; j = j + 1$ **do**
7:                 $c_{w_j}^i \leftarrow R^5(p_{w_j}^i)$
8:                 $\mathcal{C}_{w_j}[i] \leftarrow c_{w_j}^i$ ▷ Push back $c_{w_j}^i$ into sequence table
9:             **end for**
10:         **end for**
11:         **for** $k = 0; k < 4; k = k + 1$ **do**
12:             Initialize 2 hash tables $\mathcal{T}_{w_0}, \mathcal{T}_{w_1}$
13:             **for** $i = 0; i < 2^{25}; i = i + 1$ **do**
14:                 **for** $j = 0; j < 2; j = j + 1$ **do**
15:                     $\mathcal{T}_{w_j}[\text{MC}^{-1}(c_{w_j}^i)_{ID_k}] \leftarrow \text{index}(c_{w_j}^i)$ ▷ Insert the index of $c_{w_j}^i$ into hash table
16:                 **end for**
17:             **end for**
18:             **for** $i = 0; i < 2^{32}; i = i + 1$ **do**
19:                 **if** there is a collision pair with indexes (i_0, i_1) and $i_0 \neq i_1$ **then**
20:                     $c_{w_0}^{i_1} \leftarrow C_{w_0}[i_1]$, $c_{w_1}^{i_0} \leftarrow C_{w_1}[i_0]$ ▷ $(c_{w_0}^{i_0}, c_{w_1}^{i_1})$ and $(c_{w_0}^{i_1}, c_{w_1}^{i_0})$ are dual pairs
21:                     **if** $c_{w_0}^{i_1} \oplus c_{w_1}^{i_0} \in M_k$ **then**   ▷ $(c_{w_0}^{i_1}, c_{w_1}^{i_0})$ is also collided
22:                         $\Delta \leftarrow \delta$
23:                     **end if**
24:                 **end if**
25:             **end for**
26:         **end for**
27:     **end for**
28:     **return** Δ
29: **end procedure**

Algorithm 5. Remove wrong (δ_1, δ_2)

1: **procedure** REMOVE$'(\Delta, w_0, w_1)$
2:     **for** each $(\delta_1, \delta_2) \in \Delta$ **do**
3:         **if** $(\delta_1 \oplus w_0 \oplus w_1, \delta_2 \oplus w_0 \oplus w_1) \notin \Delta$ **then**
4:             Remove$'$ (δ_1, δ_2) from Δ
5:         **end if**
6:     **end for**
7:     **return** Δ
8: **end procedure**

Algorithm 6. Recover $k_{r,c} \oplus k_{r+1,c+1}$ and $k_{r,c} \oplus k_{r+2,c+2}$ (Property 2)

```
1: procedure RECOVERKEYBYTE'(r, c, t)                    ▷ Recover k_{r,c} ⊕ k_{r+1,c+1} and
      k_{r,c} ⊕ k_{r+2,c+2} with 99.76% success probability
2:     Allocate w_0, w_1, w_2, w_3 s.t. w_0 ⊕ w_1 ≠ w_2 ⊕ w_3
3:     Δ_0 ← CORE'(w_0, w_1, r, c)
4:     if |Δ_0| == 0 then
5:        return ⊥                                                          ▷ Fail
6:     else
7:        Δ'_0 ← REMOVE'(Δ_0, w_0 ⊕ w_1)
8:     end if
9:     Δ_1 ← CORE'(w_2, w_3, r, c)
10:    if |Δ_1| == 0 then
11:       return ⊥
12:    else
13:       Δ'_1 ← REMOVE'(Δ_1, w_2 ⊕ w_3)
14:    end if
15:    if Δ'_0, Δ'_1 have the same value  then
16:       return (δ_1, δ_2) ← (Δ'_0, Δ'_1)        ▷ Right k_{r,c} ⊕ k_{r+1,c+1} and k_{r,c} ⊕ k_{r+2,c+2}
      must lie in both sets
17:    else
18:       return ⊥
19:    end if
20: end procedure
```

5   Conclusion

In this paper, we explore the impact of the MC coefficient property on the security of the AES variant with a secret S-Box. We provide two attacks based on Property 1 and Property 2 respectively and achieve the best record in terms of the complexity under chosen-plaintext scenario. Such attacks remind us to notice the choice of MC matrix for AES-like ciphers.

To our best knowledge, no previous attacks on the AES have taken advantage of other properties except the branch number of the MC matrix. It means that we may substitute any other MDS matrix free of Property 1 or 2^6 for the AES MC matrix without hazarding its security against other attacks. In [9], Grassi showed that about only 6.87% among all the MDS matrices have the two kinds of properties. Nevertheless, the choice of MC is still a difficult work since we should consider the performance of the cipher. The MC matrix of AES is already qualified for its pretty low weight, thus it is an interesting open question how to choose a proper MDS matrix without the particular coefficient property and achieve the same or even higher efficiency simultaneously.

Acknowledgement. We thank the anonymous reviewers for their valuable comments. This work is supported by the National Key Research and Development Project No. 2018YFA0704702, Major Scientific and Technological Innovation Project of Shandong

---

[6] Its inverse matrix should not have Property 1 or 2.

Province, China under Grant No. 2019JZZY010133, National Natural Science Foundation of China (NSFC) under Grant No. 61572293, 61502276 and 61692276.

References

1. Bardeh, N.G., Rønjom, S.: The exchange attack: how to distinguish six rounds of AES with 288.2 chosen plaintexts. In: Galbraith, S., Moriai, S. (eds.) ASIACRYPT 2019, Part III. LNCS, vol. 11923, pp. 347–370. Springer, Cham (2019). https://doi.org/10.1007/978-3-030-34618-8_12
2. Bardeh, N.G., Rønjom, S.: Practical attacks on reduced-round AES. In: Buchmann, J., Nitaj, A., Rachidi, T. (eds.) AFRICACRYPT 2019. LNCS, vol. 11627, pp. 297–310. SPringer, Cham (2019). https://doi.org/10.1007/978-3-030-23696-0_15
3. Biham, E., Shamir, A.: Differential cryptanalysis of DES-like cryptosystems. In: Menezes, A.J., Vanstone, S.A. (eds.) CRYPTO 1990. LNCS, vol. 537, pp. 2–21. Springer, Heidelberg (1991). https://doi.org/10.1007/3-540-38424-3_1
4. Bogdanov, A., Rijmen, V.: Linear hulls with correlation zero and linear cryptanalysis of block ciphers. Des. Codes Crypt. **70**(3), 369–383 (2012). https://doi.org/10.1007/s10623-012-9697-z
5. Cid, C., Murphy, S., Robshaw, M.J.B.: Small scale variants of the AES. In: Gilbert, H., Handschuh, H. (eds.) FSE 2005. LnCS, vol. 3557, pp. 145–162. Springer, Heidelberg (2005). https://doi.org/10.1007/11502760_10
6. Cui, T., Sun, L., Chen, H., Wang, M.: Statistical integral distinguisher with multi-structure and its application on AES. In: Pieprzyk, J., Suriadi, S. (eds.) ACISP 2017, Part I. LNCS, vol. 10342, pp. 402–420. Springer, Cham (2017). https://doi.org/10.1007/978-3-319-60055-0_21
7. Daemen, J., Rijmen, V.: The Design of Rijndael: AES - The Advanced Encryption Standard. Information Security and Cryptography. Springer, Heidelberg (2002). https://doi.org/10.1007/978-3-662-04722-4
8. Daemen, J., Rijmen, V.: Security of a wide trail design. In: Menezes, A., Sarkar, P. (eds.) INDOCRYPT 2002. LNCS, vol. 2551, pp. 1–11. Springer, Heidelberg (2002). https://doi.org/10.1007/3-540-36231-2_1
9. Grassi, L.: Mixcolumns properties and attacks on (round-reduced) AES with a single secret S-box. In: Smart, N. (ed.) CT-RSA 2018. LNCS, vol. 10808, pp. 243–263. Springer, Cham (2018). https://doi.org/10.1007/978-3-319-76953-0_13
10. Grassi, L., Rechberger, C., Rønjom, S.: Subspace trail cryptanalysis and its applications to AES. IACR Trans. Symmetric Cryptol. **2016**(2), 192–225 (2016)
11. Grassi, L., Rechberger, C., Rønjom, S.: A new structural-differential property of 5-round AES. In: Coron, J.S., Nielsen, J. (eds.) EUROCRYPT 2017, Part II. LNCS, vol. 10211, pp. 289–317. Springer, Cham (2017). https://doi.org/10.1007/978-3-319-56614-6_10
12. Hu, K., Cui, T., Gao, C., Wang, M.: Towards key-dependent integral and impossible differential distinguishers on 5-round AES. In: Cid, C., Jacobson Jr., M. (eds.) SAC 2018. LNCS, vol. 11349, pp. 139–162. Springer, Cham (2018). https://doi.org/10.1007/978-3-030-10970-7_7
13. Matsui, M.: Linear cryptanalysis method for DES cipher. In: Helleseth, T. (ed.) EUROCRYPT 1993. LNCS, vol. 765, pp. 386–397. Springer, Heidelberg (1994). https://doi.org/10.1007/3-540-48285-7_33
14. Rønjom, S., Bardeh, N.G., Helleseth, T.: Yoyo tricks with AES. ASIACRYPT 2017, Part I. LNCS, vol. 10624, pp. 217–243. Springer, Cham (2017). https://doi.org/10.1007/978-3-319-70694-8_8

15. Sun, B., Liu, M., Guo, J., Qu, L., Rijmen, V.: New insights on AES-Like SPN ciphers. In: Robshaw, M., Katz, J. (eds.) CRYPTO 2016, Part I. LNCS, vol. 9814, pp. 605–624. Springer, Heidelberg (2016). https://doi.org/10.1007/978-3-662-53018-4_22
16. Tiessen, T., Knudsen, L.R., Kölbl, S., Lauridsen, M.M.: Security of the AES with a secret S-box. In: Leander, G. (ed.) FSE 2015. LNCS, vol. 9054, pp. 175–189. Springer, Heidelberg (2015). https://doi.org/10.1007/978-3-662-48116-5_9

New Results on the SymSum Distinguisher on Round-Reduced SHA3

Sahiba Suryawanshi[✉], Dhiman Saha, and Satyam Sachan

de.ci.phe.red Lab, Department of Electrical Engineering and Computer Science,
Indian Institute of Technology Bhilai, Sejbahar, India
{sahibas,dhiman,satyams}@iitbhilai.ac.in

Abstract. In ToSC 2017 Saha *et al.* demonstrated an interesting property of SHA3 based on higher-order vectorial derivatives which led to self-symmetry based distinguishers referred to as SymSum and bettered the complexity w.r.t the well-studied ZeroSum distinguisher by a factor of 4. This work attempts to take a fresh look at this distinguisher in the light of the linearization technique developed by Guo *et al.* in Asiacrypt 2016. It is observed that the efficiency of SymSum against ZeroSum drops from 4 to 2 for any number of rounds linearized. This is supported by theoretical proofs. SymSum augmented with linearization can penetrate up to two more rounds as against the classical version. In addition to that, one more round is extended by inversion technique on the final hash values. The combined approach leads to distinguishers up to 9 rounds of SHA3 variants with a complexity of only 2^{64} which is better than the equivalent ZeroSum distinguisher by the factor of 2. To the best of our knowledge this is the best distinguisher available on this many rounds of SHA3.

Keywords: SHA3 · Keccak · Distinguisher · SymSum · ZeroSum · Higher-order derivatives

1   Introduction

The hash function Keccak [3] which went on to be adopted as the SHA3 [18] standard is one of the most extensively studied hash algorithms. While finding pre-images and collisions constitute the primary analysis strategies of a hash function, the paradigm of devising distinguishers give insight into the non-randomness of the construction. Further, it has been evidenced by numerous results in contemporary literature where distinguishers have been exploited to mount collision and pre-image attacks thereby amplifying their scope and impact. In case of SHA3, one of most investigated distinguisher is the ZeroSum distinguisher which is based on the fundamental result of higher-order derivatives that the $(d+1)^{th}$ derivative of a d–degree function leads to a zero function. This translates to obtaining a zero XOR-Sum for 2^{d+1} computations of a vectorial function. The main research is in the direction of tight-bounding the value of d which automatically leads to reduction in complexity of computing the ZeroSum.

© Springer Nature Switzerland AG 2020
A. Nitaj and A. Youssef (Eds.): AFRICACRYPT 2020, LNCS 12174, pp. 132–151, 2020.
https://doi.org/10.1007/978-3-030-51938-4_7

Most of the results have been reported on the internal permutation Keccak-f and/or Keccak-p. In 2009, Aumasson and Meier [1] introduced ZeroSum distinguisher on Keccak-f which penetrated up to 16 rounds by leveraging on the *inside-out* strategy. In 2011, Plasencia *et al.* [15] introduce 4 round distinguisher for Hash function rather than internal permutation function, and also give a 2 round pre-image attack and 3 round near-collision attack on SHA3-224 and SHA3-256 variants. The same year, Boura *et al.* [4] improvise ZeroSum distinguisher. They present ZeroSum distinguisher and high order differential derivative for the full Keccak-p permutation. In 2012, Duan *et al.* [6] state an advanced ZeroSum distinguisher full round Keccak-f with 2^{1579} complexity. The same year, Duc *et al.* [7] present the Unaligned Rebound Attack for 8 round distinguisher with lesser complexity. In 2013, Morawiecki *et al.* [14] present rotational cryptanalysis. It allows a preimage attack on 4-round Keccak with complexity 2^{506}. It also states distinguisher on 5 rounds Keccak-f[1600] permutation with 2^{15} complexity. In 2014 Das *et al.* analyze differential propagation properties of Keccak furthermore uses for 6 round Distinguisher with 2^{52} complexity. In 2015, Jean *et al.* [10] produce internal differential boomerang distinguisher. They generate boomerang pairs and analyze the differential property. Their distinguisher depends on round constant. So, according to where permutation starts, their query complexity varies. For Keccak-f permutation, when it starts at 0 round, with complexity 2^5, they distinguish up to 6 rounds, and with 2^{13} complexity to 7 rounds. Similarly, when permutation begins with 3rd round with complexity $2^{10.3}$, they distinguish up to 7 rounds, and with $2^{18.3}$ complexity to 8 rounds. Same year, Dinur *et al.* [5] proposed a Cube attack like a cryptanalysis technique that includes algebraic and structural analysis, which contains key recovery and MAC forgery, practical up to 6 rounds and theoretical to 9 rounds of Keccak. In 2016, Guo *et al.* [8] introduce the linearization technique called Linear Structure. It permits linearization up to 3 rounds of Keccak. It extends the ZeroSum distinguisher of Keccak-p permutation up to 15 rounds and pre-image attack up to 4 rounds.

It is evidenced from the above discussion that most of the results have been reported on Keccak-p that few on the hash function SHA3. Moreover, only a few of the distinguishers on Keccak-p can be extended on to any SHA3 variant itself. However, in 2017, Saha *et al.* [17] introduced a new distinguisher called SymSum which examines a symmetric property of the output-sum of SHA3 when evaluated on symmetric inputs. These distinguishers penetrate up to 9 rounds and theoretically achieve a 4-fold improvement over ZeroSum in terms of complexity. The prime observation was the position of the nonlinear operation χ in the sequence of sub-operations in the Keccak-p round function. Same year, Huang *et al.* [9] improvise a Cube attack named Conditional Cube attack, impose some conditions on specific bits and use Mixed Integer Linear Programming (MILP) to construct conditional cubes with complexity 2^{33}, 7 round cube distinguisher builds on SHA3-224. The same year, Qiao *et al.* [16] introduce a pre-image attack up to 5 rounds, by linearize all S-box at first round and form a 3 round differential trail for SHAKE128 and SHA3-224. They put some conditions so that it satisfies for linearization and differential trail. Same year, Li *et al.* [12] proposed a cross-linear structure for a pre-image attack. They constructed a cross-linear structure for KECCAK [400] and found a pre-image. The complexity of their attack is 2^{150} for 3 round SHA3-256. In 2019, Li *et al.* [13] proposed a pre-image attack referred to as the Allocating Approach on 4 round SHA3-256.

In this work, we investigate the SymSum property introduced by Saha *et al.* further and try to augment with observations by Guo *et al.* in their work on linear structures. In particular, we achieve a one/two-round advantage by combining SymSum with linear structures. However, the structures we use slightly differ from the ones reported in [8] since we do not have any requirement of keeping χ^{-1} to be linear. This is attributed to the fact that we are mounting the attack on the hash-function and hence cannot leverage the inside-out technique. Consequently, we can relax the constraints that were imposed for the same. Further, we show a simple trick to gain one more round by just inverting[1] the last round χ before computing the output-sum. Using all these techniques, we are able to mount SymSum distinguishers on up to 9-rounds of SHA3 variants with a complexity of only 2^{64}. We show that SymSum loses its 4-fold advantage over ZeroSum when augmented with linear structures and also furnish a proof for the same. The present SymSum distinguishers still have a 2-fold advantage making them the best available distinguishers on SHA3 which are independent of the number (≥ 1) of rounds linearized. We validate most of claims by providing experimental evidence for some of the practically verifiable distinguishers. Our results are summarized in Table 1.

Table 1. Summary of the results reported

SHA3-variant	#Rounds	ZeroSum	SymSum	Remarks
SHA3-224	8	2^{65}	2^{64}	2R Linear
SHA3-256	7	2^{33}	2^{32}	2R Linear
SHA3-384	8	2^{33}	2^{32}	2R Linear + χ^{-1}
SHA3-512	8	2^{65}	2^{64}	1R Linear + χ^{-1}
SHAKE128	9	2^{65}	2^{64}	2R Linear + χ^{-1}
	10	2^{513}	2^{511}	χ^{-1}
SHAKE256	8	2^{33}	2^{32}	2R Linear + χ^{-1}
	9	2^{257}	2^{255}	χ^{-1}
	10	2^{513}	2^{511}	χ^{-1}

Organization. Rest of the paper is organized as follows. Section 2 gives a brief description of the SHA3 and SymSum distinguisher and linear structures of KECCAK-p. Section 3 provides proof of how the efficiency of SymSum reduces when we apply linearization. The new distinguishers introduced in this work are illustrated in Sect. 4. The experiments on round-reduced SHA3 to validate the claims are

---

[1] This applies to SHA3 variants where at least one entire plane is available from the hash value.

reported in Sect. 5. A discussion on all the devised distinguishers is furnished in
Sect. 6. Finally, concluding remarks are given in Sect. 7.

2 Preliminaries

In this section, we give a brief description of the SymSum distinguisher and the
idea of linear structure in Keccak-p.

2.1 The Keccak Hash Function

The Keccak structure follows Sponge [2] construction that applies fixed-length
permutation on variable-length input and maps to variable-length output. It
gives $\mathbb{F}_2^n$ length element output from $\mathbb{F}_2^m$ length input element where n and m
are of any length. The permutation applied on finite-state $b = r + c$ bits, where
r is rate and c is capacity. Here the finite state b of Sponge construction is
the width of Keccak-f permutation. The Sponge construction has 2 phases: the
absorption and squeezing phases. Firstly the input message M padded according
to the padding rule that makes input message after padding M' multiple of r
and breaks M' into $m_1, m_2, \ldots m_k$ each of size r. Initially, state b set to all $0's$
which is initialization vector (IV) and input of f is the XORed value of the first
input message block m_1 of size r and r bits of IV then the output of f is XORed
with next input message m_2 and input to f this will happen until all the message
blocks get processed this is absorption phase. The required output digest collects
on the squeezing phase. Suppose Z is the required digest. If $Z < r$ then, it takes
first Z bits of the output of absorbing phase, otherwise, if $Z > r$ then, it needs
to input to f and get more bits repeatedly until it gets Z bits output digest.
Finally, the output digest Z is the output of the Sponge function.

Keccak-p **Permutation:** There are 7 Keccak-f permutations which are denoted
by Keccak-$f[b, n_r]$, here n_r is the number of rounds and b is the width of Keccak-f
permutation. n_r depends on b and calculated as $n_r = 12 + 2l$, here $l = \log_2(\frac{b}{25})$
where $b \in \{25, 50, 100, 200, 400, 800, 1600\}$. Keccak-$f$ permutations states can
denote as $5 \times 5 \times w$ where $w = \frac{b}{25}$ such that $w \in \{1, 2, 4, 8, 16, 32, 64\}$. Here
we use Keccak-f [1600] that require 24 rounds. Each round has 5 mapping $R = \iota \circ \chi \circ \pi \circ \rho \circ \theta$.

θ: θ mapping is a linear operation that provides diffusion. In the θ mapping $A[x, y, z]$ XORed with parities of neighbouring 2 columns in the following
manner:

$$A[x, y, z] = A[x, y, z] \oplus P[(x - 1) \bmod\ 5, *, z] \oplus P[(x + 1) \bmod 5, *, (\bmod 64)]$$

Here $P[x, *, z]$ is parity of a column that can be calculated as:

$$P[x, *, z] = \oplus_{j=0}^{4} A[x, j, z]$$

ρ: ρ mapping is another linear operation that rotates each lane by some
predefined values. Here first column and last row represent y axis and x axis
values respectively.

$$A[x, y, z] = A[x, y, z_{\lll t}] \; for \; x, y = 0, ...4$$

Here $\lll$ is a bitwise rotation.

π: π mapping is another Linear operation which permutes on slices by inter-changing lanes as:

$$A[y, (2x + 3y) \; mod \; 5, z] = A[x, y, z] \; for \; x, y = 0, ...4, z = 0, ...63$$

χ: χ is the only Non-linear operation that operates on rows independently as:

$$A[x, y, z] = A[x, y, z] \oplus (\sim A[x + 1, y, z]) \wedge A[x + 2, y, z]$$

ι: A unique RC add to lane $A[0, 0]$ depend on round number.

$$A[0, 0, *] = A[0, 0, *] \oplus RC$$

2.2 SymSum Distinguishers on SHA3

In 2017, Saha *et al.* introduced an interesting algebraic property related to SPN round functions where the non-linear transformation preceded the round-constant addition. This was used to devise a new class of distinguishers referred to as SymSum. The basic result was that the round-constants could not influence the highest degree monomials which determined the upper-bound on the degree of a vectorial function. This helped them devise a round-constant independent function by computing a special type of derivative called the m–fold vectorial derivative. They further showed that the order of this derivative can be a factor of 4 less than the ZeroSum distinguisher which actually computes the m–fold simple derivatives. To verify this property, they used self-symmetric input states as inputs and the hypothesis was that the output sum across all hash values would also preserve the self-symmetry. Self-symmetry of KECCAK can be defined as the first 32 slices are identical to the last 32 slices of the KECCAK state as shown in Fig. 1. Here σ_1 and σ_2 are identical.

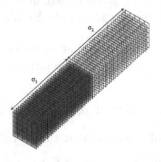

Fig. 1. Self-symmetric state of KECCAK [11]

For brevity, the main results are mentioned below, where TYPE-II as defined in [17] are monomials that are dependent on round-constants:

Lemma 1. *[17] For SPN round function $\mathcal{G}$, if the ordering of components is in such a way that the non-linear function precedes from round constant addition then $\mathcal{G}$ can express as: $\mathcal{G} = \mathcal{F} + C \times \mathcal{H}$ where $d^{\circ}\mathcal{G} = d^{\circ}\mathcal{F}$ and $d^{\circ}\mathcal{G} > d^{\circ}\mathcal{H}$ where $\mathcal{G}, \mathcal{F}, \mathcal{H} : \mathbb{F}_2^n \to \mathbb{F}_2^n$ and C is a constant.*

Theorem 1. *[17] The upper-bound on the degree of TYPE-II monomials is given by the following expression: $d^{\circ}\mathcal{F}_{s'}^q \leq d^{\circ}\mathcal{F}^q - d^{\circ}\mathcal{N}$.*

Lemma 2. *[17] The $(d^{\circ}\mathcal{F} - d^{\circ}\mathcal{N} + 1)$-fold vectorial derivative of $\mathcal{F}^q$, is a function that is independent of round constant.*

Here $d^{\circ}\mathcal{F}$, $d^{\circ}\mathcal{N}$ are the upper bounds on the degrees of function $\mathcal{G}$ and non-linear function $\mathcal{N}$ respectively and $\mathcal{F}^q$ is function after q rounds. Using the above mentioned lemmas the authors furnished a proof that SymSum distinguisher is better than ZeroSum distinguisher for SHA3 by a factor of 4.

2.3 Linear Structures

The idea of linearization as introduced by Guo *et al.* is basically a lane-wise restriction on the input space so as to handle the linear θ and non-linear χ operations of the KECCAK-p round function. The authors demonstrate linearization of the KECCAK-p permutation up to 3 rounds: 1 round backward and 2 rounds forward. It extends the ZeroSum distinguisher and also leads to new pre-image attacks. To understand the technique, one needs to look at the Boolean expression of the χ function. The primary observation is that if two consecutive variables never come together in a row then, then all output co-ordinate functions of χ become linear. The operation θ which relies on the column parity of spatially adjacent columns can be handled so that it does not diffuse the state by keeping the column parity constants across calls to KECCAK-p. The idea is captured in Fig. 2. As evident from the figure, to handle the effect of θ on the variables, the following condition is imposed where α is any constant:

$$A[1,0] \oplus A[1,1] \oplus A[1,2] \oplus A[1,3] \oplus A[1,4] = \alpha$$

This can be equivalently written as $A[1,4] = \bigoplus_{j=0}^{3} A[1,j] \oplus \alpha$. This results, in 1 round linearization of KECCAK with degree of input up to 256.

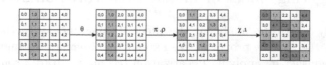

Fig. 2. KECCAK state configuration for 1-round linearization with degrees of freedom 256 [8]. Here white cells are constants, orange cells are variable with degree 1, and green cells have degree at most 1. (Color figure online)

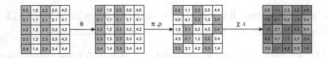

Fig. 3. KECCAK state configuration for linearization with degree of freedom 512 [8]

To increase the degree of freedom, it is possible to take variables at different columns as shown in Fig. 3 as $A[i,4] = \bigoplus_{j=0}^{3} A[i,j] \oplus \alpha_i$ where $i = 0, 2$, $j = 0, 1, 2, 3$.

For 2-round linearization, the input state should be taken as shown in the Fig. 4, here light gray cells and dark grey has value 0 and 1 respectively. To handle θ at 1 round variables need to satisfy the following condition.

$$A[1,0] \oplus A[1,1] \oplus A[1,2] \oplus A[1,3] = A[1,4] \oplus \texttt{0xf}\ldots\texttt{f}$$

$$A[2,0] \oplus A[2,1] \oplus A[2,2] \oplus A[2,3] = \texttt{0xf}\ldots\texttt{f}$$

Fig. 4. State configuration to handle χ at 2nd round [8]

At second-round θ, ρ, π permute variables, so to handle 2 round θ variables have to satisfy the following conditions.

$$A[2,0]_{\lll 62} = A[0,0] \oplus A[2,2]_{\lll 43}$$
$$A[2,1]_{\lll 6} = S[0,1]_{\lll 36} \oplus A[2,3]_{\lll 15}$$
$$A[2,2]_{\lll 43} = A[0,2]_{\lll 3}$$
$$A[2,3]_{\lll 15} = A[0,3]_{\lll 41} \oplus A[2,0]_{\lll 62}$$

3   Investigating Effect of Linear Structures on SymSum

Our first study constitutes analyzing the effect of using linear structures in conjunction with the SymSum property. We extend the ZeroSum distinguisher and SymSum distinguisher by applying linearization technique up to 2 rounds. However, we argue that because of linearization, the difference in complexities for obtaining SymSum and ZeroSum decreases from the factor of 4 to 2. We next try to furnish theoretical arguments to support this claim. Thus, we first need to look at a more general result that compares the behaviour of a SPN round function (as observed in [17]) with and without linearization. For the SPN round function without applying linear structures, the behaviour is described by Lemma 1. The following lemma captures the same while incorporating the effect of linearization.

Lemma 3. *For any SPN round function $\mathcal{G}$ iterated for n_r rounds, if $l_r(\leq n_r)$ rounds are linearized, the degrees of the linearized version $(\mathbb{G})$ and unlinearized versions $(\mathbb{G}')$ are related by the degree (λ) of the non-linear component function by the following relation:*

$$d°\mathbb{G} \leq \lambda^{l_r} \times d°\mathbb{G}' \ where \ \begin{cases} \mathbb{G} = \mathcal{G}^{n_r} \\ \mathbb{G}' = \mathcal{G}^{n_r - l_r} \circ \mathcal{G}'^{l_r} \\ \mathcal{G}' \leftarrow Linearized \ version \ of \ \mathcal{G} \end{cases}$$

Here $d°\mathbb{G}, d°\mathbb{G}'$ are the upper bounds on the degrees of $\mathbb{G}, \mathbb{G}'$ respectively.

Proof. Let us write down the degree of the unlinearized version $\mathbb{G}$. Since the degree grows exponentially (before asymptotically converging on the highest possible degree which is determined by the number of independent input variables) in the degree of the non-linear component, we can write the following expression:

$$\mathbb{G} = \mathcal{G} \circ \mathcal{G} \circ \mathcal{G} \circ \cdots n_r \ \text{times}$$
$$\implies d°\mathbb{G} \leq (d°\mathcal{G})^{n_r}$$
$$= \lambda^{n_r} \tag{1}$$

Now let us write the expression for the linearized version:

$$\mathbb{G}' = \{\mathcal{G} \circ \mathcal{G} \circ \mathcal{G} \circ \cdots (n_r - l_r) \ \text{times}\} \circ \{\mathcal{G}' \circ \mathcal{G}' \circ \mathcal{G}' \circ \cdots l_r \ \text{times}\}$$
$$\implies d°\mathbb{G}' \leq (d°\mathcal{G})^{n_r - l_r} \times (d°\mathcal{G}')^{l_r}$$
$$= \lambda^{n_r - l_r} \ [\because d°\mathcal{G}'^{l_r} = 1] \tag{2}$$

From Eq. 1 and Eq. 2 it follows that: $d°\mathbb{G} \leq \lambda^{l_r} \times d°\mathbb{G}'$.   □

With the above proof in place, we revisit Lemma 1 in the light of linearization. We argue that Lemma 1 still holds for the linearized version $\mathbb{G}'$ of $\mathbb{G}$. This implies that the degree of $\mathbb{G}'$ will be determined by monomials which are independent of round constants (TYPE-I) from monomials that involve round constants (TYPE-II). We use the same terminology as stated in [17] and redo the proof of Lemma 1.

Lemma 4. *Lemma 1 holds under linearization.*

Proof. Let us consider the SPN round function $(\mathcal{G})$ as stated above with the restriction that the non-linear operation precedes the round-constant addition (as required by Lemma 1). So, let $\mathcal{G} = \mathcal{C} \circ \mathcal{N} \circ \mathcal{L}$ where $\mathcal{C}$ represents the round constant addition, $\mathcal{N}$ is non-linear component, and $\mathcal{L}$ is the linear component. So for n_r rounds, $\mathbb{G}$ can be written as:

$$\mathbb{G} = (\mathcal{C}_{n_r} \circ \mathcal{N} \circ \mathcal{L}) \circ (\mathcal{C}_{n_r-1} \circ \mathcal{N} \circ \mathcal{L}) \circ \cdots \circ (\mathcal{C}_1 \circ \mathcal{N} \circ \mathcal{L})$$
$$= \left[(\mathcal{C}_{n_r} \circ \mathcal{N} \circ \mathcal{L}) \circ \cdots \circ (\mathcal{C}_2 \circ \mathcal{N} \circ \mathcal{L}) \circ \mathcal{C}_1 \right] \circ (\mathcal{N} \circ \mathcal{L}) \tag{3}$$

However, if *linear structures* are applied for l_r rounds then $\mathbb{G}'$ can be expressed as:

$$\mathbb{G}' = (\mathcal{C}_{n_r} \circ \mathcal{N} \circ \mathcal{L}) \circ (\mathcal{C}_{n_r-1} \circ \mathcal{N} \circ \mathcal{L}) \circ \cdots \circ (\mathcal{C}_{n_r-l_r} \circ \mathcal{N}_{n_r-l_r} \circ \mathcal{L}_{n_r-l_r})$$
$$\circ (\mathcal{C}_{l_r} \circ \mathcal{L}' \circ \mathcal{L}) \circ \cdots \circ (\mathcal{C}_1 \circ \mathcal{L}' \circ \mathcal{L})$$
$$= \left[(\mathcal{C}_{n_r} \circ \mathcal{N} \circ \mathcal{L}_q) \circ \cdots \circ (\mathcal{C}_{n_r-l_r} \circ \mathcal{N} \circ \mathcal{L}) \circ (\mathcal{C}_{l_r} \circ \mathcal{L}' \circ \mathcal{L}) \circ \cdots \circ \mathcal{C}_1 \right] \circ (\mathcal{L}' \circ \mathcal{L}) \tag{4}$$

Here $\mathcal{L}'$ is a linearized version of $\mathcal{N}$ thus $d^\circ \mathcal{L}'$ will be reduced by $(\lambda - 1)$. Due to Eq. (3) and (4), it can be observed that after 1 round, the round constant $\mathcal{C}_1$ has no effect of $\mathcal{N}$ (or $\mathcal{L}'$ in case of linearization). Now, using the strategy described in [17] to segregate monomials which are independent of round constants (**TYPE-I**) from monomials that involve round constants (**TYPE-II**) we can visualize any co-ordinate function of $\mathbb{G}'$ as $\mathcal{F}^{n_r}$:

$$\mathcal{F}^{n_r} = \mathcal{F}_{c'}^{n_r} \oplus \mathcal{F}_c^{n_r} \text{ where } \begin{cases} \textbf{TYPE-I} \in \mathcal{F}_{c'}^{n_r} \\ \textbf{TYPE-II} \in \mathcal{F}_c^{n_r} \end{cases}$$

(a) To Prove: $d^\circ \mathcal{F}_{c'}^m > d^\circ \mathcal{F}_c^m$ (Proof by induction)

Base case: Let $n_r = 1$ which implies $\mathbb{G} = \mathcal{G}^1 = \mathcal{C}_1 \circ \mathcal{N} \circ \mathcal{L}$,

However, we have to take into account the linearization. So let $l_r = 1$. Therefore $\mathbb{G}' = \mathcal{G}'^1 = \mathcal{C}_1 \circ \mathcal{L}' \circ \mathcal{L}$. Hence the degree of **TYPE-I** and **TYPE-II** monomials are:

$$d^\circ \mathcal{F}_{c'} = d^\circ (\mathcal{L}' \circ \mathcal{L}) = \lambda - (\lambda - 1) = 1$$
$$d^\circ \mathcal{F}_c = 0 \left[\because \mathcal{C}_1 \text{ is independent of } \mathcal{L}' \right]$$

Thus $d^\circ \mathcal{F}_{c'} > d^\circ \mathcal{F}_c$. Hence lemma hold for base condition i.e., at $n_r = 1$.

Inductive hypothesis: Let us assume the lemma hold for $n_r = m$ i.e., $d^\circ \mathcal{F}_{c'}^m > d^\circ \mathcal{F}_c^m$.

Inductive step: Let $n_r = m + 1$. $\mathcal{F}^{m+1} = \mathcal{C}^{m+1} \circ \mathcal{N} \circ \mathcal{L} \circ \mathcal{F}^m$

$$d^\circ \mathcal{F}_c^{m+1} \le d^\circ (\mathcal{N} \circ \mathcal{L}) \times d^\circ \mathcal{F}_c^m$$
$$< d^\circ (\mathcal{N} \circ \mathcal{L}) \times d^\circ \mathcal{F}_{c'}^m \left[\because d^\circ \mathcal{F}_{c'}^m > d^\circ \mathcal{F}_c^m \right]$$
$$\le d^\circ \mathcal{F}_{c'}^{m+1}$$

Hence, by induction, the lemma holds $\forall n_r \in \mathbb{N}$. $\qquad \square$

Our next claim is that the difference in the degrees of TYPE-I and TYPE-II monomials as stated by Saha *et al.* in [17] no longer holds as we linearize the SPN. For any value of $l_r \geq 1$, the following theorem holds instead. One can note that unlike [17], the following result is independent of the degree of the non-linear component.

Theorem 2. *With at least one round linearized, the upper-bound on the degree of TYPE-II monomials in terms of TYPE-I monomials is given by:*

$$d^\circ \mathcal{F}_c^{n_r} \leq d^\circ \mathcal{F}_{c'}^{n_r} - 1$$

Proof. We start by segregating the TYPE-II monomials further. The new sub-type is referred to as TYPE-III and represents a TYPE-II monomial which is independent of any variables and constitutes only constants terms as stated below:

$$\prod C_i \text{ where } C_i \text{ is any constant term}$$

Suppose our function is in the linear form up to l_r rounds ($l_r \geq 1$) then using notations used above:

$$\mathcal{G}'^{l_r} = (\mathcal{C}_{l_r} \circ \mathcal{L}' \circ \mathcal{L}) \circ (\mathcal{C}_{l_r-1} \circ \mathcal{L}' \circ \mathcal{L}) \circ \cdots \circ (\mathcal{C}_2 \circ \mathcal{L}' \circ \mathcal{L}) \circ (\mathcal{C}_1 \circ \mathcal{L}' \circ \mathcal{L})$$

Since there is no non-linear function, the degree of TYPE-I and TYPE-II monomials never change. Also for TYPE-II monomials, only TYPE-III monomials occur. Thus the degree of TYPE-I monomials and TYPE-II monomials should 1 and 0 (because of TYPE-III), respectively i.e., $d^\circ \mathcal{F}_c^{l_r} = 0$ and $d^\circ \mathcal{F}_{c'}^{l_r} = 1$. Now, we prove by induction.

Base Case: Let $n_r = l_r + 1$, i.e. $\mathbb{G}' = \mathcal{G} \circ \mathcal{G}'^{l_r}$ implying a single non-linear function and $d^\circ \mathcal{N} = \lambda$.

Now, TYPE-I monomials will reach the highest degree after the current round when λ TYPE-I monomials mix together under $\mathcal{N}$ in the current round. This final degree of TYPE-I is expressed as:

$$d^\circ \mathcal{F}_{c'}^{l_r+1} = \sum_{i=1}^{\lambda} [d^\circ \mathcal{F}_{c'}^{l_r}]_i$$

$$= 1 + 1 \cdots \lambda \text{ times} \quad [\because d^\circ \mathcal{F}_{c'}^{l_r} = 1]$$

$$= \lambda \tag{5}$$

Next, TYPE-II monomials reach the highest degree when $(\lambda - 1)$ TYPE-I monomials from $(\lambda - 1)$ co-ordinate functions mix with one TYPE-II monomial. Thus for TYPE-II monomials we have

$$d^\circ \mathcal{F}_c^{l_r+1} = \sum_{i=1}^{\lambda-1} [d^\circ \mathcal{F}_{c'}^{l_r}]_i + d^\circ \mathcal{F}_c^{l_r}$$

$$= \sum_{i=1}^{\lambda-1} 1 + 0 \quad [\because d^\circ \mathcal{F}_c^{l_r} = 0 \text{ (TYPE-III)} \quad d^\circ \mathcal{F}_{c'}^{l_r} = 1]$$

$$= \lambda - 1 \tag{6}$$

Hence, by Eq. (5) and (6) theorem holds for base case.

Inductive Hypothesis: Let us assume the theorem holds for $n_r = m$ rounds i.e.,

$$d^\circ \mathcal{F}_c^m \leq d^\circ \mathcal{F}_{c'}^m - 1$$

Inductive Step: Let $n_r = m+1$ then by Lemma 3 we have $d^\circ \mathcal{F}_{c'}^m \leq \lambda^{m-l_r}$ and $d^\circ \mathcal{F}_c^m \leq \lambda^{m-l_r} - 1$. Then by arguments similar to the base-case, we have degree of TYPE-I monomials as:

$$d^\circ \mathcal{F}_{c'}^{m+1} = \sum_{i=1}^{\lambda} \left[d^\circ \mathcal{F}_{c'}^m \right]_i$$

$$\leq \sum_{i=1}^{\lambda} \lambda^{m-l_r} = \lambda^{m-l_r+1} \qquad (7)$$

Similarly for TYPE-II monomials

$$d^\circ \mathcal{F}_c^{m+1} = \sum_{i=1}^{\lambda-1} \left[d^\circ \mathcal{F}_{c'}^m \right]_i + d^\circ \mathcal{F}_c^m$$

$$\leq \sum_{i=1}^{\lambda-1} \lambda^{m-l_r} + \lambda^{m-l_r} - 1$$

$$= (\lambda - 1)\lambda^{m-l_r} + \lambda^{m-l_r} - 1 = \lambda^{m-l_r+1} - 1$$

$$\leq d^\circ \mathcal{F}_{c'}^{m+1} - 1 \text{ [By Eq. 7]} \qquad (8)$$

Thus by principle of induction Theorem 2 holds $\forall n_r \in \mathbb{N}$. ☐

We now have the following corollary which forms the base of all distinguishers reported in this work. As one might realize this constitutes a deviation from the result reported in [17] as stated in Lemma 2.

Corollary 1. *With l_r linearized rounds $\left(\frac{d^\circ \mathbb{G}}{\lambda^{l_r}} \right)$-fold vectorial derivative of $\mathbb{G}$ is a function which is independent of round constants.*

The corollary easily follows from Lemma 3 and Theorem 2. Since linearized version $\mathcal{G}'$ of $\mathcal{G}$ has degree $\left(\frac{d^\circ \mathbb{G}}{\lambda^{l_r}} \right)$ and the maximum degree of TYPE-II monomials in $\mathcal{G}'$ is $\left(\frac{d^\circ \mathbb{G}}{\lambda^{l_r}} - 1 \right)$, so the $\left(\frac{d^\circ \mathbb{G}}{\lambda^{l_r}} \right)$-fold vectorial derivative of $\mathcal{G}$ will result in a round-constant independent function. Consequently, such a function would preserve the SymSum property as introduced in [17]. In the next section, we show how the above results are used to mount highly efficient and practical SymSum distinguishers on SHA3 variants.

4   Augmenting the SymSum Distinguisher

The SymSum property can be extended at varied number of rounds based on the augmentation strategies like prepending linear structures and appending the hash-inversion trick wherever applicable. This is captured by Fig. 5. In the subsequent sub-sections we explore these strategies that help us to reach highest number of rounds for some SHA3 variants.

Linear	Linear	Number of non-linear core-rounds	
Linear	Linear	Number of non-linear core-rounds	Hash Inverse
	Linear	Number of non-linear core-rounds	Hash Inverse
	Linear	Number of non-linear core-rounds	
		Number of non-linear core-rounds	Hash Inverse

Fig. 5. Various extension strategies to verify the SymSum property by augmenting 1-round, 2-round linear structures and the hash-inversion trick

4.1 Extending SymSum Using 1-Round Linearization and χ^{-1} Trick

To gain an advantage of 2 rounds for the SymSum distinguisher, we linearize the first round and perform $\chi^{-1} \circ \iota^{-1}$ on the output digest when applicable. The input set should satisfy the following conditions so that it linearizes 1 round and also satisfies the condition for SymSum distinguisher which constitutes giving self-symmetric inputs:

1. The input set is a set of inputs such that the first 32 slices of the state are the same as the last 32 slices
2. For linearization, input state has the restriction that $\forall A[i, j]$ where $i = 0, 2, \ j = 0, 1, 2, 3,$

$$A[i, 3] = \bigoplus_{j=0}^{2} A[i, j] \oplus \alpha_i \text{ for any constant } \alpha$$

0,0	1,0	2,0	3,0	4,0
0,1	1,1	2,1	3,1	4,1
0,2	1,2	2,2	3,2	4,2
0,3	1,3	2,3	3,3	4,3
0,4	1,4	2,4	3,4	4,4

0,0	1,0	2,0	3,0	4,0
0,1	1,1	2,1	3,1	4,1
0,2	1,2	2,2	3,2	4,2
0,3	1,3	2,3	3,3	4,3
0,4	1,4	2,4	3,4	4,4

(a) KECCAK state for 1-round linearization of SHAKE128 and SHA3-224

(b) Input state for 1-round linearization of SHAKE128

Fig. 6. Different slice configurations for SHA3

The χ^{-1} trick applies only to those variants of SHA3 which give at least one plane ofKECCAK state in the output hash value. Therefore, it is not applicable to SHA3-224 and SHA3-256 because they give 224 and 256 bits of hash value respectively which is less that 320 bits required for a full plane. The degree of freedom of this state will be 192 if we take the input state equivalent to the state shown in Fig. 6a. Therefore, after 1-round linearization and applying χ^{-1}

strategy, `SymSum` on `SHAKE128` can distinguish up to 9 rounds. For the other variants of `SHA3`, the input state is different because of the difference in size of capacity part. For instance, after computing the output sum for 4 rounds on `SHA3`, we get `SymSum` for 2^4 invocations. For the classical `SymSum` distinguisher, it is obtained at 2^{15} and 2^{14}. Therefore, the extended `SymSum` distinguisher has an advantage of 2 rounds, although the effectiveness reduces by the factor of 2.

4.2   Extension of `SymSum` Distinguisher up to 3 Rounds:

We now show the use of 2-round linear structures in conjunction with inverting the hash for the last round. For 2 round linearization we use the linear structure, for which we need to handle the θ, ρ, π, χ mappings of KECCAK. To handle the first round χ we take variables in 2 alternative columns so that no two variables come adjacent in χ operation, thus maintaining the linearity after the first round. We restrict other columns to 0 and/or 1, as shown in the Fig. 7 so that before χ in the second round no two adjacent lanes become variable. Additionally, because of the columns that have variables, constant values may change because of θ. To handle θ the following conditions need to be imposed:

$$A[0,0] \oplus A[0,1] \oplus A[0,2] \oplus A[0,3] = A[0,4] \oplus 0xff\ldots f$$
$$A[2,0] \oplus A[2,1] \oplus A[2,2] \oplus A[2,3] = 0xff\ldots f$$

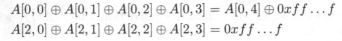

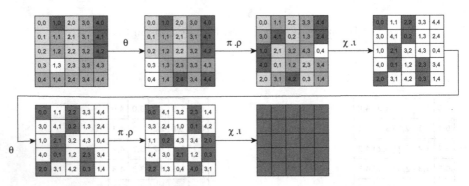

Fig. 7. KECCAK state for 2-round linearization with degree of freedom 64 [8]

Now, to linearize the second round we need to handle θ of second round. But for this the positions of the variables after first round χ need to be closely handles as would change due to ρ and π in the first round. Therefore to make two rounds linear the variables should satisfy the conditions as below:

$$A[2,0]_{\lll 62} = A[0,0] \oplus A[2,2]_{\lll 43}$$
$$A[2,1]_{\lll 6} = S[0,1]_{\lll 36} \oplus A[2,3]_{\lll 15}$$
$$A[2,2]_{\lll 43} = A[0,2]_{\lll 3}$$
$$A[2,3]_{\lll 15} = A[0,3]_{\lll 41} \oplus A[2,0]_{\lll 62}$$

It has been shown in [8] that the above system of equations has 128 degrees of freedom. However, for the SymSum property, we have the additional restriction of self-symmetric inputs which lead to revisiting the system of equations as below. The main idea is to rewrite the equations considering half of the state and then extend the solutions to the other half thereby always keeping the over-all solution self-symmetric.

$$
\begin{aligned}
A[0,0,k] \oplus A[0,1,k] \oplus A[0,2,k] \oplus A[0,3,k] &= A[0,4,k] \oplus 0xff\ldots f \\
A[2,0,k] \oplus A[2,1,k] \oplus A[2,2,k] \oplus A[2,3,k] &= 0xff\ldots f
\end{aligned}
\tag{9}
$$

Here $k \in \{0,1,\ldots,31\}$. Similarly, to make the second round linear the relations are rephrased w.r.t a 32-lane state as follows:

$$
\begin{aligned}
A[2,0,k]_{\lll 30} &= A[0,0,k] \oplus A[2,2,k]_{\lll 11} \\
A[2,1,k]_{\lll 6} &= S[0,1,k]_{\lll 4} \oplus A[2,3,k]_{\lll 15} \\
A[2,2,k]_{\lll 11} &= A[0,2,k]_{\lll 3} \\
A[2,3,k]_{\lll 15} &= A[0,3,k]_{\lll 9} \oplus A[2,0,k]_{\lll 30}
\end{aligned}
\tag{10}
$$

From the above equations, we get the first 32 slices that are as per our requirement, therefore, we take a copy of this state and make them the last 32 slices. By doing this the degree of freedom will be 64 because we have 8×32 variables and 6×32 equations. Accordingly, the degree of freedom is $8 \times 32 - 6 \times 32$. Hence for SHAKE128, we get the SymSum for 9 rounds with complexity 2^{64}.

5   Experimental Validation

In this section, we present experimental validation of some of the claims furnished above. In particular, we choose SHAKE128 as it has the smallest capacity part allowing for more control over the input. However, the attacks can easily be extended onto other SHA3 variants with proper adjustments. In the following we demonstrate an attack on 6-rounds of SHAKE128 using the 1-round linearization and hash-inverse strategy. Due to 2-round extension, the degree of 6-rounds reduces to $2^{6-2} = 16$ and by Corollary 1, the 16th order vectorial derivative will exhibit SymSum property.

Figure 6b shows input state for SHAKE128. Here orange, white, light gray lanes are variable, constant and 0's (that is also capacity part of SHAKE128) respectively. Here, we have taken first and third column as variables which satisfies the conditions as per Eq. (9). The input base message for our experiment is shown below:

```
8bd9162e  8bd9162e 1245c1c7 1245c1c7 0a3f3940 0a3f3940 eb6e955a eb6e955a 61d62226 61d62226
64cf1036  64cf1036 36da615c 36da615c 3d3b488a 3d3b488a e86d0018 e86d0018 1b16874d 1b16874d
64cf1036  64cf1036 44bbe571 44bbe571 0d0b9c27 0d0b9c27 72f3c98c 72f3c98c 53598e96 53598e96
ebc29253  ebc29253 75f22314 75f22314 92d8c5f9 92d8c5f9 372772f3 372772f3 3839af6d 3839af6d
b185e09f  b185e0
```

Table 2 shows the full KECCAK State, where **** is the variable nibble that generates individual messages by altering their values. To maintain the Self-Symmetry **** and **** should be the equivalent. To make one round linear each message generated by changing **** should satisfy the condition described above thus the value of † † †† and † † †† will modify accordingly.

Table 2. Representing Keccak State

****9162e	****9162e	1245c1c7	1245c1c7	0a3f3940	0a3f3940	eb6e955a	eb6e955a	61d62226	61d62226
64cf1036	64cf1036	36da615c	36da615c	3d3b488a	3d3b488a	e86d0018	e86d0018	1b16874d	1b16874d
64cf1036	64cf1036	44bbe571	44bbe571	0d0b9c27	0d0b9c27	72f3c98c	72f3c98c	53598e96	53598e96
† † ††9253	† † ††9253	75f22314	75f22314	92d8c5f9	92d8c5f9	372772f3	372772f3	3839af6d	3839af6d
b185e09f	b185e09f	00000000	00000000	00000000	00000000	00000000	00000000	00000000	00000000

By changing **** values of the input base message, 2^{16} individual messages were produced and inputted to 6-round SHAKE128 with output hash-size of 320. For each of the hash-values, apply $\chi^{-1} \circ \iota^{-1}$ and compute the output-sum. We witnessed ZeroSum with complexity 2^{17} and SymSum with 2^{16} that confirms the expected outcome predicted by theoretical arguments.

6   Discussion

In this work, we have extended the classical SymSum distinguisher up to 3 rounds by applying linear structures and the χ^{-1} trick. Together, we have an advantage of 3 rounds on almost all previously reported derivative based distinguishers.

One of the most important observations was the shift in the highest degree reachable by TYPE-II monomials which are fundamental to achieving a round-constant independent function thereby being the basis of the SymSum distinguisher. As dictated by Theorem 2, irrespective of the number (≥ 1) of rounds linearized SymSum loses its 4 factor advantage over ZeroSum. However, that is a little price to pay against the increase in the number of rounds penetrated. A comparison among the various approaches that extend the SymSum distinguisher is furnished in Fig. 8. The comparisons are provided for 7, 8, 9 and 10 rounds for each variant of SHA3. As one can observe for SHA3-224 and SHA3-256, the best distinguisher in terms if #Rounds is still the classical SymSum. This is due to the fact that χ^{-1} is not applicable for SHA3-224 and SHA3-256 as the output hash value length is <320 bits which is minimum requirement for applying χ^{-1} on the hash-digest. Another observation is that for SHA3-384/512 and SHAKE128/256, the maximum rounds are reached using χ^{-1} technique over classical SymSum. This is attributed to the degrees of freedom that is available when we just augment classical SymSum with χ^{-1} technique. On the other hand, linear structures lead to drastic reduction in degrees of freedom. Also, it can be noted that SymSum always enjoys a degree 2 advantage as predicted by the results discussed earlier. However, for the same number of round ZeroSum always has a better degree of freedom for well-understood reason of not having to conform to the self-symmetry constraint.

The maximum degree of freedom for different variants and approaches is depicted in Table 3. The table also shows the corresponding slice/state configuration for achieving that degree of freedom. Moreover, the constraints to be

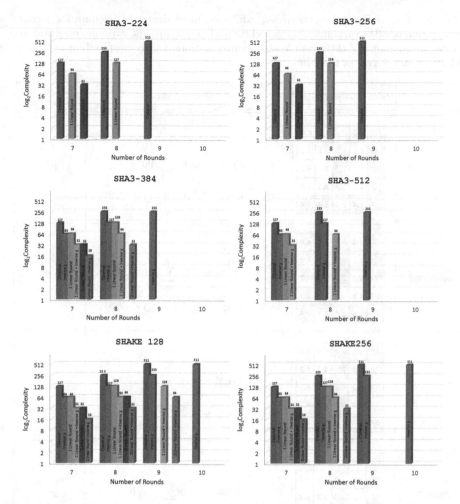

Fig. 8. Comparison of SHA3 variants for different approaches as applying χ^{-1}, 1-round linearization, 1-round linearization $+ \chi^{-1}$, 2-round linearization and 2-round linearization $+ \chi^{-1}$ with classical SymSum distinguisher

applied on the slice variables to fulfill the condition for 1-round linearization is also exhibited in the table. Similar data is furnished in Table 4 for 2-round linearization. It is worth mentioning that for SHA3-512 2-round linearization is not applicable as the rate part is substantially lower leaving very less room to formulate the necessary constraints. It is easy to appreciate that the results reported here are better than ZeroSum and classical SymSum. Interestingly, even the simple χ^{-1} trick helps classical SymSum to breach the 10-round barrier (as stated in [17]) which is now possible to be distinguished with 2^{511} calls to SHA3.

Table 3. Slice configuration, conditions and maximum degree of freedom for 1-round linearization of SHA3 variants. Orange, white and gray represent variable, constant and 0. Here we give one of the possible slice configurations and corresponding conditions and maximum degree of freedom.

Variant	Slice Configuration	Restrictions on variables	Degree of Freedom
SHAKE128	(grid 0,0–4,4)	$A[0,4] = \alpha_1 \oplus \sum_{i=0}^{3} A[0,i]$ $A[j,3] = \alpha_2 \oplus \sum_{i=0}^{2} A[j,i] \quad (j \in \{2,3\})$	2^{224}
SHAKE256	(grid 0,0–4,4)	$A[0,3] = \alpha_1 \oplus \sum_{i=0}^{2} A[0,i]$ $A[j,2] = \alpha_2 \oplus \sum_{i=0}^{1} A[j,i] \quad (j \in \{2,3\})$	2^{160}
SHA3-224	(grid 0,0–4,4)	$A[0,3] = \alpha_1 \oplus \sum_{i=0}^{2} A[0,i]$ $A[2,3] = \alpha_2 \oplus \sum_{i=0}^{2} A[2,i]$	2^{192}
SHA3-256	(grid 0,0–4,4)	$A[0,3] = \alpha_1 \oplus \sum_{i=0}^{2} A[0,i]$ $A[j,2] = \alpha_2 \oplus \sum_{i=0}^{1} A[j,i] \quad (j \in \{2,3\})$	2^{160}
SHA3-384	(grid 0,0–4,4)	$A[0,2] = \alpha_1 \oplus \sum_{i=0}^{1} A[0,i]$ $A[2,2] = \alpha_2 \oplus \sum_{i=0}^{1} A[2,i]$	2^{128}
SHA3-512	(grid 0,0–4,4)	$A[0,1] = \alpha_1 \oplus A[0,0]$ $A[j,1] = \alpha_2 \oplus A[j,0] \quad (j \in \{2,3\})$	2^{64}

Table 4. Slice configuration, conditions and degree of freedom for 2-round linearization of SHA3 variants. Orange, white, light gray and dark gray represent variable, constant, 0 and 1 respectively. Here we give one of the possible slice configurations and corresponding conditions and maximum degree of freedom. Note that this strategy is not applicable for SHA3 512

Variant	Slice Configuration	Restrictions on variables	Degree of Freedom
SHAKE128		$A[0,0] \oplus A[0,1] \oplus A[0,2] \oplus A[0,3] = \texttt{0xff}\ldots\texttt{f}$ $A[2,0] \oplus A[2,1] \oplus A[2,2] \oplus A[2,3] = \texttt{0xff}\ldots\texttt{f}$ $A[2,0]_{\lll 30} = A[0,0] \oplus A[2,2]_{\lll 11}$ $A[2,1]_{\lll 6} = A[0,1]_{\lll 4} \oplus A[2,3]_{\lll 15}$ $A[2,2]_{\lll 11} = A[0,2]_{\lll 3}$ $A[2,3]_{\lll 15} = A[0,3]_{\lll 9} \oplus A[2,0]_{\lll 30}$	2^{64}
SHAKE256		$A[i,0] \oplus A[i,1] \oplus A[i,2] = 0, \quad i = 0,2$ $A[2,0]_{\lll 30} = A[0,0] \oplus A[2,2]_{\lll 11}$ $A[2,1]_{\lll 6} = A[0,1]_{\lll 4}$ $A[2,2]_{\lll 11} = A[0,2]_{\lll 3}$	2^{32}
SHA3-224		$A[0,0] \oplus A[0,1] \oplus A[0,2] \oplus A[0,3] = A[0,4] \oplus 0$ $A[2,0] \oplus A[2,1] \oplus A[2,2] \oplus A[2,3] = 0$ $A[2,0]_{\lll 30} = A[0,0] \oplus A[2,2]_{\lll 11}$ $A[2,1]_{\lll 6} = A[0,1]_{\lll 4} \oplus A[2,3]_{\lll 15}$ $A[2,2]_{\lll 11} = A[0,2]_{\lll 3}$ $A[2,3]_{\lll 15} = A[0,3]_{\lll 9} \oplus A[2,0]_{\lll 30}$	2^{64}
SHA3-256		$A[i,0] \oplus A[i,1] \oplus A[i,2] = 0, \quad i = 0,2$ $A[2,0]_{\lll 30} = A[0,0] \oplus A[2,2]_{\lll 11}$ $A[2,1]_{\lll 6} = A[0,1]_{\lll 4}$ $A[2,2]_{\lll 11} = A[0,2]_{\lll 3}$	2^{32}
SHA3-384		$A[i,0] \oplus A[i,1] \oplus A[i,2] = 0, \quad i = 0,2$ $A[2,0]_{\lll 30} = A[0,0] \oplus A[2,2]_{\lll 11}$ $A[2,1]_{\lll 6} = A[0,1]_{\lll 4}$ $A[2,2]_{\lll 11} = A[0,2]_{\lll 3}$	2^{32}

7 Conclusion

This work aims to combine two very interesting results on SHA3 namely the SymSum property and the idea of linear structures to devise the best distinguishers on the SHA3 standard in terms of complexity and number of rounds penetrated.

The main contribution lies in studying the effect of linearization on the core SymSum property. The results show that due to the effect of linear structures the factor of four advantage that SymSum enjoys over ZeroSum is reduced to two. Theoretical arguments are provided to explain this reduction. A simple χ inversion trick is also devised on applicable variants to penetrate one round further. With the combined power of all strategies, this work reaches up to 9 rounds of certain SHA3 variants with a practically feasible complexity of 2^{64}.

References

1. Aumasson, J.P., Meier, W.: Zero-sum distinguishers for reduced Keccak-f and for the core functions of Luffa and Hamsi. Rump session of Cryptographic Hardware and Embedded Systems-CHES 2009, vol. 67 (2009)
2. Bertoni, G., Daemen, J., Peeters, M., Assche, G.V.: Sponge functions. In: EcryptHash Workshop 2007, May 2007
3. Bertoni, G., Daemen, J., Peeters, M., Assche, G.V.: The Keccak SHA-3 submission. Submission to NIST (Round 3) (2011). http://keccak.noekeon.org/Keccak-submission-3.pdf
4. Boura, C., Canteaut, A., De Cannière, C.: Higher-order differential properties of KECCAK and *Luffa*. In: Joux, A. (ed.) FSE 2011. LNCS, vol. 6733, pp. 252–269. Springer, Heidelberg (2011). https://doi.org/10.1007/978-3-642-21702-9_15
5. Dinur, I., Morawiecki, P., Pieprzyk, J., Srebrny, M., Straus, M.: Cube attacks and cube-attack-like cryptanalysis on the round-reduced Keccak sponge function. In: Oswald, E., Fischlin, M. (eds.) EUROCRYPT 2015. LNCS, vol. 9056, pp. 733–761. Springer, Heidelberg (2015). https://doi.org/10.1007/978-3-662-46800-5_28
6. Duan, M., Lai, X.: Improved zero-sum distinguisher for full round Keccak-f permutation. IACR Cryptology ePrint Archive 2011, 23 (2011)
7. Duc, A., Guo, J., Peyrin, T., Wei, L.: Unaligned rebound attack: application to Keccak. In: Canteaut, A. (ed.) FSE 2012. LNCS, vol. 7549, pp. 402–421. Springer, Heidelberg (2012). https://doi.org/10.1007/978-3-642-34047-5_23
8. Guo, J., Liu, M., Song, L.: Linear structures: applications to cryptanalysis of round-reduced KECCAK. In: Cheon, J.H., Takagi, T. (eds.) ASIACRYPT 2016, Part I. LNCS, vol. 10031, pp. 249–274. Springer, Heidelberg (2016). https://doi.org/10.1007/978-3-662-53887-6_9
9. Huang, S., Wang, X., Xu, G., Wang, M., Zhao, J.: Conditional cube attack on reduced-round Keccak sponge function. In: Coron, J.-S., Nielsen, J.B. (eds.) EUROCRYPT 2017, Part II. LNCS, vol. 10211, pp. 259–288. Springer, Cham (2017). https://doi.org/10.1007/978-3-319-56614-6_9
10. Jean, J., Nikolić, I.: Internal differential boomerangs: practical analysis of the round-reduced Keccak-*f* permutation. In: Leander, G. (ed.) FSE 2015. LNCS, vol. 9054, pp. 537–556. Springer, Heidelberg (2015). https://doi.org/10.1007/978-3-662-48116-5_26
11. Kuila, S., Saha, D., Pal, M., Roy Chowdhury, D.: Practical distinguishers against 6-round Keccak-*f* exploiting self-symmetry. In: Pointcheval, D., Vergnaud, D. (eds.) AFRICACRYPT 2014. LNCS, vol. 8469, pp. 88–108. Springer, Cham (2014). https://doi.org/10.1007/978-3-319-06734-6_6
12. Li, T., Sun, Y., Liao, M., Wang, D.: Preimage attacks on the round-reduced Keccak with cross-linear structures. IACR Trans. Symmetric Cryptol. **2017**(4), 39–57 (2017)

13. Liu, T., Sun, Y.: Preimage attacks on round-reduced Keccak-224/256 via an allocating approach. IACR Cryptology ePrint Archive 2019, 248 (2019)
14. Morawiecki, P., Pieprzyk, J., Srebrny, M.: Rotational cryptanalysis of round-reduced KECCAK. In: Moriai, S. (ed.) FSE 2013. LNCS, vol. 8424, pp. 241–262. Springer, Heidelberg (2014). https://doi.org/10.1007/978-3-662-43933-3_13
15. Naya-Plasencia, M., Röck, A., Meier, W.: Practical analysis of reduced-round KECCAK. In: Bernstein, D.J., Chatterjee, S. (eds.) INDOCRYPT 2011. LNCS, vol. 7107, pp. 236–254. Springer, Heidelberg (2011). https://doi.org/10.1007/978-3-642-25578-6_18
16. Qiao, K., Song, L., Liu, M., Guo, J.: New collision attacks on round-reduced Keccak. IACR Cryptology ePrint Archive 2017, 128 (2017)
17. Saha, D., Kuila, S., Chowdhury, D.R.: SymSum: symmetric-sum distinguishers against round reduced SHA3. IACR Trans. Symmetric Cryptol. 2017(1), 240–258 (2017)
18. Standards and Technology (NIST). SHA-3: Cryptographic hash algorithm competition. http://csrc.nist.gov/groups/ST/hash/sha-3/index.html

Cryptanalysis of FlexAEAD

Mostafizar Rahman[1]([✉]), Dhiman Saha[2], and Goutam Paul[1]

[1] Cryptology and Security Research Unit (CSRU),
Indian Statistical Institute, Kolkata, Kolkata 700108, India
mrahman454@gmail.com, goutam.paul@isical.ac.in
[2] de.ci.phe.red Lab, Department of Electrical Engineering and Computer Science,
Indian Institute of Technology, Bhilai, Raipur 492015, India
dhiman@iitbhilai.ac.in

Abstract. This paper analyzes the internal *keyed* permutation of FlexAEAD which is a round-1 candidate of the NIST LightWeight Cryptography Competition. In our analysis, we report an iterated truncated differential leveraging on a particular property of the AES S-box that becomes useful due to the particular nature of the diffusion layer of the round function. The differential holds with a low probability of 2^{-7} for one round which allows it to penetrate the same number of rounds as claimed by the designers, but with a much lower complexity. Moreover, it can be easily extended to a key-recovery attack at a little extra cost. We further report a Super-Sbox construction in the internal permutation, which is exploited using the Yoyo game to devise a 6-round deterministic distinguisher and a 7-round key recovery attack for the 128-bit internal permutation. Similar attacks can be mounted for the 64-bit and 256-bit variants. All these attacks outperform the existing results of the designers as well as other third-party results. The iterated truncated differentials can be tweaked to mount forgery attacks similar to the ones given by Eichlseder *et al*. Success probabilities of all the reported distinguishing attacks are shown to be high. All practical attacks have been experimentally verified. To the best of our knowledge, this work reports the first key-recovery attack on the internal *keyed* permutation of FlexAEAD.

Keywords: AES S-box · Distinguisher · FlexAEAD · Iterated differential · Key recovery · NIST lightweight cryptography competition · Yoyo

1 Introduction

In the modern era, the aim is to connect each of the physical devices, even the miniature ones, with the internet so that they can be monitored and controlled remotely for maximum utilization. These devices are powered with the ability of communicating among themselves. Such a huge interconnected system, consisting of numerous tiny devices, is not free from vulnerabilities. Moreover, a security breach in such systems can be catastrophic. So, a major concern in the world of

© Springer Nature Switzerland AG 2020
A. Nitaj and A. Youssef (Eds.): AFRICACRYPT 2020, LNCS 12174, pp. 152–171, 2020.
https://doi.org/10.1007/978-3-030-51938-4_8

internet-of-things is how to provide security and privacy to each system with the constraints of limited power and area. SKINNY [9], PRESENT [10], QARMA [6], KATAN and KTANTAN [11], GIFT [8] are some of the block ciphers which are designed for such constrained environments. Until recently, no standardization process has been introduced (like AES Development [2], SHA-3 Project [4], CAESAR Competition [1]) for cryptographic schemes in lightweight environments. NIST LightWeight Cryptography (LWC) competition [3] is a major step towards addressing these issues. There are a total of 57 submissions in this competition. Apart from authenticated encryption algorithms in lightweight environment, some of the designs also comprise of hash functions. Some of them have also provided new primitives for block cipher design.

FLEXAEAD is one of the round-1 candidates proposed by Nascimento and Xexéo in NIST LWC competition [17]. It is a family of lightweight authenticated encryption schemes with associated data. In this version, the processing of Associate Data (AD) has been added to the original variants [15,16,18]. There are mainly three variants of FLEXAEAD that have been listed with block sizes of 64, 128 and 256 bits. In general, a FLEXAEAD scheme is denoted by FLEXAEAD-b, with b being the block size. The size of nonce and tag is the same as block size across all variants. The length of key is 128 bits for FLEXAEAD-64 and FLEXAEAD-128 whereas it is 256 bits for FLEXAEAD-256. The nonce in FLEXAEAD is used to generate sequence numbers which are eventually XOR-ed with associated data, plaintext and intermediate-state to produce ciphertext-tag pair. The lightweight of FLEXAEAD essentially comes from the fact that for computational purposes it uses XOR operations, a look-up table for substitution layer and bit reorganizations for BlockShuffle layer. FLEXAEAD has an underlying block cipher; internal *keyed* permutation (PF_k) of 64, 128 and 256 bits. We have analyzed the PF_k function and reported several results. A brief description of PF_k has been provided in Sect. 2.1. The PF_k with x-bit state is referred to as FLEX-x.

Existing Security Claims. The designers have claimed that mounting an attack on FLEX-x based on differential and linear characteristics is more difficult than the brute force attack. According to their analysis, the probability of best differential characteristic for FLEX-64, FLEX-128 and FLEX-256 is 2^{-168}, 2^{-204} and 2^{-240} respectively. The number of chosen plaintext pairs required for a linear trail in FLEX-64, FLEX-128 and FLEX-256 are 2^{272}, 2^{326} and 2^{380} respectively [17]. Eichlseder *et al.* have claimed several forgery attacks [12,13] on FLEXAEAD. They have followed several different approaches: like changing associated data, truncating ciphertexts and reordering ciphertexts. They have reported differential characteristics for 5-round FLEX-64, 6-round FLEX-128 and 7-round FLEX-256 with probability 2^{-66}, 2^{-79} and 2^{-108} respectively. Length extension attacks based on associated data have also been shown [14]. Table 1 shows the comparison of different trail probabilities reported till date with the ones furnished in the current work. For uniformity, we have enlisted trail probabilities for same number of rounds.

Table 1. Comparison of trail probabilities of internal *keyed* permutation of FLEXAEAD

Block Size	#rounds	Trail probability	Technique	Reference
64	5	2^{-66}	Differential characteristics	[12]
	5	2^{-46}	Clustered characteristics	[12]
	5	2^{-21}	Iterated truncated differential	**This Work Sect. 3**
	5	2^{-13}	Yoyo Game	**This Work Sect. 4.3**
128	6	2^{-79}	Differential characteristics	[12]
	6	2^{-54}	Clustered characteristics	[12]
	6	2^{-21}	Iterated truncated differential	**This Work Sect. 3**
	6	1	Yoyo Game	**This Work Sect. 4.2**
256	7	2^{-108}	Differential characteristics	[12]
	7	2^{-70}	Clustered characteristics	[12]
	7	2^{-21}	Iterated Truncated Differential	**This Work Sect. 3**
	9	2^{-11}	Yoyo Game	**This Work Sect. 4.3**

Our Contributions. First of all, we report an iterated truncated differential for all the variants of PF_k using the property of AES Difference Distribution Table (DDT) where the output difference of a byte is *confined to either upper or lower nibble*. The probability of the truncated differential for one round is 2^{-7}. Its iterative nature makes it possible to penetrate more number of rounds for all FLEX-x. These differentials are further exploited to devise key-recovery attacks on all the variants.

Next, we explore the application of the Yoyo property which has been introduced by Rønjom et al. [20] on generic 2-round Substitution Permutation Networks and further extended on AES-based permutations and block ciphers [7,21]. We have been able to devise deterministic Yoyo distinguishers for 4, 6 and 8 rounds of FLEX-64, FLEX-128 and FLEX-256 respectively which are further extended by one more round to mount key recovery attacks. All key recovery attacks (reported in this work) with their respective complexities are summarized in Table 2. For the iterated truncated differential, the maximum number of rounds that is penetrable for a FLEX-x variant are enlisted in the table. The attacks with practical complexities are experimentally verified.

Further, we have used the iterated truncated differentials to mount forgery attacks on FLEXAEAD similar to the ones reported by Eichlseder et al. [12,13]. Finally, to measure the effectiveness of all distinguishers reported in this work, their theoretical success probabilities are estimated by following the approach given in [19]. The success probabilities are estimated to be high and some of them with practical complexities are experimentally verified.

Table 2. Comparison of Key Recovery Attacks. Encs, Decs, MAs refers to encryption queries, decryption queries and Memory Accesses respectively. For uniformity, memory accesses and memory complexity has been provided in terms of FLEX-128 state. 1 MA for FLEX-128 corresponds to 2 MA in FLEX-64 and 0.5 MA in FLEX-256. Memory complexity is also normalized by the same ratio.

Block size	#rounds	Data complexity		Time complexity	Memory complexity	Attack type	Section No. of Current Work
		Encs	Decs	MAs			
64	7	$2^{30.5}$		$2^{34.5}$	$2^{18.5}$	Iterated truncated differential	3.2
	5	2^{10}	$2^{16.5}$	$2^{15.5}$	2^{10}	Yoyo attack	4.3
128	16	$2^{93.5}$		$2^{108.5}$	$2^{20.5}$	Iterated truncated differential	3.2
	7	$2^{10.5}$	$2^{16.5}$	$2^{16.5}$	$2^{11.5}$	Yoyo attack	4.3
256	21	$2^{109.5}$		$2^{125.5}$	$2^{22.5}$	Iterated truncated differential	3.2
	9	2^{11}	$2^{16.5}$	$2^{17.5}$	2^{13}	Yoyo attack	4.3

All the attacks presented in this paper exploit the vulnerability that merely dividing the bytes into nibbles while using AES S-box is susceptible to differential attacks as diffusion may be slow in some scenarios. Although, FLEXAEAD is out of NIST lightweight cryptography competition, this particular vulnerability has a far-reaching impact on designing ciphers using AES S-box. Hence, it forms the basis of continued motivation for this work.

Outline. The necessary details about PF_k and Yoyo game are briefly visited in Sect. 2. Section 3 describes the *key*-recovery attacks based on Iterated Truncated Differential. Section 4 details the attacks based on Yoyo game. The success probabilities of distinguishing attacks and their experimental verification are illustrated in Sect. 5. Forgery attacks based on Iterated Differentials are described in Sect. 6. Finally, the concluding remarks are furnished.

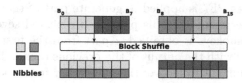

Fig. 1. Byte representation of FLEX-128 block cipher

2   Preliminaries

The analysis in this paper is regarding the PF_k of FLEXAEAD. So, first of all, a brief description of PF_k is given. Since a major part of this work uses the Yoyo strategy, for the sake of completeness, a brief description of Yoyo game and its relevant results are provided.

2.1   Internal *keyed* Permutation PF$_k$

The design strategy of PF$_k$ follows the Feistel construction. Let m be the number of bytes in a FLEX-x state ($m = x/8$). The state of FLEX-x is denoted by B and is divided into two equal halves: the bytes in the left half being numbered from $B[0]$ to $B[\frac{m}{2} - 1]$, and the ones on the right half from $B[\frac{m}{2}]$ to $B[m - 1]$. Each byte is divided into two parts representing the two nibbles with the upper half (upper nibble) being the most significant one. The other nibble is called as lower nibble. After the BlockShuffle operation, m nibbles from $B[0]$ to $B[\frac{m}{2} - 1]$ constitute the upper nibbles of each bytes whereas the nibbles from $B[\frac{m}{2}]$ to $B[m - 1]$ constitute the lower ones. The bytes at position $B[i]$ and $B[i + \frac{m}{2}]$ are referred to as a "pair of symmetric bytes". Application of BlockShuffle operation on state s in r-th round is denoted by $BS^r(s)$. Figure 1 shows the byte representation in FLEX-128 state.

Figure 2 shows the round function of FLEX-128. Each round of FLEX-x starts with the BlockShuffle operation. Then the state is bifurcated and the right half goes through subbytes operation. AES S-box is used for byte substitution. The left half is modified by XOR-ing it with the right half and applying the subbytes operation. The modified values of the left half are XOR-ed with the right half values and subbytes is applied to get new values of the right half. Then the left and right half are combined to form the new state and the next round follows. In FLEX-x there are no round keys; there are only two subkeys K_α, K_β which are used at the beginning and the end of round functions respectively. The total number of rounds for FLEX-64, FLEX-128 and FLEX-256 are 5, 6 and 7 respectively [17]. In authenticated encryption modes, three PF$_k$ are used sequentially for encrypting a block of plaintext, which makes the effective number of rounds 15, 18 and 21 in FLEXAEAD-64, FLEXAEAD-128 and FLEXAEAD-256 respectively.

Key Generation. Key generation in FLEX-x uses the PF$_k$ where the master key K is divided into two parts and used as two subkeys. State is initialized with $0^{|K|/2}$ and three times PF$_k$ is applied to generate part of the subkey to be used for encryption of the plaintext. This process is repeated several times till the required number of subkeys is obtained. Apart from the first round, each time the state is initialized with the output of the previous round. The key generation algorithm makes it difficult to recover the master key from a known subkey. The key recovery attacks presented in this paper refers to the recovery of subkeys.

2.2   Yoyo Game

By applying the Yoyo game strategy, a deterministic distinguisher for two generic Substitution-Permutation (SP) rounds have been reported [20]. This has been used to devise a 6-round FLEX-128 distinguisher and a 7-round FLEX-128 key recovery attack. To apply their results, first Zero Difference Pattern and Swapping of Words need to be defined which were originally given in [20].

Let $F : \mathbb{F}_q^n \to \mathbb{F}_q^n$ be a permutation with $q = 2^k$ and

$$F(x) = S \circ L \circ S \circ L \circ S(x).$$

Here, S is the concatenation of several smaller S-boxes operating on elements from $\mathbb{F}_q$ in parallel and L is the linear layer over $\mathbb{F}_q^n$. A *state* is defined as the vector of words $\alpha = (\alpha_0, \alpha_1, \cdots, \alpha_{n-1}) \in \mathbb{F}_q^n$.

Definition 1. Zero Difference Pattern. *[20] Let $\alpha \in \mathbb{F}_q^n$ for $q = 2^k$. The Zero Difference Pattern for α is*

$$\nu(\alpha) = (z_0, z_1, ..., z_{n-1}),$$

where $\nu(\alpha)$ takes values in $\mathbb{F}_2^n$ and $z_i = 1$ if $\alpha_i = 0$ or $z_i = 0$ otherwise.

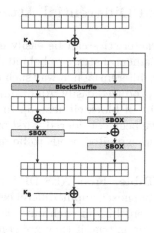

Fig. 2. Round function of FLEX-128 block cipher

Definition 2. Swapping of Words. *[20] Let $\alpha, \beta \in \mathbb{F}_q^n$ be two states and $v \in \mathbb{F}_2^n$ be a vector, then $\rho^v(\alpha, \beta)$ is a new state in $\mathbb{F}_q^n$ created from α, β by swapping components among them. The ith component of $\rho^v(\alpha, \beta)$ is defined as*

$$\rho^v(\alpha, \beta)_i = \begin{cases} \alpha_i, & \text{if } v_i = 1; \\ \beta_i, & \text{if } v_i = 0. \end{cases} \tag{1}$$

The following theorem describes the deterministic distinguisher for 2 generic SP-rounds (G_2).

Theorem 1. *[20] Let $p^0, p^1 \in \mathbb{F}_q^n$, $c^0 = G_2(p^0)$ and $c^1 = G_2(p^1)$. For any vector $v \in \mathbb{F}_2^n$, $c'^0 = \rho^v(c^0, c^1)$ and $c'^1 = \rho^v(c^1, c^0)$. Then*

$$\nu(G_2^{-1}(c'^0) \oplus G_2^{-1}(c'^1)) = \nu(p'^0 \oplus p'^1) = \nu(p^0 \oplus p^1). \tag{2}$$

The notion behind devising such distinguisher is to choose a plaintext pair according to some Zero Difference Pattern and query this plaintext pair to the cipher to obtain a ciphertext pair. Words are swapped between the two ciphertexts on the basis of the substitution layer to produce modified ciphertexts that are queried to obtain new pair of plaintexts. Theorem 1 states that the Zero Difference Pattern of the original plaintext pair and the modified plaintext pair should be the same if the cipher is of the form $S \circ L \circ S$. In the following section, details regarding iterated truncated differential attacks on PF_k are discussed.

3   Iterated Truncated Differential Attacks on PF_k

Differential of iterative characteristics can be easily exploited to penetrate full rounds of a cipher. The fundamental strategy behind devising an iterated differential is to choose the output differential in a way such that after some operations the input differential can be produced easily. Alkhzaimi *et al.* have reported such differentials for SIMON family of block ciphers [5]. In this work, iterated differentials in truncated form have considered. First of all, a particular property of AES S-box which has been exploited needs to be discussed.

Property of AES DDT Table. From AES DDT table it has been observed that the number of randomly chosen input differences that map to output differences, such that the non-zero bits in each output difference are confined to the upper nibble is 4096. Same is true if they are confined to the lower nibble. In other words,

$$\left| \left\{ (x_1, x_2) | (S(x_1) \oplus S(x_2)) \ \& \ \texttt{0xf0} \ = 0, \forall x_1, x_2 \in \mathbb{F}_{2^8} \right\} \right| = 4096,$$

$$\left| \left\{ (x_1, x_2) | (S(x_1) \oplus S(x_2)) \ \& \ \texttt{0x0f} \ = 0, \forall x_1, x_2 \in \mathbb{F}_{2^8} \right\} \right| = 4096,$$

where S is the AES S-box. Therefore, with probability $\frac{4096}{2^{16}} = 2^{-4}$ a random input difference transits to upper nibble in the output difference. With same probability, random input difference transits to lower nibble. The way this property is exploited to devise iterated truncated differential is provided in the next subsection.

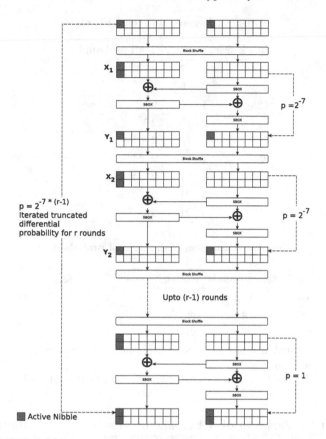

Fig. 3. Iterated Truncated Differential with One-round probability of 2^{-7}. Note that the key-addition is not shown, since it has no effect on the trail

3.1 One Round Probabilistic Iterated Truncated Differential

Refer to Fig. 3 for the iterated differential of FLEX-128. In X_1, keeping the difference in $B[0]$ ensures that in Y_1 difference are in $B[0]$ and $B[8]$. With probability 2^{-7} both differences are confined in either upper nibble or lower nibble in those bytes. Therefore, after BlockShuffle only one byte is active in X_2. In X_2 the active byte can be either $B[0]$ or $B[1]$, depending on whether the upper or lower nibbles in Y_1 are active. The iterative nature of the differential comes from the fact that in X_2 only one byte is active at the cost of 2^{-7} probability under the constraints that only one byte is active in X_1, and this particular event can be repeated an infinite number of times. Similar kinds of iterated truncated differential with the same probability exists for FLEX-64 and FLEX-256. Now, how these one round differentials are exploited to penetrate more number of rounds is discussed.

160 M. Rahman et al.

Table 3. Iterated differential trails

Block size	f	r_{max}	Trail probability
64	1	7	2^{-42}
	2	6	2^{-28}
128	1	16	2^{-105}
	2	15	2^{-91}
	3	12	2^{-63}
256	1	21	2^{-140}
	2	21	2^{-123}
	3	21	2^{-126}
	4	21	2^{-119}

Table 4. Comparison of differential probabilities

Block size	#rounds	Active S-boxes	$\mathcal{P}_D^\dagger$	$\mathcal{Q}_D^*$
64	15	28	2^{-168}	2^{-98}
128	18	34	2^{-204}	2^{-119}
256	21	40	2^{-240}	2^{-119}

† Probability of the classical differential trail claimed by the designers
* Probability of the iterated truncated differential trail

Application to Variants of PF$_k$. The one round iterated truncated differential can be applied to all the versions of PF$_k$. The iterated differential occurs with probability 2^{-7}. Depending on the blocksize, last few rounds can be made free as no byte to nibble transition is needed for those rounds.

Let the iterated truncated differential is kept free for last f rounds for FLEX-x. Then the probability of the trail is $2^{-7\times(r-f)}$. For uniform random discrete distribution, the same event will occur with probability $2^{-8\times(\frac{x}{8}-2^f)} = 2^{-(x-8\times2^f)}$. For devising a distinguisher for x-bit flex,

$$2^{-7\times(r-f)} > 2^{-(x-8\times2^f)}$$

$$\implies r < \frac{(x - 8 \times 2^f)}{7} + f. \tag{3}$$

Then, the probability of the iterated truncated differential trail for r-round FLEX-x is $2^{-7\times(r-f)}$. Table 3 shows the trail probabilities for different FLEX-x. r_{max} denotes the maximum number of rounds reachable under the constraints of fixed f. Table 4 compares the differential probabilities claim of the designers with our claim using the iterated differential. $\mathcal{P}_D$ denotes the designers' claim whereas $\mathcal{Q}_D$ denotes our claim.

Another aspect of such kind of trails is the position of active byte in each round. As mentioned in 3.1, if $B[0]$ is active in X_0, then either $B[0]$ or $B[1]$ is active in X_2. If $B[1]$ is active in X_2, then either $B[2]$ or $B[3]$ is active in X_3. In general, for FLEX-x if $B[m]$ or $B[\frac{x}{2 \times 8} + m]$ is active in X_i, then either $B[2m]$ or $B[2m + 1]$ is active in $X_{(i+1)}$. Now, the mechanism of transforming these distinguishers to key recovery attacks is detailed.

3.2   Key Recovery Using Iterated Truncated Differential

At the end of each round, the difference in a pair of symmetric bytes after S-box transits to the same nibble with probability 2^{-7}. This has been used as a filtering technique to eliminate wrong key bytes. Let the first subkey, K_α for FLEX-128 is being recovered. Using iterated truncated differential for r rounds a right pair can be identified with probability $2^{-7 \times (r-f)}$, where f is number free rounds. Suppose, in the right pair the initial difference is in $B[i]$ and $B[i+8]$. So, we guess key byte $K_\alpha[i]$ and $K_\alpha[i + 8]$. There are 2^{16} possible guesses and these are used to verify whether at the end of first-round byte to nibble transition occur. Out of 2^{16}, 2^9 key-byte candidates remain. For further filtering, two more right pairs are used. The second right pair reduces the candidate numbers to 2^2. After filtering using three different right pairs, it is expected only one candidate should remain for the key byte pair $(2^{16} \times (2^{-7})^3 = 2^{-5} < 1)$. For the remaining symmetric key bytes, the procedure is repeated 7 more times. In the end, it is expected that only one key candidate should pass the test. The other subkeys can be recovered similarly. After recovering the first subkey, the values of the plaintexts are exactly known till the second subkey whitening. The same key recovery attacks are applicable for FLEX-64 and FLEX-256. In the next subsections, details about the complexities of all attacks and experimental verification of practical ones are provided.

3.3   Complexity Evaluation

Distinguisher. To distinguish iterated truncated differential for r rounds, $2^{7 \times (r-f)}$ number of plaintext pairs are required, where f is the number of free rounds at the end. In devising the distinguishers, difference can be kept in 2 bytes only in X_1, which yields $\binom{2^{16}}{2} \approx 2^{31}$ pairs of plaintexts. For distinguishers requiring more than 2^{31} pairs, a different set of states is needed. So, the data complexity is $\frac{2^{7 \times (r-f)}}{2^{31}} \times 2^{16} = \frac{2^{7 \times (r-f)}}{2^{15}}$ encryption queries. Time complexity involves the memory accesses required to compute the specified collisions, which is the number of plaintext pairs needed, i.e., $2^{7 \times (r-f)}$. Memory complexity is 2^{16} FLEX-x states, which is the memory required for storing different states.

Consider a particular case for 21-round FLEX-256. According to Inequality 3, the value of f can be set to 4. For this case

1. Data Complexity is $\frac{2^{7 \times 17}}{2^{15}} = 2^{104}$ encryption queries..
2. Time Complexity is 2^{119} memory accesses.
3. Memory Complexity is 2^{16} FLEX-256 states $= 2^{17}$ FLEX-128 states.

Key Recovery. Complexities of key recovery attack of FLEX-x depends on distinguisher. To recover each pair of key-byte, three different right pairs are required. This procedure also needs to be repeated $\frac{x}{16}$ times for recovering the full key. Therefore, data complexity, time complexity and memory complexity of distinguisher needs to be multiplied by a factor of $3 \times \frac{x}{16}$. Moreover, candidate key-byte recovery for each pair of byte can be computed in parallel. To recover the other subkey, a plaintext, ciphertext pair (p_1, c_1) is chosen and PF_k round functions till the second subkey whitening is computed offline and XOR-ed with c_1. So, the complexities of r-round FLEX-x with f free rounds are-

1. Data Complexity is $3 \times \frac{x}{16} \times \frac{2^{7 \times (r-f)}}{2^{15}}$ encryption queries.
2. Time Complexity is $3 \times \frac{x}{16} \times 2^{7 \times (r-f)}$ memory accesses.
3. Memory Complexity is $3 \times \frac{x}{16} \times 2^{16}$ FLEX-x states.

The complexities of particular cases for 7-round FLEX-64 with $f = 1$, 16-round FLEX-128 with $f = 1$ and 21-round FLEX-256 with $f = 4$ have been listed in Table 2.

3.4 Experimental Verification

The key recovery attack using iterated differentials has been experimentally verified for 8 rounds FLEX-128 with $f = 3$. The attack initiates after a key is chosen randomly. The number of key candidates after using the first right pairs for each pair of symmetric bytes (from $(K_\alpha[0], K_\alpha[8])$ to $(K_\alpha[7], K_\alpha[15])$) are 316, 520, 632, 448, 568, 484, 368 and 356 respectively. It conforms to the theoretical analysis, which states that the number of candidates should be around 2^9. After using the second right pairs, the number of candidates is reduced to 2, 12, 4, 4, 6, 5, 2 and 5 respectively which is close to the theoretical value of 2^2. The third right pair reduces the number for all pairs of bytes to 1. The key recovery attack correctly recovers the subkeys.

In the next section, details regarding attacks on PF_k using Yoyo game strategy are provided.

4 Yoyo Attacks on PF_k

The Yoyo distinguishing attack has been briefly described in Sect. 2.2. First, the result of Yoyo game on 2-generic SP rounds has been applied for devising r-round FLEX-x deterministic distinguisher. Then cipher specific properties has been exploited to penetrate one more extra round and recover the key. Here, r is 4, 6 and 8 for FLEX-64, FLEX-128 and FLEX-256 respectively. First, details about Super-Sbox of FLEX-x is given.

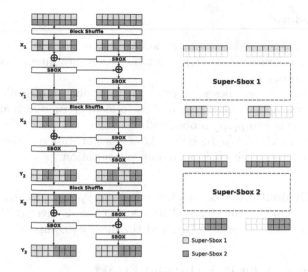

Fig. 4. Super-Sbox of FLEX-128 Block Cipher

4.1   Super-Sbox

Refer to Fig. 4 for the Super-Sbox construction in FLEX-128 block cipher. Consider the bytes $\{B[0], B[2], \cdots B[7]\}$ at X_1. Due to round function, only the symmetric bytes affect each other. So, in Y_1 every symmetric bytes depends on every symmetric bytes at X_1. Due to BS^2, $B[2i]$, $B[2i + 8]$ $(0 \le i \le 3)$ from Y_1 constitutes the $B[4i]$, $B[4i + 1]$ $(0 \le i \le 3)$ at X_2. Due to application of BS^3, $\{B[2i], B[2i + 1], B[2i + 8], B[2i + 9]\}$, $(0 \le i \le 1)$ at Y_2 affects $\{B[8i], B[8i + 1], B[8i + 2], B[8i + 3]\}$, $(0 \le i \le 1)$ at X_3. This constitutes a Super-Sbox which spans over 2.5 rounds (omitting the initial BlockShuffle). There are two 64-bit Super-Sbox in the FLEX-128 state. In similar way, FLEX-64 and FLEX-256 has 32-bit and 128-bit Super-Sbox which span over 1.5 and 3.5 rounds respectively. In the next subsection, how these Super-Sboxes are used to design deterministic Yoyo distinguishers is discussed.

4.2   Deterministic Distinguisher for r-round FLEX-x

In devising this distinguisher, Theorem 1 has been used directly. For this purpose, the $S \circ L \circ S$ layers need to be identified in this construction. The S here corresponds to Super-Sbox described in Sect. 4.1 whereas the L corresponds to the BlockShuffle layer. A pair of plaintexts is chosen such that only one of the Super-Sbox is active at X_1. Yoyo game is played using these two plaintexts to obtain a new pair of texts. The same Super-Sbox should be active in the new pair of texts and the other should be inactive. For a uniform random discrete distribution, this occurs with probability $\frac{1}{2^{\frac{x}{2}}}$. Next, attack procedures and their corresponding complexities are provided. In the attack procedure, steps pertaining to FLEX-128 has been described. Same attack strategy follows for FLEX-64 and FLEX-256.

Attack Procedure

1. Choose two 128-bit plaintexts p_1, p_2 such that, $wt(\nu(p_1 \oplus p_2)) = 1$. Inverse BlockShuffle is applied to p_1, p_2 and then they are queried to encryption oracle to obtain c_1, c_2.
2. As there is two Super-Sboxes, so only one swapping is possible. One of the Super-Sbox is swapped between c_1 and c_2 to form c_1', c_2', which are queried to decryption oracle and p_1', p_2' is obtained.
3. Check whether $wt(\nu(BS(p_1') \oplus BS(p_2'))) = 1$ or not. If it is 1, then distinguish it as FLEX-128; otherwise it is a random permutation.

Complexity Evaluation. The attack needs 2 encryption queries and 2 decryption queries; its time complexity is 2 BlockShuffle, 2 inverse BlockShuffle operation and 2 FLEX-128 state XOR, and the memory complexity is negligible.

4.3 Key Recovery for $(r + 1)$-round FLEX-x

For attacking $(r + 1)$-round FLEX-x, Yoyo distinguishing attack on r-round is composed with the one round trail of iterated truncated differential. The attack for FLEX-128 is shown in Fig. 5. With probability 2^{-7} only one Super-Sbox is active at X_2. By virtue of Yoyo game, only one Super-Sbox should be active in W_2. Due to inverse BlockShuffle, the differences should be confined to either upper nibbles or lower nibbles in Z_1; the other half should be free. With probability 2^{-8}, two symmetric bytes become free at Z_1. There are 8 (4 and 16 for FLEX-64 and FLEX-256 respectively) choices for symmetric byte positions which increases the probability to 2^{-5} (2^{-6} and 2^{-4} for FLEX-64 and FLEX-256). Therefore, at the cost of 2^{-12}, two symmetric bytes become free for the 7-round FLEX-128. Probability of the same event for 5-round FLEX-64 and 9-round FLEX-256 is 2^{-13} and 2^{-11} respectively. Now, the attack steps of FLEX-128, it's corresponding complexities and experimental verifications are discussed.

Attack Procedure

1. Choose 2^6 plaintexts such that they differ only in $B[0]$ and $B[8]$. Apply inverse BlockShuffle on them and query them to encryption oracle to obtain corresponding ciphertexts. Consider all ciphertext pairs, swap bytes between them according to the Super-Sbox output and query them to the decryption oracle to obtain new pairs of plaintexts. Check whether the pair has a pair of free symmetric bytes. At least one such pair is expected.
2. Repeat step 1 two more times to obtain two more right pairs. Let (c_1, c_2), (c_3, c_4) and (c_5, c_6) be such pairs and their corresponding plaintexts are (p_1, p_2), (p_3, p_4) and (p_5, p_6). After byte swapping, (c_1, c_2), (c_3, c_4) and (c_5, c_6) becomes (c_1', c_2'), (c_3', c_4') and (c_5', c_6'). BlockShuffle is applied on the decrypted value of these modified ciphertexts to obtain (p_1', p_2'), (p_3', p_4') and (p_5', p_6').

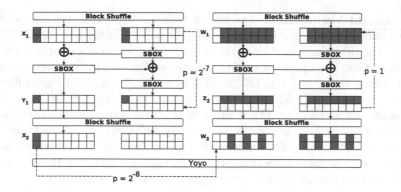

Fig. 5. 7-round Yoyo Distinguisher for FLEX-128

3. Guess key bytes 0 and 8 for K_α, run one round encryption for p'_1, p'_2 and observe whether same nibble in $B[0]$ and $B[8]$ remains free or not for the pair. Using nibble transition, out of 2^{16} candidates, 2^7 are filtered out. Then the remaining two right pairs subsequently reduces the number of candidates for $K_\alpha[0]$ and $K_\alpha[8]$ to 2^2 and 1 respectively.
4. For the remaining 7 symmetric pairs of bytes, step 3 is repeated 7 more times. At, the end 1 key candidates are expected for K_α. For each K_α, K_β is computed by using a plaintext-ciphertext pair. If there is more than one K_α, K_β pair, they are exhaustively tried for finding the right key candidate.

Complexity Evaluation. Let probability of the event that "two symmetric bytes become free" is 2^{-p}. So, for retrieving a right pair, $2^{\frac{p}{2}}$ encryption queries and 2^p decryption queries are required. For guessing each pair of key byte, 3 such right pairs are needed and to recover the key, this process need to be repeated $\frac{x}{16}$ times. Therefore, data complexity of the attack is $\frac{3 \times x}{16} \times 2^{\frac{p}{2}}$ encryption queries and $\frac{3 \times x}{16} \times 2^p$ decryption queries.

Time complexity is $\frac{3 \times x}{16} \times 2^p$ memory accesses for retrieving the stored ciphertexts.

Memory complexity is $\frac{3 \times x}{16} \times 2^{\frac{p}{2}+1}$ FLEX-x states for storing the plaintexts and ciphertexts.

The complexities of 7-round FLEX-128 key recovery attack are-

1. Data Complexity is $24 \times 2^6 \approx 2^{10.5}$ encryption queries and $24 \times 2^{12} \approx 2^{16.5}$ decryption queries.
2. Time Complexity is $2^{16.5}$ memory accesses.
3. Memory Complexity is $2^{11.5}$ FLEX-128 states.

Experimental Verification. The Yoyo attack for 7-round FLEX-128 has been experimentally verified. Initially the oracle chooses a master key randomly and computes the subkeys. Adversarial algorithm queries according to attack steps in Sect. 4.3 and retrieves right pairs. The number of key candidates corresponding to each symmetric bytes (from $(K_\alpha[0], K_\alpha[8])$ to $(K_\alpha[7], K_\alpha[15])$) after filtering with first right pairs are 502, 618, 546, 496, 510, 486, 552 and 538 respectively which conforms to the theoretical value of 2^9. The second right pairs further reduces it to 6, 7 6, 7, 7, 3, 3 and 5 respectively which is close to the theoretical value of 2^2. The third pairs reduces all these values to 1. This reduction in the number of key candidates using the right pairs conforms to the theoretical analysis. At last, the algorithm successfully recovers the subkeys.

In the next section, we discuss the success probability of distinguishing attacks reported in this work.

5 Success Probability of Distinguishing Attacks

The effectiveness of an attack depends on its success probability. First, the success probability of all reported distinguishers is computed. Then, the success probability of practical ones is experimentally verified. To deduce the theoretical estimation of success probabilities, the following theorem from [19] has been applied.

Theorem 2. *[19] Suppose, the event e happens in uniform random bitstream with probability p and in keystream of a stream cipher with probability $p(1 + q)$. Then the data complexity of the distinguisher with false positive and false negative rates α and β is given by*

$$n > \frac{\left(\kappa_1\sqrt{1-p} + \kappa_2\sqrt{(1+q)(1-p(1+q))}\right)^2}{pq^2} \tag{4}$$

where $\Phi(-\kappa_1) = \alpha$ and $\Phi(\kappa_2) = 1 - \beta$.

For computing success probability, we consider $\kappa_1 = \kappa_2$ in theorem 2, which gives us $\alpha = \beta$. Then the success probability is given by $(1 - \beta)$. Note that, in the theorem data complexity essentially refers to sample complexity. Table 5 lists the success probabilities of different distinguishers presented in this paper.

Experimental Verification. For experimental verification of success probabilities, the strategy from [21] has been followed. First, consider a blackbox which can act as either a cipher $\mathcal{C}$ or a uniform discrete random permutation $\mathcal{R}$. Then the experiment is run two times in the following ways:

1. Consider the blackbox as $\mathcal{C}$ and repeat the experiment a_c times.
2. Consider the blackbox as $\mathcal{R}$ and repeat the experiment a_r times.

Table 5. Success probabilities of various distinguishers

Distinguisher type	Block size	f	#rounds	$p \times (1 + q)$	p	Success probability
Iterated	64	1	7	2^{-42}	2^{-48}	0.8
	128	1	16	2^{-105}	2^{-112}	0.82
	256	4	21	2^{-119}	2^{-192}	0.84
Yoyo	64	n/a	5	2^{-13}	2^{-14}	0.61
	128	n/a	7	2^{-12}	2^{-13}	0.61
	256	n/a	9	2^{-11}	2^{-12}	0.61

Table 6. Confusion matrix of $\mathcal{C}$ and $\mathcal{R}$

Actual	Observed	
	$\mathcal{C}$	$\mathcal{R}$
$\mathcal{C}$	$o_c - n_{FP}$	n_{FN}
$\mathcal{R}$	n_{FP}	$o_r - n_{FN}$

Table 7. Experimental verification of success probability

Distinguisher	#rounds	f	#n	Blackbox	Detected as $\mathcal{C}$	Detected as $\mathcal{R}$	Experimental Success Probability	Estimated Success Probability
Flex-64	5	2	100	Flex-64	65	35	0.8	0.83
				$\mathcal{R}$	5	95		
Flex-64	6	2	100	Flex-64	79	21	0.76	0.77
				$\mathcal{R}$	27	73		

Let out of $(a_c + a_r)$ experiments, distinguisher decides it as $\mathcal{C}$ o_c times and as $\mathcal{R}$ o_r times. n_{FP} and n_{FN} denotes the number of false positives and false negatives respectively. Based on this parameters, the confusion matrix is shown in Table 6.

Then the success probability is calculated by:

$$Pr[Success] = \frac{(o_c - n_{FP}) + (o_r - n_{FN})}{o_c + o_r}$$

$$= \frac{(o_c - n_{FP}) + (o_r - n_{FN})}{a_c + a_r}.$$

The values of success probabilities for 5-round and 6-round Flex-64 derived using experiments and theoretical estimations are listed in Table 7.

Trade-Off Between Success Rate and Free Rounds. The iterated truncated differentials can have a different number of free rounds at the end. More number of free rounds reduces the trail complexity at the expense of success rate. For analysis, consider the case pertaining to 6-round Flex-64 with the number of free rounds 1 and 2. The success rate for both cases is listed in Table 8.

Table 8. Comparison of Success Rate for FLEX-64

f	#rounds	$p \times (1+q)$	p	Success probability
1	6	2^{-35}	2^{-48}	0.83
2	6	2^{-28}	2^{-32}	0.77

Table 9. Comparison of Success Rate for FLEX-256

f	$p \times (1+q)$	p	Success probability
1	2^{-140}	2^{-240}	0.84
2	2^{-133}	2^{-224}	0.84
3	2^{-126}	2^{-208}	0.84
4	2^{-119}	2^{-192}	0.84

For 21-round FLEX-128, the number of free rounds can take any value between 1 and 4. For each of the cases, the theoretical estimation of success probability is almost equal. The estimated success probabilities have been shown in Table 9. The difference between the distribution of random bitstream and 21-round FLEX-128 for each case is so huge, that it has a negligible effect on the success probability.

In the following section, we show how to mount forgery attacks on FLEX-AEAD variants using the idea of iterated truncated differentials.

6   Forgery Attacks on FLEXAEAD

Eichlseder *et al.* have shown forgery attacks on FLEXAEAD by applying several strategies [12]. All those strategies are also applicable using the differentials described in this paper. The main difference between these two approaches is the differential characteristics for the sequence generation. First, the differential characteristic of the sequence generation step is shown.

6.1   Differential Characteristics in Sequence Generation

A sequence of bits is used by FLEXAEAD for authenticated encryption. These sequences are generated by using PF_k, with initial state being the nonce. For details on sequence generation refer to [17]. The difference between two consecutive sequence numbers is that their last call to PF_k differ by a INC32 call. INC32 is a 32-bit word operation which acts as an XOR operation with probability 2^{-1}.

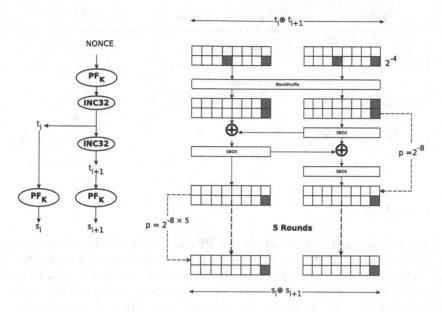

Fig. 6. Differential Characteristics of Sequence Generation for FLEXAEAD-128. Note that, plaintext difference or associated data difference can cancel out difference in $S_i \oplus S_{i+1}$ with probability 2^{-8}.

Consider, m 32-bit words in a r-round FLEX-x state. Due to INC32 with probability 2^{-m}, m nibbles at $\frac{m}{2}$ symmetric positions become active between two subsequent sequence generation steps. Due to BlockShuffle, those m active nibbles is converted to $\frac{m}{2}$ active bytes which occupies $\frac{m}{4}$ symmetric positions. In the next round, those active bytes transits to $\frac{m}{8}$ symmetric positions ($\frac{m}{4}$ active bytes) at the cost of 2^{-2m}. In the next round, $\frac{m}{16}$ symmetric positions get occupied at the cost of 2^{-m}. After repeating the process, $\left(\log_2(m) - 2\right)$ times, only one symmetric position remains occupied by the active byte. For the rest $\left(r - \log_2(m) + 2\right)$ rounds, with probability 2^{-8} for each round the position of two active nibbles in the output get fixed (Note that, in the iterated truncated differential, the position of active is not fixed and that is why the probability of 2^{-7} is paid). With 2^{-8} probability the value of the active nibbles can be fixed to a specific value.

By following this approach, the difference of two consecutive sequence numbers can be fixed to a specific value with probability 2^{-50} for FLEXAEAD-64, 2^{-60} for FLEXAEAD-128 and 2^{-80} for FLEXAEAD-256 (Corresponding complexities of forgery attacks are computed by taking the inverse of these probabilities). Differential characteristics of sequence generation for FLEXAEAD-128 is shown in Fig. 6. Once the output difference value is fixed, the techniques (*Changing Associated Data, Truncating Ciphertext, Reordering Ciphertext*) in [12] can be applied to forge ciphertext-tag pair. Comparison between several approaches regarding forgery attack is enlisted in Table 10.

Table 10. Comparison of Forgery Attacks on FLEXAEAD

Scheme	Complexity	Technique	Reference
FLEXAEAD-64	2^{50}	*Changing Associated Data*	Current Work
	2^{46}	*Truncating Ciphertext*	[12]
FLEXAEAD-128	2^{60}	*Reordering Ciphertext*	Current Work
	2^{54}		[12]
FLEXAEAD-256	2^{80}		Current Work
	2^{70}		[12]

7 Conclusion

In this work, we analyzed all variants of PF_k of FLEXAEAD. We reported a one round differential characteristic of PF_k, which due to its iterative nature was exploited to penetrate a large number of rounds. We also showed that the generalized Yoyo distinguishing attack on SPN ciphers was applicable for PF_k. While deploying Yoyo attack, a Super-Sbox construction of 1.5, 2.5 and 3.5 rounds in 64-bit, 128-bit and 256-bit PF_k respectively were reported. All these attacks were easily exploited to recover the subkeys. In addition, the iterated truncated differential attack strategy was applied to the nonce-based sequence number generator which was exploited to devise similar kinds of forgery attacks on FLEXAEAD as given by Eichlseder et al. [12]. The success probabilities of all distinguishing attacks were shown to be high. All attacks reported in this work with practical complexities were experimentally verified. All these attacks have exploited a vulnerability in the design which is based on dividing the nibbles into two parts while using AES S-box.

References

1. CAESAR Competition. https://competitions.cr.yp.to/caesar.html
2. National Institute of Standards and Technology (NIST): AES Development (1997). https://csrc.nist.gov/projects/cryptographic-standards-and-guidelines/archived-crypto-projects/aes-development
3. National Institute of Standards and Technology (NIST): Lightweight cryp- tography standardization process (2019). https://csrc.nist.gov/projects/lightweight-cryptography
4. National Institute of Standards and Technology (NIST): SHA-3 Standardization Process (2007). https://csrc.nist.gov/projects/hash-functions/sha-3-project
5. Alkhzaimi, H.A., Lauridsen, M.M.: Cryptanalysis of the SIMON Family of Block Ciphers. Cryptology ePrint Archive, Report 2013/543 (2013). https://eprint.iacr.org/2013/543

6. Avanzi, R.: The QARMA block cipher family. almost MDS matrices over rings with zero divisors, nearly symmetric even-mansour constructions with non-involutory central rounds, and search heuristics for low-latency S-boxes. IACR Trans. Symmetric Cryptol. **2017**(1), 4–44 (2017)
7. Banik, S., et al.: Cryptanalysis of ForkAES. In: Deng, R.H., Gauthier-Umaña, V., Ochoa, M., Yung, M. (eds.) ACNS 2019. LNCS, vol. 11464, pp. 43–63. Springer, Cham (2019). https://doi.org/10.1007/978-3-030-21568-2_3
8. Banik, S., Pandey, S.K., Peyrin, T., Sasaki, Y., Sim, S.M., Todo, Y.: GIFT: A small present - towards reaching the limit of lightweight encryption. In: CHES (2017)
9. Beierle, C., et al.: The SKINNY family of block ciphers and its low-latency variant MANTIS. In: CRYPTO (2016)
10. Bogdanov, A., et al.: PRESENT: an ultra-lightweight block cipher. In: Paillier, P., Verbauwhede, I. (eds.) CHES 2007. LNCS, vol. 4727, pp. 450–466. Springer, Heidelberg (2007). https://doi.org/10.1007/978-3-540-74735-2_31
11. De Cannière, C., Dunkelman, O., Knežević, M.: KATAN and KTANTAN – a family of small and efficient hardware-oriented block ciphers. In: Clavier, C., Gaj, K. (eds.) Cryptographic Hardware and Embedded Systems - CHES 2009, pp. 272–288. Springer, Berlin Heidelberg, Berlin, Heidelberg (2009). https://doi.org/10.1007/978-3-642-04138-9_20
12. Eichlseder, M., Kales, D., Schofnegger, M.: Forgery Attacks on FlexAE and Flex-AEAD. Cryptology ePrint Archive, Report 2019/679 (2019). https://eprint.iacr.org/2019/679
13. Eichlseder, M., Kales, D., Schofnegger, M.: Official Comment: FleaxAEAD. Posting on the NIST LWC mailing list (2019)
14. Mege, A.: Official Comment: FLEXAEAD. Posting on the NIST LWC mailing list (2019)
15. do Nascimento, E.M., Xexéo, J.A.M.: A flexible authenticated lightweight cipher using even-mansour construction. In: IEEE International Conference on Communications, ICC 2017, Paris, France, 21–25 May 2017, pp. 1–6 (2017)
16. do Nascimento, E.M., Xexéo, J.A.M.: A Lightweight Cipher with Integrated Authentication. In: CONCURSO DE TESES E DISSERTAÇÕES - SIMPÓSIO BRASILEIRO EM SEGURANÇA DA INFORMAÇÕO E DE SISTEMAS COMPUTACIONAIS, SBSEG, vol. 18 (2018)
17. do Nascimento, E.M., Xexéo, J.A.M.: FlexAEAD - a lightweight cipher with integrated authentication (2019). https://csrc.nist.gov/CSRC/media/Projects/Lightweight-Cryptography/documents/round-1/spec-doc/FlexAEAD-spec.pdf
18. do Nascimento, E.: Algoritmo de Criptografia Leve com Utilização de Autenticação. Ph.D. thesis, Instituto Militar de Engenharia, Rio de Janeiro (2017)
19. Paul, G., Ray, S.: On data complexity of distinguishing attacks versus message recovery attacks on stream ciphers. Des. Codes Cryptol. **86**(6), 1211–1247 (2017). https://doi.org/10.1007/s10623-017-0391-z
20. Rønjom, S., Bardeh, N.G., Helleseth, T.: Yoyo tricks with AES. In: Takagi, T., Peyrin, T. (eds.) ASIACRYPT 2017. LNCS, vol. 10624, pp. 217–243. Springer, Cham (2017). https://doi.org/10.1007/978-3-319-70694-8_8
21. Saha, D., Rahman, M., Paul, G.: New Yoyo tricks with AES-based permutations. IACR Trans. Symmetric Cryptol. **2018**(4), 102–127 (2018)

BBB Secure Nonce Based MAC Using Public Permutations

Avijit Dutta[1(✉)] and Mridul Nandi[2]

[1] Indian Institute of Technology, Kharagpur, India
avirocks.dutta13@gmail.com
[2] Indian Statistical Institute, Kolkata, India
mridul.nandi@gmail.com

Abstract. In the recent trend of CAESAR competition and NIST light-weight competition, cryptographic community have witnessed the submissions of several cryptographic schemes that are build on public random permutations. Recently, in CRYPTO 2019, Chen et al. have initiated an interesting research direction in designing beyond birthday bound PRFs from public random permutations and they proposed two instances of such PRFs. In this work, we extend this research direction by proposing a nonce-based MAC build from public random permutations. We show that our proposed MAC achieves $2n/3$ bit security (*with respect to the state size of the permutation*) and the bound is essentially tight. Moreover, the security of the MAC degrades gracefully with the repetition of the nonce.

Keywords: Faulty nonce · Mirror theory · Public permutation · Expectation method

1 Introduction

NONCE-BASED MAC. Message Authentication Code (or in short MAC) is an important cryptogaphic primitive to authenticate any digital message or packet transmitted over an insecure communication channel. When a sender wants to send a message m, she computes a MAC function with input m, the shared secret key k, and possibly an auxiliary input variable ν (called nonce), and obtains a tag t. Then she sends (ν, m, t) to the receiver. Upon receiving, receiver verifies the authenticity of (ν, m, t) by computing the MAC using (ν, m, k) and checks whether the computed tag t' matches with t.

Wegman-Carter (WC) MAC [25] is the first example of a nonce-based MAC which masks the hash value of the message with an encrypted nonce to generate the tag. WC MAC gives optimal security when the nonce is unique for every authenticated messages. However, its security is compromised if the nonce repeats even once. Wegman-Cater MAC, when instantiated with a polynomial hash, then the repetition of the nonce reveals the hash key of the polynomial hash. However, maintaining the uniqueness of the nonce for every authenticated

© Springer Nature Switzerland AG 2020
A. Nitaj and A. Youssef (Eds.): AFRICACRYPT 2020, LNCS 12174, pp. 172–191, 2020.
https://doi.org/10.1007/978-3-030-51938-4_9

messages is a challenging task in practical contexts. For example, it is difficult to maintain the uniqueness of the nonce while implementing the cipher in a stateless device or in cases where the nonce is chosen randomly from a small set. The nonce may also accidentally repeats due to a faulty implementation of the cipher or due to the fault occured by resetting of the nonce itself [4]. Therefore, the guard from the nonce repetition attack is much desired from a nonce-based MAC.

As a remedy of this, *Encrypted Wegman-Carter-Shoup* (EWCS) [11] MAC was proposed that guarantees the security even when the nonce repeats. But its security is limited only up to the birthday bound even when nonce is unique. To this end, *Encrypted Wegman-Carter with Davies-Meyer* [11] (or EWCDM) and *Decrypted Wegman-Carter with Davies-Meyer* [13] (or DWCDM) have been proposed that gives beyond the birthday bound security when nonce is unique[1] and birthday bound security when nonce repeats[2]. However, the security of both these constructions fall to the birthday bound with a single repetition of the nonce, i.e., if the nonce ever repeats accidentally, security of both the constructions immediately drops to the birthday bound.

NONCE BASED ENHANCED HASH-THEN-MASK. In FSE 2010 [21], Minematsu proposed EHtM, a beyond birthday bound secure probabilisitic MAC. It is build upon two independent n-bit keyed functions F_{k_1} and F_{k_2} and an n-bit axu hash function H_{k_h}, defined as follows:

$$\mathsf{EHtM}(m) \triangleq (r \xleftarrow{\$} \{0,1\}^n, F_{k_1}(r) \oplus F_{k_2}(r \oplus H_{k_h}(m))).$$

This construction has been further analyzed in [15] for improving its security bound. In Eurocrypt 2019, Dutta et al. [16] proposed a nonce-based variant of EHtM, called nEHtM MAC, where the random salt r is replaced by an $n - 1$ bit nonce value ν and an n-bit block cipher E_k is used as an internal primitive instead of two independent n-bit keyed functions. Schematic diagram of nEHtM is shown in Fig. 1 Similar to EWCDM and DWCDM, nEHtM gives beyond the (birthday bound) security in nonce-respecting (resp. nonce misuse) setting. But, unlike these two constructions, security of nEHtM MAC degrades gracefully with the repetition of the nonce. In other words, security of nEHtM remains beyond the birthday bound with a single repetition of the nonce (which is not true for EWCDM and DWCDM). That is, one can get adequate security from nEHtM if the repetition of the nonce occurs in a controlled way, a feature which is not present in EWCDM or DWCDM. This phenomena is formally captured by a notion, called **faulty nonce model** [16]. Informally, it says that a nonce is *faulty* if it appears in a previous signing query. It has been stated in [16] that faulty nonce model is a weaker notion than *multicollision* of nonces – a natural and a popular metric to measure the misuses of nonce. Under the notion of faulty nonce model, Dutta et al. have shown that nEHtM is secured roughly upto $2^{2n/3}$ queries.

---

[1] We call this notion *nonce-respecting* setting.
[2] We call this notion *nonce-misuse* setting.

We would like to mention here that this construction was also analyzed by Moch and List [22] in parallel to [16] in the name of HPxNP, where two independent n-bit block ciphers have been used (as they did not use the domain separation technique). However, Moch and List analyzed its security under the condition of the uniqueness of the nonce, whereas Dutta et al. [16] proved its graceful security with respect to the repetition of the nonce.

1.1 Permutation Based Cryptography

All the above discussed nonce-based MACs are build on block ciphers as their underlying primitives and even stronger, these primitives are evaluated only in the forward direction. As most of the block ciphers are designed to be efficient in both the forward and the inverse direction, block ciphers are over-hyped primitives for such purpose [10]. On the other extreme, cryptographic permutations are particularly designed with the motive to be fast in the forward direction, but not necessarily in the inverse direction. Examples of such permutation includes Keccak [2], Gimli [1], SPONGENT [5]. Moreover, in most of the cases evaluating an unkeyed public permutation is faster than evaluating a keyed block cipher, as the latter involves in evaluating the underlying key scheduling algorithm each time the block cipher is invoked in the design. With the advancement of public permutation-based designs and the efficiencies of evaluating it in the forward direction, numerous public permutation-based inverse-free hash and authenticated encryption designs have been proposed. The use of cryptographic permutation gained the momentum during SHA-3 competition [24]. Furthermore, the selection of the permutation-based Keccak sponge function as the SHA-3 standard has given a high level of confidence on using this primitive in the community. Today, permutation-based sponge construction has become a successful and a full-fledged alternative to the block cipher-based modes. In fact, in the first round of the ongoing NIST light-weight competition [23], 24 out of 57 submissions are based on cryptographic permutations, and out of 24, 16 permutation based proposals have been qualified for the second round. This statistics, beyond any doubt, clearly depicts the wide adoption of permutation based designs [1,3,7,8,12,14] in the community. In another direction, a long line of research work has been carried out in the study of designing block ciphers and tweakable block ciphers out of public random permutations. Even Mansour (EM) [17] and Iterated Even Mansour (IEM) cipher [6] are the notable approaches in this direction.

NONCE-BASED MAC BUILD FROM PUBLIC PERMUTATIONS. Nonce-based MACs using public permutations are mostly designed with sponge type of constructions. But the drawback of such designs are: (i) they do not use the full size of the permutation for guarranting security and (ii) they attain only the birthday bound security in the size of its capacity c, i.e., $c/2$ bit security (except Bettle [7], whose security bound is roughly the size of its capacity). Now, it is an admissible fact that the sponge type designs, which offer $c/2$-bit security, are good in practice when they are instantiated with large size permutations such as Keccak [2], whose state size is 1600 bits. But such large size permutations are not suitable for use in resource constrained environment. In such scneario, instead of using such large size permutations, one aims to use light-weight permutations such as SPONGENT [5] and PHOTON [18], whose state size go as low as 88 and 100 bits respectively. If we use these light-weight permutations as underlying primitives in birthday bound secure sponge type constructions, then it practically offers inadequate security. As a result, sponge type constructions instantiated with light-weight permutations are not suitable for deploying in resource constrained environment. Thus, it is natural to ask

Can we design a public permutation-based nonce-based MAC that gives an adequate security when instantiated with light-weight permutation?

This question hinted us to think of designing a MAC whose security depends on the entire size of the underlying permutation (unlike sponge type constructions whose security depends on only a part of the entire size of the underlying permutation) and the security must cross the birthday barrier. Coming up with such a design is the goal of this paper. In this direction, Chen et al. [10] have shown two instances of public permutation-based pseudo random functions that give beyond the birthday bound security with respect to the size of the permutation. We extend this line of research work by designing a public permutation-based nonce-based MAC that gives beyond the birthday bound security with respect to the size of the permutation.

OUR CONTRIBUTION. The sole contribution of this paper is to design a beyond birthday bound secure nonce-based MAC using public random permutations. To this end we propose nEHtM_p, a nonce based MAC designed using public permutations. As depicted in Fig. 1, our construction structurally resembles to the nEHtM MAC [16] where we replace its block cipher with a public random permutation and an appropriate masking of the key.

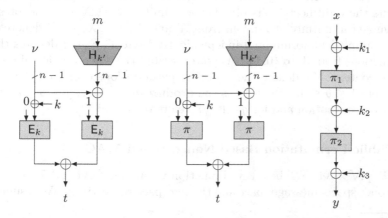

Fig. 1. (Left): nEHtM MAC based on block cipher E_k; (Middle): nEHtM_p MAC based on single public random permutation π; (Right): 2-round iterated even mansour cipher.

Note that, by instantiating the underlying block cipher of nEHtM MAC with 2-round iterated Even-Mansour cipher (as shown in Fig. 1), one can easily make the public permutation variant of nEHtM MAC, which becomes secure beyond the birthday bound (in faulty nonce model). However such transformation requires 4 permutation calls, 7 xor operations and one hash evaluation. Compared to this, nEHtM$_p$ requires only 2 permutation calls, 3 xor operations and one hash evaluation. We have shown that nEHtM$_p$ is secured roughly up to $2^{2n/3}$ queries in the nonce-respecting setting. Moreover, this security bound degrades in a graceful manner under the faulty nonce model [16]. We show the unforgeability of this construction through an extended distinguishing game and apply the expectation method to bound its distinguishing advantage. We also show that our proven security bound is tight by giving a matching attack on it with roughly $2^{2n/3}$ query complexity and 2^{2n-4} time complexity[3].

2   Preliminaries

GENERAL NOTATIONS: For $n \in \mathbb{N}$, we denote the set of all binary strings of length n and the set of all binary strings of finite arbitrary length by $\{0,1\}^n$ and $\{0,1\}^*$ respectively. We often refer the elements of $\{0,1\}^n$ as *block*. For an n-bit binary string $x = (x_{n-1} \ldots x_0)$, msb(x) denotes the first bit of x in left to right ordering, i.e. msb$(x) = x_{n-1}$. Moreover, chop$_{\mathrm{msb}}(x) \triangleq (x_{n-2} \ldots, x_0)$, i.e., chop$_{\mathrm{msb}}(x)$ returns the string x by dropping just its msb. For any element $x \in \{0,1\}^*$, $|x|$ denotes the number of bits in x and for $x, y \in \{0,1\}^*$, $x\|y$ denotes the concatenation of x followed by y. We denote the bitwise xor operation of $x, y \in \{0,1\}^n$ by $x \oplus y$. We parse $x \in \{0,1\}^*$ as $x = x_1\|x_2\|\ldots\|x_l$ where for each $i = 1, \ldots, l-1$, x_i is a block and $1 \leq |x_l| \leq n$. For a sequence of elements $(x^1, x^2, \ldots, x^s) \in \{0,1\}^*$, x_a^i denotes the a-th block of i-th element x^i. For a value s, we denote by $t \leftarrow s$ the assignment of s to variable t. For any natural number $j \in \mathbb{N}$, $\langle j \rangle_s$ denotes the s bit binary representation of integer j. For $i \in \{0,1\}^n$, left$_k(i)$ represents the leftmost k bits of i. Similarly, right$_k(i)$ represents the rightmost k bits of i. For any finite set $\mathcal{X}$, $X \leftarrow_{\$} \mathcal{X}$ denotes that X is sampled uniformly at random from $\mathcal{X}$ and $X_1, \ldots, X_s \leftarrow_{\$} \mathcal{X}$ denotes that X_i's are sampled uniformly and independently from $\mathcal{X}$. $\mathbb{F}_{\mathcal{X}}(n)$ denotes the set of all functions from $\mathcal{X}$ to $\{0,1\}^n$. We often write $\mathbb{F}(n)$ when the domain is clear from the context. We denote the set of all permutations over $\{0,1\}^n$ by $\mathbb{P}(n)$. For integers $1 \leq b \leq a$, $(a)_b$ denotes the product $a(a-1)\ldots(a-b+1)$, where $(a)_0 = 1$ by convention and for $q \in \mathbb{N}$, $[q]$ refers to the set $\{1, \ldots, q\}$.

2.1   Public Permutation Based Nonce Based MAC

Let $\mathsf{F} : \mathcal{K} \times \mathcal{N} \times \mathcal{M} \rightarrow \mathcal{T}$ be a keyed function where $\mathcal{K}, \mathcal{N}, \mathcal{M}$ and $\mathcal{T}$ are the key space, nonce space, message space and the tag space respectively. We assume that

---

[3] Time complexity does not refer to the evaluation of permutations, but only refers to the time required to find a suitable matching pair.

F makes internal calls to the public random permutations $\boldsymbol{\pi} = (\pi_1, \ldots, \pi_d)$ for $d \geq 1$, where all of the d permutations are independent and uniformly sampled from $\mathbb{P}(n)$ for some $n \in \mathbb{N}$. For simplicity, we write $\mathsf{F}_k^{\boldsymbol{\pi}}$ to denote F with uniform k and uniform $\boldsymbol{\pi}$. Based on $\mathsf{F}_k^{\boldsymbol{\pi}}$, we define the nonce-based message authentication code $\mathcal{I} = (\mathcal{I}.\mathsf{KGen}, \mathcal{I}.\mathsf{Sign}, \mathcal{I}.\mathsf{Ver})$ build from public permutations as follows: For $k \in \mathcal{K}$, the signing algorithm $\mathcal{I}.\mathsf{Sign}_k$, takes as input $(\nu, m) \in \mathcal{N} \times \mathcal{M}$ and outputs $t \leftarrow \mathsf{F}_k^{\boldsymbol{\pi}}(\nu, m)$ and the verification algorithm $\mathcal{I}.\mathsf{Ver}_k$, takes as input $(\nu, m, t) \in \mathcal{N} \times \mathcal{M} \times \mathcal{T}$ and outputs 1 if $\mathsf{F}_k^{\boldsymbol{\pi}}(\nu, m) = t$; otherwise it outputs 0.

A signing query (ν, m) by an adversary A is called a **faulty query** if A has already queried to the signing algorithm with the same nonce but with a different message. Let A be a $(\eta, q_m, q_v, p, \mathsf{t})$-adversary against the unforgeability of $\mathcal{I}$ with oracle access of the signing algorithm $\mathcal{I}.\mathsf{Sign}_k$, the verification algorithm $\mathcal{I}.\mathsf{Ver}_k$ and the d-tuple of permutations $\boldsymbol{\pi}$ and their inverses $\boldsymbol{\pi} = (\pi_1^{-1}, \ldots, \pi_d^{-1})$ such that it makes at most η faulty signing queries out of q_m signing, q_v verification and p primitive queries with running time of A at most t. A is said to be *nonce respecting* (resp. nonce misuse) if $\eta = 0$ (resp. $\eta \geq 1$). However, A may repeats nonces in its verification queries. Moreover, the primitive queries are interleaved with the signing and the verification queries. A is said to *forge $\mathcal{I}$* if for any of its verification queries (not obtained through a previous signing query), the verification algorithm returns 1. The advantage of A against the unforgeability of the nonce based MAC $\mathcal{I}$ is defined as

$$\mathbf{Adv}_{\mathcal{I}}^{\mathrm{nMAC}}(\mathsf{A}) \triangleq \Pr\left[\mathsf{A}^{\mathcal{I}.\mathsf{Sign}_k, \mathcal{I}.\mathsf{Ver}_k, \boldsymbol{\pi}, \boldsymbol{\pi}^{-1}} \text{ forges }\right],$$

where the randomness is defined over $k \leftarrow_\$ \mathcal{K}$, $\pi_1, \ldots, \pi_d \leftarrow_\$ \mathbb{P}(n)$ and the randomness of the adversary (if any). We write

$$\mathbf{Adv}_{\mathcal{I}}^{\mathrm{nMAC}}(\eta, q_m, q_v, p, \mathsf{t}) \triangleq \max_{\mathsf{A}} \mathbf{Adv}_{\mathcal{I}}^{\mathrm{nMAC}}(\mathsf{A}),$$

where the maximum is taken over all $(\eta, q_m, q_v, p, \mathsf{t})$-adversaries A. In this paper, we skip the time parameter of the adversary as we will assume throughout the paper that the adversary is computationally unbounded. This will render us to assume that the adversary is deterministic.

UPPER BOUND ON $\mathbf{Adv}_{\mathcal{I}}^{\mathrm{nMAC}}(\mathsf{A})$ ([15]). To obtain an upper bound for $\mathbf{Adv}_{\mathcal{I}}^{\mathrm{nMAC}}(\mathsf{A})$, we consider a random oracle RF that samples the tag t independently and uniformly at random from $\{0, 1\}^n$ for every nonce message pair (ν, m) and the Rej oracle always returns $\perp$ for any (ν, m, t). Then, $\mathbf{Adv}_{\mathcal{I}}^{\mathrm{nMAC}}(\mathsf{A})$ is upper bounded by

$$\max_{\mathsf{A}} \left| \Pr\left[\mathsf{A}^{\mathcal{I}.\mathsf{Sign}_k, \mathcal{I}.\mathsf{Ver}_k, \boldsymbol{\pi}, \boldsymbol{\pi}^{-1}} \Rightarrow 1\right] - \Pr\left[\mathsf{A}^{\mathsf{RF}, \mathsf{Rej}, \boldsymbol{\pi}, \boldsymbol{\pi}^{-1}} \Rightarrow 1\right] \right|, \qquad (1)$$

where $\mathsf{A}^{\mathcal{O}} \Rightarrow 1$ denotes that adversary A outputs 1 after interacting with its oracle $\mathcal{O}$ (which could be a multiple of oracles).

2.2   Almost Xor Universal and Almost Regular Hash Function

Let $\mathcal{K}_h$ and $\mathcal{X}$ be two non-empty finite sets and H be a keyed function H : $\mathcal{K}_h \times \mathcal{X} \to \{0,1\}^n$. Then, H is said to be an ϵ_{axu}-almost xor universal (axu) hash function, if for any distinct $x, x' \in \mathcal{X}$ and for any $\Delta \in \{0,1\}^n$,

$$\Pr\left[K_h \xleftarrow{\$} \mathcal{K}_h : \mathsf{H}_{K_h}(x) \oplus \mathsf{H}_{K_h}(x') = \Delta\right] \leq \epsilon_{\mathrm{axu}}.$$

Moreover, H is said to be an ϵ_{reg}-almost regular (ar) hash function, if for any $x \in \mathcal{X}$ and for any $\Delta \in \{0,1\}^n$,

$$\Pr\left[K_h \xleftarrow{\$} \mathcal{K}_h : \mathsf{H}_{K_h}(x) = \Delta\right] \leq \epsilon_{\mathrm{reg}}.$$

2.3   Expectation Method

The Expectation Method of Hoang and Tessaro [19] was used to derive a tight multi-user security bound of the key-alternating cipher. This technique has subsequently been used in [16,20]. Let A be a computationally unbounded deterministic distinguisher that interacts with either of the two worlds: $\mathbf{O}_{\mathrm{re}}$ or $\mathbf{O}_{\mathrm{id}}$, where these oracles are possibly randomized stateful systems. After the interaction, A returns a single bit. This interaction between A and the system results in an ordered sequence of queries and responses which is summarized in $\tau = ((x_1, y_1), (x_2, y_2), \ldots, (x_q, y_q))$, called a *transcript*, where x_i is the i-th query of A and y_i is the corresponding response of the system to which A interacts with. Let D_{re} (resp. D_{id}) be the random variable that takes a transcript resulting from the interaction between A and $\mathbf{O}_{\mathrm{re}}$ (resp. $\mathbf{O}_{\mathrm{id}}$). A transcript τ is said to be *attainble* if $\Pr[\mathsf{D}_{\mathrm{id}} = \tau] > 0$. Let Θ denotes the set of all attainable transcripts.

Let $\Phi : \Theta \to [0, \infty)$ be a non-negative function which maps any attainable transcript to a non-negative real value. Suppose there is a set of good transcripts $\mathsf{GoodT} \subseteq \Theta$ such that for any $\tau \in \mathsf{GoodT}$,

$$\frac{\Pr\left[\mathsf{D}_{\mathrm{re}} = \tau\right]}{\Pr\left[\mathsf{D}_{\mathrm{id}} = \tau\right]} \geq 1 - \Phi(\tau). \tag{2}$$

Then, the statistical distance between D_{re} and D_{id} can be bounded as

$$\Delta(\mathsf{D}_{\mathrm{re}}, \mathsf{D}_{\mathrm{id}}) \leq \mathbf{E}[\Phi(\mathsf{D}_{\mathrm{id}})] + \Pr[\mathsf{D}_{\mathrm{id}} \in \mathsf{BadT}], \tag{3}$$

where $\mathsf{BadT} \triangleq \Theta \setminus \mathsf{GoodT}$ is the set of all bad transcripts. In other words, the advantage of A in distinguishing $\mathbf{O}_{\mathrm{re}}$ from $\mathbf{O}_{\mathrm{id}}$ is bounded by $\mathbf{E}[\Phi(\mathsf{D}_{\mathrm{id}})] + \Pr[\mathsf{D}_{\mathrm{id}} \in \mathsf{BadT}]$. In the rest of the paper, we write Θ, GoodT and BadT to denote the set of attainable, set of good and set of bad transcripts respectively.

2.4   Sum-Capture Lemma

We use the sum capture lemma by Chen et al. [9]. Informally, the result states that for a random subset $\mathcal{S}$ of $\{0,1\}^n$ of size q and for any two arbitrary subsets

$\mathcal{A}$ and $\mathcal{B}$ of $\{0,1\}^n$, the size of the set $\{(s,a,b) \in \mathcal{S} \times \mathcal{A} \times \mathcal{B} : s = a \oplus b\}$ is at most $q|\mathcal{A}||\mathcal{B}|/2^n$, except with negligible probability. In our setting, $\mathcal{S}$ is the set of tag values t_i, which are sampled with replacement from $\{0,1\}^n$.

Lemma 1 (Sum-Capture Lemma). *Let $n, q \in \mathbb{N}$ such that $9n \leq q \leq 2^{n-1}$. Let $\mathcal{S} = \{t_1, \ldots, t_q\} \subseteq \{0,1\}^n$ such that t_i's are with replacement sample of $\{0,1\}^n$. Then, for any two subsets $\mathcal{A}$ and $\mathcal{B}$ of $\{0,1\}^n$, we have*

$$\Pr[|\{(t,a,b) \in \mathcal{S} \times \mathcal{A} \times \mathcal{B} : t = a \oplus b\}| \geq q|\mathcal{A}||\mathcal{B}|/2^n + 3\sqrt{nq|\mathcal{A}||\mathcal{B}|}] \leq \frac{2}{2^n}, \quad (4)$$

where the randomness is defined over the set $\mathcal{S}$.

3   Solving a System of Affine (Non)-equations

In this section, we present a lower bound on the number of solutions of a system of bi-variate affine equations and bi-variate affine non-equations over a finite number of unknown variables which are without replacement samples of $\{0,1\}^n$. This result will become handy for analysing the security of our proposed construction.

INITIAL SETUP: Consider an undirected edge-labelled acylic graph $G = (\mathcal{V} \triangleq \{Y_1, \ldots, Y_\alpha\}, \mathcal{F} \sqcup \mathcal{F}', \mathcal{L})$ with edge labelling function $\mathcal{L} : \mathcal{F} \sqcup \mathcal{F}' \to \{0,1\}^n$, where the edge set is partitioned into two disjoint sets $\mathcal{F}$ and $\mathcal{F}'$. For an edge $\{Y_i, Y_j\} \in \mathcal{F}$, we write $\mathcal{L}(\{Y_i, Y_j\}) = \lambda_{ij}$ (and so $\lambda_{ij} = \lambda_{ji}$) and $\mathcal{L}(\{Y_i, Y_j\}) = \lambda'_{ij}$ for all $\{Y_i, Y_j\} \in \mathcal{F}'$. Let $G^= \triangleq (\mathcal{V}, \mathcal{F}, \mathcal{L}_{|\mathcal{F}})$ denotes the subgraph of G, where $\mathcal{L}_{|\mathcal{F}}$ is the function $\mathcal{L}$ restricted over the set $\mathcal{F}$. We say G is **good** if it satisfies the following two conditions: (i) for all paths P_{st} in graph $G^=$, $\mathcal{L}(P_{st}) \neq 0$. where $\mathcal{L}(P_{st}) \triangleq \sum_{e \in P_{st}} \mathcal{L}(e) = Y_s \oplus Y_t$ and P_{st} is a path of $G^=$ between vertex s and t and (ii) for all cycles C in G such that the edge set of C contains exactly one non-equation edge $e' \in \mathcal{F}'$, $\mathcal{L}(C) \neq \mathbf{0}$, where $\mathcal{L}(C) \triangleq \sum_{e \in C} \mathcal{L}(e)$. For such a good graph G, the induced system of equations and non-equations is defined as:

$$\mathcal{E}_G = \begin{cases} Y_i \oplus Y_j & = \lambda_{ij} \ \forall \ \{Y_i, Y_j\} \in \mathcal{F}, \\ Y_i \oplus Y_j & \neq \lambda'_{ij} \ \forall \ \{Y_i, Y_j\} \in \mathcal{F}', \end{cases}$$

The set of components in G is denoted by $\mathsf{comp}(G) = (\mathsf{C}_1, \ldots, \mathsf{C}_k)$, μ_i denotes the size of (i.e. the number of vertices in) the i-th component C_i and $\mu_{\max} = \max\{\mu_1, \ldots, \mu_k\}$ is the size of the largest component of G. ρ_i the total number of vertices upto the i-th component with the convention that $\rho_0 = 0$ (Fig. 2).

Definition 1 (Injective Solution). *With respect to the system of equations and non-equations $\mathcal{E}_G$ (as defined above), an injective function $\Phi : \mathcal{V} \to \mathcal{R}$, where $\mathcal{R} \subseteq \{0,1\}^n$, is said to be an injective solution if $\Phi(Y_i) \oplus \Phi(Y_j) = \lambda_{ij}$ for all $\{Y_i, Y_j\} \in \mathcal{F}$ and $\Phi(Y_i) \oplus \Phi(Y_j) \neq \lambda'_{ij}$ for all $\{Y_i, Y_j\} \in \mathcal{F}'$.*

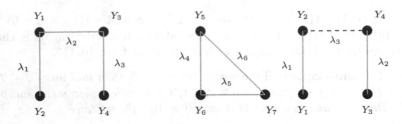

Fig. 2. (Left): Graph is a tree of size 4; (Middle): Graph is a cycle of size 3; (Right): Graph with equation edges and non-equation edge. Continuous red edge represents equation edge and dashed blue edge represents non-equation edge. (Color figure online)

Theorem 1. *Let $\mathcal{U} = \{u_1, \ldots, u_\sigma\}$ be a non-empty finite subset of $\{0,1\}^n$, for some $\sigma \geq 0$. Let $G = (\mathcal{V}, \mathcal{F} \sqcup \mathcal{F}', \mathcal{L})$ be a good graph with α vertices such that $|\mathcal{F}| = q_m, |\mathcal{F}'| = q_v$. Let $\mathsf{comp}(G^=) = (\mathsf{C}_1, \ldots, \mathsf{C}_k)$ and $|\mathsf{C}_i| = \mu_i$, $\rho_i = (\mu_1 + \cdots + \mu_i)$. Then the total number of injective solutions, chosen from a set $\mathcal{Z} = \{0,1\}^n \setminus \mathcal{U}$ of size $2^n - \sigma$, for the induced system of equations and non-equations $\mathcal{E}_G$ is at least:*

$$\frac{(2^n - \sigma)_\alpha}{2^{nq_m}} \left(1 - \sum_{i=1}^{k} \frac{6(\rho'_{i-1})^2 \binom{\mu_i}{2}}{2^{2n}} - \frac{2q_v}{2^n} \right), \tag{5}$$

provided $\rho'_k \mu_{\max} \leq 2^n/4$ where $\rho'_i = \rho_i + \sigma$.

Proof. We proceed the proof by counting the number of solutions in each of the k components. Let $\tilde{\mu}_{ij}$ denotes the number of edges from $\mathcal{F}'$ connecting vertices between i-th and j-th component of $G^=$ and μ'_i to be the number of edges in $\mathcal{F}'$ incident on $v_i \in \mathcal{V} \setminus G^=(\mathcal{V})$. For the first component, the number of solutions is at least exactly $(2^n - \mu_1\sigma)$. We fix such a solution and count the number of solutions for the second component. which is $(2^n - \mu_1\mu_2 - \tilde{\mu}_{1,2} - \mu_2\sigma)$. This is because, let $Y_{i_{\mu_1+1}}$ be an arbitrary vertex of the second component and let $y_{i_{\mu_1+1}}$ be a solution of it. This solution is valid if the following conditions hold:

- $y_{i_{\mu_1+1}} \notin \mathcal{U}$.
- $y_{i_{\mu_1+1}}$ does not take μ_1 values $(y_{i_1}, \ldots, y_{i_{\mu_1}})$ from the first component.
- It must discard $\mu_1(\mu_2 - 1)$ values $(y_{i_1} \oplus \mathcal{L}(P_j), \ldots, y_{i_{\mu_1}} \oplus \mathcal{L}(P_j))$ for all possible paths P_j from a fixed vertex to any other vertex in the second component.
- It must discard $p(\mu_2 - 1)$ values as $(y_{i_{\mu_1+1}} \oplus \mathcal{L}(P_j)) \notin \mathcal{Y}$ for all possible paths P_j from $Y_{i_{\mu_1+1}}$ to any other vertices in the second component.
- $y_{i_{\mu_1+1}}$ does not take $\tilde{\mu}_{12}$ values to compensate for the fact that the set of values is no longer a group.

Summing up all the conditions, the number of solutions for the second component is at least $(2^n - \mu_1\mu_2 - \mu_2\sigma - \tilde{\mu}_{12})$. In general, the total number of solutions for the i-th component is at least $\prod_{i=1}^{k} \left(2^n - \rho_{i-1}\mu_i - \mu_i\sigma - \sum_{j=1}^{i-1} \tilde{\mu}_{ij} \right)$.

Suppose there are k' vertices that do not belong to the set of vertices of the subgraph $G^=$. Fix such a vertex Y_{ρ_k+i} and let us assume that μ'_{ρ_k+i} blue dashed edges are incident on it. If y_{ρ_k+i} is a valid solution to the variable Y_{ρ_k+i}, then we must have (a) y_{ρ_k+i} should be distinct from the previous ρ_k assigned values, (b) y_{ρ_k+i} should be distinct from the $(i-1)$ values assigned to the variables that do not belong to the set of vertices of the subgraph $G^=(\mathcal{V})$, (c) y_{ρ_k+i} should be distinct from the values of $\mathcal{U}$, and (d) y_{ρ_k+i} should not take those μ'_{ρ_k+i} values. Therefore, the total number of solutions is at least

$$h_\alpha \geq \prod_{i=1}^{k}\left(2^n - \rho_{i-1}\mu_i - \mu_i\sigma - \sum_{j=1}^{i-1}\tilde{\mu}_{ij}\right)\cdot\prod_{i\in[k']}(2^n - \rho_k - \sigma - i + 1 - \mu'_{\rho_k+i}). \quad (6)$$

Let $\chi_i \triangleq (\tilde{\mu}_{i1} + \ldots + \tilde{\mu}_{i,i-1}), q''_v \triangleq (\mu'_{\rho_k+1} + \ldots + \mu'_{\rho_k+k'})$ and $\rho'_i = \rho_i + \sigma$. After a simple algebraic calculation on Eq. (6), we obtain

$$h_\alpha \frac{2^{nq}q_m}{(2^n - \sigma)_\alpha} \geq \underbrace{\prod_{i=1}^{k}\frac{(2^n - \rho'_{i-1}\mu_i - \chi_i)2^{n(\mu_i-1)}}{(2^n - \rho'_{i-1})_{\mu_i}}}_{\text{D.1}}\underbrace{\prod_{i=1}^{k'}\frac{(2^n - \rho'_k - i + 1 - \mu'_{\rho_k+i})}{(2^n - \rho'_k - i + 1)}}_{\text{D.2}}.$$

By expanding $(2^n - \rho'_{i-1})_{\mu_i}$ we have $(2^n - \rho'_{i-1})_{\mu_i} \leq 2^{n\mu_i} - 2^{n(\mu_i-1)}\left(\rho'_{i-1}\mu_i + \binom{\mu_i}{2}\right) + 2^{n(\mu_i-2)}A_i$, where $A_i = \left(\binom{\mu_i}{2}(\rho'_{i-1})^2 + \binom{\mu_i}{2}(\mu_i - 1)\rho'_{i-1} + \binom{\mu_i}{2}\frac{(\mu_i-2)(3\mu_i-1)}{12}\right)$.

<u>BOUNDING D.1.</u> With a simplification on the expression of D.1, we have

$$\text{D.1} \geq \prod_{i=1}^{k}\left(1 - \frac{A_i}{2^{2n} - 2^n(\rho'_{i-1}\mu_i + \binom{\mu_i}{2}) + A_i} - \frac{2^n\chi_i}{2^{2n} - 2^n(\rho'_{i-1}\mu_i + \binom{\mu_i}{2}) + A_i}\right)$$

$$\overset{(4)}{\geq} \prod_{i=1}^{k}\left(1 - \frac{2A_i}{2^{2n}} - \frac{2\chi_i}{2^n}\right) \overset{(5)}{\geq} \left(1 - \sum_{i=1}^{k}\frac{6(\rho'_{i-1})^2\binom{\mu_i}{2}}{2^{2n}} - \frac{2q'_v}{2^n}\right),$$

where (4) follows from the fact that $2^n(\rho'_{i-1}\mu_i + \binom{\mu_i}{2}) - A_i \leq 2^{2n}/2$, which holds true when $\rho'_k\mu_{max} \leq 2^n/4$, (5) holds true due to the fact that $A_i \leq 3(\rho'_{i-1})^2\binom{\mu_i}{2}$ and $(\chi_1 + \ldots + \chi_k) = q'_v$, the total number of blue dashed edges across the components of $G^=$ and $\mu_1 + \ldots + \mu_k \leq \alpha$.

<u>BOUNDING D.2.</u> For bounding D.2, we have

$$\text{D.2} \geq \prod_{i=1}^{k'}\left(1 - \frac{\mu'_{\rho_k+i}}{(2^n - \rho'_k - i + 1)}\right) \overset{(6)}{\geq} \left(1 - \sum_{i=1}^{k'}\frac{2\mu'_{\rho_k+i}}{2^n}\right) \overset{(7)}{\geq} \left(1 - \frac{2q''_v}{2^n}\right),$$

where (6) follows due to the fact that $(\rho'_k + i - 1) \leq 2^n/2$ and (7) follows as we denote $(\mu'_{\rho_k+1} + \cdots + \mu'_{\rho_k+k'}) = q''_v$, the total number of blue dashed edges incident on the vertices outside of the set $G^=(\mathcal{V})$.

COMBINING D.1 AND D.2. Finally, by combining the expression of D.1 and D.2, we have

$$h_\alpha \frac{2^{nq_m}}{(2^n - \sigma)_\alpha} \geq \left(1 - \sum_{i=1}^{k} \frac{6(\rho'_{i-1})^2 \binom{\mu_i}{2}}{2^{2n}} - \frac{2q_v}{2^n}\right),$$

where $q_v = q'_v + q''_v$, the total number of non-equation edges in G. $\square$

4   Security of nEHtM in Public Permutation Model

In this section, we first state that nEHtM_p achieves $2n/3$-bit security in public permutation model in the faulty nonce model. Followed by this, we demonstrate a matching attack in Subsect. 4.2 to show the security bound is tight.

4.1   Security of nEHtM$_p$

We show that nEHtM_p is secure against all adversaries that makes roughly $2^{2n/3}$ queries in the faulty nonce model. However, similar to nEHtM, the construction posses a birthday bound forging attack when the number of faulty nonces reaches to an order of $2^{n/2}$ [16].

Theorem 2. *Let $\mathcal{M}$ and $\mathcal{K}_h$ be two finite and non-empty sets. Let $\pi \leftarrow_\$ \mathbb{P}(n)$ be an n-bit public random permutation and $\mathsf{H} : \mathcal{K}_h \times \mathcal{M} \to \{0,1\}^{n-1}$ be an $(n-1)$-bit ϵ_{axu}-almost xor universal and ϵ_{reg}-almost regular hash function. Moreover, $K \leftarrow_\$ \{0,1\}^{n-1}$ be an $n-1$ bit random key and η be a fixed parameter. Then the forging advantage for any $(\eta, q_m, q_v, 2p)$-adversary against the construction $\mathsf{nEHtM}_p[\pi, \mathsf{H}, K]$ that makes at most η faulty queries out of q_m signing, q_v verit-ication and altogether $2p$ primitive queries, is given by*

$$\mathbf{Adv}^{\mathrm{MAC}}_{\mathsf{nEHtM}_p}(\eta, q_m, q_v, 2p) \leq \frac{12\eta^2}{2^{2n}}\left(q_m + 2p\right)^2 + \left(p + q_m\right)\left(\frac{192pq_m}{2^{2n}} + \frac{48pq_m^2 \epsilon_{\mathrm{axu}}}{2^{2n}}\right)$$

$$+ \frac{48q_m^3}{2^{2n}} + \frac{12q_m^4 \epsilon_{\mathrm{axu}}}{2^{2n}} + \frac{2q_v}{2^n} + \frac{p^2 \epsilon_{\mathrm{reg}}}{2^n}\left(3q_m + 2q_v\right) + \frac{q_m}{2^n}$$

$$+ \epsilon_{\mathrm{axu}}\left(\frac{4q_m^3}{2^n} + 2\eta q_m + \frac{pq_m^2}{2^n} + \frac{q_m^2}{2^{n+1}} + (\eta+1)q_v\right)$$

$$+ \epsilon_{\mathrm{reg}}(2\eta p + p\sqrt{3nq_m}) + \frac{2p^2 q_m}{2^{2n}} + \frac{2 + 2\eta}{2^n} + \frac{2p\sqrt{3nq_m}}{2^n}.$$

By assuming $\epsilon_{\mathrm{axu}} \approx 2/2^n$ and $\epsilon_{\mathrm{reg}} \approx 2/2^n$, the above bound is simplified to

$$\mathbf{Adv}^{\mathrm{MAC}}_{\mathsf{nEHtM}_p}(\eta, q_m, q_v, 2p) \leq \frac{80q_m^3}{2^{2n}} + \frac{4(q_m + q_v)}{2^n} + \frac{4p\sqrt{3nq_m}}{2^n} + \frac{12\eta^2}{2^{2n}}\left(q_m + 2p\right)^2$$

$$+ (p + q_m)\left(\frac{200pq_m}{2^{2n}} + \frac{96pq_m^2}{2^{3n}} + \frac{4\eta}{2^n}\right) + \frac{2\eta q_v}{2^n} + \frac{4p^2 q_v}{2^{2n}}$$

$$+ \frac{2}{2^n} + \frac{2\eta}{2^n}.$$

We defer the proof of this theorem in Sect. 5. The forging advantage of nEHtM_p for $\eta \leq 2^{n/3}$, $q_m \leq 2^{2n/3}$ and $p \leq 2^{2n/3}$ is thus given by

$$\mathbf{Adv}^{\mathrm{MAC}}_{\mathsf{nEHtM}_p}(q_m, q_v, 2p) \leq \left(\frac{29q_m}{2^{2n/3}} + \frac{6q_v}{2^{2n/3}} + \frac{28p}{2^{2n/3}} \right) + \frac{296p^2q_m}{2^{2n}} + \frac{296pq_m^2}{2^{2n}} + \frac{4p^2q_v}{2^{2n}} + \frac{4}{2^{2n/3}}.$$

4.2 Matching Attack on nEHtM_p

In this section we show a matching attack on nEHtM_p with $2^{2n/3}$ signing queries and total $2^{2n/3} + 2$ primitive queries. For carrying out the attack, we consider the following version of Polyhash function, a specific instantiation of an axu and ar hash function: for a message m, if the size of m is not a multiple of n, where n is the key size of the hash function, then we first apply an injective padding (e.g., 10^*) on it to generate a padded message m'. Then the output of the hash function for m' is computed as follows:

$$\mathsf{Poly}_{k_h}(m') = k_h^{l+1} \oplus k_h^l \cdot m_l' \oplus k_h^{l-1} m_{l-1}' \oplus \ldots \oplus k_h \cdot m_1',$$

where l denotes the number of message blocks of m' and m_i' denotes the i-th message block of m'. Now, it is easy to see that the hash function is $(l_{\max}+1)/2^n$-secure axu and ar hash function, where $l_{\max}$ is the maximum number of message blocks allowed. With this instance of the hash function of nEHtM_p, we mount the following attack. To begin with, we exploit bad event B.1 to mount the attack on the construction. We construct a deterministic adversary A that forges nEHtM_p by making $2^{2n/3}$ signing queries and total $2^{2n/3} + 2$ many primitive queries to π as follows:

Attack Algorithm:

1. A first chooses a single block message m consisting of all zeroes, i.e., $m = 0^n$.
2. Then A makes $2^{2n/3}$ signing queries with (ν_j, m) and obtains the tag t_j for $j \in [2^{2n/3}]$, where $\nu_j = 0^{n/3-1} \| \langle j \rangle_{2n/3}$.
3. A makes $2^{2n/3-1}$ forward primitive queries to π with x_j^1 and obtains the output y_j^1 for $j \in [2^{2n/3-1}]$, where $x_j^1 = 0 \| \langle j \rangle_{2n/3-1} \| 0^{n/3}$.
4. A makes again $2^{2n/3-1}$ forward primitive queries to π with x_j^2 and obtains the output y_j^2 for $j \in [2^{2n/3-1}]$, where $x_j^2 = 1 \| \mathsf{left}_{n/3-1}(\langle j \rangle_{2n/3-1}) \| 0^{n/3} \| \mathsf{right}_{n/3}(\langle j \rangle_{2n/3-1})$.
5. Then, A finds a tripet $(i, j, l) \in [2^{2n/3}] \times [2^{2n/3-1}] \times [2^{2n/3-1}]$ such that $t_i = y_j^1 \oplus y_l^1$.
6. A makes two additional forward primitive queries to π with $x_\star^1 = x_j^1 \oplus 0 \| 1^{n-1}$ and $x_\star^2 = x_k^2 \oplus 0 \| 1^{n-1}$. Let the received response be $y_\star^1$ and $y_\star^2$ respectively.
7. Finally, A forges with $(\nu_i \oplus 1^{n-1}, m, y_\star^1 \oplus y_\star^2)$.

ANALYSIS OF THE FORGING ADVANTAGE. We first note that the structure of ν_j, x_j^1 and x_j^2 are as follows:

$$\nu = \left\{ \underbrace{0\ 0\ \ldots\ 0}_{n/3-1} \| \underbrace{\star\ \star\ \ldots\ \star}_{n/3} \| \underbrace{\star\ \star\ \ldots\ \star}_{n/3} \right\}, \quad x^1 = \left\{ 0 \| \underbrace{\star\ \star\ \ldots\ \star}_{n/3-1} \| \underbrace{\star\ \star\ \ldots\ \star}_{n/3} \| \underbrace{0\ 0\ \ldots\ 0}_{n/3} \right\}.$$

$$x^2 = \left\{ 1 \| \underbrace{\star\ \star\ \cdots\ \star}_{n/3-1} \| \underbrace{0\ 0\ \cdots\ 0}_{n/3} \| \underbrace{\star\ \star\ \cdots\ \star}_{n/3} \right\}.$$

Note that, the number of elements (ν_i, x_j^1) that satisfy the relation $0\|(\nu_i \oplus k) = x_j^1$ is exactly $2^{n/3}$. As a result, the expected number of triplets (i, j, ℓ) that satisfy $0\|(\nu_i \oplus k) = x_j^1$ and $1\|(\nu_i \oplus k_h^2) = x_\ell^2$ is exactly 1. For this particular triplet (i, j, ℓ) that satifies the relation, A makes two additional forward primitive queries to π with $x_\star^1 = x_j^1 \oplus \Delta$ and $x_\star^2 = x_\ell^2 \oplus \Delta$, where $\Delta = 0\|1^{n-1}$. Thus, if A makes a forging query with $\nu_i \oplus 1^{n-1}$ (which is distinct from all other nonces that belong to the signing queries) and with the same message $m = 0^n$, then we have

$$\pi(0\|(\nu_i \oplus 1^{n-1} \oplus k)) \oplus \pi(1\|(\nu_i \oplus 1^{n-1} \oplus k_h^2))$$
$$= \pi((0\|(\nu_i \oplus k)) \oplus \Delta) \oplus \pi((1\|(\nu_i \oplus k_h^2)) \oplus \Delta) = \pi(x_\star^1) \oplus \pi(x_\star^2) = y_\star^1 \oplus y_\star^2$$

which makes $(\nu_i \oplus 1^{n-1}, m, y_\star^1 \oplus y_\star^2)$ a valid and succesful forging attempt. Note that, the number of signing queries required is $2^{2n/3}$ and the total number of primitive queries required is $2^{2n/3} + 2$. However, the time complexity of this attack is 2^{2n-2}.

5   Proof of Theorem 2: MAC Security of nEHtM$_p$

Due to Eq. (1), we bound the distinguishing advantage instead of bounding the forging advantage of nEHtM$_p$. For this, we consider any information theoretic deterministic distinghisher A that has access to the following oracles in either the real world or in the ideal world: in the real world it has access to $(\mathsf{nEHtM}_p.\mathsf{Sig}_{(k,k_h)}^\pi, \mathsf{nEHtM}_p.\mathsf{Ver}_{(k,k_h)}^\pi, \pi, \pi^{-1})$; in the ideal world it has access to $(\mathsf{RF}, \mathsf{Rej}, \pi, \pi^{-1})$. We summarize the interactions of the distinguisher with its oracle in a transcript $\tau_m \cup \tau_v$, where $\tau_m \triangleq \{(\nu_1, m_1, t_1), \ldots, (\nu_{q_m}, m_{q_m}, t_{q_m})\}$ is the MAC transcript and $\tau_v \triangleq \{(\nu_1', m_1', t_1', b_1'), \ldots, (\nu_{q_v}', m_{q_v}', t_{q_v}', b_{q_v}')\}$ is the verification transcript. Primitives queries to π are summarized in two lists in the form of $\tau_p^{(1)} \triangleq \{(x_1^1, y_1^1), \ldots, (x_p^1, y_p^1)\}$ and $\tau_p^{(2)} \triangleq \{(x_1^2, y_1^2), \ldots, (x_p^2, y_p^2)\}$, where $\mathsf{msb}(x_i^1) = 0$ and $\mathsf{msb}(x_i^2) = 1$. We assume that none of the transcripts contain any duplicate elements and after the interaction, we reveal the keys k, k_h to the distinguisher (before it output its decision), which happens to be the keys used in the construction for the real world and uniformly sampled dummy keys for the ideal world. The complete view is denoted by $\tau' = (\tau_m, \tau_v, \tau_p^{(1)}, \tau_p^{(2)}, k, k_h)$.

5.1   Definition and Probability of Bad Transcripts

For the notational simplicity, we denote $\mathsf{H}_{k_h}(m_i) = \mathsf{H}_i$. $\hat{x}_i^b$ denotes $\mathsf{chop}_{\mathsf{msb}}(x_i^b)$ for $b = 1, 2$. We also define three sets: (a) $\mathcal{T} \triangleq \{t_i : (\nu_i, m_i, t_i) \in \tau_m\}$, (b) $\mathcal{Y}_1 \triangleq \{y_i^1 : (x_i^1, y_i^1) \in \tau_p^{(1)}\}$ and (c) $\mathcal{Y}_2 \triangleq \{y_i^2 : (x_i^2, y_i^2) \in \tau_p^{(2)}\}$. The main idea of identifying bad events is to avoid the input collision of the permutation with primitive queries as that will determine the corresponding tag; hence losing the randomness of the tag, which in turn, will help the adversary to distinguish the output from random.

Definition 2 (Bad Transcript for nEHtM$_p$). *Given a parameter $\xi \in \mathbb{N}$, where $\xi \geq \eta$, an attainable transcript $\tau' = (\tau_m, \tau_v, \tau_p^{(1)}, \tau_p^{(2)}, k, k_h)$ is called a* **bad** *transcript if any one of the following holds:*

- B.1 : $\exists\, i \in [q_m], j, \ell \in [p]$ such that $\nu_i \oplus k = \hat{x}_j^1, \nu_i \oplus \mathsf{H}_i = \hat{x}_\ell^2$.
- B.2 : $\exists\, i, j, \ell \in [q_m], i \neq j, i \neq \ell$ such that $\nu_i = \nu_j$ and $\nu_i \oplus \mathsf{H}_i = \nu_\ell \oplus \mathsf{H}_\ell$.
- B.3 : $\exists\, i \neq j \in [q_m], \ell \in [p]$ such that $\nu_i \oplus k = \hat{x}_\ell^1$ and $\nu_i \oplus \mathsf{H}_i = \nu_j \oplus \mathsf{H}_j$.
- B.4 : $\exists\, i \neq j \in [q_m], \ell \in [p]$ such that $\nu_i = \nu_j$ and $\nu_i \oplus \mathsf{H}_i = \hat{x}_\ell^2$.
- B.5 : $\exists\, i \neq j \in [q_m]$ such that $\nu_i = \nu_j$ and $t_i = t_j$.
- B.6 : $\exists\, i \neq j \in [q_m]$ such that $\nu_i \oplus \mathsf{H}_i = \nu_j \oplus \mathsf{H}_j$ and $t_i = t_j$.
- B.7 : $\#\{(t_i, y_j^1, y_\ell^2) \in \mathcal{T} \times \mathcal{Y}_1 \times \mathcal{Y}_2 : t_i = y_j^1 \oplus y_\ell^2\} \geq p^2 q_m/2^n + p\sqrt{3 n q_m}$.
- B.8 : $\exists\, i \in [q_m], j, \ell \in [p]$ such that $\nu_i \oplus k = \hat{x}_j^1, y_j^1 \oplus t_i = y_\ell^2$.
- B.9 : $\exists\, i \in [q_m], j, \ell \in [p]$ such that $\nu_i \oplus \mathsf{H}_i = \hat{x}_j^2, y_j^2 \oplus t_i = y_\ell^1$.
- B.10 : $\{i_1, \ldots, i_{\xi+1}\} \subseteq [q_m]$ such that $\nu_{i_1} \oplus \mathsf{H}_{i_1} = \nu_{i_2} \oplus \mathsf{H}_{i_2} = \ldots = \nu_{i_{\xi+1}} \oplus \mathsf{H}_{i_{\xi+1}}$ *(the optimal value of ξ shall be determined later in the proof).*
- B.11 $\exists\, a \in [q_v], \exists\, i \in [q_m]$ such that $\nu_i = \nu_a', \nu_i \oplus \mathsf{H}_i = \nu_a' \oplus \mathsf{H}_a'$ and $t_i = t_a'$.
- B.12 $\exists\, a \in [q_v], \exists\, j, \ell \in [p]$ such that $\nu_a' \oplus k = \hat{x}_j^1, \nu_a' \oplus \mathsf{H}_a' = \hat{x}_\ell^2$ and $t_a' = y_j^1 \oplus y_\ell^2$.
- B.13 $\exists\, i \in [q_m]$ such that $t_i = 0^n$.

Lemma 2. *Let D_{id} and BadT be defined as in Sect. 2.3. Then*

$$\Pr[\mathsf{D}_{\mathrm{id}} \in \mathsf{BadT}] \leq \frac{p^2 \epsilon_{\mathrm{reg}}}{2^n}(3q_m + 2q_v) + \epsilon_{\mathrm{axu}}\left(\frac{q_m^2}{2\xi} + 2\eta q_m + \frac{pq_m^2}{2^n} + \frac{q_m^2}{2^{n+1}} + (\eta+1)q_v\right)$$
$$+ \epsilon_{\mathrm{reg}}(2\eta p + p\sqrt{3 n q_m}) + \frac{2p^2 q_m}{2^{2n}} + \frac{2+2\eta}{2^n} + \frac{2p\sqrt{3 n q_m}}{2^n} + \frac{q_m}{2^n}.$$

Proof of the lemma can be found in Sect. 6.

5.2 Analysis of Good Transcripts

For a good transcript $\tau' = (\tau_m, \tau_v, \tau_p^{(1)}, \tau_p^{(2)}, k_h, k)$, the ideal interpolation probability is

$$\mathsf{p}_{\mathrm{id}}(\tau') \triangleq \Pr[\mathsf{D}_{\mathrm{id}} = \tau'] = \frac{1}{|\mathcal{K}_h|} \cdot \frac{1}{2^{n-1}} \cdot \frac{1}{2^{n q_m}} \cdot \frac{1}{(2^n)_{2p}}. \tag{7}$$

Computing Real Interpolation Probability. To compute the real interpolation probability, we regroup the elements of $\tau_m, \tau_p^{(1)}$ and $\tau_p^{(2)}$ into three new transcripts $\hat{\tau}_m, \hat{\tau}_p^{(1)}$ and $\hat{\tau}_p^{(2)}$ in the following way: initially the new transcripts are set to the old one. Now, for each $(\nu_i, m_i, t_i) \in \tau_m$, if (a) $\nu_i \oplus k = \hat{x}_j^1$, then

$\hat{\tau}_m \leftarrow \tau_m \setminus \{(\nu_i, m_i, t_i)\}$ and $\hat{\tau}_p^{(2)} \leftarrow \hat{\tau}_p^{(2)} \cup \{1\|(\nu_i \oplus H_i), t_i \oplus y_j^1\}$; if (b) $\nu_i \oplus H_i = \hat{x}_j^2$, then $\hat{\tau}_m \leftarrow \tau_m \setminus \{(\nu_i, m_i, t_i)\}$ and $\hat{\tau}_p^{(1)} \leftarrow \hat{\tau}_p^{(1)} \cup \{0\|(\nu_i \oplus k), t_i \oplus y_j^2\}$. Since τ' is a good transcript, it does not meet any of the bad conditions listed in Definition 2. We know that if $\nu_i \oplus k = \hat{x}_j^1$, then $\nu_i \oplus H_i$ cannot collide with $\hat{x}_\ell^2$ (due to ¬B.1) and $y_j^1 \oplus t_i$ cannot collide with y_ℓ^2 (due to ¬B.8). Similarly for $\hat{\tau}_p^{(2)}$. This way, we will end up with soundly defined $\hat{\tau}_p^{(1)}$ and $\hat{\tau}_p^{(2)}$ and a set of signing queries $\hat{\tau}_m$ that does not collide with any tuple in $\hat{\tau}_p^{(1)}$ or $\hat{\tau}_p^{(2)}$.

Let $s_1, s_2 \leq p$ be the number of signing queries that collides with any element of $\tau_p^{(1)}$ and $\tau_p^{(2)}$ respectively. Therefore, $p_1 \overset{\Delta}{=} |\hat{\tau}_p^{(1)}| = p + s_2$, $p_2 \overset{\Delta}{=} |\hat{\tau}_p^{(2)}| = p + s_1$ and $q'_m \overset{\Delta}{=} |\hat{\tau}_m| = q_m - s_1 - s_2$. We denote $q'_p = p_1 + p_2 = 2p + s_1 + s_2$. We say that a permutation π is *compatible with* $\hat{\tau} \overset{\Delta}{=} \hat{\tau}_m \cup \tau_v \cup \hat{\tau}_p^{(1)} \cup \hat{\tau}_p^{(2)}$ if the following holds:

- for all $(\nu_i, m_i, t_i) \in \hat{\tau}_m, \pi(0\|(\nu_i \oplus k)) \oplus \pi(1\|(\nu_i \oplus H_i)) = t_i$
- forall $a \in [q_v], \pi(0\|(\nu'_a \oplus k)) \oplus \pi(1\|(\nu'_a \oplus H'_a)) \neq t'_a$
- for all $(x_i^1, y_i^1) \in \hat{\tau}_p^{(1)}, \pi(x_i^1) = y_i^1$
- for all $(x_i^2, y_i^2) \in \hat{\tau}_p^{(2)}, \pi(x_i^2) = y_i^2$.

Therefore, the remaining part is to count the number of compatible permutations π. As a result, we have

$$\mathsf{p_{re}}(\tau') \overset{\Delta}{=} \Pr[\mathsf{D_{re}} = \hat{\tau}] = \frac{1}{|\mathcal{K}_h|} \cdot \frac{1}{2^{n-1}} \cdot \frac{h_\alpha}{(2^n)_{p_1 + p_2 + \alpha}}, \tag{8}$$

where h_α denotes the number of injective solutions to the following system of equations and non-equations ($\mathcal{E}^= \cup \mathcal{E}^{\neq}$), with α many distinct variables. For notational simplicity, we denote $\pi(0\|\nu_i \oplus k)$ as U_i and $\pi(1\|\nu_i \oplus H_i)$ as V_i.

$$\mathcal{E}^= = \begin{cases} U_1 \oplus V_1 = t_1 \\ U_2 \oplus V_2 = t_2 \\ \quad\vdots \\ U_{q'_m} \oplus V_{q'_m} = t_{q'_m} \end{cases} \qquad\qquad \mathcal{E}^{\neq} = \begin{cases} U'_1 \oplus V'_1 \neq t'_1 \\ U'_2 \oplus V'_2 \neq t'_2 \\ \quad\vdots \\ U'_{q_v} \oplus V'_{q_v} \neq t'_{q_v} \end{cases}$$

where $q'_m = q_m - s_1 - s_2$. It is to be noted here that $\mathcal{E}^= \cup \mathcal{E}^{\neq}$ is defined over α many distinct variables. Therefore, some variables in $\mathcal{E}^= \cup \mathcal{E}^{\neq}$ may collide to each other. Thus, from Eq. (7) and Eq. (8), we have,

$$\frac{\mathsf{p_{re}}(\tau')}{\mathsf{p_{id}}(\tau')} = \underbrace{\frac{2^{ns_1}}{(2^n - 2p)_{s_1}}}_{\text{A.1}} \cdot \underbrace{\frac{2^{ns_2}}{(2^n - 2p - s_1)_{s_2}}}_{\text{A.2}} \cdot \underbrace{\frac{h_\alpha \cdot 2^{nq'_m}}{(2^n - 2p - s_1 - s_2)_\alpha}}_{\text{A.3}}. \tag{9}$$

Note that, A.1 ≥ 1 and A.2 ≥ 1. Therefore, we are left to bound A.3. Note that, the induced graph G of $\mathcal{E}^= \cup \mathcal{E}^{\neq}$ has α many vertices. Moreover, $|\mathcal{F}| = q_m$ and $|\mathcal{F}'| = q_v$. It is easy to verify that as τ' is a good transcript, G is a good graph.

Therefore, by putting $\sigma = q_p'$ in Theorem 1, we have

$$h_\alpha \geq \frac{(2^n - 2p - s_1 - s_2)\alpha}{2^n q_m'} \cdot \left(1 - \sum_{i=1}^{k} \frac{6(\rho_{i-1}')^2 \binom{\mu_i}{2}}{2^{2n}} - \frac{2q_v}{2^n}\right). \qquad (10)$$

From Eq. (8) and Eq. (10), we have

$$\frac{\mathsf{p_{re}}(\tau')}{\mathsf{p_{id}}(\tau')} \geq \left(1 - \sum_{i=1}^{k} \frac{6(\rho_{i-1}')^2 \binom{\mu_i}{2}}{2^{2n}} - \frac{2q_v}{2^n}\right) \overset{(1)}{\geq} 1 - \underbrace{\left(\sum_{i=1}^{k} \frac{24(q_m' + q_p')^2 \binom{\mu_i}{2}}{2^{2n}} + \frac{2q_v}{2^n}\right)}_{\Phi(\tau')},$$

where the simplification for (1) follows from the fact $\rho_{i-1}' = \alpha + q_p' \leq 2(q_m' + q_p')$. Now, from Sect. 6.2 of [16] we have

$$\mathbf{E}\left[\sum_{i=1}^{k} \binom{\mu_i}{2}\right] \leq (q_m')^2 \epsilon_{\mathrm{axu}}/2 + \eta^2/2 + 2q_m'. \qquad (11)$$

By applying the expectation method of Sect. 2.3 on Eq. (11), we have

$$\mathbf{E}[\Phi(\mathsf{D_{id}})] \leq \frac{12(q_m' + q_p')^2}{2^{2n}}\left((q_m')^2 \epsilon_{\mathrm{axu}} + \eta^2 + 4q_m'\right) + \frac{2q_v}{2^n}. \qquad (12)$$

By doing a simple algebra on Eq. (12) and by assuming $q_m' \leq q_m, q_p' \leq 4p$, we have

$$\mathbf{E}[\Phi(\mathsf{D_{id}})] \leq \left(\frac{12 q_m^4 \epsilon_{\mathrm{axu}}}{2^{2n}} + \frac{12 \eta^2 q_m^2}{2^{2n}} + \frac{48 q_m^3}{2^{2n}} + \frac{48 p q_m^3 \epsilon_{\mathrm{axu}}}{2^{2n}} + \frac{48 \eta^2 p q_m}{2^{2n}} + \frac{192 p q_m^2}{2^{2n}}\right.$$
$$\left. + \frac{48 p^2 q_m^2 \epsilon_{\mathrm{axu}}}{2^{2n}} + \frac{48 \eta^2 p^2}{2^{2n}} + \frac{192 p^2 q_m}{2^{2n}} + \frac{2q_v}{2^n}\right). \qquad (13)$$

<u>FINALIZING THE PROOF.</u> We have assumed that $\xi \geq \eta$ and from the condition of Theorem 1, we have $\xi \leq 2^n/(8q_m' + 2q_p') \leq 2^n/8q_m'$. By assuming $\eta \leq 2^n/8q_m'$ (otherwise the bound becomes vacuously true) we choose $\xi = 2^n/8q_m'$. Hence, the result follows by applying Eq. (3), Lemma 2, Eq. (13) and $\xi = 2^n/8q_m'$.

6   Proof of Lemma 2

By the union bound,

$$\Pr[\mathsf{D_{id}} \in \mathsf{BadT}] \leq \sum_{i=1}^{7} \Pr[\mathsf{B.i}] + \Pr[\mathsf{B.8} \mid \overline{\mathsf{B.7}}] + \Pr[\mathsf{B.9} \mid \overline{\mathsf{B.7}}] + \sum_{i=10}^{13} \Pr[\mathsf{B.i}]. \quad (14)$$

In the following, we bound the probabilities of all the bad events individually. The lemma will follow by adding the individual bounds.

Bounding B.1. For any possible signing query $(\nu_i, m_i, t_i) \in \tau_m$ and a pair of any possible primitive queries $(x_j^1, y_j^1) \in \tau_p^{(1)}$ and $(x_\ell^2, y_\ell^2) \in \tau_p^{(2)}$, the only randomness in the equation $\nu_i \oplus k = \hat{x}_j^1$ is k and the randomness in the equation $\nu_i \oplus H_i = \hat{x}_\ell^2$ is k_h, the hash key. In the ideal world, k and k_h are dummy keys, sampled uniformly and independently from their respective space. Therefore, for a fixed choice of i, j and ℓ, the probability of the event is $\epsilon_{\text{reg}}/2^{n-1}$, where ϵ_{reg} is the regular advantage of the underlying hash function. Summing over all possible choices of i, j and ℓ we have

$$\Pr[\text{B.1}] \leq \frac{2p^2 q_m \epsilon_{\text{reg}}}{2^n}. \tag{15}$$

Bounding B.2. Let $\mathcal{N}$ be the set of all query indices i for which there is a $j \neq i$ such that $\nu_i = \nu_j$. It is easy to see that $|\mathcal{N}| \leq 2\eta$. Event B.2 occurs if for some $j \in \mathcal{N}$, $\nu_j \oplus H_j = \nu_\ell \oplus H_\ell$ for some $\ell \neq j$. For any such fixed i, j, ℓ, the probability of the event is at most ϵ_{axu}, where ϵ_{axu} is the almost xor universal advantage of the underlying hash function. The number of such choices of (i, j, ℓ) is at most $2\eta q_m$. Hence,

$$\Pr[\text{B.2}] \leq 2\eta q_m \epsilon_{\text{axu}}. \tag{16}$$

Bounding B.3. For any two signing queries $(\nu_i, m_i, t_i), (\nu_j, m_j, t_j) \in \tau_m$ and a primitive query $(x_\ell^1, y_\ell^1) \in \tau_p^{(1)}$, the only randomness in the equation $\nu_i \oplus k = \hat{x}_\ell^1$ is k and the randomness in the equation $H_i \oplus H_j = \nu_i \oplus \nu_j$ is k_h. In the ideal world, k and k_h are dummy keys, sampled uniformly and independently from their respective space. Therefore, for a fixed choice of i, j and ℓ, the probability of the event is $\epsilon_{\text{axu}}/2^{n-1}$, where ϵ_{axu} is the almost xor universal advantage of the underlying hash function. Summing over all possible choices of i, j and ℓ we have

$$\Pr[\text{B.3}] \leq \frac{p q_m^2 \epsilon_{\text{axu}}}{2^n}. \tag{17}$$

Bounding B.4. For any two signing queries $(\nu_i, m_i, t_i), (\nu_j, m_j, t_j) \in \tau_m$ and a primitive query $(x_\ell^2, y_\ell^2) \in \tau_p^{(2)}$, the only randomness in the equation $\nu_i \oplus H_i = \hat{x}_\ell^2$ is k_h. In the ideal world, k_h is sampled uniformly from $\mathcal{K}_h$. Therefore, for a fixed choice of i, j and ℓ, the probability of the event is ϵ_{reg}. The number of choices of $i \neq j \in [q_m]$ such that $\nu_i = \nu_j$ is at most 2η and the number of choices of ℓ is at most p. Summing over all possible choices of i, j and ℓ we have

$$\Pr[\text{B.4}] \leq 2\eta p \epsilon_{\text{reg}}. \tag{18}$$

Bounding B.5. For a fixed choice of indices i and j, the probability of the event is at most $1/2^n$. Number of choices of i and j such that $\nu_i = \nu_j$ is at most 2η. Summing over all possible choices of i and j we have

$$\Pr[\text{B.5}] \leq \frac{2\eta}{2^n}. \tag{19}$$

Bounding B.6. Similar to B.5, for a fixed choice of indices i and j, the probability of the event is at most $\epsilon_{\text{axu}}/2^n$, as the event $\nu_i \oplus H_i = \nu_j \oplus H_j$ is independent over $t_i = t_j$. Summing over all possible choices of i and j we have

$$\Pr[\text{B.6}] \leq \frac{q_m^2 \epsilon_{\text{axu}}}{2^{n+1}}. \tag{20}$$

Bounding B.7. Event B.7 is bounded by Lemma 1, where we take $\mathcal{A} = \mathcal{Y}_1$ and $\mathcal{B} = \mathcal{Y}_2$.

$$\Pr[\text{B.7}] \leq \frac{2}{2^n}. \tag{21}$$

Bounding B.8 | $\overline{\text{B.7}}$. Let $\mathsf{C} \triangleq p^2 q_m/2^n + p\sqrt{3nq_m}$. As we are bounding the event B.8 | $\overline{\text{B.7}}$, number of i, j and ℓ that satisfies $t_i = y_j^1 \oplus y_\ell^2$ is at most C. For a fixed choice of indices i, j and ℓ, the probability of the event is at most $1/2^{n-1}$. Hence, by summing over all possible choices of i, j and ℓ, we have

$$\Pr[\text{B.8} \mid \overline{\text{B.7}}] \leq \frac{2p^2 q_m}{2^{2n}} + \frac{2p\sqrt{3nq_m}}{2^n}. \tag{22}$$

Bounding B.9 | $\overline{\text{B.7}}$. Bounding B.9 | $\overline{\text{B.7}}$ is identical to that of B.8 | $\overline{\text{B.7}}$. For a fixed choice of indices i, j and ℓ, the probability of the event is at most ϵ_{reg}. Summing over all possible choices of i, j and ℓ we have

$$\Pr[\text{B.9} \mid \overline{\text{B.7}}] \leq \frac{p^2 q_m \epsilon_{\text{reg}}}{2^n} + p\sqrt{3nq_m}\epsilon_{\text{reg}}. \tag{23}$$

Bounding B.10. Event B.10 occurs if there exist $\xi + 1$ distinct signing query indices $\{i_1, \ldots, i_{\xi+1}\} \subseteq [q_m]$ such that $\nu_{i_1} \oplus H_{i_1} = \ldots = \nu_{i_{\xi+1}} \oplus H_{i_{\xi+1}}$. This event is thus a $(\xi + 1)$-multicollision on the ϵ_{univ}-universal hash function[4] mapping (ν, m) to $\nu \oplus H_{k_h}(m)$ (as H_{k_h} is an ϵ_{axu}-almost-xor universal). Therefore, by applying the multicollision theorem of universal hash function (Theorem 1) of [16], we have

$$\Pr[\text{B.10}] \leq q_m^2 \epsilon_{\text{axu}}/2\xi. \tag{24}$$

Bounding B.11. For some $a \in [q_v]$ and $i \in [q_m]$, if $\nu_i = \nu_a'$, $\nu_i \oplus H_i = \nu_a' \oplus H_a'$ and $t_i = t_a'$, then $m_i \neq m_a'$ (as the distinguisher is non-trivial). Hence the probability that $\nu_i \oplus H_i = \nu_a' \oplus H_a'$ holds is at most ϵ_{axu}, due to the axu probability of the hash function. Now, for any choice of $a \in [q_v]$, there can be at most $(\eta + 1)$ indices i such that $\nu_i = \nu_a'$. Hence, the required probability is bounded as

$$\Pr[\text{B.11}] \leq (\eta + 1)q_v \epsilon_{\text{axu}}. \tag{25}$$

Bounding B.12. For any possible verification query $(\nu_a', m_a', t_a') \in \tau_v$ and a pair of any possible primitive queries $(x_j^1, y_j^1) \in \tau_p^{(1)}$ and $(x_\ell^2, y_\ell^2) \in \tau_p^{(2)}$, the only

---

[4] A hash function H_{k_h} is said to be an ϵ_{univ}-universal hash function if for all $x \neq x'$, $\Pr[H_{k_h}(x) = H_{k_h}(x')] \leq \epsilon_{\text{univ}}$.

randomness in the equation $\nu'_a \oplus k = x^1_j$ is k and the randomness in the equation $\nu'_a \oplus H'_a = x^2_\ell$ is k_h. In the ideal world, k and k_h are dummy keys, sampled uniformly and independently from their respective spaces. Therefore, for a fixed choice of a, j and ℓ, the probability of the event is $\epsilon_{\text{reg}}/2^{n-1}$. Summing over all possible choices of a, j and ℓ we have

$$\Pr[\text{B.12}] \leq \frac{2q_v p^2 \epsilon_{\text{reg}}}{2^n}. \tag{26}$$

Bounding B.13. For a fixed choice of i, the probability that $t_i = 0^n$ is exactly 2^{-n}. Summing over all possible choices of i we have

$$\Pr[\text{B.13}] \leq \frac{q_m}{2^n}. \tag{27}$$

The proof follows from Eq. (14)–Eq. (27).   □

Acknowledgement. We would like to thank all the anonymous reviewers of Africacrypt 2020. Mridul Nandi is supported by NTRO Project.

References

1. Bernstein, D.J., et al.: GIMLI: a cross-platform permutation. In: Fischer, W., Homma, N. (eds.) CHES 2017. LNCS, vol. 10529, pp. 299–320. Springer, Cham (2017). https://doi.org/10.1007/978-3-319-66787-4_15
2. Bertoni, G., Daemen, J., Peeters, M., Van Assche, G.: Keccak. In: Johansson, T., Nguyen, P.Q. (eds.) EUROCRYPT 2013. LNCS, vol. 7881, pp. 313–314. Springer, Heidelberg (2013). https://doi.org/10.1007/978-3-642-38348-9_19
3. Beyne, T., Chen, Y.L., Dobraunig, C., Mennink, B.: Elephant. NIST LWC (2019)
4. Böck, H., Zauner, A., Devlin, S., Somorovsky, J., Jovanovic, P.: Nonce-disrespecting adversaries: practical forgery attacks on GCM in TLS. In: 10th USENIX Workshop on Offensive Technologies, WOOT 2016, Austin, TX, USA, 8–9 August 2016 (2016)
5. Bogdanov, A., Knezevic, M., Leander, G., Toz, D., Varici, K., Verbauwhede, I.: SPONGENT: the design space of lightweight cryptographic hashing. IEEE Trans. Comput. **62**(10), 2041–2053 (2013)
6. Bogdanov, A., Knudsen, L.R., Leander, G., Standaert, F.-X., Steinberger, J., Tischhauser, E.: Key-alternating ciphers in a provable setting: encryption using a small number of public permutations. In: Pointcheval, D., Johansson, T. (eds.) EUROCRYPT 2012. LNCS, vol. 7237, pp. 45–62. Springer, Heidelberg (2012). https://doi.org/10.1007/978-3-642-29011-4_5
7. Chakraborti, A., Datta, N., Nandi, M., Yasuda, K.: Beetle family of lightweight and secure authenticated encryption ciphers. IACR Trans. Cryptogr. Hardw. Embed. Syst. **2018**(2), 218–241 (2018)
8. Chakraborty, B., Nandi, M.: Orange. NIST LWC (2019)
9. Chen, S., Lampe, R., Lee, J., Seurin, Y., Steinberger, J.P.: Minimizing the two-round even-mansour cipher. In: Garay, J.A., Gennaro, R. (eds.) CRYPTO 2014. LNCS, vol. 8616, pp. 39–56. Springer, Heidelberg (2014). https://doi.org/10.1007/978-3-662-44371-2_3

10. Chen, Y.L., Lambooij, E., Mennink, B.: How to build pseudorandom functions from public random permutations. In: Boldyreva, A., Micciancio, D. (eds.) CRYPTO 2019, Part I. LNCS, vol. 11692, pp. 266–293. Springer, Cham (2019). https://doi.org/10.1007/978-3-030-26948-7_10
11. Cogliati, B., Seurin, Y.: EWCDM: an efficient, beyond-birthday secure, nonce-misuse resistant MAC. In: Robshaw, M., Katz, J. (eds.) CRYPTO 2016, Part I. LNCS, vol. 9814, pp. 121–149. Springer, Heidelberg (2016). https://doi.org/10.1007/978-3-662-53018-4_5
12. Daemen, J., Hoffert, S., Peeters, M., Van Assche, G., Van Keer, R.: Xoodyak, a lightweight cryptographic scheme. NIST LWC (2019)
13. Datta, N., Dutta, A., Nandi, M., Yasuda, K.: Encrypt or decrypt? To make a single-key beyond birthday secure nonce-based MAC. In: Shacham, H., Boldyreva, A. (eds.) CRYPTO 2018, Part I. LNCS, vol. 10991, pp. 631–661. Springer, Cham (2018). https://doi.org/10.1007/978-3-319-96884-1_21
14. Dobraunig, C., Eichlseder, M., Mendel, F., Schläffer, M.: Ascon v1.2. NIST LWC (2019)
15. Dutta, A., Jha, A., Nandi, M.: Tight security analysis of ehtm MAC. IACR Trans. Symmetric Cryptol. 2017(3), 130–150 (2017)
16. Dutta, A., Nandi, M., Talnikar, S.: Beyond birthday bound secure MAC in faulty nonce model. In: Ishai, Y., Rijmen, V. (eds.) EUROCRYPT 2019, Part I. LNCS, vol. 11476, pp. 437–466. Springer, Cham (2019). https://doi.org/10.1007/978-3-030-17653-2_15
17. Even, S., Mansour, Y.: A construction of a cipher from a single pseudorandom permutation. J. Cryptol. 10(3), 151–161 (1997). https://doi.org/10.1007/s001459900025
18. Guo, J., Peyrin, T., Poschmann, A.: The PHOTON family of lightweight hash functions. In: Rogaway, P. (ed.) CRYPTO 2011. LNCS, vol. 6841, pp. 222–239. Springer, Heidelberg (2011). https://doi.org/10.1007/978-3-642-22792-9_13
19. Hoang, V.T., Tessaro, S.: Key-alternating ciphers and key-length extension: exact bounds and multi-user security. In: Robshaw, M., Katz, J. (eds.) CRYPTO 2016, Part I. LNCS, vol. 9814, pp. 3–32. Springer, Heidelberg (2016). https://doi.org/10.1007/978-3-662-53018-4_1
20. Hoang, V.T., Tessaro, S.: The multi-user security of double encryption. In: Coron, J.-S., Nielsen, J.B. (eds.) EUROCRYPT 2017, Part II. LNCS, vol. 10211, pp. 381–411. Springer, Cham (2017). https://doi.org/10.1007/978-3-319-56614-6_13
21. Minematsu, K.: How to thwart birthday attacks against MACs via small randomness. In: Hong, S., Iwata, T. (eds.) FSE 2010. LNCS, vol. 6147, pp. 230–249. Springer, Heidelberg (2010). https://doi.org/10.1007/978-3-642-13858-4_13
22. Moch, A., List, E.: Parallelizable MACs based on the sum of PRPs with security beyond the birthday bound. In: Deng, R.H., Gauthier-Umaña, V., Ochoa, M., Yung, M. (eds.) ACNS 2019. LNCS, vol. 11464, pp. 131–151. Springer, Cham (2019). https://doi.org/10.1007/978-3-030-21568-2_7
23. NIST. Lightweight cryptography (2018). https://csrc.nist.gov/Projects/Lightweight-Cryptography. Accessed 01 Aug 2019
24. Rogaway, P., Bellare, M., Black, J.: SHA-3 standard. ACM Trans. Inf. Syst. Secur. (TISSEC) 6(3), 365–403 (2003)
25. Wegman, M.N., Carter, L.: New hash functions and their use in authentication and set equality. J. Comput. Syst. Sci. 22(3), 265–279 (1981)

Elliptic Curves

On Adaptive Attacks Against
Jao-Urbanik's Isogeny-Based Protocol

Andrea Basso[1], Péter Kutas[1], Simon-Philipp Merz[2], Christophe Petit[1],
and Charlotte Weitkämper[1(✉)]

[1] University of Birmingham, Birmingham, UK
a.basso@cs.bham.ac.uk, p.kutas@bham.ac.uk, christophe.f.petit@gmail.com,
c.weitkaemper@pgr.bham.ac.uk
[2] Royal Holloway, University of London, Egham, UK
simon-philipp.merz.2018@rhul.ac.uk

Abstract. The k-SIDH protocol is a static-static isogeny-based key
agreement protocol. At Mathcrypt 2018, Jao and Urbanik introduced
a variant of this protocol which uses non-scalar automorphisms of special elliptic curves to improve its efficiency.

In this paper, we provide a new adaptive attack on Jao-Urbanik's
protocol. The attack is a non-trivial adaptation of Galbraith-Petit-Shani-
Ti's attack on SIDH (Asiacrypt 2016) and its extension to k-SIDH by
Dobson-Galbraith-LeGrow-Ti-Zobernig (IACR eprint 2019).

Our attack provides a speedup compared to a naïve application of
Dobson et al.'s attack to Jao-Urbanik's scheme, exploiting its inherent
structure. Estimating the security of k-SIDH and Jao-Urbanik's variant
with respect to these attacks, k-SIDH provides better efficiency.

Keywords: Elliptic curves · Isogenies · k-SIDH · Adaptive attack

1   Introduction

With the expected advent of quantum computers, current public key cryptography algorithms based on discrete logarithm and factorization problems will have
to be replaced by stronger, so-called post-quantum cryptography algorithms.
Isogeny-based cryptography is among the leading approaches currently considered for post-quantum cryptography. A major protocol in isogeny-based cryptography is the SIDH key exchange protocol [7], whose principles underlie the
SIKE algorithm recently submitted to the NIST post-quantum standardization
process [6,8].

In internet communication contexts, key exchange protocols are often used in
a semi-static mode, where the server uses the same *static* secret key to establish
any new session key with a client. Galbraith et al. have shown that the basic
SIDH protocol is vulnerable to adaptive attacks in these contexts [4]. In SIKE
the attacks are defeated by using a variant of the Fujisaki-Okamoto transform.

The k-SIDH protocol is an alternative countermeasure to Galbraith et al.'s
attack suggested by Azarderakhsh et al. [2]. The protocol has the additional

© Springer Nature Switzerland AG 2020
A. Nitaj and A. Youssef (Eds.): AFRICACRYPT 2020, LNCS 12174, pp. 195–213, 2020.
https://doi.org/10.1007/978-3-030-51938-4_10

advantage to allow for static-static key exchange (where both parties use static keys), but it comes at the cost of a significant efficiency loss as it essentially involves running k^2 instances of the SIDH protocol in parallel for an integer $k > 1$, with $k = 92$ suggested by the authors. Very recently, Dobson et al. described an adaptive attack against the 2-SIDH protocol [3]. Their attack also generalizes to the k-SIDH protocol with $k > 2$, though the required number of instances of the protocol with the server is exponential in k.

Our Contributions. In this paper, we provide a new adaptive attack on a variant of the k-SIDH protocol suggested by Jao and Urbanik [10]. The Jao-Urbanik protocol introduces some redundancy in k-SIDH's secret keys using the non-trivial automorphisms of curves with j-invariants 0 or 1728 to increase efficiency. While the authors of the protocol conjectured that the inherent structure could be exploited in attacks and chose larger security parameters to account for this, we provide a concrete attack.

Our attack borrows from Galbraith et al. and Dobson et al.'s attacks, but it crucially differs from them in the following ways:

- We use the underlying relationship between the kernel generators of corresponding curves to match up triples of candidate curves instead of exhaustively searching over all possibilities when querying for the first key bits.
- Instead of separately computing the key bits and pullbacks at any step of the attack, we combine these stages by guessing the key bits and computing candidate pullbacks first to then validate any possible combination using the oracle.
- Contrasting to the attack in [3], we manage to compute precise pullbacks at each step instead of having to keep track of multiple candidates which are indistinguishable to the attacker.
- Overall, we significantly reduce the number of oracle queries by exploiting the structure underlying the Jao-Urbanik protocol.

We show that our attack requires to run $\mathcal{O}(32^{k/3})$ instances of the protocol with the server, if the Jao-Urbanik protocol is instantiated with secret isogenies of degree a power of two. This is almost a cube root speedup compared to Dobson et al.'s attack on the same instantiation.

While our attack does not break the security level for the parameter sets recommended by Jao and Urbanik, we give estimated attack costs for their parameters. Under consideration of currently known attacks against k-SIDH and Jao-Urbanik's protocol, we conclude that the former provides a better efficiency-security trade-off.

Outline. The remaining of this paper is organized as follows. To begin with, we give some background on isogenies and supersingular isogeny protocols in Sect. 2. We then recall the Dobson et al. attack on k-SIDH in Sect. 3 and the Jao-Urbanik protocol in Sect. 4. We continue by describing our attack on Jao-Urbanik's scheme in Sect. 5, and conclude the paper in Sect. 6. The Appendix includes an extension of our attack.

2   Preliminaries

For a full treatment of background information on elliptic curves we refer to Silverman [9].

2.1   Isogenies

Let $\mathbb{F}_q$ be a finite field of characteristic p. In the following we assume $p > 3$ and therefore an elliptic curve E over $\mathbb{F}_q$ can be defined by its short Weierstrass form

$$E(\mathbb{F}_q) = \{(x, y) \in \mathbb{F}_q^2 \mid y^2 = x^3 + Ax + B\} \cup \{\mathcal{O}_E\},$$

where $A, B \in \mathbb{F}_q$ and $\mathcal{O}_E$ is the point $(X : Y : Z) = (0 : 1 : 0)$ on the projective curve $Y^2 Z = X^3 + AXZ^2 + BZ^3$. The set of points on an elliptic curve forms an abelian group with $\mathcal{O}_E$ being the identity element. The *j-invariant* of an elliptic curve is

$$j(E) = 1728 \frac{4A^3}{4A^3 + 27B^2},$$

and there is an isomorphism $f : E \to E'$ between the curves E and E' if and only if $j(E) = j(E')$.

Given two elliptic curves E_1 and E_2 over a finite field $\mathbb{F}_q$, an *isogeny* is a morphism $\phi : E_1 \to E_2$ such that $\phi(\mathcal{O}_{E_1}) = \mathcal{O}_{E_2}$. The condition implies that isogenies are also group homomorphisms. If there exists an isogeny $\phi : E_1 \to E_2$, then there exists a unique isogeny $\hat{\phi} : E_2 \to E_1$, called the *dual* isogeny, such that $\phi \circ \hat{\phi} = [n]$ (where $[n]$ denotes the multiplication-by-n map on E_2). If there exists a non-constant isogeny between two curves, then they are called *isogenous*. The *degree* of an isogeny ϕ is its degree when treated as an algebraic map. If the isogeny is separable (which is always the case in this work), the degree is equal to the size of the kernel of ϕ. An isogeny from E to itself is called an endomorphism. Endomorphisms of an elliptic curve form a ring under addition and composition. If E is defined over a finite field then the endomorphism ring is either an order in an imaginary quadratic number field (such curves are called *ordinary*) or an order in the quaternion algebra ramified at p (the characteristic of the finite field) and at infinity. The latter curves are called *supersingular*. In this paper we will only consider supersingular elliptic curves.

Since an isogeny defines a group homomorphism $E_1 \to E_2$, its kernel is a subgroup of E_1. Conversely, any subgroup $S \subset E_1$ determines a (separable) isogeny $\phi : E_1 \to E_2$ with $\ker(\phi) = S$ and $E_2 = E_1/S$. Furthermore, if the degree of the isogeny is smooth, Vélu's formulae [11] provide a polynomial time algorithm for computing the isogeny (as a rational map) from its kernel.

The following lemma [9, Chapter III, Corollary 4.11] describes how the isogenies corresponding to two subgroups can be related if one subgroup contains the other:

Lemma 1. *Let E_i, $i = 1, 2, 3$ be elliptic curves and let $\phi : E_1 \to E_2$ and $\psi : E_1 \to E_3$ be two isogenies such that $ker(\phi) \subseteq ker(\psi)$. Then there exists an isogeny $\lambda : E_2 \to E_3$ such that $\psi = \lambda \circ \phi$ which is unique up to isomorphism.*

2.2   SIDH

In this subsection, we recall Jao and De Feo's original scheme [7].

Let E be a supersingular elliptic curve. In the setup, one chooses two small primes ℓ_A and ℓ_B and a prime p which is of the form $p = \ell_A^{e_A} \ell_B^{e_B} f - 1$, where f is a small cofactor and e_A and e_B are large integers. Let P_A, Q_A be generators of the $\ell_A^{e_A}$-torsion and let P_B, Q_B be generators of the $\ell_B^{e_B}$-torsion of E. Then the protocol is as follows:

1. Alice chooses a random cyclic subgroup of $E[\ell_A^{e_A}]$ of order $\ell_A^{e_A}$. As P_A, Q_A form a basis of the $\ell_A^{e_A}$-torsion, there exist integers x_A, y_A such that $A = [x_A]P_A + [y_A]Q_A$ generates this subgroup. Similarly, Bob chooses a random cyclic subgroup of $E[\ell_B^{e_B}]$ of order $\ell_B^{e_B}$ generated by $B = [x_B]P_B + [y_B]Q_B$ for some x_B, y_B.
2. Alice computes the isogeny $\phi_A : E \to E/\langle A \rangle$ and Bob computes the isogeny $\phi_B : E \to E/\langle B \rangle$.
3. Alice sends the curve $E/\langle A \rangle$ and the points $\phi_A(P_B)$ and $\phi_A(Q_B)$ to Bob and Bob similarly sends $(E/\langle B \rangle, \phi_B(P_A), \phi_B(Q_A))$ to Alice.
4. Alice and Bob both use the images of the torsion points to compute the shared secret which is the curve $E/\langle A, B \rangle$ (e.g. Alice can compute $\phi_B(A) = [x_A]\phi_B(P_A) + [y_A]\phi_B(Q_A)$ and $E/\langle A, B \rangle = E_B/\langle \phi_B(A) \rangle$).

Due to efficiency reasons in [7], the authors suggested the use of $\ell_A = 2$ and $\ell_B = 3$. They also suggested to use the starting curve E with j-invariant 1728. In [1], the authors use a variant of the Fujisaki-Okamoto transform [5] to obtain an IND-CCA secure key encapsulation mechanism. For concrete parameters of the scheme the reader is referred to [1].

Note that by [4, Lemma 2.1], it is possible for Alice (and analogously for Bob) to always choose the secret integers x_A, y_A such that one of them equals 1 given that the generators P_A, Q_A of the 2^{e_A}-torsion are independent. Hence it suffices to choose a single secret instead of two integers. In practice, this is usually done for efficiency reasons, and we will also use the convention in the following.

In [4] Galbraith et al. propose an adaptive attack against SIDH, showing that SIDH is not suitable for static-static key exchange; see Sect. 2.4 for a description of the GPST attack.

2.3 k-SIDH

Now we recall the k-SIDH scheme of Azarderakhsh et al. [2]. This protocol is a modification of the original SIDH which is potentially secure against active attacks. The protocol is as follows. Both parties agree on a curve E as well as a basis of the 2^{e_A}-torsion and a basis of the 3^{e_B}-torsion. Alice chooses k different secret integers $\alpha^{(1)}, \ldots, \alpha^{(k)}$ modulo 2^{e_A} and Bob chooses k different secret integers $\beta^{(1)}, \ldots, \beta^{(k)}$ modulo 3^{e_B}. Let h be a preimage resistant hash function. The steps of the protocol are the following:

1. Alice computes the curves $E_A^{(r)} = E/\langle P_A + [\alpha^{(r)}]Q_A\rangle$ and the corresponding isogenies $\phi_{A,r}$.
2. Bob computes the curves $E_B^{(r)} = E/\langle P_B + [\beta^{(r)}]Q_B\rangle$ and the corresponding isogenies $\phi_{B,r}$.
3. Alice sends $E_A^{(r)}$, $\phi_{A,r}(P_B)$, $\phi_{A,r}(Q_B)$ to Bob and Bob sends $E_B^{(r)}$, $\phi_{B,r}(P_A)$, $\phi_{B,r}(Q_A)$ to Alice.
4. Alice and Bob perform the SIDH key exchange for every pair $E_A^{(r)}, E_B^{(s)}$ and compute the corresponding j-invariant $j_{r,s}$.
5. The shared secret is the hash $h(j_{1,1}||j_{1,2}||\ldots||j_{k,k})$ of all the j-invariants.

2.4 The GPST Attack on Static SIDH

The adaptive GPST attack actively recovers the static SIDH key α of a party, say Alice, where $\langle P_A + [\alpha]Q_A\rangle$ is the subgroup corresponding to her secret isogeny. An attacker uses the key exchange protocol as an oracle to recover Alice's static key bit-wise. For simplicity, we set $n := e_A$ in the following.

Definition 1 (Oracle in static SIDH). *Upon receipt of an elliptic curve E, two linearly independent points $R, S \in E[2^n]$ of order 2^n and another elliptic curve E', the oracle responds 1 if $j(E/\langle R + [\alpha]S\rangle) = j(E')$ and 0 otherwise.*

To recover Alice's secret key, an attacker first generates the ephemeral key $(E_B, R := \phi_B(P_A), S := \phi_B(Q_A))$ honestly as specified by the SIDH key exchange. Then, they query the oracle on $(E_B, R, S + [2^{n-1}]R, E_{AB})$, which reveals whether $E_B/\langle R + [\alpha](S + [2^{n-1}]R)\rangle$ is isomorphic to $E_B/\langle R + [\alpha]S\rangle$. By the following lemma, this reveals the least significant bit of the static secret α.

Lemma 2 *[4, Lemma 2]. For linearly independent $R, S \in E[2^n]$ of order 2^n, α is even if and only if $\langle R + [\alpha](S + [2^{n-1}]R)\rangle = \langle R + [\alpha]S\rangle$.*

Afterwards, the attacker can proceed iteratively for all but the last two bits. Assume the attacker has recovered the i least significant bits of α, i.e. the partial key $K_i := \sum_{k=0}^{i-1} \alpha_k 2^k$ such that $\alpha = K_i + \alpha_i 2^i + \alpha' 2^{i+1}$. To learn the next bit $\alpha_i \in \{0, 1\}$, the attacker queries the oracle on

$$\left(E_B, [\theta](R - [2^{n-i-1}][K_i]S), [\theta]([1 + 2^{n-i-1}]S), E_{AB}\right). \tag{1}$$

Here, θ is a suitable scaling parameter to avoid detection of the attack by Weil pairing validation. We omit further details as this has no relevance to the methods presented in this paper, and we refer to the original paper [4] for the computational details. In this exposition we omit such factors for simplicity.

The bit α_i is deduced from the oracle's answer using the following lemma.

Lemma 3 *([4]). The oracle call (1) returns 1 if and only if $\alpha_i = 0$.*

Proof. The curve computed by Alice is E_B/G' where $G' = \langle R' + [\alpha]S'\rangle = \langle (R - [2^{n-i-1}][K_i]S) + [\alpha]([1 + 2^{n-i-1}]S)\rangle = \langle R + [\alpha]S + [\alpha - K_i][2^{n-i-1}]S)\rangle$. This is equal to G if and only if $\alpha_i = 0$. □

The last two bits $\alpha_{n-2}, \alpha_{n-1}$ should be brute-forced, as there is no suitable scaling parameter θ to avoid detection by Weil pairing validation. Note that this does not require any oracle query.

3   The DGLTZ Attack

The DGLTZ attack [3] follows roughly the same methodology as the GPST one.

In this section, let $\alpha^{(r)}$ denote Alice's k secret keys associated to the kernel generators $A^{(r)} = R + [\alpha^{(r)}]S$ for some points R, S spanning $E[2^n]$. For simplicity we will largely only use two secret keys α, β with corresponding kernel generators A, B. Then we denote by α_i the i-th bit of $\alpha = K_i^{(a)} + \alpha_i 2^i + \alpha' 2^{i+1}$, where $K_i^{(a)}$ is the i-th partial key, and analogously for β. Dobson et al. first justify the existence of the following oracle.

Definition 2 (Oracle in k-SIDH). *Let H be some public hash function. Upon receipt of an elliptic curve E, two points R, S spanning $E[2^n]$ and a hash value h, the oracle reveals whether $h = H\big(j(E/\langle R+[\alpha^{(1)}]S\rangle), \ldots, j(E/\langle R+[\alpha^{(k)}]S\rangle)\big)$.*

Note that this oracle provides information related to the k-tuple of static secret keys $(\alpha^{(1)}, \ldots, \alpha^{(k)})$, but it does not immediately reveal information on each individual secret key separately.

To compensate for this limited information, multiple oracle queries will be made using the same malicious points but different hash values. After obtaining the curves $E_{A^{(i)}} := E/\langle A^{(i)}\rangle$ from Alice's public keys, the attacker successively recovers the next bit of all the different secrets simultaneously. This is done by using malicious points in oracle queries as in the GPST attack, guessing all the j-invariants computed by Alice as a result of these malicious points, and verifying each guess with an oracle query.

The attacker recovers the first bit of all secrets with queries of the form $(E, R, [1+2^{n-1}]S, H(j_1|| \ldots ||j_k))$, where the j_i are guesses on the k shared secret curves computed by Alice. Candidate tuples for the guess can be restricted by the following lemma.

Lemma 4. *Let α be any of Alice's secret keys. Consider the isogeny path from E to E_A, and replace the last step in this path by the only other possible step that leaves the path non-backtracking. Let E_A' be the final curve of this path. Let $s \in \{0,1\}$. Let $R' := R - [s][2^{n-1}]S$ and $S' := [1 + 2^{n-1}]S$. Then the SIDH key computed by Alice is either E_A or E_A'. Moreover, it is E_A if and only if $\alpha_0 = s$.*

The number of candidate tuples is 7^k as for each secret there are 7 possible curves they have to query (the respective $E_{A^{(i)}}$ and six curves which are 4-isogenous to it). In the iterative step the attacker uses queries of the form $(E, R - [K_i^{(a)}][2^{n-i-1}]S, [1+2^{n-i-1}]S, H(j_1|| \ldots ||j_k))$, which correspond to the following elliptic curves: $E/\langle A+[\alpha_i][2^{n-1}]S\rangle$, $E/\langle B+[K_i^{(b)}-K_i^{(a)}][2^{n-i-1}]S+[\beta_i][2^{n-1}]S\rangle$. If to recover the next bits one wanted to perform a similar exhaustive search as for the first bit computation, then one would need an exponential amount of queries even for $k = 2$ as the distance (in the isogeny graph) from the second curves to E_A increases as i grows. To remedy this, the authors observe that $E/\langle B + [K_i^{(b)} - K_i^{(a)}][2^{n-i-1}]S + [\beta_i][2^{n-1}]S\rangle$ is 2-isogenous to $E_i/\langle \psi_{B,i}(B + [K_i^{(b)} - K_i^{(a)}][2^{n-i-1}]S + [\beta_i][2^{n-1}]S)\rangle$ where E_i is the $(n - i)$-th curve in the isogeny path from E to E_B and $\psi_{B,i}$ is the corresponding partial isogeny. In order to be able to compute these curves, one has to compute certain intermediate points on E_i (which the authors refer to as "pullbacks"), namely $\psi_i(B)$ and $[2^{n-i}]\psi_i(S)$. This pullback-computation is required after each key bit has been recovered, and at the i-th step makes use of the known partial keys with the following query:

$$\left(E, R - [K_{i+1}^{(a)}][2^{n-i-1}]S, [1 + 2^{n-i-1}]S, H(j_1, \ldots, j_k)\right).$$

It can be computed that the corresponding curve is $E_{i+1}/\langle \psi_{B,i+1}(B + [K_{i+1}^{(b)} - K_{i+1}^{(a)}][2^{n-i-1}]S)\rangle$ (and not 2-isogenous to it as in the previous stage). Naïvely, the attacker would query the oracle with all the possibilities for $\psi_{B,i+1}(B)$ and $[2^{n-i-1}]\psi_{B,i+1}(S)$. Note however that when the oracle returns 1, there will be two possibilities for the correct pullbacks which, due to the oracle model, cannot be distinguished. One could either have found $\psi_{B,i+1}(B)$ and $[2^{n-i-1}]\psi_{B,i+1}(S)$ or $\psi_{B,i+1}(B)+C$ and $[2^{n-i-1}]\psi_{B,i+1}(S)+C$, where C generates the kernel of the isogeny from E_{i+1} to E_i. Thus the authors choose one pullback $\psi_{B,i}(B)$ for B and then have to keep a 2-element set of candidates for $[2^{n-i-1}]\psi_{B,i+1}(S)$. The computation of bits uses 24^k queries[1] and the pullback computation uses 16^k queries under certain technical conditions which are addressed in the appendix of [3]. At each step, the intermediate isogenies are computed using the following lemma:

Lemma 5. *Let* $A^{(i)} = P + [\alpha^{(i)}]Q$ *be the generator of the subgroup corresponding to the i-th secret isogeny and let* $\psi_j^{(i)} := \phi_n^{(i)} \circ \phi_{n-1}^{(i)} \circ \cdots \circ \phi_{j+1}^{(i)}$. *Then, we have*

$$\ker \phi_j^{(i)} = \langle [2^{j-1}]\psi_j^{(i)}(A^{(i)})\rangle, \qquad \ker \hat{\phi}_j^{(i)} = \langle [2^{n-1}]\psi_{j-1}^{(i)}(Q)\rangle.$$

4 The Jao-Urbanik Protocol

In this section, we present the Jao-Urbanik protocol [10], the main target of our attack.

To reduce the cost associated to k-SIDH [2], Jao and Urbanik propose to exploit the existence of non-trivial automorphisms on certain elliptic curves for a non-interactive key exchange by using distinct isogenies between isomorphic curves. As in the original SIDH proposal [7], the authors suggest choosing parameters as follows: Let ℓ_A and ℓ_B be two small primes, e_A and e_B integers such that $\ell_A^{e_A} \approx \ell_B^{e_B}$; then choose a small cofactor f such that $p = \ell_A^{e_A}\ell_B^{e_B}f \pm 1$ is prime. To simplify our description, we will again set $\ell_A = 2$ and $\ell_B = 3$ (as widely used in discussions of SIDH) when describing the protocol here.

The only elliptic curves with non-trivial automorphisms are curves with j-invariants $j \in \{0, 1728\}$; note these are all supersingular over $\mathbb{F}_p$ for $p = 2^{e_A}3^{e_B}f - 1$ since $p \equiv 2 \pmod 3$ and $p \equiv 3 \pmod 4$. As Jao and Urbanik

---

[1] Note that this estimation is not given in [3].

primarily suggest to use the former, we focus on curves with $j(E) = 0$ in this exposition. For such curves, there exists an automorphism η_6 of order six defined by $\eta_6(x,y) = (\zeta_3 x, -y)$ for ζ_3 a primitive third root of unity. Thus, η_6 further satisfies $\eta_6^2 = \eta_6 - 1$.

The existence of these automorphisms can be exploited in the following way. If $G \subseteq E$ is a subgroup, $\eta_6(G)$ and $\eta_6^2(G)$ are also subgroups of E and we may assume that all three are distinct[2]. Hence, the isogenies from E associated to the kernels $G, \eta_6(G)$ and $\eta_6^2(G)$, respectively, are all distinct while the corresponding quotients are isomorphic. For example, consider $\phi : E \to E/G$; the map $\phi \circ \eta_6^{-1} : E \to E/G$ has kernel $\eta_6(G)$ and hence we have $E/G \cong E/\eta_6(G)$. In an SIDH-setting when Alice sends a public key $(E_A, \phi_A(P_B), \phi_A(Q_B))$, we can thus view this as Alice actually having sent three distinct but related public keys. These keys all have isomorphic target curves $E/\langle A \rangle \cong E/\langle \eta_6(A) \rangle \cong E/\langle \eta_6^2(A) \rangle$, and hence share the same j-invariant, but the corresponding isogenies are not isomorphic. The same applies to any of Bob's public keys.

Lemma 6. *Suppose a base curve E with $j(E) = 0$ together with the parameters as suggested by Jao and Urbanik [10] is used for SIDH. Then a single exchange of Alice's and Bob's SIDH public keys $pk_A = (E_A, \phi_A(P_B), \phi_A(Q_B))$ and $pk_B = (E_B, \phi_B(P_A), \phi_B(Q_A))$, where $\{P_A, Q_A = \eta_6(P_A)\}$ and $\{P_B, Q_B = \eta_6(P_B)\}$ are bases of $E[2^{e_A}]$ and $E[3^{e_B}]$ respectively, yields three shared secret (isomorphism classes of) curves.*

It follows that per public key pair, Alice and Bob obtain three shared secret curves, each identified by its j-invariant, as a secret in the Jao-Urbanik version of SIDH; see Fig. 1. Hence, in the k'-SIDH setting where each party sends k' public keys, using the Jao-Urbanik technique results in a shared secret

$$h = \mathrm{Hash}(j_{1,1}||j'_{1,1}||j''_{1,1}|| \cdots ||j_{k',k'}||j'_{k',k'}||j''_{k',k'}),$$

obtained by hashing the concatenation of the j-invariants corresponding to the $k = 3(k')^2$ shared secret curves instead of the $(k')^2$ curves as in standard k'-SIDH.

4.1   Parameter Selection

In [10, Section 4] Jao and Urbanik discuss the security of their scheme for general $\ell := \ell_A$. They correctly identify that the relationship between the curves can be exploited for an attack but do not consider this extra structure fully when providing an estimate on the security of the scheme. Based on their brief analysis, they suggest the use of $k' = 18$ keys for $\ell = 11$ when 256-bit security is required. We believe the proposed parameters are safe but that their security analysis could be elaborated on.

---

[2] We have $\eta_6(G) = G$ exactly when $G \subset \ker(\eta_6 + k)$ for some odd k. Note that this is impossible since $\eta_6^2 - \eta_6 + 1 = 0$ implies that $\deg(\eta_6) = \mathrm{tr}(\eta_6) = 1$ so that $\deg(\eta_6 + k) = (\eta_6 + k)(\bar{\eta}_6 + k) = \deg(\eta_6) + k\,\mathrm{tr}(\eta_6) + k^2 = 1 + k + k^2$ is odd and hence not divisible by 2^{e_A}.

$$\boxed{\text{Alice}} \qquad\qquad\qquad \boxed{\text{Bob}}$$

$$A \subseteq E[2^{e_A}] \qquad\qquad\qquad B \subseteq E[3^{e_B}]$$
$$\text{with } A = \langle P_A + [\alpha]\eta_6(P_A)\rangle \qquad\qquad \text{with } B = \langle P_B + [\beta]\eta_6(P_B)\rangle$$

$$\phi_A : E \to E/A = E_A, \qquad\qquad \phi_B : E \to E/B = E_B,$$
$$R_A := \phi_A(P_B), S_A := \phi_A(\eta_6(P_B)) \qquad R_B := \phi_B(P_A), S_B := \phi_B(\eta_6(P_A))$$

$$pk_A = \big(E_A, R_A, S_A\big) \qquad\qquad pk_B = \big(E_B, R_B, S_B\big)$$

$$\xrightarrow{\qquad\qquad pk_A \qquad\qquad}$$
$$\xleftarrow{\qquad\qquad pk_B \qquad\qquad}$$

$$E_B/\langle[\alpha]R_A + S_A\rangle \qquad \cong E_{AB} \cong \qquad E_A/\langle[\beta]R_B + S_B\rangle$$
$$E_B/\langle -R_A + [\alpha+1]S_A\rangle \qquad \cong E_{A\eta_6(B)} \cong \qquad E_A/\langle -[\beta+1]R_B + [\beta]S_B\rangle$$
$$E_B/\langle -[\alpha+1]R_A + [\alpha]S_A\rangle \qquad \cong E_{A\eta_6^2(B)} \cong \qquad E_A/\langle -R_B + [\beta+1]S_B\rangle$$

Shared secret:
$$h = \text{Hash}\big(j(E_{AB}), j(E_{A\eta_6^2(B)}), j(E_{A\eta_6(B)})\big)$$

Fig. 1. Jao-Urbanik's protocol using one key and automorphism η_6; public parameters: $E : y^2 = x^3 + 1$ with $j(E) = 0$ defined over field of characteristic $p = f2^{e_A}3^{e_B} - 1$, bases $\{P_A, \eta_6(P_A)\}$ of $E[2^{e_A}]$ and $\{P_B, \eta_6(P_B)\}$ of $E[3^{e_B}]$.

In their discussion, the authors do not disclose a precise attack model and consider an oracle which receives a list of curves and returns true if all of them are on the secret isogeny path $E \to E/\langle A\rangle$.[3] However, using such an oracle, the attack proposed by Jao-Urbanik is not optimal. We will show that the extra structure can be exploited further by realizing that all intermediate curves on the three paths associated to one secret are isomorphic. Furthermore, in [3] it is demonstrated that using the straightforward generalization of the GPST oracle to k-SIDH would lead to an exponential-time attack even for $k = 2$. In order to go around this issue, Dobson et al. compute extra points which increases the complexity of the attack substantially. In other words, in the k-SIDH setting, the cost of the call to an oracle which returns true if and only if all the guessed curves are on the correct path is not constant but exponential in k. This observation clearly applies to the Jao-Urbanik scheme as well.

4.2 Current Impact of DGLTZ on Jao-Urbanik Protocol

Applying the DGLTZ attack to the Jao-Urbanik protocol is not straightforward. The DGLTZ attack assumes that all the secret kernels are of the form $\langle[\alpha]P+Q\rangle$ which is not the case in the Jao-Urbanik scheme due to the following. To one

---

[3] Note that the GPST attack [4] shows how to implement a similar oracle for SIDH.

secret the following three kernels are associated: $\langle [\alpha]P + Q \rangle$, $\langle -P + [\alpha + 1]Q \rangle$, $\langle -[\alpha+1]P + [\alpha]Q \rangle$. The parity of the coefficient of Q in the second and the third kernel is different, thus in particular, it is impossible that both of them are odd (hence for every λ-multiple of the kernel the coefficient of Q will be even). This difficulty could potentially be overcome, however a number of $\mathcal{O}(24^k)$ queries, where $k = 3k'$ and k' is the number of secrets, will still be required.

Our aim is that instead of treating the three curves independently we use that the three kernels are related and propose an attack in the next section which uses $\mathcal{O}(32^{\frac{k}{3}})$ queries, thus providing a nearly cube root speedup.

5   Adaptive Attack Against the Jao-Urbanik Scheme

In this section, we describe our adaptive attack on the η_6 case of the Jao-Urbanik protocol [10]. Thus, the starting curve E has j-invariant 0 and admits an automorphism of order 6, η_6. We want to attack Alice's $\ell_A^{e_A}$-torsion, so for simplicity, we again write $\ell := \ell_A$ and $n := e_A$, and set $\ell = 2$ in our exposition. See Subsect. 5.4 for a discussion on how this attack generalizes to larger ℓ. Let P and $Q = \eta_6(P)$ be such that $\{P, Q\}$ form a basis of $E[2^n]$ and let α be one of Alice's secret keys, to which we associate the following three kernel generators

$$A = [\alpha]P + Q, \qquad A' = \eta_6(A) = -P + [\alpha + 1]Q,$$
$$A'' = \eta_6^2(A) = -[\alpha + 1]P + [\alpha]Q,$$

and the three isogenies

$$\psi_{A,0} : E \to E_A = E/\langle A \rangle, \qquad \psi'_{A,0} : E \to E'_A = E/\langle A' \rangle,$$
$$\psi''_{A,0} : E \to E''_A = E/\langle A' \rangle.$$

Similarly, we denote with γ any other secret key different from α. The associated kernels are generated by C, C', C'', the curves are E_C, E'_C, E''_C and in general the notation corresponding to γ will have a subscript C. When there is no doubt about the corresponding secret key or when a property holds for all keys, we may drop the subscript.

The isogeny $\psi_{A,0}$ can be decomposed into n individual 2-isogenies. We index intermediate curves by $E_{A,i}$, with $E_{A,0} = E_A$ and $E_{A,n} = E$. The intermediate isogenies are denoted by $\phi_{A,i} : E_{A,i} \to E_{A,i-1}$. We also call $\psi_{A,i}$ the composition $\phi_{A,n} \circ \ldots \circ \phi_{A,i+1}$. We introduce similar notations for E'_A and E''_A, and denote by η_i the isomorphism between E_A and E'_A (see Lemma 8). We summarize all notations in Fig. 2.

We define

$$A_i = \psi_{A,i}(A), \quad P_i = \psi_{A,i}(P).$$

Our attack is a non-trivial adaption of the GPST and DGLTZ attacks [3,4]. It similarly has two stages. Firstly, we compute the first bit of each key (see Subsect. 5.2) and we recover the "pullbacks" A_1, A'_1, A''_1 and $[2^{n-1}]P_1$, $[2^{n-1}]P'_1$, $[2^{n-1}]P''_1$ (for every secret A). In the second stage, we show inductively that given the first i bits of every key and A_i, $[2^{n-i}]P_{A,i}$ (for every secret A), we

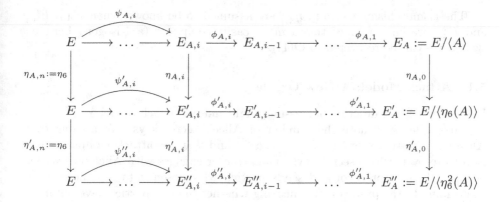

Fig. 2. Isogeny paths between the relevant curves.

can deduce the $(i+1)$-th bit and the new pullbacks (see Subsect. 5.3). In other words, if we write

$$\alpha = 2^{i+1}\alpha' + 2^i\alpha_i + K_{A,i},$$

where $K_{A,i}$ indicates the known part of the key, we can recover α_i from knowledge of the i-th pullbacks.

This is not dissimilar to what is done in the DGLTZ attack, but our attack exploits the additional structure between the shared secrets in the Jao-Urbanik protocol to recover the exact pullbacks at each step (instead of keeping two candidates) and reduce the number of queries needed for bit recovery. We thus show that the security of the Jao-Urbanik protocol with k' secret keys is only slightly better than the security of k'-SIDH, thus greatly decreasing the benefits of the Jao-Urbanik protocol. A more detailed study of the complexity of our attack can be found at the end of Subsect. 5.3.

We present our attack only by querying with points on the starting curve E, as in the DGLTZ attack. Appendix A presents a method to extend our attack to an arbitrary curve, which can also be applied to the DGLTZ attack.

We start by showing essential properties of the partial isogenies $\psi_{A,i}$, $\psi'_{A,i}$, $\psi''_{A,i}$ and of the corresponding curves $E_{A,i}$, $E'_{A,i}$, $E''_{A,i}$ in the following two lemmas.

Lemma 7. *For simplicity, denote subscripts of the form A,i by i. Then,*

$$\ker(\psi_i) = \langle [2^i]A\rangle, \qquad \ker(\psi'_i) = \langle [2^i]A'\rangle, \qquad \ker(\psi''_i) = \langle [2^i]A''\rangle,$$
$$\ker(\phi_i) = \langle [2^{i-1}]A_i\rangle, \qquad \ker(\phi'_i) = \langle [2^{i-1}]A'_i\rangle, \qquad \ker(\phi''_i) = \langle [2^{i-1}]A''_i\rangle,$$
$$\ker(\hat{\phi}_i) = \langle [2^{n-1}]P_{i-1}\rangle, \quad \ker(\hat{\phi}'_i) = \langle [2^{n-1}]P'_{i-1}\rangle, \quad \ker(\hat{\phi}''_i) = \langle [2^{n-1}]P''_{i-1}\rangle.$$

Lemma 8. *Let notation be as above. Then $E_{A,i}$, $E'_{A,i}$ and $E''_{A,i}$ are isomorphic.*

Proof. We have that $\ker(\psi_{A,i}) \subseteq \ker(\psi'_{A,i} \circ \eta_{A,n})$. Thus, there exists an isogeny $\eta_{A,i} : E_{A,i} \to E'_{A,i}$ such that $\psi'_{A,i} \circ \eta_{A,n} = \eta_{A,i} \circ \psi_{A,i}$. By examining the degrees, we find that $\deg \eta_{A,i} = 1$ and thus $\eta_{A,i}$ is an isomorphism. The same reasoning holds for $E''_{A,i}$. $\qquad\square$

The isomorphisms $\eta_{A,i}$ and $\eta'_{A,i}$ are assumed to be known when $E_{A,i}$, $E'_{A,i}$ and $E''_{A,i}$ are known, since they can be easily computed (a 1-isogeny between two curves can be recovered in $\mathcal{O}(1)$).

5.1   Attack Model: A New Oracle

In this section, we describe our assumptions and our attack model.

Firstly, let k' denote the number of Alice's secret keys. We assume that Alice has a static set of keys $\alpha^{(1)}, \ldots, \alpha^{(k')}$ and that the attacker impersonates Bob to recover Alice's secret keys. The attacker engages with Alice on sessions of Jao-Urbanik's protocol and sends particularly chosen data, not necessarily conforming to the protocol. By checking whether the two parties have obtained the same shared secret, the attacker may recover information on Alice's keys. We model this information leakage in terms of an oracle and represent each interaction with Alice as an oracle query.

An adaption of the second oracle presented in [3] to the η_6 variant of the Jao-Urbanik protocol gives an oracle $O'(E^{(1)}, \ldots, E^{(k')}, R^{(1)}, S^{(1)}, \ldots, R^{(k')}, S^{(k')}, h)$ that returns *true* if

$$h = \mathrm{Hash}(j_{1,1}||j_{1,2}||\cdots||j_{k',k'-1}||j_{k',k'}),$$

where $j_{r,s}$ denotes the concatenation of

$$j\left(E^{(r)}/\langle[\alpha^{(r)}]R^{(s)} + S^{(s)}\rangle\right),\ j\left(E^{(r)}/\langle-R^{(s)} + [\alpha^{(r)}+1]S^{(s)}\rangle\right),$$
$$j\left(E^{(r)}/\langle-[\alpha^{(r)}+1]R^{(s)} + [\alpha^{(r)}]S^{(s)}\rangle\right).$$

Similarly to what is done for the third oracle in [3], we can simplify the oracle by assuming that the attacker generates one secret key and sends repeated copies of the same curve and points. Note that any information that can be recovered with querying with distinct curves can also be recovered by querying with repeated copies of the same curve.

Hence, we obtain the following oracle

$$O(E, R, S, h) = O'(E, \ldots, E, R, S, \ldots, R, S, h), \tag{2}$$

which is the one we use in our attack. As noted in [3], the attacker could change one curve at each iteration, but all but one curves ($k' - 1$, in this case) have to remain constant across iterations for the attack to succeed.

5.2   Exploiting the Additional Structure: First Step

Let us focus on one of Alice's secrets α. The attack extends straightforwardly to all the keys. In order to recover the first bits of α, the attacker sends the modified points $P' = [1 + 2^{n-1}]P$, $Q' = Q$, so that Alice uses the following kernels in her computation of the shared secret:

1. $\hat{A} = \langle [\alpha]P' + Q' \rangle = \langle [\alpha]P + Q + [\alpha_0][2^{n-1}]P \rangle$,
2. $\hat{A}' = \langle -P' + [\alpha+1]Q' \rangle = \langle -P + [\alpha+1]Q + [2^{n-1}]P \rangle$,
3. $\hat{A}'' = \langle -[\alpha+1]P' + [\alpha]Q' \rangle = \langle -[\alpha+1]P + [\alpha]Q - [\alpha_0+1][2^{n-1}]P \rangle$.

Note that, depending on the value of the least significant bit α_0, either the first or third curve computed has not been altered by using the modified points. Thus the attacker already knows one of $j(\hat{E}_A)$ or $j(\hat{E}_{A''})$, where $\hat{E}_A = E/\langle \hat{A} \rangle$, although they do not know at this stage which one of the two.

The attacker now computes $\mathcal{E}_A^*$, the sets containing all six proper 4-neighbors of the curves E_A in Alice's public key, and their respective j-invariants. If $\alpha_0 = 0$, $\langle [\alpha]P' + Q' \rangle = \langle A \rangle$, and hence the first curve Alice obtains is isomorphic to her original E_A. The second curve is independent of α_0 and is a 4-neighbor of E_A', since they share the 2-neighbor $E/\langle 2A' \rangle$. Similarly, the third curve is a 4-neighbor of E_A'' since they share 2-neighbor $E/\langle 2A'' \rangle$. Note that the intermediate 2-neighbors in this construction are isomorphic since their kernel generators differ only by an application of η_6. Hence, the three curves E_A, $E/\langle -P'+[\alpha+1]Q' \rangle$ and $E/\langle -[\alpha+1]P'+[\alpha]Q' \rangle$ are the three distinct 2-neighbors of $E/\langle 2A \rangle$ (distinctness follows from simple computations on the kernel generators), as depicted in Fig. 3.

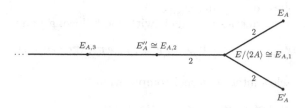

Fig. 3. The isogeny paths between E_A, E_A' and E_A''.

Analogously if $\alpha_0 = 1$, we find that the three computed curves all share a common 2-neighbor. The attacker proceeds analogously for the choices of any other curve. This allows the attacker to match up candidate curves for E_A, E_A' and E_A'' among the 4-neighbors of E_A, depending on which combination of first key bits they are querying for at the time: the attacker may choose any curve in $\mathcal{E}_A^*$ as a candidate curve for E_A', depending on the guessed bit they may select E_A or E_A'' to be equal to E_A and then select the unique curve in $\mathcal{E}_A^*$ which is also a 4-neighbor of E_A' as a candidate for the remaining curve. Querying the oracle for all possible combinations ($12^{k/3}$ combinations, six for each neighbor and one for the curve itself) gives the attacker the first bit of each secret.

Now, given the position of E_A, E_A' and E_A'' in the isogeny graph, we know that $E/\langle 2A \rangle$ must be the first intermediate curve $E_{A,1}$ and similarly E_A'' must be $E_{A,2}$. This means the attacker can easily recover the first two intermediate curves without additional oracle queries, unlike what happens in the DGLTZ attack. Since the isogenies between E_A and $E_{A,1}$ (i.e. $\phi_{A,1}$) and between $E_{A,1}$ and $E_{A,2}$ (i.e. $\phi_{A,2}$) are known, the attacker can compute the first pullbacks of

A and $[2^{n-1}]P$ (up to odd scalar multiplication) by setting A_1 to be a generator of $\ker(\phi_{A,1})$ and $[2^{n-1}]P_{A,1}$ a generator of $\ker(\hat{\phi}_{A,2})$ (see Lemma 7). Finally, the attacker obtains the pullbacks $A_1' = \eta_{A,1}(A_1)$ and $A_1'' = \eta_{A,1}'(A_1)$. This approach can be easily repeated for every following curve.

5.3   Intermediate Bit and Pullback Computation

Suppose we have recovered the first i bits of each key and have the relevant pullbacks. Let α be one of Alice's secrets keys and let γ denote any other secret key.

Now, we want to recover the $(i+1)$-th bit and compute the new pullbacks. In the DGLTZ attack, the bit recovery and pulling back are two separate stages, but in order to exploit the additional structure of Jao-Urbanik's scheme, we combine them together.

The attacker does not actively recover the $(i+1)$-th key bits, but instead tries all the $2^{k'}$ possibilities and uses the pullback queries to validate both the bit guesses and the pullback candidates.

Using Lemma 7, it is possible to compute $\hat{\phi}_{i+1}$ and thus recover ϕ_{i+1}. With this information, the attacker can obtain candidates for the pullbacks of A and P. The same applies to ϕ_{i+1}' and ϕ_{i+1}''.

The attacker then queries the oracle with the following points

$$P' = [1 + 2^{n-i-1}]P, \quad Q' = Q - [K_{A,i}][2^{n-i-1}]P.$$

These are the oracle's internal kernel computations

$$\langle [\alpha]P' + Q' \rangle = \langle A + [\alpha_i][2^{n-1}]P \rangle,$$

$$\langle -P' + [\alpha+1]Q' \rangle = \langle A' - [K_{A,i}^2 + K_{A,i} + 1][2^{n-i-1}]P$$
$$+ [K_{A,i}][\alpha_i][2^{n-1}]Q \rangle,$$

$$\langle -[\alpha+1]P' + \alpha Q' \rangle = \langle A'' - [K_{A,i}^2 + K_{A,i} + 1][2^{n-i-1}]P$$
$$- [K_{A,i} + 1][\alpha_i][2^{n-1}]P \rangle,$$

$$\langle [\gamma]P' + Q' \rangle = \langle C + [K_{C,i} - K_{A,i}][2^{n-i-1}]P$$
$$+ [\gamma_i][2^{n-1}]P \rangle,$$

$$\langle -P' + [\gamma+1]Q' \rangle = \langle C' - [K_{C,i}K_{A,i} + K_{A,i} + 1][2^{n-i-1}]P$$
$$- [K_{A,i}][\gamma_i][2^{n-1}]P \rangle,$$

$$\langle -[\gamma+1]P' + [\gamma]Q' \rangle = \langle C'' - [K_{C,i}K_{A,i} + K_{A,i} + 1][2^{n-i-1}]P$$
$$- [K_{A,i} + 1][\gamma_i][2^{n-1}]P \rangle.$$

All kernels can be shifted with ψ_{i+1} (e.g. $E/\langle C + [K_{C,i} - K_{A,i}][2^{n-i-1}]P + [\gamma_i][2^{n-1}]P \rangle = E_{C,i+1}/\langle C_{i+1} + [K_{C,i} - K_{A,i}][2^{n-i-1}]P_{C,i+1} + [\gamma_i][2^{n-1}]P \rangle$) similarly to the DGLTZ attack by applying [9, Chapter III, Corollary 4.11.]. Now, since the candidate pullbacks for A_{i+1} (preimages of A_i via $\phi_{A,i}$), C_{i+1} (preimages of C_i via $\phi_{C,i}$), $[2^{n-i-1}]P_{C,i+1}$ (preimages of $[\frac{1}{2}][2^{n-i}]P_{C,i}$), $[2^{n-i-1}]P_{A,i+1}$ (preimages of $[\frac{1}{2}][2^{n-i}]P_{A,i}$) and their isomorphic correspondents are known, the attacker can query the oracle with the hash values of all $2^{k'}2^{k'}8^{k'}$ possibilities (2 for each bit, 2 for the kernel generator pullback candidates and $4 \cdot 2$ for the P pullback candidates). Note that the attacker may try a candidate for the first curve and then shift it to the second curve using the isomorphisms η_i or η_i' (therefore reducing an a priori complexity of 32^k to $32^{k'}$). We show that if we find a match, then we have found the correct pullbacks for C_{i+1} and $P_{C,i+1}$ as well as the correct key bits for C. First we prove a simple lemma about parities.

Lemma 9. *Let $K_{A,i}$, $K_{C,i}$ be natural numbers. Then,*

1. $K_{A,i}^2 + K_{A,i} + 1$ *is odd.*
2. *It is not possible that all of $(K_{A,i} - K_{C,i})$, $(K_{A,i}K_{C,i} + K_{A,i} + 1)$ and $(K_{A,i}K_{C,i} + K_{C,i} + 1)$ have the same parity.*

Proof. The first claim is trivial. For the second claim, observe that the sum of these quantities is even, thus it is not possible that all three of them are odd. If $K_{A,i} - K_{C,i}$ is even, then $K_{A,i}$ and $K_{C,i}$ have the same parity and then $K_{A,i}K_{C,i} + K_{A,i} + 1 = K_{A,i}(K_{C,i} + 1) + 1$ is odd.   □

Now, we prove our main lemma.

Lemma 10. *If the oracle query returns* true, *then we have found γ_i, C_{i+1} and $P_{C,i+1}$.*

Proof. Suppose the attacker guesses that α_i is 0. It is clear from the above computation that we always get at least one match when we substitute C_{i+1}, γ_i and $P_{C,i+1}$. If $\gamma_i = 0$, then it follows from the computation of [3, Claim 1], that the number of matches for the first curve is exactly two. The other match corresponds to choosing $C_{i+1} + [2^i]C_{i+1}$ as the preimage of C_i and $[2^{n-i-1}]P_{C,i+1} + [2^i]C_{i+1}$ as the preimage of $[\frac{1}{2}][2^{n-i}]P_{C,i}$. Due to Lemma 9, it is not possible that $(K_{A,i} - K_{C,i})$, $(K_{A,i}K_{C,i} + K_{A,i} + 1)$ and $(K_{A,i}K_{C,i} + K_{C,i} + 1)$ are all odd. Assume for instance that $(K_{A,i} - K_{C,i})$ is odd and $(K_{A,i}K_{C,i} + K_{A,i} + 1)$ is even. Then we show that the second curve will not match as its kernel will be generated by $C_{i+1}' + [K_{C,i}K_{A,i} + K_{A,i} + 1][2^{n-i-1}]P_{C,i+1} + [2^i]C_{i+1}$. Hence it will be 4-isogenous to the queried curve. The other cases follow similarly.

When $\gamma_i = 1$, then there will be another match for the first curve. Namely when we pull back $[\frac{1}{2}][2^{n-i}]P_i$ as $[2^{n-i-1}]P_{i+1} + [2^{n-1}]P_{i+1}$. However, again a similar calculation to [3, Claim 1] (one has to distinguish cases depending on the parity of $K_{A,i}$ and $K_{C,i}$) shows that either the second or the third curve will not match. The calculations when the attacker guesses α_i to be 1 are analogous.   □

Lemma 10 implies that for all secrets except α we know the correct bits and pullbacks (as otherwise we cannot receive 1 from the oracle). However, we have seen that the coefficient $K_{A,i}^2 + K_{A,i} + 1$ is odd, thus there will be multiple matches.

In order to retrieve α_i and the corresponding pullbacks we do another query with different points, switching $K_{A,i}$ with $K_{C,i}$. For this, we can use the previously computed pullbacks and thus only query the oracle 32 times (corresponding to the 32 possibilities for the pullbacks and the bit). Since the correct pullbacks are computed, we are able to recover the isogenies $\phi_{A,i+1}$ and $\phi_{C,i+1}$ using Lemma 7. Finally, since the next intermediate curves are computed we compute the isomorphisms between them. Thus, we have proven the following theorem.

Theorem 1.

1. *There exists an algorithm that recovers the first bit of each secret using $\mathcal{O}(12^{k'}) = \mathcal{O}(12^{\frac{k}{3}})$ queries to the oracle defined in (2).*
2. *There exists an algorithm that recovers the intermediate bits and pullbacks using $\mathcal{O}(32^{k'}) = \mathcal{O}(32^{\frac{k}{3}})$ queries to the oracle defined in (2).*

5.4   Attack Costs for General ℓ

So far, we have demonstrated our attack on the Jao-Urbanik protocol with parameter choice $\ell = 2$ for simplicity. However, in their proposal, the authors suggest the use of $\ell = 11$ or $\ell = 13$ and further compute that $k' = 18$ keys are necessary to obtain security against Grover's algorithm for $\ell = 11$; see [10, Section 4]. Thus we briefly assess the cost of our attack and the DGLTZ attack for arbitrary ℓ. We divide the discussion into two parts. First, we estimate the number of queries needed for computing the first key bits and later the number of queries needed in the iterative step.

The complexity estimate of our attack is a straightforward generalization of Theorem 1. During the recovery of the first bit of every key, we query - as before - for any of the $\ell^{k'}$ possible first ℓ-adic digit combinations by first fixing the curve (either E_A or E_A'' using notation as in Subsect. 5.2) corresponding to the guessed key digit to be the curve given in Alice's public key. Then we select any of the $\ell(\ell+1)$ ℓ^2-neighbors of the correct curve to be E_A' and choose one of the remaining $\ell-1$ curves which are ℓ^2-isogneous to both previously selected curves as the third curve associated to a given key. Hence, for each possible combination of first key digits we have $\left(\ell(\ell+1)(\ell-1)\right)^{k'}$ choices of curves. Thus, there exists an algorithm which recovers the first digit of each secret using $\mathcal{O}(\ell^{k'}\ell^{3k'}) = \mathcal{O}(\ell^{4k'}) = \mathcal{O}(\ell^{\frac{4k}{3}})$ oracle queries.

For the iterative step, we again first guess the i-th ℓ-adic digits and then compute candidate preimages for the first curve and shift them to the other two curves using the respective isomorphisms. There are $\ell^{k'}$ possibilities for the digits and $\ell^{2k'}$ possibilities for each preimage. This implies that we need $\mathcal{O}(\ell^{5k'})$ queries in total.

Hence, for general ℓ, we can summarize our findings in the following theorem.

Theorem 2.

1. *There exists an algorithm that recovers the first digit of each secret using $\mathcal{O}(\ell^{4k'}) = \mathcal{O}(\ell^{\frac{4k}{3}})$ queries to the oracle defined in (2).*

2. *There exists an algorithm that recovers the intermediate digits and pullbacks using $\mathcal{O}(\ell^{5k'}) = \mathcal{O}(\ell^{\frac{5k}{3}})$ queries to the oracle defined in (2).*

5.5   Comparison of k'-SIDH and Jao-Urbanik's Protocol

Theorem 2 does not break the security parameters suggested by Jao and Urbanik. However, in order to assess the security gain of Jao-Urbanik's protocol, we compare it with the security of k'-SIDH for arbitrary ℓ. Since the DGLTZ method requires an extra step which computes the i-th digits and then uses that information to compute candidate pullbacks, the overall complexity of the attack is $\ell^{4k'}$ for k'-SIDH. The following table gives an overview of the number of SIDH-instances and public keys occurring when executing the different protocols, as well as the respective cost of attacking the ℓ-torsion (Table 1).

Table 1. Comparisons between Jao-Urbanik's scheme and k-SIDH

	# SIDH instances	# Public key exchanges	Attack cost
Jao-Urbanik with k' keys	$3(k')^2$	$(k')^2$	$\mathcal{O}(\ell^{5k'})$
k-SIDH with $k = k'$	$(k')^2$	$(k')^2$	$\mathcal{O}(\ell^{4k'})$
k-SIDH with $k = \frac{5}{4}k'$	$(\frac{5}{4}k')^2 \approx 1.56(k')^2$	$\approx 1.56(k')^2$	$\mathcal{O}(\ell^{4\frac{5}{4}k'}) = \mathcal{O}(\ell^{5k'})$

Therefore, we can observe that the Jao-Urbanik protocol with k' secrets is as secure as $\frac{5k'}{4}$-SIDH when comparing necessary oracle queries. Consequently, it is more efficient to use $\frac{5k'}{4}$-SIDH than the Jao-Urbanik scheme with k' keys and the same ℓ when measuring security with respect to the currently known attacks, as the former has a computational cost equivalent to $3(k')^2$ SIDH exchanges, whereas the latter has a computational cost equivalent to $1.56(k')^2$ SIDH exchanges. Note that the Jao-Urbanik scheme maintains a moderate advantage in public key size, since it requires sharing k' keys, compared to the $\frac{5}{4}k'$ keys shared in k-SIDH.

6   Conclusion

We have introduced an adaptive attack against Jao-Urbanik's protocol with parameter $\ell = 2$. While Jao and Urbanik suggest using $\ell = 11$ or $\ell = 13$, our attack can be extended to that case as briefly described in the previous section. The complexity of such an attack increases significantly, possibly reaching levels where the protocol is secure for the specified parameter sets. However, even in that case, our attack provides a nearly cubic speedup compared to a generic application of Dobson et al.'s attack against the Jao-Urbanik scheme. Assessing security of k-SIDH and Jao-Urbanik's variant of it with respect to currently known attacks, we conclude that Jao-Urbanik's protocol does not seem to offer a sufficient security improvement over k-SIDH with the same number of secret keys to justify the roughly two times more computations needed.

We leave a more thorough examination of whether a combination of stages in an attack on k-SIDH can evoke further optimizations to future work. Any potential improvements in the attack cost would then make it necessary to reevaluate the efficiency-security trade-off when comparing k-SIDH and the Jao-Urbanik protocol.

Acknowledgments. We would like to thank David Jao and David Urbanik for their valuable comments and feedback on this work. Furthermore, we are grateful to Samuel Dobson, Steven D. Galbraith, Jason LeGrow, Yan Bo Ti, and Lukas Zobernig for their helpful clarifications regarding the DGLTZ attack.

Work by the second and fourth authors was supported by an EPSRC New Investigator grant (EP/S01361X/1).

A   Querying with E_B

The following lemma shows how to lift from the path $E_B \to E_{AB}$ to the path $E \to E_A$.

Lemma 11. *Let $\psi_{A,i}$ be the partial isogeny from E to E_i and let $\psi_{A,i}^B$ be the corresponding partial isogeny from E_B to E_{AB}. Let A be the kernel of the isogeny from E to E_A and let $A_B = \phi_B(A)$. Let E_i be the i-th curve in the isogeny path from E to E_A and E_i^B be the i-th curve in the isogeny path from E_B to E_{AB}. Let $\delta_i : E_i^B \to E_i$ be the isogeny which is the SIDH lift of ϕ_B. Assume we know $\psi_i'(A_B)$ and $\psi_i'(\phi_B(Q))$. Then we can compute $[3^n]\psi_i(A)$ and $[3^n]\psi_i(Q)$.*

Proof. The proof follows from the observation that $\delta_i \circ \psi_i' = \psi_i \circ \hat{\phi}_B$.   □

The Lemma can be applied to compute the relevant pullbacks on the isogeny paths from E to E_A, E' to E_A' and E'' to E_A'' in the following manner. First one computes a pullback candidate on the path starting from E_B. Then it is lifted with the above lemma to the path starting from E (using the fact that 3^n is odd). Then it can further be shifted to the other two isomorphic curves. Finally these points can be shifted back with ϕ_B.

References

1. Azarderakhsh, R., et al.: Supersingular isogeny key encapsulation. Submission to the NIST Post-Quantum Standardization project (2017)
2. Azarderakhsh, R., Jao, D., Leonardi, C.: Post-quantum static-static key agreement using multiple protocol instances. In: Adams, C., Camenisch, J. (eds.) SAC 2017. LNCS, vol. 10719, pp. 45–63. Springer, Cham (2018). https://doi.org/10.1007/978-3-319-72565-9_3
3. Dobson, S., Galbraith, S.D., LeGrow, J., Ti, Y.B., Zobernig, L.: An adaptive attack on 2-SIDH (2019). http://eprint.iacr.org/2019/890
4. Galbraith, S.D., Petit, C., Shani, B., Ti, Y.B.: On the security of supersingular isogeny cryptosystems. In: Cheon, J.H., Takagi, T. (eds.) ASIACRYPT 2016. LNCS, vol. 10031, pp. 63–91. Springer, Heidelberg (2016). https://doi.org/10.1007/978-3-662-53887-6_3

5. Hofheinz, D., Hövelmanns, K., Kiltz, E.: A modular analysis of the Fujisaki-Okamoto transformation. In: Kalai, Y., Reyzin, L. (eds.) TCC 2017. LNCS, vol. 10677, pp. 341–371. Springer, Cham (2017). https://doi.org/10.1007/978-3-319-70500-2_12

6. Jao, D., et al.: SIKE: Supersingular isogeny key encapsulation (2017). http://sike.org/

7. Jao, D., De Feo, L.: Towards quantum-resistant cryptosystems from supersingular elliptic curve isogenies. In: Yang, B.-Y. (ed.) PQCrypto 2011. LNCS, vol. 7071, pp. 19–34. Springer, Heidelberg (2011). https://doi.org/10.1007/978-3-642-25405-5_2

8. National Institute of Standards and Technology: NIST post-quantum cryptography project (2017). http://csrc.nist.gov/groups/ST/post-quantum-crypto/

9. Silverman, J.H.: The Arithmetic of Elliptic Curves, vol. 106. Springer, New York (2009). https://doi.org/10.1007/978-0-387-09494-6

10. Urbanik, D., Jao, D.: New techniques for SIDH-based NIKE (accepted at Math-Crypt 2018, to appear in J. Math. Cryptol.; personal communication)

11. Vélu, J.: Isogénies entre courbes elliptiques. CR Acad. Sci. Paris Séries A **273**, 305–347 (1971)

A SAT-Based Approach for Index Calculus on Binary Elliptic Curves

Monika Trimoska[✉], Sorina Ionica, and Gilles Dequen

Laboratoire MIS, Université de Picardie Jules Verne, Amiens, France
{monika.trimoska,sorina.ionica,gilles.dequen}@u-picardie.fr

Abstract. Logical cryptanalysis, first introduced by Massacci in 2000, is a viable alternative to common algebraic cryptanalysis techniques over boolean fields. With XOR operations being at the core of many cryptographic problems, recent research in this area has focused on handling XOR clauses efficiently. In this paper, we investigate solving the point decomposition step of the index calculus method for prime-degree extension fields $\mathbb{F}_{2^n}$, using SAT solving methods. We experimented with different SAT solvers and decided on using WDSAT, a solver dedicated to this specific problem. We extend this solver by adding a novel symmetry breaking technique and optimizing the time complexity of the point decomposition step by a factor of $m!$ for the $(m+1)^{\text{th}}$ summation polynomial. While asymptotically solving the point decomposition problem with this method has exponential worst time complexity in the dimension l of the vector space defining the factor base, experimental running times show that the presented SAT solving technique is significantly faster than current algebraic methods based on Gröbner basis computation. For the values l and n considered in the experiments, the WDSAT solver coupled with our symmetry breaking technique is up to 300 times faster than MAGMA's F4 implementation, and this factor grows with l and n.

Keywords: Discrete logarithm · Index calculus · Elliptic curves · Point decomposition · Symmetry · Satisfiability · DPLL algorithm

1 Introduction

The index calculus algorithm originally denoted a technique to compute discrete logarithms modulo a prime number, but it now refers to a whole family of algorithms adapted to other finite fields and some algebraic curves. It includes the Number Field Sieve (NFS) [23], dedicated to logarithms in $\mathbb{Z}_q$ and the algorithms of Gaudry [15] and Diem [8] for algebraic curves defined over $\mathbb{F}_{q^n}$, where $q = p^k$. Index calculus algorithms proceed in two main steps. The *sieving* (or *point decomposition*) step concentrates most of the number theory and algebraic geometry needed overall. By splitting random elements over a well-chosen factor base, it produces a large sparse matrix, the rows of which are "relations". In a second phase, the *matrix step* produces "good" combinations of the relations by

© Springer Nature Switzerland AG 2020
A. Nitaj and A. Youssef (Eds.): AFRICACRYPT 2020, LNCS 12174, pp. 214–235, 2020.
https://doi.org/10.1007/978-3-030-51938-4_11

finding a non-trivial vector in the kernel of this matrix. This, in turn, enables the efficient computation of any discrete logarithm on the input domain. A crucial step of the index calculus on elliptic curves is to solve the *point decomposition problem* (PDP), by generating sufficiently many relations among suitable points on the curve. Using the so-called summation polynomials attached to the curve, this boils down to solving a system of polynomial equations whose solutions are the coordinates of points. The resulting algorithm has complexity $O(q^{2-2/n})$, but this hides an exponential factor in n which comes from the hardness of solving the point decomposition problem.

Consequently, when q is large, $n \geq 3$ is small and $\log q > cm$ for some constant c, the Gaudry-Diem algorithm has a better asymptotic complexity than generic methods for solving the discrete logarithm problem and Gröbner basis algorithms have become a well-established technique [18] to solve these systems. Since a large number of instances of PDP needs to be solved, most of the research in the area has focused on improving the complexity of this step. Several simplifications such as symmetries and polynomials with lower degree obtained from the algebraic structure of the curve have been proposed [10].

When we consider elliptic curves defined over $\mathbb{F}_{2^n}$ with n prime, solving the PDP system via Gröbner bases quickly becomes a bottleneck, and index calculus algorithms are slower than generic attacks, from a theoretical and a practical point of view. Moreover, it is not known how to define the factor base in order to exploit all the symmetries coming from the algebraic structure of the curve, without increasing the number of variables when solving PDP [36]. Finally, note that for random systems, pure Gröbner basis algorithms are both theoretically and practically slower than simpler methods, typically exhaustive search [6,24], hybrid methods [2] and SAT solvers. It is thus natural that we turn our attention towards combinatorics tools to solve the PDP in characteristic 2.

Until recent years, SAT solvers have been proven to be a powerful tool in the cryptanalysis of symmetric schemes. They were successfully used for attacking secret key cryptosystems such as Bivium, Trivium, Grain, AES [16,17,22,30,31]. However, their use in public key cryptosystems has rarely been considered. A prominent example is the work of Galbraith and Gebregiyorgis [14], where they explore the possibility of replacing available Gröbner basis implementations with generic SAT solvers (such as MiniSat), as a tool for solving the polynomial system for the PDP over binary curves. They observe experimentally that the use of SAT solvers may potentially enable larger factor bases to be considered.

In this paper, we take important steps towards fully replacing Gröbner basis techniques for solving PDP with constraint programming ones. First, we model the point decomposition problem as a logical formula, with a reduced number of clauses, when compared to the model used in [14]. We compare different SAT solvers and decide that the recently introduced WDSat solver [35] is most adapted to this problem and yields the fastest running times. Secondly, we propose a symmetry breaking technique and we implement it as an extension of this solver. We show that by using the extended solver, the proven worst-case complexity of solving a PDP is $O(\frac{2^{ml}}{m!})$, where m is the number of points in the decomposition and l is the dimension of the vector space defining the factor base. This is to be compared against the Gröbner basis algorithm proposed in [11], whose runtime $O(2^{\omega n/2})$ (with $n \sim ml$ and ω the linear algebra constant) is proven under heuristic assumptions.

We experimented with the index calculus attack on the discrete logarithm for elliptic curves over prime-degree binary extension fields. We obtain an important speedup in comparison with the best currently available implementation of Gröbner bases (F4 [11] in MAGMA [4]) and generic solvers [1,31,32]). Consequently, we were able to display results for a range of parameters l and n that were not feasible with previous approaches. In addition, our experiments show that Gröbner bases cannot compete with SAT solvers techniques in terms of memory requirements. To illustrate, a system solved with the extended WDSAT solver using only 17 MB of memory requires more than 200 GB when using the Gröbner basis method.

However, our experiments suggest that this improved PDP resolution does not render the index calculus attack faster than generic methods for solving the ECDLP in the case of prime-degree extension fields $\mathbb{F}_{2^n}$.

This paper is organized as follows. Section 2 gives an overview of the index calculus algorithm on elliptic curves, introduces the PDP problem and briefly recalls algebraic and combinatorial techniques used in the literature to solve this problem. Section 3 details the logical models used in our experiments. Section 4 explains the symmetry breaking technique that we implemented in a SAT solver. In Sect. 5 we give worst time complexity estimates for solving a PDP instance and derive the complexity of our SAT-based index calculus algorithm. Finally, Sect. 6 presents benchmarks obtained with our implementation. We compare this against results obtained using MAGMA's F4 implementation and several available best generic SAT-solvers, such as MINISAT [32] and CRYPTOMINISAT [31].

2   An Overview of Index Calculus

In 2008 and 2009, Gaudry [15] and Diem [8] independently proposed a technique to perform the point decomposition step of the index calculus attack for elliptic curves over extension fields, using Semaev's summation polynomials [27]. Since this paper focuses on binary elliptic curves, we introduce Semaev's summation polynomials here directly for these curves.

Let $\mathbb{F}_{2^n}$ be a finite field and E be an elliptic curve with j-invariant different from 0, defined by an equation

$$E : y^2 + xy = x^3 + ax^2 + b, \tag{1}$$

with $a, b \in \mathbb{F}_{2^n}$. Using standard notation, we take $\bar{\mathbb{F}}_{2^n}$ to be the algebraic closure of $\mathbb{F}_{2^n}$ and $E(\mathbb{F}_{2^n})$ (resp. $E(\bar{\mathbb{F}}_{2^n})$) to be the set of points on the elliptic curve defined over $\mathbb{F}_{2^n}$ (resp. $\bar{\mathbb{F}}_{2^n}$). Let $\mathcal{O}$ be the point at infinity on the elliptic curve. For $m \in \mathbb{N}$, the m-th summation polynomial is a multivariate polynomial in $\mathbb{F}_{2^n}[X_1, \ldots, X_m]$ with the property that, given points $P_1, \ldots, P_m \in E(\bar{\mathbb{F}}_{2^n})$, then $P_1 \pm \ldots \pm P_m = \mathcal{O}$ if and only if $S_m(\mathbf{x}_{P_1}, \ldots, \mathbf{x}_{P_m}) = 0$. We have that

$$S_2(X_1, X_2) = X_1 + X_2, \qquad\qquad (2)$$
$$S_3(X_1, X_2, X_3) = X_1^2 X_2^2 + X_1^2 X_3^2 + X_1 X_2 X_3 + X_2^2 X_3^2 + b,$$

and for $m \geq 4$ we have the following recursive formula:

$$S_m(X_1, \ldots, X_m) = \qquad\qquad (3)$$
$$Res_X(S_{m-k}(X_1, \ldots, X_{m-k-1}, X), S_{k+2}(X_{m-k}, \ldots, X_m, X)).$$

The polynomial S_m is symmetric and has degree 2^{m-2} in each of the variables. Let V be a vector subspace of $\mathbb{F}_{2^n}/\mathbb{F}_2$, whose dimension l will be defined later. We define the factor basis $\mathcal{B}$ to be:

$$\mathcal{B} = \{(\mathbf{x}, \mathbf{y}) \in E(\mathbb{F}_{2^n}) | \mathbf{x} \in V\}.$$

Heuristically, we can easily see that the factor base has approximatively 2^l elements. Given a point $R \in E(\mathbb{F}_{2^n})$, the point decomposition problem is to find m points $P_1, \ldots, P_m \in \mathcal{B}$ such that $R = P_1 \pm \ldots \pm P_m$. Using Semaev's polynomials, this problem is reduced to the one of solving a multivariate polynomial system.

Definition 1. *Given $s \geq 1$ and an l-dimensional vector subspace V of $\mathbb{F}_{2^n}/\mathbb{F}_2$ and $f \in \mathbb{F}_{2^n}[X_1, \ldots, X_m]$ any multivariate polynomial of degree bounded by s, find $(x_1, \ldots, x_m) \in V^m$ such that $f(x_1, \ldots, x_m) = 0$.*

Using the fact that $\mathbb{F}_{2^n}$ is an n-dimensional vector space over $\mathbb{F}_2$, the equation $f(\mathbf{x}_1, \ldots, \mathbf{x}_m) = 0$ can be rewritten as a system of n equations over $\mathbb{F}_2$, with ml variables. In the literature, this is called a *Weil restriction* [15] or *Weil descent* [26]. The probability of having a solution to this system depends on the ratio between n and l. Roughly, when $n/l \sim m$ the system has a reasonable chance to have a solution.

Recent work on solving the decomposition problem has focused on using advanced methods for Gröbner basis computation such as Faugère's F_4 and F_5 algorithms [11,12]. This is a natural approach, given that similar techniques for small degree extension fields in characteristic >2 yielded index calculus algorithms which are faster than the generic attacks on the DLP.

A common technique when working with Semaev's polynomials is to use a symmetrization process to further reduce the degree of the polynomials appearing in the PDP system. In short, since S_m is symmetric, we can rewrite it in terms of the elementary symmetric polynomials $e_1 = \sum_{1 \leq i_1 \leq m} X_{i_1}$, $e_2 = \sum_{1 \leq i_1, i_2 \leq m} X_{i_1} X_{i_2}$, ..., $e_m = \prod_{1 \leq i \leq m} X_i$. We denote by S'_{m+1} the polynomial obtained after symmetrizing $\bar{S}_{m+1}$ in the first m variables, i.e. we have $S'_{m+1} \in \mathbb{F}_{2^n}[e_1, \ldots, e_m, X_{m+1}]$.

In [36], the authors report on experiments carried on systems obtained using a careful choice of the vector space V and application of the symmetrization process. Using MAGMA's F_4 available implementation, we experimented with both the symmetric and the non-symmetric version for PDP systems and found, as in [36], that the symmetric version yields better results. Therefore, in order to set the notation, we detail this approach here.

Let t be a root of a defining polynomial of $\mathbb{F}_{2^n}$ over $\mathbb{F}_2$. Following [36], we choose the vector space V to be the l-dimensional subspace generated by $1, t, t^2, \ldots, t^{l-1}$. Assuming that $m(l-1) \leq n$ we can write:

$$
\begin{aligned}
e_1 &= d_{1,0} + \ldots + d_{1,l-1}t^{l-1} \\
e_2 &= d_{2,0} + \ldots + d_{2,2l-2}t^{2l-2} \\
&\ldots \\
e_m &= d_{m,0} + \ldots + d_{m,m(l-1)}t^{m(l-1)},
\end{aligned}
\tag{4}
$$

where the $d_{i,j}$ with $1 \leq i \leq m$, $0 \leq j \leq i(l-1)$ are binary variables. After choosing $\mathbf{x}_{m+1} \in \mathbb{F}_{2^n}$ and substituting $e_1, \ldots, e_m$ as in Eq. (4), we get:

$$
S'_{m+1}(e_1, \ldots, e_m, \mathbf{x}_{m+1}) = f_0 + \ldots + f_{n-1}t^{n-1},
$$

where f_i, $0 \leq i \leq n-1$ are polynomials in the binary variables $d_{i,j}$, $1 \leq i \leq m$, $0 \leq j \leq i(l-1)$. After a Weil descent, we obtain the following polynomial system

$$
f_0 = f_1 = \ldots = f_{n-1} = 0.
\tag{5}
$$

One can see that with this approach, the number of variables is increased by a factor m, but the degrees of the polynomials in the system are significantly reduced. Further simplification of this system can be obtained if the elliptic curve has a rational point of order 2 or 4 [14]. Since this is a restriction, we did not implement this approach and used the system in Eq. (5) as the starting point for our SAT model of the point decomposition problem.

2.1   Solving the Decomposition Problem Using SAT Solvers

Before presenting our approach for finding solutions to the PDP using SAT solvers, we give preliminaries on the Satisfiability problem, its terminology and solving techniques. A SAT solver is a special-purpose program to solve the SAT problem. Using SAT solvers as a cryptanalytic tool requires expressing the cryptographic problem as a Boolean formula in conjunctive normal form (CNF). The basic building block of a CNF formula is a *literal*, which is either a propositional variable or its negation. An OR -*clause* is a non-exclusive disjunction ($\vee$) of literals $x_1 \vee x_2 \vee \ldots \vee x_k$. A CNF formula is a unique OR-clause or a conjunction ($\wedge$) of at least two OR-clauses. An *interpretation* of a given propositional formula consists in assigning a truth value (TRUE/FALSE) to each of its variables. A CNF formula is said to be *satisfiable* if there exists at least one interpretation under which the formula is TRUE, and it is said to be *unsatisfiable* otherwise. The propositional satisfiability problem (SAT) is the problem of determining whether a (usually CNF) formula is satisfiable.

In the remainder of this paper, we will refer to an OR-clause simply by a clause, since CNF is the standard form used in SAT solvers. A clause where the operation between literals is an exclusive OR, will be referred to as a XOR-clause. The use of the logical XOR operator ($\oplus$) is common in cryptography. When working on cryptographic problems the CNF form can be extended to a CNF-XOR form, which is a conjunction of both OR-clauses and XOR-clauses.

A straightforward method for solving the SAT problem is to complete the truth table associated with the formula in question. This is equivalent to an exhaustive search method and thus impractical. Luckily, in some cases, a *partial* assignment on the set of variables can determine whether a clause is satisfiable. Assigning l, a literal from the partial assignment, to TRUE will lead to:

1. Every clause containing l is removed (since the clause is satisfied).
2. In every clause that contains $\neg l$ this literal is deleted (since it can not contribute to the clause being satisfied).

The second rule above can lead to obtaining a clause composed of a single literal, called a *unit* clause. Since this is the only literal left that can satisfy the clause, it must be set to TRUE and therefore *propagated*. The described method is called *unit propagation*. The reader can refer to [3] for more details.

A *conflict* occurs when it exists at least one clause with all literals assigned to FALSE in the formula. If this case is a consequence of a direct assignment, or eventually of Unit Propagation, this has to be undone. This is commonly known as *backtracking*.

Example 1. For instance, these two atomic operations can be illustrated with the following example built of a set of 5 clauses numbered C_1 to C_5:

$$C_1 : \neg x_1 \vee x_2 \vee \neg x_4$$
$$C_2 : x_1 \vee x_3 \vee x_4$$
$$C_3 : x_1 \vee \neg x_3$$
$$C_4 : x_1 \vee x_3$$
$$C_5 : x_2 \vee x_4$$

Assigning the variable x_1 to FALSE leads the clause C_1 to be satisfied by the literal x_1. Another consequence is that the clauses C_2, C_3 and C_4 cannot be satisfied by the literal x_1. Hence, x_1 can be deleted from these clauses. Then, C_3 is a unit clause composed of the literal $\neg x_3$ and as a consequence, x_3 has to be assigned to FALSE. We say that the truth value of x_3 is inferred through unit propagation.

When we set x_3 to its inferred value FALSE, we apply the second rule to clauses C_2 and C_4. As a consequence, clause C_4 can not be satisfied by any of its literals. This constitutes a conflict and it invokes a backtracking procedure. The backtracking procedure consists in going back to the state that the formula was in before the last assumption was made. In our example, the last assumption was that x_1 is FALSE and thus, we go back to the initial state.

The basic backtracking search with unit propagation that we described composes the Davis-Putnam-Logemann-Loveland (DPLL) algorithm [7], which is a state-of-the-art complete SAT solving technique. DPLL works by trying to assign a truth value to each variable in the CNF formula, recursively building a binary search tree of height equivalent (at worst) to the number of variables. After each variable assignment, the formula is simplified by unit propagation. If a *conflict* is met, a backtracking procedure is launched and the opposite truth value is assigned to the last assigned literal. If the opposite truth value results in conflict as well, we backtrack to an earlier assumption or conclude that the formula is *unsatisfiable* - when there are no earlier assumptions left. The number of conflicts is a good measure for the time complexity of a SAT problem solved using a DPLL -based solver. If the complete search tree is built, the worst-case complexity is $O(2^v)$, where v is the number of variables in the formula. Figure 1 illustrates the binary search tree resulting from the resolution of Example 1.

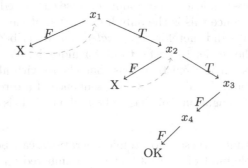

Fig. 1. Binary search tree constructed with the DPLL algorithm.

A common variation of the DPLL is the conflict-driven clause learning (CDCL) algorithm [29]. In this variation, each encountered conflict is described as a new clause which is *learnt* (added to the formula). State-of-the-art CDCL solvers, such as MINISAT [32] and GLUCOSE [1], have been shown to be a powerful tool for solving CNF formulas. However, they are not equipped to handle XOR-clauses and thus parity constraints have to be translated into CNF. Since handling CNF-clauses derived from XOR constraints is not necessarily efficient, recent works have concentrated on coupling CDCL solvers with a XOR-reasoning module. Furthermore, these techniques can be enhanced by Gaussian elimination, as in the works of Soos *et al.* (resulting in the CRYPTOMINISAT solver) [30,31], Han and Jiang [17], Laitinen *et al.* [21,22].

3   Model Description

This section gives in full detail the three models we used in our experiments: the algebraic one used by Yun-Ju *et al.* [36], the CNF model used by Galbraith and Gebregiyorgis [14] and the model we propose.

3.1   The Algebraic Model

Since the logical models are constructed starting from the algebraic one, we present first the model used when solving the PDP problem using Gröbner basis. The elementary symmetric polynomials e_i are written in terms of the $d_{i,j}$ binary variables, as in Eq. (4). Similarly, since we look for a set of solutions $(\mathbf{x}_1, \ldots, \mathbf{x}_m) \in V^m$, the X_i variables are written formally as follows:

$$X_1 = c_{1,0} + \ldots + c_{1,l-1}t^{l-1}$$
$$X_2 = c_{2,0} + \ldots + c_{2,l-1}t^{l-1}$$
$$\ldots$$
$$X_m = c_{m,0} + \ldots + c_{m,l-1}t^{l-1},$$

where $c_{i,j}$, with $1 \leq i \leq m$, $0 \leq j \leq l-1$, are binary variables. Using Eq. (4), we derive the following equations:

$$d_{1,0} = c_{1,0} + \ldots + c_{m,0}$$
$$d_{1,1} = c_{1,1} + \ldots + c_{m,1} \tag{6}$$
$$\ldots$$
$$d_{m,m(l-1)} = c_{1,l} \cdot \ldots \cdot c_{m,l}.$$

The remaining equations correspond to polynomials f_i, $0 \leq i \leq n-1$, obtained via the Weil descent on S'_{m+1}. Recall that these are polynomials in the binary variables $d_{i,j}$. We now describe how we derive logical formulas from this system.

3.2   The CNF-XOR Model

When creating constraints from a boolean polynomial system, the multiplication of variables becomes a conjunction of literals and the sum of multiple terms becomes a XOR-clause. From the two sets of equations in the algebraic model, we obtain two sets of XOR-clauses, where the terms are single literals or conjunctions. To illustrate, the logical formula derived from Eq. (6) is as follows:

$$\neg d_{1,0} \oplus c_{1,0} \oplus \ldots \oplus c_{m,0}$$
$$\neg d_{1,1} \oplus c_{1,1} \oplus \ldots \oplus c_{m,1} \tag{7}$$
$$\ldots$$
$$\neg d_{m,m(l-1)} \oplus (c_{1,l} \wedge \ldots \wedge c_{m,l}).$$

SAT solvers adapted for XOR reasoning in the literature perform on XOR clauses obtained by xoring single literals, and not conjunctions of several ones. To follow this paradigm, we have to transform the system above further. We substitute all conjunctions in a XOR clause by a newly added variable. For example, let c' be the variable substituting a conjunction $(c_{i_1,j_1} \wedge c_{i_2,j_2} \wedge ... \wedge c_{i_k,j_k})$. We have $c' \Leftrightarrow (c_{i_1,j_1} \wedge c_{i_2,j_2} \wedge ... \wedge c_{i_k,j_k})$, which rewrites as

$$
\begin{aligned}
&(c' \vee \neg c_{i_1,j_1} \vee \neg c_{i_2,j_2} \vee ... \vee \neg c_{i_k,j_k}) \wedge \\
&(\neg c' \vee c_{i_1,j_1}) \wedge \\
&(\neg c' \vee c_{i_2,j_2}) \wedge \\
&\quad ... \\
&(\neg c' \vee c_{i_k,j_k})
\end{aligned}
\tag{8}
$$

For clarity, variables introduced by substitution of monomials containing exclusively the variables $c_{i,j}$ will be denoted c' and clauses derived from these substitutions are said to be in the X-substitutions set of clauses. Similarly, substitutions of the monomials containing only the $d_{i,j}$ variables are denoted by d' and the resulting set is referred to as the E-substitutions set of clauses.

After substituting conjunctions, we will refer to the set of clauses obtained from Eq. (7) as the E-X-relation set of clauses. Finally, the equations corresponding to polynomials f_i, $0 \leq i \leq n - 1$, are derived in the same manner and the resulting clauses will be referred to as the F set of clauses.

That concludes the four sets of clauses in our SAT model. This model does not represent a CNF formula, since the E-X-relation set and the F set are made up of XOR-clauses. Hence, it will be referred to as the CNF-XOR model.

Proposition 1. *Assigning all $c_{i,j}$ variables, for $1 \leq i \leq m$ and $0 \leq j \leq l-1$, leads to the assignment of all variables in the CNF-XOR model through unit propagation.*

Proof. Let us examine the unit propagation process for each set of clauses separately.

1. Clauses in the X-substitutions set are obtained by transforming $c' \Leftrightarrow (c_{i_1,j_1} \wedge c_{i_2,j_2} \wedge ... \wedge c_{i_k,j_k})$. We note that on the right of these equivalences there are only $c_{i,j}$ variables and on the left, there is one single c' variable. The assignment of all of the $c_{i,j}$ variables will yield the assignment of all variables on the left of the equivalences, i.e. all c' variables.
2. Clauses in the E-X-relations set are obtained by transforming the algebraic system in (6). We observe that on the right of the equations there are only $c_{i,j}$ and c' variables and on the left there is one single $d_{i,j}$ variable. When all $c_{i,j}$ and all c' variables are assigned, all $d_{i,j}$ variables will have their truth value assigned through unit propagation on the E-X-relation set.
3. Clauses in the E-substitutions set are obtained by transforming $d' \Leftrightarrow (d_{i_1,j_1} \wedge d_{i_2,j_2} \wedge ... \wedge d_{i_k,j_k})$. Similarly as with the X-substitutions set, we have only $d_{i,j}$ variables on the right of these equivalences and one single d' variable on the left. The assignment of all of the $d_{i,j}$ variables will thus yield the assignment of all d' variables.
4. At this point, all variables in the parity constraints in the set F were assigned and we simply check whether the obtained interpretation satisfies the formula.

We conclude that variables in all four types of clauses of our CNF-XOR model were assigned through unit propagation.   □

3.3   The CNF Model

Since most modern SAT solvers read and process CNF formulas, we explain the classical technique for transforming a CNF-XOR model to a CNF model. In fact, this is also the technique used in MAGMA's available implementation for deriving a CNF model from a boolean polynomial system.

A XOR-clause is said to be satisfied when it evaluates to TRUE, i.e. when an odd number of literals in the clause are set to TRUE and the rest are set to FALSE. The CNF-encoding of a ternary XOR-clause $(x_1 \oplus x_2 \oplus x_3)$ is

$$
\begin{aligned}
(x_1 \vee \neg x_2 \vee \neg x_3) \wedge \\
(\neg x_1 \vee x_2 \vee \neg x_3) \wedge \\
(\neg x_1 \vee \neg x_2 \vee x_3) \wedge \\
(x_1 \vee x_2 \vee x_3)
\end{aligned}
\tag{9}
$$

Similarly, a XOR-clause of size k can be transformed into a conjunction of 2^{k-1} OR-clauses of size k. Since the number of introduced clauses grows exponentially with the size of the XOR-clause, it is a good practice to cut up the XOR-clause into manageable size clauses before proceeding with the transformation. To cut a XOR-clause $(x_1 \oplus \ldots \oplus x_k)$ of size k in two, we introduce a new variable x' and we obtain the following two XOR-clauses:

$$
\begin{aligned}
(x_1 \oplus \ldots \oplus x_i \oplus x') \wedge \\
(x_{i+1} \oplus \ldots \oplus x_k \oplus \neg x').
\end{aligned}
$$

In our experiments with MINISAT in Sect. 6, we used a CNF model obtained after cutting into ternary XOR-clauses, since any XOR SAT problem reduces in polynomial time to a 3-XOR SAT problem [3]. To the best of our knowledge, MAGMA's implementation adopts a size 5 for XOR clauses. The optimal size at which to cut the XOR-clauses depends on the nature of the model and can be determined by running experiments using different values. Running these experiments was out of the scope of our work, as the WDSAT solver does not use the CNF model.

We implemented all three models described in this section and we present Table 1 to serve as a comparison on the number of variables, equations and clauses. Values for the algebraic and CNF-XOR model are exact, whereas those for the CNF model are averages obtained from experiments presented in Sect. 6. The value of m is always 3.

In 2014, Galbraith and Gebregiyorgis [14] used MAGMA's implementation to compute the equivalent CNF logical formulas of the polynomial system resulting from the Weil descent of a PDP system and ran experiments using the general-purpose MINISAT solver to get solutions for these formulas. One can infer from

Table 1. The number of variables and equations/clauses for the three models.

		Gröbner model		CNF model		CNF-XOR model		
l	n	#Vars	#Equations	#Vars	#CNF-clauses	#Vars	#CNF-clauses	#XOR-clauses
6	19	51	52	5019	19577	767	2364	52
7	23	60	62	8223	32201	1101	3466	62
8	23	69	68	11036	43210	1510	4835	68
9	37	78	88	20969	82721	2000	6495	88
10	47	87	104	32866	130040	2577	8470	104
11	59	96	122	49538	196434	3247	10784	122

Table 1 that the model they used has a significantly larger number of clauses and variables when compared to the CNF-XOR model. This motivated our choice of the CNF-XOR model for this work.

4 Breaking Symmetry

Since Semaev's summation polynomials are symmetric, if $\{\mathbf{x}_1, \ldots, \mathbf{x}_m\}$ is a solution, then all permutations of this set are solutions as well. These solutions are equivalent and finding more than one is of no use for the PDP. When a DPLL -based SAT solver is used (see Sect. 2.1), we observe redundancy in the binary search tree. Indeed, for $m = 3$ when a potential solution $\{\mathbf{x}_1, \mathbf{x}_2, \mathbf{x}_3\}$ has been eliminated, $\{\mathbf{x}_2, \mathbf{x}_1, \mathbf{x}_3\}$ does not need to be tried out. To avoid this redundancy, we establish the following constraint $\mathbf{x}_1 \leq \mathbf{x}_2 \leq \ldots \leq \mathbf{x}_m$, where $\leq$ is the lexicographic order on $\{\text{FALSE}, \text{TRUE}\}^l$ with FALSE $<$ TRUE.

It would be tedious to add this constraint to the model itself, since this would imply adding new clauses and complexifying the SAT model. Instead, we decided to add this constraint in the DPLL algorithm using a tree-pruning-like technique. In a classical DPLL implementation we try out both FALSE and TRUE for the truth value of a chosen variable. In our symmetry breaking variation of DPLL , in some cases, the truth value of FALSE will not be tried out as all potential solutions after this assignment would not satisfy the constraint $\mathbf{x}_1 \leq \mathbf{x}_2 \leq \ldots \leq \mathbf{x}_m$. Our variation of DPLL is detailed in Algorithm 1 and the line numbers that distinguish it from a classical DPLL algorithm are in bold. Note that one crucial difference between the two algorithms is the choice of a variable on line 4. While this choice is arbitrary in a classical DPLL algorithm, in Algorithm 1 variables need to be chosen in the order from the leading bit of $\mathbf{x}_1$ to the trailing bit of $\mathbf{x}_m$. If this is not respected, our algorithm does not yield a correct answer.

Using the notation in Sect. 3, $c_{i,j}$ corresponds to the jth bit of the ith x-vector, where $1 \leq i \leq m$ and $0 \leq j \leq l - 1$. We recall from Proposition 1 that assigning all $c_{i,j}$ variables in the CNF-XOR model leads to the assignment of all variables through unit propagation. In Algorithm 1, we decide whether to try out the truth value of FALSE for $c_{i,j}$ or not by comparing two x-vectors bit for bit,

---

Algorithm 1. Function DPLL_BR_SYM(F, *compare*) : Recursive function implementing the DPLL algorithm coupled with our symmetry breaking technique.

Input: Propositional formula F and a flag *compare*
Output: TRUE if formula is satisfiable, FALSE otherwise.

1: **if** all clauses and all XOR-clauses are satisfied **then**
2:     **return** TRUE.
3: **end if**
4: choose next $c_{i,j}$.
5: **if** $j = 0$ **then**
6:     *compare* ← TRUE.
7: **end if**
8: **if** $(i = 1)$ **or** (*compare* is FALSE) **or** ($c_{i-1,j}$ is set to FALSE) **then**
9:     (*contradiction*, F') ← ASSIGN(F, $\neg c_{i,j}$).
10:     **if** *contradiction* **then**
11:         BACKTRACK().
12:         *compare* ← FALSE.
13:     **else**
14:         **if** DPLL_BR_SYM(F', *compare*) returns FALSE **then**
15:             BACKTRACK().
16:             *compare* ← FALSE.
17:         **else**
18:             **return** TRUE.
19:         **end if**
20:     **end if**
21: **end if**
22: (*contradiction*, F') ← ASSIGN(F, $c_{i,j}$).
23: **if** *contradiction* **then**
24:     BACKTRACK().
25:     **return** FALSE.
26: **end if**
27: **return** DPLL_BR_SYM(F', *compare*).

---

in the same way that we would compare binary numbers. When we are deciding on the truth value of $c_{i,j}$ we have the following reasoning:

- If $c_{i-1,j}$ is FALSE, we try to set $c_{i,j}$ both to FALSE and TRUE (if FALSE fails). When $c_{i,j}$ is set to FALSE, all of the potential $\mathbf{x}_i$ solutions are greater than or equal to $\mathbf{x}_{i-1}$, thus we continue with the same bit comparison on the next level. However, when $c_{i,j}$ is set to TRUE, all of the potential $\mathbf{x}_i$ solutions are strictly greater than $\mathbf{x}_{i-1}$ and we no longer do bit comparison on further levels.
- If $c_{i-1,j}$ is TRUE, we only try out the truth value of TRUE for $c_{i,j}$ and we continue to do bit comparison since the potential $\mathbf{x}_i$ solutions are still greater than or equal to $\mathbf{x}_{i-1}$ at this point.

Lastly, we give further information which explains in full detail Algorithm 1. We use a flag denoted *compare* to instruct whether to do bit comparison at the current search tree level or not. On line 6 we reset the *compare* flag to TRUE since $c_{i,j}$, when $j = 0$, corresponds to a leading bit of the next **x**-vector. Lastly, if-conditions on line 8 have to be checked in the specified order.

The ASSIGN procedure assigns the specified literal to TRUE in a formula F, simplifies F and infers truth values for other literals. The BACKTRACK procedure is used to undo all changes made to F after the last truth-value assignment. For more details on how these procedures are handled in the WDSAT implementation, see [35].

5   Time Complexity Analysis

As we explained in Sect. 2, the time complexity of a SAT problem in a DPLL context is measured by the number of conflicts. This essentially corresponds to the number of leaves created in the binary search tree. The worst-case complexity of the algorithm is thus 2^h, where h is the height of the tree.

As per Proposition 1, we only reason on $c_{i,j}$ variables from the CNF-XOR model. Therefore, $h = ml$ and the worst-case complexity for the PDP is 2^{ml}. Furthermore, using the symmetry breaking technique explained in Sect. 4, we optimize this complexity by a factor of $m!$. Indeed, out of the $m!$ permutations of the solution set $\{\mathbf{x}_1, \ldots, \mathbf{x}_m\}$, only one satisfies $\mathbf{x}_1 \leq \mathbf{x}_2 \leq \ldots \leq \mathbf{x}_m$ (neglecting the equality). This concludes that the worst-case number of conflicts reached for one PDP computation is

$$\frac{2^{ml}}{m!}. \tag{10}$$

Going further in the time complexity analysis, we observe that to find one conflict we go through (in the worst case) all clauses in the model during unit propagation. Hence, the running time per conflict grows linearly with the number of clauses. First, let us count the number of clauses in the X-substitutions set. For every $2 \leq d \leq m$ there exist $\binom{m}{d} \cdot l^d$ monomials of degree d given by products of variables $c_{i,j}$, and they each yield $d+1$ clauses (see Eq. (8)). In total, the number of clauses in the X-substitutions set is

$$(\sum_{d=2}^{m} \binom{m}{d} \cdot l^d)(d+1).$$

Recall that degree one monomials are not substituted and thus do not produce new clauses. We can adapt this reasoning for the E-substitutions set as well.

The number of XOR-clauses in the CNF-XOR model is equivalent to the number of equations in the algebraic model. We have $\frac{m(m+1)}{2}(l-1) + m$ in the E-X-relation set and n in the F set.

Remark 1. Using this analysis, we approximate the number of clauses, denoted by C, for $m = 3$, as all experiments presented in this paper are performed using the fourth summation polynomial.

$$C \approx \binom{3}{2} \cdot 3l^2 + \binom{3}{3} \cdot 4l^3 + \left(\binom{3}{2}\right) \cdot 3(3l-2)^2 + (6l-3) + n \approx \tag{11}$$
$$\approx 4l^3 + 171l^2 - 210l + n + 69.$$

In practice, many monomials have no occurrence in the system after the Weil descent. In fact, the value in Eq. (11) is a huge overestimate and exact values for $l \in \{6, \ldots, 11\}$ are shown in Table 1.

Assuming that we take m small, we conclude that the number of clauses in our model is polynomial in l.

Let T be a constant representing the time to process one clause. The running time of the PDP is bounded by

$$C \cdot T \cdot 2^{ml}/m!.$$

This allows us to establish the following result on the complexity of our SAT-based index calculus algorithm.

Theorem 1. *The complexity of the index calculus algorithm for solving ECDLP on a curve defined over $\mathbb{F}_{2^n}$, using a factor base given by a vector space of dimension l, is $\tilde{O}(2^{n+l})$, where the $\tilde{O}$ hides a polynomial factor in l.*

Proof. In order to perform a whole ECDLP computation, one has to find 2^l linearly independent relations. Following [9], the probability that a random point can be written as a sum of m factor basis elements is heuristically approximated by $\frac{2^{ml}}{m!2^n}$. The time complexity for the full decomposition phase, using a DPLL-based solver coupled with the breaking symmetry technique is $CT2^{n+l}$. □

This worst-case complexity is to be compared to the $O(2^{\omega \frac{n}{2}+l})$ complexity of Faugère *et al.* [13]. Both approaches rely on the heuristic approximation of the probability that a random point can be decomposed in the factor base. However, we underline here that Faugère *et al.*'s proof of this result is based on an heuristic assumption on the Gröbner basis computation for PDP, while our analysis for the SAT-based approach simply relies on the rigorously proved worst case for the DPLL search tree (see Eq. (10)).

6   Experimental Results

We conducted experiments using S_4' on binary Koblitz elliptic curves [20] defined over $\mathbb{F}_{2^n}$. We experimented with Gröbner bases and SAT approaches. In [35], WDSAT is reported to outperform the Gröbner basis methods, as well as all generic SAT solvers for this particular problem. First, we confirm this by experimenting with higher parameters and results are reported in Table 2. Secondly, we extend the WDSAT solver with our symmetry breaking algorithm described in Sect. 4. Our symmetry breaking algorithm yields faster running times and we were able to perform experiments using greater parameters. Results are shown in Table 3. All tests were performed on a 2.40 GHz Intel Xeon E5-2640 processor. Our Weil descent implementation used to generate benchmarks is open source [34].

The Gröbner basis approach takes as input an algebraic model. We used the *grevlex* ordering, as this is considered to be optimal in the literature. The MIN-ISAT solver processes a CNF model input, whereas CRYPTOMINISAT (CMS) and WDSAT use the CNF-XOR model. WDSAT can also process directly an algebraic model in ANF form. Using the CNF-XOR model is a huge advantage, as it has far fewer clauses and variables than the CNF model. Gaussian elimination can be beneficial for SAT instances derived from cryptographic problems. However, it has been reported to yield slower running times for some instances, as performing the operation is very costly. For this reason, CRYPTOMINISAT and WDSAT do not include Gaussian elimination by default, but the feature can be turned on explicitly. We experimented with both variants for both XOR-able solvers.

With WDSAT we set a custom order of branching variables, which allowed us to make use of unit propagation as explained in Proposition 1 and branch only on the $c_{i,j}$ variables. CRYPTOMINISAT does not have this feature in the current version as the authors report that custom order of branching variables leads to slower running times in most cases. We added this feature to the source code of CRYPTOMINISAT and we ran tests both with a custom order as per Proposition 1 and with the order chosen by the solver.

Table 2 compares different approaches, showing results for optimal variants of each solving tool. Running times of all variants of CRYPTOMINISAT and WDSAT are given in Appendix A. We experimented with different values of n for each l and we performed tests on 20 instances for each parameter size. Half of the instances have a solution and the other half do not. We show running time and memory averages on satisfiable and unsatisfiable instances separately since these values differ between the two cases. SAT solvers stop as soon as they find a solution and if this is not the case they need to respond with certainty that a solution does not exist. Hence, running times of SAT solvers are significantly slower when there is no solution. On the other hand, [36] indicates that the computational complexity of Gröbner bases is lower when a solution does not exist.

We set a timeout of 10 h and a memory limit of 200 GB for each run. Using MINISAT, we were not able to solve the highest parameter instances ($l = 8$) within this time frame. On the other hand, Gröbner basis computations for these instances halted before timeout because of the memory limit. This data is in line with previous works. Indeed, [36] and [28] show experiments using the fourth summation polynomial with $l = 6$, whereas the highest parameter size achieved in [14] is $l = 8$.

Table 2 shows the average runtime in seconds, the average number of conflicts and the average memory use in MB. The WDSAT solver allocates memory statically, according to predefined constant memory requirements. This explains why memory averages do not vary much between the different size parameters, or between satisfiable and unsatisfiable instances.

Our experimental results show that performing Gaussian elimination on the system comes with a significant computational cost and yields a small decrease in the number of conflicts (see Table 4 in the Appendix). As this was the case for

Table 2. Comparing different approaches for solving the PDP.

Algorithm	l	n	SATisfiable			UNSATisfiable		
			Runtime	#Conflicts	Memory	Runtime	#Conflicts	Memory
Gröbner	6	17	207.220	NA	3601	142.119	NA	3291
		19	215.187	NA	3940	155.765	NA	4091
	7	19	3854.708	NA	38763	2650.696	NA	38408
		23	3128.844	NA	35203	2286.136	NA	35162
	8	23			>200 GB			>200 GB
		26[a]			>200 GB			>200 GB
MINISAT	6	17	62.702	408189	12.7	270.261	1463309	24.2
		19	229.055	1778377	23.6	388.719	2439933	29.8
	7	19	406.918	1919565	33.6	6777.431	25180492	105
		23	12945.613	61610582	152	13260.586	59289671	163
	8	23	8027.974	63384411	256	>10 h		
		26	>10 h			>10 h		
CMS with Proposition 1	6	17	15.673	61812	34.5	62.396	260843	39.3
		19	14.128	53767	33.2	64.563	259688	42.1
	7	19	176.463	484098	41.5	843.367	2077747	72.3
		23	300.021	638152	48.9	1012.412	2070190	73.6
	8	23	1700.949	2420937	76.7	11959.938	16756106	82.4
		26	3000.831	4179236	79.4	14412.193	16783213	81.8
WDSAT with Proposition 1	6	17	.601	49117	1.4	3.851	254686	1.4
		19	.470	38137	1.4	3.913	255491	1.4
	7	19	9.643	534867	16.7	44.107	2073089	16.7
		23	9.303	477632	16.7	47.347	2067168	16.7
	8	23	68.929	2646071	16.8	525.057	16666331	16.8
		26	185.480	6261107	16.9	533.607	16684378	16.9

[a] The non-prime-degree case of $n = 26$ is not handled differently. The factor base is an l-dimensional vector space and the Weil descent does not include specific reductions which can be applied to non-prime degrees.

all instances derived from the Weil descent on S'_4, we concluded that Gaussian elimination is not beneficial for this model. Choosing the WDSAT variant without Gaussian elimination as optimal, we continued experiments for bigger size parameters using this variant coupled with the symmetry breaking technique. Table 3 shows results for $l \in \{6, 7, 8, 9, 10, 11\}$ and n sizes up to 89. All values are an average of 100 runs, as running times for satisfiable instances can vary remarkably. If we compare the number of conflicts for the first three values for l in this Table to that of the basic WDSAT solver without the breaking symmetry extension in Table 2, we observe a speedup factor that rapidly approaches 6.[1] This confirms our claims in Sect. 5 that the symmetry breaking technique proposed in this paper yields a speedup by a factor of $m!$.

Comparing results for $l = 6$ and $l = 7$ in Table 3 with the equivalent results for the Gröbner basis method in Table 2, we observe that WDSAT is up to 300 times faster than Gröbner bases for the cases where there is no solution and up to

---

[1] We compare the cases where there is no solution, as these have more stable averages.

1700 times faster for instances allowing a solution. This is a rough comparison, as the factor grows with parameters l and n.

Table 3. Experimental results using the complete WDSAT solver. Running times are in seconds and memory use is in MB.

		SATisfiable			UNSATisfiable		
l	n	Runtime	#Conflicts	Memory	Runtime	#Conflicts	Memory
6	17	.220	17792	1.4	.605	43875	1.4
	19	.243	19166	1.4	.639	44034	1.4
7	19	2.205	130062	1.4	6.859	351353	1.4
	23	3.555	189940	1.4	7.478	350257	1.4
8	23	29.584	1145966	17.0	81.767	2800335	17.0
	26	39.214	1426216	17.0	85.822	2803580	17.0
9	37	447	10557129	17.1	1048	22396994	17.1
	47	609	12675174	17.2	1167	22381494	17.2
	59	611	11297325	17.3	1327	22390211	17.3
	67	677	11608420	17.4	1430	22388053	17.4
10	47	5847	95131900	17.3	11963	179019409	17.3
	59	6849	97254458	17.4	13649	179067171	17.4
	67	6530	88292215	17.4	14555	179052277	17.4
	79	7221	86174432	17.5	16294	179043408	17.5
11	59	64162	727241718	19.2	135801	1432191354	19.2
	67	70075	741222864	19.3	145357	1432183842	19.3
	79	61370	599263451	19.4	161388	1432120827	19.4
	89	85834	736610196	19.5	175718	1432099666	19.5

Lastly, we experimented with the collision search [25] generic method, using the open source code at [33]. This implementation solves the discrete log problem in the case of prime field curves. We did not adapt the code for extension fields and the computation time for scalar multiplication on the curve might vary between the two cases. Even so, this allows for a rough comparison between the running times of generic methods and the work presented in this paper. In a uni-thread environment, a whole collision search computation for parameter $n = 59$ has an average runtime of 0.8 h on our platform. Computing 2^l successful decompositions for parameters $n = 59$ and $l = 9$ would take more than 86 h according to results in Table 3. The estimated running time becomes considerably higher when we take into account unsuccessful decompositions as well. We conclude that for the case of prime-degree extension fields, even with the significant speedup that we achieved for the PDP, index calculus attacks are still not practical compared to the PCS generic method.

7 Conclusions and Future Work

Gröbner basis methods have been shown powerful in solving the PDP in the index calculus attack for elliptic curves defined over small degree extension fields in characteristic >2. In this paper, we argue that for finite fields in characteristic 2 a SAT-based approach yields better results. We started by explaining that general-purpose SAT solvers cannot yield considerably faster running times because the number of variables in a SAT model is significantly larger than the number of variables in the algebraic model.

Our first contribution is to propose a PDP CNF-XOR model with only ml core variables, whose assignment propagates all remaining variables in the model. To solve this model we use a SAT solver dedicated to solving systems derived from a Weil descent. As our second contribution, we optimized the time complexity of this solver by a factor of $m!$ using a symmetry breaking technique.

We presented experiments for the PDP on prime-degree extension fields in characteristic 2, using parameter sizes of up to $l = 11$ and $n = 89$. This presents a significant improvement over the current state-of-the-art, as experiments using $l > 8$ have never been shown before for this case. Moreover, memory is no longer a constraint for the PDP when the Gröbner basis computation is replaced with SAT solving.

For technical reasons and lack of space, we were not able to provide here a complete comparison to other existing exhaustive search-based implementations, such as the libFes library [5] based on Bouillaguet et al.'s algorithm [6] and the Joux-Vitse hybrid algorithm [19]. For a more complete set of benchmarks, including experiments with Semaev's polynomials for $m > 3$, the interested reader is referred to the first author's upcoming PhD thesis. It would also be interesting to test the performance of SAT solvers on the simplified system obtained by considering the action of 2-torsion and 4-torsion points on the factor base, as in [14].

Acknowledgements. We thank the anonymous reviewers of the Africacrypt conference for their comments. The experimental results presented here were obtained using the MatriCS platform of the Université de Picardie Jules Verne.

A Appendix

Table 4 gives runtime and memory averages for different variations of CRYPTO-MINISAT and WDSAT.

Table 4. Comparing different variations of CRYPTOMINISAT and WDSAT for solving the PDP.

Approach	l	n	SATisfiable			UNSATisfiable		
			Runtime	#Conflicts	Memory	Runtime	#Conflicts	Memory
CMS	6	17	133.983	775948	48.4	363.513	1709971	59.5
		19	560.080	3396192	64.1	1172.740	5726372	70.1
	7	19	1210.612	5713259	85.3	10258.351	26079224	117
		23	3637.032	12159752	80.4	19857.454	47086152	130
	8	23	9846.554	18509058	123	>10 h		
		26	6905.477	13269631	115	>10 h		
CMS$_{GE}$	6	17	119.866	677336	54.5	436.811	1877699	64.2
		19	224.484	1219840	58.7	615.952	2763754	76.5
	7	19	893.425	3722805	86.5	3587.929	8642108	107
		23	580.007	1753040	82.4	3253.786	8183887	132
	8	23	11265.010	19604250	155	>10 h		
		26	3933.637	7920920	157	>10 h		
CMS with Proposition 1	6	17	15.673	61812	34.5	62.396	260843	39.3
		19	14.128	53767	33.2	64.563	259688	42.1
	7	19	176.463	484098	41.5	843.367	2077747	72.3
		23	300.021	638152	48.9	1012.412	2070190	73.6
	8	23	1700.949	2420937	76.7	11959.938	16756106	82.4
		26	3000.831	4179236	79.4	14412.193	16783213	81.8
CMS$_{GE}$ with Proposition 1	6	17	17.698	62161	39.1	86.049	294428	63.2
		19	16.301	52730	39.8	88.738	293859	62.7
	7	19	220.037	479197	51.2	2551.277	2418051	72.5
		23	367.105	653673	59.4	1329.494	2380614	93.1
	8	23	2493.328	2419268	112	19058.671	19359334	164
		26	4956.952	4171674	126	19907.670	19534832	167
WDSAT with Proposition 1	6	17	.601	49117	1.4	3.851	254686	1.4
		19	.470	38137	1.4	3.913	255491	1.4
	7	19	9.643	534867	16.7	44.107	2073089	16.7
		23	9.303	477632	16.7	47.347	2067168	16.7
	8	23	68.929	2646071	16.8	525.057	16666331	16.8
		26	185.480	6261107	16.9	533.607	16684378	16.9
WDSAT $_{GE}$ with Proposition 1	6	17	9.193	48178	1.4	56.718	253123	1.4
		19	7.041	36835	1.4	58.876	252799	1.4
	7	19	169.629	528383	16.7	736.863	2062232	16.7
		23	159.101	473223	16.7	779.432	2060501	16.7
	8	23	1290.702	2630567	16.8	9124.361	16639322	16.8
		26	3404.765	6231289	16.9	9623.677	16636122	16.9

References

1. Audemard, G., Simon, L.: Predicting learnt clauses quality in modern SAT solvers. In: IJCAI 2009, Proceedings of the 21st International Joint Conference on Artificial Intelligence, Pasadena, California, USA, 11–17 July 2009, pp. 399–404 (2009)

2. Bettale, L., Faugère, J., Perret, L.: Hybrid approach for solving multivariate systems over finite fields. J. Math. Cryptol. **3**(3), 177–197 (2009). https://doi.org/10.1515/JMC.2009.009
3. Biere, A., Heule, M., van Maaren, H., Walsh, T. (eds.): Handbook of Satisfiability, Frontiers in Artificial Intelligence and Applications, vol. 185. IOS Press, Amsterdam (2009)
4. Bosma, W., Cannon, J., Playoust, C.: The Magma algebra system. I. The user language. J. Symbolic Comput. **24**(3–4), 235–265 (1997). https://doi.org/10.1006/jsco.1996.0125
5. Bouillaguet, C.: LibFES-lite (2016). https://github.com/cbouilla/libfes-lite
6. Bouillaguet, C., Cheng, C.-M., Chou, T., Niederhagen, R., Yang, B.-Y.: Fast exhaustive search for quadratic systems in $\mathbb{F}_2$ on FPGAs. In: Lange, T., Lauter, K., Lisoněk, P. (eds.) SAC 2013. LNCS, vol. 8282, pp. 205–222. Springer, Heidelberg (2014). https://doi.org/10.1007/978-3-662-43414-7_11
7. Davis, M., Logemann, G., Loveland, D.W.: A machine program for theorem-proving. Commun. ACM **5**(7), 394–397 (1962)
8. Diem, C.: On the discrete logarithm problem in elliptic curves. Compositio Mathematica **147**(1), 75–104 (2011). https://doi.org/10.1112/S0010437X10005075
9. Diem, C.: On the discrete logarithm problem in elliptic curves II. Algebra Number Theory **7**(6), 1281–1323 (2013)
10. Faugère, J.-C., Huot, L., Joux, A., Renault, G., Vitse, V.: Symmetrized summation polynomials: using small order torsion points to speed up elliptic curve index calculus. In: Nguyen, P.Q., Oswald, E. (eds.) EUROCRYPT 2014. LNCS, vol. 8441, pp. 40–57. Springer, Heidelberg (2014). https://doi.org/10.1007/978-3-642-55220-5_3
11. Faugère, J.C.: A new efficient algorithm for computing Gröbner basis (F4). J. Pure Appl. Algebra **139**(1–3), 61–88 (1999)
12. Faugère, J.C.: A new efficient algorithm for computing Gröbner basis without reduction to zero (F5). In: Proceedings of the 2002 International Symposium on Symbolic and Algebraic Computation. ISSAC 2002, pp. 75–83. ACM, New York (2002). http://doi.acm.org/10.1145/780506.780516
13. Faugère, J.-C., Perret, L., Petit, C., Renault, G.: Improving the complexity of index calculus algorithms in elliptic curves over binary fields. In: Pointcheval, D., Johansson, T. (eds.) EUROCRYPT 2012. LNCS, vol. 7237, pp. 27–44. Springer, Heidelberg (2012). https://doi.org/10.1007/978-3-642-29011-4_4
14. Galbraith, S.D., Gebregiyorgis, S.W.: Summation polynomial algorithms for elliptic curves in characteristic two. In: Meier, W., Mukhopadhyay, D. (eds.) INDOCRYPT 2014. LNCS, vol. 8885, pp. 409–427. Springer, Cham (2014). https://doi.org/10.1007/978-3-319-13039-2_24
15. Gaudry, P.: Index calculus for abelian varieties of small dimension and the elliptic curve discrete logarithm problem. J. Symb. Comput. **44**(12), 1690–1702 (2009). https://doi.org/10.1016/j.jsc.2008.08.005
16. Gérault, D., Lafourcade, P., Minier, M., Solnon, C.: Revisiting AES related-key differential attacks with constraint programming. Inf. Process. Lett. **139**, 24–29 (2018). https://doi.org/10.1016/j.ipl.2018.07.001
17. Han, C.-S., Jiang, J.-H.R.: When boolean satisfiability meets gaussian elimination in a simplex way. In: Madhusudan, P., Seshia, S.A. (eds.) CAV 2012. LNCS, vol. 7358, pp. 410–426. Springer, Heidelberg (2012). https://doi.org/10.1007/978-3-642-31424-7_31

18. Joux, A., Vitse, V.: Cover and decomposition index calculus on elliptic curves made practical. Application to a previously unreachable curve over $\mathbb{F}_p^6$. In: Pointcheval, D., Johansson, T. (eds.) EUROCRYPT 2012. LNCS, vol. 7237, pp. 9–26. Springer, Heidelberg (2012). https://doi.org/10.1007/978-3-642-29011-4_3

19. Joux, A., Vitse, V.: A crossbred algorithm for solving boolean polynomial systems. In: Kaczorowski, J., Pieprzyk, J., Pomykała, J. (eds.) NuTMiC 2017. LNCS, vol. 10737, pp. 3–21. Springer, Cham (2018). https://doi.org/10.1007/978-3-319-76620-1_1

20. Koblitz, N.: CM-curves with good cryptographic properties. In: Feigenbaum, J. (ed.) CRYPTO 1991. LNCS, vol. 576, pp. 279–287. Springer, Heidelberg (1992). https://doi.org/10.1007/3-540-46766-1_22

21. Laitinen, T., Junttila, T., Niemela, I.: Equivalence class based parity reasoning with DPLL(XOR). In: Czumaj, A (ed.) 2011 IEEE 23rd International Conference on Tools with Artificial Intelligence, pp. 649–658, November 2011. https://doi.org/10.1109/ICTAI.2011.103

22. Laitinen, T., Junttila, T.A., Niemelä, I.: Conflict-driven XOR-clause learning (extended version). CoRR abs/1407.6571 (2014). http://arxiv.org/abs/1407.6571

23. Lenstra, A.K., Lenstra, H.W., Manasse, M.S., Pollard, J.M.: The number field sieve. In: Lenstra, A.K., Lenstra, H.W. (eds.) The development of the number field sieve. LNM, vol. 1554, pp. 11–42. Springer, Heidelberg (1993). https://doi.org/10.1007/BFb0091537

24. Lokshtanov, D., Mikhailin, I., Paturi, R., Pudlák, P.: Beating brute force for (quantified) satisfiability of circuits of bounded treewidth. In: Proceedings of the Twenty-Ninth Annual ACM-SIAM Symposium on Discrete Algorithms. SODA 2018, New Orleans, LA, USA, 7–10 January 2018, pp. 247–261 (2018). https://doi.org/10.1137/1.9781611975031.18

25. van Oorschot, P.C., Wiener, M.J.: Parallel collision search with cryptanalytic applications. J. Cryptol. **12**(1), 1–28 (1999). https://doi.org/10.1007/PL00003816

26. Petit, C., Quisquater, J.-J.: On polynomial systems arising from a Weil descent. In: Wang, X., Sako, K. (eds.) ASIACRYPT 2012. LNCS, vol. 7658, pp. 451–466. Springer, Heidelberg (2012). https://doi.org/10.1007/978-3-642-34961-4_28

27. Semaev, I.A.: Summation polynomials and the discrete logarithm problem on elliptic curves. IACR Cryptology ePrint Archive 2004, 31 (2004). http://eprint.iacr.org/2004/031

28. Shantz, M., Teske, E.: Solving the elliptic curve discrete logarithm problem using Semaev polynomials, Weil descent and Gröbner basis methods – an experimental study. In: Fischlin, M., Katzenbeisser, S. (eds.) Number Theory and Cryptography. LNCS, vol. 8260, pp. 94–107. Springer, Heidelberg (2013). https://doi.org/10.1007/978-3-642-42001-6_7

29. Silva, J.P.M., Sakallah, K.A.: Conflict analysis in search algorithms for satisfiability. In: ICTAI, pp. 467–469. IEEE Computer Society (1996)

30. Soos, M.: Enhanced Gaussian elimination in DPLL-based SAT solvers. In: Pragmatics of SAT (2010)

31. Soos, M., Nohl, K., Castelluccia, C.: Extending SAT solvers to cryptographic problems. In: Kullmann, O. (ed.) SAT 2009. LNCS, vol. 5584, pp. 244–257. Springer, Heidelberg (2009). https://doi.org/10.1007/978-3-642-02777-2_24

32. Sörensson, N., Eén, N.: A SAT solver with conflict-clause minimization. In: Proceedings of the Theory and Applications of Satisfiability Testing (2005)

33. Trimoska, M., Ionica, S., Dequen, G.: Parallel Collision Search Implementation (2019). https://github.com/mtrimoska/PCS

34. Trimoska, M., Ionica, S., Dequen, G.: EC Index Calculus Benchmarks (2020). https://github.com/mtrimoska/EC-Index-Calculus-Benchmarks
35. Trimoska, M., Ionica, S., Dequen, G.: Parity (XOR) reasoning for the index calculus attack. CoRR abs/2001.11229 (2020). https://arxiv.org/abs/2001.11229
36. Huang, Y.-J., Petit, C., Shinohara, N., Takagi, T.: Improvement of Faugère *et al.*'s method to solve ECDLP. In: Sakiyama, K., Terada, M. (eds.) IWSEC 2013. LNCS, vol. 8231, pp. 115–132. Springer, Heidelberg (2013). https://doi.org/10.1007/978-3-642-41383-4_8

Post Quantum Cryptography

Hash-Based Signatures Revisited: A Dynamic FORS with Adaptive Chosen Message Security

Mahmoud Yehia, Riham AlTawy$^{(\boxtimes)}$, and T. Aaron Gulliver

Department of Electrical and Computer Engineering, University of Victoria,
Victoria, BC V8P 5C2, Canada
`raltawy@uvic.ca`

Abstract. FORS is the underlying hash-based few-time signing scheme in SPHINCS$^+$, one of the nine signature schemes which advanced to round 2 of the NIST Post-Quantum Cryptography standardization competition. In this paper, we analyze the security of FORS with respect to adaptive chosen message attacks. We show that in such a setting, the security of FORS decreases significantly with each signed message when compared to its security against non-adaptive chosen message attacks. We propose a chaining mechanism that with slightly more computation, dynamically binds the *Obtain Random Subset* (ORS) generation with signing, hence, eliminating the offline advantage of adaptive chosen message adversaries. We apply our chaining mechanism to FORS and present DFORS whose security against adaptive chosen message attacks is equal to the non-adaptive security of FORS. In a nutshell, using SPHINCS$^+$-128s parameters, FORS provides 75-bit security and DFORS achieves 150-bit security with respect to adaptive chosen message attacks after signing one message. We note that our analysis does not affect the claimed security of SPHINCS$^+$. Nevertheless, this work provides a better understanding of FORS and other HORS variants, and furnishes a solution if new adaptive cryptanalytic techniques on SPHINCS$^+$ emerge.

Keywords: Digital signatures · Hash-based signature schemes · Post-Quantum Cryptography · Adaptive chosen message attacks

1 Introduction

The current digital signature infrastructure adopts schemes that rely on the hardness of factoring or finding discrete logarithms in finite groups [12,18,24]. Given recent advances in physics which point towards the eventual construction of large scale quantum computers [1], these hard problems will be solved in polynomial time using Shor's algorithm [25]. Lattice-based, coding-based, and multivariate signatures are considered quantum resilient schemes in the Q1 model [7]. However, either their exact security with respect to quantum attacks is still not clear [5,11] or their communication/storage complexity is impractical to a multitude of applications, e.g., megabyte keys for the matrices of McEliece-based cryptosystems [27]. On the other hand, hash-based digital signatures have moderately sized keys (order of kilobytes), and their quantum security relies solely

© Springer Nature Switzerland AG 2020
A. Nitaj and A. Youssef (Eds.): AFRICACRYPT 2020, LNCS 12174, pp. 239–257, 2020.
https://doi.org/10.1007/978-3-030-51938-4_12

on that of hash functions based on Grover's algorithm. They have been proven to offer simple quantum resilient security properties [26]. Note that the proofs in [26] follow the Q1 model where no superposition queries to quantum oracles are allowed [7].

Hash-based signature algorithms are comprised of two schemes, an underlying signing scheme and an extension algorithm. The former algorithm defines the main signing procedure where a key pair can be used to sign one (Lamport [19], Winternitz one time signature scheme (WOTS), WOTS++ [8,14]) or a few messages (e.g., Biba [21], HORS [23], HORS++ [22], PORS [2], and FORS [4]), after which a new key pair should be generated to maintain security against forgery attacks. More precisely, the security of hash-based few time (HBFT) signature schemes decreases after revealing each signature, and hence their bit-security is given under the condition that re-keying is required after r signatures. Accordingly, translating this constraint to acceptable attack models implies that a maximum of r queries are allowed to the signing oracle.

The extension algorithm is a top level construction that employs several instances of underlying signing schemes (OTS and HBFT) in a Merkle tree structure. Such an algorithm enables signing multiple messages where signatures are verified with one public key (Merkle root). Extension algorithms can be stateful such as Merkle Signature Scheme MSS [20], eXtended Merkle Signature Scheme (XMSS) [9], XMSS+ [15], Multi Tree XMSS (XMSS^{MT}) [16], and XMSS with tightened security (XMSS-T) [17], or stateless such as SPHINCS [5], SPHINCS$^+$ [4,6], and Gravity SPHINCS [3]. Stateless signature algorithms conform to the basic definition of digital signatures where no state updates are required to guarantee security, and only keys are needed to securely generate valid signatures at any time.

The security of hash-based signature algorithms relies on the security of the underlying basic signing schemes. SPHINCS is a hyper-tree construction that uses WOTS and HORS trees for signing. In [2], Aumasson and Endignoux investigated the subset-resilience problem [23] and showed that HORS is vulnerable to weak-message attacks where an adaptive adversary looks for messages that produce smaller Obtain Random Subsets (ORSs). Consequently, they reported a 7-bit decrease in the expected security of SPHINCS against classical attacks. Moreover, they proposed PORS, a variant of HORS which employs a pseudo-random bit generator (PRNG) instead of a hash function to obtain random subsets with distinct elements, thus avoiding the effect of weak messages. However, PORS is not secure against adaptive chosen message attacks where an adversary is able to generate random subsets for as many messages as they want, and select a set of r message for online queries. Finally, FORS, another HORS variant, was proposed and is currently adopted in SPHINCS$^+$, a round 2 candidate in the NIST Post-Quantum Cryptography standardization competition [4,10]. Compared to PORS, FORS mitigates weak-message attacks by increasing the size of the keys by a factor of κ where κ is the number of random subsets, and the overall signature size is also increased when it is integrated in a hyper-tree structure. On its own, the security of FORS against adaptive chosen message attacks decreases significantly with each signed message, which currently has no known effect on the security of SPHINCS$^+$ because it employs a pseudorandomly generated randomizer that is publicly sent along with the signature, and is used as a key for the hash function in FORS to obtain the random subsets. However, if cryptanalytic techniques are devised which can annihilate how this public randomizer is utilized or can break its generation procedure, then SPHINCS$^+$ will be vulnerable to adaptive chosen message attacks. Hence, given the significance of SPHINCS$^+$ as a candidate for standardization, we believe our analysis of its underlying signature scheme, FORS, is important, along with DFORS which offers a drop-in strengthened candidate.

Our Contribution. In what follows, we summarize the contributions of this paper.

- We analyze the security of FORS against adaptive chosen message adversaries. We show that its bit security with respect to adaptive chosen message attacks decreases significantly when compared to its security in a nonadaptive setting. We adopt the adaptive chosen message attack model defined by Reyzin and Reyzin [23] and used in the analysis of HORS and PORS.
- We propose a hash chaining mechanism that binds the process of generating a message ORS with signing it, which eliminates the offline adversarial advantage and makes ORS generation feasible only for the signing entity. We apply the chaining scheme to FORS and present Dynamic Forest Of Random Subsets (DFORS), a new HORS variant that resists adaptive chosen message attacks. We show that the bit-security of DFORS with respect to adaptive chosen message attacks is more than that of FORS by a factor of $r + 1$, where r is the number of signed messages per key under a given security level.
- We analyze the security of DFORS with respect to adaptive chosen message adversaries, discuss its limitations, and report its theoretical computational and communication performance. Finally, we compare DFORS with FORS and other HORS variants.

2   Preliminaries

In what follows, we provide the notation and definitions used throughout the paper. FORS can be seen as a generalized instance of HORS and it inherits most of the specifications of HORS. Accordingly, for completeness, we provide a brief overview of the HORS signature scheme.

2.1   Notation

Let n denote our security parameter. Consider a finite key space $\mathbb{K}$, message space of arbitrary length $\mathbb{M}$, the two hash families H and G where $H = \{H_k : \{0,1\}^* \rightarrow \{0,1\}^{\kappa\tau} | k \in \mathbb{K}\}$, and $G = \{G_k : \{0,1\}^* \rightarrow \{0,1\}^n | k \in \mathbb{K}\}$. H_k (resp. G_k) is an $\kappa\tau$-bit (resp. n-bit) keyed one-way function. Let the $\kappa\tau$-bit message digest of an arbitrary length message $m \in \mathbb{M}$ be divided into κ elements, each of length τ bits, such that the integer representation of a given element is a subset of $\{0, 1, \ldots, t - 1\}$, where $t = 2^\tau$. We refer to the set $\{0, 1, \ldots, t - 1\}$ by T, and the subset of κ-elements of the set T is denoted by $S_\kappa(T)$. Let $ORS_\kappa(m)$ denote an *Obtain Random Subset* function which returns a κ element subset from the $\kappa\tau$-bit hash value of a message m, formally defined as follows

$$ORS_\kappa(m) : H_k(m) \rightarrow S_\kappa(T) | k \in \mathbb{K}$$

The notion of ORS functions was introduced by Reyzin and Reyzin when HORS was proposed [23]. It has been shown that the security of the scheme is reduced to the subset resilience problem [23]. More precisely, for a given bit-security level, at most r messages can be signed before re-keying is required, otherwise an adversary can find a message whose ORS is covered by the union of the ORSs of the r messages.

Definition 1. *The messages $(m_1, m_2, \ldots, m_r, m_{r+1})$ are in an r-subset-cover relation, C_κ^r, if the Obtain Random Subset of message m_{r+1} $(ORS_\kappa(m_{r+1}))$ is a subset of the union of all Obtain Random Subsets of the r-messages, $ORS_\kappa(m_1) \cup ORS_\kappa(m_2) \cup \ldots \cup ORS_\kappa(m_r)$, formally*

$$C_\kappa^r(m_1, m_2, \ldots, m_{r+1}) \Leftrightarrow ORS_\kappa(m_{r+1}) \subseteq \bigcup_{i=1}^{r} ORS_\kappa(m_i).$$

If finding the above cover relation for a given ORS function is infeasible, then it is said that such a function is r-subset resilient.

Definition 2. *An ORS function is r-subset-resilient if for any polynomial time adversary $\mathcal{A}^{(1^n, \kappa, t)}$, the probability of finding $(m_1, m_2, \ldots, m_{r+1})$ such that $ORS_\kappa(m_{r+1})$ is a subset of $ORS_\kappa(m_1) \cup ORS_\kappa(m_2) \cup \ldots \cup ORS_\kappa(m_r)$ is negligible, Formally*

$$\Pr[(m_1, m_2, \ldots, m_{r+1}) \leftarrow \mathcal{A}^{(1^n, \kappa, t)} : C_\kappa^r(m_1, m_2, \ldots, m_{r+1})] \leq negl(n, t).$$

Definition 3. *An ORS function is r-target-subset-resilient, if for any polynomial time adversary $\mathcal{A}$ who is given the ORSs of r messages $\bigcup_{i=1}^{r} ORS_\kappa(m_i)$, it is infeasible to find a message m_{r+1} such that its κ-element $ORS_\kappa(m_{r+1})$ is a subset of the union of ORSs of the r messages, formally*

$$\Pr[(m_{r+1}) \leftarrow \mathcal{A}^{(1^n, \kappa, t, m_1, m_2, \ldots, m_r)} : C_\kappa^r(m_1, m_2, \ldots, m_{r+1})] \leq negl(n, t).$$

2.2 Hash to Obtain Random Subset (HORS) Few-Time Digital Signature Scheme

In HORS [23], the signer randomly generates t secret keys each of n-bit length, $(SK = sk_0, sk_1, \ldots, sk_{t-1})$. Using a one-way function $f : \{0,1\}^n \rightarrow \{0,1\}^n$, the signer computes the public key, $PK = (pk_0 = f(sk_0), pk_1 = f(sk_1), \ldots, pk_{t-1} = f(sk_{t-1}))$. For signing an arbitrary length message $m \in \mathbb{M}$, $ORS_\kappa(m) = \{h_0, h_1, \ldots, h_{\kappa-1}\}$ is evaluated by dividing the $\kappa\tau$-bit message digest value of $H_K(m)$ into κ elements, each of length τ bits. Each element is represented by an integer h_i where $0 \leq i \leq \kappa - 1$ and $h_i \in \{0, 1, \ldots, t - 1\}$, $t = 2^\tau$. To generate the signature, σ, the signer reveals the secret keys whose indices correspond to the integer representation of the κ elements in the ORS, i.e., $\sigma = (sk_{h_0}, sk_{h_1}, \ldots, sk_{h_{\kappa-1}})$. For verification, the verifier computes $ORS_\kappa(m) = \{h_0, h_1, \ldots, h_{\kappa-1}\}$, then checks if $f(sk_{h_i}) = pk_{h_i}$, otherwise verification fails. The description of HORS is given in Algorithm 3 in Appendix A.

Security. Assuming that f is a one-way function, the security of HORS is reduced to the hardness of the (target) subset-resilience problem [23]. It has been shown that the probability of finding a message (m_{r+1}) such that $ORS_\kappa(m_{r+1})$ is covered by the obtained random subsets of the r previously signed messages is $(r\kappa/t)^\kappa$ which corresponds to the probability of κ randomly chosen elements being a subset of the revealed $r\kappa$ secret keys. The corresponding bit-security is then

$$\log_2(t/r\kappa)^\kappa = \kappa(\log_2 t - \log_2 r - \log_2 \kappa).$$

In [2], it was proven that the security of HORS with respect to adaptive chosen message attacks is

$$\frac{\kappa}{r+1}(\log_2 t - \log_2 r - \log_2 \kappa) + \frac{\log_2 r!}{r+1},$$

(see Appendix B). A practical example of a weak-message attack was also given where an adaptive adversary finds messages that map to subsets with repeated indices which results in smaller subsets, i.e., number of distinct elements $< \kappa$. Such subsets are easier to cover and consequently, a 7-bit decrease in the expected security of SPHINCS against classical attacks was reported.

Variants. HORS++ [22] was introduced to provide security against adaptive attacks. A one-to-one mapping function $S(m)$ that belongs to a cover-free family [13] is utilized to ensure that for any $r + 1$ messages $S(m_{r+1}) \not\subseteq \bigcup_{i=1}^r (S(m_i))$. Three constructions for $S(m)$ based on polynomials over finite fields, error correcting codes, and algebraic curves over finite fields were presented. Consequently, HORS++ increases the signature size and the size of the secret keys to achieve the same security level of HORS against non-adaptive chosen message attacks. Moreover, the computational efficiency is decreased due to the computation of $S(m)$. Later, PORS was suggested to replace HORS in SPHINCS where the idea of having distinct elements in subsets of weak messages was enforced by use of a pseudorandom bit generator to obtain the subsets [2]. However, although PORS mitigates weak-message attacks, it is still vulnerable to adaptive chosen message attacks under the definition given in Appendix B. Lastly, FORS was proposed and used in SPHINCS+ [4], where security against weak-message attacks is achieved by increasing the key size from t values to κt values such that each index out of the κ indices in the ORS reveals a secret key from a different pool of t secret keys. Accordingly, when integrated in a tree structure the size of the signature also increases.

3   FORS Security Analysis

Unlike HORS which generates t secret keys from which the secret keys that are indexed by ORS(m) are released, FORS generates (κt) secret keys and dedicates t secret keys for each index out of the κ indices. By doing so, FORS mitigates weak message attacks because even if two elements in $ORS(m)$ are equal, they index values from different secret key pools. The n-bit public key of FORS is the hash of the concatenation of κ Merkle tree roots. Each root is associated with a binary hash tree whose leaves are the hashes of t secret key elements in a given pool. Accordingly, one FORS instance has κ trees, each of height $\log t = \tau$.

Figure 1 depicts the signatures of message 100 011 110 using (a) HORS and (b) FORS, where $\kappa = 3$ and $t = 8$. In FORS, the first 3 bits, i.e., 100, of the message selects sk_4, the secret key corresponding to the 4-th leaf indexed from the left and starting from 0 in the first tree along with its authentication path to $root_0$. Similarly, the second (resp. third) 3 bits of the message selects sk_3 (resp. sk_6) from the second (resp. third) tree with the authentication path to $root_1$ (resp. $root_2$). In HORS, the three 3-bit parts of the message index sk_4, sk_3, and sk_6 from the same tree, and with each selected secret key a 3 node authentication path is selected, hence the overlap in the node (colored in pale red and gray) at the pre-root level. More details about hash trees and authentication path calculations are provided in Sect. 4.

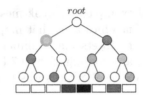

(a) HORS signature within a binary tree construction

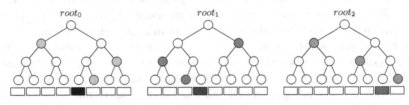

(b) FORS signature within κ binary trees construction

Fig. 1. HORS and FORS signatures of the message 100 011 110 where $\kappa = 3$ and $t = 8$. The 8 rectangles under each tree depict the eight secret keys whose hashes are stored in the corresponding leaf nodes.

It can be verified from Fig. 1 that if two 3-bit parts of the message are equal, then the same secret key value is revealed in HORS. This fact is exploited in the weak messages attack where an adversary searches for messages that have as many repeated indices as possible, which lead to ORSs containing fewer distinct elements, and thus can be easily covered with the ORSs of the revealed r messages. However, this problem is mitigated in FORS because repeated indices select secret keys from different pools. In what follows, we investigate the security of FORS with respect to non-adaptive chosen message attacks.

3.1 FORS in a Non-adaptive Setting

Reyzin and Reyzin introduced clear attack models for analyzing HBFT signature schemes against (non) adaptive chosen message attacks [23]. Such models are used in the analysis of all HORS-variants, i.e., PORS, and FORS. Specifically, in a non-adaptive setting, also referred to by r-target subset resilience problem (see Definition 3), an adversary is required to first choose r messages $m_1, m_2, \ldots, m_r$, after which they are provided with key k of H_k and allowed to select a message m_{r+1} and evaluate $H_k(m_{r+1})$. A successful non-adaptive chosen message attack happens when the adversary is able to find C_κ^r, i.e., find a message m_{r+1} that is in an r-subset cover relation with $m_1, m_2, \ldots, m_r$. This scenario corresponds to an attacker who is trying to forge a signature after observing all r allowed signatures per key, or an adversary who is allowed r queries at a time before being supplied with k to verify any of the returned signatures. Few-time signature schemes are expected to maintain their security against forgery attacks even after releasing all r signatures.

Finding C_κ^r in FORS. Given an adversary who observed the signatures of r messages, finding a message m_{r+1} that is in an r−subset cover relation with the other r messages ($C_\kappa^{r\text{-FORS}}(m_1, m_2, \ldots, m_{r+1})$) has probability of success $(r/t)^\kappa$ [6], which is equal to the probability that each $\log t$-bit element out of the κ elements in $ORS(m_{r+1})$ is covered by an element at the same position of the ORSs of the other r messages, i.e., $h_i(m_{r+1}) \in \bigcup_{j=1}^r h_i(m_j)$ for $0 \leq i \leq \kappa - 1$, where $h_i(m_j)$ denotes the i-th ORS element of the j-th message. Accordingly, the corresponding bit-security against non-adaptive chosen message attacks is given by

$$\log_2(t/r)^\kappa = \kappa(\log_2 t - \log_2 r).$$

3.2   Adaptive Chosen Message Attack Against FORS

In this setting, an adversary is given the hash key k and allowed to evaluate H_k for any message of their choice before selecting $r + 1$ messages. This attack also indicates the r-subset resilience of the signature algorithm (see Definition 2). The definition of adaptive chosen message attack is given in Appendix B. Applying the same analysis to FORS, given the key k of H_k, an adversary $\mathcal{A}$ generates the ORSs of $q > r$ messages offline, where $H_k(m_i) = h_0||h_1||\ldots||h_{\kappa-1}$ and $ORS(m_i) = \{h_0, h_1, \ldots, h_{\kappa-1}\}$, for $0 \leq i \leq q - 1$ $\mathcal{A}$ searches for all possible combinations of $(r + 1)$ message sets from the set of q messages. For any given $r+1$ messages combination, the probability that message m_{r+1} is covered by the remaining r messages (i.e., $C_\kappa^{r\text{-FORS}}(m_1, m_2, \ldots, m_{r+1})$), is $(r/t)^\kappa$. Accordingly, $\mathcal{A}$ obtains $\binom{q}{r+1}$ sets of $r + 1$ messages and each set gives $\binom{r+1}{r}$ possible choices for m_{r+1}. Therefore, the probability of $\mathcal{A}$ successfully generating $C_\kappa^{r\text{-FORS}}$ is bounded from above by

$$\text{Succ}^{C_\kappa^{r\text{FORS}}}(\mathcal{A}) \leq \binom{q}{r+1}\binom{r+1}{r}(r/t)^\kappa,$$

$$\text{Succ}^{C_\kappa^{r\text{-FORS}}} \leq q\binom{q-1}{r}(r/t)^\kappa,$$

$$\text{Succ}^{C_\kappa^{r\text{-FORS}}}(\mathcal{A}) \leq \frac{q.(q-1)\ldots(q-r)}{r!}(r/t)^\kappa.$$

which can be approximated by

$$\mathsf{Succ}^{C_{\kappa}^{r\text{-FORS}}}(\mathcal{A}) \leq \frac{q^{r+1}}{r!}(r/t)^{\kappa}.$$

Assuming a success probability close to 1, the above equation can be expressed as

$$(r+1)\log_2 q - \log_2 r! + \kappa(\log_2 r - \log_2 t) = 0.$$

Then the bit security of FORS with respect to adaptive chosen message attacks is given by

$$\frac{\kappa}{r+1}(\log_2 t - \log_2 r) + \frac{\log_2 r!}{r+1}.$$

One may conclude that due to the offline adversarial advantage given to $\mathcal{A}$ (i.e., knowledge of k implies the feasibility of evaluating ORSs for more than r messages of their choice), FORS bit security against adaptive chosen message attacks decreases by a factor of $(r+1)$ when compared to the non-adaptive setting. Note that, currently there is no attack against SPHINCS$^+$ that can utilize the offline adversarial privileges and produce $r + 1$ messages in an r-subset cover relation. This is because SPHINCS$^+$ uses a fixed pseudorandom generation of the key k to get the obtained random subset $ORS_{\kappa}(H_k(m))$. We also note that k is message dependent and is sent in the clear with each signature so verification takes place. Accordingly, in the event of attacks on the process by which k is evaluated from m, a dramatic decrease in the security of SPHINCS$^+$ will follow. Consequently, in the following section we present a technique that is robust against adaptive chosen message attacks on FORS. Our mechanism annihilates the adversarial offline advantages associated with knowing the hash key k.

4   Dynamic Forest of Random Subsets (DFORS)

In this section we present Dynamic Forest Of Random Subsets DFORS, a new HORS-variant that mitigates the offline advantage of an adversary which leads to the adaptive chosen message attack on FORS (discussed in Sect. 3). The main feature of DFORS is that the generation of the ORS is performed concurrently with signing such that each signature element is utilized to generate the next element of the ORS. In other words, signing and ORS generation are bound together using a chaining mechanism that utilizes the revealed secret keys. This procedure ensures that given a message, only the signer is able to efficiently generate an ORS. By doing so, even if an adversary has knowledge of k, they are not able to compute ORSs of a given message of their choice unless they have some secret key knowledge. In what follows we give a detailed specification of DFORS.

4.1   DFORS Parameters

DFORS uses the following parameters.

   n : The security parameter and the bit-length of (i) the secret seed $SK.seed$, (ii) secret keys $sk_{i,j}$ ($0 \leq i \leq t - 1$, $0 \leq j \leq \kappa - 1$), (iii) public key $PK.root$, and (iv) the output of the used one way function F, and hash function G.

κ : The number of (i) sub-strings of the input message, (ii) secret key pools where each contains t secret keys, and (iii) hash trees.

τ : The bit length of a sub-string of the input message and the hash tree height.

t : the number of secret keys per pool and the number of leaves in each hash tree, $t = 2^\tau$.

The input message for DFORS is of length $\kappa \log t = \kappa\tau$ bits. To achieve n-bit security when signing r messages, we have $\kappa\tau > n$ (see Sect. 5.1).

4.2   Key Generation

In what follows, we give the specifications of the secret and public key generation procedures. Moreover, DFORS is described in Algorithm 2.

Secret Key Generation. Let $SK.seed$ denote an n-bit secret seed that is sampled at random. Given a pseudorandom function, $PRF : \{0,1\}^n \times \{0,1\}^n \rightarrow \{0,1\}^n$, the n-bit κt secret key values $sk_{i,j}$, $0 \leq i \leq t-1$, $0 \leq j \leq \kappa - 1$ are generated by

$$sk_{i,j} = PRF(SK.seed, i + jt),$$

where each set of t secret keys belong to one of the κ pools.

Hash Trees and Public Key Generation. Using one-way function $F :$ $\{0,1\}^n \rightarrow \{0,1\}^n$ applied on the secret keys $sk_{i,j}$, $0 \leq i \leq t-1$, $0 \leq j \leq \kappa-1$, the leaf nodes of the κ hash trees are generated, $L_{i,j} = F(sk_{i,j})$. Every t leaves, $L_{*,j}$, are combined together in a Merkle tree construction to form the j-th (out of κ) tree. Then, the roots of these κ trees, $root_0, root_1, \ldots, root_{\kappa-1}$, are concatenated to form an input to the hash function to get the n-bit public key expressed as

$$PK.root = G_k(root_0 || root_1 || \ldots || root_{\kappa-1}).$$

Binary Hash Tree. DFORS uses the XMSS binary Merkle tree construction [9]. The height of the binary hash tree is τ. It has $\tau + 1$ levels, $t = 2^\tau$ leaf nodes (each of size n bits) on level 0, i.e., $L_i, 0 \leq i \leq t - 1$, and an n-bit root node on level τ. We denote the nodes in level j by $N_{i,j}$ where $0 \leq i < 2^{\tau-j}$, $0 \leq j \leq \tau$ and $N_{i,0} = L_i$. To construct the tree, the hash function G and a $2n$-bit mask, q, per hash evaluation are used. These bit masks are introduced to provide second-preimage resistance. The rationale for using different bit masks for each hash evaluation is to mitigate multi-target attacks [17]. For details on generating the hash keys $K_{i,j}$ and bit masks $q_{i,j}$, the reader is referred to [4,17]. Formally, for $0 < j \leq \tau$, a node $N_{i,j}$ is given by

$$N_{i,j} = G_{k_{i,j}}((N_{2i,j-1} || N_{2i+1,j-1}) \oplus q_{i,j}).$$

Figure 2 shows a simplified example of one of the κ trees in DFORS with $t = 8$. Assuming it is the j-th tree, it depicts the nodes in the authentication path (colored in gray) associated with revealing $sk_{3,j}$.

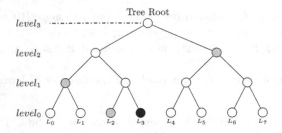

Fig. 2. A binary hash tree with the nodes in the authentication path (colored in gray) for leaf node L_3 (colored in black)

4.3   Signing and ORS Generation

We denote by $Z(h)$ a function that takes as input $\kappa\tau$ bits, h, and outputs the j-th τ bits of h, where $j = h \bmod \kappa$. Formally, $Z : \{0,1\}^{\kappa\tau} \to \{0,1\}^\tau$, and letting $h = h_0||h_1||\ldots||h_{\kappa-1}$, for $0 \le j \le \kappa - 1$

$$Z(h) : h_j \leftarrow \{h_0||h_1||\ldots||h_{\kappa-1}\}, j = h \bmod \kappa.$$

The signing algorithm takes as input the message m, the secret seed $SK.seed$, and the hash key k. It constructs the κ trees as explained above in Sect. 4.2. To compute the κ random subset $ORS_\kappa(m) = (b_0, b_1, \ldots, b_{\kappa-1})$, the algorithm first evaluates $H_k(m) = h^0$, then computes $Z(h^0) = b_0$. The first element in the signature, sig_0, is comprised of i) the secret key of index b_0 in the first pool, $\sigma_0 = sk_{b_0,0}$, and ii) the corresponding authentication path $Auth_0$, thus $sig_0 = \sigma_0, Auth_0$. Next, h^0 and $sk_{b_0,0}$ are used to choose the second random element, $Z(h^1) = b_1$, where $h^1 = H_{sk_{b_0,0}}(h^0||h^0)$. The second signature element, sig_1, is the secret key of index b_1 in the second pool, $\sigma_1 = sk_{b_1,1}$, and its corresponding authentication path $Auth_1$, $sig_1 = \sigma_1, Auth_1$. In general, the i-th element of the $ORS_\kappa(m)$ is given by $Z(h^i) = b_i$ where $h^i = H_{sk_{b_{i-1},i-1}}(h^0||h^{i-1})$. The i-th signature element, sig_i, is the secret key value of index b_i in the i-th pool and its corresponding authentication path $Auth_i$, $sig_i = \sigma_i, Auth_i$, where $\sigma_i = sk_{b_i,i}$. The above process is repeated until κ elements are generated $(b_0, b_1, \ldots, b_{\kappa-1})$. Finally, the signature is given by

$$\Sigma = (sig_0, sig_1, \ldots, sig_{\kappa-1}) = (sk_{b_0}, Auth_0, sk_{b_1}, Auth_1, \ldots, sk_{b_{\kappa-1}}, Auth_{\kappa-1})$$

$$= (\sigma_0, Auth_0, \sigma_1, Auth_1, \ldots, \sigma_{\kappa-1}, Auth_{\kappa-1}).$$

The ORS generation and signing process is illustrated in Fig. 3.

The authentication path of a leaf L_i contains all the sibling nodes of the nodes in the path from the leaf L_i to the tree root. It is required so that the verifier can successfully generate the root in order to verify the signature element σ_i related to the leaf node L_i. Figure 2 shows a simple hash tree with the authentication path for leaf L_3 colored in black and the authentication path nodes colored in gray, $Auth_i = (L_2, N_{0,1}, N_{1,2})$.

$$h^0 = H_k(m)$$

$$\rightarrow \boxed{\; h_0^0 \;|\; h_1^0 \;|\; \cdots \;|\; h_{j_0}^0 = b_0 \;|\; \cdots \;|\; h_{\kappa-1}^0 \;}$$

$$h^1 = H_{sk_{b_0}}(h^0 \,\|\, h^0)$$

$$\rightarrow \boxed{\; h_0^1 \;|\; \cdots \;|\; h_{j_1}^1 = b_1 \;|\; \cdots \;|\; h_{\kappa-1}^1 \;}$$

$$\vdots$$

$$b_{\kappa-2}$$

$$h^{\kappa-2} = H_{sk_{b_{\kappa-3}}}(h^0 \,\|\, h^{\kappa-3}) \rightarrow \boxed{\; h_0^{\kappa-2} \;|\; h_1^{\kappa-2} \;|\; \cdots \;|\; h_{j_{\kappa-2}}^{\kappa-2} \;|\; \cdots \;|\; h_{\kappa-1}^{\kappa-2} \;}$$

$$b_{\kappa-1}$$

$$h^{\kappa-1} = H_{sk_{b_{\kappa-2}}}(h^0 \,\|\, h^{\kappa-2}) \rightarrow \boxed{\; h_0^{\kappa-1} \;|\; \cdots \;|\; h_{j_{\kappa-1}}^{\kappa-1} \;|\; \cdots \;|\; h_{\kappa-1}^{\kappa-1} \;}$$

$$ORS_\kappa(m)$$

$$\rightarrow \boxed{\; b_0 \;|\; b_1 \;|\; \cdots \;|\; b_{\kappa-2} \;|\; b_{\kappa-1} \;}$$

Fig. 3. The DFORS procedure to compute $ORS_\kappa(m)$, where $j_i = h^i \bmod \kappa$, $b_i = h_{j_i}^i$, and sk_{b_i} is the b_i-th secret key in the i-th secret key pool.

4.4   Signature Verification

The verification algorithm takes as input the message m, the public key $PK.root$, the hash key K, and the signature $\Sigma = (\sigma_0, Auth_0, \sigma_1, Auth_1, \ldots, \sigma_{\kappa-1}, Auth_{\kappa-1})$. It computes $H_k(m) = h^0$, then $Z(h^0) = b_0$ to get the leaf index of the first hash tree. Then, it applies the one-way function F to the signature element σ_0 of the signature Σ to get the leaf node L_{b_0} in the first tree. The authentication path $Auth_0$ and the leaf L_{b_0} are used to compute the root of the first tree. The leaf index b_0 is required so that the verifier knows which node is concatenated on the right and on the left. The tree root calculation procedure is described in Algorithm 1. Generally, the verification algorithm computes the i-th tree root by applying Algorithm 1 on σ_i, $Auth_i$, and the leaf index b_i where $b_i = Z(h^i)$, and $h^i = H_{\sigma_{i-1}}(h^0\|h^{i-1})$. This process is repeated until κ tree roots are computed which are then concatenated to form an input to the hash function G. If the output of G is equal to $PK.root$, the signature is valid, otherwise verification fails.

Algorithm 1. Tree Root Computation

Input: Leaf node L_i, Leaf index i, Auth. Path $= (A_0, A_1, \ldots, A_{\tau-1})$.
Output: The Tree Root N_τ.

Set $N_0 \leftarrow L_i$
for $1 \leq j \leq \tau$ **do**
    if $\lfloor i/2^{j-1} \rfloor \equiv 0 \bmod 2$ **then**
        $N_j = G_{k_{i,j}}(N_{j-1}\|A_{j-1} \oplus q_{i,j})$
    else
        $N_j = G_{k_{i,j}}(A_{j-1}\|N_{j-1} \oplus q_{i,j})$
    end if
end for
Return (N_τ)

Algorithm 2. DFORS Algorithm

---

procedure KEY GENERATION(t, κ)

    $SK.seed \xleftarrow{R} \{0,1\}^n$

    for $0 \le j \le \kappa - 1$ **do**

        for $0 \le i \le t - 1$ **do**

            $sk_{i,j} \leftarrow PRF(SK.seed, i + jt)$

            $L_{i,j} \leftarrow F(sk_{i,j})$

        end for

    end for

    Compute the roots of the κ tree as described in section 4.2

    $PK.root \leftarrow G(root_0 \| root_1 \| \ldots \| root_{\kappa-1})$

    Output $(SK.seed, PK.root)$

end procedure

---

procedure SIGNING$(m, SK.seed, k, \kappa, t)$

    Generate the κ binary hash trees as in key generation procedure

    $h^0 \leftarrow H_k(m), \quad h^0 = h_0^0 \| h_1^0 \| \ldots \| h_{\kappa-1}^0$

    $b_0 \leftarrow Z(h^0) = h_{j_0}^0, \; j_0 = h^0 \bmod \kappa$

    $sig_0 \leftarrow (\sigma_0, Auth_0)$, Where $\sigma_0 = sk_{b_0,0}$

    for $1 \le i \le \kappa - 1$ **do**

        $h^i \leftarrow H_{sk_{b_{i-1},i-1}}(h^0 \| h^{i-1}), \; h^i = h_0^i \| h_1^i \| \ldots \| h_{\kappa-1}^i$

        $b_i \leftarrow Z(h^i) = h_{j_i}^i, \; j_i = h^i \bmod \kappa$

        $sig_i \leftarrow (\sigma_i, Auth_i)$, where $\sigma_i = sk_{b_i,i}$

    end for

    $\Sigma \leftarrow (\sigma_0, Auth_0, \sigma_1, Auth_1, \ldots, \sigma_{\kappa-1}, Auth_{\kappa-1})$

    Output (Σ, m)

end procedure

---

procedure VERIFICATION$(m, PK.root, k, \Sigma = (\sigma_0, Auth_0, \sigma_1, Auth_1, \ldots, \sigma_{\kappa-1}, Auth_{\kappa-1}))$

    $h^0 \leftarrow H_k(m), \; h^0 = h_0^0 \| h_1^0 \| \ldots \| h_{\kappa-1}^0$

    $b_0 \leftarrow Z(h^0) = h_{j_0}^0, \; j_0 = h^0 \bmod \kappa$

    $L_{b_0} \leftarrow F(\sigma_0)$

    $root_0 \leftarrow$ Algorithm 1 $(L_{b_0,0}, b_0, Auth_0)$

    for $1 \le i \le \kappa - 1$ **do**

        $h^i \leftarrow H_{\sigma_{i-1}}(h^0 \| h^{i-1}), \; h^i = h_0^i \| h_1^i \| \ldots \| h_{\kappa-1}^i$

        $b_i \leftarrow Z(h^i) = h_{j_i}^i, \; j_i = h^i \bmod \kappa$

        $L_{b_i} \leftarrow F(\sigma_i)$

        $root_i \leftarrow$ Algorithm 1 $(L_{b_i,i}, b_i, Auth_i)$

    end for

    if $G(root_0 \| root_1 \| \ldots \| root_{\kappa-1}) = PK.root$ **then**

        $out = 1$

    else

        $out = 0$

    end if

    Output (out)

end procedure

---

5 Security and Efficiency

In what follows, we analyze the security of DFORS and demonstrate the effect of the dynamic chaining on the security of FORS. Afterwards, the computational cost of the DFORS key generation, signing, and verification algorithms are presented. The bit size of the signature and keys are also given.

5.1   DFORS Security Analysis

In this section, we present a detailed analysis of DFORS with respect to weak-message attacks and r-target subset resilience adversaries. More precisely, since the proposed chaining technique does not allow an adaptive adversary who has knowledge of k to compute the ORSs of any message of their choice before asking the signing oracle for its signature, DFORS is essentially r-subset resilient. Hence, our analysis focuses on its security when an adversary is given the signatures of r messages.

Weak-Message Attacks. DFORS inherits FORS mitigation to weak-message attacks [6] because it specifies an independent key pool for each index in the ORS. Consequently, even if an ORS element is repeated, the corresponding revealed secret keys will be different.

r-Target Subset Resilience. According to Definition 3, we assume an adversary $\mathcal{A}$ when given the ORSs of r messages will return m_{r+1} where $C_\kappa^r(m_1, m_2, \ldots, m_{r+1})$. In what follows, we show that the success probability of $\mathcal{A}$ is bounded from above by $(r/t)^\kappa$. Note that since ORS generation is secret key dependent, the ORS function of DFORS is intrinsically r-subset resilient. In other words, the value of any random ORS element, b_i, depends on the previously revealed signature element $\sigma_{i-1} = sk_{b_{i-1}}$ and the original message m. Accordingly, without any oracle queries, $\mathcal{A}$ has no feasible function to evaluate ORSs of messages of their choice. On the other hand, if $\mathcal{A}$ is given the signatures of r messages or they queried r messages of their choice, they need to find a message m_{r+1} such that each element in its obtained random subset, $ORS_\kappa^{\mathsf{DFORS}}(m_{r+1}) = (b_0, b_1, \ldots, b_{\kappa-1})$, is covered by the elements at the same corresponding positions in the ORSs of the other r messages

$$C_\kappa^r(m_1, m_2, \ldots, m_{r+1}) \Leftrightarrow b_i(m_{r+1}) \in \bigcup_{j=1}^{r} b_i(m_j), 0 \leq i \leq \kappa - 1.$$

Due to the chaining process in generating $b_0, b_1, \ldots, b_{\kappa-1}$, $\mathcal{A}$ generates the ORSs sequentially. At any position i, if $b_i(m_{r+1}) \notin \cup_{j=1}^r b_i(m_j)$, then $\mathcal{A}$ fails. In addition, they cannot evaluate $b_{i+1} = Z(H_{sk_{b_i}}(h^0 \| h^i))$ when sk_{b_i} is not revealed by any of signatures of the r messages, Generally, for the i-th position in $ORS_\kappa^{\mathsf{DFORS}}(m_{r+1})$

$$b_i(m_{r+1}) \notin \bigcup_{j=1}^{r} b_i(m_j) \Rightarrow sk_{b_i} \notin \bigcup_{j=1}^{r} \sigma_i(m_j),$$

where $\sigma_i(m_j)$ and $b_i(m_j)$ denote the i-th signature element and i-th ORS element of the j-th message, respectively. Thus, the probability that $\mathcal{A}$ finds $C_\kappa^r(m_1, m_2, \ldots, m_{r+1})$ successfully is equal to their probability of finding a message m_{r+1} such that $\forall i \in \{0, 1, \ldots, \kappa - 1\}$, each of the $\log t$-bit $b_i(m_{r+1}) \in \{b_i(m_1), b_i(m_2), \ldots, b_i(m_r)\}$. Since $\mathcal{A}$ is given r messages, the probability of finding a cover for one $b_i(m_{r+1})$ is $(r/t)^{i+1}$ because this implies that $\forall j < i; b_j(m_{r+1}) \in \{b_j(m_1), b_j(m_2), \ldots, b_j(m_r)\}$. Thus, the probability of finding a cover for all the κ elements in $ORS_\kappa^{\mathsf{DFORS}}$ is equal to the probability of finding a cover for the last element, $b_{\kappa-1}(m_{r+1})$, which is $(r/t)^\kappa$. Therefore

$$\mathrm{Succ}^{C_\kappa^{r\text{-DFORS}}}(\mathcal{A}) \leq (r/t)^\kappa,$$

so the corresponding DFORS bit-security against adaptive chosen message attacks is

$$\log_2(t/r)^\kappa = \kappa(\log_2 t - \log_2 r).$$

Compared to the adaptive chosen message attack security of FORS (See Sect. 3), the bit security of DFORS is higher by a factor of $(r + 1)$. The extra cost is performing $\kappa - 1$ more calls to the hash function. Unlike FORS, the signing procedure cannot be parallelized because of the chaining mechanism.

5.2   Theoretical Efficiency

Key Generation. This procedure requires κt PRF function computations to generate the t secret values for κ pools, κt one-way function F computations to compute the leaf nodes of the hash trees, and $\kappa(t - 1) + 1$ hash function G evaluations to evaluate the κ hash trees and get the public key $PK.root$.

Signing. This procedure requires κt PRF function computations, κt one-way function F computations, κt hash function (H and G) to compute the κ hash trees ($\kappa(t - 1)$ hash G calls), and κ hash H calls to get $ORS_\kappa(m)$. Note that the whole tree structure is computed with each signature, otherwise, the scheme storage requirements will be huge.

Verification. This procedure requires κ one-way function F computations that compute the trees leaves, $\kappa(\tau + 1)$ hash function (H and G) evaluations to reconstruct the κ trees roots from the revealed secret values and the authentication paths ($\kappa\tau$ calls to G), and κ calls H to get $ORS_\kappa(m)$.

Signature Size. The signature contains κ secret key elements and $\kappa\tau$ tree node for the associated authentication paths. Thus, the signature size is $\kappa n(\tau + 1)$ bits, where n is the bit size of each secret keys and hash tree node.

Length of Keys. The size of the secret key, $SK.root$, is equal to that of the public key, $PK.root$, and it is n bits.

The computational complexities of the above procedures are given in Table 2.

5.3   Comparison with HORS Variants

DFORS inherits all the advantageous security properties of FORS. Additionally, it is secure against adaptive chosen message attacks. In fact, for the same parameters the bit-security of DFORS with respect to adaptive chosen message adversaries is equal to that of FORS under non-adaptive chosen message attacks. Table 1 gives a comparison between the bit security level of FORS and DFORS in an adaptive adversarial setting. We use the recommended parameters (i.e., n, τ, and κ) for all six instances of SPHINCS$^+$.

Table 1. DFORS and FORS security levels for an adaptive chosen message attack using the SPHINCS$^+$ parameters for different numbers of signed messages

SPHINCS$^+$ instance	τ	κ	FORS				DFORS			
			$r=1$	$r=2$	$r=4$	$r=8$	$r=1$	$r=2$	$r=4$	$r=8$
SPHINCS$^+$-128s	15	10	75	47	27	15	150	140	130	120
SPHINCS$^+$-128f	9	30	135	80	43	22	270	240	210	180
SPHINCS$^+$-192s	16	14	112	70	40	22	224	210	196	182
SPHINCS$^+$-192f	8	33	132	77	41	20	264	231	198	165
SPHINCS$^+$-256s	14	22	154	95	54	29	308	286	264	242
SPHINCS$^+$-256f	10	30	150	90	49	25	300	270	240	210

Table 2. Comparison between HORS, PORS, FORS, and DFORS

Algorithm	KGen (# OWF)[†]	Signing cost	Verification cost	Signature size[‡]	SK/PK size[‡]	Adaptive security
HORST	t PRF t OWF $t-1$ Hash	t PRF t OWF t Hash	κ OWF $\kappa(\log t - x) +$ 2^{x}[††] Hash	$\kappa(\log t -$ $x + 1) +$ 2^{x}[††]	1	NO
PORS[‡‡]	t PRF t OWF $t-1$ Hash	$t+\kappa$ PRF t OWF t Hash	κ OWF $\kappa(\log t - x -$ $1) + 2^{x}$[††] Hash	$\kappa(\log t -$ $\lfloor \log \kappa \rfloor + 1)$	1	NO
FORS	κt PRF κt OWF $\kappa(t-1)+1$ Hash	κt PRF κt OWF $\kappa(t-1)+1$ Hash	κ OWF $\kappa \log t + 1$ Hash	$\kappa(\log t + 1)$	1	NO
DFORS	κt PRF κt OWF $\kappa(t-1)+1$ Hash	κt PRF κt OWF κt Hash	κ OWF $\kappa(\log t + 1)$ Hash	$\kappa(\log t + 1)$	1	YES

† OWF denotes one-way function.
‡ Size is given as a factor of n bits.
†† $x = \lceil \log \kappa \rceil$ for optimal signature size in case of HORST and for the upper bound on the signature size in PORS.
‡‡ Verification cost and signature size are the upper bound values.

Table 1 shows the significant effect of increasing the number of signed messages, r, on the bit security of FORS. On the other hand, this effect is very reasonable with DFORS. For instance, when $r = 1$, an adaptive attack on FORS is equivalent to a collision attack on the underlying $\kappa\tau$-bit hash function H which has a complexity of $2^{\kappa\tau/2}$ evaluations. However, due to the r-subset resilience of DFORS where finding a covered ORS requires successive dependency on the signature elements, an adversary must find a second preimage of the ORS in the revealed secret keys, hence the complexity is $2^{\kappa\tau}$ evaluations.

Table 2 presents a comparison between DFORS and other HORS variants with respect to their computational efficiency, signature and key sizes, and security against adaptive chosen message attacks.

6   Conclusion

We analyzed the security of FORS, the underlying hash-based few-time signing scheme of SPHINCS$^+$, with respect to adaptive chosen message attacks. We showed that as the number of signed messages, r, increases, its bit-security with respect to adaptive chosen message adversaries decreases significantly compared to its non-adaptive counterpart. As a solution, we proposed DFORS, which builds on FORS but utilizes a secret key dependent ORS function. Such a function binds the process of generating the ORS with signing which makes it feasible only for the signer. Accordingly, we showed that the bit security of DFORS against adaptive chosen message attacks is more than that of FORS by a factor of $r + 1$. Note that our analysis does not affect the claimed security of SPHINCS$^+$ but rather provides a better understanding of the security of its underlying signing scheme and offers a mechanism that can be adopted by most HORS variants to provide security against adaptive chosen message attacks.

Acknowledgment. The authors would like to thank the reviewers for their valuable comments that helped improve the quality of the paper.

A   HORS Specification

The HORS key generation, signing, and verification procedures are given in Algorithm 3.

Algorithm 3. HORS Algorithm

---

procedure KEY GENERATION(t)
    Generate the secret key SK at random, $SK = (sk_0, sk_1, \ldots, sk_{t-1})$
    Compute the public key $PK = pk_0, pk_1, \ldots, pk_{t-1} = f(sk_0), f(sk_1), \ldots, f(sk_{t-1})$
    Output (SK, PK)
end procedure

---

procedure SIGNING(m, κ, SK, k)
    Compute $h = H_k(m)$, $h = h_0 || h_1 || \ldots || h_{\kappa-1}$.
    $ORS_\kappa(m) = \{h_0, h_1, \ldots, h_{\kappa-1}\}$.
    $\sigma = (\sigma_0, \sigma_1, \ldots, \sigma_{\kappa-1}) = (sk_{h_0}, sk_{h_1}, \ldots, sk_{h_{\kappa-1}})$
    Output (σ)
end procedure

---

procedure VERIFICATION(m, κ, σ, PK, k)
    Compute $h = H_k(m)$, $h = h_0 || h_1 || \ldots || h_{\kappa-1}$
    $ORS_\kappa(m) = \{h_0, h_1, \ldots, h_{\kappa-1}\}$
    for $0 \le i \le \kappa - 1$ **do**
        if $f(\sigma_i) = pk_{h_i}$ **then**
            $out = 1$
        else
            $out = 0$
            break
        end if
    end for
    Output (out)
end procedure

B   Adaptive Chosen Message Attack against HORS

In [23], the following adaptive chosen message attack against HORS was defined. Let $\mathcal{A}$ be an adaptive chosen message adversary against HORS such that given the key k, $\mathcal{A}$ can compute the hash of any message m and $ORS_\kappa(m)$ offline. Given a security parameter, n, under the birthday paradox, $\mathcal{A}$ can find $r + 1$ messages in a cover relation C_κ^r with which to query the signing oracle, formally

$$\Pr[k \leftarrow K, (m_1, m_2, \ldots, m_{r+1}) \leftarrow \mathcal{A}(k) : C_\kappa^r(m_1, m_2, \ldots, m_{r+1})] \le negl(n).$$

Aumasson and Endignoux [2] subsequently presented an adaptive chosen message attack against HORS and proved that the security level decreases by a factor of $r + 1$ when compared to non adaptive chosen message attacks. Their attack is as follows. Given an adversary $\mathcal{A}$ and a key k, the hash value $H_k(m)$ for any message of their choice can be computed, and say there are $q > r$ messages. For all possible combinations of $(r+1)$ messages from the q messages, $\mathcal{A}$ searches for $C_\kappa^{r-HORS}(m_1, m_2, \ldots m_{r+1})$ such that

$$C_\kappa^{r-HORS} \Leftrightarrow ORS(m_{r+1}) \in \bigcup_{j=1}^{r} ORS(m_j).$$

For any given subset, the probability of being an r-subset-cover relation is $(r\kappa/t)^{\kappa}$. The number of $(r+1)$-message combinations which $\mathcal{A}$ can construct from the q messages are $\binom{q}{r+1}$ and each combination can form $\binom{r+1}{r}$ choices. Accordingly, their probability of success in defeating the r-subset resilience (SR) is given by

$$Succ_{HORS}^{r-SR}(\mathcal{A}) \leq \binom{q}{r+1}\binom{r+1}{r}(\frac{r\kappa}{t})^{\kappa} \leq q\binom{q-1}{r}(\frac{r\kappa}{t})^{\kappa}.$$

Assuming a success probability close to 1, the security level of HORS against an adaptive chosen message attack is

$$\frac{\kappa}{r+1}(\log_2 t - \log_2 \kappa - \log_2 r) + \frac{\log_2 r!}{r+1}.$$

References

1. Arute, F., et al.: Quantum supremacy using a programmable superconducting processor. Nature **574**(7779), 505–510 (2019)
2. Aumasson, J.-P., Endignoux, G.: Clarifying the subset-resilience problem. IACR Cryptology ePrint Archive, p. 909 (2017)
3. Aumasson, J.-P., Endignoux, G.: Improving stateless hash-based signatures. In: Smart, N.P. (ed.) CT-RSA 2018. LNCS, vol. 10808, pp. 219–242. Springer, Cham (2018). https://doi.org/10.1007/978-3-319-76953-0_12
4. Bernstein, D., et al.: SPHINCS+-submission to the NIST post-quantum project (2017)
5. Bernstein, D.J., et al.: SPHINCS: practical stateless hash-based signatures. In: Oswald, E., Fischlin, M. (eds.) EUROCRYPT 2015. LNCS, vol. 9056, pp. 368–397. Springer, Heidelberg (2015). https://doi.org/10.1007/978-3-662-46800-5_15
6. Bernstein, D.J., Hülsing, A., Kölbl, S., Niederhagen, R., Rijneveld, J., Schwabe, P.: The SPHINCS+ signature framework. In: Proceedings of the ACM SIGSAC Conference on Computer and Communications Security, pp. 2129–2146 (201 9)
7. Bonnetain, X., Hosoyamada, A., Naya-Plasencia, M., Sasaki, Y., Schrottenloher, A.: Quantum attacks without superposition queries: the offline simon's algorithm. In: Galbraith, S.D., Moriai, S. (eds.) ASIACRYPT 2019. LNCS, vol. 11921, pp. 552–583. Springer, Cham (2019). https://doi.org/10.1007/978-3-030-34578-5_20
8. Buchmann, J., Dahmen, E., Ereth, S., Hülsing, A., Rückert, M.: On the security of the Winternitz one-time signature scheme. In: Nitaj, A., Pointcheval, D. (eds.) AFRICACRYPT 2011. LNCS, vol. 6737, pp. 363–378. Springer, Heidelberg (2011). https://doi.org/10.1007/978-3-642-21969-6_23
9. Buchmann, J., Dahmen, E., Hülsing, A.: XMSS - a practical forward secure signature scheme based on minimal security assumptions. In: Yang, B.-Y. (ed.) PQCrypto 2011. LNCS, vol. 7071, pp. 117–129. Springer, Heidelberg (2011). https://doi.org/10.1007/978-3-642-25405-5_8
10. Centre, NCSR: Round 2 submissions - Post-quantum cryptography (2019). https://csrc.nist.gov/projects/post-quantum-cryptography/round-2-submissions
11. Ducas, L., Durmus, A., Lepoint, T., Lyubashevsky, V.: Lattice signatures and bimodal Gaussians. In: Canetti, R., Garay, J.A. (eds.) CRYPTO 2013. LNCS, vol. 8042, pp. 40–56. Springer, Heidelberg (2013). https://doi.org/10.1007/978-3-642-40041-4_3

12. ElGamal, T.: A public key cryptosystem and a signature scheme based on discrete logarithms. IEEE Trans. Inf. Theory **31**(4), 469–472 (1985)
13. Erdös, P., Frankl, P., Füredi, Z.: Families of finite sets in which no set is covered by the union of r others. Isr. J. Math. **51**(1), 79–89 (1985)
14. Hülsing, A.: W-OTS+ – shorter signatures for hash-based signature schemes. In: Youssef, A., Nitaj, A., Hassanien, A.E. (eds.) AFRICACRYPT 2013. LNCS, vol. 7918, pp. 173–188. Springer, Heidelberg (2013). https://doi.org/10.1007/978-3-642-38553-7_10
15. Hülsing, A., Busold, C., Buchmann, J.: Forward secure signatures on smart cards. In: Knudsen, L.R., Wu, H. (eds.) SAC 2012. LNCS, vol. 7707, pp. 66–80. Springer, Heidelberg (2013). https://doi.org/10.1007/978-3-642-35999-6_5
16. Hülsing, A., Rausch, L., Buchmann, J.: Optimal parameters for XMSS^{MT}. In: Cuzzocrea, A., Kittl, C., Simos, D.E., Weippl, E., Xu, L. (eds.) CD-ARES 2013. LNCS, vol. 8128, pp. 194–208. Springer, Heidelberg (2013). https://doi.org/10.1007/978-3-642-40588-4_14
17. Hülsing, A., Rijneveld, J., Song, F.: Mitigating multi-target attacks in hash-based signatures. In: Cheng, C.-M., Chung, K.-M., Persiano, G., Yang, B.-Y. (eds.) PKC 2016. LNCS, vol. 9614, pp. 387–416. Springer, Heidelberg (2016). https://doi.org/10.1007/978-3-662-49384-7_15
18. Johnson, D., Menezes, A., Vanstone, S.: The elliptic curve digital signature algorithm (ECDSA). Int. J. Inf. Secur. **1**(1), 36–63 (2001)
19. Lamport, L.: Constructing digital signatures from a one-way function. Technical report, CSL-98, SRI International Palo Alto (1979)
20. Merkle, R.C.: A certified digital signature. In: Brassard, G. (ed.) CRYPTO 1989. LNCS, vol. 435, pp. 218–238. Springer, New York (1990). https://doi.org/10.1007/0-387-34805-0_21
21. Perrig, A.: The BiBa one-time signature and broadcast authentication protocol. In: Proceedings of the ACM Conference on Computer and Communications Security, pp. 28–37 (2001)
22. Pieprzyk, J., Wang, H., Xing, C.: Multiple-time signature schemes against adaptive chosen message attacks. In: Matsui, M., Zuccherato, R.J. (eds.) SAC 2003. LNCS, vol. 3006, pp. 88–100. Springer, Heidelberg (2004). https://doi.org/10.1007/978-3-540-24654-1_7
23. Reyzin, L., Reyzin, N.: Better than BiBa: short one-time signatures with fast signing and verifying. In: Batten, L., Seberry, J. (eds.) ACISP 2002. LNCS, vol. 2384, pp. 144–153. Springer, Heidelberg (2002). https://doi.org/10.1007/3-540-45450-0_11
24. Rivest, R.L., Shamir, A., Adleman, L.: A method for obtaining digital signatures and public-key cryptosystems. Commun. ACM **21**(2), 120–126 (1978)
25. Shor, P.W.: Algorithms for quantum computation: discrete logarithms and factoring. In: Proceedings of the Annual Symposium on Foundations of Computer Science, pp. 124–134 (1994)
26. Song, F.: A note on quantum security for post-quantum cryptography. In: Mosca, M. (ed.) PQCrypto 2014. LNCS, vol. 8772, pp. 246–265. Springer, Cham (2014). https://doi.org/10.1007/978-3-319-11659-4_15
27. Li, Y.X., Deng, R.H., Wang, X.M.: On the equivalence of McEliece's and Niederreiter's public-key cryptosystems. IEEE Trans. Inf. Theory **40**(1), 271–273 (1994)

LMS vs XMSS: Comparison of Stateful Hash-Based Signature Schemes on ARM Cortex-M4

Fabio Campos[1(✉)], Tim Kohlstadt[1(✉)], Steffen Reith[1(✉)], and Marc Stöttinger[2(✉)]

[1] Department of Computer Science,
RheinMain University of Applied Sciences, Wiesbaden, Germany
campos@sopmac.de, tim.kohlstadt@student.hs-rm.de, steffen.reith@hs-rm.de
[2] Continental AG, Hanover, Germany
marc.stoettinger@continental-corporation.com

Abstract. Stateful hash-based signature schemes are among the most efficient approaches for post-quantum signature schemes. Although not suitable for general use, they may be suitable for some use cases on constrained devices. LMS and XMSS are hash-based signature schemes that are conjectured to be quantum secure. In this work, we compared multiple instantiations of both schemes on an ARM Cortex-M4. More precisely, we compared performance, stack consumption, and other figures for key generation, signing and verifying. To achieve this, we evaluated LMS and XMSS using optimised implementations of SHA-256, SHAKE256, Gimli-Hash, and different variants of KECCAK. Furthermore, we present slightly optimised implementations of XMSS achieving speedups of up to $3.11\times$ for key generation, $3.11\times$ for signing, and $4.32\times$ for verifying.

Keywords: LMS · XMSS · Implementation · Hash-based signatures · Digital signature · Post-quantum cryptography

1 Introduction

Digital-signature schemes are among the most important and widely used cryptographic primitives. Schemes used in practice today (RSA [30], DSA [14], ECDSA [20], and EdDSA [4]) are based on assumptions regarding the computational difficulty of solving certain mathematical problems. Due to Shor's algorithm [32] and its variants, some of these problems, such as integer factorisation and discrete logarithms, can be efficiently solved on a quantum computer. Since the National Institute of Standards and Technology (NIST) started a project (NIST-PQC[1]) to evaluate and standardise post-quantum cryptographic algorithms, many solutions have been proposed. Hash-based signature schemes (HBS) are among the most attractive candidates for quantum-safe

---

Author list in alphabetical order; see https://www.ams.org/profession/leaders/culture/CultureStatement04.pdf.

[1] https://csrc.nist.gov/Projects/Post-Quantum-Cryptography.

A. Nitaj and A. Youssef (Eds.): AFRICACRYPT 2020, LNCS 12174, pp. 258–277, 2020.
https://doi.org/10.1007/978-3-030-51938-4_13

signature schemes. Every signature scheme requires a hash function to reduce a message to a small representation that can be easily signed. While other signature schemes rely on additional computational hardness assumptions, hash-based approaches only needs a secure hash function. HBS have been intensively analysed [5,10,13,16,27] and the two schemes discussed in this work are currently undergoing a standardisation process [18,26]. The Leighton-Micali Signature system (LMS) [26] and the eXtended Merkle Signature Scheme (XMSS) [18] have been proposed in the Internet Engineering Task Force (IETF) as quantum-secure HBS. NIST proposed [11] to approve the use of LMS and XMSS and their multi-tree variants Hierarchical Signature System (HSS) and multi-tree XMSS ($XMSS^{MT}$), respectively. This recommendation suggests the use of some of the parameter sets from the RFCs and defines some new parameter sets. It considers SHA-256 or SHAKE256 as underlying hash functions, with outputs of 192-bit or 256-bit length. HBS provide through the choice of parameters several trade-offs between time and size. Hence, the parameter selection has a major impact on how feasible it is to deploy HBS on resource-constrained environments such as embedded microcontrollers. In this work, we chose a subset of parameters from the suggested sets of the NIST recommendation which are suitable for embedded devices.

Due to the popularity and widespread use of Cortex-M4 microcontrollers in different applications, NIST recommended it to submission teams as an optimisation target for the second round of NIST-PQC. The pqm4[2] project [22] investigates the feasibility and performance of the proposed NIST-PQC approaches on microcontrollers. It provides a framework for testing and benchmarking NIST-PQC submissions on a Cortex-M4 microcontroller. It includes reference and optimised implementations of key-encapsulation mechanisms and signature schemes. The implementations and measurements in our work were realised within the pqm4 framework.

Related Work. Many aspects regarding the implementations of HBS have been studied in the literature. Rohde, Eisenbarth, Dahmen, Buchmann, Paar [31] presented the first implementation of GMSS [8], an improvement of Merkle's hash-based signature scheme, on an 8-bit smart-card microprocessor. Hülsing, Busold, Buchmann [17] implemented a variant of XMSS on a 16-bit smart card. A comparison between stateful and stateless HBS was given by Hülsing, Rijneveld, Schwabe [19]. For this, the authors implemented SPHINCS and $XMSS^{MT}$ on an ARM Cortex M3. Van der Laan, Poll, Rijneveld, de Ruiter, Schwabe, Verschuren [23] presented an implementation of XMSS on the Java Card platform. Kannwischer, Rijneveld, Schwabe, Stoffelen [22] presented the pqm4 framework for testing, speed benchmarking, and measurement of stack consumption of NIST-PQC submissions on an ARM Cortex-M4 microcontroller. Kampanakis, Fluhrer [21] provided the only comparison between LMS and XMSS on a x86-architecture regarding their security assumptions, signature/public key sizes, performance, and some other aspects.

Our Contribution. This paper aims at comparing stateful HBS on microcontrollers. To achieve this, LMS and XMSS and their multi-tree variants were compared on an ARM

---

[2] https://github.com/mupq/pqm4.

Cortex-M4. For this, we provide an adapted implementation of LMS for the Cortex-M4, which represents the first implementation to date to the best of the authors' knowledge. We evaluated suitable parameter sets for constrained devices from the NIST recommendation for stateful hash-based signature schemes [11]. Furthermore, deviating from the RFC 8391 [18], we slightly modified the reference implementation of XMSS, leading to noticeable speedups. We provide a comparative performance and stack consumption analysis for several parameter sets of the instantiated versions of LMS and XMSS. Thereby we instantiate both HBS with several optimised hash functions. All software and results described in this paper are available in the public domain. It is publicly available at https://doi.org/10.5281/zenodo.3631571. Further, we refer to the respective projects included in our implementation for licensing information.

Organisation. The remainder of this document is structured as follows. First, we start by giving preliminary information on hash-based signature schemes. In Sect. 3, we reflect the main structural differences between LMS and XMSS. Details about the implemented hash functions and the approaches to speed up XMSS are presented in Sect. 4. Our implementation results are given in Sect. 5. Next, we discuss the results and draw a conclusion in Sect. 6. Finally, Appendix A contains further evaluated results.

2   Hash-Based Signature Schemes

While the security of other post-quantum cryptographic approaches like isogeny-based cryptography is still object to further research, hash-based schemes come with well-understood security assumptions.

Both discussed stateful schemes in this work use a tree construction along with a variant of a one-time signature schemes (OTS). Unlike in stateless schemes, in LMS and XMSS the signer needs to keep track of which key pairs have already been used. Therefore, the current state (index) is stored in the secret key, indicating which key pair to use next. XMSS provides methods to decrease the worst case runtime by keeping state information beyond the index [9]. To allow a fair comparison, this have not been considered in this work.

2.1   One-Time Signature Schemes

Many techniques have been proposed for constructing OTS schemes [7,24,27]. One of the most prominent OTS is the Winternitz OTS (WOTS) scheme [27], which is relatively efficient, has been used in practice and allows space/time trade-offs. LMS and XMSS use variants of WOTS.

Winternitz One-Time Signature Scheme. The main idea of all WOTS variants is to use a function chain to sign multiple bits starting from random inputs. The key generation is processed as shown in Algorithm 1, where n is the security parameter, w is (a power of 2) the "Winternitz parameter", and $f : \{0,1\}^* \to \{0,1\}^n$ defines a one-way function. Thereby, f^{w-1} should be interpreted as the $(w-1)$-th iteration of the one-way function f. Increasing the value of the Winternitz parameter w will linearly shrink the size of a signature and increase exponentially the effort to perform key generation, signing and verification. Thus, the Winternitz parameter w enables space/time trade-offs.

Algorithm 1: Key generation.

Input : security parameter n, Winternitz paramater w.
Output: one-time key pair: (secret key X, public key Y).

1 $\ell_1 \leftarrow \lceil n/\log_2(w) \rceil$
2 $\ell_2 \leftarrow \lfloor \log_2(\ell_1(w-1))/\log_2(w) \rfloor + 1$
3 $\ell \leftarrow \ell_1 + \ell_2$
4 **for** $i = 0, ..., \ell - 1$ **do**
5 $\quad x_i \overset{\$}{\leftarrow} \{0,1\}^n$ // sampled uniformly at random
6 $\quad y_i \leftarrow f^{w-1}(x_i)$
7 **return** $((x_0, x_1, ..., x_{\ell-1}), (y_0, y_1, ..., y_{\ell-1}))$

In order to protect against trivial attacks, a checksum C is computed and signed along with the message, as shown in Algorithm 2 in line 5–7. A signature is computed by mapping the i-th chunk of M' to one intermediary value of the respective function chain, by iterating the one-way function M'_i times. As shown in Algorithm 3, in WOTS the public key can be calculated directly from the signature.

Algorithm 2: Signing.

Input : message M, secret key X, security parameter n, Winternitz parameter w.
Output: signature σ.

1 $\ell_1 \leftarrow \lceil n/\log_2(w) \rceil$
2 $\ell_2 \leftarrow \lfloor \log_2(\ell_1(w-1))/\log_2(w) \rfloor + 1$
3 $\ell \leftarrow \ell_1 + \ell_2$
4 $(M_0, M_1, ..., M_{\ell_1-1}) \leftarrow \mathbf{split}(M)$ // split M into $\log_2(w)$-bit chunks
5 $C \leftarrow \sum_{i=0}^{\ell_1-1} w - 1 - M_i$
6 $C \leftarrow \mathbf{pad}(C)$ // pad C with zeros if necessary
7 $M' \leftarrow M \parallel C$ // concatenate M and C
8 $(M'_0, M'_1, ..., M'_{\ell-1}) \leftarrow \mathbf{split}(M')$ // split M' into $\log_2(w)$-bits chunks
9 **for** $i = 0, ..., \ell - 1$ **do**
10 $\quad \sigma_i \leftarrow f^{M_i}(x_i)$
11 **return** $(\sigma_0, \sigma_1, ..., \sigma_{\ell-1})$

According to [13], assuming f is a collision-resistant one-way function, this scheme is existentially unforgeable under chosen-message attacks. XMSS makes use of the variant WOTS$^+$. WOTS$^+$, proposed by Hülsing [16], introduced a slight modification of the chaining function by adding a random bitmask r_i for each iteration, such that $f^0(x) = x$, and $f^i(x) = f(f^{i-1}(x) \oplus r_i)$ for $i > 0$. This modification eliminates the requirement for a collision resistant hash function.

Algorithm 3: Verifying.

Input : signature σ, message M, public key Y, security parameter n, Winternitz
parameter w.

Output: valid or invalid.

1 $\ell_1 \leftarrow \lceil n/\log_2(w) \rceil$
2 $\ell_2 \leftarrow \lfloor \log_2(\ell_1(w-1))/\log_2(w) \rfloor + 1$
3 $\ell \leftarrow \ell_1 + \ell_2$
4 $(M_0, M_1, ..., M_{\ell_1-1}) \leftarrow \mathbf{split}(M)$ // split M into $\log_2(w)$-bit chunks
5 $C \leftarrow \sum_{i=0}^{\ell_1-1} w - 1 - M_i$
6 $C \leftarrow \mathbf{pad}(C)$ // pad C with zeros if necessary
7 $M' \leftarrow M \,||\, C$ // concatenate M and C
8 $(M'_0, M'_1, ..., M'_{\ell-1}) \leftarrow \mathbf{split}(M')$ // split M' into $\log_2(w)$-bits chunks
9 **for** $i = 0, ..., \ell-1$ **do**
10   **if** $((f^{w-1-M'_i}(\sigma_i)) \neq y_i)$ **then**
11          $\lfloor$ **return** invalid

12 **return** valid

2.2 Many-Time Signature Schemes

Merkle trees enable the use of a single long-term public key created from a large set of OTS public keys. In the following we will only briefly describe the methods for the construction of many-time schemes and refer to [26] and [18] for further details on the respective approach.

Merkle Trees. Based on the idea of one-time signature schemes Merkle's approach [27] is to construct a balanced binary tree (a so-called *Merkle Tree*) using a given hash function to enable the use of a single public key (root of the tree) for verifying several messages. A signer generates 2^h one-time key pairs (X_j, Y_j) where $0 \leq j < 2^h$ for a selected $h \in \mathbb{N}$ and $h \geq 2$. The leaves of the tree are represented by the public keys X_j of the OTS which are derived from the secret keys Y_j for $0 \leq j < 2^h$. Parameter h defines the height of the resulting binary tree whose inner nodes are represented by the value computed as $n = f(n_l \,||\, n_r)$, where n_l and n_r are the values of the left and right children of n. To verify a signature at leaf with index i, one additionally needs the authentication path of i which is a sequence of h nodes. This authentication path contains the siblings of all the nodes on the path between leaf i and the root. Thus summarizing, a signature on a message m contains the one-time signature on m produced using X_j, the authentication path, and the index j to indicate which key pair of the OTS was used.

Multi-trees. Rather than scaling up a single tree, LMS and XMSS define single and multi-tree (hypertree) variants of their signature schemes. In the multi-tree variant, the trees on the lowest layer are used to sign messages and the trees on higher layers are used to sign the roots of the trees on the layer below. Considering a hypertree of total height h that has d layers of trees of height h/d, the top layer $d-1$ contains one tree,

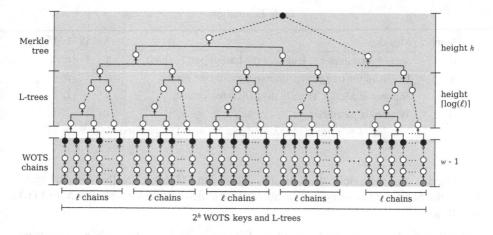

Fig. 1. Overview with L-trees and WOTS chains (adopted from [34], Fig. 1). Grey nodes are the private keys and the black nodes the public keys of the WOTS chains. The black node at the top is the public key.

layer $d - 2$ contains $2^{(h/d)}$ trees, and so on. Finally, the lowest layer contains $2^{(h-(h/d))}$ trees. In order to generate the public key, only the single tree at the top of the structure needs to be generated. This requires generating the OTS keys along the bottom of this tree. The lower trees are generated deterministically as required. Thus, for a given h, key generation in a hypertree is faster than in a single tree. A signature consists of all the signatures on the way to the highest tree. Hence, the signature size increases and signing and verifying takes slightly longer. The root of the top-level tree is the public key. For further details on the multi-tree variants of LMS and XMSS, we refer to [26] and [18], respectively.

3 Comparison

Roughly speaking, LMS and XMSS have a very similar construction. Both schemes use Merkle trees [27] along with a variant of WOTS. For this reason, we will focus on the most relevant structural differences of the schemes.

LMS and XMSS use different notations to specify equivalent parameters. As shown in Table 1, we define a common notation for parameters used in this work. For further details on the definition of the parameters, we refer to [26] and [18].

3.1 Prefixes and Bitmasks

In order to move away from collision resistance and towards collision resilience, within LMS and XMSS whenever an input is hashed, a specific prefix is added to the input. In the case of XMSS as mentioned in Sect. 2.1, WOTS⁺ [16] requires a random bitmask for each chaining iteration as additional input. Although LMS and XMSS apply different mechanisms to strengthen the security, the underlying constructions are very similar.

Table 1. Notation.

Symbol	Meaning	XMSS	LMS
n	Security parameter $\simeq$ length of the hash digest (in bits)	n	n
h	Height of the tree or hypertree in a multi-tree variant	h	h
d	Number of Merkle Trees in the multi-tree variant	d	L
w	Winternitz parameter	w	2^w
ℓ	Number of Winternitz chains used in a single OTS operation	len	p

To describe this principle theoretically, Bernstein, Hülsing, Kölbl, Niederhagen, Rijneveld, Schwabe [5] introduced an abstraction called *tweakable hash functions* (**Th**) as follows.

Definition 1 *(Tweakable hash function): Let $n, \alpha \in \mathbb{N}, \mathcal{P}$ be the public parameters space, and $\mathcal{T}$ be the tweak space. A tweakable hash function is an efficient function*

$$\mathbf{Th} : \mathcal{P} \times \mathcal{T} \times \{0,1\}^\alpha \to \{0,1\}^n, \quad \mathsf{MD} \leftarrow \mathbf{Th}(P,T,M)$$

mapping an α-bit message M to an n-bit hash value MD using a public parameter $P \in \mathcal{P}$, also called function key, and a tweak $T \in \mathcal{T}$.

Thus, a tweakable hash function adds specific context information (tweak) and public parameters (function key) to the input. According to this definition, the constructions within LMS and XMSS can roughly be described as follows.

Construction 1 *(Prefix construction/LMS): Given a hash function $H : \{0,1\}^{2n+\alpha} \to \{0,1\}^n$, we construct* **Th** *with $\mathcal{P} = \mathcal{T} = \{0,1\}^n$, as*

$$\mathbf{Th}(P,T,M) = H(P||T||M).$$

Construction 2 *(Prefix and bitmask construction/XMSS): Given two hash functions $H_1 : \{0,1\}^{2n} \times \{0,1\}^\alpha \to \{0,1\}^n$ with $2n$-bit keys, and $H_2 : \{0,1\}^{2n} \to \{0,1\}^\alpha$, we construct* **Th** *with $\mathcal{P} = \mathcal{T} = \{0,1\}^n$, as*

$$\mathbf{Th}(P,T,M) = H_1(P||T,M^\oplus), \text{ with } M^\oplus = M \oplus H_2(P||T).$$

As defined in Construction 2, while XMSS additionally generates distinct random inputs for each invocation of the hash function, LMS provides inputs with predictable changes to the hash function. Construction 1 reduces the effort, but comes in return at the cost of stronger security assumptions. For further details on the security model of LMS and XMSS, we refer to [21] and for further security notions for the defined constructions, we refer to [5].

3.2 WOTS Public Key Compression

Both schemes combine the public keys (final values) of a WOTS chain into an n-bit value. While LMS hashes them together as a single message (see Fig. 2), XMSS uses a tree (called L-tree) to compress these values (see Fig. 1). The construction in XMSS obviously leads to a higher number of hash operations.

4 LMS and XMSS on the Cortex-M4

In the case of XMSS[3], we removed all file-based procedures and implemented an interface to the pqm4 framework. For this, we used a slightly modified version of the pqm4 framework. This modification allows updating the secret key during the signing process by not passing the secret key as a constant. Thus, we enable the signing algorithm to be stateful. For further practical considerations around statefulness in this context, we refer to [25]. To port the reference implementation of LMS[4] to Cortex-M4, apart from smaller modifications, we integrated the single-thread version, and turned floating-point operations off.

4.1 Implemented Hash Functions

Primarily for the purpose of speedup and to achieve a broader comparison range, we integrated two more lightweight hash functions in addition to those recommended by NIST [11] (SHA-256 and SHAKE256) and already available in pqm4. In particular, we additionally evaluated LMS and XMSS using different variants of KECCAK and Gimli-Hash.

KECCAK-f[800]. KECCAK-f describes a family of permutations originally specified in [1]. The KECCAK-p permutations within KECCAK-f are specified by a fixed width of the permutation (b) and the respective number of rounds (n_r) required. Furthermore, the permutation is denoted by KECCAK-$p[b, n_r]$, where $b \in \{25, 50, 100, 200, 400, 800, 1600\}$ and $n_r \in \{12, 14, 16, 18, 20, 22, 24\}$. Thus, according to [28], KECCAK-f[800], a permutation with 800 bits of width, applies to KECCAK-p[800, 22]. For further details on KECCAK, we refer to [1] and [28].

In the case of KECCAK-f[800], we additionally considered a KECCAK permutation with only 12 rounds (KECCAK-p[800, 12] similar to River Keyak[5]) to reduce the computational workload per hash invocation. Evidently, a reduced number of rounds provides a smaller safety margin than the full 22 rounds recommended for KECCAK-f[800] [28]. Nevertheless, since the best known practical collision attack against SHA-3 exists only up to 5 rounds [15], the margin provided by 12 rounds is still comfortable. In a similar manner, Aumasson [2] proposed a general revision of the number of rounds of widely used symmetric primitives to speed up the standards without increasing the security risk. Furthermore to achieve a certain security level, we set the capacity $c = 256$ as specified in River Keyak (see footnote 5).

Gimli-Hash. The family of hash functions Gimli-Hash is built on top of a 384-bit permutation called Gimli. The Gimli permutation [6] was designed to achieve high security with high performance. According to the authors, the proposed permutation is distinguished from other permutation-based primitives for its high cross-platform performance. Furthermore, one of the core idea of Gimli was to define one standard that

---

[3] https://github.com/XMSS/xmss-reference, commit fb7e3f8.

[4] https://github.com/cisco/hash-sigs, commit 5efb1d0.

[5] https://keccak.team/files/Keyakv2-doc2.2.pdf.

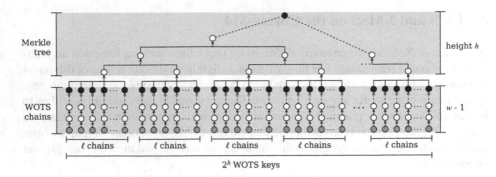

Fig. 2. Overview without L-trees (adopted from [34], Fig. 1). Grey nodes are the private keys and the black nodes the public keys of the WOTS chains. The black node at the top is the public key.

achieves high performance in lightweight as well as in non-lightweight environments. Due to the selected design, Gimli fits into 14 easily usable integer registers on 32-bit ARM microcontrollers. Gimli-Hash works on a 48-byte state with a rate of 16-byte.

We chose Gimli-Hash as an exemplary approach for the current round-2 candidates in NIST's Lightweight Cryptography Standardisation[6] process. It is of practical importance to investigate the performance of the remaining candidates.

4.2 Speeding up XMSS

In this section, we discuss three methods for speeding up XMSS deviating from RFC 8391 [18]. The first described technique replaces the tree-based WOTS public-key compression with a single hash call. This approach was first proposed in SPHINCS+ [3]. The second one, a structure omitting the use of bitmasks (the so-called "simple" version) was proposed in the round-2 submission of SPHINCS+ [3] at NIST-PQC. Finally, we describe a technique called "hash pre-computation". This approach was first mentioned by Kampanakis, Fluhrer [21] and first described by Wang, Jungk, Wälde, Deng, Gupta, Szefer, Niederhagen [34]. Thereby, recurring intermediate results of a certain type of hash calls are temporarily stored and reused in the subsequent hash calls.

All these methods lead to speedups during key generation, signing and verifying. However, during the signature verification, the hash pre-computation method only leads to small speedups in certain parameter sets. Although the methods presented in the following can also be implemented in other cases, in this work we will mainly focus on the parameter sets from Table 3. Other approaches, which lead to possible speedups in both LMS and XMSS, were intentionally not considered in this work.

Other acceleration methods, such as storing some top nodes in the secret key [12], applying a more efficient tree traversal scheme [33] (already part of the XMSS reference implementation[7] and our implementation), or instantiating the schemes with shorter hash functions, were intentionally not considered in this work. Although these methods

---

[6] https://csrc.nist.gov/projects/lightweight-cryptography.
[7] https://github.com/XMSS/xmss-reference, commit fb7e3f8.

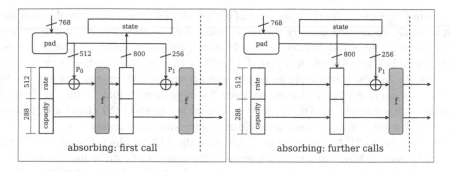

Fig. 3. Hash pre-computation within KECCAK-f[800] with a rate of 512 bits.

lead to significant speedups, they can be applied in LMS and XMSS and therefore have no fundamental impact in our comparison.

The instantiation of the different parameter sets is managed by conditional compilation. In the case of XMSS, the modifications presented in this section are also controlled by preprocessing allowing to compile different versions of XMSS.

Tree-Less WOTS+ Public Key Compression. As described in SPHINCS+ [3], we compress the end nodes of the WOTS chains (black nodes in Fig. 2) with a single call to a tweakable hash function, as shown in Fig. 2. A tree-based compression (see L-trees in Fig. 1) is slower than using a single call to a tweakable hash function with the concatenated digest of all end nodes of the WOTS chains (see black nodes in Fig. 2) as input.

Bitmask-Less Hashing. In this construction no bitmasks are generated and XORed with the input of the tweakable hash functions. In this case, the tweakable hash function is defined according to Construction 1 instead of Construction 2 (see Sect. 3.1). For the resulting implications for security by applying Construction 1 in XMSS, we strongly refer to [5].

Hash Pre-computation. Within XMSS, for a given key pair and a security parameter n, the first $2n$-bit block (n-bit domain separator and n-bit hash-function key) of the input to the pseudo-random function (of type $\mathcal{F} : \{0,1\}^{3n} \rightarrow \{0,1\}^n$) is the same for all calls. Considering this fact, we store the digest of the first $2n$-bit block at the first call to the pseudorandom function (PRF) and skip this effort by reusing this result in all further calls. This approach can easily be applied whenever the internal block size/rate of the used hash function is less than or equal to $2n$ bits. Depending on the internal block size of the used hash function, the number of saved calls to the internal compression respectively permutation function (**Speedup**$_{PRF}$) can be calculated as follows. Let $B_{bits} \geq 2n$ bits be the internal block size/rate in bits and #call$_{PRF}$ be the number of calls to the PRF, then

$$\mathbf{Speedup}_{PRF}(B_{bits}, \#\text{call}_{PRF}) = \lfloor 2n \text{ bits}/B_{bits} \rfloor * \#\text{call}_{PRF}.$$

As in Fig. 3 exemplified for the case of KECCAK-f[800] and $n = 256$, this method can basically be applied in every sponge construction, by reducing the rate to $2n$ bits whenever the rate is longer than $2n$ bits. Hence, even in the case $n = 256$, it can be implemented in SHAKE256 (KECCAK-f[1600]) by reducing the width of the rate from 1088 bits to $2n$ bits. However, in hash calls apart from the PRF invocations this would increase the number of permutations required for inputs longer than $2n$ bits. A "hybrid approach" (not considered in this paper) with variable rate width (512 bits for PRF calls and 1088 for other hashing cases) could lead to a possible acceleration.

In the case of SHA-256 and $n = 256$, where the 512-bit block fits into a 512 bit SHA-256 internal block, this approach reduces the number of calls to the compression function by half. According to the standard definition [28] in KECCAK-f[800] with a capacity of 256-bit length, the length of the rate should be 544 bits. In order to enable hash pre-computation, we reduced the length of the rate to 512 bits. In other words, the rate within an instantiation of XMSS using KECCAK-f[800] applying hash pre-computation is 512 bits long, while a version without hash pre-computation makes use of the whole 544 bits. This modified design with a longer capacity obviously has no negative influence on the security of the hash function. In the case of KECCAK-f[800], this approach reduces the number of required permutations by half. Since the rate in the sponge construction within Gimli-Hash is 128 bits long, it results in saving 4 permutation runs per PRF invocation.

From now on as shown in Table 2, we call an implementation of XMSS with L-trees using Construction 2 (see Sect. 3.1) without hash pre-computation XMSS_ROBUST, the variant without L-trees using Construction 1 XMSS_SIMPLE, and the one without L-trees applying Construction 1 and hash pre-computation XMSS_SIMPLE+PRE. The multi-tree variants are called XMSS^{MT}ROBUST, XMSS^{MT}SIMPLE, and XMSS^{MT}SIMPLE+PRE, respectively. XMSS_ROBUST and XMSS^{MT}ROBUST represent the current version of XMSS from RFC 8391[8].

Table 2. Implemented variants of XMSS.

Design	Multi-tree	Tree-less WOTS+	Bitmask-less hashing	Pre-computation
XMSS_ROBUST				
XMSS_SIMPLE		•	•	
XMSS_SIMPLE+PRE		•	•	•
XMSS^{MT}ROBUST	•			
XMSS^{MT}SIMPLE	•	•	•	
XMSS^{MT}SIMPLE+PRE	•	•	•	•

5   Evaluation

We measured the performance of our implementations on a commercially available microcontroller. We use the widely available board STM32F4DISCOVERY featuring a 32-bit ARM Cortex-M4 with FPU core, 1-Mbyte Flash ROM, and 192-Kbyte RAM.

---

[8] https://tools.ietf.org/html/rfc8391.

Table 3. Selected parameter sets.

Scheme	n	w	h	Layer	Signature size (bits)
LMS	256	16	5	1	2352
LMS	256	256	5	1	1296
LMS	256	16	10	1	2512
LMS	256	256	10	1	1456
XMSS	256	16	5	1	2340
XMSS	256	16	10	1	2500
HSS	256	16	10	2	4756
HSS	256	256	10	2	2644
XMSS^{MT}	256	16	10	2	4642

The reference implementation of LMS[9] and XMSS[10] provided the basis for our implementation. The methods used for cycle counter reading, device communication at runtime, and hardware-based random byte generation were provided by the pqm4[11] framework. This framework in turn includes the libopencm3[12] library for providing these methods. All test instances were compiled with GNU Tools for ARM Embedded Processors 9-2019-q4-major[13] (gcc version 9.2.1 20191025 (release) [ARM/arm-9-branch revision 277599]) using the flags:
`-O3 -mthumb -mcpu=cortex-m4 -mfloat-abi=hard -mfpu=fpv4-sp-d16`.

We additionally evaluated LMS and XMSS using optimised assembly implementations of KECCAK-f[800] (`KeccakP-800-u2-armv7m-le-gcc`) from the eXtended Keccak Code Package[14] and of the Gimli[15] (`arm-m4` version) permutation.

In this work, LMS and XMSS share the same implementations to perform the hash computations, clock-cycle measurement, and stack analysis, hence yielding an unbiased comparison. The selection of the evaluated parameter sets is based on the recommendation of NIST [11]. The parameter sets from Table 3 were implemented in combination with Gimli-Hash, KECCAK (KECCAK-p[800, 22] and KECCAK-p[800, 12]), SHAKE256, and SHA-256. The resulting signature size for each parameter set is also shown in Table 3.

As shown in Table 4, the implemented modifications in XMSS and XMSS^{MT} lead to significant speedups. XMSS_SIMPLE achieves a speedup of up to 3.03× for key generation and signing, and up to 4.32× for verifying. In combination with the hash precomputation approach, key generation and signing achieve accelerations up to 3.11 times. However, when applying the hash pre-computation method, a speedup only

---

[9] https://github.com/cisco/hash-sigs, commit 5efb1d0.

[10] https://github.com/XMSS/xmss-reference, commit fb7e3f8.

[11] https://github.com/mupq/pqm4, commit 8136c82.

[12] https://libopencm3.org/.

[13] https://developer.arm.com/.

[14] https://github.com/XKCP/XKCP, commit 035a8ff.

[15] https://gimli.cr.yp.to/impl.html, version 2017.06.27.

Table 4. Speedup in XMSS and XMSS^{MT} exemplary with SHA-256.

Design	w	h	Layer	Key gen[a]	Sign[a]	Verify[a]
XMSS_ROBUST	16	5	1	738.46	747.85	13.84
XMSS_SIMPLE	16	5	1	243.25	247.72	3.20
Speedup factor[b]				3.03	3.01	4.32
XMSS_SIMPLE+PRE	16	5	1	237.27	241.02	3.73
Speedup factor[b]				3.11	3.10	3.71
XMSS_ROBUST	16	10	1	23631.70	23642.03	13.07
XMSS_SIMPLE	16	10	1	7784.50	7788.56	3.67
Speedup factor[b]				3.03	3.03	3.56
XMSS_SIMPLE+PRE	16	10	1	7586.15	7589.49	4.20
Speedup factor[b]				3.11	3.11	3.11
XMSS^{MT}ROBUST	16	10	2	738.43	1498.06	27.67
XMSS^{MT}SIMPLE	16	10	2	243.49	494.55	7.77
Speedup factor[c]				3.03	3.03	3.56
XMSS^{MT}SIMPLE+PRE	16	10	2	237.26	481.73	7.77
Speedup factor[c]				3.11	3.11	3.56

[a] All results (apart from speedup) are given in 10^6 clock cycles.
[b] Compared to XMSS_ROBUST.
[c] Compared to XMSS^{MT}ROBUST.

occurs in certain parameter sets, mostly when the number of rounds of the hash function and the number of calls to the PRF are large enough to compensate for the additional effort. In the case of verification, a speedup through hash pre-computation occurred rarely (see Table 9 and Table 10).

Table 5. Number of hash operations for SHA-256, $n = 256$, and $w = 16$.

	LMS	XMSS_SIMPLE	Ratio[a]	HSS	XMSS^{MT}SIMPLE	Ratio[b]
Key gen	1105990	1100800	0.99	34566	34400	0.99
Sign	2216417	2202194	0.99	112542	104371	0.93
Verify	2217208	2202686	0.99	113493	105359	0.93

[a] XMSS_SIMPLE/LMS
[b] XMSS^{MT}SIMPLE/LMS

Reducing the number of rounds in KECCAK-f[800] to 12 instead of 22 yields a speedup of up to roughly 1.66× for key generation and signing, and 1.72× for verifying in all implemented variants of XMSS, and up to roughly 1.70× for key generation and signing, and 1.76× for verifying in all implemented variants of LMS (see Table 9, Table 10, and Table 11).

Table 6. Performance comparison for SHA-256, $n = 256$, $w = 16$, and $h = 10$.

	LMS	XMSS_ROBUST	Ratio[a]	XMSS_SIMPLE	Ratio[b]	XMSS_SIMPLE+PRE	Ratio[c]
Key gen[d]	3774.88	23631.70	6.26	7792.23	2.06	7586.15	2.01
Sign[d]	3791.15	23642.03	6.23	7796.39	2.05	7596.24	2.00
Verify[d]	2.65	13.07	4.93	3.57	1.34	4.20	1.58

[a] XMSS_ROBUST/LMS
[b] XMSS_SIMPLE/LMS
[c] XMSS_SIMPLE+PRE/LMS
[d] All results (apart from ratio) are given in 10^6 clock cycles.

Structurally, XMSS_SIMPLE, the variant without L-trees using Construction 1, differs only marginally from LMS. To confirm this analysis, we measured the number of hash operations required in LMS and XMSS_SIMPLE. As Table 5 shows, XMSS_SIMPLE and XMSS^{MT} SIMPLE hash operations are almost equivalent to LMS and HSS, respectively. As shown in Table 6, although the changes in XMSS result in a slightly smaller number of hash calls than in LMS, LMS unexpectedly requires fewer clock cycles for all tested cases. We further measured the time spent performing hash operations for each scheme. The results of this measurement are given in Table 7. In both schemes, at least 85% of the time was spent on performing the hash computations. XMSS spends 15% of the evaluated time on computing other operations, while LMS spends up to 94% of time on hashing.

Table 7. Percentage of time on hashing for SHA-256, $n = 256$, $w = 16$, $h = 10$, and $d = 2$.

	HSS	XMSS^{MT} SIMPLE
Key gen	92%	85%
Sign	92%	85%
Verify	94%	85%

During key generation, the stack consumption of XMSS is on average slightly higher than for LMS. However, as shown in Table 8, the difference during signing and verification is 1.6× and almost 4× as high, respectively.

Table 8. Stack memory usage (bytes) for XMSS^{MT} and HSS using Gimli-Hash.

Scheme	Hash type	w	h	Layer	Key gen	Sign	Verify
XMSS^{MT} ROBUST	Gimli-Hash	16	5	2	3560	3704	3604
XMSS^{MT} SIMPLE	Gimli-Hash	16	5	2	3512	3656	3600
XMSS^{MT} SIMPLE+PRE	Gimli-Hash	16	5	2	3484	3672	3572
HSS	Gimli-Hash	16	5	2	3528	2268	936
HSS	Gimli-Hash	256	5	2	3528	2268	980

The round-reduced version of KECCAK (KECCAK-p[800, 12]) achieved the best performance (see Table 9, Table 10, and Table 11) while Gimli-Hash the lowest stack consumption (see Table 12).

A complete overview of our results can be found in Appendix A.

6 Conclusion

We showed that the current reference implementation of LMS with some required modifications achieves good performance results on a Cortex-M4. Further, we presented that the implemented modifications in XMSS lead to a significant speedup. Although the XMSS_SIMPLE version of XMSS is structurally very similar to LMS, LMS still achieves significantly better performance. Therefore, these performance differences are not based on properties of the schemes but rather on properties of the reference implementation. In addition, the currently discussed correct selection of safety margins for round-based symmetric cryptographic primitives is also considered in this work. In considering the fact that post-quantum approaches are more resource intensive than those currently in use, it is worth considering round-reduced and lightweight designs and concepts of hash functions in an embedded environment.

Our results based on reference implementations should merely give an idea on how practical the evaluated stateful schemes could be in an embedded environment.

Acknowledgment. The work presented in this paper has been partly funded by the German Federal Ministry of Education and Research (BMBF) under the project "QuantumRISC" (16KIS1034) [29].

A Further Results

A.1 Speed and Stack Memory

Speed is measured in CPU clock cycles. Stack memory (bytes) excludes the space required to store key material, messages, and in the case of hash pre-computation the intermediate state.

Table 9. Speed in clock cycles for XMSS and LMS for $h = 5$.

Design	Hash type	w	h	d	Key gen	Sign	Verify
XMSS_ROBUST	Gimli-Hash	16	5	1	1048850892	1063994437	17850167
XMSS_SIMPLE	Gimli-Hash	16	5	1	345097734	351135622	4843341
XMSS_SIMPLE+PRE	Gimli-Hash	16	5	1	35652023	341236863	4991976
LMS	Gimli-Hash	16	5	1	210439959	226186258	4601931
LMS	Gimli-Hash	256	5	1	1688484184	1808265632	38644523
XMSS_ROBUST	KECCAK-p[800, 22]	16	5	1	1162653236	1179847660	19384572
XMSS_SIMPLE	KECCAK-p[800, 22]	16	5	1	380333946	387149205	5183652
XMSS_SIMPLE+PRE	KECCAK-p[800, 22]	16	5	1	369894358	375718141	5838576
LMS	KECCAK-p[800, 22]	16	5	1	180384764	193651049	4108963
LMS	KECCAK-p[800, 22]	256	5	1	1445029158	1550179966	35721222
XMSS_ROBUST	KECCAK-p[800, 12]	16	5	1	699127232	709176591	11945544
XMSS_SIMPLE	KECCAK-p[800, 12]	16	5	1	230594112	234234392	3625308
XMSS_SIMPLE+PRE	KECCAK-p[800, 12]	16	5	1	**225063121**	**228715963**	**3444956**
LMS	KECCAK-p[800, 12]	16	5	1	**106406966**	**114348011**	**2325050**
LMS	KECCAK-p[800, 12]	256	5	1	848547880	909533298	20963781
XMSS_ROBUST	SHAKE256	16	5	1	1569880839	1593969977	25282729
XMSS_SIMPLE	SHAKE256	16	5	1	515089881	523679528	7643266
LMS	SHAKE256	16	5	1	482690432	519083330	10541350
LMS	SHAKE256	256	5	1	3882760965	4165192023	92414919
XMSS_ROBUST	SHA-256	16	5	1	738461396	747855715	13842083
XMSS_SIMPLE	SHA-256	16	5	1	243254582	247726301	3207473
XMSS_SIMPLE+PRE	SHA-256	16	5	1	237275019	241026688	3735483
LMS	SHA-256	16	5	1	117988963	126516806	2576515
LMS	SHA-256	256	5	1	941182086	1009663117	23252036

Table 10. Speed in clock cycles for XMSS and LMS for $h = 10$.

Design	Hash type	w	h	d	Key gen	Sign	Verify
XMSS_ROBUST	Gimli-Hash	16	10	1	33564541776	33577999022	19809084
XMSS_SIMPLE	Gimli-Hash	16	10	1	11043410042	11048855367	5499037
XMSS_SIMPLE+PRE	Gimli-Hash	16	10	1	10741004533	10746291644	5350407
LMS	Gimli-Hash	16	10	1	6732401742	6760950108	4735761
LMS	Gimli-Hash	256	10	1	54029816692	54252236257	41774596
XMSS_ROBUST	KECCAK-p[800, 22]	16	10	1	37206439782	37224119943	19141666
XMSS_SIMPLE	KECCAK-p[800, 22]	16	10	1	12156299702	12162295897	6023986
XMSS_SIMPLE+PRE	KECCAK-p[800, 22]	16	10	1	11836857885	11842845219	5754294
LMS	KECCAK-p[800, 22]	16	10	1	5770801259	5795821406	4082342

(continued)

Table 10. (*continued*)

Design	Hash type	w	h	d	Key gen	Sign	Verify
LMS	KECCAK-p[800, 22]	256	10	1	46239422162	46435056305	35772292
XMSS_ROBUST	KECCAK-p[800, 12]	16	10	1	22373006810	22383060343	12090021
XMSS_SIMPLE	KECCAK-p[800, 12]	16	10	1	7379129292	7382968494	**3460242**
XMSS_SIMPLE+PRE	KECCAK-p[800, 12]	16	10	1	**7202125901**	**7205678899**	3591854
LMS	KECCAK-p[800, 12]	16	10	1	**3403971523**	**3418764578**	**2445893**
LMS	KECCAK-p[800, 12]	256	10	1	27152481832	27267386528	20218474
XMSS_ROBUST	SHAKE256	16	10	1	50237912742	50263977292	23600738
XMSS_SIMPLE	SHAKE256	16	10	1	16483247517	16490948379	8606414
LMS	SHAKE256	16	10	1	15443962652	15509782696	10611902
LMS	SHAKE256	256	10	1	124246229161	124768084452	92485431
XMSS_ROBUST	SHA-256	16	10	1	23631706453	23642038600	13071813
XMSS_SIMPLE	SHA-256	16	10	1	7784507955	7788564498	3676358
XMSS_SIMPLE+PRE	SHA-256	16	10	1	7586158652	7589495830	4201201
LMS	SHA-256	16	10	1	3774882103	3791157911	2658884
LMS	SHA-256	256	10	1	30117102840	30244495755	22424231

Table 11. Speed in clock cycles for XMSS^{MT} and HSS for $h = 10$ with 2 layers.

Design	Hash type	w	h	d	Key gen	Sign	Verify
XMSS^{MT}ROBUST	Gimli-Hash	16	10	2	1048850426	2132881606	33496306
XMSS^{MT}SIMPLE	Gimli-Hash	16	10	2	345098305	701246056	10713254
XMSS^{MT}SIMPLE+PRE	Gimli-Hash	16	10	2	335652685	681899583	10564618
HSS	Gimli-Hash	16	10	2	210440071	478103461	5782431
HSS	Gimli-Hash	256	10	2	1688484230	3829196649	49449332
XMSS^{MT}ROBUST	KECCAK-p[800, 22]	16	10	2	1162646143	2359535503	41171355
XMSS^{MT}SIMPLE	KECCAK-p[800, 22]	16	10	2	379877664	772410324	11268039
XMSS^{MT}SIMPLE+PRE	KECCAK-p[800, 22]	16	10	2	369895178	751777787	11335455
HSS	KECCAK-p[800, 22]	16	10	2	180384846	410370171	4730609
HSS	KECCAK-p[800, 22]	256	10	2	1445029240	3283683503	41004008
XMSS^{MT}ROBUST	KECCAK-p[800, 12]	16	10	2	699115534	1420918009	23592244
XMSS^{MT}SIMPLE	KECCAK-p[800, 12]	16	10	2	230594929	468987052	**6745119**
XMSS^{MT}SIMPLE+PRE	KECCAK-p[800, 12]	16	10	2	**225063940**	**457454439**	6882114
HSS	KECCAK-p[800, 12]	16	10	2	**106407050**	**242305287**	**2781069**
HSS	KECCAK-p[800, 12]	256	10	2	848547971	1926719634	24063701
XMSS^{MT}ROBUST	SHAKE256	16	10	2	1569879645	3190288610	50539786
XMSS^{MT}SIMPLE	SHAKE256	16	10	2	515090566	1046239697	16371600
HSS	SHAKE256	16	10	2	482690353	1095714785	12421365
HSS	SHAKE256	256	10	2	3882761056	8805213845	117271251
XMSS^{MT}ROBUST	SHA-256	16	10	2	738439917	1498069037	27673083
XMSS^{MT}SIMPLE	SHA-256	16	10	2	243495342	494559179	7775017
XMSS^{MT}SIMPLE+PRE	SHA-256	16	10	2	237269504	481736648	7775063
HSS	SHA-256	16	10	2	117989078	268526114	3082339
HSS	SHA-256	256	10	2	941182212	2140447370	26690663

Table 12. Stack memory usage (bytes) for XMSS and LMS for $h \in \{5, 10\}$, and for XMSS^{MT} and HSS.

design	hash type	w	h	layer	key gen	sign	verify
XMSS_ROBUST	Gimli-Hash	16	5	1	3784	3832	3604
XMSS_SIMPLE	Gimli-Hash	16	5	1	**3712**	**3760**	**3556**
XMSS_SIMPLE+PRE	Gimli-Hash	16	5	1	3728	3776	3572
LMS	Gimli-Hash	16	5	1	**3528**	**2240**	**876**
LMS	Gimli-Hash	256	5	1	3528	2240	876
XMSS_ROBUST	KECCAK-$p[800, x]^{a}$	16	5	1	3896	3944	3720
XMSS_SIMPLE	KECCAK-$p[800, x]^{a}$	16	5	1	3824	3872	3672
XMSS_SIMPLE+PRE	KECCAK-$p[800, x]^{a}$	16	5	1	3840	3888	3688
LMS	KECCAK-$p[800, x]^{a}$	16	5	1	3644	2356	988
LMS	KECCAK-$p[800, x]^{a}$	256	5	1	3644	2356	988
XMSS_ROBUST	SHAKE256	16	5	1	4224	4272	4088
XMSS_SIMPLE	SHAKE256	16	5	1	4176	4200	4024
LMS	SHAKE256	16	5	1	3844	2532	1164
LMS	SHAKE256	256	5	1	3844	2532	1164
XMSS_ROBUST	SHA-256	16	5	1	4032	4080	3912
XMSS_SIMPLE	SHA-256	16	5	1	3984	4032	3832
XMSS_SIMPLE+PRE	SHA-256	16	5	1	3976	4016	3840
LMS	SHA-256	16	5	1	3764	2460	1044
LMS	SHA-256	256	5	1	3740	2460	1084
XMSS_ROBUST	Gimli-Hash	16	10	1	4128	4016	3604
XMSS_SIMPLE	Gimli-Hash	16	10	1	**4056**	**3944**	**3600**
XMSS_SIMPLE+PRE	Gimli-Hash	16	10	1	4072	3960	3616
LMS	Gimli-Hash	16	10	1	**3556**	**2268**	**832**
LMS	Gimli-Hash	256	10	1	4072	3960	876
XMSS_ROBUST	KECCAK-$p[800, x]^{a}$	16	10	1	4240	4128	3720
XMSS_SIMPLE	KECCAK-$p[800, x]^{a}$	16	10	1	4168	4056	3672
XMSS_SIMPLE+PRE	KECCAK-$p[800, x]^{a}$	16	10	1	4184	4072	3688
LMS	KECCAK-$p[800, x]^{a}$	16	10	1	3644	2356	988
LMS	KECCAK-$p[800, x]^{a}$	256	10	1	3668	2356	988
XMSS_ROBUST	SHAKE256	16	10	1	4592	4480	4088
XMSS_SIMPLE	SHAKE256	16	10	1	4520	4408	4040
LMS	SHAKE256	16	10	1	3860	2532	1164
LMS	SHAKE256	256	10	1	3844	2532	1164
XMSS_ROBUST	SHA-256	16	10	1	4400	4288	3896
XMSS_SIMPLE	SHA-256	16	10	1	4328	4216	3848
XMSS	SHA-256	16	10	1	4320	4208	3848
LMS	SHA-256	16	10	1	3780	2460	1044
LMS	SHA-256	256	10	1	3780	2460	1084
XMSS^{MT} ROBUST	Gimli-Hash	16	5	2	3560	3704	3604
XMSS^{MT} SIMPLE	Gimli-Hash	16	5	2	3512	**3656**	3600
XMSS^{MT} SIMPLE+PRE	Gimli-Hash	16	5	2	**3484**	3672	**3572**
HSS	Gimli-Hash	16	5	2	**3528**	**2268**	**936**
HSS	Gimli-Hash	256	5	2	3528	2268	980
XMSS^{MT} ROBUST	KECCAK-$p[800, x]^{a}$	16	5	2	3672	3816	3760
XMSS^{MT} SIMPLE	KECCAK-$p[800, x]^{a}$	16	5	2	3624	3768	3712
XMSS^{MT} SIMPLE+PRE	KECCAK-$p[800, x]^{a}$	16	5	2	3640	3784	3688
LMS	KECCAK-$p[800, x]^{a}$	16	5	2	3644	2364	1052
LMS	KECCAK-$p[800, x]^{a}$	256	5	2	3668	2364	1092
XMSS^{MT} ROBUST	SHAKE256	16	5	2	4024	4168	4112
XMSS^{MT} SIMPLE	SHAKE256	16	5	2	3976	4080	4024
LMS	SHAKE256	16	5	2	3844	2540	1268
LMS	SHAKE256	256	5	2	3844	2564	1268
XMSS^{MT} ROBUST	SHA-256	16	5	2	3832	3976	3896
XMSS^{MT} SIMPLE	SHA-256	16	5	2	3784	3920	3832
XMSS^{MT} SIMPLE+PRE	SHA-256	16	5	2	3776	3920	3840
HSS	SHA-256	16	5	2	3764	2468	1148
HSS	SHA-256	256	5	2	3740	2468	1188

^{a} Values valid for KECCAK-$p[800, 22]$ and KECCAK-$p[800, 12]$.

References

1. Keccak implementation overview version 3.0. https://keccak.team/obsolete/Keccak-implementation-3.0.pdf. Accessed 30 Apr 2019
2. Aumasson, J.P.: Too much crypto. Cryptology ePrint Archive, Report 2019/1492 (2019). https://eprint.iacr.org/2019/1492. (version: 20200103:101600)
3. Bernstein, D.J., et al.: SPHINCS+ - Submission to the NIST post-quantum project (2017). https://sphincs.org/data/sphincs+-specification.pdf
4. Bernstein, D.J., Duif, N., Lange, T., Schwabe, P., Yang, B.Y.: High-speed high-security signatures. J. Cryptogr. Eng. 2(2), 77–89 (2012). https://doi.org/10.1007/s13389-012-0027-1
5. Bernstein, D.J., Hülsing, A., Kölbl, S., Niederhagen, R., Rijneveld, J., Schwabe, P.: The SPHINCS+ signature framework. In: Wang, X.F., Katz J. (eds.) Conference on Computer and Communications Security (CCS 2019), pp. 17–43. ACM (2019, to appear)
6. Bernstein, D.J., et al.: GIMLI : a cross-platform permutation. In: Fischer, W., Homma, N. (eds.) CHES 2017. LNCS, vol. 10529, pp. 299–320. Springer, Cham (2017). https://doi.org/10.1007/978-3-319-66787-4_15
7. Bleichenbacher, D., Maurer, U.M.: Optimal tree-based one-time digital signature schemes. In: Puech, C., Reischuk, R. (eds.) STACS 1996. LNCS, vol. 1046, pp. 361–374. Springer, Heidelberg (1996). https://doi.org/10.1007/3-540-60922-9_30
8. Buchmann, J., Dahmen, E., Klintsevich, E., Okeya, K., Vuillaume, C.: Merkle signatures with virtually unlimited signature capacity. In: Katz, J., Yung, M. (eds.) ACNS 2007. LNCS, vol. 4521, pp. 31–45. Springer, Heidelberg (2007). https://doi.org/10.1007/978-3-540-72738-5_3
9. Buchmann, J., Dahmen, E., Schneider, M.: Merkle tree traversal revisited. In: Buchmann, J., Ding, J. (eds.) PQCrypto 2008. LNCS, vol. 5299, pp. 63–78. Springer, Heidelberg (2008). https://doi.org/10.1007/978-3-540-88403-3_5
10. Buchmann, J., Dahmen, E., Hülsing, A.: XMSS - a practical forward secure signature scheme based on minimal security assumptions. In: Yang, B.-Y. (ed.) PQCrypto 2011. LNCS, vol. 7071, pp. 117–129. Springer, Heidelberg (2011). https://doi.org/10.1007/978-3-642-25405-5_8
11. Cooper, D., Apon, D., Dang, Q., Davidson, M., Dworkin, M., Miller, C.: Recommendation for stateful hash-based signature schemes. Technical report, National Institute of Standards and Technology (2019)
12. Dahmen, E., Okeya, K., Takagi, T., Vuillaume, C.: Digital signatures out of second-preimage resistant hash functions. In: Buchmann, J., Ding, J. (eds.) PQCrypto 2008. LNCS, vol. 5299, pp. 109–123. Springer, Heidelberg (2008). https://doi.org/10.1007/978-3-540-88403-3_8
13. Dods, C., Smart, N.P., Stam, M.: Hash based digital signature schemes. In: Smart, N.P. (ed.) Cryptography and Coding 2005. LNCS, vol. 3796, pp. 96–115. Springer, Heidelberg (2005). https://doi.org/10.1007/11586821_8
14. ElGamal, T.: A public key cryptosystem and a signature scheme based on discrete logarithms. IEEE Trans. Inf. Theory 31(4), 469–472 (1985)
15. Guo, J., Liao, G., Liu, G., Liu, M., Qiao, K., Song, L.: Practical collision attacks against round-reduced SHA-3. J. Cryptol. 33(1), 228–270 (2019). https://doi.org/10.1007/s00145-019-09313-3
16. Hülsing, A.: W-OTS+ – shorter signatures for hash-based signature schemes. In: Youssef, A., Nitaj, A., Hassanien, A.E. (eds.) AFRICACRYPT 2013. LNCS, vol. 7918, pp. 173–188. Springer, Heidelberg (2013). https://doi.org/10.1007/978-3-642-38553-7_10
17. Hülsing, A., Busold, C., Buchmann, J.: Forward secure signatures on smart cards. In: Knudsen, L.R., Wu, H. (eds.) SAC 2012. LNCS, vol. 7707, pp. 66–80. Springer, Heidelberg (2013). https://doi.org/10.1007/978-3-642-35999-6_5

18. Hülsing, A., Butin, D., Gazdag, S., Rijneveld, J., Mohaisen, A.: XMSS: extended Merkle signature scheme. RFC **8391**, 1–74 (2018). https://doi.org/10.17487/RFC8391
19. Hülsing, A., Rijneveld, J., Schwabe, P.: ARMed SPHINCS. In: Cheng, C.-M., Chung, K.-M., Persiano, G., Yang, B.-Y. (eds.) PKC 2016. LNCS, vol. 9614, pp. 446–470. Springer, Heidelberg (2016). https://doi.org/10.1007/978-3-662-49384-7_17
20. Johnson, D., Menezes, A., Vanstone, S.: The elliptic curve digital signature algorithm (ECDSA). Int. J. Inf. Secur. **1**(1), 36–63 (2001). https://doi.org/10.1007/s102070100002
21. Kampanakis, P., Fluhrer, S.: LMS vs XMSS: comparison of two hash-based signature standards. IACR Cryptology ePrint Archive: Report 2017/349 (2017)
22. Kannwischer, M.J., Rijneveld, J., Schwabe, P., Stoffelen, K.: PQM4: post-quantum crypto library for the ARM Cortex-M4. https://github.com/mupq/pqm4
23. van der Laan, E., Poll, E., Rijneveld, J., de Ruiter, J., Schwabe, P., Verschuren, J.: Is Java card ready for hash-based signatures? In: Inomata, A., Yasuda, K. (eds.) IWSEC 2018. LNCS, vol. 11049, pp. 127–142. Springer, Cham (2018). https://doi.org/10.1007/978-3-319-97916-8_9
24. Lamport, L.: Constructing digital signatures from a one-way function. Technical report, Technical Report CSL-98, SRI International Palo Alto (1979)
25. McGrew, D., Kampanakis, P., Fluhrer, S., Gazdag, S.-L., Butin, D., Buchmann, J.: State management for hash-based signatures. In: Chen, L., McGrew, D., Mitchell, C. (eds.) SSR 2016. LNCS, vol. 10074, pp. 244–260. Springer, Cham (2016). https://doi.org/10.1007/978-3-319-49100-4_11
26. McGrew, D.A., Curcio, M., Fluhrer, S.R.: Leighton-Micali hash-based signatures. RFC **8554**, 1–61 (2019). https://doi.org/10.17487/RFC8554
27. Merkle, R.C.: A certified digital signature. In: Brassard, G. (ed.) CRYPTO 1989. LNCS, vol. 435, pp. 218–238. Springer, New York (1990). https://doi.org/10.1007/0-387-34805-0_21
28. National Institute of Standards and Technology: FIPS 202: Permutation-Based Hash and Extendable-Output Functions (2015)
29. QuantumRISC: QuantumRISC – Next Generation Cryptography for Embedded Systems (16KIS1034) (2020). https://www.quantumrisc.org/
30. Rivest, R.L., Shamir, A., Adleman, L.: A method for obtaining digital signatures and public-key cryptosystems. Commun. ACM **21**(2), 120–126 (1978)
31. Rohde, S., Eisenbarth, T., Dahmen, E., Buchmann, J., Paar, C.: Fast hash-based signatures on constrained devices. In: Grimaud, G., Standaert, F.-X. (eds.) CARDIS 2008. LNCS, vol. 5189, pp. 104–117. Springer, Heidelberg (2008). https://doi.org/10.1007/978-3-540-85893-5_8
32. Shor, P.W.: Polynomial-time algorithms for prime factorization and discrete logarithms on a quantum computer. SIAM Rev. **41**(2), 303–332 (1999)
33. Szydlo, M.: Merkle tree traversal in log space and time. In: Cachin, C., Camenisch, J.L. (eds.) EUROCRYPT 2004. LNCS, vol. 3027, pp. 541–554. Springer, Heidelberg (2004). https://doi.org/10.1007/978-3-540-24676-3_32
34. Wang, W., et al.: XMSS and Embedded Systems - XMSS Hardware Accelerators for RISC-V. Cryptology ePrint Archive, Report 2018/1225 (2018). https://ia.cr/2018/1225 (version: 20190522:113021)

Lattice Based Cryptography

Round Optimal Secure Multisignature Schemes from Lattice with Public Key Aggregation and Signature Compression

Meenakshi Kansal$^{(\boxtimes)}$ and Ratna Dutta

Indian Institute of Technology Kharagpur, Kharagpur, India
{kansal,ratna}@maths.iitkgp.ernet.in

Abstract. This paper presents the *first* construction for an efficient multisignature (MS) in the *lattice* setting, achieving *signature compression* and *public key aggregation* simultaneously with *single round* signature generation. The multisignature size in our construction is the same as that of a single signature. The verification of a multisignature can be performed with the aggregated public key and the verifier gets convinced that the message has been signed by all the signers. More positively, our aggregated public key size is also the same as that of a single signer.

Additionally, we extend our multisignature to an accountable subgroup multisignature (ASM) that permits any subset of potential signers to sign a common message with the property that the signature reveals the identities of the signers to any verifier. Our ASM scheme enjoys the same efficiency as that of our MS scheme without incurring any loss in the security reduction. We design our schemes in the plain public key model where there is no need to verify individual public keys. Our constructions are built in the standard lattice and are proven to be secure under the hardness of the short integer solution (SIS) problem in the random oracle model.

Keywords: Multisignature · Accountable subgroup multisignature · Public key aggregation · Lattice · Short integer solution

1 Introduction

Multisignature. In today's digital world, reducing bandwidth is a desirable and challenging task, especially for low energy devices. For instance, sensors and cell phones have restricted battery life. Multisignature is a powerful cryptographic primitive that helps to reduce the bandwidth taken by N signatures from $\mathcal{O}(N)$ to $\mathcal{O}(1)$. A multisignature scheme provides a group of signers the ability to sign collaboratively a common message in such a way that the size of the multisignature remains the same as that of a single signature and the verifier gets convinced that the message has been signed by all the signers. Multisignature becomes more efficient when the public keys can be aggregated to have size

© Springer Nature Switzerland AG 2020
A. Nitaj and A. Youssef (Eds.): AFRICACRYPT 2020, LNCS 12174, pp. 281–300, 2020.
https://doi.org/10.1007/978-3-030-51938-4_14

asymptotically equivalent to that of the public key of an individual signer and can be verified with the aggregated public key.

Accountable Subgroup Multisignature. Accountable subgroup multisignature, introduced by Micali et al. [17], enables a subset S of a set of potential signers G to jointly produce a multisignature on a given message such that it satisfies *flexibility* and *accountability*. Flexibility means that any subset S of G can sign the document and the verification is then upto the verifier whether the subset S is sufficient to approve the document (message) which is signed jointly by the signers in S. For instance, consider a case as taken in [17], when a company X signs a contract of a company Y. Suppose a subset S of X containing chief operating officer, chief financial officer and chief marketing officer sign the contract and sends the signature to Y. If Y prefers to have the signature of the chief executive officer then Y may reject the signature. Accountability refers to the fact that the set S is known to the verifier.

Application of Multisignature and Accountable Subgroup Multisignature. Multisignatures find applications in areas where storage and bandwidth costs are subject to minimization. Recently, multisignature has gained attention due to the popularity of the distributed applications that supports decentralize trust such as blockchain. Blockchain is a promising technology in the new financial era where digital currency like Bitcoin is the central currency with no intermediaries trusted parties such as bank to process transactions. Multisignature can reduce the size of blockchains [16]. In blockchain, a number of users agree (sign) on a specific message and put the signature to a block. It is desirable to aggregate these signatures into a single signature to reduce the size of the block. Furthermore, since all the public keys need to be written to the blockchain, it is also required to aggregate all the public keys into a single public key such that the aggregated public key has the same size as that of a single public key.

In Bitcoin, multisig is the hash of l public keys and a number k with $1 \leq k \leq l$. Multisignature can reduce the multisig Bitcoin address. The multisig in real life offers a feature that participation of all the l signers is not required to spend funds from the multisig address, but a sufficient number k of participation is sufficient. Accountable subgroup multisignature is a solution that allows a subset S of k signers take part in the signature generation instead of all l signers where $\binom{l}{k}$ is large [4]. The subset S may be decided by the verifier from the flexibility property of the accountable subgroup multisignature [17].

Our Contribution. As pointed by Micali et al. [17], many proposed multisignature schemes are vulnerable to rogue key attacks (for instance Harn [10], Li et al. [14]) or their security requires trusted generation of each key (for instance Ohta et al. [19], Ohta et al. [20]). They constructed the first multisignature scheme in [17] without trusted key generation. However, it requires an interactive initialization session among all the signers where each signer proves to the other signers that it possesses the secret key for the given public key. This model does not support dynamic setting and is not suited for large groups. Later, Boldyreva [3] introduced the concept of *knowledge of secret key* (KOSK) to overcome the interactive initialization round in the key registration process. The KOSK assumption utilizes *non-interactive zero knowledge proof of knowledge* (ZKPoK) involving heavy computation. Consequently, it is highly desirable to construct multisignature scheme in the plain public key model where the special registration of public key is not required.

Table 1. Comparative summary of multisignature resistant to rogue key attack and secure in the ROM

MS	Communication		R_s	Storage		Computation		Security assumption	Model
	|apk|	|msig|		|pk|	|sk|	Sign	Verify		
[4]	$\|G_2\|$	$\|G_1\|$	1	$\|G_2\|$	$\|\mathbb{Z}_q\|$	1E	2P	co-DH	PPK
[5]	$\|G\|$	$2\|G\| + 3\|\mathbb{Z}_q\|$	2	$\|G\| + 2\|\mathbb{Z}_q\|$	$\|\mathbb{Z}_q\|$	5E	6E	DL	PoP
[6]	$\|G\|$	$2\|G\|$	1	$\|G\| + 2\|\mathbb{Z}_q\|$	$\mathcal{O}((\log T)^2)$	4E	3P + 1E	l-wBDHI$_3^*$	PoP
[16]	$\|G\|$	$\|G\| + \|\mathbb{Z}_q\|$	3	$\|G\|$	$\|\mathbb{Z}_q\|$	2E	1E	DL	PPK
[7]	–	$\mathcal{O}(n)$	3	$\mathcal{O}(n)$	$\mathcal{O}(n)$	2PM	$(N+1)$PM	Ring-SIS	PPK
Ours	$\mathcal{O}(n^2)$	$\tilde{\mathcal{O}}(n^2)$	1	$\tilde{\mathcal{O}}(n^2)$	$\tilde{\mathcal{O}}(n^2)$	2MM	2MM	SIS	PPK

Table 2. Comparative summary of accountable subgroup multisignature resistant to rogue key attack and secure in the ROM

ASM	Communication		Rounds		Storage			Computation		Security assumption	Model
	|apk|	|msig|	R_s	R_g	|pk|	|sk|	|mk|	Sign	Verify		
[4]	$\|G_2\|$	$\|G_1\| + \|G_2\|$	1	1	$\|G_2\|$	$\|\mathbb{Z}_q\|$	$\|\mathbb{Z}_q\|$	1E	3P	ψ-co-DH	PPK
Ours	$\mathcal{O}(n^2)$	$\mathcal{O}(n^2)$	1	1	$\tilde{\mathcal{O}}(n^2)$	$\tilde{\mathcal{O}}(n^2)$	$\mathcal{O}(n^2)$	1MM	$(2+L)$MM	SIS	PPK

\|apk\|: size of the aggregated public key, \|msig\|: size of the compressed signature, \|pk\|: size of a public key, \|sk\|: size of a secret key, \|mk\|: size of group membership key, co-DH: computational Diffie-Hellman, DL: discrete logarithm, l-wBDHI$_3^*$: weak bilinear Diffie-Hellman inversion problem for type-3 pairings, SIS: short integer solution, G, G_1, G_2 are groups of prime order q, \|G\|: bit size of an element of the group G, T: max number of time periods in forward secrecy, λ: security parameter, $n = \mathcal{O}(\lambda)$, R_s: number of rounds in the signature generation algorithm, PPK: plain public key model, PoP: proof of possession, E: number of exponentiations, P: number of pairings, R_g: number of rounds in the group membership key generation algorithm, N: number of signers, L: size of the subgroup, Model: model to prevent rogue key attack, PM: number of polynomial multiplications, MM: number of matrix multiplications.

This paper constructs the *first* lattice based multisignature scheme supporting public key aggregation in the *plain public key model*. Specifically, we design a multisignature scheme MS and an accountable subgroup multisignature scheme ASM that exhibit signature compression as well as public key aggregation. The verifier only requires an aggregated public key instead of all the public keys to verify a multisignature. Each signer in MS takes part in the multisignature generation and uses public keys of all the participating signers. On the other hand, each signer in our ASM uses aggregated public key along with a group membership key to issue a multisignature. We require only a single round interactive protocol among all the participating signers in a group G to generate a group membership key which can be used to issue an accountable subgroup multisignature for any subset of signers $S \subseteq G$. Both our constructions achieve simulation based security in the plain public key model against adversaries making bounded number of queries to signatures and hashes. The security of our MS and ASM is derived under the hardness of *short integer solution* (SIS) problem following the security model of Boneh et al. [4].

As shown in Table 1, 2, our MS and ASM schemes are computationally efficient as we have used matrix addition and multiplication. These are linear operations and are very efficient compared to exponentiations and pairings used in [4–6,16]. Our construction enjoys the same round complexity as in the work of Boneh et al. [4]. Similar to the existing works, the multisignature size in our designs are independent of the number of signers involved. Since, our designs are based on lattice, the storage and communication overheads are more (see Table 1, 2) compared to the pairing based multisignature schemes [4–6,16].

The only lattice based multisignature scheme is by Bansarkhani et al. [7] which compresses signature but does not support public key aggregation. It is based on the signature scheme of Guneysu et al. [8,9]. The verifier requires public keys of all the signers. The scheme uses ideal lattice and chooses secret keys from polynomial rings where coefficients are bounded. The scheme is secure under the hardness of ring-SIS problem. It involves three rounds of communication between a signer and cosigner to generate a multisignature. In contrast, our scheme requires only one round of communication between a signer and the designated signer, is built on standard lattice, the verifier requires only an aggregated public key instead of public keys of all the signers and is proven to be secure under the hardness of SIS problem.

Overview of Our Technique. In our MS construction, a trusted third party generates the public parameter set $\mathcal{Y}$ that contains a public matrix $\mathbf{A} \in \mathbb{Z}_q^{n \times m}$ along with hash functions $H_0 : \{0,1\}^* \to \mathbb{Z}_q^{m \times n}$, $H_1 : \{0,1\}^* \to D_{\mathbb{Z}_q,\sigma}^{m \times n}$ and $H_2 : \{0,1\}^* \to D_{\mathbb{Z}_q,\sigma}^{n \times n}$ modeled as random oracles in the security proof. Here $D_{\mathbb{Z}_q,\sigma}^{k \times l} = \{\mathbf{M} \in \mathbb{Z}_q^{k \times l} : ||\mathbf{M}|| \leq \sigma\sqrt{k}\}$. Each user generates its own public-secret key pair (pk, sk). The signer i chooses a short matrix $\mathbf{V}_i \in \mathbb{Z}_q^{m \times m}$ with $||\mathbf{V}_i|| \leq \sigma\sqrt{m}$ as its secret key sk_i and sets its own public key as $\mathsf{pk}_i = \mathbf{Y}_i = \mathbf{A} \cdot \mathbf{V}_i \in \mathbb{Z}_q^{n \times m}$ where σ is specified in the public parameter set $\mathcal{Y}$. Note that finding $\mathsf{sk}_i = \mathbf{V}_i$ from $\mathsf{pk}_i = \mathbf{Y}_i$ is the SIS problem. As each signer generates its own public-secret key pair, the adversary is allowed to generate public and secret keys of users in the security game except for the challenged signer i^*. The adversary is given access to the signing oracle corresponding to the signer $i^* \in G$. Let G be a group of signers involved in generating a multisignature on a message M and $\mathcal{PK}$ is the set of public key of the signers in G who have participated in this multisignature generation. Each signer $i \in G$ uses its secret key sk_i together with the public keys of all the signers in G to generate a signature $\mathbf{T}_{i,M} = H_0(M, \mathcal{PK}) + \mathsf{sk}_i \cdot H_1(\mathsf{pk}_i, \mathcal{PK}) \cdot H_2(M)$ on M and sends $\mathbf{T}_{i,M}$ to the designated signer. The designated signer aggregates all the received signatures $\mathbf{T}_{i,M}$ into a multisignature $\mathbf{T}_M = \sum_{i \in G} \mathbf{T}_{i,M}$ and outputs $\mathsf{msig}_{\mathcal{PK},M} = (\mathbf{T}_M, \mathsf{pkag}_{\mathcal{PK}}, G, M)$. Anyone can aggregate the public keys in $\mathcal{PK}$ into an aggregated public key

$\mathsf{pkag}_{\mathcal{PK}} = \sum_{i \in G} \mathsf{pk}_i \cdot H_1(\mathsf{pk}_i, \mathcal{PK}) \in \mathbb{Z}_q^{n \times n}$. A verifier verifies a multisignature $\mathsf{msig}_{\mathcal{PK},M} = (\mathbf{T}_M, \mathsf{pkag}_{\mathcal{PK}}, G, M)$ using the aggregated public key $\mathsf{pkag}_{\mathcal{PK}}$. It outputs 1 if $\mathbf{A} \cdot \mathbf{T}_M = \mathbf{A} \cdot |G| \cdot H_0(M, \mathcal{PK}) + \mathsf{pkag}_{\mathcal{PK}} \cdot H_2(M)$ and $||\mathbf{T}_M|| \leq |G| \cdot (||H_0(M, \mathcal{PK})|| + \sigma^3 m \sqrt{n})$. Otherwise, it outputs 0.

While the adversary makes a signature generation query, the simulator simulates the signature for the challenged signer i^*. The ranges of H_1 and H_2 have been specified with bounds to preserve the security. While simulating the signature $\mathbf{T}_{i^*,M}$ for i^* without knowing its secret key, the simulator calls for $H_1(\mathsf{pk}_{i^*}, \mathcal{PK})$ query, $H_2(M)$ query, chooses $\mathbf{T}_{i^*,M} \in \mathbb{Z}_q^{n \times m}$ and finds the value of $H_0(M, \mathcal{PK})$ satisfying the equation $\mathbf{A} \cdot \mathbf{T}_{i^*,M} = \mathbf{A} \cdot H_0(M, \mathcal{PK}) + \mathsf{pk}_{i^*} \cdot H_1(\mathsf{pk}_{i^*}, \mathcal{PK}) \cdot H_2(M)$. As there is no bound restriction on the range of H_0, one can find $H_0(M, \mathcal{PK})$ using the Gauss elimination method or any other linear algebra method. Using the generalized forking lemma, we finally show that if the adversary is able to forge a multisignature, then the simulator finds $\mathbf{V}^* \in \mathbb{Z}_q^{m \times m}$ satisfying $\mathbf{A} \cdot \mathbf{V}^* = 0 \bmod q$ with $||\mathbf{V}^*|| \leq \sigma \sqrt{m}$. Thus the simulator solves an instance of SIS problem and we have the following theorem.

Theorem 1 *(Informal). The scheme* MS *is unforgeable in the random oracle model if the* SIS *problem is hard.*

The public parameter set $\mathcal{Y}$ in our ASM scheme uses a matrix $\mathbf{A} \in \mathbb{Z}_q^{n \times m}$ and hash functions $H_0 : \{0,1\}^* \rightarrow \mathbb{Z}_q^{m \times n}$, $H_1 : \{0,1\}^* \rightarrow D_{\mathbb{Z}_q,\sigma}^{m \times n}$, $H_2 : \{0,1\}^* \rightarrow \mathbb{Z}_q^{n \times n}$ and $H_3 : \{0,1\}^* \rightarrow D_{\mathbb{Z}_q,\sigma}^{n \times n}$ where H_0, H_1, H_2 are modeled as random oracles in the security proof. The key generation and the key aggregation are performed as in our MS scheme. All the members in a group of signers G take part in the group membership key protocol. Let $\mathcal{PK}$ be the set of public keys of the signers in G. Each member $i \in G$ uses its secret key sk_i together with the public keys of other signers in G, computes $\mathbf{M}_{j,i} = H_2(\mathsf{pkag}_{\mathcal{PK}}, j) + \mathsf{sk}_i \cdot H_1(\mathsf{pk}_i, \mathcal{PK}) \cdot H_3(j)$ for all $j \in G$ and sends $\mathbf{M}_{j,i}$ to all $j \in G$ parallely where $\mathsf{pkag}_{\mathcal{PK}} = \sum_{i \in G} \mathsf{pk}_i \cdot H_1(\mathsf{pk}_i, \mathcal{PK}) \in \mathbb{Z}_q^{n \times n}$. After receiving $\mathbf{M}_{i,j}$ from all signers $j \in G$, the i-th signer generates its group membership key $\mathsf{mk}_{i,\mathcal{PK}} = \sum_{j \in G} \mathbf{M}_{i,j}$. Let S be a subset of G and L be the set of all public keys in S. Each signer $i \in S$ using its secret key sk_i together with the public keys of all the signers in G computes $\mathbf{T}_{i,M} = \mathsf{sk}_i \cdot H_0(\mathsf{pkag}_{\mathcal{PK}}, M) + \mathsf{mk}_{i,\mathcal{PK}}$ and sends $\mathbf{T}_{i,M}$ to the designated signer. The designated signer aggregates all the received signatures $\mathbf{T}_{i,M}$ into a multisignature $\mathbf{T}_M = \sum_{i \in G} \mathbf{T}_{i,M}$ and outputs $\mathsf{accmsig}_{L,M} = (\mathbf{T}_M, \mathsf{spkag}_L, \mathsf{pkag}_{\mathcal{PK}}, G, M, S)$ where $\mathsf{spkag}_L = \sum_{i \in S} \mathsf{pk}_i \cdot H_0(\mathsf{pkag}_{\mathcal{PK}}, M)$ is the aggregated subgroup public key. The verifier using the aggregated public key $\mathsf{pkag}_{\mathcal{PK}}$ and aggregated subgroup public key spkag_L, outputs 1 if $\mathbf{A} \cdot \mathbf{T}_M = \mathsf{spkag}_L + |G| \cdot \sum_{i \in S} \mathbf{A} \cdot H_2(\mathsf{pkag}_{\mathcal{PK}}, i) + \mathsf{pkag}_{\mathcal{PK}} \cdot \sum_{i \in S} H_3(i)$ and $||\mathbf{T}_M|| \leq |S| \cdot \sigma \sqrt{m} \cdot H_0(\mathsf{pkag}_{\mathcal{PK}}, M) + |G| \cdot \max_{i \in S} ||H_2(\mathsf{pkag}_{\mathcal{PK}}, i)|| + |S| \cdot |G| \cdot \sigma^3 m \sqrt{n}$. Otherwise, it outputs 0.

The adversary is given access to the group membership key query for the challenged signer $i^* \in G$. The simulator and the adversary take part in the group membership key generation protocol where the simulator simulates the group membership key for the challenged signer i^*. The ranges of H_1 and H_3 have been specified with bounds to preserve the security. While simulating $\mathbf{M}_{j,i^*}$ for i^* without knowing its secret key, the simulator chooses $\mathbf{M}_{j,i^*}$ such that $||\mathbf{M}_{j,i^*}|| \leq \sigma\sqrt{m}$ for each $j \in G$, queries to $H_1(\mathsf{pk}_j, \mathcal{PK})$ oracle for each $j \in G$, finds $H_2(\mathsf{pkag}_{\mathcal{PK}}, j)$ satisfying $\mathbf{A} \cdot \mathbf{M}_{j,i^*} = \mathbf{A} \cdot H_2(\mathsf{pkag}_{\mathcal{PK}}, j) + \mathbf{Y}_{i^*} \cdot H_1(\mathsf{pk}_{i^*}, \mathcal{PK}) \cdot H_3(j)$. There is no bound on the range of H_2 and thus can be found using any linear algebra method. The adversary is also given signature oracle to query for the challenged signer $i^* \in G$. The simulator models the random oracle H_0 to simulate the signature for the challenged signer i^*. Finally, we apply generalized forking lemma to show that forging an accountable subgroup multisignature yields a solution to an SIS instance and proved the following theorem.

Theorem 2 *(Informal). The scheme* ASM *is unforgeable in the random oracle model if the* SIS *problem is hard.*

Related Work. The first construction of multisignature was presented by Itakura and Nakamura [12]. Multisignature schemes require homomorphic properties of arithmetic operations involved in standard signatures. Unfortunately, the same homomorphic properties that permits aggregation of signatures into multisignatures can enable a rogue key attack on such schemes. Infact, the multisignature schemes in early literature [10,11,13,14,18–20] were broken mostly by mounting a rogue-key-attack. In this attack, a cheating group member sets its public key as a function of the public key of an honest signer of the group enabling it to forge multisignature easily. Many solutions were proposed to prevent rogue key attack like *key registration model, knowledge of secret key* (KOSK) assumption, *proof of possession* (PoP) assumption etc. These approaches have higher complexity and are unrealistic assumptions on the public key infrastructure (PKI). The key registration model is parameterized by the key registration and the adversarial behaviour is restricted by the security game based on the successful or unsuccessful registration. In this model, the client registers with the certifying authority through the key registration protocol and the adversary can access the key registration oracle. Okamoto [19] and Micali [17] developed proper security framework for multisignature. They also built constructions for multisignatures and analyzed the security in the respective proposed models. In contrast to [19], the security model of [17] addresses attacks in the key generation phase. To prevent rogue key attack, Micali et al. [17] allows all the signers to engage in an interactive protocol to generate public and secret keys. This scheme is not dynamic in the sense that all the signers require to be fixed at the setup phase.

The constructions in Boldyreva et al. [3], Lu et al. [15], on the other hand, use KOSK assumption to achieve security against rogue key attack. When the adversary provides a public key for a signer, it is required to provide a matching secret key. In KOSK setting, a user has to prove the knowledge of secret key to the certifying authority during public key registration. However, PKI has yet not realized the KOSK assumption. Bellare and Neven [2] pointed out that a scheme is secure under the KOSK assumption face the upgradation of existing PKI as it would require client and certifying authority to possess *zero knowledge proof of knowledge* (ZKPoK) with *extraction guarantees* in *fully concurrent settings*. The utilization of non interactive zero knowledge proof of knowledge requires heavy computation.

To avoid the KOSK assumption for preventing rogue key attack, Ristenpart and Yilek [21] modified the multisignature scheme of Boldyreva et al. [3] and proved it is secure under the PoP assumption. Unlike KOSK, the PoP setting does not ask to prove the knowledge of secret key, but it attests that a client has the access to the public and secret key pair. One of the simplest ways to achieve PoP in signature schemes is by sending the signature on the message requested by the certifying authority.

Bellare and Neven [2] had overcome the KOSK assumption and proposed a multisignature scheme in the plain public key model. In plain public key model, the users do not need to prove the knowledge or possession of their secret keys. The multisignature scheme of Micali et al. [17] is the first scheme that is secure in the plain public key model. Downfall of this scheme is that the set of the potential signers becomes static once the key setup phase is done. On the other hand, the multisignature of Bellare and Neven [2] does not require a dedicated key setup algorithm and is secure in the plain public key model. However, this scheme requires several rounds of communication between the signers.

Recently, many multisignature schemes [4–6,16] have been proposed. The scheme by Boneh et al. [4] is the first compact multisignature scheme secure under the computational co-Diffie-Hellman problem with both signature compression and public key aggregation. Further, they have constructed the first short accountable subgroup multisignature scheme under the hardness of computational Ψ-co-Diffie-Hellman problem in the *random oracle model* (ROM). Drijvers et al. [6] proposed a construction for pairing based multisignature secure under a variant of the bilinear Diffie-Hellman inversion problem in the ROM. The work in Drijvers et al. [5] pointed out serious issues in the two round multisignature schemes without pairings and presented a variant of Bagherzandi et al. [1] scheme secure under the discrete logarithm assumption in the ROM. Maxwell [16] gave the first multisignature scheme secure in the palin public key model. It is based on Schnorr signature and is secure under the hardness of discrete logarithm problem. All the aforementioned schemes are secure only on the classical machine and are not quantum computer resistant. The construction of Bansarkhani et al. [7] is the only multisignature scheme that is secure under the hardness of computational problems from lattice that are not succeptiable to quantum attacks. The scheme is secure in the ROM under the ring-SIS problem. However, the scheme is interactive involving three rounds during the signature generation and does not support public key aggregation.

Drijvers et al. [6] proposed a multisignature scheme with forward secrecy to address adaptive corruption. The adversary can corrupt committee members after they have certified (signed) a message and use their signing keys to certify (sign) a different message. Forward secure multisignatures prevent this attack and enables signers to update their secret keys over time without changing their respective verification keys.

2 Preliminaries

Notation. We provide below some of the notation that will be used: $\mathbf{a} \in \Delta^n$ means that $\mathbf{a}$ is a column vector of dimension $n \times 1$ with elements from the set Δ. For a vector $\mathbf{x} = (x_1, x_2, \ldots, x_n) \in \Delta^n$, $||\mathbf{x}|| = \sqrt{x_1^2 + \ldots + x_n^2}$ denotes the Euclidean norm. Let $\mathbf{X} = (\mathbf{x}_1, \mathbf{x}_2, \ldots, \mathbf{x}_n)$ be a matrix with n columns in Δ^m then $||\mathbf{X}|| = \max_{1 \le k \le n} ||\mathbf{x}_k||$. We say that a function f is negligible in λ if $f = \lambda^{-\omega(1)}$.

Definition 1 (Lattice). *A full rank matrix $\mathbf{B} \in \mathbb{Z}_q^{n \times m}$ is a basis of an m dimensional lattice Λ if $\Lambda = \{\mathbf{y} \in \mathbb{Z}^m \mid \exists \mathbf{x} \in \mathbb{Z}^m, \mathbf{y} = \mathbf{B} \cdot \mathbf{x}\}$. For any integer $q \ge 2$, a matrix $\mathbf{A} \in \mathbb{Z}_q^{n \times m}$ and a vector $\mathbf{u} \in \mathbb{Z}_q^n$ define $\Lambda_q^\perp(\mathbf{A}) = \{\mathbf{v} \in \mathbb{Z}_q^m \mid \mathbf{A} \cdot \mathbf{v} = \mathbf{0} \bmod q\}$ and $\Lambda_q^{\mathbf{u}}(\mathbf{A}) = \{\mathbf{v} \in \mathbb{Z}_q^m \mid \mathbf{A} \cdot \mathbf{v} = \mathbf{u} \bmod q\}$.*

Definition 2 (Discrete Gaussian Distribution). *The discrete Gaussian distribution over a lattice Λ with center $\mathbf{c} \in \mathbb{R}^m$ and parameter σ is $D_{\Lambda,\sigma,\mathbf{c}}(\mathbf{y}) = \frac{\rho_{\sigma,\mathbf{c}}(\mathbf{y})}{\rho_{\sigma,\mathbf{c}}(\Lambda)}$ for all $\mathbf{y} \in \Lambda$. Here $\rho_{\sigma,\mathbf{c}}(\mathbf{y}) = exp(-\pi \frac{||\mathbf{y}-\mathbf{c}||^2}{\sigma^2})$ and $\rho_{\sigma,\mathbf{c}}(\Lambda) = \sum_{\mathbf{y} \in \Lambda} \rho_{\sigma,\mathbf{c}}(\mathbf{y})$. If $\mathbf{c} = 0$, we simply denote it by $D_{\Lambda,\sigma}$.*

Definition 3 (Short Integer Solution (SIS) Problem). *Given a uniformly random matrix $\mathbf{A} \in \mathbb{Z}_q^{n \times m}$ and a real number β, the SIS problem is to find a vector $\mathbf{v} \in \mathbb{Z}_q^m$ such that $\mathbf{A} \cdot \mathbf{v} = \mathbf{0} \bmod q$ and $||\mathbf{v}|| \le \beta$.*

Generalized Forking Lemma [5]. Let us consider an algorithm $\mathcal{A}$ that takes $\mathsf{in}_\mathcal{A}$ as input and interacts with a random oracle $\mathcal{O}$. Let $\Omega = \{r \mid r = (\hat{r}, h_1, h_2, \ldots, h_{q_H})\}$ be the randomness space and let $r|_j = (h_1, h_2, \ldots, h_{j-1})$. Here $\hat{r}$ is the random tape of $\mathcal{A}$, q_H is the maximum allowable number of random oracle queries and h_j is the response to j-th random oracle query. The execution of $\mathcal{A}$ is termed success if it outputs $(I, \{\mathsf{out}_i\}_{i \in I})$ where I is a non empty subset of $\{1, 2, \ldots, q_H\}$. The input $\mathsf{in}_\mathcal{A}$ is generated by the input generator IG. The working of the algorithm $\mathcal{FL}_\mathcal{A}$ is explained below in Algorithm 1. We say that $\mathcal{FL}_\mathcal{A}$ succeeds if it does not output *fail*.

Lemma 1 (Generalized Forking Lemma [5]). *Let IG be a randomized input generation algorithm and $\mathcal{A}$ be a randomized algorithm running in time τ with access to a random oracle $\mathcal{O}$ such that $\mathcal{A}$ succeeds with probability ϵ. If $q > \frac{8nq_H}{\epsilon}$, then $\mathcal{FL}_\mathcal{A}(\mathsf{in}_\mathcal{A})$ runs in time atmost $\tau \cdot \frac{8n^2 q_H}{\epsilon} \cdot ln(\frac{8n}{\epsilon})$ and succeeds with probability atleast $\frac{\epsilon}{8}$, where the probability is over the choice of $\mathsf{in}_\mathcal{A} \leftarrow$ IG and over the coins of $\mathcal{FL}_\mathcal{A}$.*

Algorithm 1. Generalized Forking Algorithm $\mathcal{FL}_{\mathcal{A}}(\mathsf{in}_{\mathcal{A}})$

1: $(I, \{\mathsf{out}_i\}_{i \in I}, aux) \leftarrow \mathcal{A}^{\mathcal{O}}(\mathsf{in}_{\mathcal{A}}, r)$ where $r = (\hat{r}h_1, h_2, \ldots, h_{q_H})$;
2: **if** $I = \emptyset$ **then**
3:     output *fail*;
4: **else**
5:     Aux $\leftarrow aux$;
6:     Let $I = \{i_1, i_2, \ldots, i_n\}$ such that $i_1 \le i_2 \le \ldots \le i_n$;
7:     **for** $t = 1$ to n **do**
8:         $success_t \leftarrow 0$; $k_t \leftarrow 0$; $k_{max} \leftarrow \frac{8nq_H}{\epsilon} \cdot ln(\frac{8n}{\epsilon})$;
9:         **repeat**
10:             $r'' \in \Omega$ such that $r''|_{i_t} = r|_{i_t}$;
11:             Let $r'' = (\hat{r}, h_1, h_2, \ldots, h_{i_t-1}, h''_{i_t}, \ldots, h''_{q_H})$; (Note that $h''_j \ne h_j$ for $j = i_t$ to q_H)
12:             $(I'', \{\mathsf{out}''_i\}_{i \in I''}, aux) \leftarrow \mathcal{A}^{\mathcal{O}}(\mathsf{in}_{\mathcal{A}}, r'')$;
13:             Aux $\leftarrow$ Aux $\cup aux$;
14:             **if** $(h''_{i_t} \ne h_{i_t}$ and $I'' \ne \emptyset$ and $i_t \in I'')$ **then**
15:                 $\mathsf{out}'_{i_t} \leftarrow \mathsf{out}''_{i_t}$; $success_t \leftarrow 1$;
16:             **end if**
17:             $k_t \leftarrow k_t + 1$;
18:         **until** $success_t = 1$ or $k_t > k_{max}$
19:     **end for**
20:     **if** $(success_t = 1$ for all $t = 1, 2, \ldots, n)$ **then**
21:         **output** $(I, \{\mathsf{out}_i\}_{i \in I}, \{\mathsf{out}'_i\}_{i \in I}, \mathsf{Aux})$
22:     **else**
23:         output *fail*
24:     **end if**
25: **end if**

2.1   Multisignature - Syntax, Definition and Security Model

Syntax of Multisignature. The multisignature scheme allows a group of signers with public keys $\{\mathsf{pk}_{i_1}, \mathsf{pk}_{i_2}, \ldots, \mathsf{pk}_{i_t}\}$ to issue a multisignature 'msig' on a message M in such a way that the verifier agrees that all the N signers have signed the message M. Let there be a designated signer who combines all the signatures of the signers into a single multisignature. The designated signer may be one of the signers or an external party.

At high level, we define a multisignature scheme $\mathsf{MS} = \{\mathsf{pg}, \mathsf{kg}, \mathsf{kag}, \mathsf{sg}, \mathsf{vrf}\}$ as consisting of *parameter generation algorithm* pg, *key generation algorithm* kg and *key aggregation algorithm* kag together with an interactive *signature generation* protocol sg and a deterministic *verification* algorithm vrf. A trusted third party, called the *key generation center* (KGC), generates the public parameter set $\mathcal{Y} \leftarrow \mathsf{MS}.\mathsf{pg}$. A user generates its public-secret key pair $(\mathsf{pk}, \mathsf{sk}) \leftarrow \mathsf{MS}.\mathsf{kg}$. The public keys are made public while the secret keys are kept secret to the users. The signer i uses secret key sk_i to generate signature $\mathbf{T}_{i,M}$ on a message M and sends $\mathbf{T}_{i,M}$ to the *"designated signer"*. The designated signer aggregates all the received signatures $\mathbf{T}_{i,M}$ on the message M into a multisignature $\mathsf{msig}_{\mathcal{PK},M}$. Here $\mathcal{PK}$ is the set of public key of the signers participated in this multisignature generation. The key aggregation algorithm $\mathsf{MS}.\mathsf{kag}$ can be run by anyone to aggregate the public keys in a set $\mathcal{PK}$ into a single public key $\mathsf{pkag}_{\mathcal{PK}}$. The verifier using the aggregated public key $\mathsf{pkag}_{\mathcal{PK}}$, runs the algorithm $\mathsf{MS}.\mathsf{vrf}$ and returns 0, indicating the multisignature $\mathsf{msig}_{\mathcal{PK},M}$ is not properly generated or 1, assuring that $\mathsf{msig}_{\mathcal{PK},M}$ is correct. More concretely, we have the following.

- MS.pg(1^λ) → $\mathcal{Y}$. It is a probabilistic polynomial time (PPT) algorithm run on a security parameter λ and outputs the public parameter set $\mathcal{Y}$.
- MS.kg($\mathcal{Y}, i$) → ($\mathsf{pk}_i, \mathsf{sk}_i$). For each user i, this PPT algorithm returns the public and secret key pair ($\mathsf{pk}_i, \mathsf{sk}_i$) on input the user i and the public parameter set $\mathcal{Y}$. The public key pk_i is made public while the secret key sk_i is kept secret to the user.
- MS.kag($\mathcal{Y}, \mathcal{PK}$) → $\mathsf{pkag}_{\mathcal{PK}}$. Let $\mathcal{PK}$ be the set of public keys of signers. This is a deterministic algorithm and it aggregates the public keys in $\mathcal{PK}$ into a single public key $\mathsf{pkag}_{\mathcal{PK}}$. It outputs the aggregated public key $\mathsf{pkag}_{\mathcal{PK}}$ which asymptotically has the same size as a single public key.
- MS.sg($\mathcal{Y}, \mathcal{PK}, \mathcal{SK}, M$) → $\mathsf{msig}_{\mathcal{PK},M}$. With input the public parameter set $\mathcal{Y}$, the set of public and secret keys ($\mathcal{PK}, \mathcal{SK}$) of the signers and a message M, this single round protocol executes as follows. Let $\mathcal{PK} = \{\mathsf{pk}_{i_1}, \mathsf{pk}_{i_2}, \ldots, \mathsf{pk}_{i_l}\}$, $\mathcal{SK} = \{\mathsf{sk}_{i_1}, \mathsf{sk}_{i_2}, \ldots, \mathsf{sk}_{i_l}\}$ and $I_{\mathcal{PK}} = \{i_1, i_2, \ldots, i_l\}$. The signer $i \in I_{\mathcal{PK}}$ uses $\mathcal{PK}$ along with its secret key sk_i to generate a signature $\mathbf{T}_{i,M}$ on M and sends $\mathbf{T}_{i,M}$ to the designated signer. The designated signer aggregates all the signatures $\mathbf{T}_{i,M}, i \in I_{\mathcal{PK}}$ on M into a single multisignature $\mathsf{msig}_{\mathcal{PK},M}$.
- MS.vrf($\mathcal{Y}, \mathsf{msig}_{\mathcal{PK},M}$) → (0 or 1). On input the public parameter set $\mathcal{Y}$, a multisignature $\mathsf{msig}_{\mathcal{PK},M}$, this deterministic algorithm returns 1 if $\mathsf{msig}_{\mathcal{PK},M}$ is valid. Otherwise, it returns 0.

Completeness. A multisignature scheme should satisfy completeness. That is, for any $\mathcal{Y} \leftarrow$ MS.pg(1^λ), for any N, if we have ($\mathsf{pk}_i, \mathsf{sk}_i$) $\leftarrow$ MS.kg($\mathcal{Y}, i$) for $i = 1, 2, \ldots, N$, for any message M and for any set of public keys $\mathcal{PK} = \{\mathsf{pk}_1, \mathsf{pk}_2, \ldots, \mathsf{pk}_N\}$ with corresponding set of secret keys $\mathcal{SK} = \{\mathsf{sk}_1, \mathsf{sk}_2, \ldots, \mathsf{sk}_N\}$, if $\mathsf{msig}_{\mathcal{PK},M} \leftarrow$ MS.sg($\mathcal{Y}, \mathcal{PK}, \mathcal{SK}, M$) then MS.vrf($\mathcal{Y}, \mathsf{msig}_{\mathcal{PK},M}$) outputs 1.

Security Under Unforgeability. The unforgeability experiment $\mathsf{Exp}_{\mathcal{F}}^{\mathsf{unforg}}(\lambda)$ between a simulator $\mathcal{S}$ and a forger $\mathcal{F}$ is described in Fig. 1 following the model of Boneh et al. [4] that considers the infeasibility to forge multisignature with atleast one honest signer. The forger has given polynomially many access to the signature queries on any message M with any set of public keys $\mathcal{PK}$.

Definition 4. *We say that a multisignature is unforgeable if* $\mathsf{Adv}_{\mathcal{F}}^{\mathsf{unforg}}(\lambda) = \Pr[\mathsf{Exp}_{\mathcal{F}}^{\mathsf{unforg}}(\lambda) = 1] \leq \mathsf{negl}(\lambda)$ *for every PPT adversary* $\mathcal{F}$ *in the experiment* $\mathsf{Exp}_{\mathcal{F}}^{\mathsf{unforg}}(\lambda)$ *defined in Fig. 1 where* $\mathsf{negl}(\lambda)$ *is a negligible function in* λ.

3   The MS

Our multisignature MS = (pg, kg, kag, sg, vrf) works as follows.

- MS.pg(1^λ) → $\mathcal{Y}$. A trusted third party, called key generation center (KGC), generates the system parameters $\mathcal{Y} \leftarrow (n, q, m, \sigma, H_0, H_1, H_2, \mathbf{A})$.
    - choose n of size $\mathcal{O}(\lambda)$, q of size $\mathcal{O}(n^3)$ and $m \geq 2n\lceil \log q \rceil$,
    - pick the standard deviation σ of the discrete Gaussian distribution $D_{\Lambda,\sigma}$ of size $\Omega(\sqrt{n \log q} \log n)$,

1. The simulator $\mathcal{S}$ generates system parameters $\mathcal{Y}$ and a challenge public key pk_{i^*} for user i^*. The simulator $\mathcal{S}$ runs the forger $\mathcal{F}$ on $(\mathcal{Y}, \mathsf{pk}_{i^*})$.
2. The forger $\mathcal{F}$ is allowed to make signature queries to $\mathcal{S}$ on $(M_l, \mathcal{PK}_l)$, $1 \leq l \leq q_s$ where M_l is a message and $\mathcal{PK}_l$ is a set of public keys with $\mathsf{pk}_{i^*} \in \mathcal{PK}_l$ i.e., $\mathcal{F}$ has access to the oracle $O^{(\mathcal{Y}, \cdot, \cdot, \cdot)}$ that simulates the honest signer i^* with the public keys in $\mathcal{PK}_l$ and produce a signature $\mathbf{T}_{i^*, M}$ on M.
3. Finally, $\mathcal{F}$ outputs a forgery $\mathsf{msig}^*_{\mathcal{PK}, M}$ on a message M for a set of public keys $\mathcal{PK}$.
4. The simulator $\mathcal{S}$ returns 1 if the following conditions hold:
   (a) $\mathsf{MS.vrf}(\mathcal{Y}, \mathsf{msig}^*_{\mathcal{PK}, M}) \rightarrow 1$,
   (b) $\mathsf{pk}_{i^*} \in \mathcal{PK}$.
   (c) $M \neq M_l$ for $1 \leq l \leq q_s$.
   Otherwise, $\mathcal{S}$ returns 0.
5. The forger $\mathcal{F}$ wins the game if $\mathcal{S}$ returns 1.

Fig. 1. Unforgeability game $\mathsf{Exp}^{\mathsf{unforg}}_{\mathcal{F}}(\lambda)$

- select a matrix $\mathbf{A} \in \mathbb{Z}_q^{n \times m}$ over $\mathbb{Z}_q$ and sample cryptographically secure hash functions $H_0 : \{0,1\}^* \rightarrow \mathbb{Z}_q^{m \times n}$, $H_1 : \{0,1\}^* \rightarrow D^{m \times n}_{\mathbb{Z}_q, \sigma}$ and $H_2 : \{0,1\}^* \rightarrow D^{n \times n}_{\mathbb{Z}_q, \sigma}$ where $D^{k \times l}_{\mathbb{Z}_q, \sigma} = \{\mathbf{M} \in \mathbb{Z}_q^{k \times l} : ||\mathbf{M}|| \leq \sigma \sqrt{k}\}$.

- $\mathsf{MS.kg}(\mathcal{Y}, i) \rightarrow (\mathsf{pk}_i, \mathsf{sk}_i)$. The signer i runs this algorithm using $\mathcal{Y}$ to generate its own public and secret key pair $(\mathsf{pk}_i, \mathsf{sk}_i)$ by performing the following steps.
  - choose a short matrix $\mathbf{V}_i \in D^{m \times m}_{\mathbb{Z}_q, \sigma}$ and compute $\mathbf{Y}_i = \mathbf{A} \cdot \mathbf{V}_i \bmod q \in \mathbb{Z}_q^{n \times m}$,
  - set the public key $\mathsf{pk}_i = \mathbf{Y}_i \in \mathbb{Z}_q^{n \times m}$ and secret key $\mathsf{sk}_i = \mathbf{V}_i \in D^{m \times m}_{\mathbb{Z}_q, \sigma}$.
  The public key pk_i is made public and the secret key sk_i is kept secret to the signer i.

- $\mathsf{MS.kag}(\mathcal{Y}, \mathcal{PK}) \rightarrow \mathsf{pkag}_{\mathcal{PK}}$. This deterministic algorithm outputs the aggregated public key $\mathsf{pkag}_{\mathcal{PK}} = \sum_{i \in I_{\mathcal{PK}}} \mathsf{pk}_i \cdot H_1(\mathsf{pk}_i, \mathcal{PK}) \in \mathbb{Z}_q^{n \times n}$ by extracting H_1 from $\mathcal{Y}$ where $\mathcal{PK} = \{\mathsf{pk}_{i_1}, \mathsf{pk}_{i_2}, \ldots, \mathsf{pk}_{i_l}\}$ and $I_{\mathcal{PK}} = \{i_1, i_2, \ldots, i_l\}$ is the index set of $\mathcal{PK}$.

- $\mathsf{MS.sg}(\mathcal{Y}, \mathcal{PK}, \mathcal{SK}, M) \rightarrow \mathsf{msig}_{\mathcal{PK}, M}$. It is an interactive protocol among the signers $i \in I_{\mathcal{PK}}$ where $\mathcal{PK} = \{\mathsf{pk}_{i_1}, \mathsf{pk}_{i_2}, \ldots, \mathsf{pk}_{i_l}\}$ is the set of public keys of the signers with $\mathsf{pk}_i = \mathbf{Y}_i$, $\mathcal{SK} = \{\mathsf{sk}_{i_1}, \mathsf{sk}_{i_2}, \ldots, \mathsf{sk}_{i_l}\}$ is the corresponding set of secret keys with $\mathsf{sk}_i = \mathbf{V}_i$ and $I_{\mathcal{PK}} = \{i_1, i_2, \ldots, i_l\}$ is the index set of $\mathcal{PK}$. The protocol executes the following steps where $\mathbf{A}, n, m, \sigma, H_0, H_1, H_2$ are extracted from $\mathcal{Y}$.
  - each signer $i \in I_{\mathcal{PK}}$ generates a signature $\mathbf{T}_{i, M}$ on a message $M \in \{0, 1\}^*$ using its secret key $\mathsf{sk}_i = \mathbf{V}_i$ as $\mathbf{T}_{i, M} = H_0(M, \mathcal{PK}) + \mathsf{sk}_i \cdot H_1(\mathsf{pk}_i, \mathcal{PK}) \cdot H_2(M)$ and sends $\mathbf{T}_{i, M}$ to the designated signer. Note that

$$||\mathbf{T}_{i, M}|| \leq ||H_0(M, \mathcal{PK})|| + ||\mathsf{sk}_i|| \cdot ||H_1(\mathsf{pk}_i, \mathcal{PK})|| \cdot ||H_2(M)||$$
$$\leq ||H_0(M, \mathcal{PK})|| + \sigma^3 m \sqrt{n}$$

as $\mathsf{sk}_i \in D^{m \times m}_{\mathbb{Z}_q, \sigma}$, $H_1(\mathsf{pk}_i, \mathcal{PK}) \in D^{m \times n}_{\mathbb{Z}_q, \sigma}$ and $H_2(M) \in D^{n \times n}_{\mathbb{Z}_q, \sigma}$,

- the designated signer in turn verifies whether $||\mathbf{T}_{i,M}|| \leq ||H_0(M, \mathcal{PK})|| + \sigma^3 m \sqrt{n}$ and $\mathbf{A} \cdot \mathbf{T}_{i,M} = \mathbf{A} \cdot H_0(M, \mathcal{PK}) + \mathbf{Y}_i \cdot H_1(\mathsf{pk}_i, \mathcal{PK}) \cdot H_2(M)$,
- if the verification fails, the designated signer does not accept the signature and returns $\perp$. Otherwise, it issues the multisignature $\mathsf{msig}_{\mathcal{PK},M} = \left(\mathbf{T}_M, \mathsf{pkag}_{\mathcal{PK}}, I_{\mathcal{PK}}, M\right)$ where $\mathbf{T}_M = \sum_{i \in I_{\mathcal{PK}}} \mathbf{T}_{i,M} \bmod q$.

- MS.vrf($\mathcal{Y}, \mathsf{msig}_{\mathcal{PK},M}) \rightarrow$ (0 or 1). On input the multisignature $\mathsf{msig}_{\mathcal{PK},M} = (\mathbf{T}_M, \mathsf{pkag}_{\mathcal{PK}}, I_{\mathcal{PK}}, M)$, it outputs 1 if $\mathbf{A} \cdot \mathbf{T}_M = \mathbf{A} \cdot |I_{\mathcal{PK}}| \cdot H_0(M, \mathcal{PK}) + \mathsf{pkag}_{\mathcal{PK}} \cdot H_2(M)$, $||\mathbf{T}_M|| \leq |I_{\mathcal{PK}}| \cdot (||H_0(M, \mathcal{PK})|| + \sigma^3 m \sqrt{n})$. Otherwise, it returns 0.

The proof of the following Theorem 3 is immediate from the construction.

Theorem 3. *The scheme* MS *is complete.*

3.1   Security Proof

Theorem 4. *The scheme* MS *is* $(t_{\mathcal{F}}, q_s, q_H, \epsilon_{\mathcal{F}})$-*unforgeable in the random oracle model if* SIS *problem is* $((t_{\mathcal{F}} + t_{q_H} + t_{q_s} + t_{extra}) \cdot 8q_H^2 \cdot \epsilon_{\mathcal{F}} \cdot \log(8q_H/\epsilon_{\mathcal{F}}), \frac{\epsilon_{\mathcal{F}}}{8q_H})$-*hard. In other words, suppose that there exists a forger* $\mathcal{F}$ *running in time* $t_{\mathcal{F}}$ *can break the security under unforgeability of our scheme* MS *with non-negligible advantage* $\epsilon_{\mathcal{F}}$ *making* q_s *signature queries and* q_H *hash queries. Then there exists an algorithm* $\mathcal{S}$ *running in time* $(t_{\mathcal{F}} + t_{q_H} + t_{q_s} + t_{extra}) \cdot 8q_H^2 \cdot \epsilon_{\mathcal{F}} \cdot \log(8q_H/\epsilon_{\mathcal{F}})$, *that for a given* $\mathbf{P} \in \mathbb{Z}_q^{n \times m}$ *finds a nonzero* $\mathbf{V} \in \mathbb{Z}_q^{m \times m}$ *satisfying* $||\mathbf{V}|| \leq \sigma \sqrt{m}$ *and* $\mathbf{P} \cdot \mathbf{V} = \mathbf{0} \bmod q$ *with non negligible advantage* $\frac{\epsilon_{\mathcal{F}}}{8q_H}$. *Here* $m \geq 2n\lceil \log q \rceil$, σ *is of size* $\Omega(\sqrt{n \log q} \log n)$, q *is of size* $\mathcal{O}(n^3)$, t_{q_H}, t_{q_s} *respectively denote the time taken to answer hash and signature queries and* t_{extra} *is extra time taken by the algorithm* $\mathcal{S}$.

Proof. We assume that there exists a forger $\mathcal{F}$ that wins the unforgeability game played with a simulator $\mathcal{S}$ given in Definition 4 with probability $\epsilon_{\mathcal{F}}$.

1. Given an SIS instance $\mathbf{P} \in \mathbb{Z}_q^{n \times m}$ with $m \geq 2n\lceil \log q \rceil$, q is of size $\mathcal{O}(n^3)$, σ is of size $\Omega(\sqrt{n \log q} \log n)$, the simulator $\mathcal{S}$ sets $\mathcal{Y} = (n, q, m, \sigma, H_0, H_1, H_2, \mathbf{A})$ by setting $\mathbf{A} = \mathbf{P}$ and $H_0 : \{0, 1\}^* \rightarrow \mathbb{Z}_q^{m \times n}$, $H_1 : \{0, 1\}^* \rightarrow D_{\mathbb{Z}_q, \sigma}^{m \times n}$ and $H_2 : \{0, 1\}^* \rightarrow D_{\mathbb{Z}_q, \sigma}^{n \times n}$ where $D_{\mathbb{Z}_q, \sigma}^{k \times l} = \{\mathbf{M} \in \mathbb{Z}_q^{k \times l} : ||\mathbf{M}|| \leq \sigma \sqrt{k}\}$. The simulator $\mathcal{S}$ generates a random matrix $\mathsf{pk}_{i^*} = \mathbf{Y}_{i^*}$ and randomness $\rho = \{\xi, \mathcal{C}\}$ where $\mathcal{C} = \{\mathbf{C}_1, \mathbf{C}_2, \ldots, \mathbf{C}_{q_H}\}$, $\xi \in \mathbb{Z}_q^{m \times n}$ and each $\mathbf{C}_i \in D_{\mathbb{Z}_q, \sigma}^{m \times n}$ for $i = 1, 2, \ldots, q_H$. The simulator $\mathcal{S}$ speculates a random index $k \in \{1, 2, \ldots, q_H\}$. More precisely, $\mathcal{S}$ guesses that $\mathcal{F}$ makes k-th H_2 query on a message that is used by $\mathcal{F}$ to output a valid forgery. It then runs $\mathcal{F}$ on input $\mathsf{pk}_{i^*} \in \mathbb{Z}_q^{n \times m}$, randomness ρ and system parameters $\mathcal{Y} = (n, q, m, \sigma, H_0, H_1, H_2, \mathbf{A})$.
2. The forger $\mathcal{F}$ is allowed to make q_H many hash and q_s many signature queries which are simulated as follows.

H_1 **Query.** The simulator $\mathcal{S}$ maintains a list L_{H_1} containing elements of the form $(x, H_1(x))$. If the tuple $x = (\mathsf{pk}_i, \mathcal{PK}_l)$, $1 \le l \le q_H$ is already answered then $\mathcal{S}$ returns from the list L_{H_1}. If it is queried for the first time, $\mathcal{S}$ chooses a random value from the set $\{\mathbf{C}_1, \mathbf{C}_2, \ldots, \mathbf{C}_{q_H}\}$ for $H_1(\mathsf{pk}_{i^*}, \mathcal{PK})$ for $\mathsf{pk}_{i^*} \in \mathcal{PK}$ if $\mathsf{pk}_{i^*} \in \mathcal{PK}$ and $i = i^*$. Otherwise, it returns random value from $D_{\mathbb{Z}_q, \sigma}^{m \times n}$. Finally, the simulator stores $((\mathsf{pk}_i, \mathcal{PK}), H_1(\mathsf{pk}_i, \mathcal{PK}))$ in the list L_{H_1}.

H_2 **Query.** On receiving the query on a message M_l, $1 \le l \le q_H$ if it already queried then the simulator returns from the list L_{H_2}. Otherwise, $\mathcal{S}$ honestly generates and returns $H_2(M_l)$ to the forger $\mathcal{F}$. The simulator stores $(M_l, H_2(M_l))$ in the list L_{H_2}.

H_0 **Query.** The simulator maintains a list L_{H_0} containing elements of the form $(x, H_0(x))$ where $x = (M_l, \mathcal{PK}_l)$. If the message has already been queried then it returns from the list L_{H_0}. Otherwise, the simulator performs the following steps to answer H_0 query on any message M_l.

- choose $\mathbf{T}_{i^*, M_l} \in D_{\mathbb{Z}_q, \sigma}^{m \times n}$ uniformly,
- query $H_1(\mathsf{pk}_{i^*}, \mathcal{PK}_l)$ and $H_2(M)$ to the random oracles H_1 and H_2 respectively,
- find $\mathbf{B} \in \mathbb{Z}_q^{m \times n}$ (using Gauss elimination method or any linear algebra method) satisfying the equation $\mathbf{A} \cdot \mathbf{B} = \mathbf{A} \cdot \mathbf{T}_{i^*, M_l} - \mathbf{Y}_{i^*} \cdot H_1(\mathsf{pk}_{i^*}, \mathcal{PK}_l) \cdot H_2(M_l)$,
- return $H_0(M_l, \mathcal{PK}_l) = \mathbf{B}$ to $\mathcal{F}$ and store $((M_l, \mathcal{PK}_l), H_0(M_l, \mathcal{PK}_l))$ in the list L_{H_0} and $((M_l, \mathcal{PK}_l), \mathbf{T}_{i^*, M_l})$ in the list L_{good}.

The distribution of $\mathbf{T}_{i^*, M_l}$ is identical to the real protocol. Note that in the real protocol, $\|\mathbf{T}_{i, M_l}\| \le \sigma^3 m \sqrt{n}$ and as we have chosen $\mathbf{T}_{i^*, M_l} \in D_{\mathbb{Z}_q, \sigma}^{m \times n}$ giving $\|\mathbf{T}_{i^*, M_l}\| \le \sigma \sqrt{m} \le \sigma^3 m \sqrt{n}$.

Signature Generation Query. When $\mathcal{F}$ makes a signature query on a message M_l, with signers $\mathcal{PK}_l$, $1 \le l \le q_s$ the simulator firstly checks whether $\mathsf{pk}_{i^*} \in \mathcal{PK}_l$. If not, it aborts. Otherwise, $\mathcal{S}$ checks whether $(M_l, H_2(M_l)) \in L_{H_2}$ with $l = k$ where $k \in \{1, 2, \ldots, q_H\}$ is fixed at the beginning of the game. If yes, it aborts. Otherwise, $\mathcal{S}$ checks whether $((M_l, \mathcal{PK}_l), \mathbf{T}_{i^*, M_l}) \in L_{\mathsf{good}}$. If yes, then return $\mathbf{T}_{i^*, M_l}$. If not, then $\mathcal{S}$ calls H_0 query on $(M_l, \mathcal{PK}_l)$ and return $\mathbf{T}_{i^*, M_l}$.

3. With the above knowledge, the forger $\mathcal{F}$ outputs a forgery $\mathsf{msig}_{\mathcal{PK}, M}^* = (\mathbf{T}_M^*, \mathsf{pkag}_{\mathcal{PK}}, I_{\mathcal{PK}}, M)$ on a message M. If it is a valid forgery then $\mathbf{A} \cdot \mathbf{T}_M^* = \mathbf{A} \cdot |I_{\mathcal{PK}}| \cdot H_0(M, \mathcal{PK}) + \sum_{i \in \mathcal{PK}} \mathsf{pk}_i \cdot H_1(\mathsf{pk}_i, \mathcal{PK}) \cdot H_2(M)$.

4. The algorithm $\mathcal{S}$ returns $fail$ if (a) $\mathsf{msig}_{\mathcal{PK}, M}^*$ is not a valid forgery. (b) $\mathsf{pk}_{i^*} \notin \mathcal{PK}$. (c) $M = M_l$ for some $1 \le l \le q_s$.

As $\mathsf{pk}_{i^*} \in \mathcal{PK}$ for a valid forgery, $H_1(\mathsf{pk}_{i^*}, \mathcal{PK}) = \mathbf{C}_t$ for some t, $1 \le t \le q_H$. The simulator $\mathcal{S}$ computes $\mathsf{pkag}_{\mathcal{PK}} = \sum_{i \in I_{\mathcal{PK}}} \mathsf{pk}_i \cdot H_1(\mathsf{pk}_i, \mathcal{PK})$ where pk_i is the public key corresponding to the signer $i \in I_{\mathcal{PK}}$ and $H_1(\mathsf{pk}_i, \mathcal{PK})$ are simulated as in the H_1 query for each $\mathsf{pk}_i \in \mathcal{PK}$. Let $\mathbf{E}_j = H_1(\mathsf{pk}_j, \mathcal{PK})$ for $\mathsf{pk}_j \in \mathcal{PK}$.

Then the algorithm $\mathcal{S}^{\mathcal{F}}(\text{in}_{\mathcal{S}} = \mathbf{P}, \rho)$ outputs $(\{t\}, \{(\text{msig}_{\mathcal{PK},M}, \mathcal{PK}, \text{pkag}_{\mathcal{PK}}, \mathbf{E}_1, \cdots, \mathbf{E}_{|I_{\mathcal{PK}}|})\})$ where $\rho = (\xi, \mathbf{C}_1, \mathbf{C}_2, \ldots, \mathbf{C}_{q_H})$.

We prove the theorem by constructing an algorithm $\mathcal{B}$ that, on input an SIS instance $\mathbf{A} \in \mathbb{Z}_q^{n \times m}$ and the above constructed simulator $\mathcal{S}$, solves the SIS problem. Particularly, $\mathcal{B}$ runs the generalized forking lemma $\mathcal{FL}_{\mathcal{S}}$ on $\mathcal{S}^{\mathcal{F}}(\text{in}_{\mathcal{S}} = \mathbf{P}, \rho)$ given in Sect. 2. The algorithm $\mathcal{B}$ outputs fail if $\mathcal{FL}_{\mathcal{S}}$ outputs $(0, \bot)$. On the other hand, $\mathcal{B}$ outputs a solution $\mathbf{V}^*$ of the SIS instance as follows if $\mathcal{FL}_{\mathcal{S}}$ outputs $(\{t\}, \{\text{out}_1\}, \{\text{out}_2\})$. Here $\text{out}_1 = \{(\text{msig}^*_{\mathcal{PK},M}, \mathcal{PK}, \mathbf{E}_1, \ldots, \mathbf{E}_{|I_{\mathcal{PK}}|})\}$, $\text{out}_2 = (\{(\text{msig}'_{\mathcal{PK}',M}, \mathcal{PK}', \mathbf{E}'_1, \ldots, \mathbf{E}'_{|I_{\mathcal{PK}'}|})\})$ with $\text{msig}^*_{\mathcal{PK},M} = (\mathbf{T}^*_M, \text{pkag}_{\mathcal{PK}}, I_{\mathcal{PK}}, M)$ and $\text{msig}'_{\mathcal{PK},M} = (\mathbf{T}'_M, \text{pkag}_{\mathcal{PK}'}, I_{\mathcal{PK}'}, M)$ are obtained from two executions of $\mathcal{S}$ with randomness ρ and ρ' such that $\rho|_t = \rho'|_t$ i.e., $\rho = (\xi, \mathbf{C}_1, \mathbf{C}_2, \ldots, \mathbf{C}_{t-1}, \mathbf{C}_t, \ldots, \mathbf{C}_{q_H})$ and $\rho' = (\xi, \mathbf{C}_1, \mathbf{C}_2, \ldots, \mathbf{C}_{t-1}, \mathbf{C}'_t, \ldots, \mathbf{C}'_{q_H})$. In other words, the arguments of this query are identical ($\mathcal{PK} = \mathcal{PK}'$) but $\mathbf{E}_{i^*} = H_1(\text{pk}_{i^*}, \mathcal{PK}) = \mathbf{C}_t$ and $\mathbf{E}'_{i^*} = H_1(\text{pk}_{i^*}, \mathcal{PK}') = \mathbf{C}'_t$ with $\mathbf{E}_{i^*} \neq \mathbf{E}'_{i^*}$. Also $\text{pkag}_{\mathcal{PK}} = \sum_{i \in I_{\mathcal{PK}}} \text{pk}_i \cdot \mathbf{E}_i$ and $\text{pkag}'_{\mathcal{PK}} = \sum_{i \in I_{\mathcal{PK}}} \text{pk}_i \cdot \mathbf{E}'_i$. Since $\mathbf{E}_j = \mathbf{E}'_j$ for all $j \in I_{\mathcal{PK}}$ except $j = i^*$ before the forking point and therefore $\text{pkag}_{\mathcal{PK}} - \text{pkag}'_{\mathcal{PK}} = \text{pk}_{i^*} \mathbf{E}_{i^*} - \text{pk}'_{i^*} \mathbf{E}'_{i^*}$.

$\mathcal{B}$ extracts $\mathbf{T}^*_M$ and $\mathbf{T}'_M$ from $\text{msig}^*_{\mathcal{PK},M}$ and $\text{msig}'_{\mathcal{PK},M}$ respectively, sets $\mathbf{V}^* = \mathbf{T}^*_M - \mathbf{T}'_M = \text{sk}_{i^*} \cdot (\mathbf{E}_{i^*} - \mathbf{E}'_{i^*}) \cdot H_2(M)$ where $||\mathbf{V}^*|| \leq \sigma\sqrt{m}$, $||\mathbf{E}_{i^*}|| \leq \sigma\sqrt{m}$, $||\mathbf{E}'_{i^*}|| \leq \sigma\sqrt{m}$ and $||H_2(M)|| \leq \sigma\sqrt{n}$. Thus $||\mathbf{V}^*|| \leq \sigma^4 m\sqrt{n}$. Also note that $\mathbf{A} \cdot \mathbf{T}^*_M = \mathbf{A} \cdot \mathbf{T}'_M \bmod q$. This implies $\mathbf{A} \cdot \mathbf{V}^* = 0 \bmod q$. Hence, $\mathbf{V}^*$ is a solution to the SIS instance.

The probability of success of $\mathcal{S}$ is the probability that (i) $\mathcal{F}$ succeeds to output a valid forgery with probability $\epsilon_{\mathcal{F}}$ and (ii) $(M_k, H_2(M_k)) \in L_{H_2}$ with $M_k = M$ i.e., $\mathcal{F}$ has asked the k-th H_2 query on M. Here the index k is guessed at prior by $\mathcal{S}$ before H_2 queries are made. The algorithm $\mathcal{S}$ chooses the correct index with probability $\frac{1}{q_H}$. Thus the success probability of $\mathcal{S}$ is $\frac{\epsilon_{\mathcal{F}}}{q_H}$.

The running time of $\mathcal{S}$ is that of $\mathcal{F}$ plus the time taken to answer the queries and the additional computation $\mathcal{S}$ makes. Let t_{q_H}, t_{q_s} be the time taken to answer hash and sign queries. Let t_{extra} be extra time taken by $\mathcal{S}$. Therefore, the run time of $\mathcal{S}$ is $t_{\mathcal{F}} + t_{q_H} + t_{q_s} + t_{extra}$. By the generalized forking lemma, if $q > \frac{8q_H}{\epsilon_{\mathcal{F}}}$, the running time of $\mathcal{B}$ is $(t_{\mathcal{F}} + t_{q_H} + t_{q_s} + t_{extra}) \cdot 8q_H^2/\epsilon_{\mathcal{F}} \cdot ln(\frac{8q_H}{\epsilon_{\mathcal{F}}})$ and the success probability of $\mathcal{B}$ is atleast $\frac{\epsilon_{\mathcal{F}}}{8q_H}$. $\square$

4   Accountable Subgroup Multisignature

Syntax of Accountable Subgroup Multisignature. Let $\mathcal{PK} = \{\text{pk}_1, \text{pk}_2, \ldots, \text{pk}_l\}$ denotes the set of public keys of a group of signers $I_{\mathcal{PK}} = \{1, 2, \ldots, l\}$ and $\mathcal{SK}_{\mathcal{PK}} = \{\text{sk}_1, \text{sk}_2, \ldots, \text{sk}_l\}$ be the set of corresponding secret keys of the set $\mathcal{PK}$. Let $L = \{\text{pk}_{i_1}, \text{pk}_{i_2}, \ldots, \text{pk}_{i_k}\}$ be the set of public keys of a subgroup of signers $I_L = \{i_1, i_2, \ldots, i_k\}$ and $\mathcal{SK}_L = \{\text{sk}_{i_1}, \text{sk}_{i_2}, \ldots, \text{sk}_{i_k}\}$ be the set of corresponding secret keys of the set L. The accountable subgroup multisignature scheme allows a subgroup $I_L \subseteq I_{\mathcal{PK}}$ to issue an accountable subgroup multisignature accmsig on a message M in such a way that the verifier agrees that all the k signers in I_L have signed the message M. Let there be a designated signer who combines all the signatures of signers into a single accountable subgroup multisignature. The designated signer may be one of the signers or an external party.

An accountable subgroup multisignature scheme ASM = {pg, kg, kag, gmk, sg, vrf} consists of *parameter generation algorithm* pg, *key generation algorithm* kg and *key aggregation algorithm* kag together with an interactive *group membership key protocol* gmk, *signature generation* protocol sg and a deterministic *verification* algorithm vrf. A trusted third party, called the *key generation center* (KGC), generates the public parameter set $\mathcal{Y} \leftarrow$ AMS.pg. A user generates its public-secret key pair (pk, sk)←ASM.kg. The public keys are made public while the secret keys are kept secret to the users. All signer $i \in I_{\mathcal{PK}}$ with its own secret key sk_i execute the protocol ASM.gmk among themselves and generates a group membership key $mk_{i,\mathcal{PK}}$ $i \in I_{\mathcal{PK}}$. In signature generation protocol ASM.sg, each signer $i \in I_L \subseteq I_{\mathcal{PK}}$ uses its secret key sk_i and group membership key $mk_{i,\mathcal{PK}}$ to generate signature $\mathbf{T}_{i,M}$ on a message M and sends $\mathbf{T}_{i,M}$ to the designated signer. The designated signer aggregates all the received signatures $\mathbf{T}_{i,M}$ for $i \in I_L$ on the message M into an accountable subgroup multisignature $accmsig_{\mathcal{PK},L,M}$. The key aggregation algorithm ASM.kag can be run by anyone to aggregate the public keys in a set $\mathcal{PK}$ into a single public key $pkag_{\mathcal{PK}}$. The verifier runs the algorithm ASM.vrf and returns 0, if the multisignature $accmsig_{\mathcal{PK},L,M}$ is not properly generated or 1 if $accmsig_{\mathcal{PK},L,M}$ is correct. More concretely, description of these algorithms are given below.

- ASM.pg(1^λ) → $\mathcal{Y}$. It is a PPT algorithm run by a KGC on a security parameter λ to generate the public parameter set $\mathcal{Y}$.
- ASM.kg($\mathcal{Y}, i$) → (pk_i, sk_i). Each user i runs this algorithm with input the public parameter set $\mathcal{Y}$ to generate the public and secret key pair (pk_i, sk_i). The secret key sk_i is kept secret to the user i while the public key pk_i is made publicly available.
- ASM.kag($\mathcal{Y}, \mathcal{PK}$) → $pkag_{\mathcal{PK}}$. This is a deterministic algorithm and it aggregates the public keys in $\mathcal{PK}$ into a single public key $pkag_{\mathcal{PK}}$. It outputs the aggregated public key $pkag_{\mathcal{PK}}$ which asymptotically has the same size as a single public key.
- ASM.gmk($\mathcal{Y}, \mathcal{PK}, \mathcal{SK}_{\mathcal{PK}}$) → $mk_{i,\mathcal{PK}}$. With input the public parameter set $\mathcal{Y}$, the set of public keys $\mathcal{PK}$ of the signers, the set of secret keys $\mathcal{SK}_{\mathcal{PK}}$ of the signers in $I_{\mathcal{PK}}$, this interactive protocol runs among all signers in $I_{\mathcal{PK}}$ and generates group membership key $mk_{i,\mathcal{PK}}$ for each $i \in I_{\mathcal{PK}}$.
- ASM.sg($\mathcal{Y}, L, \mathcal{PK}, \mathcal{SK}_L, \mathcal{G}_L, M$) → $accmsig_{\mathcal{PK},L,M}$. With input the public parameter set $\mathcal{Y}$, the set of public keys $\mathcal{PK}$ of signers, the set of secret keys $\mathcal{SK}_L$ of signers in I_L, the set of group membership keys $\mathcal{G}_L = \{mk_{i,\mathcal{PK}}|i \in I_L \subseteq I_{\mathcal{PK}}\}$ and a message M, this interactive protocol works as follows. The signer $i \in I_L$ uses its secret key sk_i and group membership key $mk_{i,\mathcal{PK}}$ to generate a signature $\mathbf{T}_{i,M}$ on M and sends $\mathbf{T}_{i,M}$ to the designated signer. The designated signer aggregates all the signatures $\mathbf{T}_{i,M}$ for $i \in I_L$ on a message M into a single accountable subgroup multisignature $accmsig_{\mathcal{PK},L,M}$.

- ASM.vrf($\mathcal{Y}$, accmsig$_{\mathcal{PK},L,M}$) $\rightarrow$ (0 or 1). On input the public parameter set $\mathcal{Y}$ and an accountable subgroup multisignature accmsig$_{\mathcal{PK},L,M}$, this deterministic algorithm returns 1 if the accountable subgroup multisignature accmsig$_{\mathcal{PK},L,M}$ is valid. Otherwise, it returns 0.

---

1. The simulator $\mathcal{S}$ generates system parameters $\mathcal{Y}$ and a challenge public key pk_{i*}. The simulator $\mathcal{S}$ runs the forger $\mathcal{F}$ on $(\mathcal{Y}, pk_{i*})$.
2a. The forger $\mathcal{F}$ is allowed to make group membership key queries on a set of public keys $\mathcal{PK}_l$, $1 \leq l \leq q_m$ where $\mathcal{PK}_l$ is a set of public keys with $pk_{i*} \in \mathcal{PK}_l$ i.e., $\mathcal{F}$ has access to the oracle $O^{(\mathcal{Y}, \mathcal{PK}_l, \cdot)}$ in which $\mathcal{S}$ plays the role of the honest signer i^*. The simulator stores the resulting membership key $mk_{i*, \mathcal{PK}_l}$ but does not return it to $\mathcal{F}$.
2b. The forger $\mathcal{F}$ is allowed to make signature queries on $(M_l, \mathcal{PK}_l)$ where M_l is a message and $\mathcal{PK}_l$ is a set of public keys with $pk_{i*} \in \mathcal{PK}_l$, $1 \leq l \leq q_s$. That is, $\mathcal{F}$ has access to the oracle $O^{(\mathcal{Y}, \cdot, \mathcal{PK}_l, \cdot, \cdot, M_l)}$. The simulator plays the role of the honest signer i^* and produce a signature $\mathbf{T}_{i^*, M_l}$ on M_l.
3. Finally, $\mathcal{F}$ outputs a forgery accmsig$^*_{\mathcal{PK},L,M}$ on a message M for $L \subseteq \mathcal{PK}$ where $\mathcal{PK}$ is a set of public keys of a group of signers.
4. The simulator $\mathcal{S}$ returns 1 if the following conditions hold:
   (a) ASM.vrf($\mathcal{Y}$, accmsig$^*_{\mathcal{PK},L,M}$) $\rightarrow$ 1,
   (b) $pk_{i*} \in L$,
   (c) $M \neq M_l$ $1 \leq l \leq q_s$.
   Otherwise, $\mathcal{S}$ returns 0.
5. The forger $\mathcal{F}$ wins the game if $\mathcal{S}$ returns 1.

Fig. 2. Unforgeability game $\mathsf{Exp}_{\mathcal{F}}^{unf}(\lambda)$

Completeness. An accountable subgroup multisignature scheme should satisfy completeness. That is, for any $\mathcal{Y} \leftarrow$ ASM.pg(1^λ), $(pk_i, sk_i) \leftarrow$ ASM.kg($\mathcal{Y}, i$) with $i \in I_{\mathcal{PK}}$ where $I_{\mathcal{PK}}$ is the index set for the set of public keys $\mathcal{PK}$, $\mathcal{SK}_{\mathcal{PK}}$ is the corresponding set of secret keys, any message M, any subset $L \subset \mathcal{PK}$ with the set of secret keys $\mathcal{SK}_L$, group membership keys $\mathcal{G}_L = \{mk_{i,\mathcal{PK}} | i \in I_L \subseteq I_{\mathcal{PK}}\}$ where $mk_{i,\mathcal{PK}} \leftarrow$ ASM.gmk($\mathcal{Y}, \mathcal{PK}, \mathcal{SK}_{\mathcal{PK}}$), if accmsig$_{\mathcal{PK},L,M} \leftarrow$ ASM.sg($\mathcal{Y}, L, \mathcal{PK}, \mathcal{SK}_L, \mathcal{G}_L, M$) then ASM.vrf($\mathcal{Y}$, accmsig$_{\mathcal{PK},L,M}$) outputs 1.

Security Model. We consider the infeasibility to forge accountable subgroup multisignature with atleast one honest signer following the security model of Boneh et al. [4]. The forger has given access to q_g many group membership key queries along with q_s many signature queries on any message with any set of public keys $\mathcal{PK}$ and any subgroup of signers $I_L \subseteq I_{\mathcal{PK}}$. The unforgeability game $\mathsf{Exp}_{\mathcal{F}}^{unf}(\lambda)$ between a forger $\mathcal{F}$ and a simulator $\mathcal{L}$ is described in Fig. 2.

Definition 5. *We say that an accountable subgroup multisignature is unforgeable if* $\mathsf{Adv}_{\mathcal{F}}^{unf}(\lambda) = \Pr[\mathsf{Exp}_{\mathcal{F}}^{unf}(\lambda) = 1] \leq negl(\lambda)$ *for every PPT adversary $\mathcal{F}$ in the experiment $\mathsf{Exp}_{\mathcal{F}}^{unf}(\lambda)$ defined in Fig. 2 where $negl(\lambda)$ is a negligible function in λ.*

4.1 The ASM

We describe our accountable subgroup multisignature $\mathsf{ASM} = \{\mathsf{pg}, \mathsf{kg}, \mathsf{kag}, \mathsf{gmk}, \mathsf{sg}, \mathsf{vrf}\}$ below.

- $\mathsf{ASM.pg}(1^\lambda) \to \mathcal{Y}$. The key generation center (KGC) generates the system parameters $\mathcal{Y} \leftarrow (n, q, m, \sigma, H_0, H_1, H_2, H_3, \mathbf{A})$ as follows.
  - parameters $n, q, m, \sigma, H_0, H_1, \mathbf{A}$ are generated as in the algorithm $\mathsf{MS.pg}(1^\lambda)$ of Sect. 3,
  - sample cryptographically secure hash functions $H_2 : \{0,1\}^* \to \mathbb{Z}_q^{n \times n}$ and $H_3 : \{0,1\}^* \to D_{\mathbb{Z}_q,\sigma}^{n \times n}$ where $D_{\mathbb{Z}_q,\sigma}^{k \times l} = \{\mathbf{M} \in \mathbb{Z}_q^{k \times l} : ||\mathbf{M}|| \leq \sigma\sqrt{k}\}$.
- $\mathsf{ASM.kg}(\mathcal{Y}, i) \to (\mathsf{pk}_i, \mathsf{sk}_i)$. The signer i generates its own public and secret key pair $(\mathsf{pk}_i, \mathsf{sk}_i)$ same as in the algorithm $\mathsf{MS.kg}(\mathcal{Y}, i)$ of Sect. 3. The secret key $\mathsf{sk}_i = \mathbf{V}_i \in D_{\mathbb{Z}_q,\sigma}^{m \times m}$ is kept secret to the signer i and the public key $\mathsf{pk}_i = \mathbf{Y}_i \in \mathbb{Z}_q^{n \times m}$ is made public. Note that $\mathbf{Y}_i = \mathbf{A} \cdot \mathbf{V}_i \bmod q$.
- $\mathsf{ASM.kag}(\mathcal{Y}, \mathcal{PK}) \to \mathsf{pkag}_{\mathcal{PK}}$. This deterministic algorithm outputs the aggregated public key $\mathsf{pkag}_{\mathcal{PK}} = \sum_{i \in I_{\mathcal{PK}}} \mathsf{pk}_i \cdot H_1(\mathsf{pk}_i, \mathcal{PK}) \in \mathbb{Z}_q^{n \times n}$.
- $\mathsf{ASM.gmk}(\mathcal{Y}, \mathcal{PK}, \mathcal{SK}_{\mathcal{PK}}) \to \mathsf{mk}_{i,\mathcal{PK}}$. It is a single round protocol between the signers in $I_{\mathcal{PK}}$ where $\mathcal{PK} = \{\mathsf{pk}_{i_1}, \mathsf{pk}_{i_2}, \ldots, \mathsf{pk}_{i_l}\}$ is a set of public keys with $\mathsf{pk}_i = \mathbf{Y}_i$ and $\mathcal{SK}_{\mathcal{PK}} = \{\mathsf{sk}_{i_1}, \mathsf{sk}_{i_2}, \ldots, \mathsf{sk}_{i_l}\}$ is the collection of corresponding secret keys with $\mathsf{sk}_i = \mathbf{V}_i$. All signers $i \in I_{\mathcal{PK}}$ utilize the public parameter set $\mathcal{Y} = (n, q, m, \sigma, H_0, H_1, H_2, H_3, \mathbf{A})$ and parallely execute the following.
  - generate $\mathsf{pkag}_{\mathcal{PK}} \leftarrow \mathsf{ASM.kag}(\mathcal{Y}, \mathcal{PK})$ where $\mathsf{pkag}_{\mathcal{PK}} = \sum_{i \in I_{\mathcal{PK}}} \mathsf{pk}_i \cdot H_1(\mathsf{pk}_i, \mathcal{PK})$,
  - compute $\mathbf{M}_{j,i} = H_2(\mathsf{pkag}_{\mathcal{PK}}, j) + \mathsf{sk}_i \cdot H_1(\mathsf{pk}_i, \mathcal{PK}) \cdot H_3(j)$ for all $j \in I_{\mathcal{PK}}$,
  - send $\mathbf{M}_{j,i}$ to signer j with $||\mathbf{M}_{j,i}|| \leq ||H_2(\mathsf{pkag}_{\mathcal{PK}}, j)|| + \sigma^3 m\sqrt{n}$.
  - On receiving $\mathbf{M}_{i,j} \setminus \{i\}$ from all signers $j \in I_{\mathcal{PK}}$, the i-th signer verifies $||\mathbf{M}_{i,j}|| \leq ||H_2(\mathsf{pkag}_{\mathcal{PK}}, i)|| + \sigma^3 m\sqrt{n}$. If the verification fails, it returns $\perp$. Otherwise, it computes the group membership key
    $$\mathsf{mk}_{i,\mathcal{PK}} = \sum_{j \in I_{\mathcal{PK}}} \mathbf{M}_{i,j} = \sum_{j \in I_{\mathcal{PK}}} \left[H_2(\mathsf{pkag}_{\mathcal{PK}}, i) + \mathsf{sk}_j \cdot H_1(\mathsf{pk}_j, \mathcal{PK}) \cdot H_3(i) \right]$$
- $\mathsf{ASM.sg}(\mathcal{Y}, L, \mathcal{PK}, \mathcal{SK}_L, \mathcal{G}_L, M) \to \mathsf{accmsig}_{\mathcal{PK},L,M}$. It is a one round protocol run between the members of the set I_L where $L \subseteq \mathcal{PK} = \{\mathsf{pk}_{i_1}, \mathsf{pk}_{i_2}, \ldots, \mathsf{pk}_{i_l}\}$ is the set of public keys of the signers in I_L with $\mathsf{pk}_i = \mathbf{Y}_i$. The set $\mathcal{SK}_L$ is the collection of corresponding secret keys of the signers in I_L with $\mathsf{sk}_i = \mathbf{V}_i$. Each signer $i \in I_L$ performs the following steps by extracting $(n, q, m, \sigma, H_0, H_1, H_2, H_3, \mathbf{A})$ from $\mathcal{Y}$.
  - generate $\mathsf{pkag}_{\mathcal{PK}} \leftarrow \mathsf{ASM.kag}(\mathcal{Y}, \mathcal{PK})$ where $\mathsf{pkag}_{\mathcal{PK}} = \sum_{i \in I_{\mathcal{PK}}} \mathsf{pk}_i \cdot H_1(\mathsf{pk}_i, \mathcal{PK})$,
  - compute $\mathbf{T}_{i,M} = \mathsf{sk}_i \cdot H_0(\mathsf{pkag}_{\mathcal{PK}}, M) + \mathsf{mk}_{i,\mathcal{PK}}$ with $||\mathbf{T}_{i,M}|| \leq \sigma\sqrt{m} \cdot H_0(\mathsf{pkag}_{\mathcal{PK}}, M) + |I_{\mathcal{PK}}| \cdot ||H_2(\mathsf{pkag}_{\mathcal{PK}}, i)|| + |I_{\mathcal{PK}}| \cdot \sigma^3 m\sqrt{n}$,
  - send $\mathbf{T}_{i,M}$ to the designated signer.

Note that $||\mathbf{T}_{i,M}|| \leq \sigma\sqrt{m} \cdot H_0(\mathsf{pkag}_{\mathcal{PK}}, M) + |I_{\mathcal{PK}}| \cdot ||H_2(\mathsf{pkag}_{\mathcal{PK}}, i)|| + |I_{\mathcal{PK}}| \cdot \sigma^3 m\sqrt{n}$.

The designated signer verifies whether $||\mathbf{T}_{i,M}|| \leq \sigma\sqrt{m} \cdot H_0(\mathsf{pkag}_{\mathcal{PK}}, M) + |I_{\mathcal{PK}}| \cdot ||H_2(\mathsf{pkag}_{\mathcal{PK}}, i)|| + |I_{\mathcal{PK}}| \cdot \sigma^3 m\sqrt{n}$. If not, it aborts and returns $\perp$. Otherwise, the designated signer combines all the signatures $\mathbf{T}_{i,M}, i \in I_L$ to produce $\mathbf{T}_M = \sum_{i \in I_L} \mathbf{T}_{i,M}$ with $||\mathbf{T}_M|| \leq |I_L| \cdot \sigma\sqrt{m} \cdot H_0(\mathsf{pkag}_{\mathcal{PK}}, M) + |I_{\mathcal{PK}}| \cdot \max_{i \in I_L} ||H_2(\mathsf{pkag}_{\mathcal{PK}}, i)|| + |I_L| \cdot |I_{\mathcal{PK}}| \cdot \sigma^3 m\sqrt{n}$. The designated combiner also aggregates the public keys in L and generates aggregated subgroup public key $\mathsf{spkag}_L = \sum_{i \in I_L} \mathsf{pk}_i$. It finally returns the accountable subgroup multisignature

$\mathsf{accmsig}_{\mathcal{PK},L,M} = (\mathbf{T}_M, \mathsf{spkag}_L, \mathsf{pkag}_{\mathcal{PK}}, I_{\mathcal{PK}}, I_L, M)$.

- $\mathsf{ASM.vrf}(\mathcal{Y}, \mathsf{accmsig}_{\mathcal{PK},L,M}) \to (0 \text{ or } 1)$. On receiving an accountable subgroup multisignature $\mathsf{accmsig}_{\mathcal{PK},L,M} = (\mathbf{T}_M, \mathsf{spkag}_L, \mathsf{pkag}_{\mathcal{PK}}, I_{\mathcal{PK}}, I_L, M)$, a verifier runs this deterministic algorithm using the public parameter set $\mathcal{Y}$ and returns 1 if

  - $\mathbf{A} \cdot \mathbf{T}_M = \mathsf{spkag}_L \cdot H_0(\mathsf{pkag}_{\mathcal{PK}}, M) + |I_{\mathcal{PK}}| \cdot \sum_{i \in I_L} \mathbf{A} \cdot H_2(\mathsf{pkag}_{\mathcal{PK}}, i) + \mathsf{pkag}_{\mathcal{PK}} \cdot$
    $\sum_{i \in I_L} H_3(i)$ where $\mathsf{spkag}_L = \sum_{i \in I_L} \mathsf{pk}_i$ and $\mathsf{pkag}_{\mathcal{PK}} = \sum_{i \in I_{\mathcal{PK}}} \mathsf{pk}_i \cdot H_1(\mathsf{pk}_i, \mathcal{PK})$
  - $||\mathbf{T}_M|| \leq |I_L| \cdot \sigma\sqrt{m} \cdot H_0(\mathsf{pkag}_{\mathcal{PK}}, M) + |I_{\mathcal{PK}}| \cdot \max_{i \in I_L} ||H_2(\mathsf{pkag}_{\mathcal{PK}}, i)|| + |I_L| \cdot |I_{\mathcal{PK}}| \cdot \sigma^3 m\sqrt{n}$. Otherwise, the verifier returns 0.

The proof of the following theorem is immediate from the construction.

Theorem 5. *The scheme* ASM *described above is complete.*

Theorem 6. *The scheme* ASM *is unforgeable in the random oracle model if the* SIS *problem is hard.*

Proof **(Sketch).** We assume that there exists a forger $\mathcal{F}$ that wins the unforgeability game played with a simulator $\mathcal{S}$ given in Definition 5 with probability $\epsilon_{\mathcal{F}}$.

1. This step is similar to the step 1 of the Theorem 4 in Sect. 3.1.
2. We give the hints of the simulation of H_0, H_1 and group membership key queries. The H_1-query on $x = (\mathsf{pk}_i, \mathcal{PK})$ is simulated from the already chosen random values $\{\mathbf{C}_1, \mathbf{C}_2, \ldots, \mathbf{C}_{q_H}\}$. for $\mathsf{pk}_i \in \mathcal{PK}$ if $i = i^*$. Otherwise a random value is returned. Let $\mathbf{bad}_1$ be the event that a query to random oracles H_0 or H_2 is made involving $\mathsf{pkag}_{\mathcal{PK}}$ before making H_1 query on $(\mathsf{pk}_i, \mathcal{PK})$ for some pk_i. The simulator $\mathcal{S}$ aborts when the event $\mathbf{bad}_1$ occurs as it cannot simulate the queries without knowing the public keys used to form $\mathsf{pkag}_{\mathcal{PK}}$. The group membership key query on $\mathcal{PK}$ is simulated only if $\mathsf{pk}_{i^*} \in \mathcal{PK}$ by finding $\mathbf{B} \in \mathbb{Z}_q^{n \times n}$ satisfying $\mathbf{A} \cdot \mathbf{M}_{i,i^*} = \mathbf{A} \cdot \mathbf{B} + \mathsf{pk}_{i^*} \cdot H_1(\mathsf{pk}_{i^*}, \mathcal{PK}) \cdot H_3(i)$ and sets $H_2(\mathsf{pkag}_{\mathcal{PK}}, i) = \mathbf{B}$. Here $\mathbf{M}_{i,i^*} \in \mathbb{Z}_q^{m \times n}$ is randomly chosen such that $||\mathbf{M}_{i,i^*}|| \leq \sigma\sqrt{m}$. Let $\mathbf{bad}_2$ be the event that a query to random oracle H_0 is made involving $\mathsf{pkag}_{\mathcal{PK}}$ before making group membership key query on $\mathcal{PK}$. The simulator $\mathcal{S}$ aborts when the event $\mathbf{bad}_2$ occurs as it cannot

simulate the H_0 query without knowing $\mathsf{mk}_{i^*,\mathcal{PK}}$. Also, H_0-query on $x = (\mathsf{pkag}_{\mathcal{PK}}, M)$ is simulated by finding $\mathbf{B} \in \mathbb{Z}_q^{n \times n}$ satisfying $\mathbf{A} \cdot \mathbf{M}_{i,i^*} = \mathbf{A} \cdot \mathbf{B} + \mathbf{Y}_{i^*} \cdot H_1(\mathsf{pk}_{i^*}, \mathcal{PK}) \cdot H_3(i)$ and sets $H_2(\mathsf{pkag}_{\mathcal{PK}}, i) = \mathbf{B}$ where $\mathbf{T}_{i^*,M} \in \mathbb{Z}_q^{m \times n}$ is randomly chosen such that $||\mathbf{T}_{i^*,M}|| \leq \sigma\sqrt{m}$.

3. With the view of all the allowed queries, $\mathcal{F}$ outputs a valid forgery.
4. The simulator $\mathcal{S}$ applies the generalized forking lemma (on H_1 query) and solves the SIS instance as we have done in the Theorem 4 in Sect. 3.1. □

The complete proof will be provided in the full version of the paper.

References

1. Bagherzandi, A., Cheon, J.H., Jarecki, S.: Multisignatures secure under the discrete logarithm assumption and a generalized forking lemma. In: Proceedings of the 15th ACM Conference on Computer and Communications Security, pp. 449–458. ACM (2008)
2. Bellare, M., Neven, G.: Multi-signatures in the plain public-key model and a general forking lemma. In: Proceedings of the 13th ACM Conference on Computer and Communications Security, pp. 390–399. ACM (2006)
3. Boldyreva, A.: Threshold signatures, multisignatures and blind signatures based on the gap-Diffie-Hellman-group signature scheme. In: Desmedt, Y.G. (ed.) PKC 2003. LNCS, vol. 2567, pp. 31–46. Springer, Heidelberg (2003). https://doi.org/10.1007/3-540-36288-6_3
4. Boneh, D., Drijvers, M., Neven, G.: Compact multi-signatures for smaller blockchains. In: Peyrin, T., Galbraith, S. (eds.) ASIACRYPT 2018. LNCS, vol. 11273, pp. 435–464. Springer, Cham (2018). https://doi.org/10.1007/978-3-030-03329-3_15
5. Drijvers, M., et al.: On the security of two-round multi-signatures. In: On the Security of Two-Round Multi-signatures. IEEE (2019)
6. Drijvers, M., Gorbunov, S., Neven, G., Wee, H.: Pixel: multi-signatures for consensus
7. El Bansarkhani, R., Sturm, J.: An efficient lattice-based multisignature scheme with applications to bitcoins. In: Foresti, S., Persiano, G. (eds.) CANS 2016. LNCS, vol. 10052, pp. 140–155. Springer, Cham (2016). https://doi.org/10.1007/978-3-319-48965-0_9
8. Güneysu, T., Lyubashevsky, V., Pöppelmann, T.: Practical lattice-based cryptography: a signature scheme for embedded systems. In: Prouff, E., Schaumont, P. (eds.) CHES 2012. LNCS, vol. 7428, pp. 530–547. Springer, Heidelberg (2012). https://doi.org/10.1007/978-3-642-33027-8_31
9. Güneysu, T., Oder, T., Pöppelmann, T., Schwabe, P.: Software speed records for lattice-based signatures. In: Gaborit, P. (ed.) PQCrypto 2013. LNCS, vol. 7932, pp. 67–82. Springer, Heidelberg (2013). https://doi.org/10.1007/978-3-642-38616-9_5
10. Harn, L.: Group-oriented (t, n) threshold digital signature scheme and digital multisignature. IEE Proc.-Comput. Digital Tech. 141(5), 307–313 (1994)
11. Horster, P., Michels, M., Petersen, H.: Meta-multisignature schemes based on the discrete logarithm problem. Information Security — The Next Decade. IAICT, pp. 128–142. Springer, Boston (1995). https://doi.org/10.1007/978-0-387-34873-5_11

12. Itakura, K., Nakamura, K.: A public-key cryptosystem suitable for digital multisignatures. NEC Res. Dev. **71**, 1–8 (1983)
13. Langford, S.K.: Weaknesses in some threshold cryptosystems. In: Koblitz, N. (ed.) CRYPTO 1996. LNCS, vol. 1109, pp. 74–82. Springer, Heidelberg (1996). https://doi.org/10.1007/3-540-68697-5_6
14. Li, C.-M., Hwang, T., Lee, N.-Y.: Threshold-multisignature schemes where suspected forgery implies traceability of adversarial shareholders. In: De Santis, A. (ed.) EUROCRYPT 1994. LNCS, vol. 950, pp. 194–204. Springer, Heidelberg (1995). https://doi.org/10.1007/BFb0053435
15. Lu, S., Ostrovsky, R., Sahai, A., Shacham, H., Waters, B.: Sequential aggregate signatures, multisignatures, and verifiably encrypted signatures without random oracles. J. Cryptol. **26**(2), 340–373 (2012). https://doi.org/10.1007/s00145-012-9126-5
16. Maxwell, G., Poelstra, A., Seurin, Y., Wuille, P.: Simple Schnorr multi-signatures with applications to bitcoin. Des. Codes Cryptogr. **87**(9), 2139–2164 (2019). https://doi.org/10.1007/s10623-019-00608-x
17. Micali, S., Ohta, K., Reyzin, L.: Accountable-subgroup multisignatures. In: Proceedings of the 8th ACM Conference on Computer and Communications Security, pp. 245–254. ACM (2001)
18. Michels, M., Horster, P.: On the risk of disruption in several multiparty signature schemes. In: Kim, K., Matsumoto, T. (eds.) ASIACRYPT 1996. LNCS, vol. 1163, pp. 334–345. Springer, Heidelberg (1996). https://doi.org/10.1007/BFb0034859
19. Ohta, K., Okamoto, T.: A digital multisignature scheme based on the Fiat-Shamir scheme. In: Imai, H., Rivest, R.L., Matsumoto, T. (eds.) ASIACRYPT 1991. LNCS, vol. 739, pp. 139–148. Springer, Heidelberg (1993). https://doi.org/10.1007/3-540-57332-1_11
20. Ohta, K., Okamoto, T.: Multi-signature schemes secure against active insider attacks. IEICE Trans. Fund. Electron. Commun. Comput. Sci. **82**(1), 21–31 (1999)
21. Ristenpart, T., Yilek, S.: The power of proofs-of-possession: securing multiparty signatures against rogue-key attacks. In: Naor, M. (ed.) EUROCRYPT 2007. LNCS, vol. 4515, pp. 228–245. Springer, Heidelberg (2007). https://doi.org/10.1007/978-3-540-72540-4_13

Sieve, Enumerate, Slice, and Lift:
Hybrid Lattice Algorithms for SVP via CVPP

Emmanouil Doulgerakis$^{(\boxtimes)}$, Thijs Laarhoven, and Benne de Weger

Eindhoven University of Technology, Eindhoven, The Netherlands
{e.doulgerakis,b.m.m.d.weger}@tue.nl, mail@thijs.com

Abstract. Motivated by recent results on solving large batches of closest vector problem (CVP) instances, we study how these techniques can be combined with lattice enumeration to obtain faster methods for solving the shortest vector problem (SVP) on high-dimensional lattices.

Theoretically, under common heuristic assumptions we show how to solve SVP in dimension d with a cost proportional to running a sieve in dimension $d - \Theta(d/\log d)$, resulting in a $2^{\Theta(d/\log d)}$ speedup and memory reduction compared to running a full sieve. Combined with techniques from [Ducas, Eurocrypt 2018] we can asymptotically get a total of $[\log(13/9) + o(1)] \cdot d/\log d$ dimensions *for free* for solving SVP.

Practically, the main obstacles for observing a speedup in moderate dimensions appear to be that the leading constant in the $\Theta(d/\log d)$ term is rather small; that the overhead of the (batched) slicer may be large; and that competitive enumeration algorithms heavily rely on aggressive pruning techniques, which appear to be incompatible with our algorithms. These obstacles prevented this asymptotic speedup (compared to full sieving) from being observed in our experiments. However, it could be expected to become visible once optimized CVPP techniques are used in higher dimensional experiments.

Keywords: Lattice sieving · Lattice enumeration · Randomized slicer · Shortest vector problem (SVP) · Closest vector problem (CVP)

1 Introduction

In recent decades, lattice-based cryptography has emerged as a front-runner for building secure and efficient cryptographic primitives in the post-quantum age. For an accurate and reliable deployment of these schemes, it is essential to obtain a good understanding of the hardness of the underlying lattice problems, such as the shortest (SVP) and closest vector problems (CVP).

To date, research on lattice algorithms has resulted in two main flavors of algorithms: *enumeration* methods, requiring $2^{O(d \log d)}$ time and $d^{O(1)}$ space to solve hard lattice problems in dimension d [5,13,15,20]; and *sieving* methods, running in expected time and space $2^{O(d)}$ [2,3,27,30]. Just a few years ago, enumeration clearly dominated benchmarks for testing these algorithms in practice [1,9,14,15], but recent improvements to sieving have allowed it to overtake

© Springer Nature Switzerland AG 2020
A. Nitaj and A. Youssef (Eds.): AFRICACRYPT 2020, LNCS 12174, pp. 301–320, 2020.
https://doi.org/10.1007/978-3-030-51938-4_15

enumeration in practice as well [4,8,11,21,28]. Some attempts have also been made to combine the best of both worlds, a.o. resulting in the tuple sieving line of work [7,18,19]. A better comprehension of how to exploit the strengths and weaknesses of each method remains an interesting open problem.

A long-standing open problem from e.g. [10,15] concerns the possibility of speeding up lattice enumeration with a batch-CVP solver: if an efficient algorithm exists that can solve a large number of CVP instances on the same lattice faster than solving each problem separately, then this algorithm can be used to solve the CVP instances appearing implicitly in the enumeration tree faster. For a long time no such efficient batch-CVP algorithms were known, until the recent line of work on approximate Voronoi cells and the randomized slicer [10,12,24] showed that, at least in high dimensions, one can indeed solve large batches faster in practice than solving each problem separately. This raises the question whether these new results can be used to instantiate this conjectured hybrid algorithm and obtain better results, in theory and in practice.

Contributions. In this work we study the feasibility of combining recent batch-CVP algorithms with lattice enumeration, and show that we heuristically obtain a $2^{\Theta(d/\log d)}$ speedup and memory reduction for solving SVP compared to the state-of-the-art lattice sieve. This improvement is proper, in the sense that this does not hide large order terms: we show that for solving SVP in dimension d, the costs are proportional to those of running a sieve in dimension $d - \Theta(d/\log d)$, making the leading constant explicit, and showing that the remaining overhead is negligible. The hybrid constructions we propose are independent of e.g. the underlying nearest neighbor data structure, and we expect that these and other heuristic improvements can be applied to the hybrid algorithms as well.

Obtaining $\Theta(d/\log d)$ dimensions *for free* may sound familiar, as Ducas [11] showed that sieving in dimension $d - \Theta(d/\log d)$ implies solving SVP in dimension d. As the asymptotic improvement of Ducas is greater than ours, to improve upon his results we need to be able to combine both techniques. The feasibility of such a combined hybrid algorithm relies on Assumption 4, which Sect. 5 aims to verify with experiments. Combining both techniques, we asymptotically obtain $0.5305d/\log_2 d$ dimensions for free, compared to Ducas' $0.4150d/\log_2 d$.

Open Problems. Besides performing more extensive experiments, which may assist in obtaining estimates for the crossover points between these hybrids and plain lattice sieving, open problems include (i) finding a way to effectively incorporate *pruning* into the enumeration parts of the proposed hybrids; (ii) further studying the theoretical and practical relevance of the proposed *nested* hybrid algorithms, and their relation with progressive sieving ideas [11,25]; and (iii) finding improvements for CVPP, potentially using a dual distinguisher. We further stress that we introduced a new heuristic, Assumption 4, which may require additional simulations to see if it is indeed valid (in high dimensions) or not.

Outline. In Sect. 2 we introduce notation and cover key ingredients of the hybrid algorithms. Sections 3–4 describe these new algorithms, and state the main heuristic results regarding the $2^{\Theta(d/\log d)}$ speedups for solving SVP. Section 5 describes experimental results, to verify the new heuristic assumption introduced in Sect. 3 and to get an idea of the performance in practice. Appendices B, C contain derivations omitted from Sect. 2.3 and Sect. 3 respectively.

2 Preliminaries

2.1 Lattice Problems

Let $\mathbf{B} = \{b_1, \ldots, b_d\} \subset \mathbb{R}^d$ be a set of linearly independent vectors, which we may also interpret as a matrix with columns b_i. The lattice generated by $\mathbf{B}$ is defined as $\mathcal{L} = \mathcal{L}(\mathbf{B}) := \{\mathbf{B}\lambda : \lambda \in \mathbb{Z}^d\}$. We write $\mathrm{vol}(\mathcal{L}) := \det(\mathbf{B}^T\mathbf{B})^{1/2}$ for the volume of a lattice $\mathcal{L}$. Given a basis $\mathbf{B}$, we write $\mathbf{B}^* = \{b_1^*, \ldots, b_d^*\}$ for its Gram-Schmidt orthogonalization. We write $D_{t+\mathcal{L},s}$ for the discrete Gaussian distribution on $t + \mathcal{L}$ with probability mass function proportional to $\rho_s(x) = \exp(-\pi\|x\|^2/s^2)$ [2]. We define $\lambda_1(\mathcal{L}) := \min_{v \in \mathcal{L}\setminus\{0\}} \|v\|$ and for $t \in \mathbb{R}^d$ we define $d(t, \mathcal{L}) := \min_{v \in \mathcal{L}} \|t - v\|$, where all norms are Euclidean norms.

Definition 1 (Shortest vector problem – SVP($\mathcal{L}$)). *Given a lattice $\mathcal{L}$, find a non-zero lattice vector $s \in \mathcal{L}$ satisfying $\|s\| = \lambda_1(\mathcal{L})$.*

Definition 2 (Closest vector problem – CVP($\mathcal{L}, t$)). *Given a lattice $\mathcal{L}$ and a vector $t \in \mathbb{R}^d$, find a lattice vector $s \in \mathcal{L}$ satisfying $\|t - s\| = d(t, \mathcal{L})$.*

In the preprocessing variant of CVP (CVPP), one is allowed to preprocess the lattice $\mathcal{L}$, and use the preprocessed data to solve a CVP instance t. This problem naturally comes up in contexts where either $\mathcal{L}$ is known long before t is known, or if a large number of CVP instances on the same lattice are to be solved.

2.2 Heuristic Assumptions

For our asymptotic analyses we will rely on a number of common heuristic assumptions, which have often been used throughout the literature.

Assumption 1 (Gaussian heuristic). *Given a full-rank lattice $\mathcal{L}$ and a region $\mathcal{A} \subset \mathbb{R}^d$, the (expected) number of lattice points in $\mathcal{A}$, denoted $|\mathcal{A} \cap \mathcal{L}|$, satisfies:*

$$|\mathcal{A} \cap \mathcal{L}| = \frac{\mathrm{vol}(A)}{\mathrm{vol}(\mathcal{L})}. \tag{1}$$

Using volume arguments, the Gaussian heuristic predicts that $\lambda_1(\mathcal{L}) = \mathrm{gh}(\mathcal{L})$ where $\mathrm{gh}(\mathcal{L}) := \sqrt{d/(2\pi e)} \cdot \mathrm{vol}(\mathcal{L})^{1/d} \cdot (1 + o(1))$. For random targets $t \in \mathbb{R}^d$, we further expect that $d(t, \mathcal{L}) = \mathrm{gh}(\mathcal{L}) \cdot (1 + o(1))$ with high probability.

Assumption 2 (Geometric series assumption [32]). *After performing lattice basis reduction on a lattice basis* **B***, the Gram-Schmidt basis* **B*** *satisfies*

$$\|\boldsymbol{b}_i^*\| = q^{i-1}\|\boldsymbol{b}_1\|, \qquad q \in (0,1). \tag{2}$$

The GSA is used in analyzing enumeration and Babai lifting (Sects. 2.3, 2.6).

Assumption 3 (Randomized slicer assumption [10]). *Let* $s \gg 0$, *and let* $X_1, X_2, \cdots \in \{0,1\}$ *denote the events that running the iterative slicer on* $t_i \sim D_{t+\mathcal{L},s}$ *returns the shortest vector* $t' \in t + \mathcal{L}$ $(X_i = 1)$ *or not* $(X_i = 0)$. *Then the random variables* X_i *are identically and independently distributed.*

This assumption is related to the randomized slicer, discussed in Sect. 2.5.

2.3 Lattice Enumeration

For constructing hybrid algorithms for solving SVP, we will combine several existing techniques, the first of which is lattice enumeration. This method, first described in the 1980s [13,20] and later significantly improved in practice [5, 15,29], can be seen as a brute-force approach to SVP: every lattice vector can be described as an integer linear combination of the basis vectors, and given some guarantees on the quality of the input basis, this results in bounds on the coefficients of the shortest vector in terms of this basis. The algorithm can be described as a depth-first tree search, requiring $d^{O(1)}$ memory and $2^{O(d \log d)}$ time. For further details, we refer the reader to e.g. [15,16,26].

For our purposes, what is important to know is that the complexity of (partial) enumeration is proportional to the number of nodes visited in the tree, and that the number of nodes at depth $k = o(d)$ for a strongly-reduced d-dimensional lattice basis is $2^{O(k \log d)}$. More precisely, we will need the following lemma. A heuristic derivation, based on estimates from [17], is given in Appendix B.

Lemma 1 (Costs of enumeration [17]). *Let* **B** *be a strongly reduced basis of a lattice. Then the number of nodes* E_k *at depth* $k = o(d)$, $k = d^{1-o(1)}$, *satisfies:*

$$\mathrm{E}_k = d^{k/2+o(k)}. \tag{3}$$

Enumerating all these nodes can be done in time $\mathrm{T}_{\mathrm{enum}}$ *and space* $\mathrm{S}_{\mathrm{enum}}$, *with:*

$$\mathrm{T}_{\mathrm{enum}} = \mathrm{E}_k \cdot d^{O(1)}, \qquad \mathrm{S}_{\mathrm{enum}} = d^{O(1)}. \tag{4}$$

2.4 Lattice Sieving

Another method for solving SVP, and which will be part of our hybrid algorithms, is lattice sieving. This method dates back to the 2000s [3,28,30] and has seen various recent improvements [4,8,11,19,21] that allowed it to surpass enumeration in the SVP benchmarks [1]. This method only requires $2^{O(d)}$ time to solve SVP in dimension d (compared to $2^{O(d \log d)}$ for enumeration), but this comes at the cost of a memory requirement of $2^{O(d)}$. The algorithm starts out by generating a large number of lattice vectors as simple combinations of the basis vectors, and then proceeds by combining suitable pairs of vectors to form shorter lattice vectors. For additional details, see e.g. [8,16,22,26].

In the context of this paper we will make use of the following result from [8], which is the current state-of-the-art for (heuristic) lattice sieving in high dimensions d. The statement below is stronger than saying that sieving merely solves SVP, as lattice sieving commonly returns a list of all short lattice vectors within radius approximately $\sqrt{4/3} \cdot \lambda_1(\mathcal{L})$. This same assumption was used in [11].

Lemma 2 (Costs of lattice sieving [8]). *Given a basis* $\mathbf{B}$ *of a lattice* $\mathcal{L}$, *the LDSieve heuristically returns a list* $L \subset \mathcal{L}$ *containing the* $(4/3)^{d/2+o(d)}$ *shortest lattice vectors, in time* T_{sieve} *and space* S_{sieve} *with:*

$$T_{\text{sieve}} = (3/2)^{d/2+o(d)}, \qquad S_{\text{sieve}} = (4/3)^{d/2+o(d)}. \tag{5}$$

With the LDSieve we can therefore solve SVP with the above complexities.

2.5 The Randomized Slicer

The third ingredient for our hybrid algorithms is the randomized slicer for solving CVP(P). This algorithm, described in [10], is an extension of the iterative slicer [33], and follows a procedure of reducing targets t with a list $L \subset \mathcal{L}$ to find shorter vectors $t' \in t + \mathcal{L}$. The goal is to find the shortest vector $t^* \in t + \mathcal{L}$ by repeatedly reducing t with L, since $t - t^*$ is the solution to CVP$(\mathcal{L}, t)$.

We will make use of two separate results from [12]. These results differ in whether one desires to solve only one or many CVP instances on the same lattice; as shown in [12], solving many CVP instances simultaneously allows for more efficient memory management, thus allowing to achieve a better overall time complexity for a given space bound. Here $\zeta = -\frac{1}{2}\log_2(1 - \frac{2(1-y)}{1+\sqrt{1-y}}) = 0.2639\ldots$ where $y = 0.7739\ldots$ is a root of $p(y) = 16y^4 - 80y^3 + 120y^2 - 64y + 9$.

Lemma 3 (Costs of the randomized slicer, single target [12]). *Given a list of the* $(4/3)^{d/2+o(d)}$ *shortest vectors of a lattice* $\mathcal{L}$ *and a target* $t \in \mathbb{R}^d$, *the randomized slicer solves CVP for* t *in time* T_{slice} *and space* S_{slice}, *with:*

$$T_{\text{slice}} = 2^{\zeta d+o(d)}, \qquad S_{\text{slice}} = (4/3)^{d/2+o(d)}. \tag{6}$$

Lemma 4 (Costs of the randomized slicer, many targets [12]). *Given a list of the* $(4/3)^{d/2+o(d)}$ *shortest vectors of a lattice* $\mathcal{L}$ *and a batch of* $n \geq (13/12)^{d/2+o(d)}$ *target vectors* $t_1, \ldots, t_n \in \mathbb{R}^d$, *the batched randomized slicer solves CVP for all targets* t_i *in total time* T_{slice} *and space* S_{slice}, *with:*

$$T_{\text{slice}} = n \cdot (18/13)^{d/2+o(d)}, \qquad S_{\text{slice}} = (4/3)^{d/2+o(d)}. \tag{7}$$

The amortized time complexity per instance equals $T_{\text{slice}}/n = (18/13)^{d/2+o(d)}$.

2.6 Babai Lifting

Finally, we will revisit the extension to lattice sieving described in [11], based on Babai's nearest plane algorithm [6]. As observed by Ducas, lattice sieving returns much more information about a lattice than just the shortest vector, and this additional information can be used to obtain a few dimensions *for free* – to solve SVP in dimension d, it suffices to run sieving on a sublattice of dimension $d - \ell$ with $\ell = \Theta(d/\log d)$, and use the resulting list of vectors in this sublattice to find the shortest vector in the full lattice.

Lemma 5 (Costs of Babai lifting [11]). *Let $\gamma > 1$, let $\mathbf{B} = \{\boldsymbol{b}_1, \ldots, \boldsymbol{b}_d\}$ be a sufficiently reduced basis of a lattice $\mathcal{L}$, and let $\mathcal{L}' \subset \mathcal{L}$ be the sublattice of $\mathcal{L}$ generated by $\mathbf{B}' = \{\boldsymbol{b}_1, \ldots, \boldsymbol{b}_{d-\ell}\}$, where:*

$$\ell = \frac{2d\log_2\gamma}{\log_2 d} \cdot (1 + o(1)). \tag{8}$$

Then, given a list L' of the $\gamma^{d+o(d)}$ shortest vectors of $\mathcal{L}'$, we can find a shortest vector of $\mathcal{L}$ through Babai lifting of L' in time $\mathrm{T_{lift}}$ and space $\mathrm{S_{lift}}$, with

$$\mathrm{T_{lift}} = \gamma^{d+o(d)}, \qquad \mathrm{S_{lift}} = \gamma^{d+o(d)}. \tag{9}$$

For $\gamma = \sqrt{4/3}$ this results in $\ell = d\log_2(4/3)/\log_2 d$ dimensions for free.

3 Sieve, Enumerate, Slice, and Lift!

Suppose we have a basis $\mathbf{B} = \{\boldsymbol{b}_1, \ldots, \boldsymbol{b}_d\}$ of a lattice $\mathcal{L} = \mathcal{L}(\mathbf{B})$, and we split it into two disjoint parts as follows, for some choice $0 \le k \le d$:

$$\mathbf{B} = \mathbf{B}_{\mathrm{bot}} \cup \mathbf{B}_{\mathrm{top}}, \quad \mathbf{B}_{\mathrm{bot}} := \{\boldsymbol{b}_1, \ldots, \boldsymbol{b}_{d-k}\}, \quad \mathbf{B}_{\mathrm{top}} := \{\boldsymbol{b}_{d-k+1}, \ldots, \boldsymbol{b}_d\}. \tag{10}$$

This defines a partition of the lattice $\mathcal{L} = \mathcal{L}_{\mathrm{bot}} \oplus \mathcal{L}_{\mathrm{top}}$ as a direct sum of the two sublattices $\mathcal{L}_{\mathrm{bot}} := \mathcal{L}(\mathbf{B}_{\mathrm{bot}})$ and $\mathcal{L}_{\mathrm{top}} := \mathcal{L}(\mathbf{B}_{\mathrm{top}})$. Let us further denote a solution $\boldsymbol{s} = \mathrm{SVP}(\mathcal{L})$ as $\boldsymbol{s} = \boldsymbol{s}_{\mathrm{bot}} + \boldsymbol{s}_{\mathrm{top}}$ with $\boldsymbol{s}_{\mathrm{bot}} \in \mathcal{L}_{\mathrm{bot}}$ and $\boldsymbol{s}_{\mathrm{top}} \in \mathcal{L}_{\mathrm{top}}$. Finding $\boldsymbol{s}$ can commonly be described as solving a CVP instance on $\mathcal{L}_{\mathrm{bot}}$:

$$\boldsymbol{s}_{\mathrm{top}} \ne \boldsymbol{0} \implies \boldsymbol{s} = \boldsymbol{s}_{\mathrm{top}} - \mathrm{CVP}(\mathcal{L}_{\mathrm{bot}}, \boldsymbol{s}_{\mathrm{top}}). \tag{11}$$

Note that the case $\boldsymbol{s}_{\mathrm{top}} = \boldsymbol{0}$ is in a sense "easy", as then $\boldsymbol{s} = \mathrm{SVP}(\mathcal{L}_{\mathrm{bot}})$. The hardest problem instances occur when $\boldsymbol{s}_{\mathrm{top}} \ne \boldsymbol{0}$, and this will be our main focus.

Lattice enumeration can be viewed as a procedure for solving SVP based on the above observations: first enumerate all target vectors $\boldsymbol{t} \in \mathcal{L}_{\mathrm{top}}$ that have the potential to satisfy $\boldsymbol{t} = \boldsymbol{s}_{\mathrm{top}}$, and then compute $\mathrm{CVP}(\mathcal{L}_{\mathrm{bot}}, \boldsymbol{t})$ for each of these targets through a continued enumeration procedure on the sublattice $\mathcal{L}_{\mathrm{bot}}$, to see which of them produces the solution to SVP on the full lattice. Observe that lattice enumeration commonly solves each of these CVP instances separately, even though each problem instance can be viewed as a CVP instance on the *same* lattice $\mathcal{L}_{\mathrm{bot}}$, but with a different target vector $\boldsymbol{t} \in \mathcal{L}_{\mathrm{top}}$.

As previously outlined in e.g. [10,15], a truly efficient CVPP algorithm would imply a way to speed up processing all these CVP instances in enumeration; one would first run a one-time preprocessing on the sublattice $\mathcal{L}_{\text{bot}}$, and then solve all the CVP instances at some level k using the preprocessed data as input for the CVP(P) oracle. The initial preprocessing step may be expensive, but these costs can be amortized over the many CVP instances that potentially have to be solved during the enumeration phase. At the time of [15] no good heuristic CVPP algorithm was known, but with the results of [10,12,24] we may now finally instantiate the above idea with the ingredients from Sects. 2.3–2.5.

3.1   Hybrid 1: Sieve, Enumerate–and–Slice

In the first hybrid, after the preprocessing (sieve) finishes, we compute closest vectors to targets $t \in \mathcal{L}_{\text{top}}$ one vector at a time. This algorithm has two phases, where the second phase combines enumeration with the randomized slicer.

1. **Sieve**: First, run a lattice sieve on $\mathcal{L}_{\text{bot}}$ to generate a list $L \subset \mathcal{L}_{\text{bot}}$.
2. **Enumerate–and–slice**: Then, run a depth-first enumeration in $\mathcal{L}_{\text{top}}$, where for each leaf $t \in \mathcal{L}_{\text{top}}$ we run the randomized slicer to find the closest vector $\text{CVP}(t) \in \mathcal{L}_{\text{bot}}$. We keep track of the shortest difference vector $t - \text{CVP}(t)$, and ultimately return the shortest one as a candidate solution for $\text{SVP}(\mathcal{L})$.[1]

To optimize the asymptotic time complexity of this algorithm, note that the cost of enumeration in $\mathcal{L}_{\text{top}}$ is $T_{\text{enum}} = 2^{O(k \log d)}$ while the costs of sieving and slicing in $\mathcal{L}_{\text{bot}}$ are $T_{\text{sieve}}, T_{\text{slice}} = 2^{O(d-k)}$. To balance these costs, and minimize the overall time complexity, we will therefore set k as follows:

$$k = \frac{\alpha \cdot d}{\log_2 d}, \qquad \text{with } \alpha > 0 \text{ constant.} \tag{12}$$

Using Lemmas 1–3, optimizing α to obtain the best overall asymptotic time complexity is a straightforward exercise, and we state the result below. A detailed derivation of the following result is given in Appendix C.

Heuristic result 1 (Sieve, enumerate–and–slice). *Let* $k = \alpha d / \log_2 d$ *with*

$$\alpha < \log_2(\tfrac{3}{2}) - 2\zeta = 0.0570\ldots \qquad (\zeta \text{ as in Lemma 3}) \tag{13}$$

Let $T_1^{(d)}$ *and* $S_1^{(d)}$ *denote the overall time and space complexities of the sieve, enumerate–and–slice hybrid algorithm in dimension* d. *Then:*

$$T_1^{(d)} = T_{\text{sieve}}^{(d-k)} \cdot (1 + o(1)), \qquad S_1^{(d)} = S_{\text{sieve}}^{(d-k)} \cdot (1 + o(1)). \tag{14}$$

Letting $\alpha \to \log_2(\tfrac{3}{2}) - 2\zeta$ in the above result, we get $k \approx 0.0570 d / \log_2 d$ with an asymptotic speedup of a factor $2^{0.0167 d / \log_2 d}$ and a memory reduction of a factor $2^{0.0118 d / \log_2 d}$ compared to running a sieve directly on $\mathcal{L}$. Note that the result does not hide subexponential or even polynomial hidden order terms; the time and space complexities are dominated by the preprocessing costs.

---

[1] The case $s_{\text{top}} = \mathbf{0}$ can be handled by checking if L contains an even shorter vector.

3.2   Hybrid 2: Sieve, Enumerate, Slice

An alternative to the above approach is to separate the enumeration and slicing procedures into two disjoint parts, and run the hybrid algorithm in three phases. The benefit of this approach (cf. Sect. 2.5) is that the *batched* slicer can then be used to achieve better amortized complexities for CVPP.

1. **Sieve:** As before, run a lattice sieve on $\mathcal{L}_{\text{bot}}$, to generate a list $L \subset \mathcal{L}_{\text{bot}}$.
2. **Enumerate:** Then, enumerate all nodes $t \in \mathcal{L}_{\text{top}}$ at depth k in the enumeration tree, and store them in a list of targets $T \subset \mathcal{L}_{\text{top}}$.
3. **Slice:** Finally, use the batched randomized slicer with the list L to solve CVP on $\mathcal{L}_{\text{bot}}$ for all targets $t \in T$, and return the shortest vector $t - \text{CVP}(t)$.

Asymptotically, the additional space required for storing the nodes from the enumeration phase will not play a large role, compared to the memory required for storing the output from the preprocessing phase. On the other hand, by using the improved batch-CVPP slicer of Lemma 4 we can use nearest neighbor searching more efficiently, without increasing the memory, leading to a bigger improvement over standard sieving than with the first hybrid algorithm.

Heuristic result 2 (Sieve, enumerate, slice). *Let* $k = \alpha d / \log_2 d$ *with*

$$\alpha < \log_2(\tfrac{13}{12}) = 0.1154\dots . \tag{15}$$

Let $\mathrm{T}_2^{(d)}$ *and* $\mathrm{S}_2^{(d)}$ *denote the overall time and space complexities of the batched sieve, enumerate, slice hybrid algorithm in dimension* d. *Then:*

$$\mathrm{T}_2^{(d)} = \mathrm{T}_{\text{sieve}}^{(d-k)} \cdot (1 + o(1)), \qquad \mathrm{S}_2^{(d)} = \mathrm{S}_{\text{sieve}}^{(d-k)} \cdot (1 + o(1)). \tag{16}$$

In the limit of $\alpha \to \log_2(\tfrac{13}{12})$ we get $k \approx 0.1154 d / \log_2 d$ dimensions *for free*, leading to an asymptotic speedup of a factor $2^{0.0338 d / \log_2 d + o(d / \log d)}$ and a memory reduction of a factor $2^{0.0240 d / \log_2 d + o(d / \log d)}$ over direct sieving on $\mathcal{L}$.

3.3   Hybrid 3: Sieve, Enumerate–and–Slice, Lift

For the third and fourth hybrids, we observe that similar to lattice sieving, the slicer in the previous hybrid algorithms can actually produce much more information about the lattice than just the shortest lattice vector; for other targets $t \neq s_{\text{top}}$, as well as for "failed" outputs of the randomized slicer, the slicer will also return many short lattice vectors. This suggests that to get even more dimensions *for free*, we may be able to combine both hybrids with Babai lifting as outlined in Lemma 5.

Instead of splitting the lattice into two parts, we now split the input lattice basis into three parts $\mathbf{B} = \mathbf{B}_{\text{bot}} \cup \mathbf{B}_{\text{mid}} \cup \mathbf{B}_{\text{top}}$, where the three bases $\mathbf{B}_{\text{bot}} := \{b_1, \dots, b_\ell\}$, $\mathbf{B}_{\text{mid}} := \{b_{\ell+1}, \dots, b_{d-k}\}$, and $\mathbf{B}_{\text{top}} := \{b_{d-k+1}, \dots, b_d\}$ generate lattices $\mathcal{L}_{\text{bot}}, \mathcal{L}_{\text{mid}}, \mathcal{L}_{\text{top}}$ of dimensions ℓ, $d - k - \ell$ and k respectively. For Hybrid 3 we essentially run Hybrid 1 on $\mathcal{L}_{\text{mid}} \oplus \mathcal{L}_{\text{top}}$, and use Babai lifting to deal with the additional ℓ dimensions of $\mathcal{L}_{\text{bot}}$. This leads to the following algorithm:

1. **Sieve**: Run a lattice sieve on $\mathcal{L}_{\mathrm{mid}}$ to generate a list $L \subset \mathcal{L}_{\mathrm{mid}}$.
2. **Enumerate–and–slice**: Enumerate all nodes $t \in \mathcal{L}_{\mathrm{top}}$, and repeatedly slice each of them with the list L to find close vectors $v \in \mathcal{L}_{\mathrm{mid}}$. For each pair t, v add the vector $t - v$ to an output list $S \subset \mathcal{L}_{\mathrm{mid}} \oplus \mathcal{L}_{\mathrm{top}}$.
3. **Lift**: Finally, extend each vector $s' \in S$ to a candidate solution $s \in \mathcal{L}$ by running Babai's nearest plane algorithm. Return the shortest lifted vector.

As the slicer processes $E_k = d^{k/2+o(k)} = 2^{\alpha d/2+o(d)}$ target vectors, and requires $\rho = (16/13)^{d/2+o(d)}$ rerandomizations per target for average-case CVP to succeed (see [10,12] for details), the slicer outputs $2^{(\alpha+\log_2(16/13))\cdot d/2+o(d)}$ lattice vectors, and ideally we might hope this list contains, similar to sieving [11], (almost) all lattice vectors of norm at most $\gamma = 2^{(\alpha+\log_2(16/13))/2+o(1)} \cdot \mathrm{gh}(\mathcal{L})$.

Assumption 4 (Hybrid assumption). *The list S, output by the slicer, contains the $2^{(\alpha+\log_2(16/13))\cdot d/2+o(d)}$ shortest lattice vectors of $\mathcal{L}_{\mathrm{mid}} \oplus \mathcal{L}_{\mathrm{top}}$.*

Assuming that the above heuristic is indeed valid, we derive the following result regarding the asymptotic time and space complexities of the described hybrid algorithm. In Sect. 5 we will revisit this assumption, to study its validity[2].

Heuristic result 3 (Sieve, enumerate–and–slice, lift). *Let $k = \alpha d/\log_2 d$ and $\ell = \beta d/\log_2 d$ with*

$$\alpha < \log_2(\tfrac{3}{2}) - 2\zeta = 0.0570\ldots, \qquad \beta < \log_2(\tfrac{24}{13}) - 2\zeta = 0.3565\ldots. \qquad (17)$$

Let $\mathrm{T}_3^{(d)}$ and $\mathrm{S}_3^{(d)}$ denote the time and space complexities of the sieve, enumerate–and–slice, lift hybrid algorithm in dimension d. Then, under Assumption 4:

$$\mathrm{T}_3^{(d)} = \mathrm{T}_{\mathrm{sieve}}^{(d-k-\ell)} \cdot (1+o(1)), \qquad \mathrm{S}_3^{(d)} = \mathrm{S}_{\mathrm{sieve}}^{(d-k-\ell)} \cdot (1+o(1)). \qquad (18)$$

Observe that the number of dimensions we save compared to a full sieve here is $k + \ell \approx 0.4136 d/\log_2 d$. Compared to the result of Ducas [11] of $\ell \approx 0.4150 d/\log_2 d$ this new hybrid is asymptotically slightly worse than a sieve–and–lift hybrid.

3.4 Hybrid 4: Sieve, Enumerate, Slice, Lift

Finally, combining the second hybrid with lifting, as in the third hybrid algorithm above, results in the following optimized hybrid procedure:

1. **Sieve**: Run a lattice sieve on $\mathcal{L}_{\mathrm{mid}}$ to generate a list $L \subset \mathcal{L}_{\mathrm{mid}}$.
2. **Enumerate**: Enumerate all nodes $t \in T \subset \mathcal{L}_{\mathrm{top}}$ at depth k in $\mathcal{L}$.

---

[2] After this paper was accepted, Léo Ducas and Wessel van Woerden informed us that counterexamples to Assumption 4 can be found where S only contains at most an exponentially small fraction of the shortest vectors of $\mathcal{L}_{\mathrm{mid}} \oplus \mathcal{L}_{\mathrm{top}}$. As a result, our results relying on Assumption 4 should be seen as optimistic, best-case lower bounds on the true algorithm complexities. More details can be found in the revised online version https://eprint.iacr.org/2020/487.pdf.

3. **Slice:** Run the slicer, with the list L as input, to find close vectors in $\mathcal{L}_{\mathrm{mid}}$ to the targets $t \in T$. The result is a list $S \subset \mathcal{L}_{\mathrm{mid}} \oplus \mathcal{L}_{\mathrm{top}}$.
4. **Lift:** Finally, extend each vector $s' \in S$ to a candidate solution $s \in \mathcal{L}$ by running Babai's nearest plane algorithm. Return the shortest lifted vector.

Table 1. An overview of the techniques used in the hybrids, as well as the asymptotic number of dimensions *for free* for each part and in total (last column). In sufficiently high dimensions, under Assumption 4, Hybrid 4 outperforms all other algorithms, by saving up to $0.53d/\log_2 d$ dimensions compared to sieving in the full lattice.

Algorithm	Sieve	Enum./Slice		Lift	Dimensions for free		
		(Single)	(Batch)		($\frac{k}{d}\log_2 d$)	($\frac{\ell}{d}\log_2 d$)	($\frac{k+\ell}{d}\log_2 d$)
Full sieve [8]	✓				–	–	–
Hybrid 1	✓	✓			0.0570	–	0.0570
Hybrid 2	✓		✓		0.1154	–	0.1154
Hybrid 3	✓	✓		✓	0.0570	0.3566	0.4136
SubSieve [11]	✓			✓	–	0.4150	0.4150
Hybrid 4	✓		✓	✓	0.1155	0.4150	**0.5305**

Not only does splitting the enumeration and slicing guarantee that the batched version of the slicer gets better complexities; the smaller resulting value α also means that the number of vectors output by the slicer is larger, which leads to more dimensions for free from the lifting phase. In particular, with the batched slicer the number of vectors output by the slicer is proportional to $(4/3)^{d/2+o(d)}$, and we may get as many dimensions for free in the lifting phase as [11].

Heuristic result 4 (Sieve, enumerate, slice, lift). *Let $k = \alpha d/\log_2 d$ and $\ell = \beta d/\log_2 d$ with*

$$\alpha < \log_2(\tfrac{13}{12}) = 0.1154\ldots, \qquad \beta < \log_2(\tfrac{4}{3}) = 0.4150\ldots. \tag{19}$$

Let $\mathrm{T}_4^{(d)}$ and $\mathrm{S}_4^{(d)}$ denote the time and space complexities of the sieve, enumerate, slice, and lift hybrid algorithm in dimension d. Then, under Assumption 4:

$$\mathrm{T}_4^{(d)} = \mathrm{T}_{\mathrm{sieve}}^{(d-k-\ell)} \cdot (1 + o(1)), \qquad \mathrm{S}_4^{(d)} = \mathrm{S}_{\mathrm{sieve}}^{(d-k-\ell)} \cdot (1 + o(1)). \tag{20}$$

We again stress that the above result relies on a *batched* version of the randomized slicer. With this batched hybrid algorithm with lifting, assuming the hybrid assumption holds, we can potentially get up to $k + \ell \approx 0.5305d/\log_2(d)$ dimensions *for free*, which would improve upon Ducas' $\ell \approx 0.4150d/\log_2(d)$ [11].

An overview of the techniques used in the four hybrids, as well as the number of dimensions for free in each algorithm, is given in Table 1.

4   Sieve, Enumerate, Slice, Repeat!

For the fourth hybrid, under Assumption 4 the enumeration and batched slicer together take as input a list of all vectors of norm at most $\sqrt{4/3} \cdot \mathrm{gh}(\mathcal{L}')$ of a suitable sublattice $\mathcal{L}' \subset \mathcal{L}$, and output (almost) all lattice vectors of norm at most $\sqrt{4/3} \cdot \mathrm{gh}(\mathcal{L})$ of $\mathcal{L}$. This suggests one might replace the initial sieving step on $\mathcal{L}_{\mathrm{mid}}$ by a sieve, enumerate, slice hybrid (Hybrid 2), by splitting $\mathcal{L}_{\mathrm{mid}} = \mathcal{L}_{\mathrm{mid}}^{(1)} \oplus \mathcal{L}_{\mathrm{mid}}^{(2)}$ with $\mathrm{rank}(\mathcal{L}_{\mathrm{mid}}^{(2)}) = \Theta(d/\log d)$; running a sieve on $\mathcal{L}_{\mathrm{mid}}^{(1)}$; enumerating $\mathcal{L}_{\mathrm{mid}}^{(2)}$; and then using the slicer to find a list of short vectors $L \subset \mathcal{L}_{\mathrm{mid}}$. Under Assumption 4, this substitution of the initial sieve by Hybrid 2 can be repeated many times to obtain $\Theta(d/\log d)$ dimensions for free several times.

As an alternative interpretation, rather than running enumeration on k levels directly, one additional level of nesting suggests we first run the lower $k/2$ levels of enumeration, lift the resulting target vectors to obtain short vectors in a lattice of rank $d - k/2$, and then run another $k/2$ levels of enumeration to find short vectors in the full lattice. Splitting up the enumeration this way decreases the overall enumeration costs and the number of targets for the slicing phases $(\mathrm{E}_{k/2} + \mathrm{E}_{k/2} \ll \mathrm{E}_k)$, but at the same time the list output by the first slicing phase might not be as good for the second slicing phase as what one would get from running a sieve directly; even if Assumption 4 is true, likely this still comes at a slight loss in the quality of the list, say in the first order terms.

We finally observe that the same idea of nesting does not seem to work for the sieve, lift hybrid of [11]. Although one could define a "generalized" Babai lifting procedure, lifting targets to all nearby vectors in the higher-rank lattice, from a viewpoint of enumeration we are "missing" some branches in the tree due to L only containing some nodes in the tree at level $d - \ell$. Therefore, if the

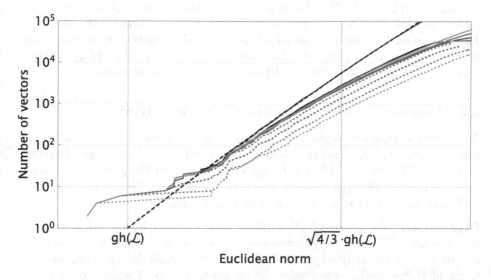

Fig. 1. The number of vectors found through a sieve (black) and sieve, enumerate, slice hybrids for $k \in \{1, 2, 3, 4\}$ (orange, green, blue, red) in dimension 60. The dashed black line, and the purple line intersecting it for large norms, indicate the true number of lattice vectors below this norm. The dashed colored lines indicate the lists obtained from running sieving in sublattices of rank $d - k$. (Color figure online)

312   E. Doulgerakis et al.

shortest vector in the lattice is actually in one of those missing branches, then a generalized lifting procedure will not succeed in finding this shortest vector.

Although we will briefly revisit the idea of nesting in the experiments in the next section, we leave a technical study of nesting for future work.

5   Experimental Results

5.1   Verifying Assumption 4

To attempt to validate (or disprove) the new heuristic assumption, we performed the following experiment. We used the 60-dimensional SVP challenge lattice with seed 0 [1], pre-reduced with BKZ-50 [31], for which $gh(\mathcal{L}) \approx 2001$ and $\lambda_1(\mathcal{L}) \approx 1943$. The black dashed line in Fig. 1 shows the expected number of lattice points below a certain norm by the Gaussian heuristic (Assumption 1). The (barely visible) purple line intersecting this line for high norms shows the actual number of lattice vectors found by a "relaxed" sieve [23], showing the accuracy of the Gaussian heuristic for large balls.

To test Assumption 4, we then ran both a standard g6k lattice sieve to produce a list L_0 (black) [4]; and sieve, enumerate, slice hybrids for $k \in \{1, 2, 3, 4\}$ by (1) running g6k on the $(d-k)$-dimensional sublattice formed by $b_1, \ldots, b_{d-k}$ to produce a list L_k, (2) running enumeration up to depth k in the full lattice to obtain targets T_k, (3) slicing each target $t \in T_k$ up to $20 \cdot (16/13)^{(d-k)/2}$ times, to obtain a list S_k, and (4) plotting the sorted norms of both L_k (dashed) and $S_k \cup L_k$ (solid) in Fig. 1. These results show that (i) as expected, the preprocessed lists L_k in rank $d-k$ become increasingly poor approximations of the sieved list L_0 as k increases, and (ii) the sliced lists $S_k \cup L_k$ together form very good approximations to the sieved list L_0. Note that, at norm $\sqrt{4/3} \cdot gh(\mathcal{L})$, all these lists are quite far off from the prediction by the Gaussian heuristic.

5.2   Assessing the Sieve, Enumerate–and–Slice Hybrid

To study the practical performance of these hybrid algorithms, we performed some preliminary experiments in dimensions 60–80, whose results are described in Table 2. This table is deferred to Appendix A due to the page limit; instead here we will describe the setup of the experiments, and discuss the results as well as conclusions that can or cannot be drawn from these results.

BKZ. To start, we used the SVP challenge lattices [1] with seed 0 in dimensions $d \in \{60, 65, 70, 75, 80\}$. We preprocessed each basis with BKZ with block size $d-10$. In case the shortest vector had a 0-coefficient for b_d when expressed in terms of $\mathbf{B}$, we would rerandomize the basis and run BKZ again, to guarantee that the preprocessed lists do not already contain the solution.

Sieve. Next, we used the g6k [35] framework to generate sieving lists in dimensions $d-k$, for $k = 0, 1, 2, 3$. We disabled the "dimensions for free" from g6k, to test the pure hybrids for their performance and limit the impact of other factors for now. The case $k = 0$ corresponds to sieving in the full lattice, and the timings in dimensions $d - k$ clearly decrease with k, as shown in Table 2. The resulting vectors were stored in an output file, and their sizes are also given in Table 2.

Enumerate. Then, we ran a full enumeration in the full lattice up to depth k, to generate the target vectors for the slicer. These were again stored in a separate file for later usage. Note that pruning would reduce the number of targets further, but (1) this would decrease the success probability of the overall algorithm, and (2) rerandomizing the lattice basis to get a high success probability would (naively) require running the costly sieving preprocessing step several times. We therefore restricted experiments to enumeration without pruning.

Slice. Finally, with the sieved list L and target vectors T as input, we identified the target $t \in T$ corresponding to the shortest vector in the lattice, and for this target we ran the randomized slicer with 10^5 trials to estimate the success probability p_{iter} of the slicer in finding the shortest vector. Table 2 shows the inverse p_{iter}^{-1} as well as the average time for each trial, which together with $|T|$ can then be used to estimate the time for the slicing as $T_{slice} \approx |T| \cdot p_{iter}^{-1} \cdot T_{iter}$.

Nested Hybrid. We also tested a simple nested hybrid from Sect. 4, with two successive (non-batched) enumerate–and–slice routines in dimension $k = 1$. In the first slicing phase, we chose the total number of iterations such that the size of the output list matches the size of a directly sieved list for $k = 1$. The rows $k = 1 + 1$ in Table 2 suggest this approach compares favorably to $k = 2$.

Conclusions. Although the results in Table 2 mainly suggest that these hybrid approaches may have a large overhead in practice, we stress that as d grows, the time complexity grows slower than a full sieve. Furthermore, for the slicer we did not use nearest neighbor techniques or batching to reduce the query times. Also, note that as $0.11d/\log_2 d < 2$ for $d < 128$ we do not expect to obtain many (additional) dimensions *for free* in dimensions $60 \leq d \leq 80$. The aforementioned reasons can provide some insight why the speedup was not observed in practice in our experiments[3].

Code in fplll. As part of this project, we implemented the iterative slicer in fplll [34], and we expect this code to be included in the library soon.

Acknowledgements. The authors thank Léo Ducas for helpful suggestions regarding the possible combination with his "dimensions for free". Emmanouil Doulgerakis is supported by the NWO under grant 628.001.028 (FASOR). Thijs Laarhoven is supported by a Veni grant from NWO under project number 016.Veni.192.005.

A   Figures and Tables

Due to the page limit, we have deferred some tables and figures to the appendix. Table 2 shows the experimental results for the experiments described in Sect. 5.

---

[3] As discussed in the footnote to Assumption 4, a possible explanation for why this may not lead to $\omega(d/\log d)$ dimensions for free is that Assumption 4 is imprecise and too optimistic.

Figures 2 and 3 present graphical overviews of the hybrid algorithms described Sects. 3 and 4, where the horizontal axis depicts the basis vectors $b_1, \ldots, b_d$ and the vertical axis corresponds to the time (with algorithms starting from the top and ending at the bottom).

Table 2. Experimental results and estimates for the costs of the hybrid algorithms, in dimensions $d \in \{60, 65, 70, 75, 80\}$ and for parameter choices $k \in \{0, 1, 2, 3\}$ as well as the nested hybrid with two iterations of $k = 1$. Single-core timings are denoted in milliseconds (ms), seconds (s), minutes (m), hours (h), and days (d). List sizes $|L|$ and estimates on the required number of rerandomizations p_{iter}^{-1} are sometimes given in multiples of one thousand (k). The last column gives estimates for the total time complexities for these algorithms, by adding up the costs for BKZ, sieving, enumeration, and slicing. The case $k = 0$ corresponds to running a sieve on the full lattice directly.

Parameters		BKZ	— Sieve —		— Enum —		— Slice —			Total
d	k	$T_{BKZ}^{(d-10)}$	$|L|$	$T_{sieve}^{(d-k)}$	$|T|$	$T_{enum}^{(k)}$	$T_{iter}^{(d-k)}$	p_{iter}^{-1}	$T_{slice}^{(d-k)}$	$T_{hyb}^{(d)}$
60	0	4 s	18k	19 s	–	–	–	–	–	23 s
	1	4 s	16k	16 s	5	0 s	3.2 ms	830	13 s	33 s
	2	4 s	13k	12 s	30	0 s	2.7 ms	530	43 s	59 s
	3	4 s	12k	9 s	155	0 s	2.4 ms	760	280 s	293 s
	1+1	4 s	13k	12 s	4	0 s	3.0 ms	500	6 s	51 s
			(16k)	(0 s)	5	0 s	3.2 ms	1820	29 s	
65	0	8 s	37k	78 s	–	–	–	–	–	1 m
	1	8 s	32k	57 s	5	0 s	6.8 ms	12.5k	7 m	8 m
	2	8 s	28k	44 s	37	0 s	6.6 ms	2.9k	12 m	13 m
	3	8 s	24k	36 s	215	0 s	5.6 ms	2.9k	58 m	59 m
	1+1	8 s	28k	44 s	4	0 s	6.6 ms	1.1k	0.5 m	6 m
			(32k)	(0 s)	5	0 s	6.8 ms	6.7k	4 m	
70	0	1 m	76k	5 m	–	–	–	–	–	6 m
	1	1 m	65k	4 m	6	0 m	20 ms	17k	35 m	40 m
	2	1 m	57k	3 m	46	0 m	16 ms	1k	12 m	16 m
	3	1 m	49k	2 m	293	0 m	13 ms	6k	381 m	384 m
	1+1	1 m	57k	3 m	5	0 m	15 ms	2k	2 m	43m
			(65k)	(0 m)	5	0 m	18 ms	25k	37 m	
75	0	2 m	155k	22 m	–	–	–	–	–	0.4 h
	1	2 m	134k	16 m	6	0 m	40 ms	25k	2 h	2 h
	2	2 m	116k	11 m	50	0 m	48 ms	20k	13 h	14 h
	3	2 m	101k	8 m	366	0 m	30 ms	12k	37 h	37 h
	1+1	2 m	116k	11 m	5	0 m	35 ms	4k	0.2 h	>8 h
			(134k)	(0 m)	6	0 m	41 ms	>100k	>7 h	
80	0	14 m	320k	74 m	–	–	–	–	–	1.5 h
	1	14 m	275k	58 m	7	0 m	95 ms	>100k	>18 h	>20 h
	2	14 m	240k	45 m	64	0 m	74 ms	>50k	>66 h	>67 h
	3	14 m	205k	36 m	506	0 m	66 ms	>50k	>19 d	>19 d

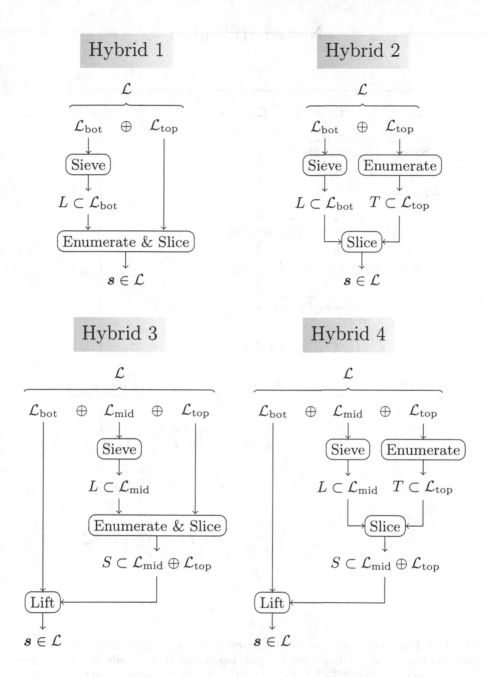

Fig. 2. A high-level description of the hybrid algorithms presented in this paper. Hybrids 1 and 3 combine enumeration and slicing, performing the randomized slicing procedure for *only one* target vector at a time. Hybrids 3 and 4 use the Babai lifting technique from [11]. The asymptotics of the slicer depend on whether targets are processed directly (left) or in batches (right). The lifting can be done directly as well, without affecting the performance of the algorithm.

Nested Hybrid

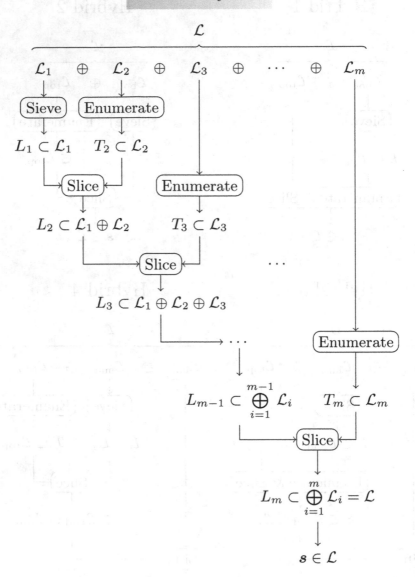

Fig. 3. A high-level description of the potential recursive hybrid algorithm, which starts on a lattice $\mathcal{L}_1$ of dimension $d - \Theta(d/\log d)$, and then repeatedly lifts the lists $L_i \subset \mathcal{L}_1 \oplus \cdots \oplus \mathcal{L}_i$ to lists $L_{i+1} \subset \mathcal{L}_1 \oplus \cdots \oplus \mathcal{L}_{i+1}$ by enumerating targets $T_{i+1} \subset \mathcal{L}_{i+1}$ and using the batched slicer with L_i as input to create L_{i+1}. Each lattice $\mathcal{L}_i$ for $i > 1$ has dimension $\Theta(d/\log d)$.

B   The Number of Nodes in the Enumeration Tree

We restate Lemma 1 and give a derivation of this claim based on results from [17] and a straightforward asymptotic expansion of the resulting formulas.

Lemma 1 (Costs of enumeration). *Let* **B** *be a strongly reduced basis of a lattice*[4] *satisfying the GSA. Then the number of nodes* E_k *in the enumeration tree at depth* $k = o(d)$*, with* $k = d^{1-o(1)}$*, heuristically satisfies:*

$$E_k = d^{k/2+o(k)}. \tag{21}$$

Enumerating all these nodes can be done in time T_{enum} *and space* S_{enum}*, with:*

$$T_{enum} = E_k \cdot d^{O(1)}, \qquad S_{enum} = d^{O(1)}. \tag{22}$$

Proof. As a starting point, we take the formula from [17, Section 6.2], which was derived using the Gaussian heuristic:

$$E_k = \frac{\pi^{k/2}}{\Gamma(k/2+1)} \cdot \frac{\|\boldsymbol{b}_1\|^k}{\prod_{i=d-k+1}^{d} \|\boldsymbol{b}_i^*\|}. \tag{23}$$

For the gamma function, we can use a very rough version of Stirling's approximation of the form $\Gamma(x) = (x/e)^{x+o(x)}$, which for the first term above gives an asymptotic scaling of $(2\pi e/k)^{k/2+o(k)} = k^{-k/2+o(k)}$. For the terms $\|\boldsymbol{b}_1\|$ and $\|\boldsymbol{b}_i^*\|$, we apply the geometric series assumption, which states that $\|\boldsymbol{b}_i^*\| = q^{i-1}$ for some $q \in (0,1)$. Using that $\sum_{i=d-k+1}^{d}(i-1) = k(2d-k-1)/2 = kd - o(kd)$ for $k = o(d)$, this reduces the above to:

$$E_k = k^{-k/2+o(k)} \cdot q^{-kd+o(kd)}. \tag{24}$$

Next, we note that for a sufficiently well-reduced basis **B**, we have $\|\boldsymbol{b}_1\| = O(\lambda_1(\mathcal{L})) = O(\sqrt{d}) \cdot \text{vol}(\mathcal{L})^{1/d}$. From the GSA, we then get:

$$\text{vol}(\mathcal{L}) = \prod_{i=1}^{d} \|\boldsymbol{b}_i^*\| = q^{d(d+1)/2}\|\boldsymbol{b}_1\|^d = q^{d(d+1)/2}d^{-d/2+o(d)} \text{vol}(\mathcal{L}). \tag{25}$$

From this we can conclude that $q = d^{-1/d+o(1/d)}$ and $q^{-kd+o(kd)} = d^{k+o(k)}$. From the assumptions that $k = d^{1-o(1)}$ and $k = o(d)$ we then get:

$$E_k = d^{-k/2+o(k)} \cdot d^{k+o(k)} = d^{k/2+o(k)}. \tag{26}$$

As for the time and space complexities of enumeration, as has been noted several times before [5,13,15] the time complexity is directly proportional to the size of the enumeration tree, while the space complexity is only polynomial in d.   □

---

[4] Similar to [11, Section 3.4], concretely we may assume **B** is quasi-HKZ reduced.

C   Asymptotics of the Hybrid Algorithms

Below we restate and give a derivation of Heuristic result 1, by analyzing the concrete time and space complexities for each phase, and arguing that with a suitable parameterization indeed the costs of the algorithm are strictly dominated by the costs of the sieve in the preprocessing phase.

Heuristic result 1 (Sieve, enumerate–and–slice). *Let $k = \alpha d / \log_2 d$ with*

$$\alpha < \log_2(\tfrac{3}{2}) - 2\zeta = 0.0570\dots. \qquad (\zeta \text{ as in Lemma 3}) \qquad (27)$$

Let $\mathrm{T}_1^{(d)}$ and $\mathrm{S}_1^{(d)}$ denote the overall time and space complexities of the sieve, enumerate–and–slice hybrid algorithm in dimension d. Then:

$$\mathrm{T}_1^{(d)} = \mathrm{T}_{\text{sieve}}^{(d-k)} \cdot (1 + o(1)), \qquad \mathrm{S}_1^{(d)} = \mathrm{S}_{\text{sieve}}^{(d-k)} \cdot (1 + o(1)). \qquad (28)$$

Proof. For the time complexities, recall that the costs of the individual parts of the algorithm, by Lemmas 1–3, are given by:

$$\mathrm{T}_{\text{sieve}} = 2^{\frac{1}{2}\log_2(\frac{3}{2})d + o(d)}, \qquad \mathrm{T}_{\text{enum}} = 2^{\frac{\alpha}{2}d + o(d)}, \qquad \mathrm{T}_{\text{slice}} = 2^{(\frac{\alpha}{2}+\zeta)d + o(d)}. \qquad (29)$$

Clearly $\mathrm{T}_{\text{enum}} = o(\mathrm{T}_{\text{slice}})$ since $\zeta > 0$. Now, due to $\alpha < \alpha_0 = \log_2(\tfrac{3}{2}) - 2\zeta$ being strictly smaller than the point where $\mathrm{T}_{\text{sieve}} \approx \mathrm{T}_{\text{slice}}$, we have $\mathrm{T}_{\text{slice}} = o(\mathrm{T}_{\text{sieve}})$ as well, giving a total time complexity of $\mathrm{T} = \mathrm{T}_{\text{sieve}} \cdot (1 + o(1))$. Finally, looking closely, we note that the cost $\mathrm{T}_{\text{sieve}}$ actually corresponds to running a standard lattice sieve in dimension $d - k$, which can be done in time $\mathrm{T}_{\text{sieve}}^{(d-k)}$ as claimed.

For the space complexities, we recall them from Lemmas 1–3 as follows:

$$\mathrm{S}_{\text{sieve}} = (4/3)^{d/2 + o(d)}, \qquad \mathrm{S}_{\text{enum}} = \text{poly}(d), \qquad \mathrm{S}_{\text{slice}} = (4/3)^{d/2 + o(d)}. \qquad (30)$$

Since $\alpha < \alpha_0$, the time complexity of the enumerate–and–slice procedure is strictly smaller than the cost of the preprocessing phase, and this will remain true even if we use a slightly smaller list as output from the preprocessing phase. So for sufficiently small $\varepsilon > 0$, we may therefore choose to use a list $L' \subset L$ for the enumerate–and–slice phase of size $|L'| = |L|^{1-\varepsilon}$, while still maintaining a time complexity $\mathrm{T}_{\text{slice}} = o(\mathrm{T}_{\text{sieve}})$. This guarantees that the overhead caused by the quasilinear-space nearest neighbor data structure, required in the third phase to achieve sublinear search costs, does not impose any overhead in the asymptotic space complexity; the memory required in the third phase will then be of size $\mathrm{S}_{\text{slice}} = (\mathrm{S}_{\text{sieve}}^{1-\varepsilon})^{1+o(1)} = o(\mathrm{S}_{\text{sieve}})$. □

For the other heuristic results, analogous derivations can be given to argue that both the time and space complexities are dominated by the initial sieving phase, as long as the parameters k (and ℓ) are below the point where the sieving and slicing (and lifting) become equally expensive. Further note that although the batched slicer has a cost of $(3/2)^{d/2+o(d)} + n \cdot (18/13)^{d/2+o(d)}$ for n targets due to the reinitializations of the costly nearest neighbor data structures [12], these costs can again be made to be $(3/2-\varepsilon)^{d/2+o(d)} + n^{1-\varepsilon} \cdot (18/13)^{d/2+o(d)}$ by slightly reducing the number of targets and the number of hash tables accordingly.

References

1. SVP Challenge (2019). https://www.latticechallenge.org/svp-challenge/
2. Aggarwal, D., Dadush, D., Regev, O., Stephens-Davidowitz, N.: Solving the shortest vector problem in 2^n time via discrete Gaussian sampling. In: Proceedings of the 47th STOC, pp. 733–742 (2015). https://doi.org/10.1145/2746539.2746606
3. Ajtai, M., Kumar, R., Sivakumar, D.: A sieve algorithm for the shortest lattice vector problem. In: Proceedings of the 33rd STOC, pp. 601–610. ACM Press (2001)
4. Albrecht, M.R., Ducas, L., Herold, G., Kirshanova, E., Postlethwaite, E.W., Stevens, M.: The general sieve kernel and new records in lattice reduction. In: Ishai, Y., Rijmen, V. (eds.) EUROCRYPT 2019. LNCS, vol. 11477, pp. 717–746. Springer, Cham (2019). https://doi.org/10.1007/978-3-030-17656-3_25
5. Aono, Y., Nguyen, P.Q.: Random sampling revisited: lattice enumeration with discrete pruning. In: Coron, J.-S., Nielsen, J.B. (eds.) EUROCRYPT 2017. LNCS, vol. 10211, pp. 65–102. Springer, Cham (2017). https://doi.org/10.1007/978-3-319-56614-6_3
6. Babai, L.: On lovasz lattice reduction and the nearest lattice point problem. Combinatorica **6**(1), 1–13 (1986). https://doi.org/10.1007/BF02579403
7. Bai, S., Laarhoven, T., Stehlé, D.: Tuple lattice sieving. In: Proceedings of the 12th ANTS 19(A), pp. 146–162 (2016)
8. Becker, A., Ducas, L., Gama, N., Laarhoven, T.: New directions in nearest neighbor searching with applications to lattice sieving. In: Proceedings of the 27th SODA, pp. 10–24. ACM-SIAM (2016)
9. Chen, Y., Nguyên, P.Q.: BKZ 2.0: Better lattice security estimates. In: Proceedings of the 17th ASIACRYPT, pp. 1–20 (2011). https://doi.org/10.1007/978-3-642-25385-0_1
10. Doulgerakis, E., Laarhoven, T., de Weger, B.: Finding closest lattice vectors using approximate Voronoi cells. In: Ding, J., Steinwandt, R. (eds.) PQCrypto 2019. LNCS, vol. 11505, pp. 3–22. Springer, Cham (2019). https://doi.org/10.1007/978-3-030-25510-7_1
11. Ducas, L.: Shortest vector from lattice sieving: a few dimensions for free. In: Nielsen, J.B., Rijmen, V. (eds.) EUROCRYPT 2018. LNCS, vol. 10820, pp. 125–145. Springer, Cham (2018). https://doi.org/10.1007/978-3-319-78381-9_5
12. Ducas, L., Laarhoven, T., van Woerden, W.: The randomized slicer for CVPP: sharper, faster, smaller, batchier. Preprint (2019)
13. Fincke, U., Pohst, M.: Improved methods for calculating vectors of short length in a lattice. Math. Comput. **44**(170), 463–471 (1985)
14. Fukase, M., Kashiwabara, K.: An accelerated algorithm for solving SVP based on statistical analysis. J. Inf. Process. **23**(1), 67–80 (2015). https://doi.org/10.2197/ipsjjip.23.67
15. Gama, N., Nguyen, P.Q., Regev, O.: Lattice enumeration using extreme pruning. In: Gilbert, H. (ed.) EUROCRYPT 2010. LNCS, vol. 6110, pp. 257–278. Springer, Heidelberg (2010). https://doi.org/10.1007/978-3-642-13190-5_13
16. Hanrot, G., Pujol, X., Stehlé, D.: Algorithms for the shortest and closest lattice vector problems. In: Proceedings of the 3rd IWCC, pp. 159–190 (2011). https://doi.org/10.1007/978-3-642-20901-7_10
17. Hanrot, G., Stehlé, D.: Improved Analysis of Kannan's Shortest Lattice Vector Algorithm. In: Menezes, A. (ed.) CRYPTO 2007. LNCS, vol. 4622, pp. 170–186. Springer, Heidelberg (2007). https://doi.org/10.1007/978-3-540-74143-5_10

18. Herold, G., Kirshanova, E.: Improved algorithms for the approximate k-list problem in euclidean norm. In: Fehr, S. (ed.) PKC 2017. LNCS, vol. 10174, pp. 16–40. Springer, Heidelberg (2017). https://doi.org/10.1007/978-3-662-54365-8_2
19. Herold, G., Kirshanova, E., Laarhoven, T.: Speed-ups and time–memory trade-offs for tuple lattice sieving. In: Abdalla, M., Dahab, R. (eds.) PKC 2018. LNCS, vol. 10769, pp. 407–436. Springer, Cham (2018). https://doi.org/10.1007/978-3-319-76578-5_14
20. Kannan, R.: Improved algorithms for integer programming and related lattice problems. In: Proceedings of the 15th STOC, pp. 193–206. ACM Press (1983)
21. Laarhoven, T.: Sieving for shortest vectors in lattices using angular locality-sensitive hashing. In: Gennaro, R., Robshaw, M. (eds.) CRYPTO 2015. LNCS, vol. 9215, pp. 3–22. Springer, Heidelberg (2015). https://doi.org/10.1007/978-3-662-47989-6_1
22. Laarhoven, T.: Search problems in cryptography. Ph.D. thesis, Eindhoven University of Technology (2016). http://repository.tue.nl/837539
23. Laarhoven, T.: Sieving for closest lattice vectors (with preprocessing). In: Avanzi, R., Heys, H. (eds.) SAC 2016. LNCS, vol. 10532, pp. 523–542. Springer, Cham (2017). https://doi.org/10.1007/978-3-319-69453-5_28
24. Laarhoven, T.: Approximate Voronoi cells for lattices, revisited. In: Proceedings of the 1st MATHCRYPT (2019). https://arxiv.org/pdf/1907.04630.pdf
25. Laarhoven, T., Mariano, A.: Progressive lattice sieving. In: Lange, T., Steinwandt, R. (eds.) PQCrypto 2018. LNCS, vol. 10786, pp. 292–311. Springer, Cham (2018). https://doi.org/10.1007/978-3-319-79063-3_14
26. Laarhoven, T., van de Pol, J., de Weger, B.: Solving hard lattice problems and the security of lattice-based cryptosystems. Cryptology ePrint Archive, Report 2012/533, pp. 1–43 (2012). http://eprint.iacr.org/2012/533
27. Micciancio, D., Voulgaris, P.: A deterministic single exponential time algorithm for most lattice problems based on Voronoi cell computations. In: Proceedings of the 42nd STOC, pp. 351–358. ACM Press (2010)
28. Micciancio, D., Voulgaris, P.: Faster exponential time algorithms for the shortest vector problem. In: Proceedings of the 21st SODA, pp. 1468–1480. ACM-SIAM (2010)
29. Micciancio, D., Walter, M.: Fast lattice point enumeration with minimal overhead. In: Proceedings of the 26th SODA, pp. 276–294 (2015). https://doi.org/10.1137/1.9781611973730.21
30. Nguyen, P.Q., Vidick, T.: Sieve algorithms for the shortest vector problem are practical. J. Math. Cryptol. **2**(2), 181–207 (2008)
31. Schnorr, C.P.: A hierarchy of polynomial time lattice basis reduction algorithms. Theoret. Comput. Sci. **53**(2), 201–224 (1987)
32. Schnorr, C.P.: Lattice reduction by random sampling and birthday methods. In: Alt, H., Habib, M. (eds.) STACS 2003. LNCS, vol. 2607, pp. 145–156. Springer, Heidelberg (2003). https://doi.org/10.1007/3-540-36494-3_14
33. Sommer, N., Feder, M., Shalvi, O.: Finding the closest lattice point by iterative slicing. SIAM J. Discrete Math. **23**(2), 715–731 (2009). https://doi.org/10.1137/060676362
34. The FPLLL development team: fplll, a lattice reduction library (2019). https://github.com/fplll/fplll
35. The g6k development team: The general sieve kernel (G6K) (2019). https://github.com/fplll/g6k

Side Channel Attacks

Online Template Attack on ECDSA:
Extracting Keys via the Other Side

Niels Roelofs, Niels Samwel$^{(\boxtimes)}$, Lejla Batina, and Joan Daemen

Radboud University, PO Box 9010, 6500 GL Nijmegen, The Netherlands
nielsroelofs95@gmail.com, {nsamwel,lejla,joan}@cs.ru.nl

Abstract. We retrieve the ephemeral private key from the power trace of a single scalar multiplication in an ECDSA signature generation and from that the signing private key using an online template attack. The innovation is that we generate the profiling traces using ECDSA signature verification on the *same* device. The attack can be prevented by randomization of the (projective) coordinates of the base point.

Keywords: Online template attacks · Scalar multiplication · ECDSA

1 Introduction

Template attacks are a very powerful type of side channel attacks, typically featuring two phases: profiling and key recovery [5]. In the profiling phase, the device's leakage is characterized as a probability distribution to make optimally use of the information present in each time sample of a leakage trace. In the attacking phase, the key is identified using the maximum likelihood principle. In the public-key cryptography application scenario, template attacks can be used to extract a private key from a single power consumption or electromagnetic emanation trace of a device performing an exponentiation of scalar multiplication [15].

In this paper we concentrate on the scalar multiplication with a known base point and a secret scalar. The goal of the adversary will be to extract the latter one. Typically, an attacker derives some bits of the secret scalar based on some well-defined positions in the trace and thereafter recovers the remainder of the scalar via lattice reduction techniques. The first phase of the attack (profiling) requires the generation of *templates* and for that the attacker ideally must be able to take traces from the same device, running scalar multiplications with chosen scalars. We call those *profiling* traces.

With classical template attacks, the required number of profiling traces to perform a successful attack can be large, depending on the noise level, set-up, implementation characteristics etc. An important innovation in this respect was the technique of the Online Template Attack (OTA) [1] that reduces the number of profiling traces to less than two times the number of scalar bits.

In real-world attack scenario's it rarely happens that an attacker can get profiling traces from the device that contains the target key. For that reason,

© Springer Nature Switzerland AG 2020
A. Nitaj and A. Youssef (Eds.): AFRICACRYPT 2020, LNCS 12174, pp. 323–336, 2020.
https://doi.org/10.1007/978-3-030-51938-4_16

one often obtains the profiling traces from a device of the same type running the same software. This is, for instance, the case if the target device is a JavaCard used for banking or used as an ID card, assuming that the attacker is able to obtain an open JavaCard from the same type. However, profiling traces obtained from a device different than the target device are not necessarily accurate due to variations between individual chips. This is the so-called issue of *portability* that has received wide coverage in many papers the last few years [3,6]. For dedicated security products such as smart cards it is often even infeasible to obtain an open device similar to the target device and profiling is simply out of the question.

In this paper we make use of a simple observation to generate profiling traces using the target device itself, thereby completely bypassing the portability discussion and the non-availability of open devices. This observation is the following: products that support the Elliptic Curve Digital Signature Algorithm (ECDSA) algorithm typically support both signature generation that includes a scalar multiplication with an ephemeral private key and signature verification that includes two scalar multiplications with scalars that are provided to the device and can hence be chosen by an attacker. The idea is simply to use scalar multiplications in the signature verification to generate profiling traces. There are still some obstacles: the scalar multiplications in signature generation and verification may make use of different algorithms. In a way, the issue of portability between devices is now replaced by a portability problem between algorithms. In this paper, we report on an attack that overcomes the difference in algorithms and succeeds in extracting the private ephemeral key from a single ECDSA signature generation trace using profiling traces from ECDSA signature verification traces on the same device.

The remainder of the paper is structured as follows. We discuss related work in Sect. 1.1 and summarize the contributions of this paper in Sect. 1.2. We provide the necessary background in Sect. 2. Section 3 focuses on the vulnerability identified and how it might actually be exploited and in Sect. 4 we introduce the actual exploitation process itself.

1.1   Related Work

There are two research directions that should be considered as relevant previous work. The first one is on portability and the other one is the work on online template attacks.

Considering the importance of portability, Elaabid and Guilley [9] show that, when precharacterized templates are outdated, the consequence can be as drastic as ranking the correct key last. The work of Choudary and Kuhn focuses on differences between devices when performing portable template attacks (considering mainly DC offset caused by temperature changes) [7]. Bhasin et al. recently compared different machine learning techniques on the efficacy with respect to portability [3]. A common point in all those works is they identified the problem and try to amortize the penalty due to portability.

Online template attacks are an adaptive template-attack technique that can recover a complete scalar from only one power trace of a scalar multiplication using this scalar [1]. The attack is characterized as online, because the templates are created after the acquisition of the target trace. The attack is not a typical template attack; i.e. no pre standard profiling template-building phase is necessary. The attack is demonstrated by acquiring one target trace from the device under attack and comparing patterns of certain identical operations from this trace with templates obtained from the attacker's device that runs the same implementation. Our work examines another dimension of online templates, as we address the portability issue at the same time by applying OTA on the same device. This strategy requires the templates creation phase to use another algorithm than the one which implementation we attack. This minor but subtle difference requires some creativity with the new attack we propose as the templates to compare and identify within the actual trace are not readily available. Our strategy is initiated by a common scenario in real-world applications where one often has only one device available and it solves the portability problem.

1.2 Contributions

In this work we show the feasibility of OTA using a single device, so templates collection and the key recovery are performed in identical conditions. This use case puts the portability discussion in perspective. We successfully extract the ephemeral private key from a single power consumption trace of an ECDSA signature generation implemented on an 8-bit microcontroller. We use the ECDSA signature verification on the same device for the online templates. The fact that the scalar multiplication in signature verification uses another algorithm than the one in signature generation does not prevent our attack.

2 Background

In this section we discuss some principles needed to understand our attack: the ECDSA signature scheme, the relevant scalar multiplication algorithms and the principle of OTA.

2.1 ECDSA

By now it is almost twenty years ago that Johnson et al. proposed the elliptic curve variant of the Digital Signature Algorithm [13]. Next to RSA [18] and Ed25519 [2] it is one of the most commonly used signature algorithms. We specify the ECDSA signing algorithm in Algorithm 1 and its verifying counterpart in Algorithm 2, along with the symbol clarification in Table 1.

In the context of side-channel analysis, in relation to elliptic curves, scalar multiplications are the standard go-to, especially if the scalar is a secret value. Namely, in the case of ECDSA, if an adversary somehow learns the value for k by exploiting some side channel during the scalar multiplication on line 3 of Algorithm 1, he can compute the private key d via line 8 of Algorithm 1 since it is the only unknown variable left.

Table 1. Symbol clarification for ECDSA related algorithms.

Symbol	Meaning	Element of
B	Base point	The elliptic curve
l	Order of base point	$\mathbb{N}$
k	Ephemeral private key	$\mathbb{Z}/l\mathbb{Z}$
d	Long-term private key	$\mathbb{Z}/l\mathbb{Z}$
D	Public key $(D = [d]B)$	$\langle B \rangle$
$H(...)$	Hash of input	$\mathbb{Z}/l\mathbb{Z}$
M	Message	$\{0,1\}^*$
(r,s)	Signature	$(\mathbb{Z}/l\mathbb{Z}, \mathbb{Z}/l\mathbb{Z})$

Algorithm 1: ECDSA signature generation.

    Input: d, l, B, M
    Output: (r, s)
1 $z \leftarrow H(M)$
2 **while** *true* **do**
3      $k \leftarrow create\_nonce(1, l-1)$
4      $(x, y) \leftarrow [k]B$
5      $r \leftarrow x \bmod l$
6   **if** $r == 0$ **then**
7 | **continue**   // new k needed
8   **end**
9      $s \leftarrow k^{-1}(z + rd) \bmod l$
10   **if** $s == 0$ **then**
11 | **continue**   // new k needed
12   **end**
13   **break**
14 **end**
15 **return** (r, s)

Algorithm 2: ECDSA signature verification.

    Input: l, r, s, B, D, M
    Output: *signature_accepted*
1 *signature_accepted* $\leftarrow 0$
2 $z \leftarrow H(M)$
3 $w \leftarrow s^{-1} \bmod l$
4 $u_1 \leftarrow zw \bmod l$
5 $u_2 \leftarrow rw \bmod l$
6 $(x, y) \leftarrow [u_1]B + [u_2]D$
7 **if** $x == r \bmod l$ **then**
8 | *signature_accepted* $\leftarrow 1$
9 **end**
10 **return** *signature_accepted*

2.2 Double-and-Add

One of the simplest fast methods for scalar multiplication is the double-and-add algorithm, see Algorithm 3.

This algorithm iterates over the scalar k, starting from the most significant bit, doubles the intermediate result in every round and conditionally adds the elliptic curve point if the scalar bit processed equals 1.

Algorithm 3: Double-and-add algorithm.

> **Input:** $(k_{n-1}, k_{n-2}, ..., k_0), P$
> **Output:** $Q = kP$
> 1 $Q \leftarrow O$
> 2 **for** $i \leftarrow n - 1$ **down to** 0 **do**
> 3 | $Q \leftarrow 2Q$
> 4 | **if** $k_i == 1$ **then**
> 5 | | $Q \leftarrow Q + P$
> 6 | **end**
> 7 **end**
> 8 **return** Q

However, this procedure is insecure to use in a cryptographic setting when k has to be kept private if a side-channel vector exists in the form of time due to the conditional statement in line 4. If different rounds within the execution of the algorithm can be distinguished from one another the secret scalar can be reconstructed bit by bit. This is not necessarily trivial. Nevertheless, to prevent such time-based attacks, one should avoid branching on secret data altogether.

2.3 Montgomery Ladder

An alternative for the double-and-add algorithm is the Montgomery ladder [16], as specified in Algorithm 4. Peter Montgomery invented it back in 1987 to speed up factorization using elliptic curves and it offers resistance against the type of side-channel attacks as discussed above.

Due to the regular structure of the algorithm, and therefore the lack of branches, the scalar multiplication occurs in constant time and even provides protection against some power analysis techniques, such as simple power analysis [14].

Still, the algorithm needs to somehow distinguish between 0 and 1 scalar bits being processed. It does so by working with two shares, X_0 and X_1. Based on the key bit, the shared a swapped in constant time by the function $cswap$. The value shares are swapped if a bit is set.

Algorithm 4 only gives a high level overview of the Montgomery ladder. In the last few decades quite some research has been done in optimizing it for speed and/or memory usage and improving its resistance against side-channel analysis. For the remainder of the paper we refer to the Montgomery ladder implementation done by Hutter et al. [12].

Algorithm 4: Montgomery ladder.

    Input: $(k_{n-1}, k_{n-2}, ..., k_0), P$
    Output: $Q = kP$
1 $X_0 \leftarrow O$
2 $X_1 \leftarrow P$
3 **for** $i \leftarrow n-1$ **down to** 0 **do**
4 | $X_1 \leftarrow X_0 + X_1$
5 | $X_0 \leftarrow 2X_0$
6 | $(X_0, X_1) = cswap(X_0, X_1, k_i)$
7 **end**
8 **return** X_0

2.4 Online Template Attack

OTA [1] can be seen as a combination a template attack [5] and doubling attacks as introduced for the scalar multiplication operation on an elliptic curve [10].

The main difference between a standard template attack and OTA is that the latter requires at most two power traces per scalar bit to recover, while in the former case it easily can be hundreds or thousands. Additionally, with OTA the process of template generation and matching can be interleaved per bit to recover. So, OTA is faster in template generation building and matching and uses significantly less storage in comparison to a standard template attack.

When looking at Algorithm 3, the key idea of OTA is the following: based on the bit value of k_{n-2}, Q will equal $2P$ or $3P$ before the doubling operation at the start of the third round of the for loop. That is because the most significant bit k_{n-1} will equal 1. Although an adversary does not know which case occurred, he can create his own profile trace, a template, for both cases. Assuming that he has access to a power consumption trace of a target doing the secret scalar multiplication and is able to identify a single doubling operation of an elliptic curve point, he can apply correlation analysis techniques to derive the correct scalar bit. That is, he compares how similar the doubling operation in the beginning of the third round of the for loop is with both of his templates in terms of power consumption. Depending on the scalar multiplication and the hardware used, it might even be possible to only generate one template and accept the corresponding correlation value based on a certain threshold value, which has to be determined empirically.

Once the value of k_{n-2} has been identified, the whole process can be repeated to determine the next bit of the scalar. The only matters that require updating are the possible input values for the doubling operation on line 3 of Algorithm 3 and the location of the doubling operation in the target trace. For example, assuming that $k_{n-2} = 0$, the template traces will represent $4P$ and $5P$.

Note that by itself it is overkill to apply OTA to the double-and-add algorithm because a simple power analysis technique will already suffice. However, in the next section we grasp the key idea of OTA and apply it to an implementation of the Montgomery ladder.

3   Spotting the Attack Vector

This section focuses on the vulnerability identified and how it might actually be exploited.

3.1   Finding the Similarity

As introduced before, for the attack to succeed, we need to find some key dependent operation in the ECDSA signing procedure, that can be mimicked with its verifying counterpart. If such a relation can be found, it allows an adversary to generate templates of that operation, one where the bit of the scalar is 0 and one where it is equal to 1.

In side channel analysis of ECDSA the typical method to achieve key extraction is to use the scalar multiplication of the ephemeral private key k with the base point B, see line 3 of Algorithm 1. If k can be reconstructed, the extraction of the private key is trivial. During the ECDSA verification procedure there are two scalar multiplications taking place as well, so those can serve as an entry point. However here arises a problem: the scalar multiplication method used during signing is the Montgomery ladder, while its counterpart uses the standard double and add algorithm. Not only do their internal computations differ, so do their coordinate systems. In our scenario we assume the usage of standard projective coordinates for the Montgomery ladder and Jacobian coordinates for the double and add algorithm. So in order to find our targeted key-dependent operation we have to dig deeper and look at the underlying field arithmetic in both cases. Once again, solving this kind of issues is the core novelty of this paper since it makes the portability discussion redundant by introducing the new OTA-like method.

Signature generation and signature verification use different scalar multiplication algorithms, thus we are not able to create templates of the whole double-and-add iteration. Instead, we aim to find an operation that is computed in both algorithms. Our requirements are: 1) In the signature generation algorithm the input value of the operation should depend on the key and 2) in the signature verification we should be able to control the input value.

The point that is doubled in the iteration depends on the key bit of the previous iteration, namely $2P$ or $2P + 1$ (see line 4 and 5 of Algorithm 4) will be doubled. We locate an operation in that step to create templates of the key bit used in the previous iteration. For the point doubling operation, the x-coordinate is squared. In the signature verification algorithm, there is also a squaring of the x-coordinate. Since the x-coordinate is part of the public key D, an attacker can control it. Therefore, this value of the x-coordinate and the squaring operation is a good candidate for the generation of templates.

For each key bit, two templates are created, one for the case where $2P$ is doubled and one where $2P + 1$ is doubled, with P the resulting point of the previous round in X_0. The template consists of a power trace of the squaring operation from the corresponding point doubling. To determine which key bit was most likely in the target trace, the Pearson correlation [4] is computed with each template where the template with the highest correlation value corresponds to the correct key bit.

3.2   Preparing the Input

Now that we have found our attack window, the question becomes how to get meaningful data as input for the identified squaring operation so that we can build our wanted templates. A first problem to overcome is to compute the possible intermediate values for X_0 in the Montgomery ladder which may serve as input for the squaring operation in the Jacobian doubling.

The issue can quite easily be solved by implementing our own Montgomery step function in SageMath[1]. After all, the input values for this step function are known, except for the secret scalar itself of course, hence two possible values for X_0 which make up the template.

However, a more serious problem arises with our values just calculated. Namely, when looking at line 6 of Algorithm 2, it only makes sense to feed our template values for X_0 via the public key D, since it is not likely that an outside adversary can manipulate the base point B to use during a signature verification. However, the complication that now arises is that typically in an ECDSA signature verification implementation as a first step a check is made whether the given D is really a public key, that is, whether the point D lies on the curve. The issue here is that it is quite feasible that both computed values for X_0 are indeed not representing a point on the curve.

To circumvent this problem, Papachristodoulou [17] came up with the idea to introduce bit flipping on the least significant bit of X_0. By flipping it, effectively a new value for X_0, say x', is computed. Together with its y' component the coordinate (x', y') might lie on the curve and hence pass the test that D is a valid public key. If (x', y') is still not a point on the curve, the bit flipping is reversed and instead the second least significant bit is flipped. This process continues just as long until a point on the curve is found. Based on experiments of Papachristodoulou and ourselves, a maximum of five tries are needed to find an elliptic curve point that actually lies on the curve.

Since we now know how and what to fill in for D in Algorithm 2, we can focus on the scalar u_2. Looking at Algorithm 3, we can think of line 3 as our Jacobian doubling with our desired squaring operation. In order to get our calculated values for X_0 into the doubling, we need the most significant bit of u_2 to be 1 so that in the beginning of the second round in the for loop our wanted operation happens. It does not really matter what happens afterwards, we only care about the power trace of the squaring operation. u_2 itself is depending on the signature tuple (r, s). So, by some simple brute forcing of either of the values we should have some random value for u_2 for the most significant bit equals 1.

Today's applications typically do not implement a simple double-and-add algorithm and execute it two times to get both scalar multiplications during ECDSA verification. Typically, they apply some kind of optimization, such as

---

[1] http://www.sagemath.org.

Non-Adjacent Form (NAF) [11] or the Straus-Shamir trick [19]. It is important to note that also these implementations are affected, because the vulnerability identified resides inside the underlying finite field arithmetic and not on the higher level scalar multiplication algorithm.

Furthermore, also realize that when creating our templates, the corresponding signature verification results do not have any meaning. It is a logical consequence of taking an intermediate result of one algorithm and use it as input for another in a different coordinate system. The takeaway here is that the verification results are irrelevant, we only care about the retrieved power traces.

4   Exploiting the Attack Vector

Now that we have introduced the entry point of our attack, we will discuss our measurement setup, after which we describe the procedure of bit extraction. We will finish with an effective countermeasure against OTA.

4.1   Measurement Setup

For a total overview of the measurement setup, see Fig. 1 and Table 2 for the symbol clarification.

The device used for our online template attack is the ChipWhisperer-Lite Classic (CWLC). It uses the Atmel Xmega 128D4 8-bit processor which runs at 32 MHz. Actually, the CWLC board consists of two parts: one with Xmega target and one main board which communicates with the target. We access the Xmega target via the main board via a USB-cable. On our computer we run Jupyter notebook to interact with the board within a specially prepared virtual machine[2] provided by the manufacturers of the CWLC.

The board itself is connected to the Waverunner 8404M-MS from Teledyne LeCroy which uses a sample rate of 25 Msamples/s in order to get a power trace. Besides that, there is also wiring from the board to the oscilloscope to plot any trigger mechanisms used. Even though the Xmega target runs our code in constant time, the triggering makes the identification process of the squaring in the trace a bit more convenient. However, it is not a necessity to use it. Finally, the oscilloscope itself is connected to another computer which runs Inspector[3], a side-channel analysis tool we will discuss in the next section.

On a completely different note, it should be mentioned that the execution time of a 256 bit elliptic curve scalar multiplication on a 8-bit architecture is a costly endeavor: approximately 60 s. In contrast, a typical home computer does it in the order of milliseconds. Additionally, the oscilloscope used can capture up to 128 Msamples. With our sampling rate of 25 Msamples/s this means that around 5 s of the signature generation can be captured. After doing some experimenting with this setup we found out that one single round of the Montgomery ladder

---

[2] https://github.com/newaetech/chipwhisperer.

[3] https://www.riscure.com/security-tools/inspector-sca/.

takes 192 ms and that the squaring we are interested in happens at a constant offset of 111.5 ms from the start of a round and takes 10.8 ms. So, this means that we can recover around 20 scalar bits with our setup. Remember, the scalar used with ECDSA signing is different and randomly chosen for every single execution so it is useless to take another target trace. However, this problem can simply by bypassed by using an oscilloscope which has bigger storage capabilities. On top of that, an adversary could try to lower the sampling rate. However, we did not test such a scenario.

4.2 Bit Extraction

Once both profiling traces have been taken for the second most significant bit, the post-processing can start. Realize that we start with the second bit, because the most significant bit will always be 1.

The basic idea is to calculate the Pearson correlation coefficient between a profile trace and every single offset of the target trace. To increase the speed of these calculations we applied the principle of window resampling with a window size of 20 with an overlap of 0.15, which leads to a sample reduction of factor 17. In our case window resampling means that the average is taken of 20 samples, which serves as 1 new sample, and that the last 3 samples of a window are reused in the next window. These numbers have been chosen empirically and are a balance between computation time and still being able to distinguish between different templates. Namely, creating the windows too big in size effective leads to a situation where every window starts to look similar which gives as a consequence that further analysis is not possible.

Table 2. Number clarification for OTA setup Fig. 1.

Number	Meaning
1	CWLC Xmega target
2	CWLC main board
3	Micro-USB connector
4	Measuring cable to oscilloscope
5	Wiring for triggering to oscilloscope
6	Computer running Jupyter notebook
7	Waverunner 8404M-MS oscilloscope
8	Processing power trace with Inspector

The concept above can be implemented quite easily with the tool Inspector from Riscure. If done so separately for both templates, we are given Fig. 2, where (a) represents the correlation analysis when the second most significant bit of the scalar equals equals 0 and (b) when it equals 1.

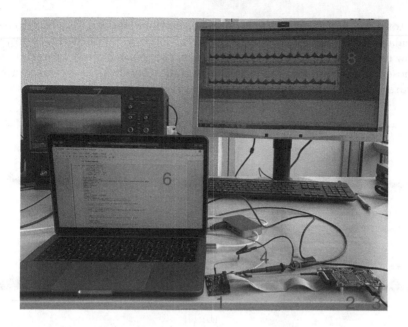

Fig. 1. Overview of the OTA attack setup.

The x-axis of both subfigures captures the time of one complete Montgomery ladder step, 192 ms. The parts in the figure marked in red refer to the area where the correlation coefficient between our template and our targeted squaring in the Montgomery ladder in the target trace should be. And indeed, there is a peak at an offset of 111.5 ms. The other correlation peaks in the figures represent points in time where either another squaring or multiplication operation in the Montgomery ladder occurs. Based on the implementation of Hutter et al. [12], we should have the eleventh peak, which is indeed the case (note the peak at an offset of 0 ms).

As a final step, the only thing that is now left to do is to compare the correlation peak values at the offset of 111.5 ms: (a) gives a correlation of 0.88 and (b) 0.61. Therefore, the conclusion can be drawn that it is more likely that the second most significant bit of the scalar equals 0. And indeed, when creating our setup we set the most significant byte of the scalar to 0×97, which gives in binary 10010111.

From here on onward, the whole procedure can be repeated for the third most significant bit and thereafter the fourth et cetera. For every scalar bit to recover new values have to be computed for X_0. They will serve as input for the templates to generate. Hereby it is important to realize that these values for X_0 depend on the previously scalar bits identified. Additionally, when trying to derive to value for the nth bit, one should look at the correlation peak at an offset of $(n-2)192 + 111.5$ ms.

In total, we repeated this procedure sixteen times and we were able to derive the scalar bit every single time without error, once we applied the appropriate window resampling parameters. Nevertheless, even if somehow a wrong bit would get chosen, the correlation values would significantly drop in successive rounds thereafter, clearly indicating that somewhere something went wrong.

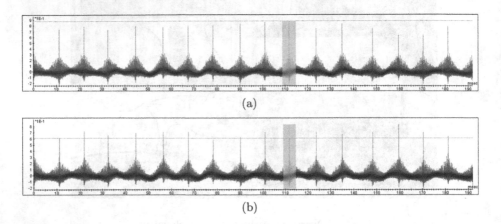

Fig. 2. Correlation results second most significant bit templates. (a) represents bit 0 and (b) bit 1.

4.3 Countermeasures

As demonstrated above, simply implementing the elliptic curve scalar multiplication in a time constant way does not provide protection against OTA. However, as Coron wrote in his influential paper [8], there are some countermeasures that can be taken in order to prevent certain types of power analysis side-channel attacks on elliptic curve cryptosystems.

One of those countermeasures described also protects against OTA: the concept of randomized projective coordinates. It is based on the concept that the projective representation of an elliptic curve point is not unique. See Eq. (1) where λ is a random scalar in $\mathbb{F}_p$, the finite field with modulo p.

$$(X, Y, Z) \leftarrow (\lambda X, \lambda Y, \lambda Z) \tag{1}$$

When this concept is applied on the base point while signing, an adversary can no longer create any meaningful templates for OTA. After all, it becomes impossible to calculate the intermediate computation value of X_0 in the Montgomery ladder which he wants to serve as input for the squaring operation during the verification process because the value is randomized.

A big advantage of this countermeasure is that it is very cheap to implement in terms of speed: it only takes three finite field multiplications. In contrast, a full

Montgomery ladder consists of several thousands of such operations. However, there is one big assumption that must not be overlooked: we assume that a device has the capability to generate randomness, an operation that by itself is far from trivial and definitely not implemented on every device out there in the world.

5 Conclusion

In this paper we demonstrated the feasibility of extracting a secret scalar used in the ECDSA verification procedure via its verifying counterpart, which does not use any secret values by itself. By itself, this is nothing the new. However, the novelty lies in the fact that a single device is used for both collecting the target trace and building the profile traces, while different scalar multiplication algorithms with different coordinate systems are used during ECDSA signing and verification.

Although we showed a rather simple but effective attack, so is its counter-measure of randomizing the coordinates of the base point. Granted, hereby we assume that the device has the ability to generate random numbers, which is definitely not always the case.

References

1. Batina, L., Chmielewski, Ł., Papachristodoulou, L., Schwabe, P., Tunstall, M.: Online template attacks. J. Cryptogr. Eng. **9**(1), 21–36 (2017). https://doi.org/10.1007/s13389-017-0171-8
2. Bernstein, D.J., Duif, N., Lange, T., Schwabe, P., Yang, B.Y.: High-speed high-security signatures. J. Cryptogr. Eng. **2**(2), 77–89 (2012). https://doi.org/10.1007/s13389-012-0027-1
3. Bhasin, S., Chattopadhyay, A., Heuser, A., Jap, D., Picek, S., Shrivastwa, R.R.: Mind the portability: a warriors guide through realistic profiled side-channel analysis. IACR Cryptol. ePrint Arch. **2019**, 661 (2019)
4. Brier, E., Clavier, C., Olivier, F.: Correlation power analysis with a leakage model. In: Joye, M., Quisquater, J.-J. (eds.) CHES 2004. LNCS, vol. 3156, pp. 16–29. Springer, Heidelberg (2004). https://doi.org/10.1007/978-3-540-28632-5_2
5. Chari, S., Rao, J.R., Rohatgi, P.: Template attacks. In: Kaliski, B.S., Koç, K., Paar, C. (eds.) CHES 2002. LNCS, vol. 2523, pp. 13–28. Springer, Heidelberg (2003). https://doi.org/10.1007/3-540-36400-5_3
6. Choudary, M.O., Kuhn, M.G.: Efficient, portable template attacks. IEEE Trans. Inf. Forensics Secur. **13**(2), 490–501 (2018)
7. Choudary, O., Kuhn, M.G.: Efficient template attacks. In: Francillon, A., Rohatgi, P. (eds.) CARDIS 2013. LNCS, vol. 8419, pp. 253–270. Springer, Cham (2014). https://doi.org/10.1007/978-3-319-08302-5_17
8. Coron, J.-S.: Resistance against differential power analysis for elliptic curve cryptosystems. In: Koç, Ç.K., Paar, C. (eds.) CHES 1999. LNCS, vol. 1717, pp. 292–302. Springer, Heidelberg (1999). https://doi.org/10.1007/3-540-48059-5_25
9. Elaabid, M.A., Guilley, S.: Portability of templates. J. Cryptogr. Eng. **2**(1), 63–74 (2012). https://doi.org/10.1007/s13389-012-0030-6

10. Fouque, P.-A., Valette, F.: The doubling attack – *why upwards is better than downwards*. In: Walter, C.D., Koç, Ç.K., Paar, C. (eds.) CHES 2003. LNCS, vol. 2779, pp. 269–280. Springer, Heidelberg (2003). https://doi.org/10.1007/978-3-540-45238-6_22
11. Hankerson, D., Vanstone, S., Menezes, A.: Guide to Elliptic Curve Cryptography. Springer, New York (2004). https://doi.org/10.1007/b97644
12. Hutter, M., Joye, M., Sierra, Y.: Memory-constrained implementations of elliptic curve cryptography in co-Z coordinate representation. In: Nitaj, A., Pointcheval, D. (eds.) AFRICACRYPT 2011. LNCS, vol. 6737, pp. 170–187. Springer, Heidelberg (2011). https://doi.org/10.1007/978-3-642-21969-6_11
13. Johnson, D., Menezes, A., Vanstone, S.: The elliptic curve digital signature algorithm (ECDSA). Int. J. Inf. Secur. **1**(1), 36–63 (2001). https://doi.org/10.1007/s102070100002
14. Kocher, P., Jaffe, J., Jun, B.: Differential power analysis. In: Wiener, M. (ed.) CRYPTO 1999. LNCS, vol. 1666, pp. 388–397. Springer, Heidelberg (1999). https://doi.org/10.1007/3-540-48405-1_25
15. Messerges, T.S., Dabbish, E.A., Sloan, R.H.: Power analysis attacks of modular exponentiation in smartcards. In: Koç, Ç.K., Paar, C. (eds.) CHES 1999. LNCS, vol. 1717, pp. 144–157. Springer, Heidelberg (1999). https://doi.org/10.1007/3-540-48059-5_14
16. Montgomery, P.L.: Speeding the Pollard and elliptic curve methods of factorization. Math. Comput. **48**(177), 243–264 (1987)
17. Papachristodoulou, L.: Masking curves: side-channel attacks on elliptic curve cryptography and countermeasures. Ph.D. thesis, Radboud University Nijmegen (2019)
18. Rivest, R.L., Shamir, A., Adleman, L.: A method for obtaining digital signatures and public-key cryptosystems. Commun. ACM **21**(2), 120–126 (1978)
19. Straus, E.G.: Addition chains of vectors (problem 5125). Am. Math. Mon. **70**(806–808), 16 (1964)

When Similarities Among Devices are Taken for Granted: Another Look at Portability

Unai Rioja[1,2]([✉]), Lejla Batina[1]([✉]), and Igor Armendariz[2]([✉])

[1] Digital Security Group, Radboud University, Nijmegen, The Netherlands
lejla@cs.ru.nl
[2] Ikerlan Technology Research Centre, Arrasate-Mondragón, Gipuzkoa, Spain
{urioja,iarmendariz}@ikerlan.es

Abstract. The original idea of profiling implies attacking one device with a leakage model generated from an "identical copy", but this concept cannot be always enforced. The leakage model is commonly generated with traces from an "open device", assuming that a model which works for one device should work for another copy as well. In practice, applying a leakage model to a different copy of the same device (commonly called portability) is a hard problem to deal with, as intrinsic differences in the devices or the experimental setups used to obtain the traces cause behavioural variations which lead to an unsuccessful attack. In this paper we propose a novel *similarity assessment* technique that allows evaluators to quantify the differences among various copies of the same device. Moreover, we support this technique with actual experiments to show that this metric is directly related to the portability issue. Finally, we derive a method that improves the performance of template attacks.

Keywords: SCA · Profiling attacks · Template attacks · Portability · SCA evaluation · DTW

1 Introduction

Nowadays profiling attacks are considered the most powerful kind of Side-Channel Attacks (SCAs). The idea behind profiling is different from the traditional concept of Differential Power Analysis (DPA) [3,4,10,19], for which the attack is separated from the device (e.g., every device that implements AES encryption is susceptible to the attacks using these techniques). In profiling attacks, the goal of the attacker is to build a leakage model of a particular device and to recover sensitive information comparing that model with the actual power consumption of the device. The first requirement to carry out this kind of SCA is to have, at least, two devices: the attacked device or the *device under test* (DUT), and another identical hardware device over which we have full control. The reason behind is that the attack requires two different stages: a profiling stage (with a "copy" of the device), in which we model the power consumption (side-channel), and an attack phase (with the "real" device), in which we use the

© Springer Nature Switzerland AG 2020
A. Nitaj and A. Youssef (Eds.): AFRICACRYPT 2020, LNCS 12174, pp. 337–357, 2020.
https://doi.org/10.1007/978-3-030-51938-4_17

generated model to obtain the secret parameter with only one or a few traces. Conversely, even though the original idea of a profiling attack is to generate the power consumption model for an "identical" copy of the attacked device, this is not always guaranteed in practice. This portability issue is often underestimated in practice, although some previous works suggest that in real-world setups small differences in the production of different devices, aging or even environmental changes during the measurements cause different behaviours of those devices, even leading to an unsuccessful attack [1,3,6,10,11,14,20,29].

In this work, our goal is to show how these dissimilarities can be addressed from the evaluation point of view, measuring how similar two different devices are and giving insights on how successful a portable profiling attack could be. Moreover, although performing this kind of attack is challenging, in this work we show the feasibility of a portable template attack in a realistic setup. We also provide some suggestions to improve the success rate of these attacks with our new point of interest (POI) selection technique.

Our main contribution is a novel *similarity assessment* technique with which, from an evaluation point of view, general similarities/dissimilarities between "identical" copies of the same device can be quantified. In addition, our work has revealed some other contributions that are all detailed as follows:

- This paper proposes the usage of the well-known Dynamic Time Warping (DTW from now on) statistical tool as a *similarity assessment* tool. Our approach shows that the warped distance between two specific graphics can quantify the similarities/dissimilarities between different devices or tracesets.
- We showcase the proposed technique with several experiments (portable template attacks with four different copies of the same device), demonstrating that the performance of the attack is directly related to this metric and hence the more similar two copies of the same device are (or two different sets of traces from the same device) the better results will be obtained.
- Finally, we propose an alternative POI selection technique which helps improving the performance of portable template attacks. This technique is also supported by the aforementioned experiments, showing how an unsuccessful portable attack can be turned into a successful attack by choosing the "best" points of interest while building the templates.

The paper is organized as follows, Sect. 2 summarizes the state of the art and the related work on this topic. Section 3 highlights the common issues with portability as a starting point for our work. Section 4 explains the details of DTW and our *similarity assessment* technique. Section 5 contains the experimental results supporting our *similarity assessment* technique and our *new POI selection* technique (which is also explained in a practical manner in this section). Finally, Sect. 6 draws the conclusions.

2   State of the Art

As mentioned above, profiling attacks are dominant in side-channel analysis nowadays. In the *profiling phase*, the model of the device can be generated by using standard classification techniques like in Template attacks [7, 28], Support Vector Machine (SVM) [15, 16, 21], Random Forest (RF) [22], regression or the Stochastic models approach [32] or recently introduced Deep learning techniques [5, 24, 27]. In the *attacking phase*, the model is applied and the secret key is guessed. Template attacks and machine learning are the two most popular approaches [23].

In this work, we focus on classical Template attacks because it is a well-known and understood technique in the field of SCA. Moreover, it should be noticed that although template attacks usually require more effort of an expert with signal processing capabilities, they allow the attacker/evaluator to focus on specific parts of the leakage keeping more control in the process (which is not always possible with deep learning techniques).

2.1 Template Attacks

Template attacks are the original form of profiling attacks as proposed for SCA by Chari et al. [7]. These attacks are based on building a multivariate model of the probability distribution of the leakage. The Probability Density Function (PDF) is usually computed assuming that the leakages follow a Gaussian distribution, as in the case of unprotected devices (devices without SCA countermeasures). This is a parametric estimation and we focus on this kind of templates technique because of its fast convergence and the fact that it is widely used and consolidated by many previous works. Nevertheless, it should be mentioned that there are other non-parametric estimations that are able to capture any distribution (which might be helpful with protected devices) like histogram and kernel-based estimators and also some other advanced tools [33].

The main goal in a "traditional" template attack is to deduce the secret (key) used to perform cryptographic operations. Thus, the attacker has to first take measurements of some device's physical property (commonly the power consumption or the electromagnetic radiation emitted by the device) during the manipulation of some intermediate value $iv = f(p, k)$ related to the plaintext p and the secret key k. In the *profiling phase* the attacker uses a set of n_p profiling traces $(T_{p,k})$ to build a Gaussian multivariate model (pdf) for each possible iv. In order to do that, the mean vector $\mu_{p,k}$ and the covariance matrix $\sum_{p,k}$ are estimated for each iv, creating the so-called *templates*. Then, in the *attack phase*, from a set of n_a real power traces and its input data (plaintext), the attacker tries to guess the correct iv value (or its Hamming Weight) by using the maximum likelihood principle. Since $iv = f(p, k)$, knowing iv and p the secret key k can be recovered.

Template attacks are optimal from an information-theoretic point of view but in practice, they have several limitations: preprocessing dependency (the effort of an expert in the field is mandatory most of the times), computational complexity problems and the need for dimensionality reduction. The latter is usually solved by selecting only a subset of the typically huge amount of samples in each power trace (Points of Interest [POI] selection [28]), applying another data-dimensionality reduction method as Principal Component Analysis (PCA)

[2,34] or Fisher's Linear Discriminant Analysis (LDA) [12,18]. Due to the high computational requirements of the other techniques, in this work, we reduce the dimensionality of the problem by selecting a few samples (Points of Interest). As we have mentioned, it also allows us to focus only on specific parts of the leakage and improve the results of the "classical" template attack (Sect. 5).

2.2 Portability

Although having two identical devices to perform a profiling attack is mandatory, in practice this is not always possible. The traces for the profiling phase and the attack phase are usually captured from the same device in most of the works on this topic [7,9,13]. Attacking a second device with a model generated with a first device is often considered trivial, while in practice this is not the case. Even if two devices are clones ("identical" copies of the same device) there always exist differences in the construction of the devices that can cause different behaviours in timing, voltage, etc. There could be different reasons for this, such as faults in the manufacturing process, aging, slight differences in the resistance and/or capacitance of the circuit, etc. Moreover, when two measurements are taken in different time moments they will often cause deviations in the acquired power traces, which could lead to an unsuccessful attack [1,11,29]. More precisely, we are referring to various small variations in the experimental setup such as I/O interference (serial port, USB, Radio, etc.), influence of the past state, memory management, garbage collection, differences in magnetic field penetration (while taking electromagnetic measurements), changes in environmental parameters (temperature, humidity, electromagnetic noise, etc.), resonance due to LC and RC oscillators, among other phenomenon.

To the best of our knowledge, there are not many papers discussing the portability of profiling attacks. The work of Elaabid et al. is introducing the portability issue and showing how waveform realignment and acquisition campaigns normalization can improve the performance of portable template attacks [11]. The work of Choudary et al. focuses on differences between devices when performing portable template attacks while attacking four different copies of the same device [8,10]. A more recent work successfully implements a portable template attack over a wireless keyboard performing AES encryption [20]. In the CHES 2018 Side Channel Contest CTF, portability was also considered, and the winning attack was able to obtain a 100% of success in all devices [14]. In [6], authors considered the usage of several devices during the various stages of a profiling attack in order to attack an RSA implementation. Bhasin et al. have recently made a comparison between different machine learning techniques using portable profiling attacks, but they only focused on machine learning techniques [3].

Our approach is orthogonal to all those works as we show a general way to find and quantify differences between clone devices, by obtaining a measurement of its dissimilarity. This metric is directly linked to portability: the more similar two devices are, the better performance the portable template attack will achieve and vice versa. Moreover, we show how this information can be used in the POI selection and we propose an improved POI selection technique, which assists in finding the optimal leakage points for different devices.

3   The Issue of Portability

As mentioned in Sect. 2.2, to perform a portable profiling attack is a challenging task, mainly because the behaviour of two theoretically identical devices could be (slightly) different in practice. After several experiments we noticed that the differences between two "identical" devices can be seen clearly in the graphics used for POI selection. Those graphics (POI graphs from now on) are generated by applying certain functions to the power traces in order to find the leaking points and select proper POIs for Template Attacks. Below we describe some of the most commonly used techniques:

Pearson Correlation Coefficient: This is a widely used metric in statistics, which assesses the linear dependence between two variables x and y [17]. It takes on a value between -1 and 1, where 0 means no (linear) correlation and 1 and -1 imply the total positive and negative linear correlation respectively. We compute the Pearson correlation coefficient between the data manipulated by the target device and the power consumption traces of the device while processing the data. For a sample of the entire population, the coefficient is defined by Eq. (1):

$$Correlation(x,y) = \frac{\sum_{i=1}^{N}((x_i - \bar{x})(y_i - \bar{y}))}{\sqrt{\sum_{i=1}^{N}(x_i - \bar{x})^2}\sqrt{\sum_{i=1}^{N}(y_i - \bar{y})^2}} \tag{1}$$

SOSD: SOSD or sum of squared differences was proposed for POIs in [13] and is defined by Eq. (2), where $\bar{x}_{y_i}$ is the mean of the power traces and the manipulated data is equal to y_i. Its value is always positive and highlights big differences in means.

$$SOSD(x,y) = \sum_{i,j>i}(\bar{x}_{y_i} - \bar{x}_{y_j})^2 \tag{2}$$

SOST: This is the normalized version of SOSD [13], which is equivalent to the pairwise Student's t-test. It is defined by Eq. (3), where n_{y_i} and n_{y_j} are the number of traces where y is equal to y_i and y_j respectively.

$$SOST(x,y) = \sum_{i,j>i}((\bar{x}_{y_i} - \bar{x}_{y_j})/\sqrt{\frac{\sigma_{y_i}^2}{n_{y_i}} + \frac{\sigma_{y_j}^2}{n_{y_j}}})^2 \tag{3}$$

SNR: Signal-to-noise ratios are commonly used in electrical engineering and signal processing. In the context of a side-channel attack, the SNR of a point of a power trace can be computed by Eq. (4), where P_{exp} is the exploitable power consumption and $P_{sw.noise}$ and $P_{el.noise}$ correspond to the noise component (switching noise and electronic noise). In a nutshell, it quantifies how much information is leaking from a point of the power trace. For a deeper explanation of the SNR calculation we refer to [25].

$$SNR = \frac{Var(P_{exp})}{Var(P_{sw.noise} + P_{el.noise})} \tag{4}$$

If we compare two POI graphs generated with traces from two "identical" copies of the same device, significant differences between them could be observed. The spikes do not occur at the same time and with the same shape (or strength), which can influence the portability of an attack. In Figs. 1, 2 and 3 these differences can be noticed. Figure 1 shows the power traces of two copies of the same device during some internal computations in which an 8-bit sensitive value is stored in memory (Voltage vs Time (samples)). In Fig. 2 the leaking part of the signal (the exact point in which the 8-bit data is stored) is shown. Also, Fig. 3 shows the output of the aforementioned POI selection functions of both devices. It is important to note that there are significant differences in the magnitude and shape of both graphs. Those differences are very problematic when porting a template attack: the POIs selected to generate the templates in the first device will not match with the optimal POIs in the second device. Thus, the portable template attack will probably fail. When performing a Template attack, the highest points of the spikes that appear in the POI selection graph are usually selected as POIs, in order to reduce the dimensionality of the multivariate leakage model and make the attack feasible. However, as these points are selected taking into account only the profiling device, a big spike for one device could be a "valley" in others. Moreover, if the spikes match, the results could still be bad if the value in the POI graph is too low. We should ideally select spikes with a value that is high enough to represent leakage. In conclusion, two devices

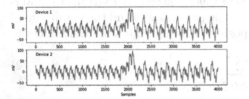

Fig. 1. Differences between devices: Power trace

Fig. 2. Differences between devices: Leaking part of the power trace

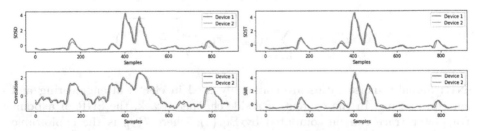

Fig. 3. Differences between POI selection functions

can be "identical" copies, but in practice there are often remarkable differences between their leaking points. When we build templates from one device and then try to attack another one, it is crucial that the selected POI represents a significant leakage in both devices. Otherwise, the behaviour modeled with the Gaussian multivariate distribution will not apply to the second device and the attack will fail.

4 Similarity Assessment

In order to quantify how different two "identical" copies of a device are, a *similarity assessment* technique is proposed next, which is based on the Dynamic Time Warping (DTW) statistical tool.

4.1 Dynamic Time Warping

DTW is a well-known algorithm to measure similarity between two temporal sequences and find the most similar points between them. In other words, this technique is able to quantify the similarity between two signals (even if they are not completely aligned) and obtain the optimal match (alignment). In Figs. 4 and 5 the difference between the "traditional" euclidean distance and the warped distance is demonstrated. Originally, DTW was used in speech recognition [30] but later on, it has been proved its applicability in several fields like gesture recognition, robotics, manufacturing, etc. This technique has been applied also in the SCA field with the elastic alignment [35] as a special kind of alignment using DTW (FastDTW [31], more precisely). This kind of alignment was proposed in order to address cryptographic implementations with random delay countermeasures. Afterwards, Muijrers et al. proposed another alignment algorithm which can deal with this countermeasure [26]. This method can align traces with less computational effort than elastic alignment (DTW algorithm is relatively computationally costly, depending on the length of the path). However, we now propose the usage of DTW algorithm for an entirely different task: assessing differences between tracesets or devices. Our approach is to use DTW to quantify how similar two devices are by measuring the similarity of two temporal sequences representing the leakage of each device.

Warp Path and Warped Distance are the two main outcomes of the DTW calculation. The former indicates the best alignment between two shapes while the latter is a measure of the similarity between signals. In our case, the DTW algorithm is applied to two discrete time signals (traces), $X = x_1, x_2, \ldots, x_i, \ldots, x_{|X|}$ and $Y = y_1, y_2, \ldots, y_j, \ldots, y_{|Y|}$. In order to compute the warp path and warped distance, the DTW algorithm calculates a *cost matrix*: an $|X|$-by-$|Y|$ matrix containing the distances between all samples of X and Y. Figure 6 shows an example of the cost matrix (and its warp path) of the two example curves shown in Figs. 4 and 5. Each element of the matrix (i, j) represents the distance $D(i, j)$ between samples x_i and y_i (the darker the cell is, the largest distance). The warping path (in dark blue), connects the cells with smaller

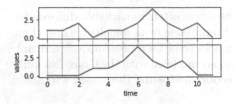

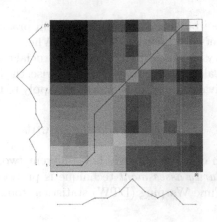

Fig. 4. Euclidian distance

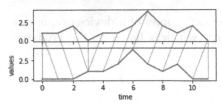

Fig. 5. Warped distance

Fig. 6. Cost matrix and warp path (Color figure online)

distance starting from $(1,1)$ to $(|X|,|Y|)$, and indicates the optimal alignment between those two curves (shown graphically in Fig. 5). The cumulative distances of the warping path is what we call warped distance (our similarity indicator between two time series). Formally speaking, the warping path W between two traces X and Y can be defined as:

$$W(X,Y) = (w_0, w_1, \ldots, w_K) \quad \text{where} \quad \max(|X|, |Y|) \leq K < |X| + |Y|$$

Here, K is the length of the warp path and $w_k = (i,j)$ the kth element of the path. Also, this path has to follow several constraints. For $w_k = (i_k, j_k)$ and $w_{k-1} = (i_{k-1}, j_{k-1})$ being two consecutive elements of the warp path, the constraints are:

– **Monotonicity:** $i_{k-1} \leq i_k$ and $j_{k-1} \leq j_k$
– **Continuity:** $i_k - i_{k-1} \leq 1$ and $j_k - j_{k-1} \leq 1$
– **Bound:** $w_1 = (1,1)$ and $w_K = (|X|, |Y|)$

The **boundary condition** ensures that every index of both time series is used in the warp path computation while **monotonicity** and **continuity** constraints assure that we do not skip any sample and we do not go backwards in time. Several paths could satisfy these conditions but the minimum-distance path is considered as the optimal warp path, where the distance is:

$$Dist(W) = \sum_{k=1}^{k=K} w_k$$

This minimum distance is what we call warped distance, a similarity measure between two time series. To find the minimum distance warp path, the distance D of each cell has to be computed. Dynamic programming can solve this problem in a very effective manner, so the value of a cell in the cost matrix is:

$$D(i,j) = d(i,j) + \min[D(i-1,j), D(i,j-1), D(i-1,j-1)]$$

Where d is usually computed as the typical Euclidean distance $d(i,j) = d(x_i, y_j) = (x_i - y_j)^2$ between samples x_i and y_i and D is known as the cumulative distance (the euclidean distance $d(i,j)$ plus the minimum of the cumulative distances of the contiguous cells).

4.2   Similarity Assessment Technique

Once the basis of the DTW technique have been clarified, our *similarity assessment technique* can be explained. In order to assess how similar two devices are, we propose the following steps:

1. **Step 1: Obtain POI graphics of both devices.** A set of n_{POI} traces will be captured from both devices. These traces must be taken when the device is manipulating a certain sensitive variable, which must have a random value each time in order to properly characterize the leakage. Once both sets of traces are taken ($n_{POI(1)}$ and $n_{POI(2)}$), two POI graphs are obtained by applying one of the POI selection functions mentioned in Sect. 3.

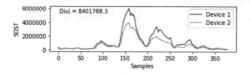

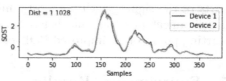

Fig. 7. SOST graph of devices 1 & 2 (Without Standardization)

Fig. 8. SOST graph of devices 1 & 2 (With Standardization)

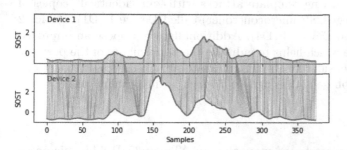

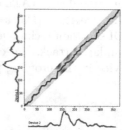

Fig. 9. Warped distance between Device 1 and Device 2

Fig. 10.   Warp   path between Device 1 and 2

2. **Step 2: Standardize both graphics.** Zero-mean and normalization are standard preprocessing techniques that are mandatory to apply after almost every SCA acquisition. Our case is not an exception: an standardization of both graphs before applying DTW can be helpful since DTW usually interprets those differences as huge dissimilarities. Figures 7 and 8 show how the distance value changes enormously depending on whether we apply this technique or not, even though both graphs are quite similar in shape. Our experimental results show how a portable template attack can be successful if the shapes of its POI graphs are similar enough, even if there are magnitude differences (as shown in Sect. 5). In other words, it is more important how the device leaks its information than the quantity of the leakage (as long as the leakage is big enough). Thus, we propose to standardize each POI graph using Eq. (5), where z is the re-scaled sample, x_i is the sample to scale and μ and σ are the mean and the standard deviation of the trace (Fig. 8).

$$z = \frac{x_i - \mu}{\sigma} \tag{5}$$

3. **Step 3: Compute the DTW algorithm** in order to obtain the minimum distance path (as explained above). In other words, by computing the cumulative of the distances of the minimum distance warping path we obtain the *distance between both graphs*: a quantitative measurement of the similarity/dissimilarity of both time sequences.

Additionally, the graphical representation of the warped distance and warping path (Fig. 9) can be helpful in the POI selection since DTW highlights the parts of the signal which are most similar between devices. To see graphically misalignment problems and behavioural differences between devices is a good starting point for an improved POI selection.

5   Experimental Results

In order to support our *similarity assessment* technique, we have performed realistic experiments involving template attacks with four "identical" copies of the same device (ATmega328P microcontroller) called Device 1 (D1), Device 2 (D2), Device 3 (D3) and Device 4 (D4). Additionally, we propose an improved POI selection technique which helps to enhance the performance of the portable template attack. We consider two main template attack use cases: using one device in the profiling phase and using two devices in the profiling phase.

5.1   Setup

The target is a development board mounting an ATmega328P 8-bit microcontroller working at 16 MHz clock frequency. We are storing random data (8-bit values) in flash memory using a memcpy() operation (in a random address each time). During that operation, we measure the power consumption of the device with a Tektronix CT1 current probe attached to a 20 GS/s digital oscilloscope

Table 1. Portable template attack experiments using Device 1 (D1) for profiling.

POI	Rank (D1 vs D1)	Rank (D1 vs D2)	Rank (D1 vs D3)	Rank (D1 vs D4)
[97, 158, 220, 294]	1	46	**17**	**18**

(LeCroy Waverunner 9104) triggered by the microcontroller, which rises a GPIO signal when the internal computation starts. Each power trace is formed by 400 samples taken at 1 GHz with 8-bit resolution. As an attacker, our goal is to obtain the exact 8-bit value loaded in flash memory using template attacks. A set of n_p profiling traces are taken from the profiling device(s) (storing random 8-bit values) and labeled with the stored value. The traces are preprocessed by aligning them and applying the aforementioned standardization technique. Then, a SOST function is ran in order to find possible POIs. 256 templates are built by computing the mean and co-variance matrix for each labeled group (in the selected POIs), using the pooled matrix optimization method. In the *attacking phase* a set of n_a power traces of the attacking device storing a fixed 8-bit value are taken. Then the multivariate model is applied and the 8-bit value is guessed using the maximum likelihood principle. Each label will obtain a confidence value and the 256 labels will be ranked. We consider the attack successful when the correct candidate obtains a rank of 25 or less (the correct candidate is in the top 10% of candidates). We assume that then, the correct value could be guessed using (optimized) brute force.

5.2 Use Case 1: Template Attack Using One Device in Profiling Phase

"Raw" Template Attack

In the *profiling phase* 20 000 power traces of D1 are taken and labeled with the stored value. The traces are preprocessed and the SOST function is run in order to find possible POI (Fig. 8, Device 1). Four significant spikes can be seen, corresponding to the different moments in which the copied variable leaks (production, travel across a bus, load into register, etc.). Thus, four POI are selected, one for each significant spike [97, 158, 220, 294] and the model using 256 templates is built. In the *attacking phase* 1 000 power traces of the same device (D1) storing a fixed value are taken. Then the multivariate model is applied and the 8-bit value is guessed. In Table 1 we can see that the rank of the correct candidate in this attack (D1 vs D1) is 1 after 1 000 traces (successful attack). In order to perform a more realistic template attack, 1 000 power traces from a second device (D2) storing the same fixed 8-bit value are taken. Then the model computed before with traces from D1 is applied and the fixed value is guessed. As it can be seen in Table 1, the attack is unsuccessful (the rank of the correct candidate in this attack (D1 vs D2) is 46) because the multivariate model of D1 does not apply to D2. The process is repeated with devices D3 and D4 (results appear in Table 1). In this case the attack is successful (the rank of the correct candidate is less than 25), but the results are not optimal. To enhance the model we apply our *similarity assessment* technique and the *improved POI selection* technique.

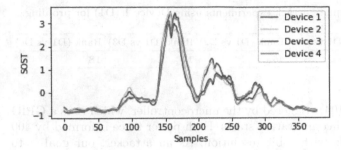

Devices	Distance
D1 vs D2	1,1028
D1 vs D3	2,4159
D1 vs D4	2,7628
D2 vs D3	2,4792
D2 vs D4	2,7153
D3 vs D4	0,9128

Fig. 11. SOST graphics of each one of the four analyzed devices and distances between them

Improving the Results

First and foremost, we apply our *similarity assessment* method. Thus, 20 000 power traces of the second device storing random 8-bit values are taken and labeled with the stored value. The traces are preprocessed and the SOST function is run (Figs. 7 and 11, Device 2). The same process is repeated with D3 and D4. Then, once we have the four POI selection graphs (Fig. 11, one for each device), we run the DTW algorithm to compute the warped distance between D1 and the rest (Fig. 11, D1 vs D2, D1 vs D3, D1 vs D4). Note that we also calculate other distances (D2 vs D3, D2 vs D4, D3 vs D4) to measure the similarities among the four devices. These results lead to the following conclusions: Devices D3 and D4 are the most similar ones since their distance is the smallest one. Thus, the distances between D1 & D3 and D1 & D4 are similar, and this fact validates the results of the attacks D1 vs D3 and D1 vs D4, which are also similar (Fig. 1). D2 is the most similar device to D1, but the attack is not successful. The reason is that the selected POIs are not optimal for this device, as shown below.

Improved POI Selection: To improve the effectiveness of the attack we suggest the following steps:

1. **Analyze the performance of each POI individually** to find which points correspond to good leaking points (when we port the model to another device, or even in the same device) and which ones are perturbing the model. In order to do that, we build templates using only one of the aforementioned POI each time [97, 158, 220, 294]. Then, we apply the templates to each device (D1, D2, D3 and D4). The results are presented in Table 2, where it can be seen that the POIs with better performance for D2 (the one with the worst results) are the second and the third POIs.
2. **Try different combinations of the POI with better performance** to guess which combination has best results. Theoretically, the optimal solution would be a combination of all of them, but in practice it is not always the case. To avoid trying all possible combinations, points with better performance in all cases (identified in previous step) must be selected. Also,

Table 2. *Improved POI selection* (when Device 1 (D1) is used for profiling.)

Step	POI	Rank (D1 vs D1)	Rank (D1 vs D2)	Rank (D1 vs D3)	Rank (D1 vs D4)	GS
1	1st POI [97]	**9**	121	121	121	38.32
	2nd POI [158]	**1**	70	170	161	35.19
	3rd POI [220]	**3**	98	53	53	24.87
	4th POI [294]	50	136	121	121	41.18
2	POI 1+3+4	**1**	140	13	14	27.01
	POI 2+3	**1**	45	72	65	17.44
	POI 1+2+3	**1**	36	49	42	**12.68**
	POI 1+2	**1**	56	116	110	25.50
	POI 3+4	**3**	148	37	38	31.73
3	[92, 153, 218]	**1**	**2**	**16**	**15**	2.48

the warped distance graphic (Fig. 9) can be used to identify the most similar parts of these signals and choose the POI combinations accordingly. In this case, we have tried the following combinations: 1+3+4, 2+3, 1+2+3, 1+2 and 3+4. Results can be seen in Table 2 (Step 2). To help identifying which combination works best in all devices we recommend to compute what we call *Goodness Score* (Table 2, column GS). This metric is computed by adding the ranks of each row weighted by a coefficient ($GS = Rank_{D_1} * C_{D_1} + Rank_{D_2} * C_{D_2} + Rank_{D_3} * C_{D_3} + Rank_{D_4} * C_{D_4}$). The value of the coefficients is obtained dividing the rank of the first attack in the Table 1, by the number of possible combinations (256), so we obtain coefficients from 0 to 1 with the emphasis put on the devices with worse result. The lower GS value, the better performance (generally speaking). Note that the combination with the best performance (in all devices) includes those three points of interest (1+2+3).

3. **Adjust the selected POI:** once we have found the best combination, we can try to tune each POI moving the selected point in a small number of samples (and adding another one near if necessary) and check if the results improve. Based on experience, points that are not exactly at the peak sometimes provide better results because the behaviour of the devices is more similar in those points. Summing up, we identified the most suitable zones to select POIs in previous step, and we are now tuning the exact value of these POIs. In our case, after a few trials we obtained very good results with [92, 153, 218] (Table 2, Step 3).

After applying the proposed techniques, we can conclude the following:

– **Not all POIs have the same performance with all devices:** For instance, in Table 2 we can see how the templates built with the 2nd POI have better performance attacking D2 than devices D3 or D4. However, with the 3rd and 4th POIs we obtain a better performance attacking devices D3

Table 3. Portable template attacks experiments using Device 3 (D3) for profiling.

Step	POI	Rank (D3 vs D3)	Rank (D3 vs D4)	Rank (D3 vs D1)	Rank (D3 vs D2)	GS
0	[97, 158, 220, 294]	1	7	114	130	
1	1st POI [97]	15	131	153	153	149.47
	2nd POI [158]	5	30	75	75	72.32
	3rd POI [220]	16	22	206	206	197.01
	4th POI [294]	2	117	135	135	131.88
2	POI 1+3+4	1	43	194	191	184.56
	POI 2+3	1	8	105	105	100.30
	POI 1+2+3	1	9	111	117	109.09
	POI 1+2	2	22	70	66	**65.30**
	POI 3+4	3	42	196	196	187.97
3	[90, 153, 156]	8	1	16	8	11.25

and D4. The same happens with combinations of those POIs: POI 1+2 has better performance for D2 than others, while profiling with POI 1+3+4 has good results for devices D3 and D4 but not for D2, etc.

- **DTW's wrapping distance can assess the similarity between devices.** After selecting proper POI, we can see how the results of the Template attacks and the *similarity assessment* technique are directly linked. In Fig. 11 we notice how devices D3 and D4 have the smallest distance between them, which means that they are very similar (Table 2 shows how the results of the attacks are almost the same for both). Another example is that if we compare the distance between D1 and the rest, the device with shortest distance is D2, and the performance of the portable attack is generally better with that device. Again, distances from devices D3 and D4 are similar, as well as the results of the portable attacks.

Extending the Problem to Other Device

With the aim of confirming the results shown above we repeat the same process, but using D3 for generating the templates (Results shown in Table 3). The conclusions obtained when profiling with D1 are now validated. Devices D3 and D4 are very similar and hence the attack using the 4 POIs located in the 4th spike of Device 3's SOST is effective for D4 but unsuccessful for D1 and D2. After analysing the performance of each POI and its combinations we obtain the same conclusion: the POIs that work for D4 (the most similar device) do not work properly for the rest of devices (D1 and D2). Only after adjusting the POI with the best performance in devices D1 and D2 (POI 1+2) and adding another point near the second POI, we can obtain good results in those devices, but at the cost of sacrificing some performance for devices D3 and D4. In conclusion, it is important to get a balance and find POIs that represent leakage in all devices.

In this case, we had to select POIs that are not optimal for attacking D4 but allowed us to successfully attack devices D1 and D2. Thus, the templates generated with the improved POI selection are suitable for attacking each one of those four devices.

Extending the Problem to Different Measurements of the Same Device
With this experiment, we want to show that measurements taken at different times may have substantial differences caused by slight changes in the device or its environment. With D3, the previous process is repeated two times, obtaining two sets of 20 000 random traces and two sets of 1 000 fixed traces. After comparing both SOST graphs (Fig. 12) it can be noticed that, although both graphs are very similar there are slight differences between both traces. In order to check whether those differences affect the performance, we carry out two different attacks. In the first one, we build templates and implement the attack with traces from the first measurement set (D3) while in the second attack we use traces from the second measurement set (D3*) with the model from the first measurement. The attack is successful in both cases, but the correct candidate ranks as 1 in the first attack and as 4 in the second one, showing the worse performance in the later.

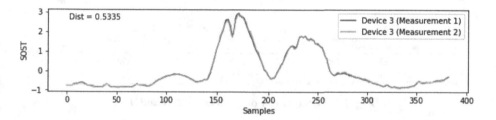

Fig. 12. SOST graph of the 1st and 2nd measurements (Device 3).

5.3   Use Case 2: Template Attack Using Two Devices in Profiling Phase

In order to improve the performance of the portable template attack, we try building templates with two different devices and attacking a third one. Thus, a model is built with 20 000 profiling traces from D1 and 20 000 profiling traces from D2. The traces are preprocessed as in previous experiments and the SOST function is calculated (Fig. 13, Device 1+2). This figure, when compared with the SOST of each device separately (Fig. 11), suggests that the new SOST is a combination of the other two. We select 7 POIs in each one of the significant spikes ([95, 142, 153, 173, 207, 218, 237]) and generate the 256 templates. In the *attacking phase* 1 000 power traces of devices D1 and D2 storing a fixed 8-bit value are used (500 from each one). Then the model is applied and the fixed value is guessed. The results of this non-portable attack using two devices for profiling are excellent and they can be seen in Table 4 (Step 0, [D1+D2] vs [D1+D2]). For the portable attack, the model is applied to 1 000 power traces from D3 storing the same fixed value. As it can be seen in Table 4 (Step 0), the results are quite bad because the model does not suit this device. The same happens with D4. As in the first use case, the *similarity assessment* method is applied. Thus, 20 000 power traces from the third and fourth device storing random 8-bit values are taken and labeled with the stored value. The traces are preprocessed and the SOST function is calculated (Fig. 13, D3 and D4). We can see that both shapes are completely different and hence the attack is not successful because we are not selecting representative POIs for all the devices. To improve the POI selection, we apply our technique, as shown in Sec. 5.2. First, we analyze the performance of each POI individually (Table 4, Step 0). Note that the results are almost the same in D3 and D4 because these devices are very similar. Then, different combinations of the 7 POIs are tested (Table 4, Step 2). The combination which throws best results is 2+3+6. After that, we try to adjust the POI of interest, achieving the attack using the points [143, 157, 217] (Table 4, Step 3).

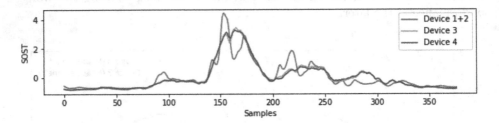

Fig. 13. SOST graph of devices 1+2, 3 and 4

Extending the Problem to Other Devices

In order to consolidate the results shown above we repeat the same process, using devices D1 and D3 for templates generation. First of all, the SOST graph of the profiling traceset (20 000 random traces form D1 and 20 000 random traces from D3) is computed (Fig. 14). In this case, the model is built with traces from two devices which have significant differences, as we have seen in previous experiments. Then, a multivariate model is built using 10 POI located in each one of the significant spikes of the SOST ([90, 104, 115, 155, 166, 178, 216, 234, 267, 296]). The results appear in Table 5 (Step 0). Note that the results are quite good without applying our improved POI selection because we have constructed a model with devices which are similar to the attacked devices (Devices D1 & D2 and D3 & D4 are very similar). Nevertheless, the results with D2 are not as good as expected, so we perform our improved POI selection. After analyzing the performance of each POI individually, we can notice that, in general, all points work better for one device than for the other. Thus, we try different

Table 4. Portable template attacks experiments using Device 1 (D1) and Device 2 (D2) for profiling.

Step	POI	Rank ([D1+D2] vs [D1+D2])	Rank ([D1+D2] vs D3)	Rank ([D1+D2] vs D4)	GS
0	[95, 142, 153, 173, 207, 218, 23]	1	42	41	
1	1° POI	1	114	114	36.96
	2° POI	4	61	61	19.79
	3° POI	6	56	43	16.10
	4° POI	8	74	74	24.02
	5° POI	92	201	201	65.53
	6° POI	2	58	58	18.81
	7° POI	9	56	56	18.19
2	POI36	2	16	18	5.52
	POI23467	1	20	19	6.33
	POI3467	1	26	24	8.11
	POI367	1	22	21	6.98
	POI67	2	54	55	17.68
	POI236	1	15	14	**4.71**
	POI346	1	24	24	7.79
3	[143, 157, 217]	1	4	5	1.46

POI combinations to find the optimal one. In this case, we try to select points that provide good results in both devices, avoiding points that work especially bad in a certain device. The combination which provides the best results is POI 1+3+4+5+6+7+9. Finally, after adjusting the selected POI, we obtain excellent results with [91, 115, 153, 168, 181, 216, 266] (Table 5, Step 3).

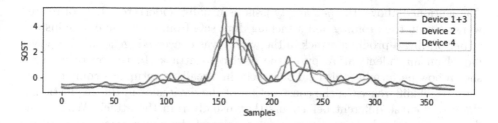

Fig. 14. SOST graph of devices 1+3, 2 and 4

Table 5. Portable template attacks experiments using Device 1 (D1) and Device 3 (D3) for profiling.

Step	POI	Rank ([D1+D3] vs [D1+D3])	Rank ([D1+D3] vs D2)	Rank ([D1+D3] vs D4)	GS
0	[90, 104, 115, 155, 166, 178, 216, 234, 267, 296]	1	25	1	
1	1° POI [90]	34	18	97	2.27
	2° POI [104]	15	119	61	11.92
	3° POI [115]	16	122	27	12.08
	4° POI [155]	13	49	5	4.86
	5° POI [166]	6	72	52	7.26
	6° POI [178]	3	88	37	8.75
	7° POI [216]	11	51	41	5.18
	8° POI [234]	1	199	22	19.52
	9° POI [267]	24	86	44	8.66
	10° POI [296]	4	126	77	12.62
2	POI 5+7+9	2	34	12	3.38
	POI 1+5+7+9	1	29	12	2.88
	POI 1+4+5+6+9	1	34	20	3.40
	POI 1+3+4+5+6+7	1	25	1	2.45
	POI 1+3+4+5+6+9	2	35	4	3.44
	POI 1+3+4+5+6+7+9	1	19	1	**1.86**
	POI 3+4+5+6+7+9	1	21	1	2.06
	POI 3+5+6+7+9	1	30	9	2.97
3	[91, 115, 153, 168, 181, 216, 266]	1	2	1	0.20

6   Conclusions

As mentioned above, the portability issue is usually underrated. Lots of related works obtain the profiling and attacking data sets from the same device instead of performing a profiling attack in the way it was conceived: generating a power model on an "identical" copy of the device to attack. In this work we have shown how performing this kind of attacks in a realistic setup is a complex task, since slight differences in the construction of the devices or in the acquisition of the traces cause different behaviours that usually ruin the attack. While some devices maximize leakage in a particular point of the power traces, the leakage of another "identical" copy of the device can be (slightly) shifted. Therefore, it is crucial to take into account these variations and to generate the models using the points where the leakage exist in all devices. In this paper we present a way to understand better how variations between devices occur, and we describe how to build models that allows finding and exploiting the common leakage. The experimental results show how our *similarity assessment* measurement (warped distance) is directly related to portability, since the portable template attacks have better performance in the most similar devices (devices with a smaller distance between them). The experimental results also confirm that our *improved POI selection* technique helps in finding the POIs which represent leakage in several devices and in avoiding the ones that perturb the model, making it not applicable to a particular device. Moreover, we have shown how building multivariate leakage models with several devices also enhances the performance of the attack, even more if the model is generated with devices with behavioural differences.

In conclusion, the proposed *similarity assessment* technique allows evaluation laboratories to identify behavioural differences between devices and quantify them, and improves the POI selection in template attacks, as shown in the different use cases presented.

References

1. Akkar, M.-L., Bevan, R., Dischamp, P., Moyart, D.: Power analysis, what is now possible. In: Okamoto, T. (ed.) ASIACRYPT 2000. LNCS, vol. 1976, pp. 489–502. Springer, Heidelberg (2000). https://doi.org/10.1007/3-540-44448-3_38
2. Archambeau, C., Peeters, E., Standaert, F.-X., Quisquater, J.-J.: Template attacks in principal subspaces. In: Goubin, L., Matsui, M. (eds.) CHES 2006. LNCS, vol. 4249, pp. 1–14. Springer, Heidelberg (2006). https://doi.org/10.1007/11894063_1
3. Bhasin, S., Chattopadhyay, A., Heuser, A., Jap, D., Picek, S., Shrivastwa, R.R.: Mind the portability: a warriors guide through realistic profiled side-channel analysis. In: Network and Distributed System Security Symposium, January 2020. https://doi.org/10.14722/ndss.2020.24390
4. Brier, E., Clavier, C., Olivier, F.: Correlation power analysis with a leakage model. In: Joye, M., Quisquater, J.-J. (eds.) CHES 2004. LNCS, vol. 3156, pp. 16–29. Springer, Heidelberg (2004). https://doi.org/10.1007/978-3-540-28632-5_2
5. Cagli, E., Dumas, C., Prouff, E.: Convolutional neural networks with data augmentation against jitter-based countermeasures. In: Fischer, W., Homma, N. (eds.) CHES 2017. LNCS, vol. 10529, pp. 45–68. Springer, Cham (2017). https://doi.org/10.1007/978-3-319-66787-4_3
6. Carbone, M., et al.: Deep learning to evaluate secure RSA implementations. Cryptology ePrint Archive, Report 2019/054 (2019)
7. Chari, S., Rao, J.R., Rohatgi, P.: Template attacks. In: Kaliski, B.S., Koç, K., Paar, C. (eds.) CHES 2002. LNCS, vol. 2523, pp. 13–28. Springer, Heidelberg (2003). https://doi.org/10.1007/3-540-36400-5_3
8. Choudary, M.O., Kuhn, M.G.: Efficient, portable template attacks. IEEE Trans. Inf. Forensics Secur. **13**(2), 490–501 (2018). https://doi.org/10.1109/TIFS.2017.2757440
9. Choudary, O., Kuhn, M.G.: Efficient template attacks. In: Francillon, A., Rohatgi, P. (eds.) CARDIS 2013. LNCS, vol. 8419, pp. 253–270. Springer, Cham (2014). https://doi.org/10.1007/978-3-319-08302-5_17
10. Choudary, O., Kuhn, M.G.: Template attacks on different devices. In: Prouff, E. (ed.) COSADE 2014. LNCS, vol. 8622, pp. 179–198. Springer, Cham (2014). https://doi.org/10.1007/978-3-319-10175-0_13
11. Elaabid, M., Abdelazizand Guilley, S.: Portability of templates. J. Cryptogr. Eng. **2**(1), 63–74 (2012). https://doi.org/10.1007/s13389-012-0030-6

12. Fisher, R.: The statistical utilization of multiple measurements. Ann. Eugen. (Cambridge) **8**, 376–386 (1935). https://doi.org/10.1111/j.1469-1809.1938.tb02189.x
13. Gierlichs, B., Lemke-Rust, K., Paar, C.: Templates vs. Stochastic methods. In: Goubin, L., Matsui, M. (eds.) CHES 2006. LNCS, vol. 4249, pp. 15–29. Springer, Heidelberg (2006). https://doi.org/10.1007/11894063_2
14. Gohr, A., Jacob, S., Schindler, W.: CHES 2018 side channel contest CTF - solution of the AES challenges. IACR Cryptology ePrint Archive (2019)
15. Heuser, A., Zohner, M.: Intelligent machine homicide. In: Schindler, W., Huss, S.A. (eds.) COSADE 2012. LNCS, vol. 7275, pp. 249–264. Springer, Heidelberg (2012). https://doi.org/10.1007/978-3-642-29912-4_18
16. Hospodar, G., Gierlichs, B., De Mulder, E., Verbauwhede, I., Vandewalle, J.: Machine learning in side-channel analysis: a first study. J. Cryptogr. Eng. **1**, 293–302 (2011). https://doi.org/10.1007/s13389-011-0023-x
17. James, G., Witten, D., Hastie, T., Tibshirani, R.: An Introduction to Statistical Learning: With Applications in R. JABES **19**, 556–557 (2014). https://doi.org/10.1007/s13253-014-0179-9
18. Johnson, R.A., Wichern, D.W. (eds.): Applied Multivariate Statistical Analysis. Prentice-Hall Inc., Upper Saddle River (1988)
19. Kocher, P., Jaffe, J., Jun, B.: Differential power analysis. In: Wiener, M. (ed.) CRYPTO 1999. LNCS, vol. 1666, pp. 388–397. Springer, Heidelberg (1999). https://doi.org/10.1007/3-540-48405-1_25
20. Kim, K., Kim, T.H., Kim, T., Ryu, S.: AES wireless keyboard: Template attack for eavesdropping. In: Black Hat Asia, Singapore (2018)
21. Lerman, L., Bontempi, G., Markowitch, O.: Side channel attack: an approach based on machine learning. In: Constructive Side-Channel Analysis and Secure Design, COSADE (2011)
22. Lerman, L., Bontempi, G., Markowitch, O.: A machine learning approach against a masked AES. J. Cryptogr. Eng. **5**(2), 123–139 (2015). https://doi.org/10.1007/s13389-014-0089-3
23. Lerman, L., Poussier, R., Markowitch, O., Standaert, F.X.: Template attacks versus machine learning revisited and the curse of dimensionality in side-channel analysis: extended version. J. Cryptogr. Eng. **8**(4), 301–313 (2018). https://doi.org/10.1007/s13389-017-0162-9
24. Maghrebi, H., Portigliatti, T., Prouff, E.: Breaking cryptographic implementations using deep learning techniques. SPACE **2016**, 3–26 (2016). https://doi.org/10.1007/978-3-319-49445-6_1
25. Mangard, S., Oswald, E., Popp, T.: Power Analysis Attacks: Revealing the Secrets of Smart Cards. Springer, Boston (2007). https://doi.org/10.1007/978-0-387-38162-6
26. Muijrers, R.A., van Woudenberg, J.G.J., Batina, L.: RAM: rapid alignment method. In: Prouff, E. (ed.) CARDIS 2011. LNCS, vol. 7079, pp. 266–282. Springer, Heidelberg (2011). https://doi.org/10.1007/978-3-642-27257-8_17
27. Picek, S., Samiotis, I.P., Kim, J., Heuser, A., Bhasin, S., Legay, A.: On the performance of convolutional neural networks for side-channel analysis. In: Chattopadhyay, A., Rebeiro, C., Yarom, Y. (eds.) SPACE 2018. LNCS, vol. 11348, pp. 157–176. Springer, Cham (2018). https://doi.org/10.1007/978-3-030-05072-6_10
28. Rechberger, C., Oswald, E.: Practical template attacks. In: Lim, C.H., Yung, M. (eds.) WISA 2004. LNCS, vol. 3325, pp. 440–456. Springer, Heidelberg (2005). https://doi.org/10.1007/978-3-540-31815-6_35

29. Renauld, M., Standaert, F.-X., Veyrat-Charvillon, N., Kamel, D., Flandre, D.: A formal study of power variability issues and side-channel attacks for nanoscale devices. In: Paterson, K.G. (ed.) EUROCRYPT 2011. LNCS, vol. 6632, pp. 109–128. Springer, Heidelberg (2011). https://doi.org/10.1007/978-3-642-20465-4_8

30. Sakoe, H., Chiba, S.: Dynamic programming algorithm optimization for spoken word recognition. IEEE Trans. Acoust. Speech Signal Process. **26**(1), 43–49 (1978). https://doi.org/10.1109/TASSP.1978.1163055

31. Salvador, S., Chan, P.: Toward accurate dynamic time warping in linear time and space. Intell. Data Anal. **11**, 561–580 (2007). https://doi.org/10.3233/IDA-2007-11508

32. Schindler, W., Lemke, K., Paar, C.: A stochastic model for differential side channel cryptanalysis. In: Rao, J.R., Sunar, B. (eds.) CHES 2005. LNCS, vol. 3659, pp. 30–46. Springer, Heidelberg (2005). https://doi.org/10.1007/11545262_3

33. Schneider, T., Moradi, A., Standaert, F.-X., Güneysu, T.: Bridging the gap: advanced tools for side-channel leakage estimation beyond Gaussian templates and histograms. In: Avanzi, R., Heys, H. (eds.) SAC 2016. LNCS, vol. 10532, pp. 58–78. Springer, Cham (2017). https://doi.org/10.1007/978-3-319-69453-5_4

34. Standaert, F.-X., Archambeau, C.: Using subspace-based template attacks to compare and combine power and electromagnetic information leakages. In: Oswald, E., Rohatgi, P. (eds.) CHES 2008. LNCS, vol. 5154, pp. 411–425. Springer, Heidelberg (2008). https://doi.org/10.1007/978-3-540-85053-3_26

35. Woudenberg, J., Witteman, M., Bakker, B.: Improving differential power analysis by elastic alignment. CT-RSA **6558**, 104–119 (2011). https://doi.org/10.1007/978-3-642-19074-2_8

Cryptanalysis

A Tale of Three Signatures: Practical Attack of ECDSA with wNAF

Gabrielle De Micheli[1(✉)], Rémi Piau[1,2], and Cécile Pierrot[1]

[1] Université de Lorraine, CNRS, Inria, LORIA, F-54000 Nancy, France
`gabrielle.de-micheli@inria.fr`
[2] ENS Rennes, Rennes, France

Abstract. Attacking ECDSA with wNAF implementation for the scalar multiplication first requires some side channel analysis to collect information, then lattice based methods to recover the secret key. In this paper, we reinvestigate the construction of the lattice used in one of these methods, the *Extended Hidden Number Problem* (EHNP). We find the secret key with only 3 signatures, thus reaching a known theoretical bound, whereas best previous methods required at least 4 signatures in practice. Given a specific leakage model, our attack is more efficient than previous attacks, and for most cases, has better probability of success. To obtain such results, we perform a detailed analysis of the parameters used in the attack and introduce a preprocessing method which reduces by a factor up to 7 the total time to recover the secret key for some parameters. We perform an error resilience analysis which has never been done before in the setup of EHNP. Our construction find the secret key with a small amount of erroneous traces, up to 2% of false digits, and 4% with a specific type of error.

Keywords: Public key cryptography · ECDSA · Side channel attack · Windowed non-adjacent form · Lattice techniques

1 Introduction

The Elliptic Curve Digital Signature Algorithm (ECDSA) [13], first proposed in 1992 by Scott Vanstone [26], is a standard public key signature protocol widely deployed. ECDSA is used in the latest library TLS 1.3, email standard OpenPGP and smart cards. It is also implemented in the library OpenSSL, and can be found in cryptocurrencies such as Bitcoin, Ethereum and Ripple. It benefits from a high security based on the hardness of the elliptic curve discrete logarithm problem and a fast signing algorithm due to its small key size. Hence, it is recognized as a standard signature algorithm by institutes such as ISO since 1998, ANSI since 1999, and IEEE and NIST since 2000.

The ECDSA signing algorithm requires scalar multiplications of a point P on an elliptic curve by an ephemeral key k. Since this operation is time-consuming and often the most time-consuming part of the protocol, it is necessary to use

© Springer Nature Switzerland AG 2020
A. Nitaj and A. Youssef (Eds.): AFRICACRYPT 2020, LNCS 12174, pp. 361–381, 2020.
https://doi.org/10.1007/978-3-030-51938-4_18

an efficient algorithm. The Non Adjacent Form (NAF) and its windowed variant (wNAF) were introduced as an alternative to the binary representation of the nonce k to reduce the execution time of the scalar multiplication. Indeed, the NAF representation does not allow two non-zero digits to be consecutive, thus reducing the Hamming weight of the representation of the scalar. This improves on the time of execution as the latter is dependent on the number of non-zero digits. The wNAF representation is present in implementations such as in Bitcoin, as well as in the libraries Cryptlib, BouncyCastle and Apple's Common-Crypto. Moreover, until very recently (May 2019), wNAF was present in all three branches of OpenSSL.

However, implementing the scalar multiplication using wNAF representation and no added layer of security makes the protocol vulnerable to side-channel attacks. Side-channel attacks were first introduced about two decades ago by Kocher et al. [14], and have since been used to break many implementations, and in particular some cryptographic primitives such as AES, RSA, and ECDSA. They allow to recover secret information throughout observable leakage. In our case, this leakage corresponds to differences in the execution time of a part of the signing algorithm, observable by monitoring the cache.

For ECDSA, cache side-channel attacks such as FLUSH&RELOAD [28,29] have been used to recover information about either the sequence of operations used to execute the scalar multiplication, or for example in [8] the modular inversion. For the scalar multiplication, these operations are either a multiplication or an addition depending on the bits of k. This information is usually referred to as a double-and-add chain or the trace of k. A trace is created when a signature is produced by ECDSA and thus we talk about signatures and traces in an equivalent sense. At this point, we ask how many traces need to be collected to successfully recover the secret key. Indeed, from an attacker's perspective, the least traces necessary, the more efficient the attack is. This quantity depends on how much information can be extracted from a single trace and how combining information of multiple traces is used to recover the key. We work on the latter to minimize the number of traces needed.

The nature of the information obtained from the side channel attack allows to determine what kind of method should be carried out to recover the secret key. Attacks on ECDSA are inspired by attacks on a similar cryptosystem, DSA. In 2001, Howgrave-Graham and Smart [12] showed how knowing partial information of the nonce k in DSA can lead to a full secret key recovery. Later, Nguyen and Shparlinski [19] gave a polynomial time algorithm that recovers the secret key in ECDSA as soon as some consecutive bits of the ephemeral key are known. They showed that using the information leaked by the side channel attack, one can recover the secret key by constructing an instance of the Hidden Number Problem (HNP) [4]. The basic structure of the attack algorithm is to construct a lattice which contains the knowledge of consecutive bits of the epheremal keys, and by solving CVP or SVP, to recover the secret key. This type of attack has been done in [3,8,26,28]. However, these results considered perfect traces, but obtaining traces without any misreadings is very rare. In 2018,

Dall et al. [6] included an error-resilience analysis to their attack: they showed that key recovery with HNP is still possible even in the presence of erroneous traces.

In 2016, Fan, Wang and Cheng [7] used another lattice-based method to attack ECDSA: the Extended Hidden Number Problem (EHNP) [11]. EHNP mostly differs from HNP by the nature of the information given as input. Indeed, the information required to construct an instance of EHNP is not sequences of consecutive bits, but the positions of the non-zero coefficients in any representation of some integers. This model, which we consider in this article as well, is relevant when describing information coming from FLUSH&RELOAD or PRIME&PROBE attacks for example, the latter giving a more generic scenario with no shared data between the attacker and the victim. In [7], the authors are able to extract 105.8 bits of information per signature on average, and thus require in theory only 3 signatures to recover a 256-bit secret key. In practice, they were able to recover the secret key using 4 error-free traces.

In order to optimize an attack on ECDSA various aspects should be considered. By minimizing the number of signatures required in the lattice construction, one minimizes the number of traces needed to be collected during the side-channel attack. Moreover, reducing the time of the lattice part of the attack, and improving the probability of success of key recovery allows to reduce the overall time of the attack. In this paper, we improve on all three of these aspects. Furthermore, we propose the first error-resilience analysis for EHNP and show that key recovery is still possible with erroneous traces too.

Contributions: In this work, we reinvestigate the attack against ECDSA with wNAF representation for the scalar multiplication using EHNP. We focus on the lattice part of the attack, *i.e.*, the exploitation of the information gathered by the side-channel attack. We first assume we obtain a set of error-free traces from a side-channel analysis. We preselect some of these traces to optimize the attack. The main idea of the lattice part is then to use the ECDSA equation and the knowledge gained from the selected traces to construct a set of modular equations which include the secret key as an unknown. These modular equations are then incorporated into a lattice basis similar to the one given in [7], and a short vector in it will contain the necessary information to reconstruct the secret key. We call "experiment" one run of this algorithm. An experiment succeeds if the algorithm recovers the secret key.

A New Preprocessing Method. The idea of selecting good traces beforehand has already been explored in [27]. The authors suggest three rules to select traces that improve the attack on the lattice part. Given a certain (large) amount of traces available, the lattice is usually built with a much smaller subset of these traces. Trying to identify beforehand the traces that would result in a better attack is a clever option. The aim of our new preprocessing—that completely differs from [27]—is to regulate the size of the coefficients in the lattice, and this results in a better lattice reduction time. For instance, with 3 signatures, we were able to reduce the total time of the attack by a factor of 7.

Analyzing the Attack. Several parameters intervene while building and reducing the lattice. We analyze the performance of the attack with respect to these parameters and present the best parameters that optimize either the total time or the probability of success.

First, we focus on the attack time. Note that when talking about the overall time of the attack, we consider the average time of a single experiment multiplied by the number of trials necessary to recover the secret key. We compare[1] our times with the numbers reported in [7, Table 3] with method C. Indeed, methods A and B in [7] use extra information that comes from choices in the implementation which we choose to ignore as we want our analysis to remain as general as possible. The comparison is justified as we consider the same leakage model, and compare timings when running experiments on similar machines. For 4 signatures, our attack is slightly slower[2] than timings in [7]. However, when considering more than 4 signatures, our attack is faster. We experiment up to 8 signatures to further improve our overall time. In this case, our attack runs at best in 2 min and 25 s. Timings for 8 signatures are not reported in [7], and the case of 3 signatures was never reached before our work. In Table 1, we compare our times with the fastest times reported by [7]. We choose their fastest times but concerning our results we choose to report experiments which are faster (not the fastest) with, if possible, better probability than theirs.

Table 1. Comparing attack times with [7], for 5000 experiments.

Number of signatures	Our attack		[7]	
	Time	Success (%)	Time	Success (%)
3	39 h	0.2	–	–
4	1 h 17 min	0.5	41 min	1.5
5	8 min 20 s	6.5	18 min	1
6	≈ 5 min	25	18 min	22
7	≈ 3 min	17.5	34 min	24
8	≈ 2 min	29	–	–

The overall time of the attack is also dependent on the success probability of key recovery. From Table 2, one can see that our success probability is higher than [7], except for 7 signatures. They have 68% of success with their best parameters whereas we only reach 45% in this case.

---

[1] In order to have a fair comparison with our methodology, the times reported in [7] with which we compare ourselves have to be multiplied by the number of trials necessary for their attack succeed, thus increasing their total time by a lot. Using 5 signatures, their best total time would be around 15 h instead of 18 min.

[2] For 4 signatures, no times are reported without method A. Thus, we have no other choice than to compare our times with theirs, using A. Yet their time for 4 signatures without A should at least be the time they report with it.

For the sake of completeness, we mention that in [21], the authors use HNP to recover the secret key using 13 signatures. Their success probability in this case is around 54% and their overall time is close to 20 s, hence much faster. However, as their leakage model is different, we do not further mention their work.

Finding the Key with Only Three Signatures. Overall, combining a new preprocessing method, a modified lattice construction and a careful choice of parameters allows us to mount an attack which works in practice with only 3 signatures. However, the probability of success in this case is very low. We were able to recover the secret key only once with BKZ-35 over 5000 experiments. This result is difficult to quantify as a probability but we note that finding the key a single time over 5000 experiments is still much better than randomly finding a 256-bit integer. If we assume the probability is around 0.02%, as each trial costs 200 s in average, we can expect to find the secret key after 12 days using a single core. Note that this time can be greatly reduced when parallelizing the process, *i.e.*, each trial can be run on a separate core. On the other hand, if we use our preprocessing method, with 3 signatures we obtain a probability of success of 0.2% and a total time of key recovery of 39 h, thus the factor 7 of improvement mentioned above. Despite the low probability of success, this result remains interesting nonetheless. Indeed, the authors in [7] reported that in practice, the key couldn't be recovered using less than 4 signatures and we improve on their result.

Table 2. Comparing success probability with [7], for 5000 experiments.

Number of signatures	Our attack		[7]	
	Success (%)	Time	Success (%)	Time
3	0.2	39 h	–	–
4	4	25 h 28 min	1.5	41 min
5	20	2 h 42 min	4	36 min
6	40	1 h 4 min	35	1 h 43 min
7	45	2 h 36 min	68	3 h 58 min
8	45	5 h 2 min	–	–

Resilience to Errors. We also investigate the resilience to errors of our attack. Such an analysis has not yet been done in the setup of EHNP. It is important to underline that collecting traces without any errors using any side-channel attack is very hard. Previous works used perfect traces to mount the lattice attack. Thus, it required collecting more traces. As pointed out in [7], more or less twice as many signatures are needed if errors are considered. In practice, this led [7] to gather in average 8 signatures to be able to find the key with 4 perfect traces. We experimentally show that we are still able to recover the secret key even in the presence of faulty traces. In particular, we find the key using only 4 faulty traces, but with a very low probability of success. As the percentage of incorrect digits in the trace grows, the probability of success decreases and thus more signatures are required to successfully recover the secret key. For instance, if 2% of the digits are wrong among all the digits of a given set of traces, it is still possible to recover the key with 6 signatures. This result is valid if errors are uniformly distributed over the digits. However, we have a better probability to recover the key if errors consist in 0-digit faulty readings, *i.e.*, 0 digits read as non-zero. In other words, the attack could work with a higher percentage of errors, around 4%, if we could ensure from the side channel attack and some preprocessing methods that none of the non-zero digits have been flipped to 0.

Organization: Sect. 2 gives background on ECDSA and the wNAF representation. In Sect. 3, we explain how to transform EHNP into a lattice problem. We explicit the lattice basis and analyze the length of the short vectors found in the reduced basis. In Sect. 4, we introduce our preprocessing method which allows us to reduce the overall time of our attack. In Sect. 5, we give experimental results. Finally, in Sect. 6, we give an error resilience analysis.

2   Preliminaries

2.1   Elliptic Curves Digital Signature Algorithm

The ECDSA algorithm is a variant of the Digital Signature Algorithm, DSA, [17] which uses elliptic curves instead of finite fields. The parameters used in ECDSA are an elliptic curve E over a finite field, a generator G of prime order q and a hash function H. The private key is an integer α such that $1 < \alpha < q - 1$ and the public key is $p_k = [\alpha]G$, the scalar multiplication of G by α.

To sign a message m using the private key α, randomly select an ephemeral key $k \leftarrow_R \mathbb{Z}_q$ and compute $[k]G$. Let r be the x-coordinate of $[k]G$. If $r = 0$, select a new nonce k. Then, compute $s = k^{-1}(H(m) + \alpha r) \bmod q$ and again if $s = 0$, select a new nonce k. Finally, the signature is given by the pair (r, s).

In order to verify a signature, first check if $r, s \in \mathbb{Z}_q$, otherwise the signature is not valid. Then, compute $v_1 = H(m) \cdot s^{-1} \bmod q$, $v_2 = r \cdot s^{-1} \bmod q$ and $(x, y) = [v_1]G + [v_2]p_k$. Finally, the signature is valid if $x \equiv r \pmod{q}$.

We consider a 128-bit level of security. Hence α, q and k are 256-bit integers.

2.2   WNAF Representation

The ECDSA algorithm requires the computation of $[k]G$, a scalar multiplication. In [10], various methods to compute fast exponentiation are presented. One family of such methods is called window methods and comes from NAF representation. Indeed, the NAF representation does not allow two non-zero digits to be consecutive, thus reducing the Hamming weight of the representation of the scalar. The basic idea of a window method is to consider chunks of w bits in the representation of the scalar k, compute powers in the window bit by bit, square w times and then multiply by the power in the next window. The window methods can be combined with the NAF representation of k. For any $k \in \mathbb{Z}$, a representation $k = \sum_{j=0}^{\infty} k_j 2^j$ is called a NAF if $k_j \in \{0, \pm 1\}$ and $k_j k_{j+1} = 0$ for all $j \geq 0$. Moreover, every k has a unique NAF representation. The NAF representation minimizes the number of non-zero digits k_j. It is presented in Algorithm 1.

The NAF representation can be combined with a sliding window method to further improve the execution time. For instance, in OpenSSL (up to the latest versions using wNAF 1.1.1b), the window size usually chosen was $w = 3$, which is the value we set for all our experiments. The scalar k is converted into wNAF form using Algorithm 2. The sequence of digits m_i belongs to the set $\{0, \pm 1, \pm 3, \ldots, \pm(2^w - 1)\}$. Let k be the sum of its non-zero digits, renamed k_i. More precisely, we get $k = \sum_{j=1}^{\ell} k_j 2^{\lambda_j}$, where ℓ is the number of non-zero digits, and λ_j represents the position of the digit k_j in the wNAF representation.

Example 1. In binary, we can write $23 = 2^4 + 2^2 + 2^1 + 2^0 = (1, 0, 1, 1, 1)$ whereas in NAF-representation, we have $23 = 2^5 - 2^3 - 2^0 = (1, 0, -1, 0, 0, -1)$. With $w = 3$, the wNAF representation gives $23 = 2^4 + 7 \times 2^0 = (1, 0, 0, 0, 7)$.

```
Input:   k ∈ Z⁺
Output:  NAF representation of k
i = 0;
while k > 0 do
    if k (mod 2) = 1 then
        kᵢ = 2 − (k (mod 4));
        k = k − kᵢ;
    else
        kᵢ = 0;
    end
    k = k/2;
    i = i + 1;
end
return kᵢ₋₁, kᵢ₋₂, ..., k₁, k₀
```
Algorithm 1: NAF algorithm

```
Input: k ∈ Z⁺, w ∈ N
Output: (m₀, m₁, ..., mₙ), i.e., k
         in its wNAF
         representation
i = 0;
while k > 0 do
    if k (mod 2) = 1 then
        mᵢ = k (mod 2^(w+1));
        if mᵢ ≥ 2^w then
            mᵢ = mᵢ − 2^(w+1);
        end
        k = k − mᵢ;
    else
        mᵢ = 0;
    end
    k = k/2;
    i = i + 1;
end
```
Algorithm 2: wNAF representation

2.3 Lattice Reduction Algorithms

A $\mathbb{Z}$-lattice is a discrete additive subgroup of $\mathbb{Z}^n$. It is usually specified by a *basis matrix* $B \in \mathbb{Z}^{n \times n}$. The lattice $L(B)$ generated by B consists of all integer combinations of the row vectors in B. The determinant of a lattice is the absolute value of the determinant of a basis matrix: $\det L(B) = |\det B|$. The discreteness property ensures that there is a vector v_1 reaching the minimum non-zero value for the euclidean norm. Let us write $||v_1||_2 = \lambda_1$. Let λ_i be the ith successive minimum of the lattice. The LLL algorithm [15] takes as an input a lattice basis, and returns in polynomial time in the lattice dimension n a reduced lattice basis whose vectors b_i satisfy the worst-case approximation bound $||b_i||_2 \leq 2^{(n-1)/2}\lambda_i$. In practice, for random lattices, LLL obtains approximation factors such that $||b_1||_2 \leq 1.02^n \lambda_1$ as noted by Nguyen and Stehlé [18]. Moreover, for random lattices, the Gaussian heuristic implies that $\lambda_1 \approx \sqrt{n/(2\pi e)} \det(L)^{1/n}$.

The BKZ algorithm [22,24] is exponential in some given block-size β and polynomial in the lattice dimension n. It outputs a reduced lattice basis whose vectors b_i satisfy the approximation $||b_i||_2 \leq i\gamma_\beta^{(n-i)/(k-1)}\lambda_i$ [23], where γ_β is the Hermite constant. In practice, Chen and Nguyen [5] observed that BKZ returns vectors such that $b_1 \leq (1 + \epsilon_\beta)^n \lambda_1$ where ϵ_β depends on the block-size β. For random lattices, they get $1 + \epsilon_\beta = 1.01$ for a block-size $\beta = 85$.

3   Attacking ECDSA Using Lattices

Using some side-channel attack, one can recover information about the wNAF representation of the nonce k. In particular, it allows us to know the positions of the non-zero coefficients in the representation of k. However, the value of these coefficients are unknown. This information can be used in the setup of the Extended Hidden Number Problem (EHNP) to recover the secret key. For many messages m, we use ECDSA to produce signatures (r, s) and each run of the signing algorithm produces a nonce k. We assume we have the corresponding trace of the nonce, that is, the equivalent of the double-and-add chain of kG using wNAF. The goal of the attack is to recover the secret α while optimizing either the number of signatures required or the total time of the attack.

3.1   The Extended Hidden Number Problem

The Hidden Number Problem (HNP) allows to recover a secret element $\alpha \in \mathbb{Z}_q$ if some information about the most significant bits of random multiples of $\alpha \pmod{q}$ are known for some prime q. Boneh and Venkatesan show how to recover α in polynomial time with probability greater than $1/2$. In [11], the authors extend the HNP and present a polynomial time algorithm for solving the instances of this extended problem. The Extended Hidden Number Problem is defined as follows. Given u congruences of the form

$$a_i\alpha + \sum_{j=1}^{\ell_i} b_{i,j}k_{i,j} \equiv c_i \pmod{q}, \tag{1}$$

where the secret α and $0 \leqslant k_{i,j} \leqslant 2^{\eta_{ij}}$ are unknown, and the values η_{ij}, a_i, $b_{i,j}$, c_i, ℓ_i are known for $1 \leqslant i \leqslant u$ (see [11], Definition 3), one has to recover α in polynomial time. The EHNP can then be transformed into a lattice problem and one recovers the secret α by solving a short vector problem in a given lattice.

3.2   Using EHNP to Attack ECDSA

From the ECDSA algorithm, we know that given a message m, the algorithm outputs a signature (r, s) such that

$$\alpha r = sk - H(m) \pmod{q}. \tag{2}$$

The value $H(m)$ is just some hash of the message m. We consider a set of u signature pairs (r_i, s_i) with corresponding message m_i that satisfy Eq. (2). For each signature pair, we have a nonce k. Using the wNAF representation of k, we write $k = \sum_{j=1}^{\ell} k_j 2^{\lambda_j}$, with $k_j \in \{\pm 1, \pm 3, \ldots, \pm(2^w - 1)\}$ and the choice of w depends on the implementation. Note that the coefficients k_j are unknown, however, the positions λ_j are supposed to be known via some side-channel leakage. It is then possible to represent the ephemeral key k as the sum of a known part, and an unknown part. As the value of k_j is odd, one can write $k_j = 2k'_j + 1$, where $-2^{w-1} \leqslant k'_j \leqslant 2^{w-1} - 1$. Using the same notations as in [7], set $d_j = k'_j + 2^{w-1}$, where $0 \leq d_j \leq 2^w - 1$. In the rest of the paper, we will denote by μ_j the window-size of d_j. Note that here, $\mu_j = w$ but this window-size will be modified later. This allows to rewrite the value of k as

$$k = \sum_{j=1}^{\ell} k_j 2^{\lambda_j} = \bar{k} + \sum_{j=1}^{\ell} d_j 2^{\lambda_j+1}, \tag{3}$$

with $\bar{k} = \sum_{j=1}^{\ell} 2^{\lambda_j} - \sum_{j=1}^{\ell} 2^{\lambda_j+w}$. The expression of $\bar{k}$ represents the known part of k. By substituting k in Eq. (3), we get a system of modular equations:

$$\alpha r_i - \sum_{j=1}^{\ell_i} 2^{\lambda_{i,j}+1} s_i d_{i,j} - (s_i \bar{k}_i - H(m_i)) \equiv 0 \pmod{q} \tag{4}$$

where the unknowns are α and the $d_{i,j}$. The known values are ℓ_i, which is the number of non-zero digits in k for the ith sample, $\lambda_{i,j}$, which is the position of the jth non-zero digit in k for the ith sample and $\bar{k}$ defined above. Equation (4) is then used as input to EHNP, following the method explained in [11]. The problem of finding the secret key is then reduced to solving the short vector problem in a given lattice presented in the following section.

3.3   Constructing the Lattice

Before giving the lattice basis construction, we redefine Eq. (4) to reduce the number of unknown variables in the system. This will allow us to construct a lattice of smaller dimension. Again, we use the same notations as in [7].

Eliminating One Variable. One straightforward way to reduce the lattice dimension is to eliminate a variable from the system. In this case, one can eliminate α

from Eq. (4). Let E_i denote the ith equation of the system. Then by computing $r_1E_i - r_iE_1$, we get the following new modular equations

$$\sum_{j=1}^{\ell_1} \underbrace{(2^{\lambda_{1,j}+1}s_1r_i)}_{:=\tau_{j,i}} d_{1,j} + \sum_{j=1}^{\ell_i} \underbrace{(-2^{\lambda_{i,j}+1}s_ir_1)}_{:=\sigma_{i,j}} d_{i,j}$$
$$- \underbrace{r_1(s_i\bar{k}_i - H(m_i)) + r_i(s_1\bar{k}_1 - H(m_1))}_{:=\gamma_i} \equiv 0 \pmod{q}.$$

(5)

Using the same notations as in [7], we define $\tau_{j,i} = 2^{\lambda_{1,j}+1}s_1r_i$, $\sigma_{i,j} = -2^{\lambda_{i,j}+1}s_ir_1$ and $\gamma_i = r_1(s_i\bar{k}_i - H(m_i)) + r_i(s_1\bar{k}_1 - H(m_1))$ for $2 \leqslant i \leqslant u$, $1 \leqslant j \leqslant \ell_i$. Even if α is eliminated from the equations, if we recover some $d_{i,j}$ values from a short vector in the lattice, we can recover α using any equation in the modular system (4). We now use Eq. (5) to construct the lattice basis.

From a Modular System to a Lattice Basis. Let $\mathcal{L}$ be the lattice constructed for the attack, and we have $\mathcal{L} = \mathcal{L}(\mathcal{B})$ where the lattice basis $\mathcal{B}$ is given below. Let $m = \max_{i,j} \mu_{ij}$ for $1 \leqslant j \leqslant \ell_i$ and $2 \leqslant i \leqslant u$. We set a scaling factor $\Delta \in \mathbb{N}$ to be defined later. The lattice basis is given by

$$\mathcal{B} = \begin{pmatrix}
\overbrace{\Delta 2^m q \quad 0}^{Eq\ (5), i=2} & \overbrace{0}^{\cdots Eq\ (5), i=u} & 0 & & & & \\
0 & \ddots & \vdots & & & & \\
0 & \cdots & \Delta 2^m q & 0 & & & \\
\Delta 2^m \tau_{1,2} & \cdots & \Delta 2^m \tau_{1,u} & 2^{m-\mu_{1,1}} & & & \\
\vdots & & \vdots & & 0 & \ddots & \\
\Delta 2^m \tau_{\ell_1,2} & \cdots & \Delta 2^m \tau_{\ell_1,u} & & 2^{m-\mu_{1,\ell_1}} & & \\
\Delta 2^m \sigma_{2,1} & 0 & 0 & & & 2^{m-\mu_{2,1}} & \\
\vdots & & \vdots & & & & \ddots \\
\Delta 2^m \sigma_{2,\ell_2} & & \vdots & & & & 2^{m-\mu_{2,\ell_2}} \\
0 & \ddots & 0 & & & & \vdots \\
\vdots & & \Delta 2^m \sigma_{u,1} & & & & 2^{m-\mu_{u,1}} \\
\vdots & & \vdots & & & & \ddots \\
0 & 0 & \Delta 2^m \sigma_{u,\ell_u} & 0 & & & 2^{m-\mu_{u,\ell_u}} \\
\Delta 2^m \gamma_2 & \cdots & \Delta 2^m \gamma_u & 2^{m-1} & \cdots & & 2^{m-1} \quad 2^{m-1}
\end{pmatrix}$$

Let $n = (u-1) + T + 1 = T + u$, with $T = \sum_{i=1}^{u} \ell_i$, be the dimension of the lattice. The $u - 1$ first columns correspond to Eq. (5) for $2 \leq i \leq u$. Each of the remaining columns, except the last one, corresponds to a d_{ij}, and contains coefficients that allow to regulate the size of the d_{ij}. The determinant of $\mathcal{L}$ is given by $\det \mathcal{L} = q^{u-1}(\Delta 2^m)^{u-1} 2^{\sum_{i,j}(m-\mu_{i,j})} 2^{m-1}$.

The lattice is built such that there exists $w \in \mathcal{L}$ which contains the unknowns $d_{i,j}$. To find it, we know there exists some values $t_2, t_3, \ldots, t_u$ such that if $v = (t_2, \ldots, t_u, d_{1,1}, \ldots, d_{u,\ell_u}, -1)$, we get $w = v\mathcal{B}$, and

$$w = (0, \ldots, 0, d_{1,1} 2^{m-\mu_{1,1}} - 2^{m-1}, \ldots, d_{u,\ell_u} 2^{m-\mu_{u,\ell_u}} - 2^{m-1}, -2^{m-1}).$$

If we are able to find w in the lattice, then we can reconstruct the secret key α. In order to find w, we estimate its norm and make sure w appears in the reduced basis. After reducing the basis, we look for vectors of the correct shape, *i.e.*, with sufficiently many zeros at the beginning and the correct last coefficient, and attempt to recover α for each of these.

How the Size of Δ Affects the Norms of the Short Vectors. In order to find the vector w in the lattice, we reduce $\mathcal{B}$ using LLL or BKZ. For w to appear in the reduced basis, one should at least set Δ such that

$$||w||_2 \leqslant (1.02)^n (\det L)^{1/n}. \tag{6}$$

The vector w we expect to find has norm $||w||_2 \leqslant 2^{m-1}\sqrt{T+1}$. From Eq. (6), one can deduce the value of Δ needed to find w in the reduced lattice:

$$\Delta \geqslant \frac{(T+1)^{(T+u)/(2(u-1))} 2^{\frac{1+\sum \mu_{i,j}-(u+T)}{u-1}}}{q(1.02)^{\frac{(T+u)^2}{u-1}}} := \Delta_{th}.$$

In our experiments, the average value of ℓ_i for $1 \leqslant i \leqslant u$ is $\tilde{\ell} = 26$, and thus $T = u \times \tilde{\ell}$ on average. Moreover, the average value of μ_{ij} is 7 and so on average $\sum \mu_{ij} = 7 \times u \times \tilde{\ell}$. Hence, if we compute Δ_{th} for $u = 3, \ldots, 8$, with these values, we obtain $\Delta_{th} \ll 1$, which does not help us to set this parameter. In practice, we verify that $\Delta = 1$ allows us to recover the secret key. In Sect. 5, we vary the size of Δ to see whether a slightly larger value affects the probability of success.

Too Many Small Vectors. While running BKZ on $\mathcal{B}$, we note that for some specific sets of parameters the reduced basis contains some undesired short vectors, *i.e.*, vectors that are shorter than w. This can be explained by looking at two consecutive rows in the lattice basis given above, say the jth row and the $(j+1)^{th}$ row. For example, one can look at rows which correspond to the $\sigma_{i,j}$ values but the same argument is valid for the rows concerning the $\tau_{j,i}$. From the definitions of the σ values we have $\sigma_{i,j+1} = -2^{\lambda_{i,j+1}+1} \cdot s_i r_1 = -2^{\lambda_{i,j+1}+1} \cdot (\frac{\sigma_{i,j}}{-2^{\lambda_{i,j}+1}})$. So $\sigma_{i,j+1} = 2^{\lambda_{i,j+1}-\lambda_{i,j}} \cdot \sigma_{i,j}$. Thus the linear combination given by the $(j+1)^{th}$ row minus $2^{\lambda_{i,j+1}-\lambda_{i,j}}$ times the jth row gives a vector

$$(0, \cdots, 0, -2^{\lambda_{i,j+1}-\lambda_{i,j}+m-\mu_{i,j}}, 2^{m-\mu_{i,j+1}}, 0, \cdots, 0). \tag{7}$$

Yet, this vector is expected to have smaller norm than w. Some experimental observations are detailed in Sect. 5.

Differences with the Lattice Construction Given in [7]. Let $\mathcal{B}'$ be the lattice basis constructed in [7]. Our basis $\mathcal{B}$ is a rescaled version of $\mathcal{B}'$ such that $\mathcal{B} = 2^m \Delta \mathcal{B}'$. This rescaling allows us to ensure that all the coefficients in our lattice basis are integer values. Note that [7] have a value δ in their construction which corresponds to $1/\Delta$. In this work, we give a precise analysis of the value of Δ, both theoretically and experimentally in Sect. 5, which is missing in [7].

4   Improving the Lattice Attack

4.1   Reducing the Lattice Dimension: The Merging Technique

In [7], the authors present another way to further reduce the lattice dimension, which they call the merging technique. It aims at reducing the lattice dimension by reducing the number of non-zero digits of k. The lattice dimension depends on the value $T = \sum_{i=1}^{u} \ell_i$, and thus reducing T reduces the dimension. To understand the attack, it suffices to know that after merging, we obtain some new values ℓ' corresponding to the new number of non-zero digits and λ'_j the position of these digits for $1 \leqslant j \leqslant \ell'$. After merging, one can rewrite $k = \bar{k} + \sum_{j=1}^{\ell'} d'_j 2^{\lambda'_j + 1}$, where the new d'_j have a new window size which we denote μ_j, i.e., $0 \leqslant d'_j \leqslant 2^{\mu_j} - 1$.

We present our merging algorithm based on Algorithm 3 given in [7]. Our algorithm modifies directly the sequence $\{\lambda_j\}_{j=1}^{\ell}$, whereas [7] work on the double-and-add chains. This helped us avoid some implementation issues such as an index outrun present in Algorithm 3 [7], line 7. To facilitate the ease of reading of (our) Algorithm 3, we work with dynamic tables. Let us first recall various known methods we use in the algorithm: $push\_back(e)$ inserts an element e at the end of the table, $at(i)$ outputs the element at index i, and $last()$ returns the last element of the table. We consider tables of integers indexed in $[0; S-1]$, where S is the size of the table.

Input: v_λ, a table of size n with the positions of non-zero digits in the trace sorted in increasing order and $n \geqslant 1$, a window size w.
Output: $v_{\lambda'}$, a table of size $n' \leqslant n$ containing the merged λ values and table v_μ of same size n', with the values of the window size μ_i.
Initialisation
$i \leftarrow 1;$
$v_{\lambda'} \leftarrow$ empty array;
$v_\mu \leftarrow$ empty array;
Processing
$v_{\lambda'}.push\_back(v_\lambda.at(0));$
while $i < n$ **do**
    | $dist \leftarrow v_\lambda.at(i) - v_\lambda.at(i-1);$
    | **if** $dist > w + 1$ **then**
    | | $v_\mu.push\_back(v_\lambda.at(i-1) - v_{\lambda'}.last() + w);$
    | | $v_{\lambda'}.push\_back(v_\lambda.at(i));$
    | **end**
    | $i \leftarrow i + 1;$
end
$v_\mu.push\_back(v_\lambda.at(n) - v_{\lambda'}.last() + w);$
return $(v_{\lambda'}, v_\mu)$

Algorithm 3: Merging algorithm

A useful example of the merging technique is given in [7]. From 3 to 8 signatures the approximate dimension of the lattices using the elimination and merging techniques are the following: $80, 110, 135, 160, 190$ and 215. Each new lattice dimension is roughly 54% of the dimension of the lattice before applying these techniques, for the same number of signatures. For instance, with 8 signatures we would have a lattice of dimension 400 on average, far too large to be easily reduced. For the traces we consider, after merging the mean of the ℓ_i is 26, the minimum being 17 and the maximum 37 with a standard deviation of 3. One could further reduce the lattice dimension by preprocessing traces with small ℓ_i. However, the standard deviation being small, the difference in the reduction times should not be affected too much.

4.2   Preprocessing the Traces

The two main pieces of information we can extract and use in our attack are first the number of non-zero digits in the wNAF representation of the nonce k, denoted ℓ and the weight of each non-zero digit, denoted μ_j for $1 \leqslant j \leqslant \ell$. Let $\mathcal{T}$ be the set of traces we obtained from the side-channel leakage representing the wNAF representation of the nonce k used while producing an ECDSA signature. We consider the subset $S_a = \{t \in \mathcal{T} \mid \max_j \mu_j \leqslant a, 1 \leqslant j \leqslant \ell\}$. We choose to preselect traces in a subset S_a for small values of a. The idea behind this preprocessing is to regulate the size of the coefficients in the lattice. Indeed, when selecting u traces for the attack, by upper-bounding $m = max_{i,j}\mu_{i,j}$ for $2 \leqslant i \leqslant u$, we force the coefficients to remain smaller than when taking traces at random.

We work with a set $\mathcal{T}$ of 2000 traces such that for all traces $11 \leq \max_j \mu_j \leq 67$. The proportion of signatures corresponding to the different preprocessing subsets we consider in our experiments are: 2% for S_{11}, 18% for S_{15} and 44% for S_{19}. The effect of preprocessing on the total time is explained in Sect. 5.

5   Performance Analysis

Traces from the Real World. We work with the elliptic curve secp256k1 but none of the techniques introduced here are limited to this specific elliptic curve. We consider traces from a FLUSH&RELOAD attack, executed through hyperthreading, as it can virtually recover the most amount of information.[3]

To the best of our knowledge, the only information we can recover are the positions of the non-zero digits. We are not able to determine the sign or the value of the digits in the wNAF representation. In [7], the authors exploit the

---

[3] In practice, measurements done during the cache attack depend on the noise in the execution environment, the threat model and the target leaky implementation. For instance, FLUSH&RELOAD ran from another core would be noisy. PRIME&PROBE would give the same information, with a more generic scenario. In an SGX scenario, it would recover the largest amount of information but in a user/user threat model it would be too noisy to lead to practical key recovery.

fact that the length of the binary string of k is fixed in implementations such as OpenSSL, and thus more information can be recovered by comparing this length to the length of the double-and-add chain. In particular, they were able to recover the MSB of k, and in some cases the sign of the second MSB. We do not consider this extra information as we want our analysis to remain general.

We report calculations ran on error-free traces where we evaluate the total time necessary to recover the secret key and the probability of success of the attack. Our experiments have two possible outputs: either we reconstruct the secret key α and thus consider the experiment a success, or we do not recover the secret key, and the experiment fails. In order to compute the success probability and the average time of one reduction, we run 5000 experiments for some specific sets of parameters using either Sage's default BKZ implementation [25] or a more recent implementation of the latest sieving strategies, the General Sieve Kernel (G6K) [1]. The experiments were ran using the cluster Grid'5000 on a single core of an Intel Xeon Gold 6130. The total time is the average time of a single reduction multiplied by the number of trials necessary to recover the key. The number of trials necessary to recover the secret key corresponds the number of experiments ran until we have a success for a given set of parameters. For a fixed number of signatures, we either optimize the total time or the success probability. We report numbers in Tables 3, 4 when using BKZ.[4]

Table 3. Fastest key recovery with respect to the number of signatures.

Number of signatures	Total time	Parameters			Probability of success (%)
		BKZ	Preprocessing	Δ	
3	39 h	35	S_{11}	$\approx 2^3$	0.2
4	1 h 17	25	S_{15}	$\approx 2^3$	0.5
5	8 min 20	25	S_{19}	$\approx 2^3$	6.5
6	3 min 55	20	S_{all}	$\approx 2^3$	7
7	2 min 43	20	S_{all}	$\approx 2^3$	17.5
8	2 min 25	20	S_{all}	$\approx 2^3$	29

Comments on G6K: We do not report the full experiments ran with G6K since using this implementation does not lead to the fastest total time of our attack: around 2 min using 8 signatures for BKZ and at best 5 min for G6K.

---

[4] In [7], the authors use an Intel Core i7-3770 CPU running at 3.40 GHz on a single core. In order for the time comparison to be meaningful, we ran experiments with a machine of comparable performance to estimate the timings of a single reduction. As we obtained similar timings with an older machine than used in [7], the variations we find when comparing ourselves to them solely come from the lattice construction and the reduction algorithm being used rather than hardware differences.

Table 4. Highest probability of success with respect to the number of signatures.

Number of signatures	Probability of success (%)	Parameters			Total time
		BKZ	Preprocessing	Δ	
3	0.2	35	S_{11}	$\approx 2^3$	39 h
4	4	35	S_{all}	$\approx 2^3$	25 h 28
5	20	35	S_{all}	$\approx 2^3$	2 h 42
6	40	35	S_{all}	$\approx 2^3$	1 h 04
7	45	35	S_{all}	$\approx 2^3$	2 h 36
8	45	35	S_{all}	$\approx 2^3$	5 h 02

However, G6K allows to reduce lattices with much higher block-sizes than BKZ. For comparable probabilities of success, G6K is faster. Considering the highest probability achieved, on one hand, BKZ-35 leads to a probability of success of 45%, and a single reduction takes 133 min. On the other hand, to reach around the same probability of success with G6K, we increase the block-size to 80, and a single reduction is only around 45 min on average. This is an improvement by a factor of 3 in the reduction time.

Only 3 Signatures. Using $\Delta \approx 2^3$ and no preprocessing, we recovered the secret key using 3 signatures with BKZ-35 only once and three times with BKZ-40. When using pre-processing S_{11}, BKZ-35 and $\Delta \approx 2^3$, the probability of success went up to 0.2%. Since all the probabilities remain much less than 1% an extensive analysis would have taken too long. Thus, in the rest of the section, the number of signatures only varies between 4 and 8. However, we want to emphasize that it is precisely this detailed analysis on a slightly higher number of signatures that allowed us to understand the impact of the parameters on the performance of the attack and resulted in finding the right ones allowing to mount the attack with 3 signatures.

Varying the Bitsize of Δ. In Fig. 1, we analyze the total time of key recovery as a function of the bitsize of Δ. We fix the block-size of BKZ to 25 and take traces without any preprocessing. We are able to recover the secret key by setting $\Delta = 1$, which is the lowest theoretical value one can choose. However, we observed a slight increase in the probability of success by taking a larger Δ. Without any surprise, we note that the total time to recover the secret key increases with the bitsize of Δ as the coefficients in the lattice basis become larger.

Analyzing the Effect of Preprocessing. We analyze the influence of our preprocessing method on the attack time. We fix BKZ block-size to 25. The effect of preprocessing is influenced by the bitsize of Δ and we give here an analyze for $\Delta \approx 2^{25}$ since the effect is more noticeable.

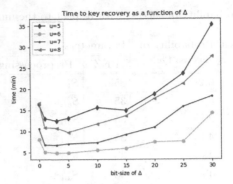

Fig. 1. Analyzing the overall time to recover the secret key as a function of the bitsize of Δ. We report the numbers BKZ-25 and no preprocessing. The optimal value for Δ is around 2^3 except for $u = 8$ where it is 2^5.

The effect of preprocessing is difficult to predict since its behavior varies depending on the parameters, having both positive and negative effects. On the one hand, we reduce the size of all the coefficients in the lattice, thus reducing the reduction time. On the other hand, we generate more potential small vectors[5] with norms smaller than the norm of w. For this reason, the probability of success of the attack decreases since the vector w is more likely to be a linear combination of vectors already in the reduced basis. For example, with 7 signatures we find in average w to be the third or fourth vector in the reduced basis without preprocessing, whereas with S_{11} it is more likely to appear in position 40.

The positive effect of preprocessing is most noticeable for $u = 4$ and $u = 5$, as shown in Fig. 2. For instance, using S_{15} and $u = 4$ lowers the overall time by a factor up to 5.7. For $u = 5$, we gain a factor close to 3 by using either S_{15} or S_{19}. For $u > 5$, using preprocessed traces is less impactful. For large Δ such as $\Delta \approx 2^{25}$, we still note some lower overall times when using S_{15} and S_{19}, up to a factor 2. When the bitsize gets smaller, reducing the size of the coefficients in the lattice is less impactful.

Balancing the Block-size of BKZ. Finally, we vary the block-size in the BKZ algorithm. We fix $\Delta \approx 2^3$ and use no preprocessing. We plot the results in Fig. 3 for 6 and 7 signatures. For other values of u, the plot is very similar and we omit them in Fig. 3. Without any surprise, we see that as we increase the block-size, the probability of success increases, however the reduction time increases significantly as well. This explains the results shown in Table 3 and Table 4: to reach the best probability of success one needs to increase the block-size in BKZ (we did not try any block-size greater than 40), but to get the fastest key recovery attack, the block-size is chosen between 20 and 25, except for 3 signatures where the probability of success is too low with these parameters.

---

[5] In the sense of vectors exhibited in (7).

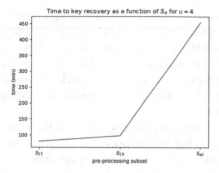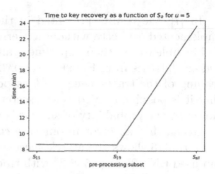

Fig. 2. Overall time to recover the secret key as a function of the preprocessing subset for 4 and 5 traces. The other parameters are fixed: $\Delta \approx 2^{25}$ and BKZ-25.

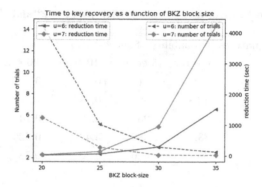

Fig. 3. Analyzing the number of trials to recover the secret key and the reduction time of the lattice as a function of the block-size of BKZ. We consider the cases where $u = 6$ and $u = 7$. The dotted lines correspond to the number of trials, and the continued lines to the reduction time in seconds.

6 Error Resilience Analysis

It is not unexpected to have errors in the traces collected during side-channel attacks. Obtaining error-free traces requires some amount of work on the signal processing side. Prior to [6], the presence of errors in traces was either ignored or preprocessing was done on the traces until an error-free sample was found, see [2,9]. In [6], it is shown the lattice attack still successfully recovers the secret key even when traces contain errors. An error in the setup given in [6] corresponds to an incorrect bound on the size of the values being collected. In our setup, a trace without errors corresponds to a trace where every single coefficient in the wNAF representation of k has been identified correctly as either non-zero or not. The probability of having an error in our setup is thus much higher. Side-channel attacks without any errors are very rare. Both [21] and [6] give some analysis of the attacks FLUSH&RELOAD and PRIME&PROBE in real life scenarios.

In [7], the results presented in the paper assume the FLUSH&RELOAD is implemented perfectly, without any error. In particular, to obtain 4 perfect traces and be able to run their experiment and find the key, one would need to have in average 8 traces from FLUSH&RELOAD – the probability to conduct to a perfect reading of the traces being 56% as pointed out in [21]. In our work, we show that it is possible to recover the secret key using only 4, even erroneous, traces. However, the probability of success is very low.

Recall that an error in our case corresponds to a flipped digit in the trace of k. Table 5 shows the attack success probability in the presence of errors. We ran used BKZ-25 and $\Delta \approx 2^3$ with traces taken from S_{all}. We average over 5000 experiments. We write $\ll 1$ when the attack succeeded less than five times over 5000 experiments, thus making it difficult to evaluate the probability of success.

Table 5. Error analysis using BKZ-25, $\Delta \approx 2^3$ and S_{all}.

Number of signatures	Probability of success (%)				
	0 error	5 errors	10 errors	20 errors	30 errors
4	0.28	$\ll 1$	0	0	0
5	4.58	0.86	0.18	$\ll 1$	0
6	19.52	5.26	1.26	0.14	$\ll 1$
7	33.54	10.82	3.42	0.32	$\ll 1$
8	35.14	13.26	4.70	0.58	$\ll 1$

The attack works up to a resilience to 2% of errors. Indeed, for $u = 6$, we recovered the secret key with 30 errors, *i.e.*, 30 flipped digits over 6×257 digits.

Different Types of Errors. There exists two possible types of errors. In the first case, a coefficient which is zero is evaluated as a non-zero coefficient. In theory, this only adds a new variable to the system, *i.e.*, the number ℓ of non-zero coefficients is overestimated. This does not affect the probability of success much. Indeed, we just have an overly-constrained system. We can see in Fig. 4 that the probability of success of the attack indeed decreases slowly as we add errors of this form. With errors only of this form, we were able to recover the secret key up to nearly 4% of errors, (for instance with $u = 6$, using BKZ-35). The other type of errors consists of a non-zero coefficients which is misread as a zero coefficient. In this case, we lose information necessary for the key recovery and thus this type of error affects the probability of success far more importantly as can also be seen in Fig. 4. In this setup, we were not able to recover the secret key when more than 3 errors of this type appear in the set of traces considered.

Strategy. If the signal processing method is hesitant between a non-zero digit or 0, we would recommend to favor putting a non-zero instead of 0 to increase the chance of having an error of type $0 \rightarrow$ non-zero, for which the attack is a lot more tolerant.

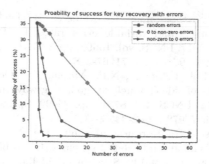

Fig. 4. Probability of success for key recovery with various types of errors when using $u = 8$, BKZ-25, $\Delta \approx 2^3$, and no preprocessing.

7   Conclusion and Countermeasures

In the last decades, most implementations of ECDSA have been the target of microarchitectural attacks, and thus existing implementations have either been replaced by more robust algorithms, or layers of security have been added.

For example, one way of minimizing leakage from the scalar multiplication is to use the Montgomery ladder scalar-by-point multiplication [16], much more resilient to side-channel attacks due to the regularity of the operations. However, this does not entirely remove the risk of leakage [28]. Additional countermeasures are necessary.

When looking at common countermeasures, many implementations use blinding or masking techniques [20], for example in BouncyCastle implementation of ECDSA. The former consists in blinding the data before doing any operations, and masking techniques randomize all the data-dependent operations by applying random transformations, thus making any leakage inexploitable.

However, it is important to keep in mind these lattices attacks as they can be applied at any level of an implementation that leaks the correct information.

Acknowledgement. We would like to thank Nadia Heninger for discussions about possible lattice constructions, Medhi Tibouchi for answering our side-channel questions, Alenka Zajic and Milos Prvulovic for providing us with traces from OpenSSL that allowed us to confirm our results on a deployed implementation, Daniel Genkin for pointing us towards the Extended Hidden Number Problem, and Pierrick Gaudry for his precious support and reading. Experiments presented in this paper were carried out using the Grid'5000 testbed, supported by a scientific interest group hosted by Inria and including CNRS, RENATER and several universities as well as other organizations.

References

1. Albrecht, M.R., Ducas, L., Herold, G., Kirshanova, E., Postlethwaite, E.W., Stevens, M.: The general sieve kernel and new records in lattice reduction. Cryptology ePrint Archive, Report 2019/089 (2019). https://eprint.iacr.org/2019/089

2. Angel, J., Rahul, R., Ashokkumar, C., Menezes, B.: DSA signing key recovery with noisy side channels and variable error rates. In: Patra, A., Smart, N.P. (eds.) INDOCRYPT 2017. LNCS, vol. 10698, pp. 147–165. Springer, Cham (2017). https://doi.org/10.1007/978-3-319-71667-1_8

3. Benger, N., van de Pol, J., Smart, N.P., Yarom, Y.: "Ooh Aah... Just a Little Bit" : a small amount of side channel can go a long way. In: Batina, L., Robshaw, M. (eds.) CHES 2014. LNCS, vol. 8731, pp. 75–92. Springer, Heidelberg (2014). https://doi.org/10.1007/978-3-662-44709-3_5

4. Boneh, D., Venkatesan, R.: Hardness of computing the most significant bits of secret keys in diffie-hellman and related schemes. In: Koblitz, N. (ed.) CRYPTO 1996. LNCS, vol. 1109, pp. 129–142. Springer, Heidelberg (1996). https://doi.org/10.1007/3-540-68697-5_11

5. Chen, Y., Nguyen, P.Q.: BKZ 2.0: better lattice security estimates. In: Lee, D.H., Wang, X. (eds.) ASIACRYPT 2011. LNCS, vol. 7073, pp. 1–20. Springer, Heidelberg (2011). https://doi.org/10.1007/978-3-642-25385-0_1

6. Dall, F., et al.: Cachequote: Efficiently recovering long-term secrets of SGX EPID via cache attacks (2018)

7. Fan, S., Wang, W., Cheng, Q.: Attacking OpenSSL implementation of ECDSA with a few signatures. In: Weippl, E.R., Katzenbeisser, S., Kruegel, C., Myers, A.C., Halevi, S. (eds.) ACM CCS 2016, pp. 1505–1515. ACM Press, October 2016

8. García, C.P., Brumley, B.B.: Constant-time callees with variable-time callers. In: Kirda, E., Ristenpart, T. (eds.) USENIX Security 2017, pp. 83–98. USENIX Association, August 2017

9. Genkin, D., Pachmanov, L., Pipman, I., Tromer, E., Yarom, Y.: ECDSA key extraction from mobile devices via nonintrusive physical side channels. In: Weippl, E.R., Katzenbeisser, S., Kruegel, C., Myers, A.C., Halevi, S. (eds.) ACM CCS 2016, pp. 1626–1638. ACM Press, October 2016

10. Gordon, D.M.: A survey of fast exponentiation methods. J. Algorithms **27**(1), 129–146 (1998)

11. Hlaváč, M., Rosa, T.: Extended hidden number problem and its cryptanalytic applications. In: Biham, E., Youssef, A.M. (eds.) SAC 2006. LNCS, vol. 4356, pp. 114–133. Springer, Heidelberg (2007). https://doi.org/10.1007/978-3-540-74462-7_9

12. Howgrave-Graham, N.A., Smart, N.P.: Lattice attacks on digital signature schemes. Des. Codes Cryptol. **23**(3), 283–290 (2001)

13. Johnson, D., Menezes, A., Vanstone, S.: The elliptic curve digital signature algorithm (ECDSA). Int. J. Inf. Secur. **1**(1), 36–63 (2001)

14. Kocher, P., Jaffe, J., Jun, B.: Differential power analysis. In: Wiener, M. (ed.) CRYPTO 1999. LNCS, vol. 1666, pp. 388–397. Springer, Heidelberg (1999). https://doi.org/10.1007/3-540-48405-1_25

15. Lenstra, A.K., Lenstra, H.W., Lovász, L.: Factoring polynomials with rational coefficients. Math. Ann. **261**(4), 515–534 (1982)

16. Montgomery, P.L.: Speeding the pollard and elliptic curve methods of factorization. Math. Comput. **48**(177), 243–243 (1987)

17. National Institute of Standards and Technology: Digital Signature Standard (DSS) (2013)

18. Nguyen, P.Q., Stehlé, D.: LLL on the average. In: Hess, F., Pauli, S., Pohst, M. (eds.) ANTS 2006. LNCS, vol. 4076, pp. 238–256. Springer, Heidelberg (2006). https://doi.org/10.1007/11792086_18

19. Nguyen, P.Q., Shparlinski, I.E.: The insecurity of the elliptic curve digital signature algorithm with partially known nonces. Des. Codes Cryptol. **30**(2), 201–217 (2003)

20. Osvik, D.A., Shamir, A., Tromer, E.: Cache attacks and countermeasures: the case of AES. In: Pointcheval, D. (ed.) CT-RSA 2006. LNCS, vol. 3860, pp. 1–20. Springer, Heidelberg (2006). https://doi.org/10.1007/11605805_1
21. van de Pol, J., Smart, N.P., Yarom, Y.: Just a little bit more. In: Nyberg, K. (ed.) CT-RSA 2015. LNCS, vol. 9048, pp. 3–21. Springer, Cham (2015). https://doi.org/10.1007/978-3-319-16715-2_1
22. Schnorr, C.P.: A hierarchy of polynomial time lattice basis reduction algorithms. Theoret. Comput. Sci. **53**(2–3), 201–224 (1987)
23. Schnorr, C.P.: Block reduced lattice bases and successive minima. Comb. Probab. Comput. **3**, 507–522 (1994)
24. Schnorr, C.P., Euchner, M.: Lattice basis reduction: Improved practical algorithms and solving subset sum problems. Math. Program. **66**(2), 181–199 (1994)
25. The FPLLL development team: FPLLL, a lattice reduction library (2016)
26. Vanstone, S.: Responses to NIST's proposals (1992)
27. Wang, W., Fan, S.: Attacking OpenSSL ECDSA with a small amount of side-channel information. Sci. China Inf. Sci. **61**(3), 032105 (2017)
28. Yarom, Y., Benger, N.: Recovering OpenSSL ECDSA nonces using the FLUSH+RELOAD cache side-channel attack. IACR Cryptol. ePrint Archive **2014**, 140 (2014)
29. Yarom, Y., Falkner, K.: FLUSH+RELOAD: A high resolution, low noise, L3 cache side-channel attack. In: Proceedings of the 23rd USENIX Conference on Security Symposium, SEC 2014, Berkeley, CA, USA, pp. 719–732. USENIX Association (2014)

Attacking RSA Using an Arbitrary Parameter

Muhammad Rezal Kamel Ariffin[1,2]([✉])[ID], Amir Hamzah Abd Ghafar[1][ID], and Muhammad Asyraf Asbullah[1,3][ID]

[1] Institute for Mathematical Research, Universiti Putra Malaysia,
43400 UPM Serdang, Selangor Darul Ehsan, Malaysia
rezal@upm.edu.my
[2] Department of Mathematics, Faculty of Science, Universiti Putra Malaysia,
43400 UPM Serdang, Selangor Darul Ehsan, Malaysia
[3] Centre of Foundation Studies for Agricultural Science, Universiti Putra Malaysia,
43400 UPM Serdang, Selangor Darul Ehsan, Malaysia

Abstract. In this paper, we introduce a parameter u that is related to N via an arbitrary relation. By knowing the parameter along with RSA public key pairs, (N, e), we conduct two new attacks on the RSA cryptosystem. The first attack works on the equation $eX - uY = Z - \phi_b$ where ϕ_b is the best known lower bound of $\phi(N)$. It combines the continued fraction method and Coppersmith's method to factor N in polynomial time. The second attack shows that given (N_i, e_i) for $1 \leq i \leq k$ and a fixed X, we can simultaneously factor the k RSA moduli. It manipulates the result from diophantine approximation to enable the conditions of Coppersmith's method. These attacks show that there are more possible weak RSA key pairs.

Keywords: RSA cryptosystem · Cryptanalysis · Coppersmith's method · Diophantine approximation

1 Introduction

The RSA cryptosystem [16] is one of the vital components in transferring data securely over the internet. This cryptosystem is comprised of three main algorithms. Namely, key generation algorithm, encryption algorithm and decryption algorithm. While the details of encryption and decryption algorithms can be viewed in [16], for the key generation algorithm, one must generate two different primes p and q where $q < p < 2p$. The product of the primes, N is known as RSA modulus. Using the value of the modulus, the RSA public exponent,e is chosen such that $e < \phi(N)$ and $\gcd(e, \phi(N)) = 1$ where $\phi(N)$ is Euler's totient function. Then, the corresponding RSA private exponent, d is computed via the RSA key relation,

$$d \equiv e^{-1} \pmod{\phi(N)}. \tag{1}$$

The RSA public key, (N, e) and secret parameters $(p, q, \phi(N), d)$ are said to be the outputs of the algorithm. The security strength of RSA is embedded in

© Springer Nature Switzerland AG 2020
A. Nitaj and A. Youssef (Eds.): AFRICACRYPT 2020, LNCS 12174, pp. 382–399, 2020.
https://doi.org/10.1007/978-3-030-51938-4_19

the difficulty to factor its RSA modulus, $N = pq$ since p and q are n–bit primes where n is typically set to be 1024. The problem to factor N in polynomial time is dubbed the integer factorization problem and the best algorithm to solve it still runs in sub-exponential time [4]. However, previous attacks on RSA showed that a small size of d can compromise the security of RSA [2,10,17]. This type of attack is known as small private exponent attacks and it manipulates the form of (1) by using suitable approximation of $\phi(N)$. This type of attack may generalize by using the following equation.

$$ex - uy = z \qquad (2)$$

for suitable integers x, y, z [11–13]. These attacks usually combine the continued fraction method and Coppersmith's method to formulate a new strategy in factoring N.

In this paper, we present two new attacks upon RSA. These new attacks do not depend on the RSA diophantine key equation as previous research did. To initiate the attack, first we define a parameter u that can be computed from the best known upper and lower bounds of $\phi(N)$. However it should be noted that u can be an arbitrary value that is suitably larger than N. Using u, we show an attack upon RSA that works when there exist integers X, Y and Z verifying the equation $eX - uY = Z - \phi_b$ such that

$$1 \leq Y < X < \frac{u}{2\left(\phi(N) - \phi_b\right)}, \quad \phi(N) + \frac{p-q}{p+q} N^{1/4} < N - 2N^{1/2},$$

$$|Z - \phi(N)| < \frac{p-q}{p+q} N^{1/4}$$

where ϕ_b is the best known lower bound of $\phi(N)$. The first attack combines the continued fraction method in [17] and Coppersmith's method in [6] upon the equation $eX - uY = Z - \phi_b$. Note that this equation is not derived from the RSA key equation.

The second attack generalizes the result from the first attack. We assume that the adversary is given k instances of weak RSA moduli $N_i = p_i q_i$ with its corresponding public exponent e_i. We show that if there exist an integer $X < N^\delta$ and k integers $Y_i < N^\delta$ and $|Z_i - \phi(N_i)| < \frac{p_i - q_i}{p_i + q_i} N^{1/4}$ such that $e_i X - Y_i u_i = Z_i - \phi_b$ for $i = 1, \ldots, k$, and $|Z_i - \phi_{b_i}| < \lambda N^{\delta + \frac{1}{4}}$ where $\lambda < \frac{3}{2}\left(2^{\frac{k+5}{4}} - 3\right)$ then $N_i = p_i q_i$ can be factored in polynomial time.

From these two attacks, we realized there are about $N^{\frac{1}{2} - \epsilon}$ many pairs of (N, e) that are probable candidates of weak keys of RSA. This may expose some of the RSA users into using weak RSA public key pairs, (N, e).

The paper is organized as follows. In Sect. 2, a brief introduction to the continued fractions expansion via Legendre's Theorem, the lattice basis reduction and also simultaneous Diophantine approximation. Section 3 and Sect. 4 presents the first and second attacks, respectively. Section 5 compares our findings against previous findings with respect to their conditions. Then, the conclusion of our work is presented in Sect. 6.

2   Preliminaries

We first show the theorem of continued fractions below:

Theorem 1 (Legendre's theorem). *Let R is a rational number. Let x and y are integers where $y \neq 0$ and $gcd(x, y) = 1$. Suppose*

$$\left| R - \frac{x}{y} \right| < \frac{1}{2y^2}$$

Then $\frac{x}{y}$ is a convergent of the continued fraction expansion of R.

Proof. See [7].

To find the private keys of RSA using the weak RSA public keys (N, e), we use Coppersmith's method [5] to find the integer roots of a univariate or bivariate polynomials modulo N. Particularly, given a large integer N, let

$$F(x) = x^n + a_{n-1}x^{n-1} + \ldots + a_1 x + a_0.$$

If there exists $x_0 < N^{1/n}$ such that $F(x_0) \equiv 0 \pmod{N}$, then [5] showed that x_0 can be found in polynomial time with the aid of the LLL algorithm. The LLL algorithm [9] produces a different polynomial f that is related to $F(x)$ that satisfy the conditions imposed for x_0 with smaller values. Due to the smaller values, this method runs in polynomial time. Coppersmith also applied the method in [6] to factor N, given certain approximation of p as shown in the next theorem.

Theorem 2 (Coppersmith's approximation of p). *Let $N = pq$ be the product of two unknown integers such that $p < q < 2p$. Given an approximation of p with additive error term at most $N^{1/4}$, then p and q can be found in polynomial time with respect to $\log(N)$.*

Proof. See [6].

In the system of equations of k weak RSA moduli $N_i = p_i q_i$, the next theorem is required for the adversary to find p_i and q_i.

Theorem 3 (Simultaneous Diophantine Approximations). *There is a polynomial time algorithm with respect to $\log(p_i)$ where $i = 1, \ldots, n$, for given rational numbers $\alpha_1, ..., \alpha_n$ and $0 < \epsilon < 1$, to compute integers $p_1, \cdots, p_n$ and a positive integer q such that*

$$\max_i |q\alpha_i - p_i| < \epsilon \quad and \quad q \leq 2^{n(n-3)/4} \cdot 3^n \cdot \epsilon^{-n}.$$

Proof. See [15].

3   The First Attack

We first define a parameter u in the following definition.

Definition 1. *Let ϕ_a be the smallest integer value of known upper bound of $\phi(N)$. Let ϕ_b be the largest integer value of known lower bound of $\phi(N)$. Then we define $u = \phi_a + \phi_b$.*

The next remark shows how we can find the best current approximation values for ϕ_a and ϕ_b.

Remark 1. From [14] we know that $2\sqrt{N} < p + q < \frac{3}{\sqrt{2}}\sqrt{N}$. This means $N - \frac{3}{\sqrt{2}}\sqrt{N} + 1 < \phi(N) < N - 2\sqrt{N} + 1$ as $N - (p + q) + 1 = \phi(N)$. Hence the best current approximation for ϕ_a is $\left\lfloor N - 2\sqrt{N} + 1 \right\rfloor$ and the best current approximation for ϕ_b is $\left\lceil N - \frac{3}{\sqrt{2}}\sqrt{N} + 1 \right\rceil$.

It should be noted that u can be an arbitrary value that is suitably larger than N. However, in our case, we use $u = \phi_a + \phi_b$ as in Definition 1. The following lemmas and theorem show the conditions to be fulfilled by parameters in our equation so that its information can be computed in order to find an approximation of p which satisfies Theorem 2.

Lemma 1. *Let $N = pq$ be an RSA modulus with $q < p < 2q$. Suppose we know an approximation S of $p + q$ such that $S > 2N^{1/2}$, $\sqrt{S^2 - 4N} > p - q$ and*

$$|p + q - S| < \frac{p - q}{p + q} N^{1/4}.$$

Then $\tilde{P} = \frac{1}{2}\left(S + \sqrt{S^2 - 4N}\right)$ where $|p - \tilde{P}| < N^{1/4}$.

Proof. Suppose that $S > 2N^{1/2}$ and let $D = \sqrt{S^2 - 4N}$. We have

$$|(p - q)^2 - D^2| = |(p - q)^2 - S^2 + 4N| = |(p + q)^2 - S^2|.$$

Dividing by $p - q + D$, we get

$$|p - q - D| = \frac{(p + q + S)|p + q - S|}{p - q + D}$$

Next, suppose $|p + q - S| < \frac{p-q}{p+q}N^{1/4}$. Since $\frac{p-q}{p+q}N^{1/4} < N^{1/4}$, then

$$p + q + S < 2(p + q) + N^{1/4}$$
$$< 2(p + q) + 2N^{1/4}$$
$$= 2(p + q) + \frac{2N^{1/2}}{N^{1/4}}$$
$$< 2(p + q) + \frac{p + q}{N^{1/4}}$$
$$= \left(2 + \frac{1}{N^{1/4}}\right)(p + q)$$

as $2N^{1/2} < (p+q)$. Let $\sqrt{S^2 - 4N} > p - q$, then combining with $p - q + D > p - q + (p - q) = 2(p - q)$, we deduce

$$
\begin{aligned}
|p - q - D| &< \frac{\left(2 + \frac{1}{N^{1/4}}\right)(p+q)|p+q-S|}{2(p-q)} \\
&< \frac{\left(2 + \frac{1}{N^{1/4}}\right)(p+q)}{2(p-q)} \cdot \frac{(p-q)}{(p+q)} N^{1/4} \\
&= \left(1 + \frac{1}{2N^{1/4}}\right) \cdot N^{1/4} \\
&\approx N^{1/4}
\end{aligned}
$$

as $\frac{1}{2N^{1/4}}$ tends to be negligible for large N. Now, set $\tilde{P} = \frac{1}{2}(S + D)$. Finally we can have

$$
\begin{aligned}
|p - \tilde{P}| &= \left|p - \frac{1}{2}(S + D)\right| \\
&= \frac{1}{2}|p + q - S + p - q - D| \\
&\leq \frac{1}{2} \cdot |p + q - S| + \frac{1}{2}|p - q - D| \\
&< \frac{1}{2} \cdot \frac{p-q}{p+q} N^{1/4} + \frac{1}{2} N^{1/4} \\
&< N^{1/4}
\end{aligned}
$$

as $\frac{(p-q)}{(p+q)} < 1$. This terminates the proof.

Lemma 2. Let $N = pq$ be an RSA modulus with $q < p < 2q$. Let e satisfy the equation $eX - uY = Z - \phi_b$ where X, Y are positive integers with $\gcd(X, Y) = 1$. If $1 \leq Y < X < \left|\frac{u}{2(\phi(N) - \phi_b)}\right|$ and $|Z - \phi(N)| < \frac{p-q}{p+q} N^{1/4}$ then $\frac{Y}{X}$ is a convergent of $\frac{e}{u} - \frac{N^{1/4}}{2u}$.

Proof. Consider the equation

$$
eX - uY = Z - \phi_b \tag{3}
$$

Let $|Z - \phi(N)| < \frac{p-q}{p+q}N^{1/4}$. Then divide (3) by uX we get

$$\frac{e}{u} - \frac{Y}{X} = \frac{Z - \phi_b}{uX}$$

$$\leq \frac{\frac{p-q}{p+q}N^{1/4} + \phi(N) - \phi_b}{uX}$$

$$< \frac{\frac{N^{1/2}}{2N^{1/2}}N^{1/4} + \phi(N) - \phi_b}{uX}$$

$$< \frac{XN^{1/4}}{2uX} + \frac{\phi(N) - \phi_b}{uX}$$

$$\leq \frac{N^{1/4}}{2u} + \frac{\phi(N) - \phi_b}{uX} \tag{4}$$

since $q - p < N^{1/2}$, $p + q > 2N^{1/2}$ and $X > 1$. If $X < \left|\frac{u}{2(\phi(N) - \phi_b)}\right|$ then $\frac{1}{2X} > \left|\frac{2(\phi(N) - \phi_b)}{u}\right|$. As uX will always be a positive value, rearranging (4), we obtain

$$\left|\left(\frac{e}{u} - \frac{N^{1/4}}{2u}\right) - \frac{Y}{X}\right| < \left|\frac{\phi(N) - \phi_b}{uX}\right|$$

$$< \frac{1}{2X^2}$$

which satisfies Theorem 1. This terminates the proof.

Theorem 4. *Let $N = pq$ be an RSA modulus with $q < p < 2q$. Let e satisfies the equation $eX - uY = Z - \phi_b$ where X, Y are positive integers with $\gcd(X, Y) = 1$. If*

$$1 \leq Y < X < \frac{u}{2(\phi(N) - \phi_b)}, \quad \phi(N) + \frac{p-q}{p+q}N^{1/4} < N - 2N^{1/2},$$

$$|Z - \phi(N)| < \frac{p-q}{p+q}N^{1/4}$$

then N can be factored in polynomial time.

Proof. Suppose e satisfies an equation $eX - uY = Z - \phi_b$. Let X, Y and Z satisfy the conditions in Lemma 2, then we can find the values of X and Y by computing $\frac{e}{u} - \frac{N^{1/4}}{2u}$. From the values of X and Y, we define

$$S = N - (eX - uY + \phi_b) = N - Z.$$

Since $\phi(N) + \frac{p-q}{p+q}N^{1/4} < N - 2N^{1/2}$ then $S \geq N - \left(\phi(N) + \frac{p-q}{p+q}N^{1/4}\right) > N - (N - 2N^{1/2}) = 2N^{1/2}$. We also have

$$S^2 - 4N = (N - Z)^2 - 4N$$
$$= N^2 - 2NZ + Z^2 - 4N$$
$$= N(N - 2Z - 4) + Z^2$$
$$> N.$$

Thus $\sqrt{S^2 - 4N} > N^{1/2} > p - q$. We also observe that

$$
\begin{aligned}
S &= N - Z \\
&> N - \left(\frac{p-q}{p+q} N^{1/4} + \phi(N) \right) \\
&> N - \phi(N) - \frac{p-q}{p+q} N^{1/4} \\
&= p + q - 1 - \frac{p-q}{p+q} N^{1/4}
\end{aligned}
\tag{5}
$$

Rearranging (5), we get

$$
|p + q - S - 1| < |p + q - S| < \frac{p-q}{p+q} N^{1/4}
$$

which satisfies Lemma 1. Thus we can find $\tilde{P} = \frac{1}{2} \left(S + \sqrt{S^2 - 4N} \right)$ such that $|p - \tilde{P}| < N^{1/4}$. Based on Theorem 2, we can factor N in polynomial time.

Remark 2. Observe that $\frac{Y}{X}$ is a convergent of the terms $\frac{e}{u} - \frac{N^{\frac{1}{4}}}{2u}$. Since $u \approx N$, the condition $Y < X$ will always hold. The convergents of $\frac{e}{u} - \frac{N^{\frac{1}{4}}}{2u}$ will produce a sequence, where candidates of X begins from the smallest possible integer till $2u^2$. Since $1 < \frac{u}{2(\phi(N)-\phi_b)} < 2u^2$, there will exist candidates of X where $1 < X < \frac{u}{2(\phi(N)-\phi_b)}$. Moreover, since the continued fractions process ends in polynomial time, candidates for X can be tested in polynomial time. Thus, we can guarantee the existence of the pair (X, Y) satisfying the conditions of Theorem 4.

Given (N, e) the following is an algorithm to initiate factoring $N = pq$ by using the continued fraction and Coppersmith's method via the LLL algorithm. The algorithm is as follows:

Algorithm 1. Factoring RSA moduli satisfying Theorem 4.

Input: The RSA public key pair (N, e) and u.
Output: The prime factors p, q or $\perp$.
1: Compute A to be the continued fraction of $\left(\frac{e}{u} - \frac{N^{1/4}}{2u} \right)$
2: Set $Y =$ numerator of A and $X =$ denominator of A such that $\gcd(X, Y) = 1$.
3: For each convergent $\frac{Y}{X}$ of $\left(\frac{e}{u} - \frac{N^{1/4}}{2u} \right)$, compute $Z = eX - uY + \phi_b$
4: Compute $S = N - Z$ and $\tilde{P} = \frac{1}{2} \left(S + \sqrt{S^2 - 4N} \right)$
5: Consider the polynomials $F(v) = (v + \tilde{P})$
6: Construct a matrix M of coefficient vectors of elements of $\langle F(v), N \rangle$.
7: Run LLL algorithm onto M.
8: Construct the polynomials $M'(v)$ from the first row of output of Step 7.
9: Factor $M'(v)$ to obtain small root v_0.
10: Compute $p = v_0 + \tilde{P}$ and $q = \frac{N}{p}$.
11: **if** $q \in \mathbb{Z}$, **then** output p, q.
12: **else** Algorithm fails or $\perp$.

Remark 3. Due to the fact that the equation being manipulated given by $eX - uY = Z - \phi_b$ does not represent the RSA key equation, we do not need an upper bound of the decryption exponent d for the attack to work properly. Indeed, there is no need to discuss the bound for d, since neither d nor its generalized parameter is in our equation. Upon factoring $N = pq$, one is able to retrieve $d \approx N$. This is a major finding. All previous results related to studying the RSA key equation has the condition the maximum bound of d is given by $d < N^{1/2}$.

The following is an example to illustrate Algorithm 1.

Example 1. We use RSA-129 modulus in this example. Specifically, we are given

$$N = 3511053077638484246715947902716191465 99$$

and

$$e = 943837024474969735510396386229690517$$

Then we compute

$$\phi_a = \left\lfloor N - 2\sqrt{N} + 1 \right\rfloor$$
$$= 3511053077638484246341191817901629222 35$$

and

$$\phi_b = \left\lceil N - \frac{3}{\sqrt{2}}\sqrt{N} + 1 \right\rceil$$
$$= 3511053077638484246318459049421244601 15$$

which values are used to compute

$$u = \phi_a + \phi_b$$
$$= 7022106155276968492659650867322873823 50.$$

Then we obtain the continued fraction expansion of $\frac{e}{u} - \frac{N^{1/4}}{2u}$ which is

$$\left[0, \frac{1}{743}, \frac{1}{744}, \frac{228}{169631}, \ldots, \frac{19879}{14789889}, \frac{1040411704253353285}{77406175462588273 8716}, \ldots \right]$$

Taking $\frac{Y}{X} = \frac{19879}{14789889}$, then we compute

$$Z = eX - uY + \phi_b$$
$$= 3511053077638484246327850920525015070 78.$$

Then we compute

$$S = N - Z$$
$$= 38809698219117639522$$

and

$$\tilde{P} = \frac{1}{2}\left(S + \sqrt{S^2 - 4N}\right)$$
$$= 24448940821740240387$$

Let $F(v) = (v + \tilde{P})$ and $V = 8000000$, be the upper bound of the unknown $|p - \tilde{P}|$. We consider the polynomials, $N^2, NF(v), F(v)^2, vF(v)^2$ and $v^2F(v)^2$ and build a matrix, M corresponding to these polynomials. Particularly,

$$M = \begin{bmatrix} N^2 & 0 & 0 & 0 & 0 \\ N\tilde{P} & N \cdot V & 0 & 0 & 0 \\ \tilde{P}^2 & 2\tilde{P}V & V^2 & 0 & 0 \\ 0 & \tilde{P}^2V & 2\tilde{P}V^2 & V^3 & 0 \\ 0 & 0 & \tilde{P}^2V^2 & 2\tilde{P}V^3 & V^4 \end{bmatrix}$$

Let M_{LLL} as the LLL-reduced matrix, we use the coefficients of the first row of M_{LLL} to construct the polynomial $M'(v)$ where

$$M'(v) = -80322272v^4 + 4316657527524354v^3 - 17123235643412959749419v^2$$
$$- 25819107876857731036710641043v + 1639490446731502573047261983372752.$$

By finding the integer roots of $M'(v)$, we obtain

$$v = 493424.$$

Observe

$$p = v + \tilde{P}$$
$$= 24448940821740733811$$

Now we can solve the factorization of N by finding

$$q = \frac{N}{p}$$
$$= 14360757397377109309.$$

Remark 4. The RSA private exponent, d corresponding with (N, e) as given in Example 1 such that $ed \equiv 1 \pmod{\phi(N)}$ is

$$d = 44601440284214524132897789887339371933 \approx N^{0.97675} \approx N.$$

Remark 5. Observe that values of X and Y in Example 1 satisfy conditions posed in Theorem 4.

Remark 6. Observe that since $1 \leq Y < X < \frac{u}{2(\phi(N)-\phi_b)}$,

$$e = \frac{Z - \phi_b + uY}{X} \geq \frac{Z - \phi_b + u}{X}$$

$$> \frac{Z - \phi_b + u}{u} \cdot 2(\phi(N) - \phi_b)$$

$$= 2(\phi(N) - \phi_b)\left(1 + \frac{Z - \phi_b}{u}\right)$$

$$> 2(\phi(N) - \phi_b) \approx N^{1/2}.$$

This means our attack only works if $e > N^{1/2}$.

3.1 Estimating Numbers of (N, e)'s Satisfying $eX - uY = Z - \phi_b$

In this section, we give an estimation of the numbers of e satisfying $eX - uY = Z - \phi_b$. The following lemma states that the public parameter $e < N$ satisfies at most one equation $eX - uY = Z - \phi_b$ where the unknown parameters X, Y and Z satisfy the conditions of Theorem 4.

Lemma 3. *Let $N = pq$ be an RSA modulus with $q < p < 2q$. For $i = 1, 2$, let e satisfies the equation $eX_i - uY_i = Z_i - \phi_b$ with $\gcd(X, Y) = 1$,*

$$1 \leq Y_i < X_i < \frac{u}{2\left(\phi(N) - \phi_b\right)}, \quad \phi(N) + \frac{p-q}{p+q}N^{1/4} < N - 2N^{1/2},$$

$$\text{and } |Z_i - \phi(N)| < \frac{p-q}{p+q}N^{1/4}.$$

Then $X_1 = X_2$, $Y_1 = Y_2$ and $Z_1 = Z_2$.

Proof. Suppose that e satisfying two equations

$$eX_1 - uY_1 = Z_1 - \phi_b \quad \text{and} \quad eX_2 - uY_2 = Z_2 - \phi_b$$

with

$$X_1, X_2 < \frac{u}{2\left(\phi(N) - \phi_b\right)} \quad \text{and} \quad |Z_1 - \phi(N)|, |Z_2 - \phi(N)| < \frac{p-q}{p+q}N^{1/4}.$$

Then, equating the term e, we have

$$\frac{Z_1 - \phi_b + uY_1}{X_1} = \frac{Z_2 - \phi_b + uY_2}{X_2} \tag{6}$$

Rearranged (6) to

$$X_2(Z_1 - \phi_b) + X_1(\phi_b - Z_2) = u(X_1 Y_2 - X_2 Y_1). \tag{7}$$

Suppose $X_1, X_2 < \frac{u}{2(\phi(N)-\phi_b)}$. Observe that

$$|Z_1 - Z_2| < \frac{2(p-q)}{p+q}N^{1/4} \quad \text{and} \quad \phi(N) - \phi_b > N^{1/4}$$

which implies $\frac{Z_1 - Z_2}{(\phi(N) - \phi_b)} < 1$. Consider the left hand side of (7),

$$X_2(Z_1 - \phi_b) + X_1(\phi_b - Z_2) < \frac{u}{2\,(\phi(N) - \phi_b)}(Z_1 - \phi_b) + \frac{u}{2\,(\phi(N) - \phi_b)}(\phi_b - Z_2)$$

$$= \frac{u}{2}\left(\frac{Z_1 - \phi_b}{(\phi(N) - \phi_b)} + \frac{\phi_b - Z_2}{(\phi(N) - \phi_b)}\right)$$

$$= \frac{u}{2}\left(\frac{Z_1 - Z_2}{(\phi(N) - \phi_b)}\right)$$

$$< u \tag{8}$$

Hence from the right hand side of (7), we deduce that $X_1Y_2 - X_2Y_1 = 0$. Since $\gcd(X_1, Y_1) = \gcd(X_2, Y_2) = 1$, it shows that $X_1 = X_2$ and $Y_1 = Y_2$. Thus, from (6), this leads to $Z_1 = Z_2$.

The following result give the estimation of the number of e's for which the Theorem 4 applies.

Lemma 4. *Let X and Y be two integers satisfying $1 \le Y < X < \frac{p-q}{p+q}N^{\frac{1}{4}}$ and $\gcd(X, Y) = 1$. Then there exists an integer Z such that $Z \equiv \phi_b - uY \pmod{X}$ and $|Z - \phi(N)| < \frac{p-q}{p+q}N^{\frac{1}{4}}$.*

Proof. Assume that X and Y are fixed with $\gcd(X, Y) = 1$. Let $Z_0 = \phi_b - uY$. Let $\beta \equiv \phi(N) - Z_0 \pmod{X}$ with $0 \le \beta < X$ and set $Z = \phi(N) - \beta$. Then

$$Z = \phi(N) - \beta \equiv Z_0 \equiv \phi_b - uY \pmod{X}.$$

Define $e = \frac{Z - Z_0}{X}$. Then $eX = Z - Z_0 = Z - \phi_b + uY$, that is $eX - uY = Z - \phi_b$. Moreover, we have

$$|Z - \phi(N)| = \beta < X < \frac{p-q}{p+q}N^{\frac{1}{4}}.$$

This terminates the proof. $\qquad\qquad\qquad\qquad\qquad\qquad\qquad\qquad\qquad\qquad\square$

Theorem 5. *Let $N = pq$ be the product of two balanced prime integers such that $p - q > c_1\sqrt{N}$. The number of possible values of the parameter $e < N$ in Theorem 4 where*

$$e = \frac{Z - \phi_b + uY}{X}$$

and $\gcd(X, Y) = 1$ with

$$1 \le Y < X < \frac{p-q}{p+q}N^{\frac{1}{4}}$$

is at least $N^{\frac{1}{2} - \epsilon}$ where $\epsilon > 0$ is arbitrarily small for suitably large N.

Proof. Let X and Y be two integers satisfying $1 \leq Y < X < \frac{p-q}{p+q}N^{\frac{1}{4}}$ and $\gcd(X, Y) = 1$. Then by Lemma 4, there exists an integer Z such that $e = \frac{Z - \phi_b + uY}{X}$ is also an integer. Let $z = Z - \phi_b$. Then

$$e = \frac{z + uY}{X}.$$

The number of the parameter e's satisfying the equation $e = \frac{z+uY}{X}$ with the conditions given in the Theorem 4 is

$$\#(e) = \sum_{X=1}^{\mathcal{N}_1} \sum_{\substack{Y=1 \\ \gcd(X,Y)=1}}^{X-1} 1, \tag{9}$$

where

$$\mathcal{N}_1 = \frac{p-q}{p+q}N^{\frac{1}{4}} \approx c_1 N^{\frac{1}{4}}$$

when p and q are balanced with $p - q > c_2\sqrt{N}$ for some positive constants c_1 and c_2.

Observe that for $1 \leq Y < X < \frac{p-q}{p+q}N^{\frac{1}{4}}$ we have the following.

$$\sum_{\substack{Y=1 \\ \gcd(X,Y)=1}}^{X-1} 1 = \phi(X) > \frac{c_3 X}{\log\log X} > \frac{c_3 X}{\log\log N}, \tag{10}$$

where c_3 is a constant (see [7], Theorem 328). Substitute (10) in (9), we obtain

$$\#(e) > \frac{c_3}{\log\log N} \sum_{X=1}^{\mathcal{N}_1} X \tag{11}$$

Next, for $\sum_{X=1}^{\mathcal{N}_1} X$, we have

$$\sum_{X=1}^{\mathcal{N}_1} X = \frac{\mathcal{N}_1(\mathcal{N}_1 + 1)}{2} > \frac{\mathcal{N}_1^2}{2} = \frac{\left(c_1 N^{\frac{1}{4}}\right)^2}{2} \tag{12}$$

Substitute (12) in (11), we obtain

$$\#(e) > \frac{c_3}{\log\log N} \times \frac{\left(c_1 N^{\frac{1}{4}}\right)^2}{2}$$

$$> \frac{c_1^2 c_3}{2\log\log N} N^{\frac{1}{2}} \tag{13}$$

$$= N^{\frac{1}{2} - \epsilon}$$

Hence a good approximation for the number of weak keys e is at least $N^{\frac{1}{2} - \epsilon}$ where $\epsilon > 0$ is arbitrarily small for suitably large N where $N^{-\epsilon} = \frac{c_1^2 c_3}{2\log\log N}$. $\square$

4   The Second Attack

In this section, we are given k RSA moduli $N_i = p_i q_i$ with its corresponding public exponent e_i and u_i where $u_i = \phi_{a_i} + \phi_{b_i}$ follows Definition 1. By using the following theorem, we can factor k RSA moduli N_i simultaneously if there exist suitable X and Y_i that satisfy conditions required in the theorem. The ability to factor these moduli simultaneously are based on the results from Theorem 2 and Theorem 3.

Theorem 6. *For $k \geq 2$, let $N_i = p_i q_i$, $1 \leq i \leq k$, be k RSA moduli. Let $N = \min_i N_i$. Let e_i, $i = 1, \ldots, k$, be k public exponents. Define $\delta = \frac{k}{2(k+1)}$. If there exist an integer $X < N^\delta$ and k integers $Y_i < N^\delta$ with $\gcd(X, Y_i) = 1$ and $|Z_i - \phi(N_i)| < \frac{p_i - q_i}{p_i + q_i} N^{1/4}$ such that $e_i X - Y_i u_i = Z_i - \phi_{b_i}$ for $i = 1, \ldots, k$, and $|Z_i - \phi_{b_i}| < \lambda N^{\delta + \frac{1}{4}}$ where $\lambda < \frac{3}{2}\left(2^{\frac{k+5}{4}} - 3\right)$ then one can factor the k RSA moduli $N_1, \cdots N_k$ in polynomial time.*

Proof. For $k \geq 2$ and $i = 1, \ldots, k$, the equation $e_i X - u_i Y_i = Z_i - \phi_{b_i}$ can be rewritten as

$$e_i X - \left(N_i - 2\sqrt{N_i} + 1 + N_i - \frac{3}{\sqrt{2}}\sqrt{N_i} + 1\right) Y_i = Z_i - \phi_{b_i}$$

as $u_i = \phi_{a_i} + \phi_{b_i}$ and $\phi_{a_i} = N_i - 2\sqrt{N_i} + 1, \phi_{a_i} = N_i - \frac{3}{\sqrt{2}}\sqrt{N_i} + 1$. This implies

$$e_i X - (2(N_i + 1)) Y_i = Z_i - \phi_{b_i} - \left(2\sqrt{N_i} + \frac{3}{\sqrt{2}}\sqrt{N_i}\right) Y_i.$$

Hence

$$\left|\frac{e_i X}{2(N_i + 1)} - Y_i\right| = \frac{\left|Z_i - \phi_{b_i} - \left(2\sqrt{N_i} + \frac{3}{\sqrt{2}}\sqrt{N_i}\right) Y_i\right|}{2(N_i + 1)}. \tag{14}$$

Let $N = \min_i N_i$ and suppose that $Y_i < N^\delta$ and $|Z_i - \phi_{b_i}| < \lambda N^{\delta + \frac{1}{4}}$. Then $|Z_i - \phi_{b_i}| < \lambda \frac{p_i - q_i}{p_i + q_i} N^{1/4} < \lambda N^{\delta + \frac{1}{4}}$. Since $2\sqrt{N_i} + \frac{3}{\sqrt{2}}\sqrt{N_i} < \frac{9}{2}\sqrt{N_i}$, we will get

$$\frac{\left|Z_i - \phi_{b_i} - \left(2\sqrt{N_i} + \frac{3}{\sqrt{2}}\sqrt{N_i}\right) Y_i\right|}{2N_i} \leq \frac{|Z_i - \phi_{b_i}| + \left(2\sqrt{N} + \frac{3}{\sqrt{2}}\sqrt{N}\right) Y_i}{2N}$$

$$< \frac{\lambda N^{\delta + \frac{1}{4}} + \left(\frac{9}{2}\sqrt{N}\right) Y_i}{2N}$$

$$< \frac{\lambda N^{\delta + \frac{1}{4}} + \frac{9}{2} N^{\delta + \frac{1}{2}}}{2N}$$

$$< \frac{\left(\frac{9}{2} + \lambda\right) N^{\delta + \frac{1}{2}}}{2N}$$

$$= \left(\frac{\frac{9}{2} + \lambda}{2}\right) N^{\delta - \frac{1}{2}}$$

Plugging in (14), we get

$$\left|\frac{e_i X}{2(N_i + 1)} - Y_i\right| < \left(\frac{\frac{9}{2} + \lambda}{2}\right) N^{\delta - \frac{1}{2}}$$

We now proceed to prove the existence of the integer X. Let $\epsilon = \left(\frac{\frac{9}{2} + \lambda}{2}\right) N^{\delta - \frac{1}{2}}$, $\delta = \frac{k}{2(k+1)}$. We have

$$N^\delta \cdot \epsilon^k = N^\delta \cdot N^{k\delta - \frac{k}{2}} \left(\frac{\frac{9}{2} + \lambda}{2}\right)^k = N^{\delta(k+1) - \frac{k}{2}} \cdot \left(\frac{\frac{9}{2} + \lambda}{2}\right)^k. \tag{15}$$

Since $\delta = \frac{k}{2(k+1)}$, (15) becomes

$$N^0 \cdot \left(\frac{\frac{9}{2} + \lambda}{2}\right)^k = \left(\frac{\frac{9}{2} + \lambda}{2}\right)^k. \tag{16}$$

Suppose $\lambda < \frac{3}{2} \left(2^{\frac{k+5}{4}} - 3\right)$ then (16) becomes

$$\left(\frac{\frac{9}{2} + \lambda}{2}\right)^k < \left(\frac{\frac{9}{2} + \frac{3}{2}\left(2^{\frac{k+5}{4}} - 3\right)}{2}\right)^k$$

$$= \left(\frac{9}{4} + \frac{3}{4}\left(2^{\frac{k+5}{4}} - 3\right)\right)^k$$

$$= \left(2^{\frac{k+5}{4}} \cdot 3 \cdot 2^{-2}\right)^k$$

$$= 2^{\frac{k(k-3)}{4}} \cdot 3^k. \tag{17}$$

Combining (15) and (17), we obtain

$$N^\delta < 2^{\frac{k(k-3)}{4}} \cdot 3^k \cdot \epsilon^{-k}$$

It follows that if $X < N^\delta$, then $X < 2^{\frac{k(k-3)}{4}} \cdot 3^k \cdot \epsilon^{-k}$. Summarizing, for $i = 1, \ldots, k$, we have

$$\left|\frac{e_i X}{2(N_i + 1)} - Y_i\right| < \epsilon, \quad X < 2^{\frac{k(k-3)}{4}} \cdot 3^k \cdot \epsilon^{-k}$$

which satisfies the conditions in Theorem 3 which will find X and Y_i for $i = 1, \ldots, k$. Next, using the equation $e_i X - u_i Y_i + \phi_{b_i} = Z_i$, we get the value of Z_i. We also observe that

$$S_i = N_i - Z_i$$

$$\geq N_i - \left(\frac{p_i - q_i}{p_i + q_i} N_i^{1/4} + \phi(N_i)\right)$$

$$= N_i - \phi(N_i) - \frac{p_i - q_i}{p_i + q_i} N_i^{1/4}$$

$$= p_i + q_i - 1 - \frac{p_i - q_i}{p_i + q_i} N_i^{1/4} \tag{18}$$

Rearranging (18), we get

$$|p_i + q_i - S_i - 1| < |p_i + q_i - S_i| < \frac{p_i - q_i}{p_i + q_i} N_i^{1/4}$$

which satisfies Lemma 1. Thus we can find $\tilde{p}_i = \frac{1}{2}\left(S_i + \sqrt{S_i^2 - 4N_i}\right)$ such that $|p_i - \tilde{p}_i| < N_i^{1/4}$. Based on Theorem 2, we can factor N_i in polynomial time.

We can build an algorithm to factor k RSA moduli N_i simultaneously. The algorithm is shown in Algorithm 1:

Algorithm 2. Factoring k RSA moduli simultaneously satisfying Theorem 6

Input: The public RSA key pairs (N_i, e_i) and u_i for $i = 2, 3, \ldots, k$.
Output: The prime factors p_i, q_i.
1: **for** $i = 2, 3, \ldots, k$ **do**
2:     Compute $\phi_{a_i} = \lfloor N_i - 2\sqrt{N_i} + 1 \rfloor$.
3:     Compute $\phi_{b_i} = \lceil N_i - \frac{3}{\sqrt{2}}\sqrt{N_i} + 1 \rceil$.
4:     Compute $u_i = \phi_{a_i} + \phi_{b_i}$.
5: **end for**
6: Set $N = \min(N_1, N_2, N_3)$.
7: Compute $\delta = \frac{k}{2(k+1)}$.
8: Compute $\lambda = \lfloor \frac{3}{2}\left(2^{\frac{k+5}{4}} - 3\right) \rfloor$.
9: Compute $\epsilon = \left(\frac{\frac{9}{2}+\lambda}{2}\right) N^{\delta - \frac{1}{2}}$.
10: Compute $C = \lceil 3^{n+1} \cdot 2^{\frac{(n+1)(n-4)}{4}} 4 \cdot \epsilon^{-n-1} \rceil$.
11: Compute lattice $\mathcal{L}$ spanned by the rows of the matrix M shown in proof of Theorem 4 in [15].
12: Compute matrix K by applying LLL algorithm onto M.
13: Compute matrix $H = KM^{-1}$.
14: Assign every element in the first row of H (starting from most left) as $X, Y_1, \ldots, Y_k$ respectively.
15: **for** $i = 2, 3, \ldots, k$ **do**
16:     Compute $S_i = N_i - Z_i = N_i - (e_i X - u_i Y_i) + \phi_{b_i}$.
17:     Compute $D_i = \lceil \sqrt{S_i^2 - 4N_i} \rceil$.
18:     Compute $\tilde{P}_i = \frac{1}{2}(S_i + D_i)$.
19:     Applying Coppersmith's method in Theorem 2 onto each P_i to output p_i.
20:     Compute $q_i = N_i / p_i$.
21:     **if** $q_i \in \mathbb{Z}$, **then** output p_i, q_i.
22:     **else** Algorithm fails or $\perp$.
23: **end for**

---

5   Comparative Analysis

In this section, we compare our findings against previous findings with respect to the form of the modified key equations and their conditions. The comparisons are illustrated in Table 1.

Table 1. Comparison of Our Methods Against Previous Findings

Findings	Manipulated equation	Conditions
Blömer and May [3]	$ex - y\phi(N) = z$	$x < \frac{1}{3}N^{1/4}$ and $\lvert z \rvert < exN^{-3/4}$
Hinek [8]	$e_i d - k_i \phi(N_i) = 1$	$d < N^{\delta}$ with $\delta = \frac{k}{2(k+1)} - \epsilon$ where ϵ depending on N
Nitaj $et\ al.$ (Theorem 5 in [15])	$e_i x - y_i \phi(N_i) = z_i$	$N = \min_i N_i,\ x < N^{\delta}$, $y_i < N^{\delta}$, $\lvert z_i \rvert < \frac{p_i - q_i}{3(p_i + q_i)} y_i N^{1/4}$ where $\delta = \frac{k}{2(k+1)}$
Nitaj $et\ al.$ (Theorem 6 in [15])	$e_i x_i - y\phi(N_i) = z_i$	$N = \min_i N_i,\ \min_i e_i = N^{\alpha}$, $x_i < N^{\delta},\ y < N^{\delta}$, $\lvert z_i \rvert < \frac{p_i - q_i}{3(p_i + q_i)} y N^{1/4}$ where $\delta = \frac{(2\alpha - 1)k}{2(k+1)}$
Ariffin $et\ al.$ (Theorem 13 in [1])	$ed - k\phi(N) = 1$	$\lvert b^2 p - a^2 q \rvert < N^{\gamma}$ $(a^2(b^4+1)p - b^2(a^4+1)q)(b^2 p - a^2 q) > 0$ $d < \frac{\sqrt{3}}{\sqrt{2}} N^{\frac{3}{4}\gamma}$
Our method: Theorem 4	$eX - uY = Z - \phi_b$	$1 \leq Y < X < \frac{u}{2(\phi(N) - \phi_b)}$, $\phi(N) + \frac{p-q}{p+q} N^{1/4} < N - 2N^{1/2}$, $\lvert Z - \phi(N) \rvert < \frac{p-q}{p+q} N^{1/4}$
Our method: Theorem 6	$e_i X - Y_i u_i = Z_i - \phi_{b_i}$	$N = \min_i N_i$, $X < N^{\delta},\ Y_i < N^{\delta}$, $\lvert Z_i - \phi(N_i) \rvert < \frac{p_i - q_i}{p_i + q_i} N^{1/4}$ $\lvert Z_i - \phi_{b_i} \rvert < \lambda N^{\delta + \frac{1}{4}}$ where $\lambda < \frac{3}{2}\left(2^{\frac{k+5}{4}} - 3\right)$ and $\delta = \frac{k}{2(k+1)}$

From Table 1, based on the references given, we can see that all earlier first 5 findings from Blömer and May [3] till Ariffin $et\ al.$ [1] type of attacks zoomed into the RSA diophantine equation either in its original or generalized form. The first 5 findings had to dictate conditions upon the decryption exponent d or its corresponding generalized parameter.

In retrospect, our equation did not utilize the RSA diophantine equation either in its original or generalized form. As a result, our strategy enables us to factor $N = pq$ for a set of weak keys with $d \approx N$. This is a new and important result. The conditions upon our parameters cannot not be compared to conditions upon parameters of earlier results. This is due do the fact that there is no relation between our parameters X and Y and the parameters d and $\phi(N)$.

6   Conclusion

We have formulated two new attacks on RSA using a method derived from past literature regarding attacks on the RSA key equation. In our method, we utilized an equation that does not represent the RSA key equation, which under our defined conditions can be utilized to factor N in polynomial time. The strategy uses a combination of continued fractions and Coppersmith's methods. Implicitly, the insertion of u into the equation will render a particular (N, e) to be a weak RSA public key pair. We also estimate the number of e's that satisfying our theorem is at least $N^{\frac{1}{2}-\epsilon}$. Finally, we have presented a case where given k weak RSA public key pairs, we can find the prime factors of each N simultaneously in polynomial time.

References

1. Ariffin, M.R.K., Abubakar, S.I., Yunos, F., Asbullah, M.A.: New cryptanalytic attack on RSA modulus $N = pq$ using small prime difference method. Cryptography **3**(1), 2 (2019)
2. Asbullah, M., Ariffin, M.: New attacks on RSA with modulus $N = p^2q$ using continued fractions. J. Phy. Conf. Ser. **622**, 012019 (2015)
3. Blömer, J., May, A.: A generalized wiener attack on RSA. In: Bao, F., Deng, R., Zhou, J. (eds.) PKC 2004. LNCS, vol. 2947, pp. 1–13. Springer, Heidelberg (2004). https://doi.org/10.1007/978-3-540-24632-9_1
4. Buhler, J.P., Lenstra, H.W., Pomerance, C.: Factoring integers with the number field sieve. In: Lenstra, A.K., Lenstra, H.W. (eds.) The Development of the Number Field Sieve. LNM, vol. 1554, pp. 50–94. Springer, Heidelberg (1993). https://doi.org/10.1007/BFb0091539
5. Coppersmith, D.: Finding a small root of a bivariate integer equation; factoring with high bits known. In: Maurer, U. (ed.) EUROCRYPT 1996. LNCS, vol. 1070, pp. 178–189. Springer, Heidelberg (1996). https://doi.org/10.1007/3-540-68339-9_16
6. Coppersmith, D.: Small solutions to polynomial equations, and low exponent RSA vulnerabilities. J. Cryptol. **10**(4), 233–260 (1997)
7. Hardy, G.H., Wright, E.M.: An Introduction to the Theory of Numbers. Oxford University Press, Oxford (1979)
8. Hinek, M.J.: On the security of some variants of RSA. Ph.D. thesis, University of Waterloo (2007)
9. Lenstra Jr., H.W.: Factoring integers with elliptic curves. Ann. Math. **126**, 649–673 (1987)
10. Maitra, S., Santanu, S.: Revisiting Wiener's attack - new weak keys in RSA. In: Wu, T.-C., Lei, C.-L., Rijmen, V., Lee, D.-T. (eds.) ISC 2008. LNCS, vol. 5222, pp. 228–243. Springer, Heidelberg (2008). https://doi.org/10.1007/978-3-540-85886-7_16
11. Nitaj, A.: Cryptanalysis of RSA using the ratio of the primes. In: Preneel, B. (ed.) AFRICACRYPT 2009. LNCS, vol. 5580, pp. 98–115. Springer, Heidelberg (2009). https://doi.org/10.1007/978-3-642-02384-2_7
12. Nitaj, A.: A new vulnerable class of exponents in RSA. JP J. Algebra Number Theory Appl. **21**(2), 203–220 (2011)
13. Nitaj, A.: New weak RSA keys. JP J. Algebra Number Theory Appl. **23**(2), 131–148 (2011)
14. Nitaj, A.: Diophantine and lattice cryptanalysis of the RSA cryptosystem. In: Yang, X.S. (ed.) Artificial Intelligence, Evolutionary Computing and Metaheuristics. Studies in Computational Intelligence, vol. 427, pp. 139–168. Springer, Heidelberg (2013). https://doi.org/10.1007/978-3-642-29694-9_7

15. Nitaj, A., Ariffin, M.R.K., Nassr, D.I., Bahig, H.M.: New attacks on the RSA cryptosystem. In: Pointcheval, D., Vergnaud, D. (eds.) AFRICACRYPT 2014. LNCS, vol. 8469, pp. 178–198. Springer, Cham (2014). https://doi.org/10.1007/978-3-319-06734-6_12

16. Rivest, R.L., Shamir, A., Adleman, L.: A method for obtaining digital signatures and public-key cryptosystems. Commun. ACM **21**(2), 120–126 (1978)

17. Wiener, M.J.: Cryptanalysis of short RSA secret exponents. IEEE Trans. Inf. Theory **36**(3), 553–558 (1990)

New Algorithms and Schemes

A New Encoding Algorithm for a Multidimensional Version of the Montgomery Ladder

Aaron Hutchinson[1(✉)] and Koray Karabina[2,3]

[1] University of Waterloo, Waterloo, Canada
a5hutchinson@uwaterloo.ca
[2] Florida Atlantic University, Boca Raton, USA
kkarabina@fau.edu
[3] National Research Council Canada, Ottawa, Canada
koray.karabina@nrc-cnrc.gc.ca

Abstract. We propose a new encoding algorithm for the simultaneous differential multidimensional scalar point multiplication algorithm d-MUL. Previous encoding algorithms are known to have major drawbacks in their efficient and secure implementation. Some of these drawbacks have been avoided in a recent paper in 2018 at a cost of losing the general functionality of the point multiplication algorithm. In this paper, we address these issues. Our new encoding algorithm takes the binary representations of scalars as input, and constructs a compact binary sequence and a permutation, which explicitly determines a regular sequence of group operations to be performed in d-MUL. Our algorithm simply slides windows of size two over the scalars and it is very efficient. As a result, while preserving the full generality of d-MUL, we successfully eliminate the recursive integer matrix computations in the originally proposed encoding algorithms. We also expect that our new encoding algorithm will make it easier to implement d-MUL in constant time. Our results can be seen as the efficient and full generalization of the one dimensional Montgomery ladder to arbitrary dimension.

Keywords: d-MUL · Scalar multiplication algorithm · Scalar encoding · Montgomery ladder

MSC: 94A60 · 11Y16

1 Introduction

Efficient and secure scalar multiplication algorithms are essential in modern cryptography. A (single dimensional) *scalar multiplication algorithm* for a group $\mathbb{G}$ is one which takes an integer α and group element $P \in \mathbb{G}$ as input and produces the element αP as output. Such an algorithm is required in numerous protocols such as Diffie-Hellman key exchange, and digital signature generation and verification.

© Springer Nature Switzerland AG 2020
A. Nitaj and A. Youssef (Eds.): AFRICACRYPT 2020, LNCS 12174, pp. 403–422, 2020.
https://doi.org/10.1007/978-3-030-51938-4_20

In such group based cryptographic schemes, scalar multiplication dominate the run time of the system, and therefore it is crucial to minimize its cost. Some cryptographic applications can further make use of *multidimensional* scalar multiplication algorithms, which take vectors $(\alpha_1, \ldots, \alpha_d)$ of integers and $(P_1, \ldots, P_d)$ of group elements as input and produces the element $\alpha_1 P_1 + \cdots + \alpha_d P_d$ as output. For example, verifying a signature in the Elliptic Curve Digital Signature Algorithm (ECDSA) requires computing a point $uP + vQ$, where P and Q are public parameters and u and v are derived from the given signature. Multidimensional scalar multiplication can also speed up single scalar multiplication with a fixed base P. For $\lambda = \lfloor |\mathbb{G}|^{1/d} \rfloor$ and $\lambda_i = \lambda^{i-1}$, one can write $\alpha = \sum_{i=1}^{d} \alpha_i \lambda_i$ for $0 \le \alpha_i < \lambda$, precompute $P_i = \lambda_i P$, and compute

$$\alpha P = (\sum_{i=1}^{d} \alpha_i \lambda_i) P = \sum_{i=1}^{d} \alpha_i P_i$$

through multiscalar multiplication with input α_i, P_i, $i = 1, \ldots, d$. If the group $\mathbb{G}$ is equipped with efficiently computable endomorphisms, one can use similar techniques to speed up single scalar multiplication with variable base P because the cost of precomputating P_i becomes negligible compared to the overall cost; see [3,4].

Scalar multiplication algorithms have been studied heavily in the past. One very interesting single dimensional algorithm is the Montgomery ladder [7]. A key difference between the Montgomery ladder and the double-and-add algorithm is that the Montgomery ladder is *regular* in the sense that every iteration of the main loop performs the same operations. It is known that irregularity of algorithms can be exploited through side-channel analysis and underlying scalars may be recovered by attackers; see [9]. Therefore, regularity is essential for security when the scalar α must be kept secret, such as in Diffie-Hellman public key derivation. Another interesting key feature of the Montgomery ladder is that it allows the use of differential point addition $(P, Q, P - Q \mapsto P + Q)$, where the knowledge of the difference of the points helps to write more efficient formulas [8]. As an example, $73P$ can be computed in seven steps by setting $[T, B] = [0, P]$, tracing the bits b_i of 73 from left to right, updating

$$[T, B] \leftarrow [2T, T + B] \text{ if } b_i = 0,$$
$$[T, B] \leftarrow [T + B, 2B] \text{ if } b_i = 1,$$

and so performing one addition and one doubling at each step; see Table 1. Note that the difference of the points to be added is always known (0 or P).

Bernstein [1] proposed a regular two dimensional differential addition chain (the DJB algorithm). The DJB algorithm computes $\alpha_1 P_1 + \alpha_2 P_2$ for ℓ-bit scalars in ℓ steps, performing two additions and one doubling at each step. In particular, the DJB algorithm initiates $T[1] \leftarrow 0$, $T[2] \leftarrow P_1$, $T[3] \leftarrow P_2$, and at each step, $[T[1], T[2], T[3]]$ is updated by doubling one $T[i]$ and adding two distinct pairs of points. Given the bit sequence of α_1 and α_2, a recursive formula was presented in [1] to encode a sequence for the update rules. Table 2 shows an example for

Table 1. Montgomery ladder for $\alpha = 73$

i	1	2	3	4	5	6	7
b_i	1	0	0	1	0	0	1
T	0	P	$2P$	$4P$	$9P$	$18P$	$36P$	$73P$
B	P	$2P$	$3P$	$5P$	$10P$	$19P$	$37P$	$74P$

Table 2. The DJB algorithm for computing $73P + 59Q$

i	1	2	3	4	5	6	7
$T[1]$	0	$P+Q$	$3P+Q$	$5P+3Q$	$9P+7Q$	$19P+15Q$	$37P+29Q$	$73P+59Q$
$T[2]$	P	$2P$	$2P+2Q$	$4P+4Q$	$10P+8Q$	$18P+14Q$	$36P+30Q$	$74P+58Q$
$T[3]$	Q	$2P+Q$	$3P+2Q$	$5P+4Q$	$9P+8Q$	$18P+15Q$	$37P+30Q$	$74P+59Q$

computing $73P + 59Q$ in seven steps, performing 1 doubling and 2 additions per step. Note that the difference of the points to be added is always known $(0, P, Q, \text{ or } P \pm Q)$.

In 2017, a generalization of the Montgomery ladder to d dimensions was made in [6] by means of an algorithm called d-MUL, originally based on an algorithm of Brown from 2006 in [2]. d-MUL uses a sequence of *state matrices* (defined in Sect. 2.1) to derive an encoding of the scalar vector $(\alpha_1, \ldots, \alpha_d)$, which is used to perform the scalar multiplication. For ℓ-bit scalars α_i, the encoding algorithm in [6] requires dealing with $(d + 1) \times d$ integer matrices with ℓ-bit integers. Even though the underlying matrix arithmetic is simple, it introduces non-trivial overhead cost, and makes it harder to resist against side-channel attacks. For example, a constant time implementation of d-MUL at the 128-bit security level in [5] reported about 10,000 cycle counts for the encoding phase. After encoding, d-MUL loops through ℓ steps, where one doubling and d (differential) addition are performed per step in a regular fashion.

A second paper [5] further explored d-MUL. The motivation in [5] is to bypass the encoding step, and immediately start scalar multiplication by a carefully chosen sequence of group operations: d additions and 1 doubling per step, for a total number of ℓ steps. In particular, a bijection was established between $2^{\ell d} d!$ different choices of (r, σ), where r is a length-ℓd bitstring and σ is a permutation on $\{1, 2, ..., d\}$, and the set of all state matrices containing (at most) ℓ-bit odd scalars $[\alpha_1, ..., \alpha_d]$. In short, by sampling r and σ at random, one can compute a point $\alpha_1 P_1 + \cdots + \alpha_d P_d$, for some α_i sampled at random among ℓ-bit odd integers without explicitly constructing α_i, or their binary representation.

When $d = 1$ and $d = 2$, the algorithms in [5], which we call *randomized d-MUL*, greatly simplify. When $d = 1$, there is only one choice of $\sigma = [1]$, and given r, the scalar multiplication algorithm starts with

$$T[1] \leftarrow 0, \ T[2] \leftarrow P;$$

bits r_i of r are traced from left to right, and $T[1]$ and $T[2]$ are updated as follows

$$[T[1], T[2]] \leftarrow [2T[r_i + 1], T[1] + T[2]].$$

Table 3 gives an example with $r = [1\ 1\ 0\ 1\ 1\ 0\ 1]$, which in the end computes $73P$. Note that the relation between the scalar and the r-sequence is not obvious. This may be compared to the Montgomery ladder computation in Table 1.

Table 3. Randomized d-MUL with $r = [1\ 1\ 0\ 1\ 1\ 0\ 1]$

i		1	2	3	4	5	6	7
r_i		1	1	0	1	1	0	1
$T[1]$	0	$2P$	$2P$	$4P$	$10P$	$18P$	$36P$	$74P$
$T[2]$	P	P	$3P$	$5P$	$9P$	$19P$	$37P$	$73P$

When $d = 2$, there are two choices of $\sigma \in \{[1, 2], [2, 1]\}$, and given r, the scalar multiplication algorithm starts with

$$T[1] \leftarrow 0,\ T[2] \leftarrow P,\ T[3] \leftarrow P + Q,\ \text{if } \sigma = [1, 2],$$
$$T[1] \leftarrow 0,\ T[2] \leftarrow Q,\ T[3] \leftarrow P + Q,\ \text{if } \sigma = [2, 1];$$

bits r_i of r are traced from left to right, and $T[1]$ and $T[2]$ are updated such that

$$[T[1], T[2], T[3]] \leftarrow [2T[r_{2i-1} + r_{2i} + 1], T[r_{2i} + 1] + T[r_{2i} + 2], T[1] + T[3]].$$

Table 4 gives an example with $\sigma = [1, 2]$ and $r = [01\ 11\ 00\ 10\ 11\ 01\ 01]$, which in the end computes $73P + 59Q$. As in the case of $d = 1$, the relation between the scalars and the r-sequence is not obvious. One may compare this computation to the DJB algorithm example in Table 2.

Table 4. Randomized d-MUL with $\sigma = [1, 2]$ and $r = [01\ 11\ 00\ 10\ 11\ 01\ 01]$

i		1	2	3	4	5	6	7
$r_{2i-1}r_{2i}$		01	11	00	10	11	01	01
$T[1]$	0	$2P$	$2P + 2Q$	$4P + 4Q$	$10P + 8Q$	$18P + 14Q$	$36P + 30Q$	$74P + 60Q$
$T[2]$	P	$2P + Q$	$3P + 2Q$	$5P + 4Q$	$9P + 8Q$	$18P + 15Q$	$37P + 30Q$	$74P + 59Q$
$T[3]$	$P + Q$	$P + Q$	$3P + 3Q$	$5P + 3Q$	$9P + 7Q$	$19P + 15Q$	$37P + 29Q$	$73P + 59Q$

The randomized d-MUL method [5] may be useful for some applications where one is interested in computing $\sum \alpha_i P_i$ for some random scalars α_i, but not for some specific (priori-fixed) values α_i. Therefore, applications of this method are limited despite it being very efficient. Deriving α_i from a given (r, σ) was made explicit but the connection between (r, σ) and the corresponding α_i in the other direction was not entirely clear in [5]. In particular, it is not known how to derive (r, σ) from given α_i other than running the original d-MUL encoding as mentioned before, which has its own efficiency and potential security drawbacks.

2   Preliminaries and Our Contributions

In this paper, we derive many theoretical results which explore the connection between (r, σ) and the scalars $(\alpha_1, \ldots, \alpha_d)$ appearing in the output of the d-MUL algorithm from [5]. We use these theoretical results to derive an efficient and compact encoding of an integer vector $(\alpha_1, \ldots, \alpha_d)$ as a bitstring, which we use to build a regular scalar multiplication algorithm similar to that of [5]. In particular, our new encoding algorithm takes the bitstring representations of α_i's and constructs a pair (r, σ) by simply sliding windows of size two from right to left. As a result, while preserving the full generality of d-MUL, we successfully eliminate the recursive integer matrix computations in the original encoding algorithm as proposed in [6]. Therefore, we expect significant time and memory savings in the encoding phase of d-MUL. We also expect that our new encoding algorithm will make it easier to implement d-MUL in constant time.

When α_i are ℓ-bit odd positive integers for $i = 1, \ldots, d$, our encoding algorithm simplifies to Algorithm 1. Note that Algorithm 1 processes two bits at a time and uses small tables, large integer matrices are not required, and there is no if/else branch in the algorithm. These are some desired features for an efficient and secure implementation of an algorithm. As an example, running Algorithm 1 with $\alpha = 73$ yields the r-sequence as in Table 3, and running it with $[\alpha_1, \alpha_2] = [73, 59]$ yields the r-sequence as in Table 4 and the permutation $\sigma = [1, 2]$. We should emphasize again that previous encoding algorithms do not offer such an efficient algorithm to construct the r-sequence from a given scalar sequence for general $d \geq 1$. Given the r-sequence and σ, point multiplication can be performed using the same rules as described above, or more generally, as described in [5]. Our algorithm in its full generalization to ℓ-bit scalars, including the point multiplication part, is presented later in this paper in Algorithm 4.

Below we give some preliminaries before formally stating the contributions and organization of this paper in Subsect. 2.2.

2.1   Preliminaries

In this subsection we summarize some key definitions and results from [6] and [5] as points of reference. Details can be found in the respective papers. We point out that d-dimensional scalar multiplication algorithms in a group $\mathbb{G}$ correspond to those in $\mathbb{Z}^d$ by identifying combinations $\alpha_1 P_1 + \cdots + \alpha_d P_d$ with the vector $(\alpha_1, \ldots, \alpha_d)$; this identification is a group isomorphism modulo the order of P_i in component i, and so we restrict to studying algorithms in $\mathbb{Z}^d$.

Notation. Throughout this paper, we will write $(b_1 b_2 \cdots b_n)_2$ for the binary representation of an integer, where b_1 is the most significant digit and b_n is the parity digit. For binary strings r_1 and r_2 we use $r_1 \| r_2$ to denote their concatenation. As usual for a matrix A, we write A_i for the ith row of A, and $A_{i,j}$ for the entry in the ith row and j^{th} column. Matrix indices always begin at 1. We use e_j to denote the unit basis row vector with a 1 in the jth column and 0 s elsewhere.

The primary structure that the d-MUL algorithm is built on is a state matrix.

Algorithm 1: New Encoding for d-MUL

Input: Odd integers $\alpha_1, \ldots, \alpha_d \in [0, 2^\ell)$, points $P_1, \ldots, P_d \in \mathbb{G}$, $\mathbb{G}$ abelian
Output: A binary sequence r of length ℓd bits and a permutation σ on $\{1, ..., d\}$

1   Let $B[i]$ be the binary representation of α_i, with extra leading 0.
2   $\sigma \leftarrow [d - i : i = 0, ..., (d-1)]$
3   $r \leftarrow [\,]$
4   **for** $k = \ell$ **down to** 1 **do**
5     $t \leftarrow [\,], r_t \leftarrow [\,]$
6   **for** $i = 1$ **to** d **do**
7      $t[i] \leftarrow (B[i][k] + B[i][k+1]) \mod 2$
8   **end**
9
10    $h \leftarrow 0$
11   **for** $i = 1$ **to** d **do**
12     $r_t[i] \leftarrow t[\sigma[i]]$
13     $h \leftarrow h + r_t[i]$
14   **end**
15
16    $r \leftarrow r_t \| r$
17    $L \leftarrow [\,]$, $c_0 \leftarrow 0$, $c_1 \leftarrow 0$
18   **for** $i = 1$ **to** d **do**
19     $w_0 \leftarrow (1 - r_t[i])$, $c_0 \leftarrow c_0 + w_0$
20     $w_1 \leftarrow r_t[i]$, $c_1 \leftarrow c_1 + w_1$
21     $sgn \leftarrow (1 - 2r_t[i])$
22     $L[h + sgn \cdot (w_0 \cdot c_0 + w_1 \cdot (c_1 - 1))] \leftarrow \sigma[i]$
23   **end**
24    $\sigma \leftarrow L$
25 **end**
26 **return** r, σ

Definition 1. *A $(d+1) \times d$ **state matrix** A is integer-valued and satisfies:*

1. *each row A_i has $i - 1$ odd entries.*
2. *for $1 \leq i \leq d$, we have $A_{i+1} - A_i \in \{e_j, -e_j\}$ for some $1 \leq j \leq d$.*

*The **difference vector** for A is $c^A := A_{d+1} - A_1$. We define a bijection $\sigma_A : \{2, \ldots, d+1\} \to \{1, \ldots, d\}$, called the **column sequence** of A, by letting $\sigma_A(i)$ be the position in which $A_i - A_{i-1}$ is nonzero. The **magnitude** of A is defined as $|A| = \max_{i,j}\{|A_{ij}|\}$.*

By "matrix" we will always mean a state matrix unless otherwise stated. All state matrices considered in this paper will have a common size of $(d+1) \times d$ for some dimension d; we will never consider matrices of different sizes simultaneously. We mostly consider matrices with non-negative values. Our interest will lie in pairs of state matrices having special properties, which we introduce shortly in Definition 3. We first state a few necessary results which were proved in [5].

Lemma 1. *For a state matrix A, the row sum $A_m + A_n$ has $|m - n|$ odd entries.*

Corollary 1. *Let A and B be state matrices such that every row in A is the sum of two rows from B. Then for every k there is some m such that $A_k = B_m + B_{m+k-1}$. In particular, $A_1 = 2B_{h+1}$, where h is the number of odd entries in the integer row vector $\frac{1}{2}A_1$.*

Theorem 1. *For a state matrix A, there is a unique state matrix B such that every row in A is the sum of two rows from B.*

Definition 2. *Let A and B be state matrices such that every row in A is the sum of two rows from B. The **addition sequence** $\{a_k\}_{k=1}^{d+1}$ for A corresponding to B is defined to be $a_k = (x_k, y_k)$, where x_k and y_k are the unique row indices for which $A_k = B_{x_k} + B_{y_k}$*

As it turns out, there are exactly 2^d many addition sequences corresponding to a $(d+1) \times d$ matrix B which each yield a different matrix A. The following definition gives a bijection between binary strings and additions sequences, which we use to encode the sequence as a binary string.

Definition 3. *Let B be a $(d+1) \times d$ state matrix and r a binary string of length d. Let h be the number of 1's in r. Define a recursive sequence $a_k = (x_k, y_k)$ of ordered pairs by $x_1 = y_1 = h + 1$ and*

$$a_k = \begin{cases} (x_{k-1}, y_{k-1} + 1) & \text{if } r_{k-1} = 0 \\ (x_{k-1} - 1, y_{k-1}) & \text{if } r_{k-1} = 1 \end{cases}$$

*for $2 \leq k \leq d + 1$. The **extension matrix** of B corresponding to r is the $(d+1) \times d$ state matrix A having addition sequence a_k with respect to the matrix B.*

Figure 1 gives an example of an extension matrix. Iterating the construction in Definition 3 allows us to built a sequence of matrices given a long binary string.

Definition 4. *Let B be a $(d+1) \times d$ state matrix. Let $r_1, \ldots, r_\ell$ be binary strings of length d, and $r = r_1 || \cdots || r_\ell$. The **extension sequence** with base B corresponding to r is a sequence $\{A^{(i)}\}_{i=1}^{\ell+1}$ of $(d+1) \times d$ state matrices defined recursively by $A^{(1)} = B$, and $A^{(i+1)}$ is the extension matrix of $A^{(i)}$ corresponding to r_i.*

This definition gives us a way of encoding an entire sequence of matrices $\{A^{(i)}\}_{i=1}^{\ell+1}$ as a simple pair (B, r). Note also that by Theorem 1 the entire sequence is uniquely determined by the final matrix A^ℓ. The idea of the randomized d-MUL algorithm in [5] is to randomly choose a $\{0, 1\}$-valued state matrix B and binary string of length ℓd, and output the last row of the last matrix of the corresponding extension sequence. The group version of the algorithm can these operations without constructing the matrix sequence explicitly by using the encoding given in Definition 4.

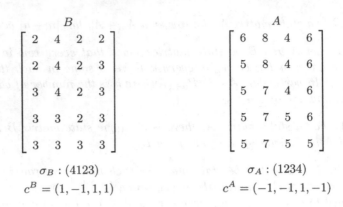

Fig. 1. Two state matrices A and B of dimension $d = 4$, along with their column sequences and difference vectors. A is the extension matrix of B corresponding to the bitstring $r = 1001$.

2.2   Contributions and Organization

The main contributions of this paper are:

1. We derive many theoretical results on state matrices and extension sequences. In particular, we determine the exact relationship between the pair (B, r) and the last row of the last matrix of the corresponding extension sequence $\{A^{(i)}\}$. This relationship is stated precisely in Theorem 4, which details how the sequence of matrices built in the algorithm of [6] can be modeled and encoded using the efficient framework of [5].
2. Using the results of Theorem 4 we detail a new version of d-MUL, a d-dimensional scalar multiplication algorithm which is a full generalization of the Montgomery ladder to d dimensions. This version of d-MUL recodes the ℓ-bit input scalars $(\alpha_1, \dots, \alpha_d)$ very efficiently into a ℓd-length bitstring r, a process only involving permuting the XOR of consecutive bits of the α_i. After recoding the scalars, we use the algorithm of [5] to perform the scalar multiplication with the careful choice of the bitstring r. In particular, this version retains the pattern of 1 point doubling $\mathbf{D}$ and d point additions $\mathbf{A}$ for each bit of the input scalars, giving an operation cost of $\ell\mathbf{D} + \ell d\mathbf{A}$ for the point addition stage. Furthermore, every addition can be performed as a differential addition. Our algorithm does not require storage of any precomputed points, unless differential additions are employed.

In Sect. 3 we state and prove many theoretical results on extension sequences of state matrices with the aim of optimizing the d-MUL algorithm. In Sect. 4 we apply the results of Sect. 3 to construct a new version of the d-MUL algorithm.

3   Theoretical Results

In this section we solve the following two problems:

1. Let $\{A^{(k)}\}_{k=1}^{\ell}$ be an extension sequence with $|A^{(1)}| = 1$. Given only the binary representation of the entries in the row vector $A_1^{(\ell)} + A_{d+1}^{(\ell)}$, find a simple expression giving the binary representations of the entries in $A_1^{(k)}$ for all $k = 1, \ldots, \ell$.
2. Let A be an extension matrix of B corresponding to the bitstring r, and let σ_A and σ_B be the column sequences for A and B, respectively. Find a simple method for determining (σ_B, r) given only (A_1, σ_A).

We make use of the solution to these two problems in the following manner. For a vector $(\alpha_1, \ldots, \alpha_d)$ of positive odd ℓ bit integers, choose a matrix $A^{(\ell)}$ such that $A_1^{(\ell)} + A_{d+1}^{(\ell)} = [\alpha_1 \cdots \alpha_d]$ and let $\{A^{(k)}\}_{k=1}^{\ell}$ be the derived extension sequence. Then using the solution to (1) we can determine $A_1^{(k)}$ for every k, and by iterating the solution to (2) we can determine all column sequences σ_k for each matrix $A^{(k)}$ as well as the bitstring r for the entire sequence $\{A^{(k)}\}_{k=1}^{\ell}$. This allows us to determine (r, σ_1) without ever having to construct any matrices. Furthermore $A^{(1)}$ is completely determined by σ_1 since $|A^{(1)}| = 1$. This entire process can then be turned into a method for constructing an efficient addition chain algorithm which uses only the bits of the α_i and the initial choice of column sequence σ_ℓ, and which has very small storage costs and encoding phase.

This section will solve problems (1) and (2) above, whose solutions yield Theorem 4 giving an equivalence of two extension sequence constructions. Section 4 will use the solutions to these problems to detail an efficient scalar multiplication algorithm similar to the original d-MUL algorithm of [6].

3.1   Determining the Bits of an Extension Sequence

The output of the addition chain constructed in Theorem 4 of [5] is always determined by the last row of the final matrix, and so it makes sense to analyze how these final rows change throughout the sequence of state matrices. Our first result of this section finds the connection between the last rows of successive matrices.

Theorem 2. *Let A be an extension matrix of B. Let $B_{d+1,i} = B_{1,i} + c_i$ and $B_{1,i} + B_{d+1,i} = (b_1 b_2 \cdots b_{n-1} 1)_2$. If $A_1 = 2B_{h+1}$, then*

$$
A_{1,i} + A_{d+1,i} = \begin{cases} (b_1 b_2 \cdots b_{n-1} 11)_2 & \textit{if } (B_{h+1,i} \textit{ is even and } c_i = -1) \\ & \textit{or } (B_{h+1,i} \textit{ is odd and } c_i = 1) \\ (b_1 b_2 \cdots b_{n-1} 01)_2 & \textit{if } (B_{h+1,i} \textit{ is even and } c_i = 1) \\ & \textit{or } (B_{h+1,i} \textit{ is odd and } c_i = -1) \end{cases}
$$

Proof. We consider two cases.

1. Suppose $B_{h+1,i}$ is even. Then

$$
\begin{aligned}
A_{1,i} + A_{d+1,i} &= 2B_{h+1,i} + (B_{1,i} + B_{d+1,i}) \\
&= 2B_{1,i} + (B_{1,i} + B_{d+1,i}) && \text{since } B_{h+1,i} \text{ is even} \\
&= B_{1,i} + B_{d+1,i} - c_i + (B_{1,i} + B_{d+1,i}) \\
&= 2 \cdot (b_1 b_2 \cdots b_{n-1} 1)_2 - c_i \\
&= (b_1 b_2 \cdots b_{n-1} 1 0)_2 - c_i
\end{aligned}
$$

2. Suppose $B_{h+1,i}$ is odd. Then

$$
\begin{aligned}
A_{1,i} + A_{d+1,i} &= 2B_{h+1,i} + (B_{1,i} + B_{d+1,i}) \\
&= 2B_{d+1,i} + (B_{1,i} + B_{d+1,i}) && \text{since } B_{h+1,i} \text{ is odd} \\
&= B_{1,i} + B_{d+1,i} + c_i + (B_{1,i} + B_{d+1,i}) \\
&= 2 \cdot (b_1 b_2 \cdots b_{n-1} 1)_2 + c_i \\
&= (b_1 b_2 \cdots b_{n-1} 1 0)_2 + c_i
\end{aligned}
$$

The result follows when considering $c_i = 1$ and $c_i = -1$ in both cases.

With this theorem we can relate the top and bottom rows in a sequence of matrices with the bits of the final matrix, as described in the following corollary.

Corollary 2. *Let* $\{A^{(i)}\}_{i=1}^{\ell}$ *be an extension sequence such that* $|A^{(1)}| = 1$. *Let* $A_{1,i}^{(\ell)} + A_{d+1,i}^{(\ell)} = (b_1^{(i)} b_2^{(i)} \cdots b_{\ell-1}^{(i)} 1)_2$. *Then for* $1 \le k \le \ell$,

(1) $A_{1,i}^{(k)} + A_{d+1,i}^{(k)} = (b_1^{(i)} b_2^{(i)} \cdots b_{k-1}^{(i)} 1)_2$,
(2) $A_{1,i}^{(k)} = (b_1^{(i)} b_2^{(i)} \cdots b_{k-1}^{(i)})_2 + b_{k-1}^{(i)}$,
(3) $A_{d+1,i}^{(k)} = (b_1^{(i)} b_2^{(i)} \cdots b_{k-1}^{(i)})_2 + 1 - b_{k-1}^{(i)}$.

with $b_0^{(i)} := 0$.

Proof. Note that (2) and (3) follow immediately from (1) since any odd integer a with binary representation $(b_1 b_2 \cdots b_{k-1} 1)_2$ can be written as $a = t + (t + 1)$ for some unique integer t, with the even integer in $\{t, t + 1\}$ expressible as $(b_1 b_2 \cdots b_{k-1})_2 + b_{k-1}$ and the odd integer expressible as $(b_1 b_2 \cdots b_{k-1})_2 + 1 - b_{k-1}$.

To prove (1), we use backwards induction on k. The base case $k = \ell$ is given by assumption. Assume that $A_{1,i}^{(k+1)} + A_{d+1,i}^{(k+1)} = (b_1^{(i)} b_2^{(i)} \cdots b_k^{(i)} 1)_2$ for some k. By Theorem 2 the binary expansion of $A_{1,i}^{(k+1)} + A_{d+1,i}^{(k+1)}$ is exactly that of $A_{1,i}^{(k)} + A_{d+1,i}^{(k)}$ with a single bit inserted between the final two bits, and so $A_{1,i}^{(k)} + A_{d+1,i}^{(k)} = (b_1^{(i)} b_2^{(i)} \cdots b_{k-1}^{(i)} 1)_2$.

The above corollary solves problem (1) posed at the beginning of this section.

3.2 Determining the Column Sequence and Bitstring from an Extension Matrix

In this subsection we solve problem (2) detailed at the introduction to this section. The following theorem provides an alternative method for describing the addition sequence for a given extension matrix, which will be needed in the results to come.

Theorem 3. *Let A be an extension matrix of B. Let $A_1 = [2\alpha_1 \; 2\alpha_2 \cdots 2\alpha_d]$, let σ_A be the column sequence for A, and let $a_k = (x_k, y_k)$ be the addition sequence for A corresponding to B. Then for $k \geq 1$ we have*

$$a_{k+1} = \begin{cases} (x_k - 1, y_k) & \text{if } \alpha_{\sigma_A(k+1)} \text{ is odd} \\ (x_k, y_k + 1) & \text{if } \alpha_{\sigma_A(k+1)} \text{ is even} \end{cases}$$

Proof. Fix $k \geq 1$. Then

$$2\alpha_{\sigma_A(k+1)} = B_{x_k, \sigma_A(k+1)} + B_{y_k, \sigma_A(k+1)} = A_{k, \sigma_A(k+1)} \equiv 0 \bmod 2$$

and

$$B_{x_{k+1}, \sigma_A(k+1)} + B_{y_{k+1}, \sigma_A(k+1)} = A_{k+1, \sigma_A(k+1)} \equiv 1 \bmod 2$$

and so we have

$$a_{k+1} = (x_k - 1, y_k)$$
$$\Longleftrightarrow B_{x_k, \sigma_A(k+1)} \equiv 1 \bmod 2 \quad \text{and} \quad B_{x_{k+1}, \sigma_A(k+1)} \equiv 0 \bmod 2$$
$$\text{(since } x_{k+1} < x_k)$$
$$\Longleftrightarrow \alpha_{\sigma_A(k+1)} \text{ is odd}$$

and similarly

$$a_{k+1} = (x_k, y_k + 1)$$
$$\Longleftrightarrow B_{y_k, \sigma_A(k+1)} \equiv 0 \bmod 2 \quad \text{and} \quad B_{y_{k+1}, \sigma_A(k+1)} \equiv 1 \bmod 2$$
$$\text{(since } y_{k+1} > y_k)$$
$$\Longleftrightarrow \alpha_{\sigma_A(k+1)} \text{ is even.}$$

We can now derive an expression for the binary string giving the addition sequence for two state matrices A and B using only the column sequence for A and the row which was doubled from B.

Corollary 3. *Let A be an extension matrix of B. Let $A_1 = [2\alpha_1 \; 2\alpha_2 \cdots 2\alpha_d]$ and let σ_A be the column sequence for A. Then*

$$r = (\alpha_{\sigma_A(2)} \bmod 2) || \cdots || (\alpha_{\sigma_A(d+1)} \bmod 2)$$

is the binary string giving the addition sequence for A corresponding to B, where $||$ denotes concatenation of bits.

Proof. Let $a_k = (x_k, y_k)$ be the addition sequence for A corresponding to B, and let $\hat{a}_k = (\hat{x}_k, \hat{y}_k)$ be the recursive sequence obtained from r using Definition 3. We show that $a_k = \hat{a}_k$ for every k by induction on k. For $k = 1$, we have $A_1 = \begin{bmatrix} 2\alpha_1 \ 2\alpha_2 \ \cdots \ 2\alpha_d \end{bmatrix} = 2B_{h+1}$ by Corollary 1, where h is the number of odds in $\begin{bmatrix} \alpha_1 \ \alpha_2 \ \cdots \ \alpha_d \end{bmatrix}$, and so $a_1 = (h+1, h+1)$. By the definition of an extension matrix, we have $\hat{x}_1 = \hat{y}_1 = 1 + \sum_{i=1}^{d} (\alpha_{\sigma_A(i+1)} \bmod 2) = 1 + \sum_{i=1}^{d} (\alpha_i \bmod 2) = 1 + h$ since σ is a bijection. Therefore $a_1 = \hat{a}_1$.

Let r_i be the ith bit in r. If $k \geq 1$, we have

$$
\hat{a}_{k+1} = \begin{cases} (\hat{x}_k - 1, \hat{y}_k) & \text{if } r_k = 1 \\ (\hat{x}_k, \hat{y}_k + 1) & \text{if } r_k = 0 \end{cases}
$$

$$
= \begin{cases} (\hat{x}_k - 1, \hat{y}_k) & \text{if } \alpha_{\sigma_A(k+1)} \text{ is odd} \\ (\hat{x}_k, \hat{y}_k + 1) & \text{if } \alpha_{\sigma_A(k+1)} \text{ is even} \end{cases} \qquad \text{by definition of } r
$$

$$
= \begin{cases} (x_k - 1, y_k) & \text{if } \alpha_{\sigma_A(k+1)} \text{ is odd} \\ (x_k, y_k + 1) & \text{if } \alpha_{\sigma_A(k+1)} \text{ is even} \end{cases} \qquad \text{by inductive hypothesis}
$$

$$
= a_{k+1} \qquad \text{by Theorem 3.}
$$

We can now relate the column sequences of the two state matrices A and B through the following definition. Lemma 2 to follow shows this relationship explicitly.

Definition 5. *Let $\sigma\colon \{2, 3, \ldots, d+1\} \to \{1, 2, \ldots, d\}$ be a bijection and let $b_1, \ldots, b_d$ be bits. Define the bijection $\tau\colon \{2, 3, \ldots, d+1\} \to \{1, 2, \ldots, d\}$ as follows:*

1. *Initialize two empty lists L_0 and L_1.*
2. *For $i = 1$ to d, append $\sigma(i+1)$ to the end of L_{b_i}.*
3. *Let $L = \text{REVERSE}(L_1) \| L_0$, where $\|$ denotes concatenation.*
4. *Define $\tau(i+1) = L(i)$ for $1 \leq i \leq d$.*

Define Ψ as the function giving τ from σ and $b_1, \ldots, b_d$; that is,

$$
\Psi(\sigma, (b_1, \ldots, b_d)) = \tau.
$$

When given a list as input, the function REVERSE returns the list in reverse order. Note that τ is a bijection since L contains each of the values $\sigma(2), \sigma(3), \ldots, \sigma(d+1)$ exactly once.

Lemma 2. *Let A be an extension matrix of B. Let σ_A and σ_B be the column sequences for A and B, respectively, and let $A_1 = \begin{bmatrix} 2\alpha_1 \ \cdots \ 2\alpha_d \end{bmatrix}$. Then*

$$
\sigma_B = \Psi\left(\sigma_A, (\alpha_{\sigma_A(2)} \bmod 2, \ldots, \alpha_{\sigma_A(d+1)} \bmod 2)\right).
$$

Proof. Let $\tau = \Psi\left(\sigma_A, (\alpha_{\sigma_A(2)} \bmod 2, \ldots, \alpha_{\sigma_A(d+1)} \bmod 2)\right)$. We begin by noting that at step 3 in defining τ we have that the size of L_1 is $|\{i : \alpha_i = 1 \bmod 2\}| = h$. Let $1 \leq k \leq d$. We examine two cases.

Suppose $\alpha_{\sigma_A(k+1)}$ is odd. Then

$$A_{k+1} = A_k + c^A_{\sigma_A(k+1)}e_{\sigma_A(k+1)} = B_{x_k} + B_{y_k} + c^A_{\sigma_A(k+1)}e_{\sigma_A(k+1)}$$

and by Theorem 3 we have $a_{k+1} = (x_{k+1}, y_{k+1}) = (x_k - 1, y_k)$ and

$$A_{k+1} = B_{x_{k+1}} + B_{y_{k+1}} = B_{x_k-1} + B_{y_k} = B_{x_k} - c^B_{\sigma_B(x_k)}e_{\sigma_B(x_k)} + B_{y_k}$$

Equating these two expressions for A_{k+1} gives $\sigma_B(x_k) = \sigma_A(k+1)$. We point out that $|\{\alpha_{\sigma_A(i)} : 2 \le i \le k+1, \alpha_{\sigma_A(i)} \text{ odd}\}| = h + 1 - x_{k+1}$ since $x_1 = h + 1$ and x_i decreases exactly when an odd α_j is found. In defining τ, step 2 would put $\sigma_A(k+1)$ into $L_{\alpha_{\sigma_A(k+1)} \bmod 2} = L_1$ and we would have $L_1(h + 1 - x_{k+1}) = \sigma_A(k+1)$. Since the order of L_1 is reversed to form L, we have $\tau(x_k) = L(x_k-1) = L(x_{k+1}) = L_1(h + 1 - x_{k+1}) = \sigma_A(k+1) = \sigma_B(x_k)$.

Suppose now $\alpha_{\sigma_A(k+1)}$ is even. Then $A_{k+1} = B_{x_k} + B_{y_k} + c^A_{\sigma_A(k+1)}e_{\sigma_A(k+1)}$ as before, and by Theorem 3 we have $a_{k+1} = (x_{k+1}, y_{k+1}) = (x_k, y_k + 1)$ and so

$$A_{k+1} = B_{x_{k+1}} + B_{y_{k+1}} = B_{x_k} + B_{y_k+1} = B_{x_k} + B_{y_k} + c^B_{\sigma_B(y_k+1)}e_{\sigma_B(y_k+1)}$$

Equating these two expressions for A_{k+1} gives $\sigma_B(y_k +1) = \sigma_A(k+1)$. Similarly to the first case we have $|\{\alpha_{\sigma_A(i)} : 2 \le i \le k+1, \alpha_{\sigma_A(i)} \text{ even}\}| = y_{k+1} - (h + 1)$ since $y_1 = h + 1$ and y_i increases exactly when an even α_j is found. Step 2 in τ's definition would put $\sigma_A(k+1)$ into $L_{\alpha_{\sigma_A(k+1)} \bmod 2} = L_0$ and we would have $L_0(y_{k+1} - (h+1)) = \sigma_A(k+1)$. Since L_0 is concatenated to the end of L_1 when forming L, we have $\tau(y_k + 1) = L(y_k) = L_0(y_k - h) = L_0(y_{k+1} - (h + 1)) = \sigma_A(k + 1) = \sigma_B(y_k + 1)$.

Since the sequence $\{x_i\}_{i=1}^{d+1}$ takes on every value in $\{1, 2, \ldots, h + 1\}$ and $\{y_i\}_{i=1}^{d+1}$ takes on every value in $\{h + 1, h + 2, \ldots, d+1\}$, we have that $\sigma_B = \tau$. This concludes the proof.

With Corollary 3 and Lemma 2, we have solved problem (2).

3.3   Alternative Construction of an Extension Sequence

We now arrive at our primary result of this section, which uses the results from the previous subsections to directly construct the binary string for an extension sequence yielding a given d-tuple.

Theorem 4. *Suppose the following are given:*

- $(\alpha_1, \alpha_2, \ldots, \alpha_d)$, *where each α_i is an odd positive integer with ℓ bits or less*
- $\sigma_\ell : \{2, 3, \ldots, d + 1\} \to \{1, 2, \ldots, d\}$ *a bijection.*

From this information, let $\alpha_i = (b_1^{(i)}b_2^{(i)}\cdots b_{\ell-1}^{(i)}1)_2$ and:

1. *Let $A^{(\ell)}$ be the state matrix having*
   i) $A_{1,i}^{(\ell)} = (b_1^{(i)}b_2^{(i)}\cdots b_{\ell-1}^{(i)})_2 + b_{\ell-1}^{(i)}$,
   ii) $A_{d+1,i}^{(\ell)} = (b_1^{(i)}b_2^{(i)}\cdots b_{\ell-1}^{(i)})_2 + 1 - b_{\ell-1}^{(i)}$,

iii) column sequence σ_ℓ.
Let $\{A^{(i)}\}_{i=1}^{\ell}$ be the unique (Theorem 1) sequence of state matrices such that every row from $A^{(i)}$ is the sum of two rows from $A^{(i-1)}$ for $1 < i \leq \ell$, and let σ_i be the column sequence for $A^{(i)}$.

2. *Define a recursive sequence by $\hat{\sigma}_\ell = \sigma_\ell$ and*

$$\hat{\sigma}_k = \Psi\left(\hat{\sigma}_{k+1}, ((b_{k-1}^{(\hat{\sigma}_{k+1}(2))} \oplus b_k^{(\hat{\sigma}_{k+1}(2))}), \ldots, (b_{k-1}^{(\hat{\sigma}_{k+1}(d+1))} \oplus b_k^{(\hat{\sigma}_{k+1}(d+1))}))\right)$$

for $1 \leq k < \ell$, where $b_0^{(i)} := 0$ and "$\oplus$"es of this difference vecto denotes XOR of bits. Let

$$r^{(k)} = (b_{k-1}^{(\hat{\sigma}_{k+1}(2))} \oplus b_k^{(\hat{\sigma}_{k+1}(2))})|| \cdots ||(b_{k-1}^{(\hat{\sigma}_{k+1}(d+1))} \oplus b_k^{(\hat{\sigma}_{k+1}(d+1))})$$

for $1 \leq k < \ell$, where $||$ denotes concatenation.

Then $\sigma_k = \hat{\sigma}_k$ for $1 \leq k \leq \ell$ and $\{A^{(i)}\}_{i=1}^{\ell}$ is the extension sequence corresponding to $r = r^{(1)}||r^{(2)}|| \cdots ||r^{(\ell-1)}$ and having a base given by a matrix having magnitude 1 and column sequence $\hat{\sigma}_1$.

Proof. We first note that for any $0 \leq k < \ell$ and $1 \leq i \leq d$, Corollary 2 gives $A_{1,i}^{(k+1)} = (b_1^{(i)}b_2^{(i)} \cdots b_{k-1}^{(i)}b_k^{(i)})_2 + b_k^{(i)}$. In both cases that $b_k^{(i)} = 0$ or $b_k^{(i)} = 1$, we see that $\frac{1}{2}A_{1,i}^{(k+1)} \bmod 2 = b_{k-1}^{(i)} \oplus b_k^{(i)}$, where $b_j^{(i)} := 0$ for $j < 1$.

We show $\sigma_k = \hat{\sigma}_k$ for all k by backwards induction on k. When $k = \ell$ we have $\sigma_\ell = \hat{\sigma}_\ell$ by definition. Suppose $\sigma_{k+1} = \hat{\sigma}_{k+1}$ for some k. Taking $A = A^{(k+1)}$ and $B = A^{(k)}$ in the supposition of Lemma 2, we conclude that

$$\sigma_k = \Psi\left(\sigma_{k+1}, (\tfrac{1}{2}A_{1,\sigma_{k+1}(2)}^{(k+1)} \bmod 2, \ldots, \tfrac{1}{2}A_{1,\sigma_{k+1}(d+1)}^{(k+1)} \bmod 2)\right)$$

$$= \Psi\left(\sigma_{k+1}, (b_{k-1}^{(\sigma_{k+1}(2))} \oplus b_k^{(\sigma_{k+1}(2))}, \ldots, b_{k-1}^{(\sigma_{k+1}(d+1))} \oplus b_k^{(\sigma_{k+1}(d+1))})\right)$$

$$= \hat{\sigma}_k$$

since $\sigma_{k+1} = \hat{\sigma}_{k+1}$.

Now we show that $A^{(k+1)}$ is the extension matrix of $A^{(k)}$ corresponding to $r^{(k)}$ for a fixed k. Taking $A = A^{(k+1)}$ and $B = A^{(k)}$ in the supposition of Corollary 3, we have that the binary string giving the addition sequence for $A^{(k+1)}$ corresponding to $A^{(k)}$ is

$$(\tfrac{1}{2}A_{1,\sigma_{k+1}(2)}^{(k+1)} \bmod 2)|| \cdots ||(\tfrac{1}{2}A_{1,\sigma_{k+1}(d+1)}^{(k+1)} \bmod 2)$$

$$= (b_{k-1}^{(\sigma_{k+1}(2))} \oplus b_k^{(\sigma_{k+1}(2))})|| \cdots ||(b_{k-1}^{(\sigma_{k+1}(d+1))} \oplus b_k^{(\sigma_{k+1}(d+1))})$$

$$= r^{(k)}$$

since we've already shown $\sigma_k = \hat{\sigma}_k$ for all k.

By definition we now have that $\{A^{(i)}\}_{i=1}^{\ell}$ is the extension sequence with base $A^{(1)}$ corresponding to r. By Theorem 4.4 of [6], $A^{(1)}$ has magnitude 1 and by definition has column sequence $\sigma_1 = \hat{\sigma}_1$. This concludes the proof of the theorem.

In the context of Theorem 4, note that

$$A_{1,i}^{(\ell)} + A_{d+1,i}^{(\ell)} = \left[(b_1^{(i)}b_2^{(i)}\cdots b_{\ell-1}^{(i)})_2 + b_{\ell-1}^{(i)}\right] + \left[(b_1^{(i)}b_2^{(i)}\cdots b_{\ell-1}^{(i)})_2 + 1 - b_{\ell-1}^{(i)}\right]$$

$$= 2 \cdot (b_1^{(i)}b_2^{(i)}\cdots b_{\ell-1}^{(i)})_2 + 1 = (b_1^{(i)}b_2^{(i)}\cdots b_{\ell-1}^{(i)}1)_2 = \alpha_i.$$

The significance of Theorem 4 is the following. The d-MUL algorithm, Algorithm 3 in [6], is performed using the method of item (1) in Theorem 4; that is, it computes the sequence $\{A^{(i)}\}_{i=1}^{\ell}$ explicitly and stores the addition sequence information for each matrix. This is a very costly operation in terms of clock cycles and storage. Theorem 4 shows that the algorithm can be performed instead using item (2) by only computing the sequence $\{\sigma_i\}_{i=1}^{\ell}$ (given by Ψ) and the bit string r, therefore bypassing any matrix or integer arithmetic and allowing us to begin computing points immediately after r has been constructed. An algorithm similar to that of Algorithm 2 of [5] can then be used to compute the same output as running the original d-MUL with the input $(a_1, \ldots, a_d)$ and a choice for σ_ℓ.

4   Optimized d-MUL

In this section we present Algorithm 4, which is essentially Algorithm 3.2 of [5] in which the bitstring r is constructed through the method of item (2) in Theorem 4 to give a desired set of output scalars. This is in contrast to choosing r uniformly at random as in [5].

In addition to using the alternative method of computation given by Theorem 4, we address a potential security issue when formulating Algorithm 4. The algorithm in [5] and many of the results in this paper have produced an integer vector with odd entries, and with the intention of subtracting off a binary vector v to yield an output vector with entries of arbitrary parity. How exactly the point corresponding to this vector v is subtracted off has not yet been discussed.

Let P_i be the points of a desired linear combination. If all 3^d elements of the set $\{c_1 P_1 + \cdots + c_d P_d : c_i \in \{0, 1\}\}$ are stored, such as when using differential additions, then the point corresponding to the binary vector v is one such point; this point may then be looked up and a single addition can be performed to complete the scalar multiplication.

If these 3^d points are not stored, then more care should be taken. If each P_i satisfying $v_i = 1$ is to be subtracted off from the output in succession, then this may leak information about the scalars of the desired linear combination (or at the very least the number of even scalars). One solution is to simply not perform the subtraction by v at all and settle for an output in which all scalars are odd. This would cut down the size of the output space by a factor of 2^d. This may or may not be acceptable for a given application of the algorithm.

We give an alternative solution to this problem now, which essentially just adds another iteration in the state matrix sequence. That is, we make the sacrifice of an additional d additions and 1 doubling for added security and a uniform output. Suppose we wish to compute the point $\alpha_1 P_1 + \cdots + \alpha_d P_d$ for arbitrary ℓ-bit α_i (not necessarily odd or positive). If any α_i is negative, we may negate α_i and P_i and treat $\alpha_i P_i$ as $(-\alpha_i)(-P_i)$. With negligible preprocessing we may therefore assume every α_i is positive. Let $(b_1^{(i)} b_2^{(i)} \cdots b_\ell^{(i)})_2$ be the binary representation of α_i, and define $\hat{\alpha}_i$ as $(b_1^{(i)} b_2^{(i)} \cdots b_\ell^{(i)})_2 + b_\ell^{(i)} - 1$. Then $\alpha_i - \hat{\alpha}_i \in \{0, 1\}$, and $2\hat{\alpha}_i + 1$ has $\ell + 1$ bits. We then apply Theorem 4 to the odd integers $2\hat{\alpha}_i + 1$ for $1 \le i \le d$ and some column sequence σ. By item (1) of the same theorem, we get a state matrix $A^{(\ell+1)}$ satisfying:

1. $A_{1,i}^{(\ell+1)} = (b_1^{(i)} b_2^{(i)} \cdots b_\ell^{(i)})_2 + b_\ell^{(i)}$,
2. $A_{d+1,i}^{(\ell+1)} = (b_1^{(i)} b_2^{(i)} \cdots b_\ell^{(i)})_2 + 1 - b_\ell^{(i)}$,
3. $A^{(\ell+1)}$ has column sequence σ.

The matrix $A^{(\ell+1)}$ therefore contains all of the original values $\alpha_1, \ldots, \alpha_d$. If σ is chosen carefully, then this matrix will contain the row $\begin{bmatrix} \alpha_1 & \alpha_2 & \cdots & \alpha_d \end{bmatrix}$. Specifically, we may choose σ as any bijection in which the indices for all odd α_i come before those which are even. The index corresponding to this row will be exactly $h := 1 + \sum(\alpha_i \mod 2)$.

We note that Theorem 4 doesn't use the last parity bits of the α_i, but in this context we are applying the theorem to the integers $2\hat{\alpha}_i + 1$. Therefore the final "1" bit of $2\hat{\alpha}_i + 1$ will be ignored, but the rest will be used to construct a bitstring r of length ℓd. That is, we use exactly the bits of $\hat{\alpha}_i$ with an extra leading "0" bit.

Details of Algorithm 4: Here we give some details regarding Algorithm 4. The notation $\mathbf{Ai}(j)$ refers to line j of Algorithm i.

1. To simplify the presentation we deal with negative integer inputs by calling Algorithm 3, SANITIZE, using the method described at the beginning of this section. This is, if α_i is negative we replace α_i by $-\alpha_i$ and P_i by $-P_i$. If working in a setting such as a Montgomery curve using XZ-coordinates, this step isn't necessary since P_i is identified with $-P_i$.
2. Similarly, we separate the process of choosing an initial column sequence σ into a different algorithm, Algorithm 2: CHOOSESEQ. We choose any permutation for which the indices of the odd α_i are placed before the indices for the even α_i. The RANDOMPERMUTATION function seen in Algorithm 2 returns a permutation of the input set chosen uniformly at random, represented in list form. The lists σ_E and σ_O are concatenated to form a single permutation.
3. The binary representation in line Algorithm 4(4) is computed with the most significant bit of $\hat{\alpha}_i$ being $b_2^{(i)}$ and the parity bit being $b_{\ell+1}^{(i)}$.
4. The loop Algorithm 4(6) follows Definition 5 while also constructing the bitstring r simultaneously.
5. The loop Algorithm 4(14) is essentially the same as that seen in the Randomized d-MUL algorithm of [5]. The conditional seen in [5] has been replaced in favor of a much simpler, compact, and equivalent assignment for both x and y.

Algorithm 2: ChooseSeq

Input: Integers $\alpha_1, \ldots, \alpha_d$
Output: Permutation on $\{1, 2, \ldots, d\}$
1 Evens $\leftarrow \{i : \alpha_i \equiv 0 \mod 2\}$
2 Odds $\leftarrow \{i : \alpha_i \equiv 1 \mod 2\}$
3 $\sigma_E \leftarrow$ RANDOMPERMUTATION(Evens)
4 $\sigma_O \leftarrow$ RANDOMPERMUTATION(Odds)
5 **return** $\sigma_O \| \sigma_E$

Algorithm 3: Sanitize

Input: Integers $\alpha_1, \ldots, \alpha_d$, points $P_1, \ldots, P_d \in \mathbb{G}$, $\mathbb{G}$ abelian
Output: Positive integers $\alpha_1, \ldots, \alpha_d$, points $P_1, \ldots, P_d \in \mathbb{G}$, $\mathbb{G}$ abelian
1 **for** $i = 1$ *to* d **do**
2   **if** $\alpha_i < 0$ **then**
3        $\alpha_i \leftarrow -\alpha_i$
4        $P_i \leftarrow -P_i$
5   **end**
6 **end**
7 **return** α, P

A special case is when all scalars α_i are positive and odd. In this case, the SANITIZE step has no effect, and CHOOSESEQ amounts to choosing any permutation on d elements. Furthermore, the $\hat{\alpha}_i$ calculated in Algorithm 4 are equal to the input α_i. This special case leads to an encoding given by the implementation-oriented Algorithm 1, where we skip sanitization and always make the same choice of initial σ. In addition, the construction of the array L is done without an if/else branch for side-channel resistance.

A basic Magma implementation of Algorithm 4 can be found here:

https://github.com/AaronHutchinson/d-MUL-Optimized-2020-

4.1 Differential Additions

This subsection aims to outline an alternate version of Algorithm 4 which utilizes differential additions. Our only sacrifice to gain knowledge of point differences is storing each column sequence σ generated in the loop on line 6 of Algorithm 4. We can compute point differences using the following theorem.

Theorem 5. *Let A be an extension matrix of B with addition sequence $\{a_k\}_{k=1}^{d+1}$. If σ is the column sequence for B and c is the difference vector for B, then $B_{y_1} - B_{x_1}$ is the zero row matrix and for $2 \leq k \leq d+1$ we have*

$$B_{y_k} - B_{x_k} = \sum_{i=x_k+1}^{y_k} c_{\sigma(i)} e_{\sigma(i)}.$$

Proof. We use induction on k. When $k = 1$ we have $x_1 = y_1$ by definition of an addition sequence, and so $B_{y_1} - B_{x_1}$ is zero. Assume that $B_{y_k} - B_{x_k} = \sum_{i=x_k+1}^{y_k} c_{\sigma(i)} e_{\sigma(i)}$ for some k with $1 \le k \le d$. We have either that $a_{k+1} = (x_k - 1, y_k)$ or $a_{k+1} = (x_k, y_k + 1)$.

Suppose that $a_{k+1} = (x_k - 1, y_k)$ so that $y_{k+1} = y_k$ and $x_{k+1} = x_k - 1$. Then

$$B_{y_{k+1}} - B_{x_{k+1}} = B_{y_k} - B_{x_k-1} = B_{y_k} - \left(B_{x_k} - c_{\sigma(x_k)} e_{\sigma(x_k)}\right)$$

$$= \left(B_{y_k} - B_{x_k}\right) + c_{\sigma(x_k)} e_{\sigma(x_k)} = \sum_{i=x_k+1}^{y_k} c_{\sigma(i)} e_{\sigma(i)} + c_{\sigma(x_k)} e_{\sigma(x_k)}$$

$$= \sum_{i=x_k}^{y_k} c_{\sigma(i)} e_{\sigma(i)} = \sum_{i=x_{k+1}+1}^{y_{k+1}} c_{\sigma(i)} e_{\sigma(i)}.$$

If $a_{k+1} = (x_k, y_k + 1)$ then $y_{k+1} = y_k + 1$ and $x_{k+1} = x_k$, and so

$$B_{y_{k+1}} - B_{x_{k+1}} = B_{y_k+1} - B_{x_k} = \left(B_{y_k} + c_{\sigma(y_k+1)} e_{\sigma(y_k+1)}\right) - B_{x_k}$$

$$= \left(B_{y_k} - B_{x_k}\right) + c_{\sigma(y_k+1)} e_{\sigma(y_k+1)}$$

$$= \left(\sum_{i=x_k+1}^{y_k} c_{\sigma(i)} e_{\sigma(i)}\right) + c_{\sigma(y_k+1)} e_{\sigma(y_k+1)}$$

$$= \sum_{i=x_k+1}^{y_k+1} c_{\sigma(i)} e_{\sigma(i)} = \sum_{i=x_{k+1}+1}^{y_{k+1}} c_{\sigma(i)} e_{\sigma(i)}.$$

This concludes the proof.

Suppose that all rows in the set $S = \{[t_1, \ldots, t_d] : t_i \in \{0, 1, -1\}\}$ are stored. Then the above theorem tells us exactly how to find the proper element of S for the difference which corresponds to a sum $B_i + B_j$. The only knowledge required to compute this row is the column sequence σ and the difference vector c. We will now show that only a slight modification of Algorithm 4 will allow us to perform differential additions.

Let α_i and $\hat{\alpha}_i$ for $i = 1, \ldots, d$ be as in Sect. 4, and let σ be any column sequence. Again by Theorem 4 we may derive a sequence $\{A^{(k)}\}_{k=1}^{\ell+1}$ of state matrices where each row in $A^{(k+1)}$ is the sum of two rows from $A^{(k)}$ and the final matrix $A^{(\ell+1)}$ satisfies:

1. $A_{1,i}^{(\ell+1)} = (b_1^{(i)} b_2^{(i)} \cdots b_\ell^{(i)})_2 + b_\ell^{(i)}$,
2. $A_{d+1,i}^{(\ell+1)} = (b_1^{(i)} b_2^{(i)} \cdots b_\ell^{(i)})_2 + 1 - b_\ell^{(i)}$,
3. $A^{(\ell+1)}$ has column sequence σ

where $(b_1^{(i)} b_2^{(i)} \cdots b_\ell^{(i)})_2$ is the binary representation of α_i. We recall that the difference vector c for any state matrix A is defined to be $A_{d+1} - A_1$. Applying Corollary 2 to our current scenario, we find that the ith entry of the difference vector for $A^{(k)}$ is exactly

$$A_{d+1,i}^{(k)} - A_{1,i}^{(k)} = \left((b_1^{(i)} b_2^{(i)} \cdots b_{k-1}^{(i)})_2 + 1 - b_{k-1}^{(i)}\right) - \left((b_1^{(i)} b_2^{(i)} \cdots b_{k-1}^{(i)})_2 + b_{k-1}^{(i)}\right)$$

$$= 1 - 2b_{k-1}^{(i)}$$

Algorithm 4: Optimized d-MUL

Input: Integers $\alpha_1, \ldots, \alpha_d \in (-2^\ell, 2^\ell)$, points $P_1, \ldots, P_d \in \mathbb{G}$, $\mathbb{G}$ abelian
Output: Group element $\alpha_1 P_1 + \cdots + \alpha_d P_d$

1 $\alpha, P \leftarrow$ SANITIZE(α, P).
2 $\sigma \leftarrow$ CHOOSESEQ(α).
3 $\hat{\alpha} \leftarrow (\alpha_1 + (\alpha_1 \mod 2) - 1, \ldots, \alpha_d + (\alpha_d \mod 2) - 1)$
4 Let $(0\, b_2^{(i)} b_3^{(i)} \cdots b_\ell^{(i)} b_{\ell+1}^{(i)})_2$ be the binary form of $\hat{\alpha}_i$, with extra leading 0.
5 Initialize an empty binary array r of length ℓd.
6 **for** $k = \ell$ down to 1 **do**
7 $\quad$ For $i = 1$ to d, assign $r_{(k-1)d+i} \leftarrow b_k^{(\sigma(i))} \oplus b_{k+1}^{(\sigma(i))}$.
8 $\quad$ Initialize empty lists L_0 and L_1 of length d.
9 $\quad$ For $i = 1$ to d, append $\sigma(i)$ to the end of $L_{b_k^{(\sigma(i))} \oplus b_{k+1}^{(\sigma(i))}}$.
10 $\quad$ Overwrite $\sigma \leftarrow$ REVERSE$(L_1) \| L_0$, where $\|$ denotes concatenation.
11 **end**
12 Initialize group elements $Q_1, \ldots, Q_{d+1}, R_1, \ldots R_{d+1}$ as $id(\mathbb{G})$.
13 For $i = 1$ to d, assign $Q_{i+1} \leftarrow Q_i + P_{\sigma(i)}$.
14 **for** $k = 1$ to ℓ **do**
15 $\quad$ $h, x, y \leftarrow r_{(k-1)d+1} + \cdots + r_{kd} + 1$
16 $\quad$ $R_1 \leftarrow 2Q_h$
17 $\quad$ **for** $i = 1$ to d **do**
18 $\quad\quad$ $x \leftarrow x - r_{(k-1)d+i}$, $y \leftarrow y + 1 - r_{(k-1)d+i}$
19 $\quad\quad$ $R_{i+1} \leftarrow Q_x + Q_y$
20 $\quad$ **end**
21 $\quad$ $Q \leftarrow R$
22 **end**
23 $h \leftarrow (\alpha_1 \mod 2) + \cdots + (\alpha_d \mod 2) + 1$
24 **return** Q_h

Therefore the entries of this difference vector are given "for free", as they only depend on the bits in position $k - 1$ of the α_i.

With this discussion in mind, Algorithm 4 may be altered so that each σ derived in the loop beginning on line 6 is saved in a table so that the column sequence for matrix $A^{(i)}$ is stored as σ_i. One may then use Theorem 5 to find the difference corresponding to each sum; it is exactly

$$A_{y_k}^{(i)} - A_{x_k}^{(i)} = \sum_{i=x_k+1}^{y_k} (1 - 2b_{i-1}^{(\sigma_i(k))}) e_{\sigma_i(k)}.$$

5 Conclusions

There are now three versions of the d-MUL algorithm: Original d-MUL (Algorithm 3 of [6]), Randomized d-MUL (Algorithm 2 of [5]), and Optimized d-MUL (Algorithm 4 in this paper). Optimized d-MUL seems to be a direct improvement over Original d-MUL, since the storage of two $(d + 1) \times d$ matrices with large entries, ℓ many arrays D, and large integer arithmetic is exchanged for the storage of a single ℓd length bitstring and the computation of ℓ many simple permutations. We therefore see no reason to use Original d-MUL over Optimized d-MUL.

We believe that Randomized d-MUL may still be preferable over Optimized d-MUL in certain special situations. If a given application only calls for a random linear combination, then it would be more efficient to employ Randomized d-MUL over Optimized d-MUL since in the former case we need only generate a random bit string rather than derive it from random scalars as in the latter case. The efficiency gain is slightly more dramatic when the scalars of the combination need not be known, since the derivation of the scalars in Randomized d-MUL is split off into an independent algorithm. On the other hand, if the setting calls for a specific linear combination to be computed from given points, we see no way to use Randomized d-MUL in such a setting and so Optimized d-MUL seems to be the best option out of these three algorithms.

Acknowledgment. This research has been partially supported by the U.S. Army Research Office (ARO) under the award number W911NF-17-1-0311. The content is solely the responsibility of the authors and does not necessarily represent the official views of the ARO. The authors thank reviewers for their comments.

References

1. Bernstein, D.: Differential addition chains. Technical report (2006). http://cr.yp.to/ecdh/diffchain-20060219.pdf
2. Brown, D.: Multi-dimensional montgomery ladders for elliptic curves. ePrint Archive: Report 2006/220. http://eprint.iacr.org/2006/220
3. Galbraith, S.D., Lin, X., Scott, M.: Endomorphisms for faster elliptic curve cryptography on a large class of curves. J. Cryptol. **24**(3), 446–469 (2010). https://doi.org/10.1007/s00145-010-9065-y
4. Gallant, R.P., Lambert, R.J., Vanstone, S.A.: Faster point multiplication on elliptic curves with efficient endomorphisms. In: Kilian, J. (ed.) CRYPTO 2001. LNCS, vol. 2139, pp. 190–200. Springer, Heidelberg (2001). https://doi.org/10.1007/3-540-44647-8_11
5. Hisil, H., Hutchinson, A., Karabina, K.: d-MUL: optimizing and implementing a multidimensional scalar multiplication algorithm over elliptic curves. In: Chattopadhyay, A., Rebeiro, C., Yarom, Y. (eds.) SPACE 2018. LNCS, vol. 11348, pp. 198–217. Springer, Cham (2018). https://doi.org/10.1007/978-3-030-05072-6_12
6. Hutchinson, A., Karabina, K.: Constructing multidimensional differential addition chains and their applications. J. Cryptogr. Eng. **9**(1), 1–19 (2017). https://doi.org/10.1007/s13389-017-0177-2
7. Montgomery, P.L.: Evaluating Recurrences of the Form $X_{m+n} = f(X_m, X_n, X_{m-n})$ via Lucas Chains (1983). https://cr.yp.to/bib/1992/montgomery-lucas.ps
8. Montgomery, P.L.: Speeding the pollard and elliptic curve methods of factorization. Math. Comput. **48**, 243–264 (1987)
9. Kocher, P., Jaffe, J., Jun, B.: Differential power analysis. In: Wiener, M. (ed.) CRYPTO 1999. LNCS, vol. 1666, pp. 388–397. Springer, Heidelberg (1999). https://doi.org/10.1007/3-540-48405-1_25

New Ideas to Build Noise-Free Homomorphic Cryptosystems

Gerald Gavin[1(✉)] and Sandrine Tainturier[2]

[1] Laboratory ERIC - University of Lyon, Lyon, France
gerald.gavin@univ-lyon1.fr
[2] Adecco, Geneva, Switzerland
sandrine-tainturier@orange.fr

Abstract. We design a very simple private-key encryption scheme whose decryption function is a rational function. This scheme is not born naturally homomorphic. To get homomorphic properties, a nonlinear additive homomorphic operator is specifically developed. The security analysis is based on symmetry considerations and we prove some formal results under the factoring assumption. In particular, we prove IND-CPA security in the generic ring model. Even if our security proof is not complete, we think that it is convincing and that the technical tools considered in this paper are interesting by themselves. Moreover, the factoring assumption is just needed to ensure that solving nonlinear equations or finding non-null polynomials with many roots is difficult. Consequently, the ideas behind our construction could be re-used in rings satisfying these properties. As motivating perspectives, we then propose to develop a simple multiplicative operator. To achieve this, randomness is added in our construction giving hope to remove the factoring assumption in order to get a pure multivariate encryption scheme.

Keywords: Homomorphic cryptosystem · Multivariate encryption scheme · Generic ring model

1 Introduction

The prospect of outsourcing an increasing amount of data storage and management to cloud services raises many new privacy concerns for individuals and businesses alike. The privacy concerns can be satisfactorily addressed if users encrypt the data they send to the cloud. If the encryption scheme is homomorphic, the cloud can still perform meaningful computations on the data, even though it is encrypted.

The theoretical problem of constructing a fully homomorphic encryption scheme (FHE) supporting arbitrary functions f, was only recently solved by the breakthrough work of Gentry [9]. More recently, further fully homomorphic schemes were presented [5,10,12,20,21] following Gentry's framework. The underlying tool behind all these schemes is the use of Euclidean lattices,

© Springer Nature Switzerland AG 2020
A. Nitaj and A. Youssef (Eds.): AFRICACRYPT 2020, LNCS 12174, pp. 423–451, 2020.
https://doi.org/10.1007/978-3-030-51938-4_21

which have previously proved powerful for devising many cryptographic primitives. A central aspect of Gentry's fully homomorphic scheme (and the subsequent schemes) is the ciphertext refreshing Recrypt operation. Even if many improvements have been made in one decade, this operation remains very costly [4,6,11,15]. Indeed, bootstrapped bit operations are still about one billion times slower than their plaintext equivalents (see [4]).

In this paper, we adopt another approach where a ciphertext is a vector c over $\mathbb{Z}_n$, n being an RSA modulus chosen at random. Given a secret multivariate rational function Φ_0/Φ_0', an encryption of $x \in \mathbb{Z}_n$ is a vector c chosen at random ensuring that $\Phi_0/\Phi_0'(c) = x$. Clearly, the expanded representations of Φ_0, Φ_0' should not be polynomial-size (otherwise the CPA attacker could recover them by solving a polynomial-size linear system). In order to get polynomial-time encryptions and decryptions, Φ_0/Φ_0' should be written in a compact form, e.g. a factored or semi-factored form. By construction, the generic cryptosystem described above is not homomorphic in the sense that the vector sum is not a homomorphic operator. This is a *sine qua non* condition for overcoming Gentry's machinery. Indeed, as a ciphertext c is a vector, it is always possible to write it as a linear combination of other known ciphertexts. Thus, if the vector sum were a homomorphic operator, the cryptosystem would not be secure at all. This simple remark suffices to prove the weakness of the homomorphic cryptosystems presented in [14,22]. In order to use the vector sum as a homomorphic operator, noise should be injected into the encryptions as done in all existing FHE [2,5,9,10,20,21]. To get homomorphic properties, we develop *ad hoc* a nonlinear additively homomorphic operator Add and we obtain a noise-free additive encryption scheme.

The factoring assumption restricts the adversary's power providing hope to base the security of our scheme on this assumption. We prove a result based on symmetry (see Lemma 1) encapsulating the idea that it is not possible to extract roots of polynomials in $\mathbb{Z}_n$ intuitively meaning that a CPA attacker can only solve linear equations. For concreteness, Lemma 1 ensures that it cannot recover non-symmetric values only given symmetric values. By construction the CPA attacker has only access to symmetric values. Thus, it suffices to prove that breaking semantic security requires to recover non-symmetric values. Compact representations of Φ_0 or Φ_0' deal with non-symmetric values implying that they cannot be recovered according to Lemma 1. However, $\Phi_0(c) = 0$ provided c encrypts 0 implying that the expanded representation of Φ_0 could be recovered by solving a linear system. This kind of attacks will be called *attacks by linearization*. This attack fails by adjusting the parameters in order that Φ_0 has an exponential number of monomials. Nevertheless, the introduction of homomorphic operators may introduce new attacks by linearization. In Sect. 5.3, we propose to formally define this class of attacks and we prove that such attacks do not exist against our scheme.

In Sect. 5.4, we propose a security analysis in the generic ring model [1,13]. In this model, the power of the CPA attacker is restricted in the sense that it can only perform arithmetic operations. Recently, some results were shown in the generic ring model. For instance, it was shown that breaking the security of RSA in the generic ring model is as difficult as factoring [1]. An emblematic counterexample against security analysis in the generic ring model deals with Jacobi's symbol J_n. For concreteness, it was shown in [13] that computing J_n is difficult in the generic ring model while it is not in general. However, this result is neither surprising nor relevant because J_n is not a rational function[1]. Indeed, we can even show that $\Phi(x) = J_n(x)$ with probability smaller than $1/2$ provided Φ is a rational function and x uniform over $\mathbb{Z}_n^*$. As far as we know, there does not exist any rational function provably difficult to compute in the generic ring model but not in general. While the analysis in the generic ring model excludes lattice-based attacks (working *outside* $\mathbb{Z}_n$), all the considered random variables are uniform over $\mathbb{Z}_n$ contrarily to noise values considered in lattice-based cryptosystems.

We propose a general result reducing the generic IND-CPA security to algebraic conditions (Proposition 7). These results essentially come from a fundamental result (see Theorem 1) shown in [1] claiming that, under the factoring assumption, it is difficult to recover non-null polynomials having many roots. We then prove generic IND-CPA security (see Proposition 8).

Although we prove some results suggesting the security of our scheme, the security proof is not complete. Moreover the performance of our scheme is not competitive with respect to other existing additively homomorphic schemes (e.g. Paillier [16], El Gamal [7], Castagnos et al. [3]). So it is legitimate to question the usefulness of this paper. In our opinion, the underlying ideas of this paper are very promising and the proposed construction can be seen as a feasibility study. We see at least two motivating perspectives from this work. The principal one would be to build a multiplicative homomorphic operator. In Sect. 6, we propose a noise-free compact-FHE. The algebraic condition proposed for the homomorphic additive encryption remains valid. This condition could be exploited to get a formal security proof at least in the generic ring model. We propose a very short security analysis at least showing that our construction has a chance to be secure. A second motivating perspective would be to remove the factoring assumption to obtain a pure multivariate encryption scheme (such a scheme is proposed in Appendix B). This assumption is required to get formal results (Proposition 1, Lemma 1 and Proposition 4) but the function Decrypt does not require the factorization of n. This gives hope to remove this assumption: this basically consists of considering Schwartz-Zippel's lemma [19] instead of Proposition 1 and adding randomness to the construction in order to maintain the truth of the formal results proved under the factoring assumption.

Notation. *We use standard Landau notations. Throughout this paper, we let λ denote the security parameter: all known attacks against the cryptographic scheme under scope should require $2^{\Omega(\lambda)}$ bit operations to mount. Let $\kappa \geq 2$ be an integer and let $n = pq$ be a randomly chosen RSA modulus. All the computations considered in this paper will be done in $\mathbb{Z}_n$.*

---

[1] It comes from the fact that $J_n(x) \mod p$ (resp. $J_n(x) \mod q$) is not a function of $x \mod p$ (resp. $x \mod q$).

- Δ_κ is the set of permutations over $\{1,\ldots,\kappa\}$
- $\Sigma_\kappa = \{\sigma_1,\ldots,\sigma_\kappa\} \subset \Delta_\kappa$ defined by $\sigma_i(j) = (i+j-2 \bmod \kappa)+1$, i.e. $\sigma_i(1) = i; \sigma_i(2) = i+1; \ldots; \sigma_i(\kappa) = i-1$.
- The cardinality of a set S will be denoted by $\#S$.
- 'Choose at random $x \in X$' will systematically mean that x is chosen according to uniform probability distribution over X.
- 'An algorithm $\mathcal{A}$ outputs a polynomial p' will systematically mean that $\mathcal{A}$ outputs a $\{+,-,\times\}$-circuit representing p.
- The inner product of two vectors v and v' is denoted by $\langle v, v' \rangle$.
- The set of all square $t-by-t$ matrices over $\mathbb{Z}_n$ is denoted by $\mathbb{Z}_n^{t\times t}$.

Remark 1. The number $M(m,d)$ of m-variate monomials of degree d is equal to $\binom{d+m-1}{d}$. In particular, $M(2\kappa,\kappa) \approx (27/4)^\kappa$.

2 Overview

In this section, we propose a high-level description of the main ideas of this paper. All the computations will be done in $\mathbb{Z}_n$, $n \geq 3$.

First Encryption Scheme. The secret key K contains 2κ randomly chosen secret vectors $s_1,\ldots,s_{2\kappa}$ belonging to $\mathbb{Z}_n^{2\kappa}$.

Encrypting $x \in \mathbb{Z}_n$ simply consists of randomly choosing $c \in \mathbb{Z}_n^{2\kappa}$ satisfying

$$\frac{\langle s_1, c\rangle}{\langle s_2, c\rangle} + \cdots + \frac{\langle s_{2\kappa-1}, c\rangle}{\langle s_{2\kappa}, c\rangle} = x \tag{1}$$

In other words, by considering the $2\kappa - by - 2\kappa$ matrix S whose i^{th} row is s_i (assuming S invertible)

$$c = S^{-1} \begin{pmatrix} r_1 x_1 \\ r_1 \\ \cdots \\ r_\kappa x_\kappa \\ r_\kappa \end{pmatrix}$$

where $(x_i, r_i)_{i=1,\ldots,\kappa}$ is randomly chosen in $(\mathbb{Z}_n \times \mathbb{Z}_n^*)^\kappa$ s.t. $x_1 + \cdots + x_\kappa = x$.

Security Analysis. By multiplying each side of (1) by $\Phi_0'(c) = \prod_{i=1}^\kappa \langle s_{2i}, c\rangle$, we get a degree-$\kappa$ polynomial equation in the form

$$\Phi_0(c) - x\Phi_0'(c) = \Phi_x(c) = \sum_{t_1+\cdots+t_{2\kappa}=\kappa} \alpha_{t_1,\ldots,t_{2\kappa}} c_1^{t_1} \cdots c_{2\kappa}^{t_{2\kappa}} = 0$$

where the coefficients $\alpha_{t_1,\ldots,t_{2\kappa}}$ are evaluations of degree-κ polynomials over S, x. As $\Phi_x(c) = 0$ if and only if c is an encryption of x, the knowledge of Φ_x is sufficient to break IND-CPA security. Moreover, by sampling sufficiently many encryptions of x, the monomials of Φ_x can be recovered by solving a linear system. However, by choosing $\kappa = \Theta(\lambda)$, the number of monomials is exponential (see Remark 1), making this attack fail.

Homomorphic Properties. The *vector sum* is not an additive homomorphic operator. But, contrarily to what we may intuitively think, this scheme has some homomorphic capabilities coming from the following observation:

$$\frac{\langle s_1, c\rangle\langle s_2, c'\rangle + \langle s_2, c\rangle\langle s_1, c'\rangle}{\langle s_2, c\rangle\langle s_2, c'\rangle} + \cdots$$

$$\cdots + \frac{\langle s_{2\kappa-1}, c\rangle\langle s_{2\kappa}, c'\rangle + \langle s_{2\kappa}, c\rangle\langle s_{2\kappa-1}, c'\rangle}{\langle s_{2\kappa}, c\rangle\langle s_{2\kappa}, c'\rangle} = x + x'$$

where c and c' are encryptions of respectively x and x'. This will be used to develop an additive homomorphic operator.

Second Encryption Scheme. This second encryption scheme is essentially the same as the first one except that we consider an operator Add achieving homomorphic additions. Given two encryptions c and c' of x and x', Add(c, c') returns an encryption c'' defined by

$$c'' = S^{-1} \begin{pmatrix} r_1 r_1'(x_1 + x_1') \\ r_1 r_1' \\ \cdots \\ r_\kappa r_\kappa'(x_\kappa + x_\kappa') \\ r_\kappa r_\kappa' \end{pmatrix}$$

where $c = S^{-1}(r_1 x_1, r_1, \ldots, r_\kappa x_\kappa, r_\kappa)$ and $c' = S^{-1}(r_1' x_1', r_1', \ldots, r_\kappa' x_\kappa', r_\kappa')$.

Security Analysis. Unfortunately, the adjunction of Add brings weaknesses. Indeed, we can mount what we will call an *attack by linearization*. For concreteness, the CPA attacker can efficiently build the vector $\tilde{c}$ defined by

$$\tilde{c} = S^{-1} \begin{pmatrix} r_1^{\phi(n)}\phi(n)x_1 \\ r_1^{\phi(n)} \\ \cdots \\ r_\kappa^{\phi(n)}\phi(n)x_\kappa \\ r_\kappa^{\phi(n)} \end{pmatrix} = S^{-1} \begin{pmatrix} \phi(n)x_1 \\ 1 \\ \cdots \\ \phi(n)x_\kappa \\ 1 \end{pmatrix}$$

by recursively applying Add over c. We let see the reader see for themselves how to use it to totally break our scheme[2]. To overcome this, the factoring assumption

---

[2] By considering 2κ randomly chosen encryptions $c_1, \ldots c_{2\kappa}$ of arbitrarily chosen plaintexts $x_1, \ldots, x_{2\kappa}$, the vectors $\tilde{c}_1, \ldots \tilde{c}_{2\kappa}$ can be generated as explained above. For any $i = 1, \ldots, 2\kappa$, it is ensured that $\langle v, \tilde{c}_i\rangle = x_i$, with $v = (s_1 + s_3 + \cdots + s_{2\kappa-1})/\phi(n)$. Hence, by solving this linear system (where the variables are the components of v), v can be recovered. This is sufficient to break the IND-CPA security of our scheme. Indeed, given a challenge encryption c, the encrypted value x can be recovered, i.e. $x = \langle v, \tilde{c}\rangle$.

should be introduced by choosing n as a RSA modulus. In this paper, we will show how to efficiently implement Add and we will prove IND-CPA security in the generic ring model under the factoring assumption assuming $\kappa = \Theta(\lambda)$. This represents the main result of this paper.

Removing the Factoring Assumption? There are many other ways to define an additive homomorphic operator. For instance, randomness can be introduced in Add to get an operator $\mathsf{Add^{rand}}$ by defining $c'' = \mathsf{Add^{rand}}(c, c')$ by

$$c'' = S^{-1} \begin{pmatrix} \rho_1(c, c') r_{\sigma(1)} r'_{\sigma'(1)} (x_{\sigma(1)} + x'_{\sigma'(1)}) \\ \rho_1(c, c') r_{\sigma(1)} r'_{\sigma'(1)} \\ \cdots \\ \rho_\kappa(c, c') r_{\sigma(\kappa)} r'_{\sigma'(\kappa)} (x_{\sigma(\kappa)} + x'_{\sigma'(\kappa)}) \\ \rho_\kappa(c, c') r_{\sigma(\kappa)} r'_{\sigma'(\kappa)} \end{pmatrix}$$

where σ, σ' are randomly (and secretely) chosen permutations of $\{1, \ldots, \kappa\}$ and $\rho_1, \ldots, \rho_\kappa$ are randomly (and secretely) chosen (e.g. quadratic) polynomials. By doing this, the above attack does not work anymore and the factoring assumption could be hopefully removed. We let it as a perspective (an example of implementation is proposed in Appendix B).

Perspective of FHEs. By the same way, one can efficiently implement operators $\mathcal{O}$ computing $c'' = \mathcal{O}(c, c')$ defined by

$$c'' = S^{-1} \begin{pmatrix} \rho_1(c, c') r_{\sigma(1)} r'_{\sigma'(1)} x_{\sigma(1)} x'_{\sigma'(1)} \\ \rho_1(c, c') r_{\sigma(1)} r'_{\sigma'(1)} \\ \cdots \\ \rho_\kappa(c, c') r_{\sigma(\kappa)} r'_{\sigma'(\kappa)} x_{\sigma(\kappa)} x'_{\sigma'(\kappa)} \\ \rho_\kappa(c, c') r_{\sigma(\kappa)} r'_{\sigma'(\kappa)} \end{pmatrix}$$

Roughly speaking, c'' *stores* κ products $x_i x_j$. By combining several such well-chosen operators (at least κ) and the additive homomorphic operator, one can build a multiplicative homomorphic operator (using the equality $xx' = \sum_{ij} x_i x'_j$).

Discussion. The first encryption scheme can be straightforwardly turned into a new noise-free cryptographic problem. The search version of this problem would consist of recovering the secret matrix S given sufficiently many encryptions of 0 and the decisional version would consist of distinguishing between encryptions of 0 and randomly chosen vectors. We believe this problem hard for any $n \geq 3$ assuming $\kappa = \Theta(\lambda)$. In our opinion, this problem could be fruitful in cryptography and could merit to be independently studied. We briefly saw natural ways to build homomorphic operators. We think that many other relevant constructions can be achieved.

3   Some Security Results Under the Factoring Assumption

Throughout this section, n denotes a randomly chosen RSA-modulus. Given a function $\phi : \mathbb{Z}_n^r \to \mathbb{Z}_n$, $z_\phi \overset{\text{def}}{=} \#\{x \in \mathbb{Z}_n^r | \phi(x) = 0\}/n^r$. Classically a polynomial will be said *null* (or identically null) if each coefficient of its expanded representation is equal to 0.

3.1   Roots of Polynomials

The following result proved in [1] establishes that it is difficult to output a polynomial ϕ such that z_ϕ is non-negligible without knowing the factorization of n. The security of RSA in the generic ring model can be quite straightforwardly derived from this result (see [1]).

Theorem 1 *(Lemma 4 of [1])*. *Assuming factoring is hard, there is no p.p.t-algorithm $\mathcal{A}$ which inputs n and which outputs[3] a $\{+,-,\times\}$-circuit representing a non-null polynomial $\phi \in \mathbb{Z}_n[X]$ such that z_ϕ is non-negligible.*

Thanks to this lemma, showing that two polynomials (*built without knowing the factorization of n*) are equal with non-negligible probability becomes an algebraic problem: it suffices to prove that they are identically equal. This lemma is a very powerful tool which is at the heart of the security proofs proposed in this paper. We extend this result to the multivariate case.

Proposition 1. *Assuming factoring is hard, there is no p.p.t algorithm $\mathcal{A}$ which inputs n and which outputs (see footnote 3) a $\{+,-,\times\}$-circuit representing a non-null polynomial $\phi \in \mathbb{Z}_n[X_1,\ldots,X_r]$ such that z_ϕ is non-negligible.*

Proof. See Appendix C.   □

3.2   Symmetry

Let $\kappa \geq 2$ and $t \geq 1$ be positive integers with polynomial size in λ. Recall that Δ_κ denotes the set of the permutations over $\{1,\ldots,\kappa\}$. Throughout this section, we will consider an arbitrary subset $\Sigma \subseteq \Delta_\kappa$. Let y_1, y_2 be randomly chosen in $\mathbb{Z}_n$. It is well-known that recovering y_1 with non-negligible probability given only $S = y_1 + y_2$ or $P = y_1 y_2$ is difficult assuming the hardness of factoring (y_1, y_2 are the roots of the polynomial $y^2 - Sy + P$). In this section, we propose to extend this. The following definition naturally extends the classical definition of symmetric polynomials.

Definition 1. *Consider the tuples of indeterminate $(Y_\ell = (X_{\ell 1}, \ldots, X_{\ell t}))_{\ell=1,\ldots,\kappa}$. A polynomial $\phi \in \mathbb{Z}_n[Y_1, \ldots, Y_\kappa]$ is Σ-symmetric if for any permutation $\sigma \in \Sigma$,*

$$\phi(Y_1, \ldots, Y_\kappa) = \phi(Y_{\sigma(1)}, \ldots, Y_{\sigma(\kappa)})$$

---

[3] With non-negligible probability (the coin toss being the choice of n and the internal randomness of $\mathcal{A}$).

Let $\mathcal{P}$ be an arbitrary p.p.t algorithm which inputs n and outputs m Σ-symmetric polynomials $s_1, \ldots, s_m$ and a non Σ-symmetric polynomial π. We show that evaluating π only given evaluations of $s_1, \ldots, s_m$ is difficult.

Lemma 1. *Let n be a randomly chosen RSA modulus and $(s_1, \ldots, s_m, \pi) \leftarrow \mathcal{P}(n)$. Assuming the hardness of factoring, there is no p.p.t algorithm which outputs $\pi(y)$ given only $s_1(y), \ldots, s_m(y)$ with non-negligible probability over the choice of $n, y \xleftarrow{\$} \mathbb{Z}_n^{\kappa t}$.*

Proof. See Appendix D.   □

4   An Additively Homomorphic Private-Key Encryption Scheme

We first propose a private-key encryption scheme. The homomorphic operator will be developed later.

Definition 2. *Let λ be a security parameter. The functions KeyGen, Encrypt, Decrypt are defined as follows:*

- *KeyGen(λ). Let η, κ be positive integers indexed by λ, let n be an η-bit RSA modulus chosen at random. Choose at random an invertible matrix $S \in \mathbb{Z}_n^{2\kappa \times 2\kappa}$ and let $T = S^{-1}$. The ith row of S is denoted by $\boldsymbol{s}_i$ and $\mathcal{L}_i$ denotes the linear function defined by $\mathcal{L}_i(\boldsymbol{v}) = \langle \boldsymbol{s}_i, \boldsymbol{v} \rangle$. Output*

$$K = \{S\} \; ; \; pp = \{n, \kappa\}$$

- *Encrypt($K, pp, x \in \mathbb{Z}_n$). Choose at random $r_1, \ldots, r_\kappa$ in $\mathbb{Z}_n^*$ and $x_1, \ldots, x_\kappa$ in $\mathbb{Z}_n$ s.t. $x_1 + \cdots + x_\kappa = x$. Output*

$$c = T \begin{pmatrix} r_1 x_1 \\ r_1 \\ \cdots \\ r_\kappa x_\kappa \\ r_\kappa \end{pmatrix}$$

- *Decrypt($K, pp, c \in \mathbb{Z}_n^{2\kappa}$). Output $x = \sum_{\ell=1}^{\kappa} \mathcal{L}_{2\ell-1}(\boldsymbol{c})/\mathcal{L}_{2\ell}(\boldsymbol{c})$.*

Throughout this paper, $pp = \{n, \kappa\}$ will be assumed to be public. The homomorphic operator(s), developed later, will be included in pp. Proving correctness is straightforward by using the relation $x = r_1 x_1/r_1 + \ldots + r_\kappa x_\kappa/r_\kappa$. The function Decrypt can be represented as the ratio of two degree-κ polynomials $\Phi_0, \Phi_0' \in \mathbb{Z}_n[X_1, \cdots, X_{2\kappa}]$ defined by

$$\Phi_0 = \sum_{\ell=1}^{\kappa} \mathcal{L}_{2\ell-1} \prod_{\ell' \neq \ell} \mathcal{L}_{2\ell'} \; ; \; \Phi_0' = \prod_{\ell=1}^{\kappa} \mathcal{L}_{2\ell} \tag{2}$$

i.e.
$$\text{Decrypt}(K, pp, \boldsymbol{c}) = \Phi_0(\boldsymbol{c})/\Phi_0'(\boldsymbol{c})$$

At this step, our scheme is not homomorphic in the sense that the vector sum is not an homomorphic operator. Indeed, $\boldsymbol{c}$ and $a \cdot \boldsymbol{c}$ encrypt the same message for any $a \in \mathbb{Z}_n^*$.

4.1   Externalizing the Generation of n

To clearly understand the role of the factoring assumption in our security proof, it is important to notice that the factorization of n is not used in KeyGen. Consequently, the generation of n could be externalized (for instance generated by an oracle) ensuring that its factorization was forgotten just after its generation. In other words, n could be a public input of KeyGen. This means that all the polynomials considered in our security analysis are built without using the factorization of n implying that they are equal to 0 with negligible probability provided they are not null (according to Proposition 1).

4.2   A Basic Attack

We present here the most natural attack consisting of solving a linear system. Let $\boldsymbol{c} \leftarrow \text{Encrypt}(K, pp, 0)$ be an encryption of 0. By definition, Φ_0 (see (2)) satisfies $\Phi_0(\boldsymbol{c}) = \prod_{\ell=1}^{\kappa} r_\ell \cdot \sum_{\ell=1}^{\kappa} x_\ell = 0$ ensuring that $\Phi_0(\boldsymbol{c}) = 0$. By considering several encryptions $\boldsymbol{c}_1, \ldots, \boldsymbol{c}_t$ of 0, we get the system of equations $\Phi_0(\boldsymbol{c}_1) = 0, \ldots, \Phi_0(\boldsymbol{c}_t) = 0$.

The expanded representation of Φ_0 could be thus recovered[4] by solving a linear system whose variables are its monomial coefficients. However, this attack fails provided $\kappa = \Theta(\lambda)$ because the expanded representation of Φ_0 is exponential-size in this case (see Remark 1). For instance, by choosing $\kappa = 13$, the attack consists of solving a linear system with approximatively $5 \cdot 10^9$ variables.

It should be noticed that the previous equation system can be seen as a nonlinear system whose variables are the coefficients of S. Proposition 4 will ensure that this system cannot be solved assuming the hardness of factoring.

4.3   The Additive Operator

Let $S \leftarrow \text{KeyGen}(\lambda)$. In this section, we will consider the quadratic polynomials $\mathcal{L}_{ij} \in \mathbb{Z}_n[U_1, \ldots, U_{2\kappa}, V_1, \ldots, V_{2\kappa}]$ defined by $\mathcal{L}_{ij}(\boldsymbol{u}, \boldsymbol{v}) = \mathcal{L}_i(\boldsymbol{u})\mathcal{L}_j(\boldsymbol{v})$.

Definition 3. *AddGen(S) outputs the expanded representation of the polynomials $q_1, \ldots, q_{2\kappa}$ defined by*

---

[4] Up to a multiplicative factor.

$$
\begin{pmatrix} q_1 \\ \cdots \\ q_{2\kappa} \end{pmatrix} = T \begin{pmatrix} \mathcal{L}_{12} + \mathcal{L}_{21} \\ \mathcal{L}_{22} \\ \cdots \\ \mathcal{L}_{2\kappa-1,2\kappa} + \mathcal{L}_{2\kappa,2\kappa-1} \\ \mathcal{L}_{2\kappa,2\kappa} \end{pmatrix}
$$

As each quadratic polynomial q_i has $O(\kappa^2)$ monomials, the running time of AddGen is $O(\kappa^4)$ (2κ sums of 2κ quadratic polynomials). The operator Add $\leftarrow$ AddGen(S) consists of evaluating the polynomials $q_1, \ldots, q_{2\kappa}$, i.e. Add($\boldsymbol{u}, \boldsymbol{v}$) = $(q_1(\boldsymbol{u}, \boldsymbol{v}), \ldots, q_{2\kappa}(\boldsymbol{u}, \boldsymbol{v}))$, leading to a running time in $O(\kappa^3)$. See Appendix A for a toy implementation of Add.

Proposition 2. *Add $\leftarrow$ AddGen(S) is a valid additive homomorphic operator.*

Proof. Straightforward (see Fig. 1).   □

$$
\mathsf{Add}\left(T \begin{pmatrix} r_1 x_1 \\ r_1 \\ \cdots \\ r_\kappa x_\kappa \\ r_\kappa \end{pmatrix}, \; T \begin{pmatrix} r'_1 x'_1 \\ r'_1 \\ \cdots \\ r'_\kappa x'_\kappa \\ r'_\kappa \end{pmatrix} \right) = T \begin{pmatrix} r_1 r'_1 (x_1 + x'_1) \\ r_1 r'_1 \\ \cdots \\ r_\kappa r'_\kappa (x_\kappa + x'_\kappa) \\ r_\kappa r'_\kappa \end{pmatrix}
$$

Fig. 1. Description of the additive operator Add $\leftarrow$ AddGen(S) showing that Decrypt($K, pp, $ Add($\boldsymbol{c}, \boldsymbol{c}'$)) = Decrypt($K, pp, \boldsymbol{c}$) + Decrypt($K, pp, \boldsymbol{c}'$).

For sake of simplicity, Add($\boldsymbol{c}, \boldsymbol{c}'$) will be sometimes denoted by $\boldsymbol{c} \oplus \boldsymbol{c}'$. One easily checks that this operator is commutative and associative legitimating the notation

$$
a \cdot \boldsymbol{c} \overset{\text{def}}{=} \underbrace{\boldsymbol{c} \oplus \boldsymbol{c} \oplus \cdots \oplus \boldsymbol{c}}_{a \text{ times}}
$$

As seen in Sect. 2, the operator Add introduces weaknesses provided the factorization of n is known.

Proposition 3. *IND-CPA security $\Rightarrow$ hardness of factoring.*

4.4   Efficiency

Encrypting/Decrypting/Add requires respectively $O(\kappa^2/\kappa^2/\kappa^3)$ modular multiplications. A ciphertext is a 2κ-vector in $\mathbb{Z}_n$, implying that the ratio of ciphertext size to plaintext size is 2κ. In terms of storage, Add contains $4\kappa^3 + 6\kappa^2$ elements of $\mathbb{Z}_n$, which leads to a space complexity in $O(|n|\kappa^3)$.

By considering $\kappa = 13$ as done in Sect. 4.2, evaluating Add requires around 10500 modular multiplications *vs* only one for Paillier's cryptosystem. Efficiency could be improved by choosing n as a prime (large or not) in constructions not requiring the factoring assumption. We propose an example of such a construction in Appendix B.

4.5   Discussion

The private-key encryption scheme is very simple. Many cryptographic constructions based on this scheme can be imagined by adding auxiliary information, e.g. the operator Add. For these reasons, we think that the security of this scheme can be seen as a new cryptographic problem and its security can be studied independently of related constructions.

The classic way (see [18]) to transform a private-key cryptosystem into a public-key cryptosystem consists of publicizing encryptions $c_1, \ldots, c_t$ of known values $x_1, \ldots, x_t$ and using the homomorphic operators to encrypt x. Let Encrypt1 denote this new encryption function. Assuming the IND-CPA security of the private-key cryptosystem, it suffices that Encrypt1(pk, x) and Encrypt(K, pp, x) are computationally indistinguishable to ensure the IND-CPA security of the public-key cryptosystem.

In our case, a function Encrypt1(pk, x) statistically indistinguishable from Encrypt(K, pp, x) can be naturally built provided $t = \Theta(\kappa)$. To encrypt x, randomly choose $a_1, \ldots, a_t \in \mathbb{Z}_n$ at random s.t. $a_1 x_1 + \cdots + a_t x_t = x$ and then output (see notation of Sect. 4.3)

$$c = a_1 \cdot c_1 \oplus \cdots \oplus a_t \cdot c_t$$

5   Security Analysis

Notation. *Let* $Y = ((X_{i\ell}, R_{i\ell})_{i=0,\ldots,t}, (S_{2\ell-1,i}, S_{2\ell,i})_{i=1,\ldots,2\kappa})_{\ell=1,\ldots,\kappa}$ *be a tuple of indeterminate used throughout this section. Typically, a polynomial* $\alpha \in \mathbb{Z}_n[Y]$ *will be evaluated over* θ_n, θ_n *containing the randomness used to build the knowledge of the CPA attacker (see Definition 4) and* $\alpha(\theta_n)$ *being a value known by the CPA attacker.*

Breaking IND-CPA security consists of recovering a p.p.t. algorithm $\mathcal{A}$ distinguishing encryptions of 0 from ones of 1, i.e. satisfying

$$|\Pr(\mathcal{A}(\mathsf{Encrypt}(K, pp, 1)) = 0) - \Pr(\mathcal{A}(\mathsf{Encrypt}(K, pp, 0)) = 0)| > \nu(\lambda) \qquad (3)$$

where $\nu(\lambda)$ is a non-negligible quantity. Throughout our security analysis, it will be assumed that

$$\kappa = \Theta(\lambda)$$

5.1   Knowledge of the CPA Attacker

For technical reasons, we propose a slight modification in Definitions 2, 3 by setting $T = \det^2 S \cdot S^{-1}$ (instead of $T = S^{-1}$): each coefficient of T can be thus expressed as a polynomial defined over S keeping true some symmetry properties encapsulated in Lemma 2. It is straightforward to show that the decrypting function and the operator Add remain correct.

There are classically two sources of randomness *behind* the knowledge of the CPA attacker. The first source of randomness is the internal randomness of KeyGen, i.e. the choice of $K = \{S\}$. The second source of randomness comes from the encryption oracle. After receiving the challenge encryption $c_0 \leftarrow$ Encrypt(K, pp, x_0), the CPA attacker requests the encryption oracle to get encryptions $c_1, \ldots, c_t$ of chosen plaintexts $x_1, \ldots, x_t \in \mathbb{Z}_n$. Without loss of generality, we will here assume that the encryptions are **random** meaning that the encryption oracle randomly chooses plaintexts $x_1, \ldots, x_t$ itself and returns these values and their encryptions $c_1, \ldots, c_t$ (drawn according to Encrypt). This assumption can be done because the CPA attacker can use the operator Add, after receiving $c_1, \ldots, c_t, x_1, \ldots, x_t$, to get encryptions of chosen plaintexts statistically indistinguishable from encryptions output by Encrypt. Clearly, it suffices to consider $t = O(\kappa)$ to ensure this. All the randomness can be encapsulated in the vector θ_n defined as follows.

Definition 4. *Let $S \leftarrow$ KeyGen(λ), let $(x_{i1}, r_{i1}, \ldots, x_{i\kappa}, r_{i\kappa})$ be the values (randomly) chosen by the encryption oracle to produce[5] c_i. For any $\ell \in \{1, \ldots, \kappa\}$, the random vector $\theta_\ell \in \mathbb{Z}_n^{4\kappa + 2(t+1)}$ is defined by*

$$\theta_\ell = ((x_{i\ell}, r_{i\ell})_{i=0,\ldots,t}, (s_{2\ell-1,i}, s_{2\ell,i})_{i=1,\ldots,2\kappa})$$

The random vector $(\theta_1, \ldots, \theta_\kappa)$ is denoted by θ_n if $x_0 = x_{01} + \cdots + x_{0\kappa}$ is uniform over $\mathbb{Z}_n$ and $\theta_n^{[x]}$ if $x_0 = x$.

It should be noticed that θ_n is drawn according to a probability statistically indistinguishable from the uniform distribution over $\mathbb{Z}_n^{\kappa\gamma}$. The knowledge of the CPA attacker can be represented as a vector $\alpha \in \mathbb{Z}_n^{\gamma'}$, with $\gamma' = O(\kappa^3)$ provided $t = \Theta(\kappa)$.

Definition 5. *The CPA attacker's knowledge $(c_0, \ldots, c_t, x_1, \ldots, x_t, \text{Add})$ can be represented by a vector $\alpha \in \mathbb{Z}_n^{\gamma'}$, the ith component of α being the evaluation of a polynomial (see footnote 8) $\alpha_i \in \mathbb{Z}_n[Y]$ over θ_n, i.e. $\alpha = (\alpha_1(\theta_n), \ldots, \alpha_{\gamma'}(\theta_n)) \stackrel{\text{def}}{=} \alpha(\theta_n)$.*

The polynomials α_i are implicitly described in previous sections. Nevertheless, we do not need to precisely define them. We will only exploit their symmetry properties. For instance, Add is not impacted by switching the two first rows of S with the two last ones. The following result generalizes it.

Lemma 2. *Each polynomial α_i is Δ_κ-symmetric (see Definition 1).*

Proof. See Appendix E.   □

---

[5] $c_i = T(r_{i1}x_{i1}, r_{i1}, \ldots, r_{i\kappa}x_{i\kappa}, r_{i\kappa})$.

5.2   A Fundamental Result Based on Symmetry

By exploiting intrinsic symmetry properties of our scheme, one can show that S cannot be recovered. Worse, non Δ_κ-symmetric polynomials cannot be evaluated over the secret matrix S.

Proposition 4. *Let (see footnote 8) $\pi \in \mathbb{Z}_n[Y]$ be a non Δ_κ-symmetric polynomial chosen by the CPA attacker $\mathcal{A}$. Assuming the hardness of factoring, $\mathcal{A}$ cannot recover $\pi(\theta_n)$ with non-negligible probability over the choice of θ_n, n.*

Proof. A direct consequence of Lemma 1 and Lemma 2. $\qquad\qquad\qquad\square$

Corollary 1. *Assume the hardness of factoring.*

1. *The secret key S cannot be recovered.*
2. *Any product of strictly less than κ coefficients of S cannot be recovered.*
3. *The polynomials $\mathcal{L}_{i_1} \times \cdots \times \mathcal{L}_{i_t}$ cannot be evaluated (thus recovered) provided $t < \kappa$.*

This result is not sufficient to ensure that $\Phi_0 = \sum_{\ell=1}^{\kappa} \mathcal{L}_{2\ell-1} \prod_{\ell' \neq \ell} \mathcal{L}_{2\ell'}$ cannot be recovered. Indeed, each monomial coefficient of Φ_0 is Δ_κ-symmetric (and thus could be recovered). However, the expanded representation of Φ_0 (or its multiples) is exponential-size provided $\kappa = \Theta(\lambda)$ and thus cannot be recovered.

By construction, Φ_0 (or its multiples) could nevertheless be efficiently represented with the linear functions $\mathcal{L}_i$ (or O(1)-products of these linear functions). However, these compact semi-factored representations do not deal with Δ_κ-symmetric quantities and they cannot be recovered according to Proposition 4. However, maybe other efficient representations of Φ_0 can exist only dealing with Δ_κ-symmetric values. We will show that it is not the case in the generic ring model (see Proposition 8) which is sufficient to prove generic IND-CPA security (see Proposition 7).

5.3   Attacks by Linearization

Proposition 4 intuitively justifies that our security analysis can be restricted to a natural class of attacks, called *attacks by linearization*, generalizing the attacks described in Sects. 2 and 4.2. For concreteness, the CPA attacker $\mathcal{A}$ can generate new vectors $v_1, \ldots, v_r$ by recursively applying the homomorphic operator Add on the challenge encryption c_0 and $c_1, \ldots, c_t$ in the hope that there exists a *small* polynomial φ s.t. $\Phi(c_0) = \varphi(v_1, \ldots, v_r)$ distinguishes between encryptions of 0 and encryptions of 1. For instance, $v_1 = c_0 \oplus c_0$, $v_2 = v_1 \oplus c_0$, $v_3 = v_2 \oplus c_1$, etc. The procedure (chosen by the attacker) which outputs $(v_1, \ldots, v_r)$ is denoted by GenVec, i.e. $\Phi(c_0) = \varphi \circ \text{GenVec}(c_0, c_1, \ldots, c_t)$. If the expanded representation of φ is small enough then the CPA attacker could recover it by solving a linear system.

Proposition 5. *Assuming the hardness of factoring, the CPA attacker cannot find[6] a procedure GenVec and a polynomial-size polynomial[7] $\varphi \in \mathbb{Z}_n[X_1, \ldots, X_{2\kappa r}]$*

---

[6] With non-negligible probability.

[7] Polynomial-size expanded representation. Note that degree-κ polynomials have an exponential number of monomials (see Remark 1) provided $\kappa = \Theta(\lambda)$.

s.t. $\varphi \circ GenVec$ satisfies

$$|Pr_{c_0 \leftarrow Encrypt(K,pp,1)}(\varphi \circ GenVec(c_0, c_1, \ldots, c_t) = 0)$$
$$- Pr_{c_0 \leftarrow Encrypt(K,pp,0)}(\varphi \circ GenVec(c_0, c_1, \ldots, c_t) = 0)| > \nu(\lambda)$$

with non-negligible probability over the choice of $(c_i \leftarrow Encrypt(K, pp, x_i))_{i=1,\ldots,t}$

Proof. See Appendix F.   □

5.4 Generic IND-CPA Security

Roughly speaking, a Generic Ring Algorithm (GRA) defined over a ring $\mathcal{R}$ (here $\mathcal{R} = \mathbb{Z}_n$) is an algorithm where only arithmetic operations $+, -, \times, /$ and equality tests are allowed (see [1]). In the special case of $\mathcal{R} = \mathbb{Z}_n$ where n is a randomly chosen RSA modulus, equality tests are not needed. This is implicitly shown in [1] as a straightforward consequence of Theorem 1. Indeed, this result ensures that two polynomials are either identically equal or equal with negligible probability. We say that our scheme is secure in the generic ring model if the CPA cannot find any distinguishing rational function.

Definition 6. *Our encryption scheme is generically IND-CPA secure if the CPA attacker cannot recover a $\{+, -, \times, /\}$-circuit representing a (rational) function ϕ satisfying*

$$\left| Pr\left(\phi \circ \alpha(\theta_n^{[1]}) = 0\right) - Pr\left(\phi \circ \alpha(\theta_n^{[0]}) = 0\right) \right| > \nu(\lambda) \tag{4}$$

where $\nu(\lambda)$ is a non-negligible quantity.

This definition can be restricted to polynomials.

Proposition 6. *Our encryption scheme is generically IND-CPA secure if the CPA attacker cannot recover a (polynomial-size) $\{+, -, \times\}$-circuit representing a polynomial ϕ satisfying (4).*

Proof. See Appendix G.1   □

To prove generic security, we will prove that the CPA attacker cannot output a non-null polynomial ϕ such that $\phi \circ \alpha(\theta_n^{[x]}) = 0$ with non-negligible probability. Without loss of generality, we will focus on the case $x = 0$. In this case, the polynomial ϕ_0 defined as follows plays a central role in our analysis.

Definition 7. *Let us consider the polynomials[8] $L_t(Y, V) = \sum_{k=1}^{2\kappa} S_{t,k} \cdot V_k$ with $V = (V_1, \ldots, V_{2\kappa})$. The polynomial $\phi_0 \in \mathbb{Z}_n[Y, V]$ is defined by*

$$\phi_0 = \sum_{\ell=1}^{\kappa} L_{2\ell-1} \prod_{\ell' \neq \ell} L_{2\ell'}$$

---

[8] Recall that $Y = ((X_{i\ell}, R_{i\ell})_{i=0,\ldots,t}, (S_{2\ell-1,i}, S_{2\ell,i})_{i=1,\ldots,2\kappa})_{\ell=1,\ldots,\kappa}.$

By construction, the polynomial ϕ_0 satisfies $\phi_0(\theta_n, v) = \Phi_0(v)$. The following proposition states that our scheme is generically IND-CPA secure if the CPA attacker cannot represent any non-null multiple of ϕ_0 from its knowledge. To simplify notation, we redefine α by $\alpha(\theta_n, v) = (\alpha_1(\theta_n), \ldots, \alpha_{\gamma'}(\theta_n), v)$.

Proposition 7. *Assuming the hardness of factoring, our scheme is generically IND-CPA secure if there does not exist any polynomial-size $\{+, -, \times\}$-circuit representing a polynomial ϕ s.t. $\phi \circ \alpha$ is a non-null multiple of ϕ_0 (see Definition 7).*

Proof. See Appendix G.2. $\qquad\qquad\qquad\qquad\qquad\qquad\qquad\qquad\qquad\qquad$ □

Consequently, generic IND-CPA security can be reduced to an algebraic problem. Indeed, it suffices to prove the non-existence of polynomials ϕ satisfying requirements of Proposition 7. The proof is based on the Δ_κ-symmetry of CPA attacker's knowledge (see Lemma 2).

Proposition 8. *Our scheme is generically IND-CPA secure assuming the hardness of factoring.*

Proof. See Appendix G.3. $\qquad\qquad\qquad\qquad\qquad\qquad\qquad\qquad\qquad\qquad\qquad$ □

This result holds as long as Lemma 2 holds. It means in particular that IND-CPA security is ensured even if other evaluations of Δ_κ-symmetric polynomials are given to the CPA attacker.

6 Perspectives

A first motivating perspective would consist of removing the factoring assumption required to prove formal results (Theorem 1, Lemma 1 and Proposition 4). This assumption defeats the whole "post-quantum" purpose of multivariate cryptography [17]. While decrypting does not require the factorization of n, this assumption allows us to prove some formal impossibility results. Randomness might be introduced in order to get a pure multivariate encryption scheme. In our opinion, the additional randomness introduced to develop the multiplicative operator (in the following of this section) could be sufficient to achieve this (such randomness should also be introduced in Add).

6.1 A Naive/Toy Construction of Mult

We here consider the case $\kappa = 2$ where S is a 4×4 matrix. Let us consider the two following quadratic operators $\mathcal{O}_1, \mathcal{O}_2$ defined by (see Sect. 4.3 for notation):

$$\mathcal{O}_1 = T \begin{pmatrix} \mathcal{L}_{11} \\ \mathcal{L}_{22} \\ \mathcal{L}_{33} \\ \mathcal{L}_{44} \end{pmatrix} ; \mathcal{O}_2 = T \begin{pmatrix} \mathcal{L}_{13} \\ \mathcal{L}_{24} \\ \mathcal{L}_{31} \\ \mathcal{L}_{42} \end{pmatrix}$$

Given two encryptions c, c' of x, x', we have

$$\mathcal{O}_1(c, c') = T \begin{pmatrix} r_1 r_1' x_1 x_1' \\ r_1 r_1' \\ r_2 r_2' x_2 x_2' \\ r_2 r_2' \end{pmatrix} ; \mathcal{O}_2(c, c') = T \begin{pmatrix} r_1 r_2' x_1 x_2' \\ r_1 r_2' \\ r_2 r_1' x_2 x_1' \\ r_2 r_1' \end{pmatrix}$$

implying that $c'' = \mathsf{Mult}(c, c') \overset{\text{def}}{=} \mathsf{Add}(\mathcal{O}_1(c, c'), \mathcal{O}_2(c, c'))$ is a valid encryption of xx'. Indeed,

$$c'' = T \begin{pmatrix} r_1^2 r_1' r_2' (x_1 x_1' + x_1 x_2') \\ r_1^2 r_1' r_2' \\ r_2^2 r_1' r_2' (x_2 x_1' + x_2 x_2') \\ r_2^2 r_1' r_2' \end{pmatrix}$$

and $\mathsf{Decrypt}(K, pp, c'') = (x_1' + x_2')x_1 + (x_1' + x_2')x_2 = (x_1' + x_2')(x_1 + x_2) = xx'$.

Roughly speaking, the $\kappa^2 = 4$ products $x_i x_j'$ are stored in two intermediate vectors output by $\mathcal{O}_1, \mathcal{O}_2$. While there are many others ways to define these operators, let us assume that their description is public[9] (or guessed by the CPA attacker). This choice of $\mathcal{O}_1, \mathcal{O}_2$ leads to an attack by linearization more efficient than the basic attack presented in Sect. 4.2.

Example of attack by linearization. Assume that c' is an encryption of 0, i.e. $x' = x_1' + x_2' = 0$. In this case[10],

$$\mathsf{Mult}(c, c') \sim T \begin{pmatrix} 0 \\ r_1^2 \\ 0 \\ r_2^2 \end{pmatrix}$$

It follows that a linear combination of $\mathcal{L}_1, \mathcal{L}_3$ can be recovered by solving a small linear system, i.e. smaller than the one involved in the basic attack. allowing the CPA attacker to distinguish the case $x' = 0$ from the case $x' \neq 0$. In order to remove such weaknesses, we will introduce randomness in our construction, i.e. the coefficients τ_{ijk} and the polynomials ρ_{ijk}.

6.2 Overview

A multiplicative operator Mult should be developed to get an FHE. Let c, c' be two encryptions of x, x'. The operator Mult developed in this section will output an encryption $c'' = \mathsf{Mult}(c, c')$ satisfying

$$c'' = T \begin{pmatrix} R_1(c, c') \cdot \sum_{ij} \tau_{ij1} x_i x_j' \\ R_1(c, c') \\ \cdots \\ R_\kappa(c, c') \cdot \sum_{ij} \tau_{ij\kappa} x_i x_j' \\ R_\kappa(c, c') \end{pmatrix}$$

---

[9] While the operators are public, their description could be not divulged.
[10] $\sim$ meaning "equal up to a multiplicative constant".

where τ_{ijk} are randomly chosen over $\mathbb{Z}_n$ s.t. $\sum_{k=1}^{\kappa} \tau_{ijk} = 1$ for any $(i,j) \in \{1,\ldots,\kappa\}^2$ and $R_1,\ldots,R_\kappa$ are randomly chosen polynomials. Clearly,

$$\mathsf{Decrypt}(K, pp, c'') = \sum_k \sum_{ij} \tau_{ijk} x_i x_j' = \sum_{ij} x_i x_j' = xx'$$

Unfortunately, unlike Add, this operator Mult cannot be efficiently represented with Δ_κ-symmetric values. We propose to represent it by using weaker symmetry properties.

The implementation of Mult is less straightforward than the one of Add. It cannot be achieved using only one quadratic operator. Indeed, it exploits the equality $xx' = \sum_{i=1}^{\kappa} \sum_{j=1}^{\kappa} x_i x_j'$ and several operators are necessary to *store* all the products $x_i x_j'$ in some intermediate vectors. The price to pay is to degrade symmetry properties. Nevertheless, we propose a construction partially keeping them.

6.3   Our Proposal

Notation. *Let $I_\kappa = \{1,\ldots,\kappa\}$ and let Γ^κ be the set of quadratic homogeneous polynomials $\rho \in \mathbb{Z}_n[X_1,\ldots,X_{2\kappa}, Y_1,\ldots,Y_{2\kappa}]$ s.t. $\rho(X,Y) = \sum_{i,j} a_{ij} X_i Y_j$.*

Given two permutations $\sigma, \sigma' \in \Delta_\kappa$, a family of polynomials $\rho \in \Gamma^\kappa$ and a vector $\tau \in \mathbb{Z}_n^\kappa$, the function $\mathsf{OGen}(S, \sigma, \sigma', \rho, \tau)$ outputs[11] the degree-4 operator $\mathcal{O}$ defined by

$$\mathcal{O} = T \begin{pmatrix} \tau_1 \; \rho_1 \mathcal{L}_{2\sigma(1)-1, 2\sigma'(1)-1} \\ \rho_1 \mathcal{L}_{2\sigma(1), 2\sigma'(1)} \\ \cdots \\ \tau_\kappa \; \rho_\kappa \mathcal{L}_{2\sigma(\kappa)-1, 2\sigma'(\kappa)-1} \\ \rho_\kappa \mathcal{L}_{2\sigma(\kappa), 2\sigma'(\kappa)} \end{pmatrix}$$

By construction,

$$\mathsf{Decrypt}(sk, \mathcal{O}(c, c')) = \tau_1 x_{\sigma(1)} x_{\sigma'(1)'} + \cdots + \tau_\kappa x_{\sigma(\kappa)} x_{\sigma'(\kappa)'}$$

We note that $\mathsf{Decrypt}(sk, \mathcal{O}(c, c'))$ does not depend on the polynomials ρ_i. These polynomials will be chosen at random in Mult. Roughly speaking, the vector $\mathcal{O}(c, c')$ stores κ (additive shares of) products $x_i x_j$. By considering several such operators (at least κ), all the products can be stored. It then suffices to homomorphically add these vectors (by using the operator Add) to get an encryption of xx'. This is detailed below.

Mult. Let $\tau = (\tau_{ijk})_{(i,j,k)\in I_\kappa^3}$ be randomly chosen such that $\sum_{k=1}^{\kappa} \tau_{ijk} = 1$ for any $(i,j) \in I_\kappa^2$. To build the operator Mult, it suffices to invoke κ^2 times the function OGen in order to generate and publicize

$$\mathcal{O}_{ij} \leftarrow \mathsf{OGen}\left(S, \sigma_i, \sigma_j, \rho_{ij}, (\tau_{\sigma_i(k), \sigma_j(k), k})_{k=1,\ldots,\kappa}\right)$$

---

[11] The expanded representation of the 2κ degree-4 polynomials $q_1,\ldots,q_{2\kappa}$ satisfying $(q_1(u, v),\ldots,q_{2\kappa}(u, v)) = \mathcal{O}(u, v)$.

for any $(i,j) \in I_\kappa^2$ where ρ_{ij} is randomly chosen over Γ^κ and $\sigma_i, \sigma_j \in \Sigma_\kappa$[12]. To homomorphically multiply c and c', it suffices to homomorphically add the vectors $\mathcal{O}_{ij}(c, c')$, i.e.

$$\mathsf{Mult}(c, c') \stackrel{\text{def}}{=} \bigoplus_{(i,j) \in I_\kappa^2} \mathcal{O}_{ij}(c, c')$$

where $\oplus$ refers to the operator Add, i.e. $u \oplus v = \mathsf{Add}(u, v)$. As evaluating $\mathcal{O}_{ij}(c, c')$ can be done in $O(\kappa^5)$, the running time of Mult is $O(\kappa^7)$.

Example. Description of the operators $\mathcal{O}_{11}, \mathcal{O}_{12}, \mathcal{O}_{12}, \mathcal{O}_{22}$ and Mult in the case $\kappa = 2$.

$$\mathcal{O}_{11}(c,c') = T \begin{pmatrix} \rho_{111}(c,c')r_1 r_1' \tau_{111} x_1 x_1' \\ \rho_{111}(c,c')r_1 r_1' \\ \rho_{112}(c,c')r_2 r_2' \tau_{222} x_2 x_2' \\ \rho_{112}(c,c')r_2 r_2' \end{pmatrix} ; \quad \mathcal{O}_{12}(c,c') = T \begin{pmatrix} \rho_{121}(c,c')r_1 r_2' \tau_{121} x_1 x_2' \\ \rho_{121}(c,c')r_1 r_2' \\ \rho_{122}(c,c')r_2 r_1' \tau_{212} x_2 x_1' \\ \rho_{122}(c,c')r_2 r_1' \end{pmatrix}$$

$$\mathcal{O}_{21}(c,c') = T \begin{pmatrix} \rho_{211}(c,c')r_1 r_2' \tau_{211} x_2 x_1' \\ \rho_{211}(c,c')r_1 r_2' \\ \rho_{212}(c,c')r_2 r_1' \tau_{122} x_1 x_2' \\ \rho_{212}(c,c')r_2 r_1' \end{pmatrix} ; \quad \mathcal{O}_{22}(c,c') = T \begin{pmatrix} \rho_{221}(c,c')r_2 r_2' \tau_{221} x_2 x_2' \\ \rho_{221}(c,c')r_2 r_2' \\ \rho_{222}(c,c')r_1 r_1' \tau_{112} x_1 x_1' \\ \rho_{222}(c,c')r_1 r_1' \end{pmatrix}$$

$$\mathsf{Mult}(c,c') \sim T \begin{pmatrix} \prod_{(i,j) \in \{1,2\}^2} \rho_{ij1}(c,c') \sum_{(i,j) \in \{1,2\}^2} \tau_{ij1} x_i x_j' \\ \prod_{(i,j) \in \{1,2\}^2} \rho_{ij1}(c,c') \\ \prod_{(i,j) \in \{1,2\}^2} \rho_{ij2}(c,c') \sum_{(i,j) \in \{1,2\}^2} \tau_{ij2} x_i x_j' \\ \prod_{(i,j) \in \{1,2\}^2} \rho_{ij2}(c,c') \end{pmatrix}$$

6.4   Security Analysis

Randomness θ_n (see Definition 4) can be easily adapted in order to integrate the polynomials ρ_{ijk} and the values τ_{ijk} used in our construction. Each value known by the CPA attacker can be still written as the evaluation of a polynomial α_i (see Definition 5) over θ_n. In this context, Proposition 7 remains true. Unfortunately, Proposition 8 cannot be naturally extended because its proof is based on the fact that the polynomials α_i are Δ_κ-symmetric. Even if Lemma 2 is not true anymore, the polynomials α_i keep symmetry properties: they are just Σ_κ-symmetric instead of being Δ_κ-symmetric. Proposition 4 can be easily adapted.

---

[12] Recall that $\sigma_i \in \Sigma_\kappa$ refers to the permutation over $\{1, \ldots, \kappa\}$ defined by $\sigma_i(1) = i; \sigma_i(2) = i + 1; \ldots; \sigma_i(\kappa) = i - 1$.

Proposition 9. *Let π be a non Σ_κ-symmetric polynomial chosen by the CPA attacker $\mathcal{A}$. Assuming the hardness of factoring, $\mathcal{A}$ cannot recover $\pi(\theta_n)$ with non-negligible probability over the choice of θ_n, n.*

Proof. In order to take into account (symmetric) constraints over the coefficients τ_{ijk}, a slight extension of Lemma 1, i.e. Lemma 3, should be used to prove this result. $\qquad\square$

It follows that Corollary 1 still holds. However, the proof of Proposition 8 intrinsically exploits Δ_κ-symmetry properties and cannot be easily adapted. While we are convinced that the introduction of the polynomials ρ_{ijk} and the coefficients τ_{ijk} protect our scheme against attacks by linearization, we did not manage to formally prove it.

Assume nevertheless that the multiplicative operator Mult can be replaced by an oracle $\mathcal{O}$ in the security analysis. In this case, the proof of Proposition 5 can be easily adapted to show the non-existence of efficient attacks by linearization.

Mult can be Replaced by an Oracle $\mathcal{O}$? We propose two (informal) reasons/modifications suggesting this.

- The operators $\mathcal{O}_{ij}$ play a symmetric role and there is no reason to publicize the permutations σ_i, σ_j involved in these operators. We can speculate on the fact that the CPA attacker cannot recover them or equivalently that it cannot distinguish between $\mathcal{O}_{ij}$ and $\mathcal{O}_{i'j'}$.
- The operators $\mathcal{O}_{ij}$ output vectors relevant under the secret key S. However, nothing justifies it and one can imagine that $\mathcal{O}_{ij}$ output vectors relevant under randomly chosen keys S_{ij}. It suffices then to generate new operators Add (adapted to these new keys) in order to (homomorphically) add these vectors. Roughly speaking, the operators $\mathcal{O}_{ij}$ and the (new) operators Add involved in Mult become chained making non-specified uses irrelevant. This also could lead to significant improvements by replacing each degree-4 operators by two quadratic operators.

Acknowledgment. The authors would like to thank the anonymous referees for their helpful comments.

A   Implementation of Add in the Case $\kappa = 1$

In this section, we provide an example of the implementation of the homomorphic scheme for $\kappa = 1$. Let $S = [s_{ij}] \in \mathbb{Z}_n^{2 \times 2}$ and $\Delta = s_{11}s_{22} - s_{12}s_{21}$.
    Add $= (q_1, q_2) \leftarrow$ AddGen(S) is defined by

$$
\begin{aligned}
\Delta \cdot q_1(\boldsymbol{u}, \boldsymbol{v}) = &(2s_{22}s_{11}s_{21} - s_{12}s_{21}^2)u_1v_1 \\
&+ s_{22}^2 s_{11}(u_1v_2 + u_2v_1) \\
&+ s_{12}s_{22}^2 u_2v_2
\end{aligned}
$$

$$\Delta \cdot q_2(\boldsymbol{u}, \boldsymbol{v}) = - s_{11} s_{21}^2 u_1 v_1$$
$$- s_{21}^2 s_{12} (u_1 v_2 + u_2 v_1)$$
$$+ (s_{11} s_{22}^2 - 2 s_{21} s_{12} s_{22}) u_2 v_2$$

B   Removing the Factoring Assumption?

We propose to implement the *randomized* operator $\mathsf{Add}^{\mathsf{rand}}$ considered in Sect. 2 (with $\sigma = \sigma' = \mathsf{Id}$). This operator can be implemented with degree-4 polynomials (provided the polynomials ρ_i are quadratic). To improve efficiency, we propose to split it into two quadratic operators Add' and Rand, i.e.

$$\mathsf{Add}^{\mathsf{rand}}(\boldsymbol{c}, \boldsymbol{c}') = \mathsf{Rand}(\mathsf{Add}'(\boldsymbol{c}, \boldsymbol{c}'))$$

- Add' exactly follows Add except that $\boldsymbol{c}'' = \mathsf{Add}'(\boldsymbol{c}, \boldsymbol{c}')$ is not relevant under S but relevant under a randomly chosen S'.
- Rand *randomizes* $\boldsymbol{c}''$ with polynomials ρ_i.

Let $S' \in \mathbb{Z}_n^{2\kappa \times 2\kappa}$ be a randomly chosen invertible matrix, $T' = S'^{-1}$ its inverse and $\mathcal{L}'_i$ the linear application defined by $\mathcal{L}'_i(\boldsymbol{u}) = \langle \boldsymbol{s}'_i, \boldsymbol{u} \rangle$ where $\boldsymbol{s}'_i$ is the ith row of S'.

Add'. It suffices now to define Add' as Add except that T is replaced by T' in Definition 3. In other words,

$$\mathsf{Add}'(\boldsymbol{c}, \boldsymbol{c}') = T' \cdot S \cdot \mathsf{Add}(\boldsymbol{c}, \boldsymbol{c}')$$

Rand. Let $\rho_1, \dots, \rho_\kappa$ be randomly chosen degree-1 polynomials.

$$\mathsf{Rand}(\boldsymbol{u}) = T \begin{pmatrix} \rho_1(\boldsymbol{u})\mathcal{L}'_1(\boldsymbol{u}) \\ \rho_1(\boldsymbol{u})\mathcal{L}'_2(\boldsymbol{u}) \\ \cdots \\ \rho_\kappa(\boldsymbol{u})\mathcal{L}'_{2\kappa-1}(\boldsymbol{u}) \\ \rho_\kappa(\boldsymbol{u})\mathcal{L}'_{2\kappa}(\boldsymbol{u}) \end{pmatrix}$$

It is straightforward to see that this new operator $\mathsf{Add}^{\mathsf{rand}}$ is correct

Security Analysis. As symmetry properties are preserved, all the results proved previously still hold under the factoring assumption. Let us now assume that n is a prime (instead of a RSA modulus). Note first that n should be a large prime, i.e. $n \approx 2^\lambda$, to avoid that $\rho_i(\boldsymbol{u}) = 0$ with non-negligible probability. Clearly, the attack by linearization exhibited in Sect. 2 is not relevant anymore. However, as the factorization of n is known, nonlinear univariate equations can be solved. Hence, our construction becomes potentially vulnerable to attacks based on Groëbner bases. We carry out some experiments on *SageMath platform* using variable elimination algorithms. It appears that computational-time required by these attacks is prohibitive even for very small values of κ, e.g $\kappa = 2$. We did not exhibit any attack working faster than the basic attack (see Sect. 4.2). Obviously further investigations should be done. In our opinion this is a nice challenge whose formulation is relatively simple.

C   Proof of Proposition 1

This result can be shown by induction over r. By Lemma 1, the result is true for $r = 1$. Let us assume the result true for any $r < t$ and let us show it for $r = t$. We can identify $\mathbb{Z}_n[X_1, \ldots, X_t]$ to $R[X_t]$ with $R = \mathbb{Z}_n[X_1, \ldots, X_{t-1}]$. Let ϕ be a a non-null polynomial $\phi \in \mathbb{Z}_n[X_1, \ldots, X_t]$ output by a p.p.t. algorithm $\mathcal{A}$, i.e. $\phi \leftarrow \mathcal{A}(n)$. ϕ can be identified by a non-null polynomial $\phi' \in R[X_1]$. Thus, by fixing $X_2, \ldots, X_t$ to randomly chosen values $x_2, \ldots, x_t \in \mathbb{Z}_n$, the polynomial $\phi_{x_2,\ldots,x_t}$ defined by $\phi_{x_2,\ldots,x_t}(x_1) = \phi(x_1, \ldots, x_t)$ is not (identically) null with overwhelming probability over the choice of $n, x_2, \ldots, x_t$ according to the induction hypothesis. Moreover, provided $\phi_{x_2,\ldots,x_t}$ is not null, $\phi_{x_2,\ldots,x_t}(x_1) = 0$ with negligible probability other choice of n, x_1 according to the induction hypothesis. This proves $\phi(x_1, \ldots, x_t) = 0$ with negligible over the choice of $n, x_1, \ldots, x_t$. $\qquad\square$

D   Proof of Lemma 1

D.1   The Proof

Let D be the uniform probability distribution of over $\mathbb{Z}_n^{\kappa t}$ The proof consists of building a polynomial factoring algorithm $\mathcal{A}$ by using a solver $\mathcal{B}$ of our problem as subroutine ($\mathcal{B}$ is assumed to solve our problem if it outputs $\pi(y)$ with non-negligible probability). Let us consider the following polynomial-time algorithm $\mathcal{A}$:

Input: $n = pq$

$(s_1, \ldots, s_m, \pi) \leftarrow \mathcal{P}(n)$

Repeat

1. *Let $y = (y_1, \ldots, y_\kappa) \leftarrow D$*
2. *Compute $\overline{s}_j = s_j(y)$ for all $j = 1, \ldots, m$.*
3. *Compute $\Pi = \pi(y)$*
4. *Apply $\mathcal{B}$ on the inputs $\overline{s}_1, \ldots, \overline{s}_m$, i.e. $\Pi_\mathcal{B} \leftarrow \mathcal{B}(\overline{s}_1, \ldots, \overline{s}_m)$*

until $\gcd(\Pi - \Pi_\mathcal{B}, n) \neq 1$

output $\gcd(\Pi - \Pi_\mathcal{B}, n)$

By construction, this algorithm is correct. Let us show that it terminates in polynomial-time. First, each step of $\mathcal{A}$ can be computed in polynomial-time implying that $\mathcal{A}$ is polynomial if the expectation of the number of steps of $\mathcal{A}$ is polynomial (or equivalently, if the probability to get $\gcd(\Pi - \Pi_\mathcal{B}, n) \neq 1$ is not negligible).

As π is not Σ-symmetric, there exists $\sigma^* \in \Sigma$ s.t. $\pi - \pi_{\sigma^*}$ is not null, where π_{σ^*} is the polynomial defined by $\pi_{\sigma^*}(y) = \pi(y_{\sigma^*(1)}, \ldots, y_{\sigma^*(\kappa)})$. Thus, according to Proposition 1, $\pi(y) \neq \pi_{\sigma^*}(y)$ with overwhelming probability. It follows that $\pi(y) \not\equiv \pi_{\sigma^*}(y) \mod p$ or $\pi(y) \not\equiv \pi_{\sigma^*}(y) \mod q$ with overwhelming probability. Without loss of generality, we assume that

$$\pi(y) \not\equiv \pi_{\sigma^*}(y) \mod q \qquad (5)$$

with overwhelming probability. Let us consider the function $h : (\mathbb{Z}_n^t)^\kappa \to (\mathbb{Z}_n^t)^\kappa$ such that $(y'_1, \ldots, y'_\kappa) = h(y_1, \ldots, y_\kappa)$ is defined by

- $y'_{\ell i} \equiv y_{\ell i} \mod p$ for any $(\ell, i) \in \{1, \ldots, \kappa\} \times \{1, \ldots, t\}$
- $y'_{\ell i} \equiv y_{\sigma^*(\ell), i} \mod q$ for any $(\ell, i) \in \{1, \ldots, \kappa\} \times \{1, \ldots, t\}$.

Clearly, $y' = (y'_1, \ldots, y'_\kappa)$ and y have the same probability over D, i.e.

$$\mathrm{Pr}_D(y) = \mathrm{Pr}_D(y')$$

Let $\Pi' = \pi(y')$. As the functions s_j are Σ-symmetric polynomials, we get $s_j(y') = s_j(y)$ for all $j = 1, \ldots, m$. It follows that

$$\mathrm{Pr}_D(\Pi_\mathcal{B} = \Pi) = \mathrm{Pr}_D(\Pi_\mathcal{B} = \Pi')$$

As $\mathcal{B}$ is assumed to solve our problem, $\mathrm{Pr}_D(\Pi_\mathcal{B} = \Pi)$ is non-negligible implying that $\mathrm{Pr}_D(\Pi_\mathcal{B} = \Pi')$ is non-negligible.

By construction $\Pi \equiv \Pi' \mod p$. Since $\Pi' \equiv \pi_{\sigma^*}(y) \mod q$, Eq. (5) implies that $\Pi \not\equiv \Pi' \mod q$ with overwhelming probability. It follows that $p = \gcd(n, \Pi - \Pi')$ with overwhelming probability. Consequently, $\mathcal{A}$ terminates (when $\Pi_\mathcal{B} = \Pi'$) in polynomial-time. $\qquad\square$

D.2   Extension

We now propose to extend this result when y is drawn under symmetric constraints. Let assume that $\mathcal{P}(n)$ outputs:

- Σ-symmetric polynomials $s_1, \ldots, s_m \in \mathbb{Z}_n[((X_{ij}, Z_{ij})_{j=1,\ldots,t})_{i=1,\ldots,\kappa}]$
- polynomials $p_1, \ldots, p_\gamma \in \mathbb{Z}_n[((Z_{ij})_{j=1,\ldots,t})_{i=1,\ldots,\kappa}]$
- a non Σ-symmetric polynomial $\pi \in \mathbb{Z}_n[((X_{ij})_{j=1,\ldots,t})_{i=1,\ldots,\kappa}]$.

We consider the probability distribution $D^{p_1,\ldots,p_\gamma,\Sigma}$ uniform over the set (assumed to be not empty)

$$\{((x_1, z_1), \ldots, (x_\kappa, z_\kappa)) \in \mathbb{Z}_n^{(t+r)\kappa} | p_i(z_{\sigma(1)}, \ldots, z_{\sigma(\kappa)}) = 0$$
$$\text{for any } (i, \sigma) \in \{1, \ldots, \gamma\} \times \Sigma\}$$

We will assume that $D^{p_1,\ldots,p_\gamma,\Sigma}$ is sampleable meaning there exists a p.p.t. algorithm $\mathcal{D}$ s.t. $\mathcal{D}(n)$ outputs a vector drawn according to a probability distribution statistically close to $D^{p_1,\ldots,p_\gamma,\Sigma}$.

Lemma 3. *Let $(s_1, \ldots, s_m, p_1, \ldots, p_\gamma, \pi) \leftarrow \mathcal{P}(n)$. There is no p.p.t algorithm which outputs $\pi(x_1, \ldots, x_\kappa)$ given only $s_1(y), \ldots, s_m(y)$ with non-negligible probability over the choice of n, $y = ((x_1, z_1), \ldots, (x_\kappa, z_\kappa)) \leftarrow D^{p_1,\ldots,p_\gamma,\Sigma}$ assuming the hardness of factoring.*

Proof. Exactly follows the proof of Lemma 1. $\qquad\square$

E   Proof of Lemma 2

Recall that we set $T = \det^2 S \cdot S^{-1}$ in order to ensure that value known by the CPA attacker can be written as the evaluation of a polynomial over θ. It remains to prove that these polynomials are Δ_κ-symmetric. First, it should be noticed that, contrarily to $\det S$, $\det^2 S$ can be written as a Δ_κ-symmetric polynomial defined over $s = (s_1, \ldots, s_{2\kappa})$ and thus $\theta_n = (\theta_1, \ldots, \theta_\kappa)$. The values $x_i = x_{i1} + \cdots + x_{i\kappa}$ are also evaluations of Δ_κ-polynomials.

By construction, each component of c_i is the evaluation over θ_n of a Δ_κ-symmetric polynomial. Indeed, c_i is the unique vector satisfying the following system

$$\text{for any } \ell = 1, \ldots, \kappa \quad \begin{cases} \langle s_{2\ell-1}, c_i \rangle = (\det S)^2 \cdot r_{i\ell} x_{i\ell} \\ \langle s_{2\ell}, c_i \rangle = (\det S)^2 \cdot r_{i\ell} \end{cases}$$

stable by permutating the tuples $(\theta_1, \ldots, \theta_\kappa)$.
Let $(q_1, \ldots, q_{2\kappa}) \leftarrow \mathsf{AddGen}(S)$. The coefficient of $u_i v_j$ in $q_k(u, v)$ is denoted by a_{kij}. By construction, the vector $a_{ij} = (a_{1ij}, \ldots, a_{2\kappa,ij})$ is the unique solution of the following linear system (the variables being a_{kij})

$$\text{for any } \ell = 1, \ldots, \kappa \quad \begin{cases} \langle s_{2\ell-1}, a_{ij} \rangle = (\det S)^2 \cdot s_{2\ell-1,i} s_{2\ell,j} + s_{2\ell,i} s_{2\ell-1,j} \\ \langle s_{2\ell}, a_{ij} \rangle = (\det S)^2 \cdot s_{2\ell,i} s_{2\ell,j} \end{cases}$$

stable by permutating the tuples $(\theta_1, \ldots, \theta_\kappa)$. It follows that a_{kij} is the evaluation over θ_n of a Δ_κ-symmetric polynomial.   □

F   Proof of Proposition 5

Lemma 4. *Let $\phi \in \mathbb{Z}_n[X_1, \ldots, X_\kappa, Y_1, \ldots, Y_\kappa]$ be a non-null polynomial such that each monomial $X_1^{e_1} \cdots X_\kappa^{e_\kappa} Y_1^{e_1'} \cdots Y_\kappa^{e_\kappa'}$ satisfies*

- $\exists i \in \{1, \ldots, \kappa\}, e_i = e_i' = 0$
- $\forall i \in \{1, \ldots, \kappa\}, e_i = 0 \Rightarrow e_i' = 0$

For any $\alpha \in \mathbb{Z}_n$, the polynomial $\phi_\alpha = \phi(X_1, \ldots, X_\kappa, Y_1, \ldots, Y_{\kappa-1}, \alpha - Y_1 - \ldots - Y_{\kappa-1})$ is not null.

Proof. Let $\phi = \sum_{i=1}^\rho a_i M_i$ where $M_i = X_1^{e_{i1}} \cdots X_\kappa^{e_{i,\kappa}} Y_1^{e_{i1}'} \cdots Y_\kappa^{e_{i,\kappa}'}$ and $a_i \in \mathbb{Z}_n^*$, let $m = \max_i e_{i,\kappa}'$.

If $m = 0$ then the result is trivially true. Thus, one can assume that $m > 0$. We have

$$\phi_\alpha = \sum_{i=0}^\rho a_i (\alpha - Y_1 - \ldots - Y_{\kappa-1})^{e_{i,\kappa}'} M_i'$$

where $M_i' = X_1^{e_{i,1}} \cdots X_\kappa^{e_{i,\kappa}} Y_1^{e_{i,1}'} \cdots Y_{\kappa-1}^{e_{i,\kappa-1}'}$.

Given an arbitrary monomial $M = X_1^{e_1} \cdots X_\kappa^{e_\kappa} Y_1^{e'_1} \cdots Y_\kappa^{e'_\kappa}$, the set $\{j \in \{1,\ldots,\kappa\} | e_j \neq 0\}$ is denoted by $E(M)$. Let i_0 s.t. $e'_{i_0,\kappa} = m$. As $\exists j \in \{1,\ldots,\kappa\}$ s.t. $e_{ij} = e_{i'j} = 0$, one can assume that $1 \notin E(M'_{i_0})$. Let us show that the monomial $Y_1^m M'_{i_0}$ belongs to ϕ_α (implying that ϕ_α is not null). To achieve this, it suffices to show that this monomial does not belong to any polynomial $(\alpha - Y_1 - \ldots - Y_{\kappa-1})^{e'_{i,\kappa}} M'_i$ with $i \neq i_0$.

Suppose that there exists $i_1 \neq i_0$ s.t. $Y_1^m M'_{i_0}$ belongs to $(\alpha - Y_1 - \ldots - Y_{\kappa-1})^{e'_{i_1,\kappa}} M'_{i_1}$. Clearly, $1 \notin E(M'_{i_0})$ implies that $1 \notin E(M'_{i_1})$ and $e'_{i_1,\kappa} \geq m$ (because the constraint $e_i = 0 \Rightarrow e'_i = 0$ implies that the exponent of Y_1 in M'_i is equal to 0). By definition of m, it follows that $e'_{i_1,\kappa} = m$ implying that $M'_{i_0} \neq M'_{i_1}$ (because $M_{i_0} = M_{i_1}$ otherwise). Thus, $Y_1^m M'_{i_0}$ does not belong to $(\alpha - Y_1 - \ldots - Y_{\kappa-1})^{e'_{i_1,\kappa}=m} M'_{i_1}$. This concludes the proof. □

Let us assume that the CPA attacker can recover a procedure GenVec and a polynomial φ of $\mathbb{Z}_n[X_1,\ldots,X_{2\kappa r}]$ such that $\deg \varphi < \kappa$ satisfying the requirements of the proposition. Let $c_1^*,\ldots,c_t^*$ be encryptions such that

$$|Pr_{c_0 \leftarrow \mathsf{Encrypt}(K,pp,1)}(\varphi \circ \mathsf{GenVec}(c_0,c_1^*,\ldots,c_t^*) = 0)$$
$$- Pr_{c_0 \leftarrow \mathsf{Encrypt}(K,pp,0)}(\varphi \circ \mathsf{GenVec}(c_0,c_1^*,\ldots,c_t^*) = 0)| > \nu(\lambda)$$

It follows that the polynomial $\overline{\varphi \circ \mathsf{GenVec}} \in \mathbb{Z}_n[R_1,\ldots,R_\kappa,X_1,\ldots,X_\kappa]$ defined by

$$\overline{\varphi \circ \mathsf{GenVec}}(R_1,\ldots,R_\kappa,X_1,\ldots,X_\kappa) = \varphi \circ \mathsf{GenVec}(Y,c_1^*,\ldots,c_t^*)$$

where[13] $Y = T(R_1 X_1, R_1, \ldots, R_\kappa X_\kappa, R_\kappa)$ is not null. By construction of GenVec, each vector v output by $\varphi \circ \mathsf{GenVec}(Y,c_1^*,\ldots,c_t^*)$ is in the form

$$v = T(p_1(R_1 X_1, X_1), p'_1(R_1 X_1, R_1), \ldots, p_\kappa(R_\kappa X_\kappa, R_\kappa), p'_\kappa(R_\kappa X_\kappa, R_\kappa))$$

where p_i, p'_i are polynomials.

Consequently, as $\deg \varphi < \kappa$, each monomial $R_1^{e_1} \cdots R_\kappa^{e_\kappa} X_1^{e'_1} \cdots X_\kappa^{e'_\kappa}$ of $\overline{\varphi \circ \mathsf{GenVec}}$ satisfies

- $\exists i \in \{1,\ldots,\kappa\}$ s.t. $e_i = e'_i = 0$
- $\forall i \in \{1,\ldots,\kappa\}$, $e_i = 0 \Rightarrow e'_i = 0$.

Let $x \in \mathbb{Z}_n$ be arbitrarily chosen. By fixing $X_1 + \cdots + X_\kappa = x$, we consider the polynomial $\overline{\varphi \circ \mathsf{GenVec}}_x \in \mathbb{Z}_n[R_1,\ldots,R_\kappa,X_1,\ldots,X_{\kappa-1}]$ equal to the polynomial $\overline{\varphi \circ \mathsf{GenVec}}(R_1,\ldots,R_\kappa,X_1,\ldots,X_{\kappa-1},x-X_{\kappa-1}-\ldots-X_1)$. By Lemma 4, this polynomial is not null. Hence, according to Proposition 1,

$$\overline{\varphi \circ \mathsf{GenVec}}_x(r_1,\ldots,r_\kappa,x_1,\ldots,x_{\kappa-1}) = 0$$

with negligible probability over the choice of $r_1,\ldots,r_\kappa \in \mathbb{Z}_n^*$ and $x_1,\ldots,x_{\kappa-1} \in \mathbb{Z}_n$ assuming factoring is hard. Thus, for any $x \in \mathbb{Z}_n$,

$$Pr_{c_0 \leftarrow \mathsf{Encrypt}(K,pp,x)}(\varphi \circ \mathsf{GenVec}(c_0,c_1^*,\ldots,c_t^*) = 0)$$

is negligible leading to a contradiction implying that $\deg \varphi \geq \kappa$. □

---

[13] $T = \det^2 S \cdot S^{-1}$.

G   Proofs of Sect. 5.4

Lemma 5. *There do not exist any polynomial $q \in \mathbb{Z}_n[X_1, \ldots, X_t]$ and symmetric polynomials $\pi_1, \ldots, \pi_t \in \mathbb{Z}_n[X_1, \ldots, X_\kappa]$ satisfying $q(\pi_1, \ldots, \pi_t) = X_1 \cdots X_\kappa$ provided $\deg \pi_i < \kappa$.*

Proof. It straightforwardly comes from the fundamental theorem of symmetric polynomials. □

G.1   Proof of Proposition 6

Given $\mathcal{C}$ be a polynomial-size $\{+, -, \times, /\}$-circuit, we denote by $\phi_\mathcal{C}$ the (rational) function computed by $\mathcal{C}$. In [1], by induction on the gates of $\mathcal{C}$, it is shown that there exists a p.p.t. algorithm $\mathcal{A}$ such that $\mathcal{A}(\mathcal{C})$ outputs two polynomial-size $\{+, -, \times\}$-circuits $\mathcal{C}', \mathcal{C}''$ satisfying $\phi_\mathcal{C} = \phi_{\mathcal{C}'}/\phi_{\mathcal{C}''}$. Let us assume that $\phi_\mathcal{C}$ satisfies (4). According to Proposition 1, if $\phi_{\mathcal{C}''} \circ \alpha(\theta_n^{[x]})$ is not null then it is equal to 0 with negligible probability. Firstly, $\phi_{\mathcal{C}''} \circ \alpha(\theta_n^{[0]})$ and $\phi_{\mathcal{C}''} \circ \alpha(\theta_n^{[1]})$ cannot be both null because $\phi_\mathcal{C}$ satisfies (4). If $\phi_{\mathcal{C}''} \circ \alpha(\theta_n^{[1]})$ is null but not $\phi_{\mathcal{C}''} \circ \alpha(\theta_n^{[0]})$ (or the converse) then $\phi_{\mathcal{C}''}$ satisfies (4). Finally, if $\phi_{\mathcal{C}''} \circ \alpha(\theta_n^{[1]})$ and $\phi_{\mathcal{C}''} \circ \alpha(\theta_n^{[0]})$ are both not null then $\phi_{\mathcal{C}'}$ satisfies (4). This proves that the CPA attacker can recover a polynomial satisfying (4). □

G.2   Proof of Proposition 7

We propose here a sketch of the proof. Details can be found in [8].

Recall that $\theta_n = ((x_{i\ell}, r_{i\ell})_{i=1,\ldots,r}, s_{2\ell-1}, s_{2\ell})_{\ell=1,\ldots,\kappa}$ is drawn according to a probability distribution over $\mathbb{Z}_n^\gamma$ (with $\gamma = 4\kappa^2 + 2(t+1)\kappa$) statistically close to the uniform one. Consider the following tuples of indeterminate:

- $V = (V_i)_{i \in \{1,\ldots,2\kappa\}}$,
- $Y = ((X_{i\ell}, R_{i\ell})_{i=0,\ldots,t}, (S_{2\ell-1,i}, S_{2\ell,i})_{i=1,\ldots,2\kappa})_{\ell=1,\ldots,\kappa}$,
- $Z = (X_1, \ldots, X_{\kappa-1}, R_1, \ldots, R_\kappa)$.

Let $T = [t_{ij}] = (\det S)S^{-1}$. The degree-$(2\kappa - 1)$ polynomial computing t_{ij} is (abusively) denoted by t_{ij}, i.e. $t_{ij}(Y) = t_{ij}$.

Let assume that the CPA attacker can recover a non-null polynomial $\phi \in \mathbb{Z}_n[X_1, \ldots, X_{\gamma'+2\kappa}]$ such that

$$\phi \circ \alpha(\theta_n, c) = 0$$

with non-negligible probability over θ_n, $c \leftarrow$ Encrypt$(K, pp, 0)$. Let $\psi, \psi', \varepsilon_1, \ldots, \varepsilon_{2\kappa}$ be polynomials defined by

- $\psi(Y, V) = \phi \circ \alpha(Y, V)$
- $\varepsilon_\ell(Y, Z) = t_{\ell,1}(Y)R_1X_1 + t_{\ell,2}(Y)R_2 + t_{\ell,3}(Y)R_2X_2 + t_{\ell,4}(Y)R_2 + \ldots + t_{\ell,2\kappa-1}(Y)R_\kappa(-X_1 - \ldots - X_{\kappa-1}) + t_{\ell,2\kappa}(Y)R_\kappa$.
- $\psi'(Y, Z) = \psi(Y, \varepsilon_1(Y, Z), \ldots, \varepsilon_{2\kappa}(Y, Z))$

Obviously, ψ is not null. By construction, $\psi'(\theta_n, x_1 \ldots, x_{\kappa-1}, r_1, \ldots, r_\kappa)$ is null with non-negligible probability. It follows that it is null according to Proposition 1. The set of polynomials ψ ensuring that ψ' is null is an ideal. To conclude, it suffices to check that this ideal is generated by ϕ_0 (see [8] for details) implying that $\phi \circ \alpha$ is a non-null multiple of ϕ_0. $\square$

G.3   Proof of Proposition 8

We here enhance the power of the attacker by letting it choose the Δ_κ-symmetric polynomials $\alpha_1, \ldots, \alpha_{\gamma'}$. Without loss of generality, we prove here that there does not exist any polynomial-size $\{+, -, \times\}$-circuit representing a polynomial ϕ satisfying $\phi \circ \alpha = \phi_0$. The extension to multiples of ϕ_0 is not difficult (but not straightforward). It should be noticed that this result is a pure algebraic result which does not rely on the factoring assumption, i.e. n could be prime.

According to notation of Definition 7, we consider the tuples $V = (V_1, \ldots, V_{2\kappa})$ and $Y = ((X_{i\ell}, R_{i\ell})_{i=1,\ldots,t}, (S_{2\ell-1,i}, S_{2\ell,i})_{i=1,\ldots,2\kappa})_{\ell=1,\ldots,\kappa}$.

As $\phi \circ \alpha(Y) = \phi_0(Y)$, the equality also holds by setting $X_{i\ell} = R_{i\ell} = 1$ for any $i = 1, \ldots, t$ and $S_{2\ell-1,i} = S_{2\ell,i}$ for any i, ℓ. We then consider the polynomials $\nu_1, \ldots, \nu_\gamma$ and ψ defined over $V, S = ((S_{\ell,i})_{i=1,\ldots,2\kappa})_{\ell=1,\ldots,\kappa}$ by

$$\nu_i(S) = \alpha_i \left((1, \ldots, 1, (S_{2\ell,i}, S_{2\ell,i})_{i=1,\ldots,2\kappa})_{\ell=1,\ldots,\kappa} \right)$$

$$\psi(S, V) = \frac{1}{\kappa} \phi_0 \left((1, \ldots, 1, (S_{2\ell,i}, S_{2\ell,i})_{i=1,\ldots,2\kappa})_{\ell=1,\ldots,\kappa}, V \right)$$

$$= \prod_{\ell=1,\ldots,\kappa} \left(\sum_{i=1}^{2\kappa} S_{2\ell,i} V_i \right)$$

Similarly to the definition of α, we consider the function

$$\nu(S, V) = (\nu_1(S), \ldots, \nu_{\gamma'}(S), V)$$

To establish our result, it suffices to show that there does not exist any (polynomial-size) polynomial ϕ such that $\phi \circ \nu = \psi$. To achieve it, we first notice that the polynomials ν_i remain Δ_κ-symmetric. Without loss of generality, we will assume that the polynomials ν_i are homogeneous (otherwise we split them into homogeneous polynomials). Moreover, as $\deg \psi = \kappa$, one can assume that $\deg \nu_i \leq \kappa$. Consider the two sets I_1, I_2 defined by

- $I_1 = \{i \in \{1, \ldots, \gamma'\} | \deg \nu_i < \kappa\}$,
- $I_2 = \{i \in \{1, \ldots, \gamma'\} | \deg \nu_i = \kappa\}$

Let
$$V_\kappa \stackrel{\text{def}}{=} \{v \in \{0, 1\}^{2\kappa} | v_1 + \cdots + v_{2\kappa} = \kappa\}$$

For a given $v \in \mathbb{Z}_n^{2\kappa}$, the polynomial ψ_v is defined by,

$$\psi_{v=(v_1, \ldots, v_{2\kappa})}(S) = \psi(S, v) = \cdot \prod_{\ell=1,\ldots,\kappa} \left(\sum_{i=1}^{2\kappa} v_i S_{2\ell,i} \right)$$

Lemma 6. *Let $v_1, \ldots, v_r \in V_\kappa$ and $a_1, \ldots, a_r \in \mathbb{Z}_n \setminus \{0\}$. The polynomial $a_1 \psi_{v_1} + \ldots + a_r \psi_{v_r}$ cannot be written as a polynomial $p((\nu_i)_{i \in I_1})$.*

Proof. By Lemma 5, one can straightforwardly show that $\psi_{(1,0,\ldots,0)}$ ($\psi_{(1,0,\ldots,0)}(S) = s_{2,1} s_{4,1} \cdots s_{2\kappa,1}$) cannot be written as a polynomial $p((\nu_i)_{i \in I_1})$. Given $\tau \in \mathbb{Z}_n^{2\kappa}$, we denote by $\nu_1^\tau, \ldots, \nu_{\gamma'}^\tau$ the polynomials $\nu_1, \ldots, \nu_{\gamma'}$ where the variables $s_{2\ell,i}$ are substituted by $\tau_i s_{2\ell,1}$ for any $1 \leq i \leq 2\kappa$ and φ_i denotes the polynomial ψ_{v_i} by doing the same substitution. It is important to notice that $\nu_1^\tau, \ldots, \nu_{\gamma'}^\tau$ are symmetric polynomials defined over $s_{2,1}, s_{4,1}, \cdots, s_{2\kappa,1}$. Moreover,

$$\varphi_i(\tau, s_{2,1}, s_{4,1}, \cdots, s_{2\kappa,1}) = q_i(\tau) s_{2,1} s_{4,1} \cdots s_{2\kappa,1}$$

where q_i is a degree-κ polynomial. It follows that

$$\sum_{i=1}^{r} a_i \varphi_i(\tau, s_{2,1}, s_{4,1}, \cdots, s_{2\kappa,1}) = q(\tau) s_{2,1} s_{4,1} \cdots s_{2\kappa,1}$$

where $q = \sum_{i=1}^{r} a_i q_i$ is a degree-κ polynomial. By definition of V_κ, each q_i contains at least one monomial which does not belong to the other polynomials $q_{j \neq i}$. It follows that q is not null.

Thus, according to the famous lemma of Schwartz and Zippel [19], $q(\tau) = 0$ with negligible probability over the choice of τ. Let τ^* such that $q(\tau^*) \neq 0$. The equality $p((\nu_i)_{i \in I_1}) = a_1 \psi_{v_1} + \ldots + a_r \psi_{v_r}$ implies that

$$p((\nu_i^{\tau^*})_{i \in I_1}) = C \cdot s_{2,1} \cdots s_{2\kappa,1}$$

with $C \neq 0$ contradicting Lemma 5. $\qquad\square$

The result is a direct consequence of this lemma. Given a polynomial ϕ, we consider the polynomial ϕ_v defined by $\phi_v(\nu_1(S), \ldots, \nu_{\gamma'}(S)) = \phi \circ \nu(S, v)$. Let us assume that $\phi \circ \nu = \psi$ implying that for each $v \in V_\kappa$, $\psi_v = \phi_v$.

Because $\deg \psi = \kappa$, we can write $\phi_v(\nu_1, \ldots, \nu_t) = \phi_v'(\nu_{i \in I_1}) + \phi_v''(\nu_{i \in I_2})$ with $\deg \phi_v'' = 1$. As $|I_2| \leq \gamma'$ is polynomial but not $\#V_\kappa$, there exist $v_1, \ldots, v_r \in V_\kappa$ s.t. the linear functions $\phi_{v_1}'', \ldots, \phi_{v_r}''$ are linearly dependant. It follows that there exist $a_1, \ldots, a_r \in \mathbb{Z}_n \setminus \{0\}$ such that

$$a_1 \phi_{v_1}''(\nu_{i \in I_2}) + \ldots + a_r \phi_{v_r}''(\nu_{i \in I_2}) = 0$$

It implies that $a_1 \phi_{v_1}'(\nu_{i \in I_1}) + \cdots + a_r \phi_{v_r}'(\nu_{i \in I_1}) = a_1 \psi_{v_1} + \ldots + a_r \psi_{v_r}$ contradicting Lemma 6. $\qquad\square$

References

1. Aggarwal, D., Maurer, U.: Breaking RSA generically is equivalent to factoring. In: Joux, A. (ed.) EUROCRYPT 2009. LNCS, vol. 5479, pp. 36–53. Springer, Heidelberg (2009). https://doi.org/10.1007/978-3-642-01001-9_2

2. Brakerski, Z., Vaikuntanathan, V.: Efficient fully homomorphic encryption from (standard) LWE. Cryptology ePrint Archive, Report 2011/344 (2011). http://eprint.iacr.org/

3. Castagnos, G., Laguillaumie, F.: Linearly homomorphic encryption from DDH. In: Nyberg, K. (ed.) CT-RSA 2015. LNCS, vol. 9048, pp. 487–505. Springer, Cham (2015). https://doi.org/10.1007/978-3-319-16715-2_26

4. Chillotti, I., Gama, N., Georgieva, M., Izabachène, M.: TFHE: fast fully homomorphic encryption over the torus. IACR Cryptology ePrint Archive, 2018:421 (2018)

5. Coron, J.-S., Naccache, D., Tibouchi, M.: Public key compression and modulus switching for fully homomorphic encryption over the integers. In: Pointcheval, D., Johansson, T. (eds.) EUROCRYPT 2012. LNCS, vol. 7237, pp. 446–464. Springer, Heidelberg (2012). https://doi.org/10.1007/978-3-642-29011-4_27

6. Ducas, L., Micciancio, D.: FHEW: bootstrapping homomorphic encryption in less than a second. In: Oswald, E., Fischlin, M. (eds.) EUROCRYPT 2015, Part I. LNCS, vol. 9056, pp. 617–640. Springer, Heidelberg (2015). https://doi.org/10.1007/978-3-662-46800-5_24

7. Elgamal, T.: A public key cryptosystem and a signature sheme based on discrete logarithms. IEEE Trans. Inf. Theory **31**, 469–472 (1985)

8. Gavin, G., Tainturier, S.: New ideas to build noise-free homomorphic cryptosystems. Cryptology ePrint Archive, Report 2019/1375 (2019). https://eprint.iacr.org/2019/1375

9. Gentry, C.: Fully homomorphic encryption using ideal lattices. In: STOC, pp. 169–178 (2009)

10. Gentry, C., Halevi, S., Smart, N.P.: Fully homomorphic encryption with polylog overhead. In: Pointcheval, D., Johansson, T. (eds.) EUROCRYPT 2012. LNCS, vol. 7237, pp. 465–482. Springer, Heidelberg (2012). https://doi.org/10.1007/978-3-642-29011-4_28

11. Gentry, C., Halevi, S., Smart, N.P.: Homomorphic evaluation of the AES circuit. In: Safavi-Naini, R., Canetti, R. (eds.) CRYPTO 2012. LNCS, vol. 7417, pp. 850–867. Springer, Heidelberg (2012). https://doi.org/10.1007/978-3-642-32009-5_49

12. Gentry, C., Sahai, A., Waters, B.: Homomorphic encryption from learning with errors: conceptually-simpler, asymptotically-faster, attribute-based. In: Canetti, R., Garay, J.A. (eds.) CRYPTO 2013, Part I. LNCS, vol. 8042, pp. 75–92. Springer, Heidelberg (2013). https://doi.org/10.1007/978-3-642-40041-4_5

13. Jager, T., Schwenk, J.: On the analysis of cryptographic assumptions in the generic ring model. In: Matsui, M. (ed.) ASIACRYPT 2009. LNCS, vol. 5912, pp. 399–416. Springer, Heidelberg (2009). https://doi.org/10.1007/978-3-642-10366-7_24

14. Kipnis, A., Hibshoosh, E.: Efficient methods for practical fully homomorphic symmetric-key encrypton, randomization and verification. Cryptology ePrint Archive, Report 2012/637 (2012). http://eprint.iacr.org/

15. Lauter, K., Naehrig, M., Vaikuntanathan, V.: Can homomorphic encryption be practical? IACR Cryptology ePrint Archive, 2011:405 (2011)

16. Paillier, P.: Public-key cryptosystems based on composite degree residuosity classes. In: Stern, J. (ed.) EUROCRYPT 1999. LNCS, vol. 1592, pp. 223–238. Springer, Heidelberg (1999). https://doi.org/10.1007/3-540-48910-X_16

17. Patarin, J.: Hidden fields equations (HFE) and isomorphisms of polynomials (IP): two new families of asymmetric algorithms. In: Maurer, U. (ed.) EUROCRYPT 1996. LNCS, vol. 1070, pp. 33–48. Springer, Heidelberg (1996). https://doi.org/10.1007/3-540-68339-9_4

18. Rothblum, R.: Homomorphic encryption: from private-key to public-key. In: Ishai, Y. (ed.) TCC 2011. LNCS, vol. 6597, pp. 219–234. Springer, Heidelberg (2011). https://doi.org/10.1007/978-3-642-19571-6_14
19. Schwartz, J.T.: Fast probabilistic algorithms for verification of polynomial identities. J. ACM **27**(4), 701–717 (1980)
20. Stehlé, D., Steinfeld, R.: Faster fully homomorphic encryption. In: Abe, M. (ed.) ASIACRYPT 2010. LNCS, vol. 6477, pp. 377–394. Springer, Heidelberg (2010). https://doi.org/10.1007/978-3-642-17373-8_22
21. van Dijk, M., Gentry, C., Halevi, S., Vaikuntanathan, V.: Fully homomorphic encryption over the integers. In: Gilbert, H. (ed.) EUROCRYPT 2010. LNCS, vol. 6110, pp. 24–43. Springer, Heidelberg (2010). https://doi.org/10.1007/978-3-642-13190-5_2
22. Xiao, L., Bastani, O., Yen, I.-L.: An efficient homomorphic encryption protocol for multi-user systems. IACR Cryptology ePrint Archive, 2012:193 (2012)

Author Index

Printed in the United States
By Bookmasters